KU-625-508

The **Rough Guide** to

Bulgaria

written and researched by

Jonathan Bousfield and Dan Richardson

with additional contributions from
Matt Willis

ROUGH
GUIDES

NEW YORK · LONDON · DELHI

www.roughguides.com

Contents

Tradition and ritual
colour section
following p.120

The Great Outdoors
colour section
following p.344

3

◀ Shoreline, Sozopol

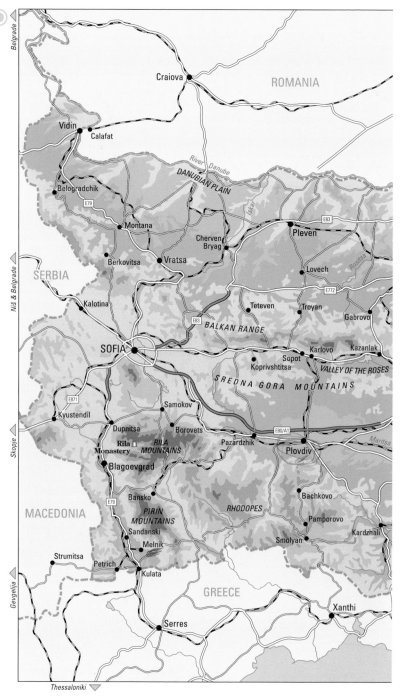

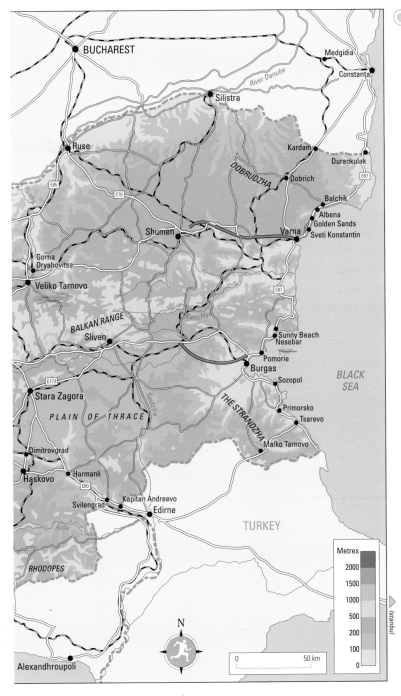

Introduction to
Bulgaria

In many ways Bulgaria is one of the success stories of the Balkans; a politically stable democracy and EU member, it also harbours one of the fastest-growing tourist industries in Europe. Yet despite the soaring popularity of its seaside resorts, Bulgaria remains a little-known destination with a great deal to discover: much of the country is like an open-air museum of Balkan culture, with beautifully decorated churches, fine mosques, wonderfully preserved rustic villages and a great deal of enduring folklore. The mountainous interior makes it one of the top hiking destinations of Europe, while over on the Black Sea coast, the white-sand beaches are just as magnificent in reality as they look in the tourist brochures.

The Bulgarians themselves have long been frustrated by their country's lack of a clearly defined image abroad. Heirs to one of Europe's great civilizations, and guardians of Balkan Christian traditions, they have a keen sense of national identity distilled by centuries of turbulent history. In a constantly repeating cycle of grandeur, decline and national rebirth, successive Bulgarian states have striven to dominate the Balkan peninsula before succumbing to defeat and foreign tutelage, only to be regenerated by patriotic resistance to outside control.

The Bulgarian nation was formed in the seventh and eighth centuries when the **Bulgars**, warlike nomads from central Asia, assumed the leadership of Slav tribes in the lower Danube basin and took them on a spree of conquest in southeastern Europe. The resulting **First Bulgarian Kingdom**, after accepting Orthodox Christianity as the state religion, became the centre of Slavonic culture and spirituality before falling victim to a resurgent **Byzantine Empire** in the eleventh century. Recovery came a century later

Fact file

• Bulgaria is a country of 7.4 million people located in the extreme southeastern corner of Europe, sharing borders with Romania, Serbia, Macedonia, Greece and Turkey.

• Roughly 84 percent of the population is made up of Bulgarians, who speak a Slavic language akin to Russian and Serbo-Croat, and practise the Orthodox Christian faith.

• There is also a sizeable Muslim population (thirteen percent of the total), comprising both *pomaks* (Bulgarians who converted to Islam from the sixteenth century onwards) and ethnic Turks. Bulgaria also plays host to an estimated 350,000 Gypsies or Roma, many of whom represent the poorest segment of the population.

• Much of Bulgaria's industry collapsed, along with the Communist system that developed it, after 1989, and the country is nowadays known for natural products such as fruit, vegetables, wine and yoghurt – along with tobacco, a mainstay of the rural south.

• Bulgaria's Black Sea coast was earmarked for intensive tourist develop-ment as early as the 1960s, although recent years have seen attempts to encourage village tourism and hiking holidays in the country's mountainous interior.

when the local aristocracy broke free from Constantinople and restored past glories in the shape of the **Second Bulgarian Kingdom**. However, the rise of Ottoman power in the fourteenth century ushered in a 500-year-long period of *Tursko robstvo* or **"Turkish bondage"**, when the achievements of the medieval era were extinguished. Bulgarian art and culture recovered during the nineteenth-century **National Revival**, and the emergence of a potent revolutionary movement prepared the ground for Bulgaria's eventual **Liberation** in 1878, achieved with the

> **Much of the country is like an open-air museum of Balkan culture**

help of Russian arms. However, Europe's other Great Powers conspired to limit the size of the infant state at the Berlin Congress of 1878, the first of a series of betrayals which denied Bulgarian claims

7

■

▼ Bar at Sunny Beach

to a territory which had long been considered an integral part of the historical Bulgarian state, **Macedonia**. In the twentieth century alone, Bulgaria went to war three times (in the Balkan Wars of 1912–13, World War I and World War II) to try and recover Macedonia, only to be defeated on each occasion. By 1945 it appeared as a country that had somehow missed out on its destiny, and rapidly turned in on itself during the subsequent deep sleep of **Communism**.

Mosques

A long Ottoman occupation left Bulgaria with some of the finest Islamic architecture in the Balkans. Mosques in areas of Muslim settlement are still in daily use, and prestige mosques such as the *Tombul dzhamiya* in Shumen are deservedly popular as tourist attractions. The basic layout of a mosque is a carpet-covered square with a mihrab cut into the eastern end facing Mecca; from this niche the *imam* or priest leads the congregation in prayer, the women grouped behind the men on a balcony or behind a low balustrade. Because the Islamic faith prohibits reproduction of the human form, the richest mosques tend to be covered in passages from the Koran and non-figurative decoration of tiles and ornamented plaster.

Today, while undoubtedly more open to the outside world and more visitor-friendly than ever before, Bulgaria remains a country in transition. Despite losing their monopoly on power in 1989, Bulgaria's ex-Communists (now renamed the Bulgarian Socialist Party) remain the most disciplined political force in the country, and with right-of-centre groupings coalescing and dissolving every few years or so, Bulgaria's political landscape remains relatively fluid.

While private enterprise and the entrepreneurial spirit have brought new energy to Bulgaria's streets, locals are quick to point out that the transition to capitalism has meant poor conditions for many. High employment levels and job security are things of the past, and the new business culture is riddled with corruption. One of the fastest-growing sectors of the Bulgarian economy is real estate, with Western buyers eagerly snapping up properties throughout the country. While sales of country cottages have brought undoubted benefits to hitherto depopulated rural areas, the real estate gold-rush has led to a spate of speculative building projects on the Black Sea coast and in inland skiing resorts, encroaching on the unspoilt landscapes and wildlife habitats for which Bulgaria is famed. Balancing economic development with conservation issues is one of Bulgaria's biggest challenges for the future.

Monasteries

During five centuries of Ottoman rule, Bulgarian national traditions were kept alive by its monasteries, which had been centres of Bulgarian-language learning since the Middle Ages. Often hidden away in mountain valleys – both for defensive reasons, and because of the tranquillity offered to hermits – the monasteries later provided the populace with both spiritual and political leadership during the nineteenth-century upsurge of patriotic feeling known as the National Revival. For today's visitor, the monasteries offer a unique atmosphere of sanctity and peace, as well as the chance to peer inside some wonderfully decorated churches. Rila, Troyan and Bachkovo are the three most-visited foundations, welcoming pilgrims all year round and attracting crowds of celebrants on major saints' days.

Yoghurt

Silkily smooth and additive-free, Bulgarian yoghurt (*kiselo mlyako*) is one of the gastronomic highlights of the country and has legendary health-giving properties to boot. Much of its reputation rests on the presence of *bacillus bulgaricus*, a naturally occurring bacterium which is said to boost the immune system. Regular consumption of yoghurt is widely believed to be one of the reasons why there is such a high proportion of centenarians in Bulgaria's highland villages. Delicious when eaten on its own or with fresh fruit, Bulgarian yoghurt also serves as the main ingredient in *tarator*, a refreshing cold soup including garlic and cucumber. Most Bulgarian yoghurt comes from cows' milk, although the tangy sheeps' milk yoghurt (*ovche mlyako*) and rich velvety buffalo yoghurt (*bivolsko mlyako*) are also well worth a try.

▼ Gourds for sale, Melnik

Where to go and when

Bulgaria has a continental climate, with long, hot, dry summers and – in the interior at least – bitterly cold winters. July and August can be oppressively hot in the big cities, and crowded on the Black Sea coast – elsewhere, you won't have to worry about being swamped by fellow visitors. Using public transport is reasonably easy throughout the year, although the highest cross-mountain routes will be closed during the coldest months.

Bulgaria's most obvious urban attractions are **Sofia**, a set-piece capital city whose centre was laid out by successive regimes as an expression of political power;

Chalga

Despite the popularity of Western rock and dance music among big-city Bulgarians, much of the country has preserved a distinctive popular culture of its own. Nowhere is this more apparent than in the music known as *chalga*, the oriental-influenced blend of eastern melodies, hip-shaking  rhythms and love-and-betrayal lyrics, largely delivered by a glamorous roster of provocatively dressed stars, such as Azis (above). Drawing inspiration from the folk-pop music of neighbouring Turkey, Greece and Serbia, the sound of *chalga* blares ubiquitously from radio stations across the country. Many urban Bulgarians look down on *chalga* as an unsophisticated, brash and vulgar form of pop that panders to the showbiz-generated fantasies of the uneducated – and most *chalga* is indeed formulaic and banal. However, the best of the genre contains a good deal more heart and soul than contemporary house and techno tunes, and if dancing on the table with your hands in the air has always been your idea of a good holiday, then *chalga* is guaranteed to set you on your way.

and the second city **Plovdiv**, home to what is arguably the finest collection of nineteenth-century architecture in the Balkans. Both are increasingly cosmopolitan places, offering a host of nightlife opportunities and cultural events.

Yet it's in the countryside rather than the cities that the real rewards of inland travel are to be found. You'll come across some of Europe's finest highland scenery in the **Rila**, **Pirin**, **Balkan**, **Sredna Gora** and **Rhodope mountain ranges**, whose valleys harbour the kind of **bucolic villages**

> It's in the countryside rather than the cities that the real rewards of inland travel are to be found

which have all but disappeared in Western Europe. Many of them are time-consuming to reach by public transport, but if traditional architecture and goat-thronged, cobbled alleys appeal, any effort will be rewarded. While the villages of **Bansko**, **Koprivshtitsa** – a living memorial to the 1876 April Rising – and **Melnik** have the best tourist facilities, more rustic out-of-the-way spots such as **Brashlyan**, **Kovachevitsa** and **Zheravna** are also well worth seeking out. In addition, the highland regions display Bulgaria's rich spiritual traditions via its many **monasteries**: Bachkovo, Rila, Rozhen and Troyan are the big four, although any number of smaller foundations make worthwhile destinations. Also in the mountains, a burgeoning winter tourist industry is taking shape in resorts such as **Bansko**, **Borovets** and **Pamporovo**, although the latter two are purpose-built package resorts which lack the charm of the former. Snow is thick on the ground from mid-December through to mid-March, and in summer the mountain resorts are taken over by climbers and ramblers.

▼ Hiking in the Pirin Mountains

However, most foreign visitors still make a beeline for the **Black Sea**, formerly the summer playground of the entire Eastern Bloc. The main resort-city of **Varna** is the liveliest place along the coast, while small peninsula settlements like **Nesebar** and **Sozopol**, though crowded in August, provide traditional fishing-village architecture as well as enticing stretches of sand. Indeed, beaches are on the whole magnificent, especially in the south, and private enterprise is more developed here than anywhere else in the country, ensuring a plentiful supply of private rooms and good seafood restaurants.

▲ Fruit and vegetable stall

Although the climate remains mild all the year round, the Black Sea becomes deserted outside the main tourist season (June–September), when many attractions and hotels shut up shop.

Elsewhere, although few places are geared up to cater to Western-style, consumer-oriented tourism, the rugged highlands that cut across the centre of the country are the best places to explore the heartland of Bulgarian history and culture. The crafts towns and monasteries of the central Balkan Range were the places where Bulgarian culture recovered during the nineteenth-century National Revival,

▲ Street scene, Sofia

and are easily explored from the dramatically situated, citadel-encrusted town of **Veliko Tarnovo**, medieval capital of the Second Bulgarian Kingdom.

Shumen, the main town of the northwest, is dour in comparison, but makes a good base from which to visit some compelling historical sites at **Madara**, **Pliska** and **Preslav**. Between the Balkan Range and the **Sredna Gora**, with its countless reminders of Bulgaria's nineteenth-century struggles against Turkish oppression, lies the **Valley of the Roses**, lined by a string of historic market towns and home to Bulgaria's renowned rose harvest in late May.

Average daily maximum temperatures in degrees centigrade

	Jan	Feb	Mar	Apr	May	Jun	Jul	Aug	Sep	Oct	Nov	Dec
Borovets	-1	1	5	9	15	19	22	23	16	12	6	1
Plovdiv	1	3	7	12	17	23	23	24	19	13	8	3
Sofia	-1	1	5	10	15	19	23	24	16	12	6	1
Varna	3	6	6	12	17	22	24	23	20	16	10	4

30

things not to miss

It's not possible to see everything that Bulgaria has to offer in one trip – and we don't suggest you try. What follows is a selective taste of the country's highlights: outstanding monasteries and churches, vibrant festivals, spectacular mountainscapes, and even good things to eat and drink. It's arranged in five colour-coded categories, so that you can browse through to find the very best things to see, do and experience. All highlights have a page reference to take you into the guide, where you can find out more.

 **Aleksandar Nevski Church, Sofia** Page **92** • The capital's most
striking edifice, built in Byzantine–Muscovite style, with an opulently decorated interior.

ACTIVITIES I CONSUME I EVENTS I NATURE I SIGHTS I

14

02 Beach bars Page **389** • In summer, impromptu beach bars are set up below the Sea Gardens in Varna, and all along the Black Sea coast.

04 Trigrad Gorge Page **353** • This spectacular gorge lies deep in the Rhodope mountains and is the site of the stupendous Devil's Throat (*Dyavolsko garlo*) cave.

03 Lazaruvane Page **49** • Across Bulgaria, St Lazarus's Day (the day before Palm Sunday) sees young girls dressing up in folk costumes to perform dances to celebrate the coming spring.

06 Birdwatching Page **207, 363 & 412** • Bulgaria is a paradise for ornithologists, particularly the unspoilt areas of Srebarna, Madzharovo and the lakes around Burgas.

08 Bachkovo monastery Page **340** • Bulgaria's second-largest monastery is beautifully set in the Rhodope mountains, and boasts equally dazzling frescoes.

05 Mount Vitosha Page **100** • An easy bus ride from Sofia, the mountain is mobbed at weekends by city folk, who come to hike the dense forests in summer, or ski the slopes in winter.

07 Tombul Dzhamiya, Shumen Page **256** • A major spiritual centre for the Turks of the northwest, this is the outstanding example of the country's Ottoman-built mosques.

09 **Sunflower fields** Page **188** • Every summer, the fields of the Balkan Range are bathed in sunflowers, a dazzling sight as you're driving by.

10 **Varna Archeological Museum** Page **379** • The Black Sea town of Varna is home to an outstanding museum of Thracian artefacts and Roman-era funerary sculpture.

11 **Apocalyptic art** Page **127, 224 & 242** • Check out nineteenth-century artist Zahari Zograf's horrific *Last Judgement* images at the monasteries of Rila, Troyan and Preobrazhenski.

13 Kukeri Page **120** • The *kukeri* – local men in animal costumes and grotesque masks – drive away evil spirits with orgiastic dances. In most parts of the country *kukeri* rites take place at Shrovetide, although the towns and villages of southwestern Bulgaria enact these rituals in early to mid-January.

12 The Shipka Pass Page **269** • Pay your respects at the Freedom Monument, where Bulgarian and Russian forces resisted a huge Turkish army in 1877.

14 Belogradchik Page **185** • Remote Belogradchik rewards a visit with its historic fortress surrounded by outlandishly twisted pinnacles of eroded sandstone.

15 **Nesebar** Page **405** • The rich Byzantine-Bulgarian civilization that thrived here in the late Middle Ages is still visible in Nesebar's narrow streets and numerous churches.

16 **Church of the Nativity, Arbanasi** Page **241** • An awe-inspiring example of the spiritual culture retained by the Bulgarians even at the height of the Ottoman occupation.

17 **Beach-hopping** Page **427** • The southern Black Sea coast is lined with vast stretches of white sand, best of all at Sinemorets.

18 Sozopol Page **416** • This ancient fishing village attracts a steady stream of day-trippers, but even in high summer there's still space to escape the crowds.

19 Orthodox Easter

Page **50** • A rewarding time to be in Bulgaria: after midnight Mass on Easter Saturday, celebrants flood out onto the streets bearing candles symbolizing the Resurrection, before smashing painted eggs.

20 Koprivshtitsa Page **273** • This highland village is renowned for its role in the April Rising of 1876, when local revolutionaries heroically failed to unseat the occupying Ottoman powers.

21 Melnik Page **158** • The walk from this ancient wine-making village over the mountains to Rozhen Monastery takes you through a strange landscape of pyramid-shaped rock formations.

22 A night in Bansko Page **147** • Restaurants in the village of Bansko cater to crowds of Sofia folk at Easter time and in high summer, with their famous grilled food and live folk music.

23 Rila Monastery Page **127** • The most-visited monastic foundation in the country – a hoard of miracle-working relics and icons in its beautifully decorated church draws pilgrims year-round.

24 The Old Quarter, Plovdiv
Page **326** • Many of the houses in this nineteenth-century quarter of town have been restored, with exquisitely carved wooden ceilings and fanciful wall paintings inside.

26 Yoghurt
Page **10** • Available everywhere, Bulgarian yoghurt (*kiselo mlyako*) is renowned for its health-giving properties. Try it with *banitsa*, a delicious flaky pastry, for a typical Bulgarian snack.

25 The Feast of the Assumption (Golyama Bogoroditsa)
Page **224, 340 & 101**
• August 15 is a big deal here, marked by processions and services at any church associated with the Holy Virgin. Head especially for the monasteries at Troyan, Bachkovo or Dragalevtsi.

27 Veliko Tarnovo
Page **228**
• Perched above the twisting River Yantra, this ancient city is home to the vast fortified complex of Tsarevets, capital of the country's thirteenth-century tsars.

28 **Thracian tombs** Pages **264 & 293** • Bulgaria's ancient inhabitants' burial mounds often preserve ornately decorated interiors – the best can be seen in Sveshtari and Kazanlak.

30 **Socialist sculpture** Page **96** • Although many of the Communist-era statues facing Bulgaria's town squares were demolished in the post-1989 period, several brazenly propagandist monuments still survive. The Soviet Army Memorial in Sofia is among the most notorious.

29 **Heritage villages** Page **155, 350, 250 & 308** • Many of Bulgaria's villages preserve the kind of stone- or timber-built farmhouses that have largely died out elsewhere in the Balkans. A number have been spruced up or rebuilt with tourism in mind – Kovachevitsa, Shiroka Laka, Bozhentsi and Zheravna are four of the most evocative.

Basics

Basics

Getting there

The easiest way to reach Bulgaria is by air, with direct flights from the UK and indirect flights from North America and Australasia. Travelling overland from Britain is a long haul, and you'll save little, if anything, going by train, although with an Inter-Rail or Eurail pass you can take in Bulgaria as part of a wider European trip. Approaching Bulgaria by car or bus from the UK involves a journey of at least 2400km and takes the best part of three days.

Air fares always depend on the **season**. Peak times for flights to Bulgaria are mid-December to early March, June to August, and around the Easter holidays; at these times be prepared to book well in advance. Fares drop during the "shoulder" seasons (May & Sept); and you'll get the best prices during the low season (mid-March & April excluding Easter, Oct to mid-Dec). Note also that flying at weekends can be slightly more expensive than midweek travel.

The best deals are usually to be found by booking through discount travel websites or the websites of the airlines themselves.

Flights from the UK and Ireland

Both British Airways and Bulgaria Air offer daily **direct flights to Sofia** – the former from London Heathrow, the latter from both Heathrow and Gatwick. In addition, low-cost airline Wizzair flies daily from London Luton to Sofia, and three times weekly from London Luton to Burgas (May–Sept only). easyJet flies daily from London Gatwick to Sofia. The journey from London to Sofia takes three hours, a little more to Burgas. Competition between the above carriers has led to a growing flexibility in prices, and a low-season return, booked over the Internet well in advance, can cost less than £100 if you avoid weekend travel. Return fares in busy periods can cost anything from £160 to £300. Getting from London to the Black Sea city of Varna involves a one-stop flight with an operator such as Bulgaria Air (via Sofia) or Malev (via Budapest) – peak-season prices hover around the £330–440 mark.

Depending on which part of the UK or Ireland you live in, **one-stop flights** via a European hub may work out cheaper than travelling to London to pick up a flight. Typical routes include Manchester to Sofia with CSA via Prague, or with Lufthansa via Frankfurt; or Glasgow to Sofia with Lufthansa via Frankfurt or Munich. Peak-season returns on these routes are around £280–330. Flying from Ireland, one-stop flights from Dublin to Sofia (again with a European airline such as CSA or Lufthansa) will cost around €400–500 return in peak season. Flights from Belfast to Bulgaria usually involve time-consuming changes and tend to be expensive; it may be cheaper to travel through Dublin or the UK mainland.

Tour operators such as Thomas Cook and Balkan Holidays operate charter flights from several regional UK airports to Varna and Burgas from May to September. These flights are usually filled with package tourists, although empty seats are often sold off cheaply to individual travellers.

Flights from the US and Canada

Although there are no direct flights from North America to Bulgaria, there are plenty of indirect routes to choose from. If you're departing from one of North America's gateway cities you'll probably only have to change planes once; otherwise, a two-stop flight is more likely.

Some of the best **fares** to Sofia from east-coast USA and Canada are offered by European airlines such as LOT (flying from New York, Chicago or Toronto via Warsaw), CSA (from New York, Washington or Toronto via Prague), Malev (from New York and

Toronto via Budapest) or Austrian Airlines (from New York or Washington via Vienna). Flying from central or west-coast USA, you're much more likely to be offered a combination of airlines and more than one change of plane en route. Given all that, the following return fares are only examples of what you might find online or by calling discount travel companies. Fares from New York can be as little as US$850 in low season, rising to US$1300 in high season; from Los Angeles US$1400 in low season and US$1950 in high season. Flying from Toronto or Montreal you'll be paying anything from Can$1800 to Can$2500 depending on season. Travellers from North America may save money by picking up a flight with a low-cost airline to London, and continuing their journey with a separate airline from there.

The choice of **package tours** to Bulgaria available in the US or Canada is limited, and they are often priced as **land-only**, excluding the cost of air fares from the US to Sofia or a starting point like London. Compare what's on offer from tour operators in Britain (see p.34) and search for a transatlantic flight yourself, and you could get a better deal.

Flights from Australia and New Zealand

There are no direct flights from Australia or New Zealand to Bulgaria, and anyway,

---

Fly less – stay longer! Travel and climate change

Climate change is the single biggest issue facing our planet. It is caused by a build-up in the atmosphere of carbon dioxide and other greenhouse gases, which are emitted by many sources – including planes. Already, flights account for around 3–4 percent of human-induced global warming: that figure may sound small, but it is rising year on year and threatens to counteract the progress made by reducing greenhouse emissions in other areas.

Rough Guides regard travel, overall, as a global benefit, and feel strongly that the advantages to developing economies are important, as are the opportunities for greater contact and awareness among peoples. But we all have a responsibility to limit our personal "carbon footprint". That means giving thought to how often we fly and what we can do to redress the harm that our trips create.

Flying and climate change

Pretty much every form of motorized travel generates CO_2, but planes are particularly bad offenders, releasing large volumes of greenhouse gases at altitudes where their impact is far more harmful. Flying also allows us to travel much further than we would contemplate doing by road or rail, so the emissions attributable to each passenger become truly shocking. For example, one person taking a return flight between Europe and California produces the equivalent impact of 2.5 tonnes of CO_2 – similar to the yearly output of the average UK car.

Less harmful planes may evolve but it will be decades before they replace the current fleet – which could be too late for avoiding climate chaos. In the meantime, there are limited options for concerned travellers: to reduce the amount we travel by air (take fewer trips, stay longer!), to avoid night flights (when plane contrails trap heat from Earth but can't reflect sunlight back to space), and to make the trips we do take "climate neutral" via a carbon-offset scheme.

Carbon-offset schemes

Offset schemes run by **climatecare.org**, **carbonneutral.com** and others allow you to "neutralize" the greenhouse gases that you are responsible for releasing. Their websites have simple calculators that let you work out the impact of any flight. Once that's done, you can pay to fund projects that will reduce future carbon emissions by an equivalent amount (such as the distribution of low-energy light bulbs and cooking stoves in developing countries). Please take the time to visit our website and make your trip climate neutral.

@**www.roughguides.com/climatechange**

travellers from down under usually visit it as part of a wider European trip. Many airlines offer **one-stop** flights from Sydney to European cities from where there are onward flights to Sofia, though you might not get a same-day connection. However, many of the cheaper deals offered by booking agents involve **two-stop** flights, calling at a major Asian hub to pick up a flight to Europe and then an onward connection to Sofia. Typical prices from Sydney are AUS$2000 for a two-stop flight in low season, rising to AUS$3000 for a one-stop flight in high season.

A handful of travel agents offer ten-day and two-week tours of Bulgaria, and can also help in fashioning tailor-made itineraries to suit your requirements.

Trains

You're unlikely to save any money travelling to Bulgaria by train; the chief reason for doing so is to visit other countries as well. The most direct **train routes** to Bulgaria involve heading across France, then though Italy, Slovenia, Croatia and Serbia (Dieppe–Paris–Milan–Venice–Zagreb–Belgrade–Sofia) or through Belgium and Germany before picking up the same route (Ostende–Brussels–Munich–Zagreb–Belgrade–Sofia). Slightly longer though equally rewarding alternatives take in Hungary (Paris/Brussels–Budapest–Belgrade–Sofia) or both Hungary and Romania (Paris/Brussels–Budapest–Bucharest–Sofia). Depending on connections, the journey takes about three days and involves two nights on the train, unless you choose to break your journey in the cities you're travelling through. Bring food, drinks and toilet paper for the duration, plus warm clothing if you're travelling from October to May (the carriages are sometimes inadequately heated).

Perhaps the most roundabout train route to Bulgaria is London–Paris–Milan–Brindisi, followed by a ferry to Patras in Greece, from where you can continue to Sofia via Athens and Thessaloniki by train or bus (one or two of each daily).

Citizens of the EU, USA, Canada, Australia and New Zealand don't need **transit visas** to travel through Croatia and Serbia; citizens of other countries should check with the relevant embassies before they leave home.

Buying a **through ticket** for these routes isn't easy: most major UK train stations can sell tickets as far as Brussels, but are rarely equipped to deal with destinations beyond. The agents who specialize in international train journeys (see "Rail Contacts" p.30) may be able to book your passage as far as Budapest or Zagreb, but are unlikely to sell tickets further east. The price of a second-class return ticket from London to Budapest using Eurostar hovers around the £220 mark – to this you'll need to add a further £40–50 to cover the remaining leg of the journey. The trip will work out slightly cheaper if you cross the Channel by ferry, but as none of the ticket agents sells through tickets on continental journeys not using Eurostar, you'll have to buy tickets as you go.

Rail passes

If you're planning to visit Bulgaria as part of a more extensive trip around Europe, it may be worth buying a **rail pass**. Bulgaria is covered in the Inter-Rail pass scheme, which is available to European residents. Non-European residents can make use of the Eurail pass (which covers Bulgaria but does not include some of the countries you might wish to travel through en route) and the Eurail Selectpass (which covers Bulgaria and neighbouring countries).

All these passes can be bought at Rail Europe in the UK; Eurail passes are available from selected agents in North America and Australia (see p.30 for details).

Inter-Rail passes come in over-26 and (cheaper) under-26 versions, and cover 31 countries, including Bulgaria and all the countries you need to travel through in order to get there. A pass for five days' travel in a ten-day period (£175 for adults, £110 for those under 26) will barely suffice to get you to Bulgaria and back; it is therefore preferable to purchase a pass for ten days' travel within a 22-day period (£225 and £168 respectively) or a pass for one month's continuous travel (£425 and £282). Inter-Rail passes do not include travel between Britain and the Continent, although pass holders are eligible for discounts on rail travel in the UK and on cross-Channel ferries.

Non-European residents qualify for the **Eurail Global pass**, which must be purchased before arrival in Europe (or from Rail Europe in London by non-residents who were unable to get it at home). The pass allows unlimited free first-class train travel in seventeen European countries, including Belgium, Germany, Austria, Hungary, Romania and Bulgaria, but not Slovenia, Croatia or Serbia – so you're effectively limited to certain cross-European routes. The pass is available in increments of fifteen days ($675), 21 days ($877) and one month ($1088). A **Eurail Global Flexi pass** will give you ten days' first-class travel in a two-month period for $798. If you're under 26, you can save money with a **Eurail Global Youthpass** ($440 for fifteen days, $708 for one month, or $519 for ten days' travel in a two-month period). Further details of these passes and other Eurail permutations can be found on ⓦ www.raileurope.com.

Rail contacts

CIT World Travel Australia ☎ 1300 361 500, ⓦ www.cittravel.com.au. Eurail and Europass rail passes.

Deutsche Bahn UK ☎ 0871/880 8066, ⓦ www.bahn.co.uk. Timetable information and through ticketing on European routes.

Europrail International Canada ☎ 1-888/667-9734, ⓦ www.europrail.net. Eurail, Europass and individual country passes.

Eurostar UK ☎ 0870/518 6186, ⓦ www.eurostar.com. Passenger train that goes from St Pancras International station in central London to Paris (2hr 15min) and to Brussels (1hr 51min), and from Ebbsfleet International station, off Junction 2 of the M25 (journey times 10min shorter). You can get tickets – including the tube journey to St Pancras International – from Eurostar itself, from most travel agents and from mainline train stations in Britain.

Inter-Rail passes give discounts on the Eurostar service.

Rail Europe UK ☎ 0870/584 8848, ⓦ www.raileurope.co.uk; US ☎ 1-877/257-2887, Canada ☎ 1-800/361-RAIL; ⓦ www.raileurope.com/us. Agents for Eurail, Inter-Rail and Eurostar.

Rail Plus Australia ☎ 1300/555 003 or 03/9642 8644, ⓦ www.railplus.com.au. Sells Eurail, Europass, Britrail and Amtrak passes.

The Man in Seat 61 ⓦ www.seat61.com. Enthusiast-run site packed with information on all aspects of international rail travel, including tips on how best to enjoy the trip to Bulgaria. Far more reliable than many official sites.

Trailfinders Australia ☎ 02/9247 7666, ⓦ www.trailfinder.com.au. Sells all Europe passes.

Trainseurope UK ☎ 0871 700 7722, ⓦ www.trainseurope.co.uk. Tickets from the UK to European destinations. Inter-Rail and other individual country passes.

Buses

It is possible to travel to **Sofia via Frankfurt** on a weekly coach operated by Eurolines, though it takes about 48 hours. With tickets costing £180 return (with five percent reductions for those under 26 or over 60), it's unlikely to be much cheaper than travelling by plane. You might save money by travelling with a London-based Bulgarian company such as Balkan Horn, which operates a twice-weekly London–Sofia–Varna service for £120 return.

Although several other bus operators run services to Sofia from elsewhere in Europe (from many cities in Germany, plus Vienna, Prague and Budapest), the near impossibility of finding out schedules or reserving seats from Britain means that you could well spend days waiting for a connection.

Useful publications

The *Thomas Cook European Timetables* details schedules of over fifty thousand trains in Europe, as well as timings of over two hundred ferry routes and rail-connecting bus services. It's updated and issued every month; the main changes are in the June edition (published end of May), which has details of the summer European schedules, and the October edition, (published end of Sept), which includes winter schedules; some also have advance summer/winter timings. The book can be purchased online (which gets you a ten percent discount) at ⓦ www.thomascooktimetables.com or from branches of Thomas Cook (see ⓦ www.thomascook.co.uk for your nearest branch) and costs £11.50. Their useful *Rail Map of Europe* (regular price £8.95) also comes with an online discount.

Citizens of the EU, USA, Canada, Australia and New Zealand don't need **transit visas** to travel through Croatia, Serbia and Romania; citizens of other countries should check with the relevant embassies before they leave home.

Bus contacts

Balkan Horn UK ☎ 020/7630 1252, ⓦ www.balkanhorn.com.
Eurolines UK ☎ 0870/580 8080, ⓦ www.nationalexpress.com/eurolines.

By car

Driving to Bulgaria may be a time-consuming and potentially exhausting endeavour, but nevertheless constitutes an exhilarating trip through the heart of Europe. Once across the Channel, the **fastest route** is through Belgium, Germany, Austria, Slovenia, Croatia and Serbia to the Bulgarian border at Dimitrovgrad/Kalotina. This route involves a lot of dull motorway driving, but does offer the chance of stopping off in fascinating cities such as Ljubljana, Zagreb and Belgrade. Other possibilities include travelling through Switzerland and Italy to the Adriatic port of Ancona, where you can take a ferry to either Split (Croatia) or Igoumenitsa (Greece); or alternatively driving through Austria, Hungary and Romania before entering Bulgaria from the north. Either way, you'll experience a rich diversity of scenery and culture.

The most convenient **Channel crossings** are on the P&O Stena services from Dover /Folkestone to Calais, or Eurotunnel's Le Shuttle Channel Tunnel option from Folkestone to Calais. Once in Calais or Ostend, you can pick up the main motorway route east through Belgium and beyond.

Ferry contacts

Irish Ferries UK ☎ 0870/517 1717, Northern Ireland ☎ 0818 300 400; ⓦ www.irishferries.com. Dublin to Holyhead; Rosslare to Pembroke.
Norfolk Line UK ☎ 0870/1642 114, ⓦ www .norfolkline-ferries.com. Dover to Dunkerque.
P&O UK ☎ 0870/598 0303, ⓦ www.poferries.com. Dover to Calais; Hull to Rotterdam; Hull to Zeebrugge; Dublin to Liverpool.
Sea Cat UK ☎ 0870/552 3523, Republic of Ireland ☎ 1800/805055; ⓦ www.seacat.co.uk. Belfast to Stranraer, Heysham and Troon; Dublin to Liverpool.

Sea France UK ☎ 0870/443 1653, ⓦ www .seafrance.com. Dover to Calais.
Stena Line UK ☎ 0870/570 7070, Northern Ireland ☎ 0870/520 4204, Republic of Ireland ☎ 1/204 7777; ⓦ www.stenaline.co.uk. Harwich to the Hook of Holland.

Channel tunnel

Eurotunnel UK ☎ 0870/535 3535, ⓦ www .eurotunnel.com. Shuttle train via the Channel Tunnel for vehicles and their passengers only. The service runs continuously between Folkestone and Coquelles, near Calais, with up to four departures per hour (only one per hour midnight–6am) and takes 35min (45min for some night departure times), though you must arrive at least 30min before departure. It is possible to turn up and buy your ticket at the tollbooths (after exiting the M20 at junction 11a), though at busy times booking is advisable. Rates depend on the time of year, time of day and length of stay; it's cheaper to travel between 10pm and 6am, while the highest fares are for weekend departures and returns in July and August.

Airlines, agents and operators

Online booking

ⓦ www.expedia.co.uk (in UK) ⓦ www.expedia .com (in US) ⓦ www.expedia.ca (in Canada)
ⓦ www.lastminute.com (in UK)
ⓦ www.opodo.co.uk (in UK)
ⓦ www.orbitz.com (in US)
ⓦ www.travelocity.co.uk (in UK) ⓦ www .travelocity.com (in US) ⓦ www.travelocity.ca (in Canada)
ⓦ www.zuji.com.au (in Australia) ⓦ www .zuji.co.nz (in New Zealand)

Airlines

Air Canada ☎ 1-888/247-2262, UK ☎ 0871/220 1111, Republic of Ireland ☎ 01/679 3958, Australia ☎ 1300/655 767, New Zealand ☎ 0508/747 767; ⓦ www.aircanada.com. Flights from most Canadian airports to a European hub, with onward connections to Sofia.
Air France US ☎ 1-800/237-2747, Canada ☎ 1-800/667-2747, UK ☎ 0870/142 4343, Australia ☎ 1300/390 190, SA ☎ 0861/340 340;

Ⓦwww.airfrance.com. One- and two-stop flights from North America and Australia to Sofia via Paris.

Air New Zealand Australia ☎13 24 76, New Zealand ☎0800/737 000, UK ☎0800/028 4149, USA ☎1800-262/1234, Canada ☎1800-663/5494; Ⓦwww.airnz.co.nz. Daily flights from Auckland to London via Los Angeles, then onward connections to Sofia.

Alitalia US ☎1-800/223-5730, Canada ☎1-800/361-8336, UK ☎0870/544 8259, Republic of Ireland ☎01/677 5171, New Zealand ☎09/308 3357, SA ☎11/721 4500; Ⓦwww.alitalia.com. Flights from UK and North American airports to Sofia, with a change of plane in Rome or Milan.

Austrian Airlines US ☎1-800/843-0002, Canada ☎1888-8174/444, UK ☎0870/124 2625, Republic of Ireland ☎1800/509 142, Australia ☎1800/642 438 or 02/9251 6155; Ⓦwww.aua.com. One-stop flights from UK, North American and Australian airports to Bulgaria via Vienna.

British Airways US and Canada ☎1-800/AIRWAYS, UK ☎0870/850 9850, Republic of Ireland ☎1890/626 747, Australia ☎1300/767 177, New Zealand ☎09/966 9777, South Africa ☎114/418 600; Ⓦwww.ba.com. Direct flights from London Heathrow and London Gatwick to Sofia, with connections from North America and Australia.

Bulgaria Air UK ☎020/7637 7637, Ⓦwww.air.bg. Direct flights from London Gatwick to Sofia, with onward connections to Burgas and Varna.

Cathay Pacific US ☎1-800/233-2742, Canada ☎1-800/2686-868, UK ☎020/8834 8888, Australia ☎13 17 47, New Zealand ☎09/379 0861, South Africa ☎11/700 8900; Ⓦwww.cathaypacific.com. Flights from Australia and New Zealand to Hong Kong, with onward connections to major European hubs then Sofia.

CSA (Czech Airlines) US ☎1-800/223-2365, Canada ☎416/363-3174, UK ☎0870/444 3747, Republic of Ireland ☎0818/200 014, Australia ☎61/82480 000; Ⓦwww.czechairlines.co.uk Flights from Dublin, London, Manchester, New York, Toronto and Washington to Sofia via Prague.

EasyJet UK ☎0905/821 0905, Ⓦwww.easyjet.com. Daily flights from London Gatwick to Sofia.

LOT (Polish Airlines) US ☎212/789-0970, Canada ☎616/236-4242, UK ☎0845/601 0949, Republic of Ireland ☎1890/359 568, Australia ☎02/9244 2466, New Zealand ☎09/308 3369; Ⓦwww.lot.com. Flights from Chicago, New York and Toronto to Sofia via Warsaw.

Lufthansa US ☎1-800/399-5838, Canada ☎1-800/563-5954, UK ☎0870/837 7747, Republic of Ireland ☎01/844 5544, Australia ☎1300/655 727, New Zealand ☎0800-945 220, SA ☎0861/842 538; Ⓦwww.lufthansa.com. Indirect flights to Sofia from Belfast, Dublin, London and Manchester, changing planes in Frankfurt or another German hub. Also flights from North America and Australia to Frankfurt with onward connections to Sofia.

Malev Hungarian Airlines US ☎1-212/566-9944, Canada ☎1-416/944 0093, UK ☎0870/909 0577, Republic of Ireland ☎01/844 4303; Ⓦwww.malev.hu. Flights from London, New York and Toronto to Sofia and Varna via Budapest.

Qantas US and Canada ☎1-800/227-4500, UK ☎0845/774 7767, Republic of Ireland ☎01/407 3278, Australia ☎13 13 13, New Zealand ☎0800/808 767 or 09/357 8900, SA ☎11/441 8550; Ⓦwww.qantas.com. Flights from Australia (with connections from New Zealand) to a European hub with onward connections to Sofia.

Thomas Cook Airlines UK ☎0870/750 5711, Ⓦwww.thomascook.com. Flights from regional UK airports to Varna and Burgas. May–Sept only.

United Airlines US ☎1-800/UNITED-1, UK ☎0845/844 4777, Australia ☎13 17 77; Ⓦwww.united.com. One- or two-stop flights from most American cities to major European hubs, with onward connections to Sofia.

Virgin Atlantic US ☎1-800/821-5438, UK ☎0870/380 2007, Australia ☎1300/727 340, SA ☎11/340 3400; Ⓦwww.virgin-atlantic.com. Flights from Los Angeles, Miami, New York and Washington to London, where you can pick up flights to Sofia with another airline.

Wizzair ☎+48 22/351 9499 and +36 1/470 9499, Ⓦwww.wizzair.com. London Luton to Sofia and Burgas.

Zoom US & Canada ☎1-866/359 9666, Ⓦwww.flyzoom.com.Flights from New York and various Canadian cities to London Gatwick.

Flight agents

ebookers UK ☎0800/082 3000, Republic of Ireland ☎01/488 3507; Ⓦwww.ebookers.com, Ⓦwww.ebookers.ie. Low fares on an extensive selection of scheduled flights and package deals.

North South Travel UK ☎01245/608 291, Ⓦwww.northsouthtravel.co.uk. Friendly, competitive travel agency, offering discounted fares worldwide. Profits are used to support projects in the developing world, especially the promotion of sustainable tourism.

Trailfinders UK ☎0845/058 5858, Republic of Ireland ☎01/677 7888, Australia ☎1300/780 212; Ⓦwww.trailfinders.com. One of the best-informed and most efficient agents for independent travellers.

STA Travel US ☎1-800/781-4040, UK ☎0871/230 0040, Australia ☎134 STA,

New Zealand ☏ 0800/474 400, SA ☏ 0861/781 781; ⓦ www.statravel.com. Worldwide specialists in independent travel; also student IDs, travel insurance, car rental, rail passes and more. Good discounts for students and those under 26.

Package deals

The most popular packages to Bulgaria are beach holidays on the Black Sea coast, or winter skiing trips in highland resorts. The **season** for summer packages runs from mid-May to late September, peaking in the first two weeks of August. The winter season runs from December to March, peaking in mid-February.

There are also a number of other options: Balkan Holidays arranges numerous **two-centre trips**, combining coastal and mountain resorts, Bulgarian and Romanian, or Bulgarian and Turkish destinations, as well as fly-drive holidays with pre-booked accommodation. East-European specialists Regent Holidays can arrange **city breaks** in Sofia, tailoring a flight-plus-accommodation deal to your needs. If you'd rather travel with a group, **tours** covering the highlights of Bulgaria in eight to ten days are a good option; operators such as Abercrombie and Kent and Worldwide Adventures Abroad offer trips in the £1000–1500 per person range.

Beach holidays

The drawback to package holidays on the Black Sea coast is the nature of the principal **resorts**. The purpose-built complexes are often over-large and some distance from the nearest town or village, ensuring that you experience little of Bulgarian life. Beaches, however, are generally spotless, and coastal waters warm, clean and safe. **Sunny Beach** (Slanchev bryag) and **Golden Sands** (Zlatni pyasatsi) are the biggest (and most soulless) of the complexes, chock-full of restaurants, bars and discos, while **Albena** is almost as huge but marginally more stylish, with excellent sports facilities. **Sveti Konstantin, Sunny Day** and **Riviera** are smaller, and come surrounded by woodlands and coves. You could also stay in the former fishing ports of **Balchik**, **Nesebar** or **Sozopol**, either in a hotel or an apartment.

Balkan Holidays is the main tour operator offering summer beach packages, although

there are plenty of other operators to choose from. Peak-season prices for holidays in the main resorts hover around £450–550 for one week, £600–700 for two, though prices can be £150–200 lower in May and September.

Skiing holidays

The purpose-built resorts of Borovets and Pamporovo are the most popular destinations with package-tour operators. Both offer good intermediate **skiing** in beautiful pine-shrouded surroundings, but neither offers a proper town centre with historic sights or shops. Bansko in the Pirin range offers more in the way of advanced skiing and is a handsome historic town to boot – although thanks to a recent boom in construction work, it is no longer the charming spot it once was.

While skiing rules, **snowboarding** is increasingly popular at the three main resorts. The **cost** of the packages depends on the date (Christmas, New Year and mid-Feb are the most expensive times), the type and standard of accommodation (hotel or chalet), and fees for lessons, equipment and lift passes. Expect to pay £600 for seven nights in mid-February, £400 in late March. Lift passes (£90) and equipment rental (£100) will cost extra.

Specialist holidays

The Rila, Pirin and Rhodope mountains offer great opportunities for **hiking**, and seven- or fourteen-day itineraries offered by adventure specialists like Exodus and Explore Worldwide usually offer a taste of the terrain in all three ranges, with cosy accommodation in rustic guesthouses and B&Bs. Hiking tours are available from May to September; the same tour operators offer snowshoeing tours in winter, which involve trekking across the mountain snowfields in specially designed footwear. Expect to pay £600 upwards for six to seven days of hiking or snowshoeing.

Bulgaria's spectacular bird life is the subject of **ornithological tours** run by several specialist companies. Since some do only one trip a year, it's vital to book well ahead. The amenities can be fairly basic despite the cost (from £1000 for ten days), but you can be sure of fantastic bird life and expert guides.

Cultural tours, accompanied by expert lecturers, are offered by ACE Study Tours and Andante. While Melnik, Rila, Plovdiv and Koprivshtitsa invariably feature on the itineraries, other sites vary. These tours are slightly pricier than birdwatching ones, but the amenities are superior.

If your heart is set on a particular activity-based or special-interest holiday not offered by any of the UK-based companies, consider booking your own flight to Sofia and asking a Bulgarian specialist agent to tailor your trip (see "Tour operators in Bulgaria" on p.35).

Tour operators

ACE Study Tours UK ☎01223/835055, ⊛www.acestudytours.co.uk. Two-week study tours of monasteries and natural beauty spots.

Adventure Center US ☎1-800/228-8747, ⊛www.adventurecenter.com. Eight-day summer hiking tours and winter snowshoeing tours around the Vitosha and Rila mountains.

Adventure Company UK ☎0845/450 5316, ⊛www.adventurecompany.co.uk. Summer hiking tours and winter snowshoeing or skiing holidays.

Avian Adventures UK ☎01384/372013, ⊛www.avianadventures.co.uk. Eight-day birdwatching tours of the Black Sea coast and Danube wetlands.

Balkan Holidays UK reservations ☎0845/130 1114, itinerary enquiries ☎020/7543 5569, ⊛www.balkanholidays.co.uk. Wide range of beach, skiing, and mountain and lake holidays; multi-country tours (Bulgaria with Romania or Turkey); plus flight-only deals and special-interest tours for independent travellers.

Balkan Travel & Tours US ☎212/594 900 or 1-800/822 1106, ⊛www.balkan-travel.com. Various seven- and ten-day tours to the major historical sights, and tailor-made arrangements for individual tourists.

Balkania Travel UK ☎020/7636 8338, ⊛www.bbfs.org.uk. Travel arm of the British-Bulgarian Friendship Society, offering birdwatching, cultural and other special-interest tours led by local experts.

Birdwatching Breaks UK ☎01381/610495, ⊛www.birdwatchingbreaks.com. Eight-day birdwatching tours with expert guides.

Cox and Kings UK ☎020/7873 5006, ⊛www.coxandkings.co.uk. Eight-day cultural tours.

Cross-Culture US ☎1-800/491 1148, ⊛www.ccjourneys.com. Nine-day tours combining Bulgaria and Romania.

Crystal Holidays UK ☎0870/405 5047, ⊛www.crystalski.co.uk. Ski packages to Borovets and Pamporovo.

Eastern Eurotours Australia ☎1800/242 353 or 07/5526 2855, ⊛www.easterneurotours.com.au. Flights, hotel accommodation, city breaks and guided tours.

Elderhostel US ☎1-800/454 5768, ⊛www.elderhostel.org. Two-week art and history tour for senior travellers.

Exodus UK ☎0870/240 5550, ⊛www.exodus.co.uk. Ten-day Rhodope Mountains tour incorporating easy hikes.

Explore Worldwide UK ☎0870/333 4001, ⊛www.explore.co.uk. Summer hiking in the Rhodope mountains and winter snowshoeing tours.

First Choice UK ☎0871/200 7799, ⊛www.firstchoice.co.uk. Ski packages to Bansko, Borovets and Pamporovo.

Inghams UK ☎020/8780 4433, ⊛www.inghams.co.uk. Ski packages to Bansko, Borovets and Pamporovo.

Isram World of Travel US ☎1-800/223-7460, ⊛www.isram.com. City breaks in Sofia.

Limosa Holidays UK ☎01263/578143, ⊛www.limosaholidays.co.uk. Offers an eleven-day birdwatching tour featuring the Rhodopes, Black Sea coast and Danube wetlands.

Mountain Travel Sobek ⊛www.mtsobek.com. Ten-day hiking trips in the Rila, Pirin and Rhodope ranges.

Naturetrek UK ☎01962/733051, ⊛www.naturetrek.co.uk. Eight-day spring and autumn birdwatching tours, plus summer tours concentrating on mountain flora and butterflies.

Neilson UK ☎0870/333 3356, ⊛www.neilson.co.uk. Ski packages to Borovets and Bansko.

Ornitholidays UK ☎01794/519445, ⊛www.ornitholidays.co.uk. Eight days' birdwatching in the autumn.

Quest Tours and Adventures US ☎1-800/621 8687, ⊛www.romtour.com. Seven-day tours of Bulgaria, and two-week Romania-Bulgaria combinations.

Ramblers Holidays UK ☎01707/331133, ⊛www.ramblersholidays.co.uk. Two-week mountains and monasteries tour covering the Rila and Pirin regions.

Regent Holidays UK ☎0845/277 3317, ⊛www.regent-holidays.co.uk. City breaks and tailor-made holidays from a long-standing eastern Europe specialist.

Walking Softly Adventures US ☎1-888/743 0723, ⊛www.wsadventures.com. Ten-day hiking tours in the Rila and Pirin ranges.

Worldwide Adventures Abroad UK ☎0114/247 3400, US ☎1-800/665 3998, ⊛www.adventures-abroad.com. Eight-day highlights of

Bulgaria tour, or two-week trips combining Bulgaria and Romania.

Tour operators in Bulgaria

Arkan Tours 4002 Plovdiv, Lerin 7A Str ☎ 359 32/640 205, ⓦ www.arkantours.com. Specialist in horse riding and cultural tours in the Sredna Gora region.

Lyuba Tours 1164 Sofia, ul. Tsanko Tserkovski 22 ☎ 359 2/963 3343, ⓦ www.lyubatours .com. Specialist in one- and two-day, small-group excursions from Sofia (check the website for current schedule), focusing on folk celebrations, archeology, and ethnographically interesting rural areas that

are difficult to get to independently. Can also fix up tailor-made cultural itineraries for groups.

Pandion 1421 Sofia, ul. Cherni Vrah 20A ☎ 359 2/963 0436, ⓦ www.birdwatchingholidays.com. All-inclusive trips with a birdwatching theme.

Penguin 1421 Sofia, ul. Orfey 9 ☎ 359 2/400 1050, ⓦ www.penguin.bg. Activity holidays, cultural tours and accommodation bookings.

Zig-Zag/Odysseia-In 1301 Sofia, bul. Stamboliiski 20-V ☎ 359 2/980 5102, ⓦ www .zigzagbg.com. Bulgaria's leading adventure tourism agency, offering all kinds of individual and group hiking tours, hotel reservations, tailor-made arrangements and car hire.

Getting around

Despite run-down station buildings and antiquated vehicles, travel between Bulgaria's major cities is reasonably cheap and comfortable. However, Bulgarian transport remains pretty slow by western European standards, a failing compounded by Bulgaria's mountainous terrain and climatic extremes (which rapidly degrade tarmac), with train journeys between the north and south being particularly prone to roundabout routes and changes.

Timetable boards *(razpisanie)* displayed in train and bus stations are invariably written in Cyrillic only, and in some provincial bus stations may not be visible at all – departure details are instead scribbled on a piece of paper stuck to the window of the ticket office. Usually, arrivals *(pristigane)* are listed on one side, and departures *(tragvane* or *zaminavane)* on the other. To make things easier we've included a rundown of regional transport under the "Travel Details" at the end of each chapter.

By train

Bulgarian State Railways *(BDZh)* can get you to most towns mentioned in this book, although trains are very slow by Western standards and delays are common on the longer routes. Intercity *(intersiti)* and express *(ekspresen vlak)* services only operate on the

main trunk routes, but on everything except the humblest branch lines you'll find so-called rapid *(barz vlak)* trains. Use these rather than the snail-like *patnicheski* (ПЪТНИЧЕСКИ; literally "passenger train", but meaning "slow" in this context) services unless you're planning to alight at some particularly insignificant halt. Generally speaking, intercity services are the only ones that carry a buffet car, so if travelling on another type of train, make sure you have enough food and drink for the journey. On timetables, the four types of services are indicated by the **abbreviations** ИС, ЕБ, Б and П express services are usually lettered in red. A **reservation** *(zapazeno myasto*; about 1Lv in addition to the basic ticket price) is compulsory on intercity and express services, and advisable for all other trains if you're travelling on summer weekends. You might

Cyrillic checklist: getting around

Bulgarian State Railways	БДЖ	Slow service	ПЪТНИЧЕСКИ ВЛАК
		Couchettes	КУШЕТ
Timetables	РАЗПИСАНИЕ	Sleepers	СПАЛЕН ВАГОН
Departures	ТРЪГВА (abbreviated to ТР or ЗАМИНАВАНЕ)	Left luggage office	ГАРДЕРОБ
		Bus station	АВТОГАРА
		Petrol station	БЕНЗИНОСТАНЦИЯ
Arrivals	ПРИСТИГАНЕ ПР	Petrol	БЕНЗИН
Tickets	БИЛЕТИ	Motoring map	ПЪТНА КАРТА
National train timetable	ПЪТЕВОДИТЕЛ	Street	УЛ.
		Square	ПЛ.
Intercity service	ИНТЕРСИТИ	Boulevard	БУЛ.
Express service	ЕКСПРЕСЕН ВЛАК	Suburb	КВ.
Rapid service	БЪРЗ ВЛАК	Block	БЛ.

find yourself paying a hefty surcharge if you board a train without one.

Though a **national timetable** (*patevoditel*) is extremely useful for frequent train travellers, the chances of obtaining one are slim, as they're snapped up immediately after publication each May. If you do get hold of a copy, note that trains running on a particular day only are indicated by a number in a circle (for example, 1 = Monday, 2 = Tuesday, and so forth). International services are printed in the Roman alphabet, rather than Cyrillic.

Long-distance/overnight trains have a wagon with reasonably priced **couchettes** (*kushet reitn*) and/or **sleepers** (*spalen vagon*). At the time of writing you can travel from Sofia to Varna by sleeper for under 40Lv/€20, which probably works out cheaper than a night's accommodation. In order to secure a bed on the train, you need to reserve a day or two in advance, and, if possible, at least a week in advance in July or August.

Commonly, a single sign halfway down the platform is all that identifies a **station** (*gara*). If you're sitting at the back, you won't see this until the train starts up again, so try to sit up front. Most stations have a **left-luggage office** (*garderob*); in the large ones you may need to complete a form before stowing your gear.

Passes

Unless you've already bought a rail pass (see p.29) to get to Bulgaria, buying a train pass to travel around the country makes little sense. Indeed, the only one currently on offer is the **Inter-Rail One/Freedom Pass**, which must be bought before you travel and allows for three, four, six or eight days' travel within any given month, but its cost (an eight-day pass will cost £112/€165/US$213 first class, £82/€120/US$156 second class or £54/€78 /US$103 for second class for those under 26) will almost certainly exceed what you'd spend on fares without a pass – especially given that many destinations in Bulgaria can only be reached by bus.

Inter Rail One/Freedom passes are available from Rail Europe in the UK and North America; see p.30 for contact details.

Buying tickets

Bulgaria's main **intercity routes** are very busy in summer and at weekends throughout the year. It is wise – if not always essential – to **book** a day or two in advance; otherwise you'll probably have to spend the journey standing in the carriage corridor. In many large towns, it's possible to **buy tickets** (*bileti*) and make advance reservations at **railway booking offices**, listed in the appropriate places in this guide. Tickets can also be bought at the station just before travel (in out-of-the-way places, a ticket window will only open a few minutes before the train is due). If you arrive at a station too late to queue up and buy a ticket, you can **pay on the train** itself, albeit with a surcharge of thirty to forty percent.

International tickets

International tickets are handled by a separate organization, the Rila Agency, whose main office is in Sofia at ul. General Gurko 5 (℡02/987 0777). Although cities like Sofia and Ruse have international ticket counters in the stations (so you can buy a ticket immediately before travel if you're pressed for time), more often, Rila offices are located some distance away from stations, and you'll need to make sure you buy your ticket well in advance. We've given addresses where appropriate in this guide.

Generally speaking, **prices** of tickets to Romania, Hungary, Greece and Turkey are quite reasonable (at the time of writing, a one-way ticket from Sofia to Bucharest costs about 60Lv/€30), but increase significantly if travelling to western Europe.

By bus

In many parts of Bulgaria it's necessary – or easier – to travel by **bus** (avtobus), especially in the Rhodopes and the Pirin, where few of the attractions are accessible by train. Each town of any size has a bus station (avtogara), or sometimes more; buses departing in different directions may well use different terminals (as detailed in this guide). Some **bus companies** operate a fleet of comfortable vehicles with air conditioning, while others – especially those in rural areas – use ancient contraptions that look as if they belong in a museum. On some routes, minibuses are used, in which case seats run out fast, so it's a good idea to arrive early.

Buying tickets

As a general rule, tickets are sold from the ticket counter until five minutes before departure, although it's advisable to buy them an hour or two in advance if travelling on a route serving major towns, especially during summer or at weekends. Note that if you're catching a **bus that originates elsewhere**, tickets are only sold when the bus arrives, in which case you need to queue outside the shuttered ticket hatch. On **rural routes**, tickets are often sold by the driver rather than at the terminal. If you're aiming for a campsite or monastery along a bus route, ask the driver for the spirkata za kampinga (or manastira), or call Spri! ("Stop!") as it comes into sight.

City buses

On **urban transport** – trams and buses in Sofia, buses and trolleybuses everywhere else – there's usually a **flat fare** (seldom more than 0.80Lv/€0.40) on all routes. In Sofia, **tickets** are bought beforehand and then punched in a machine on board, so it's sensible to buy a bunch of ten tickets (from street kiosks next to tram and bus stops) as soon as you arrive. Fare dodgers pay a spot fine. Elsewhere in Bulgaria, tickets are sold by an onboard conductor. Routes are sometimes displayed on each bus stop (spirka) together with the times of the first and last services, but many of these signs are so old that it's best to check with the locals before jumping aboard. In some regions, private companies operate, so on a few routes you'll encounter a plethora of different coloured buses and minibuses, identifiable only by a scribbled route number posted on the windscreen.

International buses

A plethora of private companies offer **international bus services** connecting Bulgaria's main towns and cities with neighbouring countries and further afield. As you'd expect, the main point of departure is Sofia – from where you can reach any country in southern and central Europe – but there are also several regional towns where you can pick up a bus to Turkey, Greece, Macedonia or Albania. Tickets are priced in leva or euros, but you can pay in most currencies at the prevailing rate of exchange. Details appear in the relevant section of this guide.

By taxi

Providing you don't get ripped off, **taxis** are a reasonably priced and useful way of getting around in towns and cities, or reaching places that aren't accessible by public transport. All licensed taxis are metered, and generally charge about 0.60Lv/€0.30 initially, plus 0.70Lv/€0.35 per kilometre thereafter during the day (twice as much at night), except for taxis on the Black Sea coast, whose rates are three to four times higher (though city taxis in Varna and Burgas charge normal rates). The minority of taxi drivers out to take advantage of foreigners tend to hang around airports, major train stations and city centre hotels, so it's best to go looking for a taxi elsewhere if you have the option. We've given phone numbers of some reputable taxi firms in the relevant sections of this guide, though it is unlikely that anyone on the other end of the line will speak English.

By car

Foreigners may drive in Bulgaria using their national **driving licence** (though, should you stay longer than six months, it must be translated and legalized). As **car theft** is endemic and Bulgaria is a major transit route for stolen vehicles, drivers bringing their own car should be sure to carry their log book (and make photocopies of it), and take every precaution against the documents and the vehicle being stolen. Use guarded parking lots wherever possible, and never leave vehicles on side streets unless fitted with wheel locks and immobilizers.

In order to drive on Bulgarian roads outside cities, towns and villages, drivers must pay a kind of **road tax** by purchasing a windscreen sticker or vignette (*vinyetka*), which is available at border points, post offices and petrol stations belonging to the Shell and OMV chains. A vignette for a car (either on its own or with a trailer) costs 10Lv/€5 for one week, 25Lv/€12.50 for one month, or 67Lv/€33.50 for one year. Note that a vignette is not necessary if all you want to do is drive around within the Sofia city limits – but possession of one is compulsory once you hit the open road.

Fuel, maps and signs

Petrol (*benzin*) in Bulgaria – cheaper than in Britain and western Europe, and more expensive than in the USA – can sometimes be hard to find. Although you'll find 24-hour **filling stations** (*benzinostantsiya*) equipped with shops and cafés on the main road exits from most large towns, and spaced 30–40km apart along the highways, they're few and far between once you get off the beaten track, so fill up wherever you can.

Names signposted along the main highways appear in both alphabets, and although the system of transliteration is not always the same as the one used in this guide, they're recognizably similar. Signs on main routes in and out of major cities are frequently misleading or contradictory, so you should expect to get lost at least once during the course of the day. In rural areas, signs are often in Cyrillic only and in many cases completely non-existent.

Roads, traffic and speed limits

Roads in Bulgaria tend to be inconsistently numbered (some highways carry two or three designations), and even trunk routes (marked in red on maps) have the same bumpy, potholed surfaces as the minor roads (indicated in yellow). There are stretches of **dual carriageway** (*magistrala*) between Sofia and Plovdiv, Sofia and Pravets, and Shumen and Varna, but travel is pretty slow going elsewhere. If following the main Sofia–Burgas, Sofia–Varna, Sofia–Vidin, Sofia–Kulata or Plovdiv–Kapitan Andreevo routes, expect to be stuck behind long files of slow-moving freight **traffic** for large stretches of the journey. Traffic on other routes can be very light, but a combination of poor road manners and abysmal surface quality should prevent you from getting anywhere quickly. Potholes, farm carts, meandering cyclists and wandering animals are regular hazards on country roads. Reckless overtaking is habitual among local drivers – particularly unnerving if you are approaching in the oncoming lane. Inadequate lighting and poor lane markings make night driving something of an adventure.

In urban areas buses have the right of way and parking is restricted to specified spots. **Speed limits** in built-up areas (60kph), on the open road (80kph), and highways (130kph) are reduced to 50kph, 70kph or 100kph for minibuses or cars with caravans or trailers.

If you see a police car approaching in your rear mirror, you are required to move over and let it pass whether it is flashing its lights or not.

Accidents, fines and theft

Motorists are legally obliged to report **accidents** and, in case of injury, render assistance where appropriate while waiting for the police (*Politsiya*). **Spot fines** for trivial offences are common practice; traffic police will frequently invent an arbitrary sum before pocketing the cash. Requests for a receipt might put a stop to this – or make things worse. If an oncoming vehicle flashes its lights at you, it is probably intended as a warning that a police patrol is waiting round the corner. It is illegal to drive with more than **0.05 milligrams of alcohol** in the blood, roughly equivalent to a pint and a half of beer or two small glasses of wine.

In the event of being in an accident or having your car stolen, the **bureaucratic procedures** are nightmarish. You will need a police report (which can take two to three days) that must be taken to the local prosecutor's office for stamping (involving another delay), and then be stamped by the local customs office, which may insist that the document is authorized by the regional office in another town. All this is done in Bulgarian, so unless you're lucky enough to find an official who speaks English, there is also the cost of hiring an interpreter to consider, not to mention accommodation costs and other related expenses for the duration. If the vehicle was brought into Bulgaria you won't be allowed to leave the country without it, even if the car is a total write-off.

Car rental

Most major international car **rental agencies** are present in Bulgaria, alongside numerous local firms. Most Bulgarian travel agents act as representatives for one firm or another; you'll also find car rental desks in the lobbies of big hotels. The big international firms offer the widest choice of new cars, but also charge the highest rates: expect to pay 100Lv/€50 a day for a small economy car for a period of five to seven days; more if you only require it for a day or two. Older (but still perfectly serviceable) cars offered by local firms work out significantly cheaper. Most local firms have smaller fleets however, and may not be able to provide the vehicle you want unless you book well in advance.

You can cut out much of the hassle of car hire by **booking in advance** from your home country with one of the major car rental companies (see below for contacts), or take advantage of some of the pre-booked car

rental deals offered by the package-holiday companies. Booked through a package company, a week with unlimited mileage in a Fiat Cinquecento can cost as little as 440Lv/€220 on the coast and 520Lv/€260 in the ski resorts.

Another option is to rent a car **with a driver**, relieving you of the worries associated with road use in a strange country. Any of the rental firms can oblige, or, if you have Bulgarian friends, it's relatively easy to find someone to drive you around for a negotiable sum. Making arrangements unofficially – or even with a regular taxi driver – you can probably get a car with a driver for 100Lv/€50 a day, plus petrol costs and any expenses if an overnight stay is required.

International car rental agencies

Avis US and Canada ☎1-800/331-1212, UK ☎0870/606 0100, Republic of Ireland ☎021/428 1111, Australia ☎13 63 33 or 02/9353 9000, New Zealand ☎09/526 2847 or 0800/655 111; ☎www.avis.com.
Budget US ☎1-800/527-0700, Canada ☎1-800/268-8900, UK ☎0870/156 5656, Australia ☎1300/362 848, New Zealand ☎0800/283 438, ☎www.budget.com.
Europcar US & Canada ☎1-877/940 6900, UK ☎0870/607 5000, Republic of Ireland ☎01/614 2800, Australia ☎393/306 160; ☎www.europcar.com.
Hertz US & Canada ☎1-800/654-3131, UK ☎020/7026 0077, Republic of Ireland ☎01/870 5777, New Zealand ☎0800/654 321; ☎www.hertz.com.
SIXT Republic of Ireland ☎1850/206 088, UK ☎0800/4747 4227, US ☎1-877/347-3227; ☎www.irishcarrentals.ie.

By air

There's little in the way of a domestic air network, with three daily flights from Sofia to Varna and one daily flight from Sofia to Burgas operated by Bulgaria Air (☎www.air.bg) the only services currently available. Given the length of the bus or train journey (six to eight hours), the one-hour flight to Varna or Burgas is worth considering, even though at around 300Lv/€150 return it works out six times more expensive.

Accommodation

A recent boom in hotel building has ensured that the main cities and resorts now offer a wide choice of accommodation in all categories. Things can be more unpredictable in the provinces, although the growth in rural B&Bs means that you can always find a cosy and characterful place to sleep if you know where to look. Backpacker-friendly hostels have mushroomed in Sofia and the major cities, although campsites are limited in number and tend towards the basic.

All accommodation in Bulgaria is rated according to the international five-star system, although this is not always an accurate guide to quality. Some perfectly cosy budget hotels have been given a one-star grading simply because their rooms are oddly shaped or the lobby area is on the small side. The four-star category on the other hand is far too broad, embracing rather ordinary establishments alongside quite luxurious places. Throughout this guide we have based our accommodation recommendations on factors such as atmosphere, comfort and value for money rather than on any star rating.

Hotels

Hotels in Bulgaria come in all shapes and sizes. Every sizeable town possesses a grey concrete hotel dating from the Communist period, and though most of these have been renovated in the last few years, a number still display their original dull brown colour schemes and threadbare carpets. Big seaside resorts such as Golden Sands and Sunny Beach date from the Communist period too. Generally speaking, if a hotel has a one- or two-star rating it probably means that it is largely unrenovated, while a rating of three stars or above suggests that it has been brought up to Western standards.

There has also been a lot of new building, with a broad range of modern **business-oriented hotels** popping up in the cities, and **resort complexes** comprising hotel rooms, apartments and swimming pools appearing on the coast and in the inland skiing resorts. Hotels featuring gyms, saunas and beauty-treatment facilities are becoming the norm in the cities and on the coast, although style-conscious boutique hotels are still something of a novelty in Bulgaria. Well-touristed areas do however feature many small-sized, family-run hotels, often offering a cosier, friendlier vibe than the bigger establishments. **Standards of service** remain unpredictable in all areas of the hotel market.

Staff who can be helpful and enthusiastic one day can turn truculent and uncommunicative the next.

Most hotels of three stars or above will have Western-style bathrooms with shower cubicles or bathtubs. Hotels in lower categories are more likely to have Bulgarian-style open showers, in which water splashes over everything else in the bathroom and drains down a central hole.

The **going rate** for a no-frills double room in a two-star hotel is 60–90Lv/€30–45. A double with minibar and air conditioning could set you back anywhere between 80–160Lv/€40–80. Doubles in big-city business-class hotels start at about 200Lv/€100. **Reservations** are essential when visiting well-touristed areas in season, and are a good idea all year in Sofia and Plovdiv.

Spa hotels

Recent years have seen a huge increase in the number of establishments describing themselves as "spa hotels". In most cases this simply means that they offer indoor swimming pool, massage facilities and a range of cosmetic treatments, and as such they can be great places in which to indulge in a bit of pampering. If you want to cultivate your health as well as your vanity, however, then there are plenty of **genuine**

Cyrillic checklist: accommodation

Accommodation bureau	КВАРТИРНО БЮРО
Campsite	КАМПИНГ
Hostel	ТУРИСТИЧЕСКА СПАЛНЯ
Hotel	ХОТЕЛ
Mountain hut	ХИЖА
Private rooms	ЧАСТНИ КВАРТИРИ
Rest-home	ПОЧИВНА СТАНЦИЯ or ПОЧИВЕН ДОМ

spa hotels – many of which are of very high quality – in towns famous for their medicinal waters, such as Velingrad (see p.357), Hisarya (p.282), Sandanski (p.156), and Kyustendil (p.120).

Guesthouses and B&Bs

Family-run **guesthouses** (*kashta za gosti*) are springing up all over Bulgaria, and in many cases offer some of the most characterful and atmospheric accommodation you are likely to find in the country. Most are in the highland areas and rural villages, although they also exist in the cities, where they might occupy a converted flat in an apartment block rather than an actual house.

The guesthouses differ greatly in terms of quality. Some are frugally furnished affairs occupying undistinguished buildings, while others – especially those that occupy well-preserved villages houses – have gone overboard with folksy furnishings and traditional fabrics. In heritage villages such as Koprivshtitsa, Kovachevitsa and Zheravna, you may well be padding about on hand-woven kilims and bedding down under sheepskin rugs. The more upmarket guesthouses offer en-suite rooms with modern bathrooms and maybe a TV, whereas elsewhere shared facilities are the rule. Almost everywhere you will receive a warm welcome, and – in the rural areas at least – locally sourced food and drink.

Expect to pay 50–60Lv/€25–30 for a double room in most rural guesthouses, slightly more in elegantly renovated historical farmhouses or in big cities. Some guesthouses serve breakfast only, although there are plenty that provide delicious home-cooked lunches and dinners for an additional price.

Private rooms

Private rooms (*chastni kvartiri*) are available along the coast and in picturesque highland villages. Usually this involves staying with a local elderly woman who will provide you with a simply furnished room with a shared bathroom in the hallway. Some hostesses shower their guests with friendliness and hospitality, although most will simply hand you the room keys and leave you to your own devices. They can sometimes be booked through local tourist offices or travel agents, although in the many cases where these don't exist, **vacancies** are advertised by hanging a sign in the window reading *kvartiri* or *stayi* ("rooms"). Private rooms rarely cost more than 20Lv/€10 per person. Breakfast isn't usually included, although the friendlier landladies may well provide it for a few extra leva.

Accommodation price codes

All accommodation in this book has been categorized according to the following **price codes**. The prices quoted are for the cheapest double room in high season, inclusive of tax Accommodation prices in Bulgaria are often quoted in euros, although you can always pay in local currency.

- ❶ under 30Lv/€15
- ❷ 30–50Lv/€15–25
- ❸ 50–70Lv/€25–35
- ❹ 70–90Lv/€35–45
- ❺ 90–120Lv/€45–60
- ❻ 120–150Lv/€60–75
- ❼ 150–200Lv/€75–100
- ❽ 200–300Lv/€100–150
- ❾ over 300Lv/€150

Hostels

Ten years ago Bulgaria couldn't muster a single backpacker-friendly hostel, yet now there are at least a dozen in central Sofia alone and the number is rising. With the provincial cities of Plovdiv, Veliko Tarnovo and Varna each boasting a handful too, it is now possible to traverse the country on a budget and swap tales with other travellers while you're at it. **Hostels** are usually located in converted flats in downtown apartment blocks, and typically feature bunk-bed dorms, although many establishments offer double or triple rooms as well. Some form of breakfast is usually available, and most have a communal kitchen. The going rate for a bed is 20Lv/€10, slightly more if you're sleeping in a double room.

Old-fashioned "**tourist dormitories**" (*turisticheska spalnya*), run by the Bulgarian Tourist Union, still exist in some towns and villages. Here you'll be offered a rickety bunk in a large dorm, and facilities will be on the simple side. Prices range from 10–15Lv /€5–7.50 per person; contact the Bulgarian Tourist Union (Balgarski Turisticheski Sayuz) at 1000 Sofia, bul. Vasil Levski 75 (☎02/873409) for details.

Campsites, mountain huts and monasteries

While most towns of interest once had a **campsite** (*kamping*) on their outskirts, many have now closed down or face an uncertain future, and it is only on the coast and in a handful of highland areas that they are still going strong. Most of these charge around 8–10Lv/€4–5 to pitch a tent, and also have two-person **bungalows** available for rent at around 20Lv/€10 a night. Note that many campsites close down in early September, as soon as the summer rush has slackened. **Camping rough** is technically illegal, although the authorities usually turn a blind eye, especially along wilder stretches of the Black Sea coast that have long been popular with tent-toting Sofians.

In highland areas favoured by hikers there are scores of **mountain huts** (*hizhi*), some primitive, others more like comfortable hotels. Costs at all but the most expensive will rarely come to more than 10–15Lv /€5–7.50 per night. Upon arrival you may have to wait for the custodian to turn up before being allocated a dorm bed. You can **reserve** beds in some parts of the country through local tourist offices or Zig-Zag in Sofia (see p.75).

The larger of Bulgaria's **monasteries** – notably Rila, Troyan and Bachkovo – provide accommodation for about 10–30Lv/€5–15 per person. The rooms are usually quite spartan, with a washbasin and maybe some form of heating, but not necessarily any hot water. Although you don't have to be an Orthodox Christian to stay in monasteries, the atmosphere remains one of spiritual retreat, so alcohol, cigarettes and late-night socializing are all frowned upon.

Food and drink

The backbone of Bulgarian cuisine is provided by the grilled meat dishes (meatballs, sausages and skewer-grilled kebabs) common to the Balkan peninsula. Pot-baked stews featuring chopped meats, vegetables and cheese help to add variety, while a rich diversity of fish and seafood is available on the coast. As you would expect from a country rich in agricultural produce, healthy salads and vegetable dishes form a major part of every restaurant menu. Bulgarian meals usually start with a stiff shot of local *rakiya* or brandy, and there is a wonderful variety of domestic wines to enjoy. Bulgarian yoghurt is famously healthy, containing beneficial bacteria unique to the region.

Bulgarian **food shops** (*hranitelni stoki*) are usually reasonably well-stocked with useful picnic ingredients: Bulgarian cheese comes as either *sirene* (salty white cheese similar to Greek feta) or the hard yellow *kashkaval*. *Kashkaval Vitosha* is made from cow's milk, *kashkaval Balkan* from ewe's milk. Traditional meat products include *pastarma* (a spicy beef salami) and *sudzhuk* and *lukanka* (flat home-cured sausages of either pork or beef). Although big-city supermarkets will offer a large choice, frequently alongside a range of imported delicatessen products, rural shops will be much more limited in choice.

A large choice of domestic and imported fruit and veg is available in the outdoor **markets** (*pazar*) that take place daily in town and village centres. Some towns have large **indoor markets** (*hali*) where stallholders offer a raft of delicatessen products. Bulgarian **bakeries** usually sell white bread (*hlyab*) although wholemeal and other speciality varieties are available in bigger supermarkets.

Breakfast, snacks, street food and pizzerias

Few restaurants or cafés offer a breakfast menu, and a typical **breakfast** for many locals tends to consist of an espresso coffee and a cigarette, followed by another round of the same if hunger still prevails. Most hotels and guesthouses provide a simple breakfast of the continental type, or a small buffet comprising ham, cheese and maybe some cereal. Otherwise, the most convenient places to pick up breakfast are street stalls and bakeries. The most common **Bulgarian snack food** is *banitsa*, a flaky pastry filled with white cheese. At its best, the *banitsa* is a delicious light bite, although it's invariably quite stodgy by the time it reaches the streets. *Mlechna banitsa* (literally "milk *banitsa*") is a richer, sweeter version made using eggs and dusted with icing sugar, while the *Rhodopska banitsa*, found only in the Rhodopes, is more like a soufflé filled with cheese. Equally popular is the *kifla*, a small bread roll usually made from slightly

Cyrillic checklist: eating and drinking

Bread	ХЛЯБ	Outdoor market	ПАЗАР
Breakfast/snack	ЗАКУСКИ	Supermarket	МАГАЗИН НА
Café	КАФЕНЕ		САМООбСЛУЖВАНЕ
Café-bar/	КАФЕ-АПЕРИТИФ	Patisserie	СЛАДКАРНИЦА
kafe-aperitiv		Restaurant	РЕСТОРАНТ
Folk restaurant	ХАН ХАНЧЕ	Self-service	ЕКСПРЕСРЕ-
Food shop	ХРАНИТЕЛНИ		СТОРАНТ
	СТОКИ	Skara-bira	СКАРА-БИЖРА
Indoor market, inn	ХАЛИ	Vegetarian	ВЕГЕТАРИАНСКИ
Mehana, tavern	МЕХАНА		

sweetened dough and with a vein of marmalade running through the middle, although you are more likely to encounter savoury variants, filled either with cheese (sas sirene), or a small hot-dog-type sausage (s krenvirsh). Similar is the sirenka, a small bread bun with a cheese filling.

Snacks such as these are typically washed down with one of two traditional **breakfast drinks**: yoghurt (kiselo mlyako); ayryan, a salty, water-diluted drinking yoghurt; and boza, a browny-coloured millet drink that tastes like liquidized breakfast cereal.

Bulgaria's **street-food scene** is dominated by grilled-meat snacks like kebabcheta (sausage-like cylinders of minced pork), and kyofteta (a burger-shaped wad of the same meat), sold from stalls in town centres, at bus stations and in busy markets. Often accompanied by a white bread bun and nothing else, they can be a cheap and filling way of enjoying local food – but are also the likeliest cause of an upset stomach on sweltering midsummer days.

The sandwiches (sandvichi) sold by most kiosks and street stalls tend towards the basic, although an increasing number of big-city cafés are beginning to offer the kind of deli sandwiches that compare favourably with Western equivalents. Pizzerias, together with kiosks offering pizza slices (pizza na parche), are a ubiquitous feature of any Bulgarian high street. Although they offer an effective, low-cost fill-up, Bulgarian pizzas don't always resemble their Italian originals, frequently featuring biscuity dough and locally inspired toppings (expect yellow kachkaval cheese instead of mozzarella, watery ham in place of prosciutto, and sliced gherkins taking the place of Mediterranean vegetables).

Restaurants and meals

Although **restaurants** (restorant) vary widely in terms of décor and service, the choice of food on offer is fairly standardized, with the same Bulgarian grills, pot-roasts and salads appearing on menus throughout the country. Restaurants dedicated to international, ethnic or speciality cuisine are on the increase in big cities and resorts, although they are hard to find elsewhere.

Smart restaurants with starched napkins and officious waiters are common in Sofia,

Black Sea resorts and in upscale hotels throughout the country. Elsewhere eating venues tend towards the informal. The most common type of eatery in Bulgaria is the **mehana** or tavern, which concentrates on a traditional repertoire of Balkan dishes, and usually features folksy touches such as embroidered tablecloths and brightly decorated tableware. The bigger mehanas frequently offer atmospheric courtyard seating and live music in the evening. Other traditional establishments that don't differ that much from a mehana are the **han** or **hanche** (literally "inn") and the krachma – a neighbourhood pub where food is served. In rural areas, a simple krachma selling beer and grilled food may be the only culinary option.

Restaurants offering French, Italian or international fusion cuisine are on the increase in Sofia and a handful of other cities, and there is also a boom in the number of stylish bar-restaurants which offer a full menu of modern European food alongside cocktails, contemporary furnishings and DJ-driven sounds. Standards are outstanding in some of these establishments, while others offer over-ambitious recipes that local kitchen staff are never quite capable of pulling off. Sofia can boast a clutch of worthwhile Armenian, Indian, Lebanese and Turkish restaurants; elsewhere, cheap and cheerful Chinese eateries provide the main source of ethnic food.

Restaurants and mehanas are usually **open** between about 11am and 11pm. Bar-restaurants in resort areas may keep going until the early hours, although hot food may only be served until around midnight. Wherever you eat, prices should be well below those charged in western Europe. The price of a main course in a mid-price restaurant or mehana can hover anywhere between 6Lv/€3 and 20Lv/€10 – the total outlay rather depends on how many extra dishes and drinks you order. You will pay more for a meal in the smattering of gourmet restaurants found in the capital and on the coast, although even here you will find a handful of economically priced dishes on the menu. For a glossary of food and dishes you'll find on a menu, see pp.479–481 of Contexts.

Soups, salads and starters

If you're looking for a quick and inexpensive stomach-filler, most restaurants and *mehanas* serve filling **soups** accompanied by copious amounts of bread. *Bob* (bean soup) and *tarator* (a refreshing cold soup made from yoghurt and cucumber) are the most common varieties, although *shkembe chorba* – the lip-smackingly spicy tripe soup which locals swear by as a hangover cure – should be tried at least once.

Salads in Bulgaria are usually composed of local vegetables, frequently organically grown and superior to Western supermarket produce in terms of flavour. Tomatoes (*domati*), cucumber (*krastavitsi*) and peppers (*piperki* or *chushki*) are the most common. *Shopska salata*, in which all of the above are topped with grated white cheese, is the classic salad order, often eaten as a starter or as the accompaniment to a stiff *rakiya*. Two yoghurt-based salads are *mlechna salata* (like *tarator* but thicker, with nuts) and *snezhanka* (pickled cucumbers covered in yoghurt). Other common starters are *parzheni chushki*, baked peppers; *lukanka*, a spicy salami-like sausage; and *sudzhuk*, a home-cured pork sausage. All of these make an excellent drink accompaniment.

Main courses

The mainstay of any Bulgarian restaurant or *mehana* menu is the **grilled meat**, of which *kebapcheta* and *kyufte* are the most common. More substantial are chops (*parzhola* or *kotlet*) or fillets (*file* or *kare*), which are invariably *teleshko* (veal), *svinsko* (pork) or *pileshko* (chicken). The same meats feature in skewer-grilled kebabs (*shishche*), which feature on the menus of the better *mehanas*. Most traditional *mehanas* also offer Bulgarian dishes baked and served in earthenware pots. The best known is **gyuveche** (which literally means "earthenware dish"), a rich stew of peppers, aubergines, and beans, to which is added diced meat (usualy pork or chicken). *Kavarma* is a spicy meat stew prepared in similar fashion. One other typical Bulgarian dish is **sache**, a metal plate loaded with chopped meat and vegetables and heated over a fire before being served sizzling to the table.

Restaurants along the coast excel in all kinds of **fish** (*riba*) – usually pan-fried or grilled – with *lefer* (bluefish), *palamud* (Black Sea bonito) and *skumriya* (mackerel) being among the most succulent. *Skumriya na keramidi* (literally "mackerel on a tile"), is baked in an earthenware container, usually with a rich tomato sauce. A plate of *tsatsa* (small white fish which are deep fried in batter and eaten whole) is a staple of coastal snack bars and goes down a treat with a cold beer. Locally farmed *midi* (mussels) are a genuine delicacy; most other forms of seafood on restaurant menus (including octopus, squid and prawns) are likely to be imported. Inland, trout (*pastarva*) and salmon (*syomga*) are the most common types of freshwater fish, although restaurants in the towns along the Danube offer a much wider range, including pan-fried fillets of *som* (catfish) and *sharan* (carp).

Main courses may be served with a set *garnitura* (usually fries and the occasional vegetable), although sometimes you'll find these items listed individually on the menu and will have to order them separately (always ask about this; otherwise you may end up being served a slab of meat or fish and nothing else). In the grander restaurants the main course will be accompanied by potatoes (*kartofi*) and a couple of vegetables. Note that bread is not always delivered directly to the table and you may have to order it specifically, indicating how many slices (*filiiki*) you want.

Vegetarian dishes

Little provision is made for vegetarians in Bulgarian restaurants, although it is always possible to improvise a meal by ordering two or three of the vegetable dishes listed on the menu as salads or starters. Fried or grilled mushrooms (*gabi* or *manatarki*), courgettes (*tikvichki*) or aubergines (*patlidzhan*) are the most common vegetable dishes, alongside peppers stuffed with egg and cheese and fried in breadcrumbs (*chushka byurek*).

Standard menus usually include an omelette (*omlet*), either with a cheese or mushroom filling, along with *kashkaval pane*, hard cheese fried in breadcrumbs or batter; *kartofi s sirene*, french fries with grated white cheese; *sirene po shopski*, cheese baked in an earthenware pot with a spicy tomato sauce; and *palneni chushki*, peppers stuffed with cheese. One popular meatless dish is *mishmash*, scrambled eggs with chopped peppers and tomatoes; and there's also a vegetarian version of the oven-baked stew *gyuveche* (ask for *postno gyuveche*). One dish indigenous to the Rhodope mountains is *patatnik*, mashed potato baked with cheese and herbs - although it is hard to find in the rest of the country.

When in doubt, use the phrase *postno yadene* (literally "fasting food") to ensure that you receive something that's genuinely meat-free.

Desserts

Typical desserts found on restaurant menus include pancakes (*palachinki*), often stuffed with jam; ice cream (*sladoled*) and seasonal fruits – melon (*papesh*) and watermelon (*dinya*) are particularly refreshing in summer. Bulgarian **yoghurt** (*kiselo mlyako*) is pretty ubiquitous, often served with honey or fruit preserve. The best restaurants will serve buffalo yoghurt (*bivolsko mlyako*) and sheep's milk yoghurt (*ovche mlyako*) as well as the regular cow's milk version. **Cakes** and **pastries** are sold throughout the day in a patisserie or *sladkarnitsa*. Many of Bulgaria's sweet dishes were originally imported from the Middle East by the Turks – the syrupy *baklava*, the nut-filled *revane*, and the gooey rich *kadaif* being the most common. Turkish Delight (*lokum*) and *halva* are also firm favourites. Betraying a more central European ancestry are the variety of cakes (*torta*), with buttercream (*maselna*), fruit (*frukti*) or chocolate (*shokoladova*) filling. *Garash*, a layered chocolate cake, is the most widely available.

Drinking

Daytime drinking takes place in a *kafene* (café) or **sladkarnitsa** (patisserie or sweet shop), where coffee, tea and soft drinks are usually accompanied by a choice of alcoholic drinks as well. These establishments vary widely in terms of size and style, ranging from order-at-the-counter affairs with a few plastic tables and chairs to swish cafés with comfy seating and a menu offering cakes, ice cream and pancakes. Sofia boasts a handful of Western-style coffee bars serving up doughnuts, sandwiches and a full range of brews – a trend that looks set to catch on elsewhere in the country.

Traditionally, **evening drinking** takes place in the *mehanas* and *krachmas* that also attract diners, although Bulgaria's cities and resorts now have bars, pubs and clubs that compare favourably with anything found in the average western European town. Here you can get domestic alcoholic and non-alcoholic drinks, as well as imported spirits and beers, and all kinds of cocktails.

Bulgarians are enthusiastic **coffee** drinkers, with a thick black *espresso* being the drink of choice. Standards vary widely from place to place however, and if you're really particular about the quality of your coffee you should aim for an establishment that has a sign in the window advertising an international brand such as Lavazza or Segafredo. *Sas mlyako* means "with milk". Cappuccinos and fancy coffees are available in cities and resorts; in smaller towns it's probably better not to ask. Bulgaria produces several excellent forms of herbal **tea** (*bilkov chay*), and this is what cafés will offer unless you specify otherwise: *cheren chay* (black tea) or *zelen chay* (green tea) are the terms to use if you want the real McCoy.

Fruit juice (*sok*) and mineral water (*mineralna voda*) are available everywhere.

Bulgarian wine

Most regions of Bulgaria can boast a centuries-old vine-growing tradition, and the impressive range of domestic grape varieties (alongside imported ones such as Cabernet Sauvignon and Merlot) ensures that there's a great deal worth sampling. In wine-growing areas, many *mehanas* and restaurants offer **home-made** wine (*domashno vino*), often straight from the cask (*nalivno*). There is never a problem ordering by the glass (*chasha*). In shops and supermarkets it's possible to pick up a good bottle of wine from between 10Lv/€5 and 20Lv/€10 a bottle.

Bulgaria's **reds** are probably the best known, with the full-bodied Melnik (from the town of the same name in the southwest), the mellower Gamza from the northwest; and the rich, dark Mavrud from the

Plovdiv-Asenovgrad region being the most worthwhile of the indigenous wines.

Melnik wine can be bought direct from local producers in Melnik itself, although there is no quality control and what you come home with will be largely a question of pot luck. If you're buying wine from supermarkets or in restaurants, the Damyanitza winery (based in the Struma valley near Melnik) produces the most dependable range of Melnik wines. The Todoroff winery, based in the village of Brestovitsa, just south of Plovdiv, produces Mavruds and Merlots of quality.

Of the **whites**, there are exceedingly drinkable Chardonnays from the eastern Bulgarian vine-growing regions of Pomorie and Novi Pazar. Traminer Han Krum, from Preslav, and Traminer Evksinograd, from the Evksinograd Palsce outside Varna, are the best of the dry whites.

Spirits

Bulgarian *rakiya* (**brandy**) is highly potent and costs little more than 12Lv/€6 a bottle. Most *rakiya* is made from grapes, and is produced anywhere where vines are cultivated. There are as many varieties of *rakiya* as there are villages in Bulgaria, and most bars, restaurants and supermarkets will have ten to twenty varieties to choose from. As a general rule, *otlezhala* (matured) *rakiya* is smoother than the non-matured variety, so buy this version if you're taking it home as a gift. Slivenska Perla and Burgas 63 are among the more respected brands. Plum brandy or *slivova rakiya* is a speciality of the Troyan region, while *kaisieva rakiya* (apricot brandy) is distilled in the villages of the Danubian plain.

Bulgarians usually begin a sit-down meal with a round of *rakiyas*, with *shopska salata* (see "Soups, salads and starters" p.45) being the standard accompaniment.

Bulgarian **mastika** (similar to Greek ouzo or Turkish raki) is drunk with water and/or ice and makes for a deliciously refreshing summer drink, although it should be treated with extreme respect unless you want to get legless at great speed.

Most bars and restaurants also offer a reasonable choice of international whiskies, vodkas and other spirits. Whatever you drink, spirits are sold by the gram. The smallest measure, *pedeset grama* (50g or 5cl), is roughly equivalent to a British double, *sto grama* (10cl) a quadruple.

Beer

Bulgarian **beer** (*bira*) is pretty unexciting but perfectly drinkable. The most popular brands are *Zagorka* from Stara Zagora, *Shumensko* from Shumen and *Kamenitza* from Plovdiv, all of which are lagers. Regional brews such as *Pirin* from Blagoevgrad, *Plevensko Pivo* from Pleven, and *Ledenika* from Vratsa also have a following, but true drinkers sniff at *Ariana* from Sofia. A 50cl bottle of regular *Kamenitza*, *Shumensko* or *Zagorka* rarely costs more than 3Lv/€1.50 in a bar or restaurant, while the slightly stronger, 33cl "export" bottles will set you back about 4–5Lv/€2–2.50. Imported German, Austrian, Czech and Danish beers are also widely available, at about twice the price. An increasing number of bars offer **draught beer** (*nalivna bira*) as well as bottled – either Bulgarian or an imported brand.

The media

Most Bulgarian hotel rooms are equipped with cable or satellite television, with CNN, BBC World and Eurosport among the most popular of the English-language channels. Newspapers and magazines in English are available in a handful of outlets in Sofia, and in seaside and mountain resorts in season, although the range of available titles is unpredictable and you won't always come across the reading matter of your choice.

Newspapers and magazines

There is a growing roster of local **English-language publications**. Weekly newspaper *The Sofia Echo* (@ www.sofiaecho.com), available from city-centre newspaper kiosks in Sofia and on the coast, is an authoritative source of local news and comment, accompanied by lifestyle and travel articles. Monthly magazine *Vagabond* (@ www .vagabond-bg.com) combines a broad and stimulating blend of interviews, travel pieces and social comment. Particularly invaluable are the small-format city guides produced by *In Your Pocket* (@ www.inyourpocket.com), available free from many hotels, restaurants and bars. Their guides to Sofia (published quarterly) and Bansko, Plovdiv and Varna (each published annually to coincide with the tourist season) provide lively, opinionated and up-to-date reviews of eating and drinking venues, as well as plenty of useful listings information.

The two principal **daily newspapers** are 24 ЧАСА (*24 Chasa*, "24 Hours") and ТРУД (*Trud* or "Work"), tabloids that mix news reporting with racy articles about Hollywood starlets or the antics of the Bulgarian mafia. Although politically independent, they're overwhelmingly conservative-nationalist in tone. Of the "serious" dailies, ДНЕВНИК (*Dnevnik*, or "Journal") is reasonably impartial and carries a smattering of cultural and lifestyle features. Its sister publication КАПИТАЛ (*Kapital*, or "Capital"), is primarily a business weekly, but also supplies in-depth political analysis and arts coverage that other publications largely lack.

The glossy **magazine** scene is extraordinarily vibrant, although many titles are locally franchised versions of established Western lifestyle publications. Among the genuinely home-grown monthlies, ЕДНО (*Edno*, or "One"), is a well-designed and highly individualistic survey of what's new in music, art, film and fashion; while ЕВА (*Eva*) is the most stylish and intelligent of the women's interest titles.

Television and radio

The state **TV channel**, Kanal 1, and independent stations bTV and Nova TV are the three main national broadcasters, although a handful of privately owned channels are sporadically available depending on area. Talk shows, phone-ins, imported soap operas and action movies form the principal diet of the TV stations, and there is a disappointing lack of domestically produced drama. **Cable** and **satellite TV** have caught on in a big way, so many households have access to Discovery, MTV or other international media brands, alongside domestic cable stations showing round-the-clock pop-folk videos.

The best way to catch up on news is the **BBC World Service** on short wave (available on different frequencies depending on the time of day: check @ www.bbc.co.uk/worldservice for details) or in Sofia on VHF (91MHz). At the time of writing this was the only English-language radio station available in Bulgaria.

Festivals

Bulgaria's festival diary is largely determined by the calendar of the Orthodox Church, with Christmas, Easter, the Assumption and a host of saints' days providing the framework for a rich tapestry of ritual and celebration. Many feast days also betray pre-Christian, pagan roots, notably the fertility-related *kukeri* rites of New Year and early spring. There's not a great deal of folklore on display in Bulgaria's big cities, but Sofia, Plovdiv and Varna all pull their weight when it comes to top-quality music and arts festivals.

Precise dates of Bulgarian festivals can be difficult to pin down, especially in rural areas. Events are often organized at short notice, and folk celebrations are frequently enacted on the nearest weekend to a particular saint's day, rather than on the day itself. The situation is made more complicated as some rural communities still celebrate saints' days according to the old-style (Julian) calendar once used by the Bulgarian Orthodox Church, thereby placing them thirteen days behind the official (Gregorian) calendar adhered to by everybody else.

Seasonal rites and religious festivals

The festive calendar begins with **New Year's Day** or St Basil's Day – also known as *survaki* – when children go from house to house offering New Year wishes to the occupants by slapping them on the back with a *survaknitsa* – a bunch of twigs adorned with brightly coloured threads and dried fruit. In southwestern Bulgaria, New Year's Day is also marked by processions of villagers wearing animal masks, a ritual similar to those performed on *Kukerov den* (see below).

On Yordanovden (Jan 6), Christ's baptism in the River Jordan is traditionally celebrated by throwing a cross into an icy river so that the village menfolk can jump in to retrieve it. This is still enacted in many areas, notably Kalofer in the Valley of the Roses. Ivanovden (Jan 7) is traditionally the day when newly married men have to be purified by ritual washing – which usually means another bout of jumping into streams and splashing around in freezing-cold water.

In wine-producing areas, vines are pruned and sprinkled with wine for good luck and casks of young wine from last year's harvest are broached on St Tryphon's Day, **Trifon zarezan** (Feb 1 in some places, Feb 14 in others). A more widespread festival associated with the start of the agricultural year in arable or pastoral regions is **Kukerov den**, the day of the *kukeri*, on the first Sunday before Lent. Processions are led through the village by dancing, leaping men dressed in animal costumes and grotesque masks, augmented by a girdle of goat or sheep bells and extravagantly tasselled trousers. In southwestern Bulgaria, the festival is conflated with *survaki* and held on New Year's Eve or New Year's Day. In Shiroka Laka in the Rhodopes, *kukeri* rites are celebrated in March; while in Eleshnitsa near Bansko they are enacted on Easter Sunday.

The advent of spring, **Baba marta** (literally, "Granny March"), is celebrated on March 1, when peasant households embark on a round of spring-cleaning, symbolically sweeping the winter months away. On the same day people present each other with **martenitsa**, good-luck charms made of red and white woollen threads with tassels or furry bobbles on the end. These are worn until the sighting of the first migrating stork or budding bush (if the latter, the charms are then hung on its branches). **Todorovden**, or St Theodor's Day, on the first Saturday of Lent, is still marked by horse races in Koprivshtitsa, Dobrinishte and Katarino, while another more widespread springtime fertility rite is **Lazaruvane**, which takes place on St Lazar's Day, or

Easter

The **Orthodox Easter** occurs roughly a week later than in western Europe, and its exact timing varies from year to year. Certain other festivals (chiefly Lent) and saints' days are also timed in relation to Easter, rather than occurring on a fixed date. The dates for the next few years are:

2008: April 27
2009: April 19
2010: April 4
2011: April 24

Lazarovden (the Sat before Palm Sunday), when village maidens considered fit for marriage perform ritual dances, songs and games. On Palm Sunday (*Tsvetnitsa* or *Varbnitsa*) itself, people buy willow branches and hang them at home in preparation for the **Easter** services in churches on Thursday night (the eve of Good Friday) and Saturday night (the eve of Easter Sunday). At the latter, the priest emerges from behind the iconostasis at midnight bearing a candle symbolizing Christ's resurrection; the congregation lights their own candles from this and files outside to walk around the church three times. Painted eggs (prepared by families beforehand) are then knocked together and eaten; the first egg to be made is always painted red to symbolize the blood of Christ and put aside – either to be buried in the fields to ensure fertility or kept in the home to bring good luck.

Last of the springtime festivals is **Gergyovden** or St George's Day (May 6), an occasion for sacrificing and roasting sheep to celebrate the end of spring. The coming of summer is traditionally marked by the feast day of **SS Konstantin and Elena** (May 21 by the New Style calendar, May 4 by the Old). Many pastoral Rhodope villages hold a festival known as the **Measuring of the Milk** or *Predoi*, which is intended to ensure good milk yields for the rest of the year. It includes the practice of milking a ewe so that the milk dribbles through the wedding ring of a young bride before falling into the pail; while in a few remote villages in the Strandzha hills, they go in for the ancient pagan custom of **fire-dancing** barefoot on hot coals.

Other church holidays tend to coincide with the changing of the seasons. **St Marina's Day** (July 17) has always been a popular midsummer feast day, and **Enyovden**, the birthday of St John the Baptist (June 24), is still regarded as the best time to pick medicinal herbs.

Orthodox saints' days

Where there are two dates below, it is because the saint's day is celebrated either on the date in the New Style Calendar (first date given) or on the date in the Old Style Calendar (second date given), or sometimes both.

Yordanovden (Jordan Day) Jan 6

Trifon Zarezan (St Tryphon's Day) Feb 14

Todorovden (St Theodor's Day) First Sat of Lent

Lazarovden (St Lazar's Day) Sat before Palm Sunday

Gergyovden (St George's Day) May 6

SS Cyril and Methodius May 11

SS Konstantin and Elena May 4 and May 24

Ilinden (St Elijah's Day) July 20 and Aug 2

Golyama Bogoroditsa (Feast of the Assumption) Aug 15 and Aug 29

St John of Rila (birthday) Aug 18

Malka Bogoroditsa (Birth of the Virgin) Sept 6 and Sept 16

Krastovden (Day of the Holy Cross) Sept 14

St John of Rila (feast day) Oct 19

Dimitrovden (St Dimitrius's Day) Oct 26

Arhangelovden (Archangels Michael and Gabriel) Nov 8

Nikulen (St Nicholas's Day) Dec 6

Koleda (Christmas) Dec 25 and Jan 6

The biggest festival of the summer is **Golyama Bogoroditsa** (Assumption of the Virgin), which occasions big gatherings at any church or monastery dedicated to her, picnics in the grounds of the Dragalevski and Lopushanski monasteries, and a parade of icons at Troyan and Bachkovo. The feast is generally observed on its New Style date (Aug 15), but Christian Gypsies celebrate it according to the Old Style calendar (Aug 29). **Malka Bogoroditsa** (Birth of the Virgin; Sept 8) is marked by a parade of icons at Rozhen Monastery.

While Melnik and other wine-growing areas celebrate their harvest on October 18, elsewhere, the end of the farming year is traditionally marked on St Dimitrius's Day, **Dimitrovden** (Oct 26).

On Easter Sunday married couples traditionally visit the best man at their wedding and have roast lamb for lunch.

Of the many other saints' days in the Orthodox calendar, three engender particularly impressive crowds and spectacles: the birthday (Aug 18) and feast day (Oct 19) of **St John of Rila** at the Rila Monastery; and the pilgrimage to **Krastova gora** on the eve of **Krastovden** (Sept 14). The mountaintop shrine of Krastova Gora is Bulgaria's chief pilgrimage site (see p.343) and attracts New Age cultists as well as mainstream Christians.

Christmas (*koleda*) is a family and neighbourly affair which most people celebrate on December 25 according to the Gregorian calendar, though traditionalists do so on January 6/7 by the Old calendar, and those who can afford it might even celebrate both. A traditional practice in villages is the *koleduvane*, whereby young men go from house to house singing carols under the leadership of a *stanenik*, who has to bake a specially decorated loaf of bread that the singers take with them on their rounds.

Muslim festivals

Bulgaria's Muslim minority is no less observant of **Islamic festivals**, converging on mosques and holy sites to celebrate the more important holidays. If you're in Bulgaria at the right time, these gatherings can be observed in Sofia and Plovdiv, or towns in areas of Muslim settlement, such as Shumen, Razgrad and Dobrich in the north; Pazardzhik, Kardzhali, Haskovo and Momchilgrad in the south.

During **Ramadan** (*Ramazan*), the month of daylight abstention from food, water, tobacco and sexual relations, cafés and restaurants still open for business, and the degree to which the fast is observed varies, but everyone enjoys the three-day **Sheker bayram** ("Sugar Holiday") at the end of Ramadan, celebrated with family get-togethers and the giving of presents and sweets to children. Another major event is the **Kurban bayram** ("Festival of the Sacrifice"), which is marked by the ritual slaughter of sheep and goats, feasting and dancing.

Outdoor feasts are an important aspect of Muslim culture in Bulgaria, and one that is shared by their Christian compatriots. Many people from both faiths come to picnic and enjoy themselves at localities revered by Muslims (usually a dervish mausoleum, or *Tekke*). Happily for everyone, the **Aliani festival of Hidrelez** at the beginning of summer coincides with the Orthodox feast

Muslim festivals

Since the Islamic calendar is lunar, dates of festivals tend to drift backwards eleven days each year relative to the Gregorian calendar, but as the **start of Ramadan** depends on the visibility of the new moon at Mecca and elsewhere, it is impossible to predict the dates of the Sheker bayram holiday, at the end of Ramadan, or the Kurban bayram, with total accuracy – so these dates are only approximate.

Sheker bayram	**Kurban bayram**
2008: 2 October	2008: December 8–11
2009: 21 September	2009: November 28–December 1
2010: 10 September	2010: November 17–20
2011: 31 August	2011: November 11–14

of Gergyovden (May 6). Foreigners are welcome to attend, but anyone squeamish about animal slaughter should stay away. Bulgarian Muslims are not averse to drinking alcohol on these occasions.

Major folk music festivals

The traditional feast-day calendar has given rise to some spectacular festivals of traditional music, with August – the month of the Assumption of the Virgin – being by far the busiest period. Most famous of Bulgaria's folk events is the **Koprivshtitsa Folklore Festival**, a huge gathering of traditional singers and musicians from all over the country, traditionally held on a mid-August weekend every five years (the next is due in 2010), although a smaller version of the festival does occur annually. Other August music festivals of national importance include the **Rozhenski sabor** at Rozhen in the Rhodopes, and **Pirin Pee** ("Pirin Sings"; see p.148) at the Predel Pass, both of which are usually held on even-numbered years.

Events which reliably take place every year include the bagpipe festival at the Rhodopi village of Gela in early August, and the celebration of western Rhodope traditions at Dorkovo (last weekend in July or first weekend in Aug). Festivals whose schedules tend to slide include a festival of Karakachani music in the Karandila region north of Sliven (either late June or early July), and an even more unpredictable **Gypsy festival** in Stara Zagora (June, July, or Aug; depending on when most of the local Gypsy bands are available to attend).

In winter, the celebration of *kukeri* rites in the southwest provides the inspiration for the International Festival of Masquerade Games in Pernik (even-numbered years) and the International Kukeri Festival in Razlog (odd-numbered years).

Urban folklore festivals featuring Bulgarian and international performers include those in Plovdiv (July), Varna (Aug) and Burgas (Aug). Folklore performances also play a major role in the **Rose Carnivals** organized in the bloom-producing towns of Karlovo and Kazanlak (both early June).

Classical music, jazz, theatre and the arts

Bulgaria's festival calendar includes plenty of serious culture. For lovers of **classical music**, the **major events** remain the Sofia Music Weeks (late-May to late-June), the March Music Days in Ruse, the international chamber music festival in Plovdiv (mid-June), and the opera festival in Plovdiv (late June–early July). In addition, there's a feast of orchestral music, opera and ballet during the **Varna Summer** (June–July), and a mixed menu of classical music, theatre, jazz and pop at Sozopol's **Apollonia Festival** (early Sept).

Biggest of the annual **jazz** events is the Bansko Jazz Festival in mid-August, although both the Varna Jazz Festival (early Aug) and the Plovdiv Jazz Nights (Sept) can boast their fair share of big-name international guests.

The best in Bulgarian **drama** can be seen at the Varna International Theatre Festival in Varna in June, and the Theatre at the Crossroads festival in Plovdiv in September, which attract new Bulgarian productions alongside top-level foreign guests.

The most enjoyable **arts festival** is Plovdiv's Night of the Museums and Galleries (last weekend in Sept), when thousands of celebrants swarm around the city's old quarter in search of art shows, chamber concerts and performances.

Events calendar

Events occuring on the cusp of two months are listed under the earlier date.

January

Kukeri processions (New Year's Eve/Jan 1) Takes place in Razlog, Sandanski, Pernik and Petrich.
Yordanovden (Jan 6) Celebrations at Koprivshtitsa and Kalofer.
New Year's Day (Old Style) (Jan 14) *Kukeri* processions in villages west of Pernik including Yardzhilovtsi, Kosharevo and Banishte.
International Kukeri festival (odd-numbered years only; Jan 13–14) Razlog
Surva International Festival of Masquerade Games (even-numbered years only; mid-or late Jan) Pernik ⓦ www.surva.org. Bulgarian *kukeri* and mummers from around the world.

February

Trifon zarezan (Feb 1 or 14) Celebrated in wine-growing areas.

March–April

Baba Marta (March 1) ("Granny March"). Donning of red-and-white good-luck charms throughout Bulgaria

Sofia Film Fest (early March); ⓦ www.cinema .bg/sff. Contemporary European cinema.

Kukeri (first weekend in March) At Shiroka Laka, and (Easter Sunday) Eleshnitsa.

March Music Days (last two weeks in March) Classical music festival in Ruse.

Todorovden (first Sat of Lent) Horse races at Koprivshtitsa, Dobrinishte and Katarino near Razlog.

Easter Nationwide church services on Thursday and Saturday night, a Great Easter Concert in Bansko, and Kukeri rites at Eleshnitsa (Easter Monday).

Lazarovden Lazaruvane displays in towns and villages throughout the country.

May

Procession of icons (25 days after Easter Sunday) From Bachkovo Monastery to Ayazmoto.

Gergyovden (May 6) Sacrifices and feasts at Chiprovtsi, Slatolin (near Montana) and the Monastery of St George near Hadzhidimovo (outside Gotse Delchev). Also Muslim/Christian gatherings at Ak Yazula Baba Tekke near Obrochiste, and Demir Baba Tekke near Sveshtari.

Measuring of the Milk (May 21) Festivals in Rhodope highland villages.

Sofia Music Weeks (late May to late June) Festival of classical music and ballet.

Festival of Humour and Satire (every 2 or 3 years); ⓦ www.humorhouse.bg. Takes place in Gabrovo.

Thrace Sings (Trakia pee) (last weekend in May) Folklore festival, Haskovo.

June

Varna International Theatre Festival (first ten days in June) ⓦ www.theatrefest-varna.org.

Fire-dancing (June 4 or nearest weekend) At Balgari in the Strandzha.

Karlovo Rose Festival (first Sat in June) With folk music and parades.

Kazanlak Rose Festival (first Sun in June) With music, dancing and carnival floats.

International chamber music festival (mid- to late June) In Plovdiv.

Folklore and crafts displays (June 24) At Etara, near Gabrovo.

Kavarna Rock Fest (last weekend in June) ⓦ www.kavarna.bg.

Plovdiv Opera Festival (late June-early July); ⓦ www.ofd-plovdiv.org. Opera by Verdi and others, in the Roman Theatre.

Karakachani festival (last weekend in June or first weekend in July) Folk music and feasting at the Blue Rocks outside Sliven.

Varna Summer (late June to end July) ⓦ www .varnasummerfest.org. Festival of classical music

July

Ilinden (New Style) (July 20 or the last Sun in July) Services at churches and monasteries named after St Elijah, as well as civic events throughout the Pirin region. Also a Christian/Muslim gathering at Demir Baba Tekke, near Sveshtari.

Plovdiv International Folk Festival (late July) Street parades followed by open-air concerts in the Roman Theatre.

Dorkovo festival (last weekend in Jul or first weekend in Aug) Festival of regional folklore (Macedonian, Pomak and Vlach) at north-Rhodope village of Dorkovo.

Veliko Tarnovo International Folklore Festival (late Jul to early Aug) ⓦ www.folklorefest.com.

Plovdiv International Folklore Festival (late Jul to early Aug).

August

Varna International Jazz Festival (first week in Aug) ⓦ www.vsjf.com.

Varna International Folk Festival (early to mid-Aug) ⓦ www.varnafolk.org.

Ilinden (Old Style) (first Sun in Aug) Ilinden bagpipe festival at Gela near Shiroka Laka.

Pirin Pee folklore festival (first or second weekend in Aug, even-numbered years only). At the Predel Pass in the Pirin Mountains.

Trakiisko Iyato (early to mid-Aug) Chamber music in the mansions of Old Plovdiv.

Bansko International Jazz Festival (mid-Aug) ⓦ www.banskojazz.org.

Folk music festival (Aug 15 or nearest weekend) In Koprivshtitsa. Big national festival every five years (next due in 2010), smaller local festival takes place annually.

Golyama Bogoroditsa (Aug 15) Parade of icons at Troyan, Rozhen, Rila and Bachkovo monasteries.

Trigrad Orphic Festival (mid-Aug) Music, from folk to rock, at Trigrad.

Birthday of St John of Rila (Aug 18) Celebrated at Rila Monastery.

Danovisti gathering (Aug 19–28) At the Seven Lakes in the Rila Mountains.

Golyama Bogoroditsa (Old Style) (Aug 28–29) Roma gathering at Bachkovo monastery.
International Folk Festival (late Aug) In Burgas.
Rozhenski sabor (mid- or late Aug, even years only) ⓦwww.rojen.info. Folklore festival at Rozhen in the Rhodopes
Milk Festival (last weekend in Aug) At Smilyan in the Rhodopes.

September

Love is Folly Film Festival (first week in Sept) Feature films from Bulgaria, Europe and beyond. Varna.
Thracian Festival (first week in Sept) Music, dancing and wrestling in Madzharovo.
Apollonia Festival (first 7–10 days of Sept); ⓦwww.apollonia.bg. Classical, jazz, rock and theatre festival

Plovdiv Jazz Nights (mid-Sept) ⓦwww.jazznight .plovdiv.bg.
Scene at the Crossroads (mid-Sept); ⓦwww .scenatepe.com. International theatre festival, Plovdiv
Malka Bogoroditsa (Sept 8) Parade of icons at Rozhen Monastery.
Krastovden pilgrimage (Sept 14) To Krastova gora.
Contemporary Art Weeks (mid-Sept to early Oct); ⓦwww.arttoday.org. Plovdiv.
Night of Museums and Galleries (last weekend in Sept); ⓦwww.gallery-night.info. Dusk-til-dawn cultural festival at Plovdiv.

October–December

Feast day of St John of Rila (Oct 19) Celebrated at Rila Monastery.
Christmas (Dec 25) Koleda.

Outdoor activities and sports

Riven by mountain chains and boasting large areas of unspoilt wilderness, Bulgaria offers enormous potential for activities such as hiking, mountain biking, climbing, caving and skiing. The country's mountains and lowlands are incredibly rich in wildlife – especially flora and birds – as the country has features of both the Balkan and Mediterranean ecosystems, and is visited by hundreds of migratory species. While many people may prefer to book a tour through a specialist operator abroad (see p.34), it's perfectly possible to arrange adventure and ecotourism trips through various agencies in Bulgaria.

Hiking

Hiking was first popularized in Bulgaria in the late nineteenth century, when it had patriotic connotations. During Communist times it was regarded as an ideal activity for citizens, and a network of trails and huts (*hizhi*) was created throughout the mountains. Though not as well-signposted as they could be, the hundreds of trails can be combined in an almost infinite variety of routes. The main hiking areas are the Pirin and Rila national parks, the central and western Rhodopes, and the Stara planina.

The **Pirin Mountains** (p.149) are the wildest, most picturesque range in Bulgaria, with 45 peaks over 2590m, deep valleys, karst massifs and more than two hundred glacial lakes, mainly in the northern part of the range, which has the finest panoramic views. Further north, the **Rila Mountains** (p.123) include the highest peak in the Balkan peninsula and Bulgaria's greatest monastery, and are characterized by magnificent coniferous forests and alpine scenery, abloom with wild flowers all year. Here too there are many lakes, including a cluster that attracts sun-worshippers. Both ranges abut the **Rhodopes** (p.338), which are lower, but arguably the loveliest range in Bulgaria, with a mixture of pine forests, crags, highland meadows and villages of stone houses, not to mention the fantastic caves and birdlife around the Trigrad Gorge.

In the **Stara planina** or Balkan Range (p.169), the fir-clad heights of the northwest are relatively uncharted, but their ill-marked trails reward the efforts of those with time to spare. Villages such as Berkovitsa and Chiprovtsi provide the best access to higher altitudes. The central Stara planina between the Valley of the Roses and the Danubian plain has better-maintained trails, and is best approached from Karlovo in the south or Cherni Osam and Apriltsi in the north.

If you're planning to go hiking independently you should visit Zig-Zag/Odysseia-In in Sofia (see p.75) first, to stock up on hiking maps (see p.62) and advice; they can also book accommodation in some areas.

Climbing and caving

Bulgaria's mountainous terrain means that the opportunities for **climbing** are practically limitless. The most popular areas with mountaineers and rock-climbers are Mount Malyovitsa (p.136) in the Rila Mountains; the karst region to the north of Mount Vihren (p.149) in the Pirin range; Lakatnik in the Iskar Gorge (p.172); Vratsa (p.175) and Belogradchik (p.185) in the western Stara planina; Samovodene near Veliko Tarnovo; and the Blue Rocks outside Sliven (p.304).

Of the hundreds of **caves** in Bulgaria (mostly in the Stara planina and western Rhodopes), a dozen have been fitted with walkways and lighting and opened to the public. The most famous are the Ledenika cave in the mountains above Vratsa (p.178); the Magura Cave near Belogradchik (p.187), with its prehistoric paintings; the Yagodina Cave in the Rhodopes, with its stalactites and cave pearls; and the awesome Devil's Throat near Trigrad (p.353). Scores of other spectacular caves are only known to Bulgarian cavers, who usually welcome contacts with their foreign counterparts.

Though no foreign operator runs climbing or caving package tours, individuals can go climbing **with a guide** from Zig-Zag/ Odysseia-In for 60–80Lv/€30–40 per person per day, plus expenses and equipment rental (if required). The most useful local caving contact is the Bulgarian Federation of Speleologists, at 1040 Sofia, bul. Vasil Levski 75 (☎02/987 8812, ⊛www.speleo-bg.com).

Mountain biking

With its wealth of dirt roads and tracks, Bulgaria is perfect for mountain biking: the challenge is to find a locality where bikes can be rented and routes have been adequately marked. From a climatic standpoint, mid-May to late October is the ideal time for biking in Bulgaria, although the season can be stretched well into the winter if you're pedalling around the foothills and avoiding snow-covered peaks. In the Pirin range, bikes can be **rented** from big hotels and travel agents in the resort of Bansko, but local trails are not (yet) signposted – it's really a question of acquiring a local hiking map and trying your luck, or getting expert advice from local enthusiasts like the *Hotel Avalon* (see p.144). In the Rhodopes, local biking association Bike Area (⊛www.bikearea.org) has published trail maps of the Velingrad and Smolyan-Momchilovtsi areas (although you may have to travel to the Zig-Zag travel agency in Sofia to pick these up). In the Stara Planina region, the *Little Spring B&B* (⊛www.littlespring.eu) in the hills above Yablanitsa (see p.213) has developed a network of local trails and also rents out bikes. Further east in the central Stara planina, some routes have been marked by the Stara Planina Tourist Association (see p.210), and bikes can be rented in tourist offices in Apriltsi, Gabrovo, Teteven, Troyan and Tryavna.

Winter sports

Bulgaria's main **skiing centres** are Borovets in the Rila mountains, Bansko in the Pirin range, and Pamporovo in the Rhodopes, and it is in these three that you will find most in the way of resort facilities. Each is undergoing rapid development, with new hotels and apartment blocks encroaching on areas of goat-nibbled pasture and pine forest. Bansko does at least have a charming historic town at its heart, and is the pick of the resorts if you want to combine your skiing with a bit of Balkan atmosphere. Mount Vitosha, immediately south of Sofia, offers low-key skiing with little in the way of infrastructure, although it does have the advantage of being within easy day-trip range of the city centre.

All these resorts have nursery slopes, pistes for beginners and intermediates, and snowboard parks. Bansko has the longest continuous downhill runs, and boasts the added attraction of at least one black run for advanced skiiers. Lift passes and equipment hire is moderately priced by Western standards, although at 120Lv/€60 per day can still be a major outlay.

Package holidays to Borovets, Bansko and Pamporovo are offered by major UK-based tour operators (see p.34), although it's reasonably easy for independent travellers to fit a couple of days skiing into a wider trip around Bulgaria. Only in peak periods such as mid-February are you likely to find all the available accommodation booked solid by tour groups.

Birdwatching

Bulgaria is great for **birdwatching**, since it is a nesting ground for most European birds in spring (May–June) and on the migratory path of many Asian birds in autumn (Sept to mid-Oct). In total there are around four hundred species that can be spotted in the country. There are plenty to see at any time, owing to the diversity of ecological niches and lower use of pesticides and insecticides than in Western Europe. Though birdlife can be seen anywhere, the richest concentrations are in the Rhodope Mountains, along the Black Sea coast and the floodplain of the River Danube.

In the **Rhodopes**, the Trigrad Gorge (see p.353) is notable for Pallid swifts, Crag martins, Pot-bellied dippers and, above all, the rare, elusive Wallcreeper, while the local caves harbour six types of bat. Although eagles, hawks and falcons can be seen all over the highlands, the best sites for observing raptors are in the Arda Gorge near Madzharovo (see p.363), which boasts rare Eastern and Imperial eagles, Egyptian, Black and Griffon vultures, Black storks, Blue Rock thrushes, Chukars, Nuthatches and Barred, Orphean and Olivaceous warblers.

The **Black Sea coast** has an even greater variety of birdlife, especially during the great autumn migration, when flocks of raptors fly over the lakes and marshes around Burgas (see p.412), which teem with Black and White storks, Marsh harriers and Mediterranean gulls, while Black-winged stilts and avocets feed in the lagoons and terns fish offshore. In spring, the salt-pans and reed-marshes sustain White and Dalmatian pelicans, Great White and Little egrets, Bearded and Penduline tits, Red-necked Phalarope and Broad-billed sandpipers. Cape Kaliakra (see p.379) is likewise good for observing birds of passage (larks, pipits, wagtails, wheatears and warblers besides larger migrants like storks and buzzards), while in spring you'll see Alpine swifts, Pied wheatears and the rare Finch's wheatear (found nowhere else in Europe). On Lake Durankulak (see p.400), Spanish sparrows breed in the nests of storks and there's a small nesting colony of Paddyfield warblers. Pygmy cormorants are also around in September, along with Ruddy and Ferruginous shelducks (the latter an endangered species).

In spring especially, another major site is **Lake Srebarna** (p.207) on the Danube floodplain, which is frequented by around eighty migratory species and has a nesting colony of Dalmatian pelicans. Its rich variety of wildfowl includes "Wheezing" Penduline tits, egrets, several kinds of warblers, and seventy types of heron. Black- and Red-necked grebes attend their floating nests, and Whiskered and White-winged Black terns drift on the open water. Further west the lowlands are home to Pygmy cormorants, Glossy ibises and Marsh harriers.

For **information** on all these sites, contact the Bulgarian Society for the Protection of Birds (for contact details see opposite), which can recommend local guides and advise on all matters ornithological.

Wildlife organizations in Bulgaria

Balkani Wildlife Society ☎02/963 1470, ⊛www.balkani.org. Federation of Bulgarian NGOs involved with nature conservation.

Bulgarian Biodiversity Foundation ☎02/980 4131, ⊛www.bbf.biodiversity.bg. Coordinates numerous regional projects throughout Bulgaria, including those at the Poda Nature Reserve outside Burgas (see p.412), and numerous others along the Black Sea coast.

Bulgarian Society for the Protection of Birds (BDZP) ☎02/971 5855, ⊛www.bspb.org. The national ornithological society, with affiliates around the country.

Conservation Centre ☎03720/280 or 304, ⓦwww.geocities.com/niccer_bg. Runs the vulture reserve in the Arda gorges near Madzharovo (see p.363).

Le Balkan ⓦwww.lebalkan.com. Coordinates projects aong the northern Black Sea coast around Shabla and Kavarna.

Zoology, botany and geology

Aside from birds, Bulgaria's fauna includes most of the Balkan and Mediterranean **reptiles** (over fifty species) and **mammals**. Mountainous areas are the habitat of bears, boars, wolves, wild cats, deer, foxes and badgers, while jackals can be found in the Strandzha, and otters and coypu in the coastal wetlands. However they are all pretty reclusive, so you shouldn't expect to see too much in the course of walking in these areas – aside from **butterflies** and **moths**, of which Bulgaria boasts some 1100 species. Of more recherché interest are the 75 species of **cave fauna**, including eight kinds of bats.

Bulgaria's **flora** is extremely diverse due to the three types of climate (continental, Mediterranean and steppe) within its borders. Almost a third of the country is covered in **trees**, with conifers (Corsican, Scots, Macedonian and white pine, fir, spruce and juniper) predominating in the high mountains of the Pirin, Rila and western Rhodopes, and deciduous trees (oak, beech, hornbeam, elm, ash, hazel and lime) in the Stara planina, Sredna gora and Strandzha. The Rila, Pirin and Rhodopes are especially rich in **wild flowers**, **herbs** and **fungi**, including some species that became extinct elsewhere in Europe centuries ago and others that are unique to Bulgaria, such as *Astragalus physocalyx*, *Glycyrrhiza glabra*, *Haberlea rhodopensis*, *Prunus laurocerasus*, *Ramondia sorbica*, *Rheum rhaponticum* and *Rhododendron ponticum*.

If geology is your passion, Bulgaria is great for **rock formations** and **minerals**. The Pirin range has some spectacular glacial and karst features, while the Rhodopes abound in odd rock formations such as the Miraculous Bridges (see p.344); the Stone Wedding and others in the

Kardzhali region (see p.363); fantastic caves like the Devil's Throat near Trigrad (see p.353); and all kinds of gemstones and crystals. In northern Bulgaria the finest rockscapes are at Belogradchik (see p.185), Vratsa (see p.175), the Iskar Gorge (see p.172) and outside Sliven (see p.304).

Football

Despite the popularity of team sports such as basketball, handball and volleyball, none can compete with football (*futbol*) in terms of the passions involved. Teams in the premier division ("A" Grupa) play on Saturday or Sunday afternoons. **Tickets** are generally cheap and sold at booths outside the grounds on the day of the match. Due to Bulgaria's harsh winters, the **football season** (mid-Aug to mid-May) is interrupted by a break in January and February. Many Bulgarian stadia are dilapidated, uncovered affairs with rickety bench seating, though the top clubs have installed plastic bucket-seating to meet UEFA safety guidelines.

While CSKA Sofia (ⓦwww.cska.bg) and Levski Sofia (ⓦwww.levski.bg) remain the most successful and popular **teams**, in recent seasons powerful private sponsors have done much to ensure high league positions for Lokomotiv Plovdiv and Liteks Lovech. Matches between all these clubs are always big occasions, as are any derbies involving teams from the capital (CSKA, Levski, Lokomotiv and Slavia).

Matches involving the **Bulgarian national team** (fourth in the World Cup in 1994, but largely ineffectual ever since) are the only ones for which advance purchase of tickets, from the stadium box office, is advisable. International matches are usually held at the Vasil Levski Stadium in Sofia.

The Bulgarian Football Association maintains an informative website with English-language content (ⓦwww.bulgarian-football.com). If you can decipher Cyrillic script, the daily sports papers *7 Dni Sport* and *Meridian Match* are the best sources of football information, and carry full details of British and other European league matches in their Monday editions.

Culture and etiquette

The first thing that any traveller to Bulgaria needs to come to terms with is that locals shake their head when they mean yes and nod when they mean no. Bulgarians who are accustomed to foreigners or who have spent time abroad frequently reverse these gestures in order to make you feel more comfortable, although this often only adds to the confusion. The best way to avoid misunderstandings is to say a firm yes ("da") or no ("ne") without moving your head in any direction – although even this takes considerable practice.

When **drinking** with Bulgarian friends bear in mind that it is common to say cheers ("na zdrave!") every time a new round of drinks arrives, and that it is obligatory to clink glasses with everyone present while making eye contact with them at the same time. Simply raising your glass in their general direction just won't do.

If invited to dinner at a Bulgarian home, it's never a bad idea to bring **flowers** for the hostess. Make sure there's an odd number of blooms; even-numbered bouquets are for funerals.

Tobacco is a major crop in Bulgaria, so **smoking** is almost a patriotic duty. Smoking is prohibited on public transport, although it is still tolerated in the corridors of trains. Restaurants and bars are obliged by law to provide no-smoking areas for clients, although in practice this may consist of one or two tables placed in close proximity to the rest. Few adults see anything amiss in smoking beside children or small babies.

Visitors to Bulgarian **churches** should be aware that bare arms (for females) and bare legs (for males) are regarded as a sign of disrespect, and should cover up accordingly. Taking photographs inside churches is often considered to be in profound bad taste: always ask first before snapping away. As far as **mosques** are concerned, non-Muslims may enter but shoes must be removed before entering, and women have to cover their heads, arms and legs. Using the Islamic greeting *salaam aleikum* ("Peace be upon you") will be appreciated as a courteous gesture, and you should avoid walking in front of someone who is kneeling in prayer, as it is considered very rude.

Topless bathing is pretty much *de rigueur* on the Black Sea coast, and nude sunbathing quite common on the quieter beaches. Generally speaking, it's acceptable to strip off anywhere on the coast providing you find a quiet cove, or a relatively isolated stretch of beach situated a discreet distance away from the main family sunbathing areas.

Travel essentials

Addresses

Like everything else in Bulgaria, addresses are normally written in the Cyrillic alphabet. In the text of this guide, they're transcribed into Roman script according to the system explained in "Language" on p.474. The most common abbreviations are УЛ. (*ul.*) for "street" (*ulitsa*), ПЛ. (*pl.*) for "square" (*ploshtad*) and БУЛ. (*bul.*) for *bulevard*, although these designations are omitted altogether when the meaning is clear from the context. In large towns, you also see the abbreviation Ж.К. (zh.k) for "housing estate". The street number of a building is given after the name of the street. Addresses in the high-rise suburbs (kvartal, abbreviated to kv, КВ) include the building number (blok, shortened to bl, БЛъб a letter denoting the entrance (vhod), Roman numerals signifying the floor (etazh), and finally the number of the apartment itself.

Costs

Bulgaria always was a relatively cheap country for tourists and, despite the shift to a market economy and accession to the EU, most of life's essentials cost considerably less here than they do in western Europe.

If you're hostelling or camping, and buying food in local markets and street stalls, you can live on 60Lv/€30/£20/US$38 a day. Staying in modest hotels and eating out regularly, 120Lv/€60/£40/ US$76 per person should be sufficient, while on a daily budget of 160Lv/€80/£55/US$105 or above you can enjoy a very good life, staying in mid-range hotels and taking taxis everywhere. Only if you require big-city four-star accommodation or above will you need more than that.

The most unpredictable factor is the cost of **accommodation**, which varies from region to region, as well as depending on the facilities, age and ownership of the place in question. Simple hotels and B&Bs can cost anywhere from 20Lv/€10/£7/US$13 to 40Lv/€20/£14/US$26 per person; while a three-star hotel will cost around 60Lv/€30/£21/US$39 per person, and four- and five-star establishments from 100Lv/€50/£35/US$65 per person. Hostels, mountain huts and campsites rarely cost more than 20Lv/€10/£7/US$13 per person, although standards do vary.

Once you've sorted out a bed for the night, your remaining daily costs can be very low. **Public transport** is cheap, with flat fares of about 1Lv/€0.50/£0.35/US$0.65 on most urban transport and inexpensive rates on intercity buses and trains; travelling second class by train, you can cross the entire country from east to west for

28Lv/€14/£10/ US$19. Providing you avoid deluxe hotel restaurants, **eating** should likewise prove economical. An average evening meal with drinks will set you back 20Lv/€10–15/£7–10/US$13–19, less if you stick to standard local food such as simple grills and salad. **Drinking** Bulgarian wine or spirits (about 14Lv/€7/£5/US$9 and 20Lv/€10/£7/US$13 a bottle respectively) will hit your liver harder than your wallet, and snatching a quick cup of coffee or a sandwich won't set you back more than about 3Lv/€1.50/£1/US$1.90.

Entrance fees to Bulgarian **museums** and tourist attractions rarely exceed 2.80–5.60Lv/€1.40–2.80/£1–2/US$1.90–3.80, although tickets to set-piece attractions (the National History Museum in Sofia, for example) will set you back something in the region of 11.20Lv/€5.60/£4/US$7.60.

Crime and personal safety

Despite an increase in theft, corruption and mafia-style organized crime over the last twenty years, Bulgaria still feels an unthreatening country in which to travel, and most tourists will have little or no contact with the Bulgarian police (Politsiya, ПОЛИЦИЯ). However, everyone is required to carry ID at all times, so it's a good idea to keep your passport handy to satisfy any policeman making a casual check.

Petty theft is common in big cities and on the coast. A few common-sense precautions will help you avoid trouble: display cameras as little as possible, never leave your valuables in your room, and keep large sums of cash in a moneybelt, out of sight. Never leave clothes or beach bags unguarded on the beach. Don't travel without insurance (see p.61), and be sure to make a photocopy of your passport. If you are robbed, go to the police immediately, and get a report detailing the things you've lost.

When travelling around Bulgaria, don't fall asleep on train journeys; try to book a couchette or sleeper if you're travelling overnight – it's always more secure than the (often unlit) regular carriages. On arrival in a new city, beware of over-friendly acquaintances plying you with food and drink, as it may be drugged.

Car theft is common, with foreign cars and 4WD vehicles particularly sought after. It's always worth paying to park in a guarded lot (*ohranen parking*), and avoid leaving your vehicle on the street unless it's equipped with immobilizers and wheel locks. Never leave anything of value on display, wherever you park.

If you're unfortunate enough to be **arrested** yourself, wait until you can explain matters to someone in English if at all possible (misunderstandings in a foreign language can only make things worse), and then request that your **consulate** be notified (see Sofia "Listings" on p.113 for addresses). Note that while consulates can be helpful in some respects, they will never lend cash to nationals who've run out of money or been robbed.

Electricity

220 volts AC; round two-pin plugs are used.

Entry requirements

Citizens of the EU, Australia, New Zealand, Canada and the USA are allowed to enter Bulgaria visa-free for a period of ninety days. Citizens of other countries should check visa requirements with their local Bulgarian embassy before travelling. If you wish to stay in Bulgaria longer than ninety days, you are officially required to apply for a residence permit at the local police station (*politseiski uchastak*, or *Ministerstvo na vatreshni raboti* – MVR, MBPЬ), although it is probably easier to simply leave the country and re-enter. If you need advice, contact your embassy (*posolstvo*) in Sofia (see p.113 for a full list).

Bulgarian embassies and consulates abroad

Usual opening hours are Mon–Fri 9.30am–noon.

Australia 33 Culgoa Circuit, O'Malley, Canberra, ACT 2606 ☎02/6286 9711, ✉bulgemb@bigpond.net.au.

Britain 186–188 Queen's Gate, London SW7 5HL ☎020/7584 9400, ⓦwww.bulgarianembassy-london.org.

Canada 325 Stewart St, Ottawa, Ontario N1K 6K5 ☎613/789 3215, ✉mailmn@storm.ca.

Ireland 22 Burlington Rd, Dublin 4 ☎1/660 3293, ⓦwww.bulgarianembassy.ie.

New Zealand No representation; visa applications should be made through the Bulgarian consulate in Australia (see above) or via local travel agents.

US 1621 22nd St N W, Washington DC 20008 ☎202/387 0174, ⓦwww.bulgaria-embassy.org.

Gay and lesbian travellers

While conservative and patriarchal culture still forms the bedrock of Bulgarian society, anti-gay prejudice is rarely aired in public. Several openly gay men are prominent in the Bulgarian media, and cross-dressing folk-pop diva Azis has become something of a Bulgarian icon. Sofia boasts a handful of dedicated gay nightlife venues, and both in the capital and on the coast there are several fashionable bars and clubs that attract a tolerant, mixed crowd. At least one hotel in Sofia openly advertises itself as being 'gay-friendly' (*Scotty's*; see p.80), setting a trend which may well continue in the coming years. Several Bulgarian gay and lesbian websites have English-language content: ⓦwww.bulgayria.com is an excellent source of listings information and travel advice, while ⓦwww.bgogemini.org and ⓦwww.queer-bulgaria.org are more oriented towards social and campaigning issues.

Health

No inoculations are required for travel in Bulgaria, although anybody planning to spend a lot of time walking in the mountains ought to consider being inoculated against tickborne encephalitis. Most visitors suffer nothing worse than diarrhoea or sunburn, so stock up on preparations like Diocalm before you leave home, and protect yourself with a good sunscreen. While salads and fresh fruit are quite safe, it's risky to eat grilled snacks in provincial restaurants with a slow turnover. Tap water is safe to drink in all parts of the country.

Of the two kinds of poisonous **snakes** in Bulgaria, the most venomous is the nose-horned viper (*Vipera ammodytes*, locally known as *pepelanka*). Although vipers instinctively shun contact with humans, you

Cyrillic checklist: health

Health centre	ПОЛИКЛИНИКА
Herbal pharmacy	БИЛКОВА АПТЕКА
Hospital	БОЛНИЦА
Pharmacy	АПТЕКА

should avoid going barefoot, turning over rocks or sticking your hands into dark crevices anywhere off the beaten track.

Minor complaints can be solved at a **pharmacy** or Apteka, but if you require a doctor (*lekar*) or dentist (*zabolekar*), head for the nearest Poliklinika or **health centre**, whose staff might speak English, German or French. Urgent cases go to **hospitals** (*bolnitsa*) courtesy of the *barza pomosht* or ambulance service (☎150 in most towns, service free), and emergency treatment is free of charge although you must pay for **medicines**. Although Bulgarian physicians are well-trained and competent, the equipment, facilities, auxiliary staff and aftercare in hospitals falls well below the standards to which Westerners are accustomed, so it's best to fly home in the case of anything serious.

Bulgaria has a strong tradition of **herbal medicine** (though none, curiously, of homeopathy), and most towns will have a *Bilkova apteka* or herbal pharmacy offering a range of natural remedies. However, you'll need to speak Bulgarian, or enlist the help of a native speaker, if you want to understand what you're being offered.

Insurance

Although emergency health care (but not the cost of medicines) is free of charge in Bulgaria,

you'd do well to take out an **insurance policy** before travelling to cover against theft, loss and illness or injury. Before paying for a new policy, however, it's worth checking whether you are already covered: some all-risks home insurance policies may cover your possessions when overseas, and many private medical schemes include cover when abroad. In Canada, provincial health plans usually provide partial cover for medical mishaps overseas, while holders of official student, teacher or youth cards in Canada and the US are entitled to meagre accident coverage and hospital inpatient benefits. Students will often find that their student health coverage extends during the vacations and for one term beyond the date of last enrolment.

After exhausting the possibilities above, you might want to contact a specialist travel insurance company, or consider the travel insurance deal Rough Guides offers (see box below). A typical travel insurance policy usually provides cover for the loss of baggage, tickets and – up to a certain limit – cash or cheques, as well as cancellation or curtailment of your journey. Most of them exclude so-called dangerous sports unless an extra premium is paid. Many policies can be chopped and changed to exclude coverage you don't need – for example, sickness and accident benefits can often be excluded or included at will. If you do take medical coverage, find out whether benefits will be paid as treatment proceeds or only after you return home, and whether there is a 24-hour medical emergency number. When securing baggage cover, make sure that the per-article limit – typically under £500 – will cover your most valuable possession. If you need to make a claim, you should keep

Rough Guides insurance

Rough Guides has teamed up with Columbus Direct to offer you travel insurance that can be tailored to suit your needs. Products include a low-cost **backpacker** option for long stays; a **short break** option for city getaways; a typical **holiday package** option; and others. There are also annual **multi-trip** policies for those who travel regularly. Different sports and activities (trekking, skiing, etc) can usually be covered if required. See our website (Ⓦwww.roughguides.com/website/shop) for eligibility and purchasing options. Alternatively, UK residents should call ☎0870/033 9988; Australians should call ☎1300/669 999 and New Zealanders should call ☎0800/55 9911. All other nationalities should call ☎+44 870/890 2843.

receipts for medicines and medical treatment, and if you have anything stolen, you must obtain an official statement from the police.

Internet

In Bulgaria, Internet cafés (most are called "clubs", although this doesn't mean that you have to be a member to use them) are now a common sight in the big cities, and rarely cost more than 2Lv/€1 an hour to use, although connection times can be slow.

With an increasing number of hotels and cafés both in Sofia and on the coast offering free **wireless Internet** access to their guests, it's worth bringing your laptop along providing you have a well-padded and secure bag to carry it around in.

Laundry

Laundrettes (*peralnya*, ПЕРАЛНЯ), let alone dry cleaners (*himichesko chistene*, ХИМИЧЕСКО ЧИСТЕНЕ), are exceedingly rare in Bulgaria, and are usually found in distant suburban housing estates where travellers are unlikely to go. At the larger hotels, it's possible to have cleaning done on the premises, but this can be quite costly. The longer you spend in the country, therefore, the more likely you are to be washing your smalls in the hotel sink.

Left luggage

Most train stations have a left-luggage office or *garderob* (ГАРДЕРОБ); in the larger towns these will be open 24hr. Bus stations will usually have a *garderob* as well, but opening

Cyrillic checklist: communications

Air mail	ВЪЗДУШНА
Envelopes	ПЛИКОВЕ
Express mail	БЪРЗА
Letters	ПИСМА
Parcels	КОЛЕТИ
Phonecard	ФОНКАРТА
Post office	ПОЩА
Poste restante	ПИСМА ДО
	ПОИСКВАНЕ
Stamps	МАРКИ
Telephone	ТЕЛЕФОН

times are more restricted and staff take more frequent breaks (*pauza* or *pochivka*). To store each item of baggage should cost no more than a few leva.

Mail

Most **post offices** (*poshta*) are open from 8.30am to 5.30pm from Monday to Saturday, although those in the larger towns tend to open an extra thirty minutes or so either side. It's not always easy to identify the right counter (*gishe*) to queue up at; look for signs advertising the sale of *marki* (stamps) or the despatch of *pisma* (letters) and *koleti* (parcels). **Stamps** are best bought at the post office, although **envelopes** (*plikove*) are sold at street kiosks. Mail can take seven to ten days to reach Britain and two to three weeks to the US; less than half that time if you send it *barza* (express) or *vazdushna* (airmail).

Poste restante services are available at the major post office in every sizeable town. Mail can be claimed by showing your passport (ask *Ima li pisma za mene* – is there any mail for me?), and letters should be addressed ПИСМА ДО ПОИСКВАНЕ, ЦЕНТРАЛНА ПОЩА, followed by the name of the town. Letters from western Europe generally take around a week to arrive in Bulgaria, those from North America two weeks, and Bulgarian postal officers are apt to misfile or return mail to the sender if it's not claimed immediately, so don't hold high hopes for poste restante communications.

When writing **letters to Bulgaria**, remember that the postcode and name of the town comes first, the street and number second, and the name of the recipient last: eg. 9000 Varna, ul. Nevazhna 40, Mr Hristo Stoichkov.

Maps

The best **general maps** available inside Bulgaria are the 1:500,000 road map (*Patna karta*) published by Kartografiya in Sofia and the 1:540, 000 road map published by Domino. Both are available in Cyrillic and Latin versions and are sold on street stalls, at petrol stations and in bookshops throughout the country. It's well worth struggling with one of the Cyrillic versions if you can, as this will help you read Cyrillic road signs when travelling in the country. Outside Bulgaria both Kümmerly and Frey and Freytag and Berndt publish 1:1,000,000 **combined maps** of Romania and Bulgaria.

The availability of **town plans** (*plan-ukazatel*) is less predictable, although a new series of city maps produced by Domino covers most urban areas in the country and can usually be found in newspaper kiosks and bookshops in the cities mapped (although it might be difficult finding a map of Varna in Plovdiv, and vice versa). Kartografiya publishes a map of Sofia that marks public transport routes that is available in Bulgarian and English versions.

In cooperation with the Bulgarian Tourist Union (BTS; БТС), Kartografiya also publishes a series of hiking maps covering the Rhodopes, Stara planina, Rila and Pirin ranges. Easily recognizable in their distinctive green covers, they can be purchased from bookshops, newspaper kiosks or from activity-based travel agents such as Zig-Zag in Sofia (see p.75).

Money

The Bulgarian currency is the **lev** (plural leva), which is divided up into 100 stotinki. Notes come in denominations of 100, 50, 20, 10, 5, 2 and 1 leva; while coins come in denominations of 2 and 1 leva, and 50, 20, 10, 5, 2 and 1 stotinki. The lev is pegged to the euro and, minor fluctuations aside, remains relatively stable against Western currencies. At the time of writing €1 buys 1.95Lv, £1 buys 2.80Lv, and US$1 buys 1.40Lv. Prices of certain services (hotel rooms, airline tickets) are often quoted in euros, although payment is usually made in leva.

You can **change** money in banks, tourist offices, at reception desks of the bigger hotels, and at private exchange bureaux. There's usually a slight difference in the **rates** offered, with private bureaux offering the most generous terms, providing you avoid the ones on main streets and well-touristed thoroughfares. Hotels offer the worst exchange rates, and should be avoided unless absolutely necessary. Don't change money with anyone who approaches you on the street.

Banking hours are usually Monday to Friday 9am–4pm. **Private exchange**

Cyrillic checklist: money and banks

Bank	БАНКА
Exchange	ОБМЯНА

bureaux are usually open until 5pm or 6pm (longer in summer), and sometimes 24 hours. On leaving the country, you can usually buy US dollars and euros (and, on occasion, sterling) from bureaux with your excess leva, but the exchange rate may be disadvantageous.

Traveller's cheques and credit cards

While it's a sensible precaution to carry a percentage of your funds in the form of **traveller's cheques**, they are certainly not convenient for everyday use, except in Sofia and the coastal and ski package resorts. Elsewhere you'll be lucky to find a private exchange that will touch them, and even banks can be reluctant to accept any but the brand to which they're affiliated.

ATMs are plentiful in city centres and in resorts but much rarer in rural areas. Most accept Visa, MasterCard, Maestro and Diners Club cards. The same cards can be used to pay for car rental, at petrol stations, top–notch restaurants and hotels, smart shops, and in supermarkets; but they are unlikely to be accepted in cafés, bars, souvenir stalls or taxis.

Opening hours and public holidays

In general, **shops** are open Monday to Friday from 8.30am (or earlier) until 6pm (or later, in the case of neighbourhood stores); on Saturdays they usually close at 2pm. Opening hours in central Sofia and in holiday resorts frequently extend to 8pm or beyond, seven days a week. In rural areas, a kind of unofficial siesta may prevail between noon and 3pm. In many towns **museums** are open Monday–Friday 9am–5pm, although in well-touristed areas they are more likely to be open at weekends (and may well close on Mon or Tues to compensate).

Public holidays

Jan 1	New Year's Day (*Nova godina*)
March 3	Liberation Day
Easter	
May 1	Labour Day
May 6	St George's Day
May 24	SS Cyril and Methodius's Day
Sep 6	Unification Day
Sept 22	Independence Day
Dec 25, 26	Christmas

Phones

GSM **mobile phones** can be used almost everywhere in Bulgaria save for mountain valleys, although you should contact your network to ensure that your **international roaming** facility is activated before you travel. Bulgaria's three main GSM operators Globul, MTel and Vivatel each sell prepaid SIM cards and top-up vouchers so you can use the local network. Some mobile phones automatically block if you insert a new SIM card into them, however, so check with your operator before trying this out.

Usage of public telephones taking **phonecards** (*fonkarta*) has dropped dramatically in Bulgaria, but they still exist on street corners, in post offices and outside major public buildings. They are operated by two separate companies: Bulfon (whose phones are orange) and Betkom (with blue phones). It's best to carry both cards as you never know

which system will be available (in some towns one has a monopoly). You can use them to make any kind of direct-dial call for the same cost as you'd pay in a telephone office or private house. Phonecards are sold at post offices and many shops and kiosks.

In the absence of a phonecard you'll have to fall back on the **telephone offices** (*telefon*, ТЕЛЕФОН) attached to post offices, where you are assigned a cabin and pay for your call afterwards. The telephone section is usually open longer than other parts of the post office, often as late as 11pm in major cities and 24 hours in Sofia. As most hotels levy extortionate surcharges on **international calls**, you'll almost always save money by going through a phone office instead.

Photography

Colour print film and memory cards for digital cameras are widely available in most big towns and along the coast, and a growing number of photo shops will develop films in one or two hours. More specialized items, such as black-and-white film, film for transparencies and camera batteries, can be difficult to find outside Sofia, so it's best to stock up before leaving home.

Time

Two hours ahead of GMT, seven hours ahead of EST. Bulgarian Summer Time lasts from the beginning of April to the end of September.

International telephone codes

To **dial abroad direct from Bulgaria**, first use the international code listed below and then the STD (area) code, remembering to omit the initial 0 from the STD code.

UK ℡0044
Ireland ℡00353
US & Canada ℡001
Australia ℡0061
New Zealand ℡0064

To **call Bulgaria from abroad**, use the following international access codes, followed by the area code (omitting the initial 0) and the local number.

From the UK & Ireland ℡00359
From the US & Canada ℡011359
From Australia & New Zealand ℡0011359

Toilets

Public toilets (*toaletni*, ТОАЛЕТНИ) are found at all train stations, most bus stations, and in central parks in towns. They're usually quite appalling, despite the presence of a caretaker or cleaner, to whom you pay a small fee (*taksa*) on entering. Many toilets will clog if you put paper down them, so take the hint if a wastebasket is provided. *Mazhe* (МЪЖЕ or М) are men; *zheni* (ЖЕНИ or Ж) or *dami* (ДАМИ, Д) are women.

Tourist information

Tourist information offices in the western European or North American sense are still in their infancy in Bulgaria, and although the State Committeee for Tourism operates an information centre in Sofia (see p.75), the provision of offices throughout the country is patchy. A smattering of tourist offices does exist in the Pirin, Stara planina, Rhodope and northern Black Sea regions, but they are all under-funded and rarely keep to their advertised working hours. Addresses are provided throughout this guide.

There are no Bulgarian tourist information offices abroad, and the State Committee for Tourism's website (Ⓦ www.bulgariatravel.org) is rather basic.

Guide

Guide

Sofia

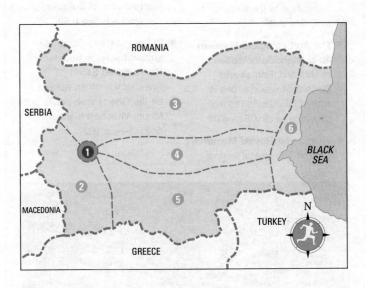

CHAPTER 1 # Highlights

* **Sofia Synagogue** Lovingly restored building with a superb interior; a fitting memorial to one of the capital's most historically important communities. See p.86

* **Zhenski pazar** A popular central market, where you can pick up everything from fresh vegetables to the kitchen sink. See p.86

* **The Archeological Museum** An outstanding collection of Thracian, Roman and Bulgarian treasures, this is a great introduction to the country's history. See p.88

* **Aleksandar Nevski Memorial Church** The capital's prime ecclesiastical monument – a magnificent neo-Byzantine edifice intended to symbolize Bulgarian–Russian friendship. See p.92

* **Boyana Church** The vibrant frescoes in this outwardly unassuming structure constitute one of the masterpieces of Bulgarian medieval art. See p.99

* **Zlatni mostove** Scramble around the huge boulders of the so-called Stone River, or launch an assault on the Cherni vrah peak, Mount Vitosha's highest point. See p.102

▲ Zhenski pazar market

Sofia

According to its motto, **SOFIA (СОФИЯ)** "grows but does not age" (*raste no ne staree*): a tribute to the mushrooming suburbs occupied by an estimated one-fifth of Bulgaria's population, and a cryptic reference to its ancient origins. Roman ruins, Byzantine churches and fine mosques attest to a long and colourful history, although the peeling stucco of its early-twentieth-century buildings lends an air of dilapidation to the capital's wide, tree-shaded boulevards.

The mixture of chaos and disorganization which characterizes most of Sofia's points of arrival makes it an unwelcoming city for first-time visitors. However, once you've settled in and begun to explore, you'll find Sofia surprisingly laid-back for a capital city. The place comes into its own on fine spring and summer evenings, when the downtown streets and their pavement cafés buzz with life. The close historical relationship between Bulgaria and Russia reveals itself in the capital's public buildings, foremost of which is the **Aleksandar Nevski Memorial Church**. The neighbouring streets harbour a modest collection of museums and galleries – enough to justify a day or two's sightseeing. Urban pursuits can be easily combined with the recreational possibilities offered by verdant **Mount Vitosha**, just 12km south of the centre. Also on the fringes of the city, the medieval frescoes at the **Boyana Church** and **Kremikovtsi Monastery** make essential viewing for anyone interested in Orthodox art. A host of new bars and clubs has given the city a raw, hedonistic edge – plus there's lots of drama and serious music, especially during the **Sofia Music Weeks**, which take place each June.

Some history

Sofia's first inhabitants were the **Serdi**, a Thracian tribe who settled here some three thousand years ago. Their Roman conquerors named it Serdica, a walled city that reached its zenith under Emperor Constantine in the early fourth century AD. Serdica owed its importance to the position it occupied on the *diagonis*, the Roman road that linked Constantinople with modern Belgrade on the Danube, providing the Balkans with its main commercial and strategic artery. However, the empire's foes also used the road as a quick route to the riches of Constantinople, and Serdica was frequently under attack – most notably from the Huns, who sacked the city in the fifth century. Once rebuilt by the emperor Justinian in the mid-sixth century, Serdica became one of the Byzantine Empire's most important strongholds in the Balkans.

Migrating Slavs began to filter into the city in the seventh century, becoming the dominant force in the region after Serdica's capture by the Bulgar Khan Krum in 809. The city continued to flourish under the

Bulgarians, although few medieval cultural monuments remain, save for the thirteenth-century **Boyana Church**. Renamed Sredets by the Slavs (and subsequently Triaditsa by the Byzantines), the city became known as Sofia sometime in the fourteenth century, most probably taking its name from the ancient **Church of Sveta Sofia** (Holy Wisdom), which still stands in the city centre. Five centuries of **Ottoman rule** began with the city's capture in 1382, during which time Sofia thrived as a market centre, though little material evidence of the Ottoman period remains save for a couple of mosques.

Economic decline set in during the nineteenth century, hastened by earthquakes in 1852. Sofia was a minor provincial centre at the time of the Liberation in 1878, when defeat of the Ottoman Empire by Russian forces paved the way for the foundation of an **independent Bulgarian state**. Sofia was chosen to become the new capital of the country in preference to more prestigious centres (such as Tarnovo in central Bulgaria) because of its geographical location: situated on a wide plain fringed by mountains, Sofia combined defensibility with the potential for future growth. It was also thought that it would occupy a central position in any Bulgarian state, which included (as was then hoped) Macedonia. The Bulgarians were keen to stamp their identity on the city right at the outset. Mosques were demolished or turned to other uses, and six thousand of the city's Turks chose to emigrate. Sofia underwent a period of rapid development, although progress sometimes sat uneasily beside backwardness and poverty. The Czech historian and educationalist Konstantin Jireček – one of many foreign experts brought in to help run the new state – dubbed Sofia *boklukopolis* ("trashville") in recognition of its chaotic post-Liberation appearance. Yet foreign observers were on the whole impressed by the way in which the Bulgarians speedily improvised a capital city out of nothing. "I had expected a semi-barbaric Eastern town," remarked Frank Cox, the *Morning Post*'s Balkan correspondent in 1913, "but I found a modern capital, small but orderly, clean and well-managed . . . but oh, so deadly dull."

Despite its increasing prosperity, Sofia didn't experience much of a *belle époque*, save for the lavish palace balls presided over by the mercurial Tsar Ferdinand, and the weekly dances at the military club. The city experienced more frenetic growth during the **post-World War II era** of "socialist construction", and a veneer of Stalinist monumentalism was added to the city centre in the shape of buildings like the **Party House**, a stern-looking expression of political authority. Sofia's rising population was housed in the endless high-rise suburbs (places with declamatory names like Mladost – "Youth", Druzhba – "Friendship", and Nadezhda – "Hope") that girdle the city today.

The factories that used to employ the inhabitants of these suburbs went into a steep decline during the 1980s and collapsed totally in the 1990s, leading to high unemployment and a drop in living standards. But Sofia has coped with

The Shops

The majority of Sofia's inhabitants are of **Shop descent** – the Shops being the original peasant population from the surrounding countryside who have migrated to the city in vast numbers over the past hundred years. Although you can still tell a Shop by his or her accent, which is flatter than standard Bulgarian – they say *desno* instead of *dyasno* for "right", *levo* instead of *lyavo* for "left" – the other cultural differences that made them a distinct group a century ago have now all but disappeared.

At the time of the Liberation many Shops – especially those living around the foothills of Mount Vitosha – still lived in an extended family community known as a **zadruga**, an arrangement once common to the entire South Slav area. In a *zadruga*, several married brothers and cousins pooled their lands and lived together under the rule of a *domovladika* (literally "head of the household"), who would apportion tasks and look after the accounts. *Zadruga* members tended to specialize in different jobs (one might be a miller, one an innkeeper, another a priest, and so on) in order to keep the community self-sufficient. The growth of Sofia disrupted the traditional rural economy and signalled the end of this system.

Some of the villages around Sofia still preserve age-old **Shop Lenten customs**. Voluyak, 10km northwest of Sofia on the Berkovitsa road, still celebrates the Dzhamala festival (forty days before Easter on odd-numbered years), when a camel (actually a wooden sled dressed in skins) is hauled through the streets before being symbolically killed and returned to life again, in what is essentially a Dionysiac death-and-rebirth ritual of ancient origins. The neighbouring village of Mramor is the Sofia district's main centre for celebrations linked with Todorovden (St Theodore's day, the first Saturday of Lent), when people from all over the Shop area congregate – usually bringing their horses and carts – for a day of feasting and carousing.

the transition from Communism to capitalism better than most Bulgarian towns. New businesses are springing up all the time (though many go bust just as quickly), jobs are easier to come by here than elsewhere, and the population has been swelled by migrants from provincial towns blighted by economic stagnation. Sofia's city council has made small but significant steps in smartening up the capital, repaving central pavements and providing key buildings with a much-needed facelift. Even so, much about contemporary Sofia remains strange or surprising: walking through the quiet, under-lit streets at night often makes you feel as if you're in a small provincial town rather than a million-strong urban sprawl.

Arrival

Sofia airport, 10km east of town, has two terminals, the dated and rather gloomy Terminal One (still used by most airlines) and the modern glass-and-steel Terminal Two (used by Bulgaria Air, British Airways and a number of other operators). Bus #84 from Terminal One and bus #284 from Terminal Two (both every 15–20min 7am–11pm) run to Orlov most on the eastern fringes of the city centre (see p.96). Tickets cost 0.70Lv from kiosks near the relevant bus stops or 0.80Lv from the driver. You must buy an extra ticket for each large item of luggage.

To get into town by **taxi**, avoid the touts in the arrivals hall and head outside to find an official taxi rank, where the yellow-liveried cars of reputable firms like OK Supertrans will take you to the centre for 15–20Lv.

By train

Trains arrive at the **Central Station** (ЦЕНТРАЛНА ГАРА; *Tsentralna gara*), a concrete barn twenty minutes' walk north of the city centre. Trams #1 and #7 will take you from the station forecourt to pl. Sveta Nedelya, within easy reach of central hotels and hostels.

For details on **leaving Sofia by train**, see "Moving on from Sofia" on p.113.

By bus

Most inter-city and international services arrive at the brand-new **Tsentralna Avtogara** adjacent to the Central Station on bul. Knyaginya Mariya Luiza, or at the **Trafik-Market** bus park just next door. However, several services from provincial towns still use a ring of smaller bus stations in the suburbs: some buses from points north and northeast of Sofia use the **Avtogara Poduyane** (АВТОГАРА ПОДУЯНЕ; sometimes referred to as Avtogara Iztok) terminal on ul. Todorini Kukli (bus #75 runs from here to Orlov most; otherwise head one block north from the station and cross to the opposite side of bul. Vladimir Vazov to catch trolleybus #1 to bul. Vasil Levski). Buses from the southwest use **Ovcha Kupel** (АВТОГАРА ОВЧА КУПЕЛ), halfway down bul. Tsar Boris III (take tram #5 to the Palace of Justice or *Sadebna palata* in the city centre, or tram #19 to the Central Station). Buses from the southeast use the **Yug** terminal (АВТОГАРА ЮГ), on bul. Dragan Tsankov, beneath the overpass known as Nadlez Darvenitsa, just beyond the *Park Hotel Moskva* (a few steps away from the Interpred metro station due to open in 2009; until then walk northwest up ul. Dragan Tsankov for 500m to pick up tram #18 to the central ul. Graf Ignatiev).

For details on **leaving Sofia by bus**, see p.113.

Information

The **National Tourist Information Centre**, at pl. Sveta Nedelya 1 (*Tsentar za natsionalna informatsiya*; Mon–Fri 9am–5pm; ℡02/987 9778, ⓦwww .bulgariatravel.org), doesn't always have the answers to specific queries about the capital, though staff members are English-speaking and friendly. They also have a limited amount of information and brochures on other parts of Bulgaria. More useful is the commercial travel agent **Zig Zag Odysseia-in**, at bul. Stamboliyski 20 (entrance round the corner on ul. Lavele; June–Sept daily 9am–7.30pm, Oct–May Mon–Fri 9am–7.30pm, ℡02/980 5102, ⓦwww .zigzagbg.com), which specializes in independent travel. Zig Zag offers accommodation bookings in Sofia and throughout Bulgaria, as well as advice on rural tourism and hiking, car hire and one-day tours; there's also a good selection of maps for sale. Staff charge a 5Lv consultation fee, but this is deducted from the price of any service you book through them.

The Domino **city map**, updated regularly and featuring public transport routes, can be bought from most newsstands and bookshops. Best of the locally produced English-language **city guides** is *Sofia In Your Pocket* (free from hostels, hotels and restaurants; also available online at ⓦwww.inyourpocket.com), an entertainingly written and above all accurate guide to the city's sights and nightlife. There's also a weekly English-language **newspaper**, the increasingly authoritative *Sofia Echo* (ⓦwww.sofiaecho.com; available from central newsstands), which offers up-to-date coverage of Bulgarian politics and business news.

City transport

Public transport is cheap and reasonably efficient, with intertwining networks of buses (*avtobus*), trolleybuses (*troleibus*) and trams (*tramvai*). Some cross-town routes are operated by privately owned **minibuses** (*marshrutki*), which are faster than regular buses but tend to be uncomfortable. A single **metro line** (*metropoliten*) runs from the western suburb of Lyulin to the Serdika station on pl. Sveta Nedelya. The line is due to be extended southeastwards to Sofia University and Borisova Gradina park sometime in 2009, when it should become enormously useful as a means of shuttling across the city centre. Most public transport services run from about 4am until 11.30pm.

The main problem for visitors is lack of information: while some bus and tram stops are well marked, others are merely corroded metal poles displaying no information about which services call there or how often. Always be prepared to ask the locals, and buy a good city map if possible.

There's a flat fare on all urban routes (currently 0.70Lv but be prepared for price rises), and **tickets** (*bileti*) for buses, trolleys and trams can be bought from street kiosks or, sometimes, from the driver (0.80Lv). All tickets must be punched on board the vehicle: inspections are frequent and there are spot fines for fare-dodgers. Officially, you're supposed to buy an extra ticket for each large item of baggage, but in practice this is rarely enforced – except on buses to and from the airport, where inspectors deliberately pick on foreigners on the grounds that they're less likely than the locals to put up an argument. If you're staying in Sofia for any length of time, a one-day ticket (*karta za edin den*; 3Lv) or a strip of ten tickets (*talon*; 6Lv) can be a sound investment, but can only be bought from kiosks. Tram, bus and trolleybus tickets are not valid on the metro (for which separate tickets must be purchased at the station counter; 0.70Lv) or in minibuses, for which you must pay the driver (around 1Lv flat fare).

Taxis

Taxis aren't particularly expensive, charging the equivalent of 0.70–0.80Lv per km until 10pm, 0.90–1Lv per km after that. Taxis hang around at most big intersections, or can be flagged down on the street – a green light in the windscreen indicates that a taxi is vacant; a red one means that it is occupied. You can order a taxi by phone (see "Listings" p.114 for recommended firms), but don't expect to get through to an English-speaker. Sofia taxi drivers don't always have a detailed knowledge of their own city, and clients may be expected to supply directions themselves. The overcharging of foreigners is fairly endemic, and there's little you can do to prevent this except check that meters are working and be firm with obvious transgressors.

Accommodation

In general, you'll find yourself paying more in Sofia than elsewhere in the country for a decent place to stay, although there are plenty of hostels and guesthouses catering for budget travellers and a growing number of mid-range choices too. The number of establishments offering rooms of international business standard is also on the increase – and prices are comparable with those in Western Europe. The Zig-Zag/Odysseia-In agency (see p.75) can organize beds in cheap hotels and hostels; it also has its own two- or three-person apartment (❸).

With the Vrana campsite 10km east of town on the main Plovdiv road increasingly gone to seed, camping isn't really an option.

Hostels

There is a wealth of hospitable, characterful and downright quirky hostels in central Sofia, with competition between them ensuring that prices remain reasonably low – 20Lv being the going rate for a dorm bed with breakfast. If the bunk-bed lifestyle doesn't appeal, many of Sofia's hostels do offer self-contained double rooms as well. Hostels fill up quickly in summer, putting pressure on both staff and facilities, so always ring in advance to secure a bed.

The hostels listed below are marked on the Central Sofia map on p.82 unless otherwise stated.

Art Hostel ul. Angel Kanchev 21A ☎02/987 0545, ⓦwww.art-hostel.com. Easy-going hostel (which also goes by the quirky name "Usually We Spend Our Time In The Garden") complete with art exhibitions in the common room, a graffiti-decorated guests-only bar, and a relaxing garden. One ten-bed and one four-bed dorm on the ground floor, and three double rooms in the self-contained apartment above. Prices include breakfast. Ask about discounts for long-term stays. Doubles ❷, dorms from 20Lv per person.

Hostel Mostel bul. Makedoniya 2A (see map, p.78) ☎0889 223 296, ⓦwww .hostelmostel.com. An anonymous-looking doorway leads through to a courtyard containing a modern reconstruction of a nineteenth-century coaching inn, complete with balustraded balconies and creaky wooden stairs. The ground floor contains a large common room with pool table, lounge seating and kitchen area, and there are five eight-bed dorms on the floor above, each with wooden floors and pastelly décor. Breakfast is included, and there is Wi-Fi coverage in the lounge. You can book a whole dorm for double or triple use in the off-season. Beds from 20Lv per person.

Hostel Sofia ul. Pozitano 16 ☎02/989 8582, ⓔhostelsofia@yahoo.com. Cramped but cosy place occupying a couple of storeys of a downtown apartment building. Friendly staff, free use of kitchen, and breakfast included. Book in advance if you can. Dorm beds 18Lv per person; reductions for stays longer than two nights.

Kervan ul. Rositsa 3 ☎02/983 9428 or 0888 374 369, ⊛www.kervanhostel.com. Set amid quiet streets just north of the Aleksandar Nevski Memorial Church, Kervan is a thoughtfully decorated place with hardwood floors and warm textiles, with five- or six-bed dorms. Very small kitchen and delightfully snug breakfast area. Laundry service for a few extra leva. Dorms 20Lv per person.

The Rooms ul. Pop Bogomil 10 ☎02/983 3508 and 0898 260 316, ⓔtheroomshostel@yahoo.com. Although it describes itself as a hostel, this is more

like a kooky guesthouse, offering self-contained rooms (a single, a couple of doubles and one triple) instead of dorms. No breakfast, but there is at least a communal kettle in the cute corner that passes for a lounge. Discounts for long-term stays. Doubles ❷

Sofia Guesthouse bul. Patriarh Evtimiy 27 ☎02/981 3656, ⊛www.sofiaguest.com. Bright, clean and airy hostel with two six-bed and two-eight-bed dorms, plus a solitary en-suite double. There's a reasonable number of toilets and showers to go around, along with a kitchen, a spacious lounge and a washing machine you can use for a small extra fee. A basic breakfast is included, and pick-up from the central train and bus stations is free. Wi-Fi coverage throughout. Double room ❸, dorm beds 20Lv.

Hotels

Sofia offers an increasingly wide choice of hotels, and good-value accommodation can be found even in the centre of the city. The business end of the market is well catered for, and a growing number of boutique hotels, mid-priced family-run establishments and guesthouses have added considerable variety to what's on offer. Places can fill up quickly in summer, so it's advisable to make **reservations** in advance.

Central Sofia

All the hotels listed below are marked on the Central Sofia map (pp.82–83).

Diter ul. Han Asparuh 65 ☎02/989 8998, ⊛www .diterhotel.com. Mid-sized hotel occupying a nicely restored pre-World War I townhouse in a central but relatively quiet neighbourhood. Rooms come in refreshingly bold colours and feature TV, a/c and multi-nozzled shower cubicles that are perfect if you're in need of a liquid massage. ❼

Grand Hotel Sofia ul. General Gurko 1 ☎02/811 0800, ⊛www.grandhotelsofia.bg. Very central five-star hogging one side of the City Garden, boasting liveried doormen and fully equipped, spacious rooms decked out in plush greens and maroons, plus a gym and sauna on-site. Ask for an "executive" double on the seventh floor or above if you want a panoramic view of downtown Sofia. Added facilities include a secure subterranean car park and a Wi-Fi zone in the lobby. Doubles from €220. ❾

Les Fleurs bul. Vitosha 21 ☎02/810 0800, ⊛www.lesfleurshotel.com. Designer hotel right on the main boulevard, whose irregularly shaped rooms feature curved walls, flat-screen TVs and intricately tiled bathrooms. Each room is named after a flower – go for a "sunflower" if you want an open-plan room with a walk-in wardrobe area, or a "daisy" if you fancy a studio apartment with

outdoor terrace and panoramic views. Doubles from €200. ❾

Kolikovski ul. Hristo Belchev 46. Modern, medium-sized establishment on a quiet corner only two minutes away from bul. Vitosha, offering en-suite rooms with TV. Standard doubles come in unobtrusive greens and ochres but for the business-class rooms you really need to like loud colours, with purple, lilac, orange and matt-black predominant. ❼

Niky ul. Neofit Rilski 16 ☎02/952 3058, ⊛www .hotel-niky.com. Excellent-value accommodation in a converted apartment block just off the main bul. Vitosha. Basic doubles are small but neat and tidy with modern showers and a/c; bigger apartment-style rooms have a kitchenette and bath. Apartments from ❻, rooms ❹

Pop Bogomil ul. Pop Bogomil 5 ☎02/983 1165, ⊛www.bulgariabedandbreakfast.com. Friendly family-run place on a quiet downtown street. Rooms are small and loudly decorated but otherwise neat and cosy, with modern fittings and TV. Some rooms come with bathtubs, others with shower. Generous breakfast for a few extra leva. ❹

Radisson SAS pl. Narodno Sabranie 4 ☎02/933 4334, ⊛www.sofia.radissonsas.com. Modern hotel

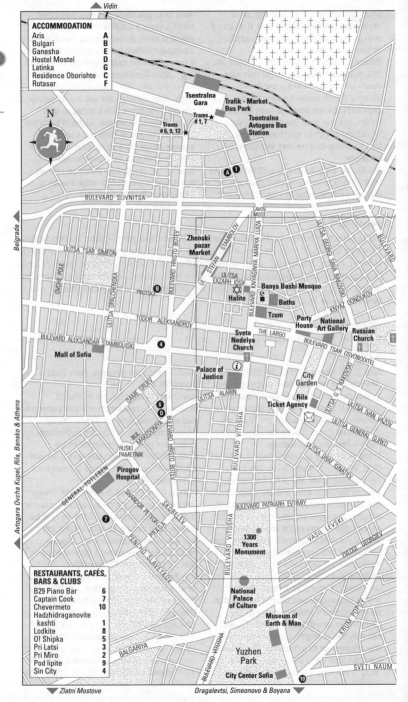

▲ Vidin

ACCOMMODATION
Aris	A
Bulgari	B
Ganesha	E
Hostel Mostel	D
Latinka	C
Residence Oborishte	F
Rotasar	G

N

Belgrade ◀

Avtogara Ovcha Kupel, Rila, Bansko & Athens ◀

Tsentralna Gara

Trafik - Market Bus Park

Trams #1, 7

Trams #6, 9, 12

Tsentralna Avtogara Bus Station

Ⓐ ❶

BULEVARD SLIVNITSA

LAVOV MOST

ULITSA TSAR SIMEON

OVCHE POLE

ULITSA OPALCHENSKA

BULEVARD HRISTO BOTEV

UL. STEFAN STAMBOLOV

Zhenski pazar Market

ULITSA EXZARH JOSIF

BULEVARD KNYAGINA MARIYA LUIZA

Banya Bashi Mosque

Halite

Baths

ULITSA GEORGI SAVA RAKOVSKI

KNYAZ DONDUKOV

BULEVARD

PIROTSKA

Ⓑ

TODOR ALEKSANDROV

Tzum

Party House

National Art Gallery

Russian Church

BULEVARD ALEKSANDAR STAMBOLIISKI

Mall of Sofia

❹

THE LARGO

Sveta Nedelya Church

BULEVARD TSAR OSVOBODITEL

DAME GRUEV

Palace of Justice

ⓘ

City Garden

ULITSA G S RAKOVSKI

❻ Ⓓ

BUL. MAKEDONIYA

ULITSA ALABIN

Rila Ticket Agency

ULITSA IVAN VAZOV

BULEVARD VITOSHA

ULITSA GENERAL GURKO

RUSKI PAMETNIK

BULEVARD HRISTO BOTEV

ULITSA GRAF IGNATIEV

GENERAL TOTLEBEN

Pirogov Hospital

SHANDOR PETYOFI

PRAGA

SKOBELEV

BULEVARD PATRIARH EVTIMIY

VASIL LEVSKI

EVLOGI GEORGIEV

❼

PENCHO SLAVEYKOV

BULEVARD VITOSHA

1300 Years Monument

RESTAURANTS, CAFÉS, BARS & CLUBS
B29 Piano Bar	6
Captain Cook	7
Chevermeto	10
Hadzhidraganovite kashti	1
Lodkite	8
O! Shipka	5
Pri Latsi	3
Pri Miro	2
Pod lipite	9
Sin City	4

National Palace of Culture

Museum of Earth & Man

KRUM POPOV

BALGARIYA

BULEVARD VITOSHA

Yuzhen Park

SVETI NAUM

City Center Sofia

❿

▼ Zlatni Mostove

▼ Dragalevtsi, Simeonovo & Boyana ▼

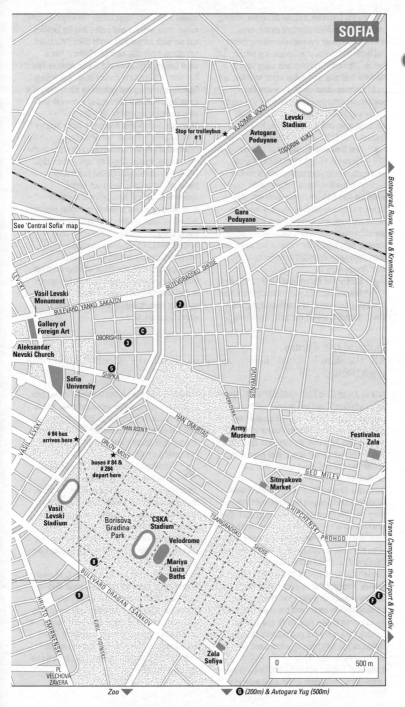

SOFIA

Stop for trolleybus #1 ★ ... VLADIMIR VAZOV

Levski Stadium

Avtogara Poduyane

TODORINI KUKI

Botevgrad, Ruse, Varna & Kremikovtsi

Gara Poduyane

See 'Central Sofia' map

BOTEVGRADSKO SHOSE

Vasil Levski Monument

BULEVARD YANKO SAKAZOV

2

Gallery of Foreign Art

OBORISHTE

C

3

Aleksandar Nevski Church

SHIPKA

5

Sofia University

CHERKOVNA

SITNYAKOVO

IVAN ASEN II

HAN OMURTAG

Army Museum

Festivalna Zala

84 bus arrives here ★

ORLOV MOST

GEO MILEV

buses # 84 & # 284 depart here ★

Sitnyakovo Market

SHIPCHENSKI PROHOD

Vasil Levski Stadium

Vrana Campsite, the Airport & Plovdiv

TSARIGRADSKO SHOSE

Borisova Gradina Park

CSKA Stadium

Velodrome

8

Mariya Luiza Baths

9

HRISTO SMIRNENSKI

BULEVARD DRAGAN TSANKOV

KIRIL VIDINSKI

F E

Zala Sofiya

PL VELCHOVA ZAVERA

0   500 m

Zoo ▼   ▼ **G** (200m) & *Avtogara Yug (500m)*

opposite the Bulgarian National Assembly, offering comfortable business-standard rooms, each offering reasonable desk-space, relaxing cream and butterscotch colour schemes, and electric kettles. "Standard" doubles face away from pl. Narodno Sabranie, so it's well worth splashing out on a "business-class" room (or one of the spectacular sixth-floor junior suites) if you want a full view of Sofia's most elegant square. Fully equipped gym, plus Wi-Fi coverage throughout. Doubles from €170, junior suites from €250. ⑨

🏃 **Red Bed and Breakfast** ul. Lyuben Karavelov 15 ☎02/988 8188, ⓦwww .redbandb.com. Spread across several upstairs sections in the Red House cultural centre (see p.95), the Red B&B offers six rooms with shared facilities in an arty informal environment. Some rooms are huge and furnished with antique wardrobes and lush fabrics, while others are sparsely decorated in the extreme, but all are neat and comfortable. Breakfast is delivered to your door. Rooms from ④

🏃 **Scotty's** ul. Ekzarh Yosif 11 ☎02/983 6777, ⓦwww.geocities.com/scottysboutiquehotel. Occupying three floors of a renovated apartment block, *Scotty's* is among the more characterful of central Sofia's mid-range hotels. The bright en-suite rooms come with tea-and-coffee-making facilities and are each named after world cities ("Auckland" has atmospheric attic ceilings; "Sydney" has a small balcony with views of Sofia synagogue). The first hotel in Bulgaria to declare itself "gay-friendly", Scotty's easy-going and welcoming atmosphere is a major plus. Breakfast delivered to your room and Wi-Fi coverage throughout. ⑤–⑥

Sheraton Sofia Hotel Balkan pl. Sveta Nedelya 5 ☎02/981 6541, ⓦwww.luxurycollection.com/sofia. Dependable five-star occupying a prime site on the city's central square. Originally built in the 1950s (when the hotel accommodated Communist big-wigs), the building has much period atmosphere, its long high-ceilinged corridors illuminated by ornate chandeliers. Fitness facilities in the basement. Doubles start at €190. ⑨

Sveta Sofia ul. Pirotska 18 ☎02/981 2634, ⓦwww.svetasofia-alexanders.com. Converted nineteenth-century townhouse on a busy pedestrianized shopping street, offering small but welcoming rooms with contemporary furnishings, neutral colours and showers – "luxe" rooms with bath cost extra. It's noisy at weekends due to wedding parties. ⑦

Outside the centre

All the hotels listed below are marked on the Central Sofia map (pp.82–83).

Aris ul. Knyaz Boris I 203 ☎02/931 3177, ⓦwww .hotel-aris.com. Clean and unfussy rooms in a medium-sized hotel in a quiet street near the central train and bus stations. Rooms come with small TV and Bulgarian-style WC with open shower. Triples and four-person apartments (comprising double bed and fold-down couch) may suit families. ⑤

Bulgari ul. Pirotska 50 ☎02/831 0060, ⓦwww .bulgarihotel.net. Located on an animated shopping street near the Zhenski pazar market, *Bulgari* offers economically priced en-suite rooms which are on the small side but otherwise excellent. Colourful artworks in the hall areas provide plenty of atmosphere, and there's Wi-Fi coverage in the lobby. ⑤

Ganesha ul. Al. Humboldt 26 ☎02/971 3815, ⓦwww.hotelganesha-bg.com. A converted apartment block on a suburban street, midway between the city centre and the airport. The neat en-suite rooms have satellite TV and a small balcony. Take bus #213 or #313 from the train station, or bus #84 from the airport, and get off at the *Hotel Pliska* stop. ④

Latinka ul. Latinka 28A ☎02/870 0848, ⓦwww .hotel-latinka-sofia.com. A mid-sized hotel in a residential area just beyond Borisova Gradina park, *Latinka* is well-placed for woodland walks and is only a 15-minute journey from the centre on tram #18. The en-suite rooms feature TV and minibar. The top-floor doubles with skylight windows are extremely cosy. ⑥

🏃 **Residence Oborishte** ul. Oborishte 63 ☎02/814 4888, ⓦwww.residence .oborishte.com. Occupying a leafy part of town that accommodates several foreign embassies, this place is more of a homely retreat than a hotel. Most accommodation is in the form of two-room apartments, and the social areas are perfect for lounging around in. Apartments from ⑧, rooms ⑦

Rotasar ul. Liditse 1 ☎02/971 4571, ⓦwww .rotasar.com. Smallish suburban hotel 4km southeast of the centre, with an intimate ambience. Rooms are decked out in warm reds and blues, all with fridge, TV and a/c. Some come with shower, others with bathtub. There are a couple of three- to four-person suites suitable for families or groups. Directions as for the *Ganesha*. ④

The City

The heart of Sofia fits compactly within the irregular octagon formed by the city's inner ring road. Most of the sights are found inside this central area within easy walking distance of each other, and the grid-like pattern of streets radiating outwards from the main point of reference, **ploshtad Sveta Nedelya** (ПЛОЩАД СВЕТА НЕДЕЛЯ), makes orientation relatively easy. It's a good idea to sample the area around Sveta Nedelya first, before embarking on a trip to the set-piece public buildings and squares to the east. Within striking distance are the refreshing open spaces of the city's main **parks**, a brisk walk or tram ride away from the centre. Expeditions to **Mount Vitosha** and the suburbs nestling in its foothills require more time and reliance on public transport.

Around ploshtad Sveta Nedelya

Ploshtad Sveta Nedelya – Sveta Nedelya square – stands at the historical centre of Sofia and still serves as its hub, straddling the capital's principal north–south thoroughfare and providing easy access to the main business and sightseeing districts. The square elongates to join **bulevard Vitosha** (БУЛ. ВИТОША), the city's main shopping street, to the south, while to the north the *Sheraton* hotel and the Tzum shopping mall guard the entrance to **pl. Nezavisimost**, a broad street-cum-square surrounded by government buildings erected during the socialist period. On the northern side of pl. Nezavisimost, **bulevard Knyaginya Mariya Luiza** (БУЛ. КНЯГИНЯ МАРИЯ ЛУИЗА) heads towards the main train station, passing the city's principal mosque, synagogue and public baths on the way.

The Church of Sveta Nedelya

Trams rattle round a paved island on which lies the **Church of Sveta Nedelya**. Standing upon the former site of Serdica's chief crossroads, the current structure is the much-rebuilt successor to a line of churches that has stood here since medieval times. During the Ottoman period it was known as the Church of Sveti Kral – the "Blessed King" – as the remains of the Serbian monarch, Stefan Urosh II Milutin (1282–1321) were brought here for safe keeping during the fifteenth century. In 1925 the church almost claimed another king, when Communist insurgents detonated bombs during a funeral mass, killing 123 people but failing to harm their intended victims, Tsar Boris III and his cabinet. Nowadays Sveta Nedelya is second only to the Aleksandar Nevski Memorial Church (see p.92) in importance as a city-centre place of worship. It's the venue of choice for society weddings on Saturdays, and is the scene of particularly well attended services on Thursdays, when special prayers are intoned to ward off black magic and the evil eye.

Inside, the broad dome hovers above a vast chamber paved with slabs of smooth marble, bordered on each side by vigorous modern frescoes. The shrouded relics of Stefan Urosh are kept in a wooden chest directly to the right of the iconostasis, which is sometimes opened for serious pilgrims if there's a priest in attendance. It's a popular prayer site among women who believe that health problems can be cured by leaving a plastic bag containing their underclothes in the chest for 24 hours.

The Chapel of Sveta Petka Paraskeva

Just off the square to the east, a low doorway on ul. Saborna leads down into the subterranean **Chapel of Sveta Petka Paraskeva**, a medieval foundation

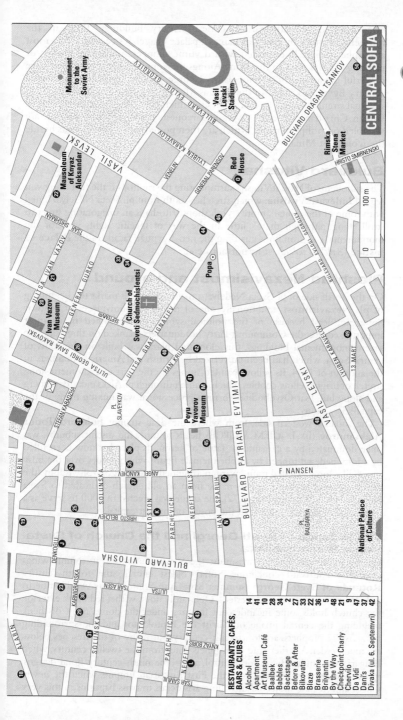

SOFIA

CENTRAL SOFIA

0 ___ 100 m

Monument to the Soviet Army

Vasil Levski Stadium

Rimska Stena Market

Mausoleum of Knyaz Aleksandar

Red House

Ivan Vazov Museum

Church of Sveti Sedmochislentsi

Peyu Yavorov Museum

National Palace of Culture

RESTAURANTS, CAFÉS, BARS & CLUBS

Alcohol	14
Apartment	41
Art Museum Café	10
Baalbek	28
Babbles	34
Backstage	2
Before & After	27
Bilkovata	33
Blaze	22
Brasserie	36
Brilyantin	48
By the Way	5
Checkpoint Charly	21
Chervilo	9
Da Vidi	47
Dani's	37
Divaka (ul. 6. Septemvri)	42

83

now dwarfed beneath early-twentieth-century buildings. Built in the thirteenth century by Tsar Kaloyan as a palace chapel, it's central Sofia's most atmospheric church, crammed with daytime shoppers muttering prayers or planting candles next to the icons. Alongside icons of Sveta Petka herself are powerful depictions of warrior–saints George, Dimitar and Mina (a fourth-century Egyptian known in the West as Menas), powerful personifications of spiritual strength in the face of adversity which have long been important to Balkan Christians. Special prayers and requests for divine intervention are scribbled onto slips of paper, which are then posted into a box that sits beside the icon of St Mina.

Bulevard Vitosha

The silhouette of Mount Vitosha surmounting the rooftops is the first thing you see on **bulevard Vitosha**, which stretches south from pl. Sveta Nedelya. Lined with some of the capital's more stylish shops, Vitosha is an invigorating street to stroll along, although there's little in the way of specific sights save for the monumental cast-iron lions guarding the neo-Egyptian facade of the **Palace of Justice** (*Sadebna palata*), at its northern end.

Ploshtad Nezavisimost and around

On the north side of pl. Sveta Nedelya, a major crossroads marks the beginning of **pl. Nezavisimost**, traditionally one of the major showpieces of postwar Sofia, not least because of the political symbolism embodied in its most imposing edifice, the Communist Party headquarters. Flanked on three sides by severe monumental buildings, this elongated plaza was built on the ruins of central Sofia, which had been pulverized by British and American bombers in the autumn of 1944. Its yellow-painted stones are the start of a kilometre-long stretch of bright yellow cobbles which, leading through pl. Aleksandar Batenberg and along bul. Tsar Osvoboditel, forms a processional way linking many of the capital's key sights.

The square's western side, from where the dead-straight **bulevard Todor Aleksandrov** (БУЛ. АЛЕКСАНДРОВ) heads towards the distant suburbs, was once dominated by a gargantuan statue of Lenin. Its place has now been filled by a lofty pedestal topped by a robed female figure, who presides over the busy streets like some celestial traffic warden. Intended as an allegory of wisdom (the city itself most probably got its name from an old church dedicated to Sveta Sofia or "Holy Wisdom"; see p.72), the statue was erected in 2000 to serve as a new, non-ideological symbol of the post-Communist capital.

The Rotunda of Sveti Georgi and the Church of Sveta Petka Samardzhiiska

On the south side of pl. Nezavisimost, the *Sheraton* hotel casts its sombre wings around a courtyard containing Sofia's oldest church, the fourth-century **Rotunda of Sveti Georgi** (summer 8am–7pm, winter hours variable due to lack of heating; donation requested). Outwardly dour, with a red brick exterior, the church holds some incandescent frescoes under the dome. Most of them, including the central image of Christ the Pantokrator and the surrounding frieze of 22 prophets, are fourteenth-century, but many of the frescoes below are much older. Another ring of prophets dates from the twelfth century, when Bulgaria was under Byzantine control, and some ninth-century floral designs, in the northern niche, date from the First Bulgarian Empire, when the newly Christianized state subjected unwilling aristocrats to mass baptisms in this very church. You can scramble around some remains of Roman-era Sofia in the plaza behind the church.

Pedestrians scurry down into the underpass which links the pl. Nezavisimost's southern and northern sides, and also gives access to **Serdika station** – the busy city-centre terminus of Sofia's metro. In the adjoining subterranean plaza is the weathered brick and stone of the **Church of Sveta Petka Samardzhiiska**, girded with concrete platforms, its tiled rooftop poking above street level. Built in the fourteenth century on the site of a late-Roman chapel, the church gained the epithet *samardzhiiska* in the nineteenth century, when it was adopted by the Saddlers' Guild as their private chapel. The church is entered via the crypt, from where spiral stairs ascend to the barrel-vaulted nave, filled with brightly coloured sixteenth-century frescoes illustrating bible scenes.

The northern side of pl. Nezavisimost is dominated by a large postwar structure that houses the Council of Ministers (Bulgaria's cabinet) and the **Tzum shopping mall**, three storeys of boutiques, cafés and banks occupying the premises of the now-defunct TzUM (ЦУМ), a state-owned department store that was once the pride of Communist-era Sofia.

The Party House

Of the buildings surrounding the Largo, the white, colonnaded supertanker of the **Party House**, or *partiinyat dom*, is by far the most arresting structure. Nowadays providing office space for members of the *Sabranie* (Bulgaria's parliament), it was originally built in the 1950s as the office of the Communist Party's Central Committee, and featured in a popular joke: a man cycles up to the building and leans his bike against it, whereupon a policeman shouts, "Hey! You can't leave that there, a high Soviet delegation is due to arrive any minute." "That's okay," replies the cyclist, "I'll chain it up".

After November 1989, public pressure mounted to have the Communists evicted from the building: initially without much result. In August 1990 anti-Communist demonstrators, enraged by the continuing presence of an enormous **red star** above the roof, despite a decree from the National Assembly ordering the removal of Communist iconography from all public buildings, attempted to torch it. The Party was finally ejected in early 1992, after which the House served briefly as a cinema before assuming its current function.

Immediately in front of the Party House, another pedestrian subway contains substantial remnants of the **Istochna porta** – the eastern gate of the Roman city of Serdica. Now surrounded by huge chunks of concrete, the bulging defensive towers which once stood guard on each side of the gate are still visible, different courses of brickwork pointing to later Byzantine and medieval Bulgarian rebuildings.

The Banya Bashi mosque and the mineral baths

North of pl. Nezavisimost, **bulevard Knyaginya Mariya Luiza** was the "most horrible street in Europe" for Arthur Symons when he was here in 1903, a "kind of mongrel East" existing "between two civilizations … a rag-heap for the refuse of both". Though it has been considerably cleaned up since then, you can see what he was getting at, if only in the dilapidated mixture of buildings that line the northerly sections of the street. However, the southern end is marked by one of the most graceful ensembles of buildings in the city, most eye-catching of which is the **Banya Bashi mosque**: a "Sultan-style" edifice with one large dome and a single minaret, built in 1576 by Hadzhi Mimar Sonah, who also designed the great mosque at Edirne in Turkey. In 1960, Bernard Newman noted "scarcely enough Turks in Sofia to make up a congregation", and in subsequent years the mosque fell into disuse as the Communist regime turned against the country's Muslim population. Now it is once again open for worship, the discreet call of the muezzin occasionally wafting above the heads of bemused city-centre shoppers.

Standing behind the mosque on the far side of a fountain-splashed park is Sofia's **Central Bath House** (*Tsentralna banya*), a stately pre-World War I structure which blends Byzantine forms with Art Nouveau-inspired decorative detail. Closed for restoration in 1986, it has yet to reopen its doors, although it has been earmarked as a potential home for the Museum of Sofia, which currently has nowhere to exhibit its vast collection. The natural mineral water that once fed the baths still spurts from public taps on the opposite side of ul. Ekzarh Yosif. Known to have beneficial effects for the digestion and immune system, the water regularly draws locals armed with bottles and jugs.

Halite and the synagogue

Facing the mosque to the west is the market hall or **Halite** (daily 7am–midnight), built at the same time as the Bath House and in a similar hybrid style. Inside, a glass roof held up by cast-iron pillars stretches above two storeys of stalls selling clothes, booze and a mouth-watering range of local deli products. A couple of salad bars and canteen-style eateries make this a good place to stop off for food between sightseeing.

Behind the market hall is the vast dome of **Sofia synagogue** (Mon–Fri 9am–5pm, Sat 9am–1pm; ring the bell and wait for the caretaker to emerge; free), an eye-catching piece of architecture designed by Viennese architect Friedrich Gruenanger in 1909. Combining Moorish and Art Nouveau elements that were much in vogue at the time, the synagogue was intended to symbolize the Jewish contribution to Bulgaria's burgeoning capital, blending in with the nearby mosque, market hall and Bath House to create an impressive assemblage of showpiece buildings. Tsar Ferdinand's presence at the opening ceremony was a clear demonstration of how much the Jewish community – which made up one fifth of the capital's population at the time – was valued by the regime. Until World War II Sofia's Jews occupied an overcrowded maze of narrow streets that stretched from here along what is now pl. Nezavisimost to the east. The area was turned to rubble by Allied bombing, although the vast majority of Sofia's Jews survived the war (see box, p.88), emigrating to Palestine in large numbers in the late 1940s. The synagogue's superbly restored interior is dominated by an enormous brass chandelier weighing over 2.25 tonnes, which hangs from a broad octagonal dome. Much of the ceiling space around it is painted to resemble a blue, star-filled sky, all framed by flowing, Art-Nouveau-inspired friezes.

Ulitsa Pirotska and the Zhenski pazar

On the southern side of the synagogue, the pedestrianized **ulitsa Pirotska** (УЛ. ПИРОТСКА) darts westwards past nineteenth-century apartment blocks, nowadays colonized by clothes boutiques and electrical goods stores. Tastefully cobbled, and with flowerbeds and cast-iron lampstands running down the middle, it's one of central Sofia's more attractive shopping streets.

The junction of Pirotska and ul. Stefan Stambolov marks the southern extent of the **Zhenski pazar** or Women's Market, an intensely crowded affair where you can find everything from fruit and vegetables to fake designer-label tracksuits and car parts. Peasants from the surrounding countryside arrive here early each

▲ Sofia synagogue

morning to sell their produce, and it's one of the few places in Sofia where the pulse of the Balkans of old can still be felt. Beyond lies one of Sofia's **older quarters**, with rutted cobblestones and low houses built around courtyards: a far cry from the modern housing estates that girdle the town.

Bulgaria's Jews

There are currently approximately five thousand Jews in Bulgaria (around half of whom live in the capital), the meagre remnants of what was historically a much larger community. Their presence in the country dates from at least the tenth century, although the most significant increase in Jewish numbers came towards the end of the fifteenth century, when the **Sephardic community** expelled by the Christian monarchs of Spain were resettled throughout the Levant and the Balkans by the considerably more tolerant Islamic rulers of the Ottoman Empire. Speaking the Ladino language (a mixture of medieval Spanish and Portuguese), the new arrivals established trading colonies in Bulgarian towns such as Nikopol, Ruse and elsewhere, although it was **Sofia** that became their cultural and social centre.

Bulgaria is one of the few European countries in which there seems to be no tradition of popular anti-Semitism. Even during the struggle to free Bulgaria from the Ottoman yoke, when non-Bulgarian ethnic groups were frequently perceived as national enemies, Jews managed to retain their status as respected members of the community. Jewish leaders dissuaded the Ottoman authorities from setting fire to Sofia in the aftermath of the Russo–Turkish war of 1877, something that wasn't forgotten by Bulgaria's post-independence leaders.

Things changed for Bulgaria's Jews in February **1940** (by which time the community numbered some 48,000), when Tsar Boris III appointed a pro-Nazi government under rabid anti-Semite Bogdan Filov, in the hope of forging an alliance with Hitler's Germany. Filov immediately set about introducing discriminatory legislation, closing down Jewish cultural institutions in January 1941, and forcing Jews to wear the yellow star in September 1942.

Uniquely in eastern Europe, however, the bulk of Bulgaria's Jews were saved from the Holocaust. Neither the sitting government nor Tsar Boris III could take much credit for this; they would have passively accepted Nazi plans to murder their Jewish subjects had not public opinion prevented them from doing so. In January **1943** the Bulgarian government responded to German demands for the deportation of Balkan Jews by promising to hand over twenty thousand Jews from Bulgarian-occupied

East of ploshtad Nezavisimost:
the Archeological Museum

At the eastern end of pl. Nezavisimost, on the corner of ul. Lege, stands an ivy-clad nine-domed building, formerly the *Buyuk Djami* or "Big Mosque", dating from 1494, and now housing the **Archeological Museum** (Arheoloshki muzey; Tues–Sun 10am–6pm; 5Lv). The attractive display of Thracian, Roman and medieval Bulgarian artefacts makes the perfect introduction to the nation's history, and is more effective than that offered by the over-hyped National History Museum (see p.98). The mosque's former prayer hall is filled with imposing Roman sarcophagi and funerary monuments, with Neolithic finds and ancient Greek vases arranged around the sides. Most personable of the major relics is the **Stela of Anaxander**, a sixth-century BC gravestone from the Greek colony of Apollonia (now Sozopol) on the Black Sea coast, which bears a relief of the deceased leaning on a staff, accompanied by his pet dog. Upstairs, past a copy of the enigmatic Madara Horseman (see p.259), there's a balconied gallery filled with frescoes removed from crumbling church walls throughout Bulgaria. Leading off one side of the gallery is a room stuffed with exquisite medieval Bulgarian jewellery. The most spectacular exhibit is on the mezzanine level just above the gallery, where the gold and silver treasures amassed by ancient Thracian chieftains is displayed. Occupying centre stage is the **Valchitran Treasure**, an elaborate 3000-year-old vessel in three parts that

Thrace and Macedonia. On discovering that there were only eleven thousand Jews from this source, they decided to make up the shortfall by rounding up Jews from Bulgaria proper. Jewish community leaders in Kyustendil complained to their MP, Dimitar Peshev, who began to rally support for the Jews among his parliamentary colleagues. Fearing a back-bench revolt, Prime Minister Filov went ahead with the deportation of the Jews from Macedonia and Thrace – all of whom perished in the death camps – but backed down from the other deportations, opting instead to intern Bulgaria's own Jews within the country itself.

Sensing that they enjoyed widespread popular sympathy, Jewish leaders in Sofia organized a mass protest on May 24, 1943. The demonstration didn't save them from internment, but it succeeded in alerting Bulgarian public opinion to their predicament. A wide cross-section of Bulgarian society, including the intelligentsia and the Orthodox Church, supported the Jews. The government henceforth remained deaf to German demands for further deportations, and the vast majority of Bulgarian Jews survived the war, returning to their homes after the Communist coup d'état of September 1944.

Communist Bulgaria presented something of a paradox to many Jews. On one hand the new order was welcomed, because it placed all citizens on an equal footing whatever their race. On the other hand, religious institutions of all kinds were persecuted, and Jews were encouraged to abandon their traditional beliefs in favour of state-sponsored atheism. Faced with the choice of staying in Bulgaria or emigrating to the new Jewish homeland in Palestine, the vast majority of Jews chose the latter, ninety percent of them leaving the country between 1948 and 1951. Those who remained were able to retain a sense of Jewish identity, although their religious and community life was now placed under the aegis of a single state-controlled organization. The latter was dissolved in 1990 and replaced by **Shalom**, a non-governmental cultural organization that has made great strides in the revival of Jewish traditions, and the renewal of contacts with Bulgarian Jews throughout the world.

was probably used for mixing sacred liquids during religious ceremonies. Elsewhere in the same room, a dazzling golden funeral mask dating from the fifth century BC bears a captivating portrait of a bearded Thracian ruler.

On the opposite side of ul. Lege from the museum stand the offices of Bulgaria's president, guarded day and night by soldiers clad in comic-opera nineteenth-century uniforms. Sightseers sometimes pause to observe the **changing of the guard**, which takes place on the hour.

Ploshtad Aleksandar Batenberg

If the Bulgarian Communist Party had a soul, it would doubtless still hover over the cobbled expanse of **ploshtad Aleksandar Batenberg** (ПЛОЩАД АЛЕКСАНДЪР БАТЕНБЕРГ), formerly pl. Deveti Septemvri or 9 September Square, where major anniversaries were celebrated with **parades**. These took place on May 1 and September 9 (the date of the Communist coup in 1944), and featured a familiar repertoire of Communist spectacle: red-scarved Young Pioneers, brigades of workers bearing portraits of their leaders, and floats carrying tableaux symbolizing the achievements of socialist construction. The anniversary of the Bolshevik Revolution (Nov 7) was marked by soldiers goose-stepping and armoured vehicles grinding across the plaza in emulation of mightier parades in Moscow. Such events – known as "spontaneous demonstrations of the people" during the Stalinist era – were a tiresome obligation for many participants. "We have seen so many of these demonstrations which humiliate human dignity, where normal people are expected to applaud some paltry mediocrity who has proclaimed himself a demigod and condescendingly waves to them from the heights of his police inviolability", wrote dissident writer Georgi Markov (criticisms like those eventually cost Markov his life, taken by a Bulgarian agent wielding a poisoned umbrella in London in 1978).

The National Art Gallery and the Ethnographic Museum

Stretching along the northern side of the square is the former royal palace, which was once so dilapidated that Tsar "Foxy" Ferdinand had to sleep under scaffolding to prevent the roof falling in on him. The palace began life as the Ottoman *Konak* where national hero Vasil Levski (see p.286) was tortured prior to his execution; it subsequently had the current Neoclassical facade tacked onto it by Ferdinand's predecessor, Knyaz Aleksandar. Inside is the **National Art Gallery** (Tues–Sun 10.30am–6pm; 3Lv; Ⓦ www.nationalartgallery-bg .org), an intriguing collection that kicks off with nineteenth-century icon painter Zahari Zograf – who created a hybrid of ancient Byzantine and modern European art – and goes on to reveal a rich seam of maverick twentieth-century Bulgarian painters. Indigenous folk styles and motifs inspired the works of Tsanko Lavrenov, whose pictures of Old Plovdiv are filled with magical-realist imagery. Bulgaria's most influential twentieth-century painter, Vladimir Dimitrov-Maistora (see p.121), was a mystic who believed that the Bulgarian peasantry possessed deep spiritual values – his portraits of peasant girls, several of which are on display here, are suffused with the aura of Orthodox icon paintings.

Housed in the same building is the **Ethnographic Museum** (Tues–Sun 10am–5.30pm; 3Lv), harbouring a multicoloured array of costumes, carpets and domestic knick-knacks from all over the country, accompanied by English-language texts. Much of the museum is taken up by high-profile themed exhibitions (there's usually a new one every year), while part of the ground floor is given over to Sofia's best-stocked souvenir shop (see "Shopping", p.111).

The south side of the square and the City Garden

On major Communist anniversaries party leaders used to take the salute from atop an austere white mausoleum on the southern side of the square, built to house the embalmed body of **Georgi Dimitrov** (1882–1949), the first leader of the People's Republic of Bulgaria. Once one of the top "tourist" sights in the capital – with reverential citizens filing through antiseptic corridors guarded by goose-stepping sentries – the mausoleum stood empty for ten years following the removal of Dimitrov's corpse in July 1990, before finally being demolished by the right-of-centre SDS government. The spot is now occupied by a rather lacklustre arrangement of flowers and shrubs, around which paths lead to the tree-shaded lawns and well-tended flowerbeds of the **City Garden** (*Gradskata gradina*), favoured preserve of chess-playing senior citizens and office workers on their lunch break. Several fountains splash opposite the **Ivan Vazov National Theatre**, a handsome Neoclassical edifice, which provides a welcome contrast to the sombre ministerial buildings on either side. At the southern end of the park, the **City Art Gallery** (Tues–Sat 10am–6pm, Sun 11am–5pm; free) offers an imaginative programme of contemporary art shows.

▲ Ivan Vazov National Theatre

Bulevard Tsar Osvoboditel and around

Bulevard Tsar Osvoboditel (БУЛ. ЦАР ОСВОБОДИТЕЛ) heads out of pl. Aleksandar Batenberg's eastern end, an attractive thoroughfare partially lined with chestnut trees. The **Natural Science Museum**, at no. 1 (daily 10am–5pm; 2Lv), was founded in 1889 by Knyaz Ferdinand I, himself a keen butterfly collector, and presents a thorough catalogue of Bulgarian and worldwide wildlife, both stuffed and pickled. Tanks containing live snakes and lizards line the stairs, domestic grass snakes vying for attention with Central American geckos, pythons and anacondas. At teatime, live rodents are lowered into the tanks of the larger reptiles. There's also a small gift shop selling minerals and fossils.

The Russian Church

Immediately beyond the Natural Science Museum, the **Russian church** (daily 8am–6.30pm) is an unmistakable, zany firecracker of a building with an exuberant exterior of bright yellow tiles, five gilded domes and an emerald spire, concealing a dark, candlewax-scented interior. Officially dedicated to St Nicholas the Blessed, the church was built in 1913 at the behest of a Tsarist diplomat, Semontovski-Kurilo, who feared his soul would be in danger if he worshipped in Bulgarian churches, which he believed to be schismatic. Pilgrims are drawn to the crypt (accessed via a doorway round the western side of the church), where prayers are uttered at the tomb of **Archbishop Serafim**. Much admired as the leader of Sofia's anti-Bolshevik, Russian émigré congregation from 1921 to 1950, Serafim now enjoys almost saintly status among the local faithful.

Towards National Assembly Square
Continuing eastward along bul. Tsar Osvoboditel, you come to a small square of greenery known popularly as **Kristal**, after the café that once stood on its southern flank. Opposite the park on the northern side of the boulevard is the Neoclassical facade of the **military club**, once the centre of post-Liberation Bulgaria's high society, and the place where the Zveno (a politically radical group of young officers) hatched several conspiracies in the interwar years.

Bul. Tsar Osvoboditel opens out into pl. Narodno sabranie – National Assembly Square. On the northern side stands a cream building housing the *Narodno sabranie* itself – Bulgaria's **National Assembly**, the facade of which bears the motto *saedinenieto pravi silata* ("unity is strength"). Directly opposite, a semi-circular plaza encloses the Monument to the Liberators, which gives pride of place to a statue of the *Tsar Osvoboditel*, or "Tsar Liberator" himself, Alexander II of Russia.

Ploshtad Aleksandar Nevski
The area immediately north of bul. Tsar Osvoboditel is dominated by **ploshtad Aleksandar Nevski** (ПЛОЩАД АЛЕКСАНДЪР НЕВСКИ), another of Sofia's set-piece squares, an expanse of greenery and paving stones (overlaying what was, in Roman times, the necropolis of Serdica) watched over by the twinkling domes of the Aleksandar Nevski Memorial Church. Entering the square from the western end, however, you first encounter the brown-brick **Church of Sveta Sofia**. Dating from late Roman times, but much rebuilt after numerous invasions and earthquakes (the last one in 1858), the church still follows the classic Byzantine plan of a regular cross with a dome at the intersection. It was turned into a mosque by the Ottomans, and locals believed that it was haunted nightly by the ghost of Constantine the Great's daughter Sofia, supposed founder of the first church to stand on this site. An air of calm reigns in the gracefully simple interior, layers of Byzantine brickwork giving some idea of the church's age. Around the back an engraved boulder marks the **grave of Ivan Vazov** (p.94), who requested that he be buried amid the daily life of his people; you'll notice his statue, seated with book in hand, in a park nearby. Set beside the southern wall of the church is the Tomb of the Unknown Soldier, guarded by a recumbent lion.

Immediately opposite Sveta Sofia, shielded by trees, a beige building sporting a stripe of brightly coloured ceramic tiles houses the Bulgarian Orthodox Church's **Holy Synod**, a fine example of the melding of Byzantine and Art-Nouveau styles which characterized so many of the public buildings built in the early twentieth century.

The Aleksandar Nevski Memorial Church
One of the finest pieces of architecture in the Balkans and certainly Sofia's crowning glory, the **Aleksandar Nevski Memorial Church** honours the 200,000 Russian casualties of the 1877–78 War of Liberation, particularly the defenders of the Shipka Pass. Financed by public subscription and built between 1882 and 1924 to the designs of St Petersburg architect Pomerantsev, it's a

magnificent structure, bulging with domes and half-domes and glittering with gold leaf donated by the Soviet Union in 1960. Within the cavernous interior, a white-bearded God glowers down from the main cupola, an angelic sunburst covers the central vault, and as a parting shot a *Day of Judgement* looms above the exit. Expressive frescoes executed by the leading Bulgarian artists of the day (including expat Czech painter Ivan Mrkvička) depict episodes from the life of Christ in rich tones, and the grandeur of the iconostasis is enhanced by twin thrones with columns of onyx and alabaster.

Orthodox congregations stand or kneel during services, although the weak and the elderly traditionally lean or sit on benches round the side. The church's capacity of five thousand is ample for daily **services** (usually in the morning at around 9.30am and in the evening at about 5pm), which can be spectacular affairs, rich with incense, candlelight and sonorous chanting.

The **crypt**, entered from the outside, contains a superb **collection of icons** (daily except Tues 10.30am–12.30pm & 2–6.30pm; 5Lv) from all over the country. They're mostly eighteenth- and nineteenth-century pieces, but look out for some medieval gems from the coastal town of Nesebar, home to a prolific icon-painting school, and source of the oldest icon on display here, a serene, white-bearded St Nicholas. Other highlights include a fourteenth-century wood-carved bas-relief from Sozopol showing saints George and Dimitar riding together against some common foe. The horsemen are regarded as brother-saints in the Balkans, not least because their feast days (May 6 for George, October 26 for Dimitar) play an important ritual role in marking the beginnings of the summer and winter cycles in the agricultural year. They're often pictured together in Bulgarian art, with St George invariably riding a white steed (symbolizing spring), Dimitar a red one (symbolizing autumn).

The National Gallery of Foreign Art

An imposing gallery on the northeastern edge of the square houses the **National Gallery of Foreign Art** (daily except Tues 11am–6pm; 3Lv; Ⓦ www.ngfa.icb.bg), an international art collection largely based on the donations of rich Bulgarians living abroad (and the occasional foreigner – Robert Maxwell was one early benefactor). The ground floor contains an impressive collection of Indian miniatures, Japanese prints and Burmese Buddhas, including one gilt example sitting cross-legged on the backs of three elephants. Upstairs, second-division French artists take up a lot of space, although there are a couple of Delacroix sketches, a small Picasso etching (*The Visions of Count d'Orgas* from 1966), and a mesmerizing *Lucifer* by German symbolist Franz von Stück. In the basement (not always open), Thracian gravestones from an ancient necropolis excavated nearby surround a reconstructed mortuary chapel dating from late Roman times.

Ulitsa G. S. Rakovski and around

Central Sofia's southeastern quarter is one of the inner city's liveliest areas, full of office workers and shoppers during the day, theatregoers and restaurant patrons in the evening. The area's main thoroughfares are **ulitsa G.S. Rakovski** (УЛ. Г. С. РАКОВСКИ), a workaday street lined with office blocks, and **ulitsa Graf Ignatiev** (УЛ. ГРАФ ИГНАТИЕВ), which is the capital's most important shopping district after bul. Vitosha. Government buildings and residential houses line the quiet streets in between, along with a couple of worthwhile literary museums.

The Ivan Vazov House-Museum

Three blocks south of bul. Tsar Osvoboditel, on the corner of ul. Rakovski and Vazov, is the **Ivan Vazov House-Museum** (Tues & Sun 1–7pm, Thurs 1–5pm, Fri & Sat 9am–5pm; 3Lv), where Bulgaria's greatest novelist lived from 1895 until his death in 1921. Most of the rooms are decked out in early nineteenth-century wallpaper and traditional Bulgarian floor coverings, making this one of the few places in town where the atmosphere of the old, post-Liberation Sofia still reigns. Downstairs a words-and-pictures display details the main events of Vazov's life, from childhood in Sopot (see p.285) through to exile in Odessa (where he wrote *Under the Yoke*, his epic novel of nineteenth-century Bulgarian life) to old age in Sofia: the dining room where he suffered a fatal heart attack is preserved in its original state. Period rooms upstairs include the writer's study, where visitors are greeted by the stuffed remains of Vazov's beloved dog, Bobi. The unfortunate hound was run over by a tram just outside the house and whisked off to the taxidermist by Vazov's youngest brother Boris.

Peyu Yavorov (1878–1914)

Man of action, poet and charismatic loner, **Peyu Kracholov** was born in the dusty provincial backwater of Chirpan. At the age of 16, he was forced by an unsympathetic father to abandon his studies and take up work as a telegraph operator. It was in the post offices of provincial towns like Sliven and Pomorie that the introverted **Yavorov** started to write the sombre, romantic symbolist poetry for which he became famous. Changing his name to Yavorov because it sounded more earthy (Yavor means "sycamore tree"), he was instantly received into Sofia's literary world, hung out with all the major writers of the day (including Vazov, who championed his work), and became editor of the top literary magazine *Misal*. A star while still in his twenties, Yavorov nevertheless yearned for more than the salon-bound cultural life of the capital. Tiring of his youthful passion for socialism, he threw himself into the struggle to free Macedonia from the Ottoman Empire, fighting as a guerrilla in the mountains and writing a biography of the movement's leader, Gotse Delchev (see p.153). The death of Delchev and the failure of the Ilinden Uprising in 1903 left Yavorov disillusioned, but he continued to serve as an unofficial ambassador for the Macedonian cause, and returned to the fray as a *voyvoda* (guerrilla leader) in the Balkan Wars, liberating the Aegean town of Kavala from Ottoman rule in 1912.

Yavorov's other great passion was writing love poetry to the two women with whom he had obsessive affairs. The first was Mina Todorova, teenage daughter of Petko Todorov, a fellow member of the *Misal* circle. Despite being an ardent admirer of Yavorov's writings, Todorov was horrified by the idea of having a penniless revolutionary poet as a son-in-law. Banned from seeing her, Yavorov wrote Mina love letters in verse, offering them to *Misal* for publication at the same time. Mina died of tuberculosis in 1910, and it was at her graveside in Paris that Yavorov struck up a friendship with the next object of his affections, Lora Karavelova. The daughter of former prime minister Petko Karavelov, Lora was one of Sofia's most modern, emancipated women, and she and Yavorov soon became the city's favourite intellectual couple. They married almost immediately, but Lora found Yavorov – already wed to Macedonia and his own writing – a distant, difficult companion. By early 1913 Lora was convinced (probably without reason) that Yavorov was having an affair with Dora Konova, the fiancée of a friend. They argued, and Lora threatened to shoot herself. Whether intentionally or not, the gun went off. Yavorov was tried for her murder – and speedily acquitted, despite the popular feeling that he was the guilty party. Abandoned by his friends and living in extreme poverty, Yavorov then turned a gun on himself, but at the first attempt lost only his eyesight. A few months later, at his second attempt, he succeeded in taking his life.

The Museum of Peyu Yavorov

Continuing south along ul. Rakovski you soon come to the **Museum of Peyu Yavorov** in a Secession-style house at no. 136 (Tues & Sun 1–7pm, Thurs 1–5pm, Fri & Sat 9am–5pm; 2Lv). One of the most compelling figures in Bulgarian literature (see box, opposite), Yavorov lived in a modest first-floor flat here for eleven months in 1913. Among the period furniture and traditional rugs are some evocative personal effects, such as the knife and binoculars given to him by Macedonian freedom fighters Gotse Delchev and Yane Sandanski. Quite by chance, the photographs of Yavorov and his wife Lora which hang in the sitting room have been separated by a large crack which has recently appeared in the wall – a poignant reminder of their tragic end.

Ulitsa Graf Ignatiev and around

Cutting across ul. Rakovski is **ulitsa Graf Ignatiev**, a partially pedestrianized thoroughfare lined with shops, named after the Russian count (and grandfather of Canadian novelist, Michael Ignatiev) who served as Russian ambassador to Constantinople in the 1870s, and persuaded Tsar Aleksandar to support Bulgarian liberation. The western half of Graf Ignatiev runs through pl. Slaveikov, a vast open-air **book market** where Bulgarian translations of the latest Western bestsellers are eagerly snapped up by local readers. Running southeast from the junction with ul. Rakovski, the street runs past the city centre's main fruit and veg market. Near here, in the small garden beside the intersection with ul. Tsar Shishman stands the **Church of Sveti Sedmochislenitsi**, literally the "Holy Seven", referring to Cyril, Methodius and their followers, the seven saints who brought Christianity to the Slavs. It was built on the site of the so-called "Black Mosque", an edifice that served as Sofia's main prison immediately after the Liberation. Prisoners used to sell handmade trinkets to passing city folk in order to pay for their food.

A block beyond the Church of Sveti Sedmochislenitsi, a statue of Bulgaria's fourteenth-century church leader Patriarh Evtimiy presides over the busy three-way junction of ul. Graf Ignatiev, bul. Vasil Levski and bul. Patriarh Evtimiy. Known colloquially as **Popa** ("the priest"), the statue is a popular meeting point upon which half the city seems to converge in the evening.

The Red House

Continuing along ul. Graf Ignatiev and taking the first left into ul. Lyuben Karavelov brings you to the rather self-consciously named **Red House Centre for Culture and Debate** at no.15 (*Chervenata kashta*; Tues–Sat 3pm–7pm; free; ⓦ www.redhouse-sofia.org), an independent gallery space that also organizes concerts, drama performances and seminars – and houses a charming B&B to boot (see p.80). The centre occupies the former home of Andrey Nikolov (1878–1940), the Vratsa-born sculptor who spent much of his adult life in Rome, and built this Italianate villa on his return to Bulgaria in 1927. A selection of Nikolov's sculptures is on permanent display in one of the Centre's gallery spaces – the smoothly sensual marble bust of a swooning female entitled *Kopnezh* ("yearning") is the item most likely to grab your attention.

For a full schedule of events at the Red House, check the website or pick up the monthly programme at the door.

Bulevard Vasil Levski and around

Heading northeast from Popa along the broad bul. Vasil Levski soon brings you to the **Mausoleum of Knyaz Aleksandar Batenberg** (Mon–Fri 9am–noon

& 2–5pm; free), occupying a small park at the corner of ul. Slavyanska. Despite being deposed in 1886 and living in exile in Graz until his death in 1893, Bulgaria's first post-Liberation ruler always wanted to be buried in Sofia, and his successor Ferdinand obliged by having the mausoleum erected in his honour. It took so long to build, however, that Aleksandar's corpse spent five years in the Rotunda of Sveti Georgi before finally taking up residence here. A neo-Baroque cupola-topped structure holds his plain marble sarcophagus, draped with a Bulgarian flag and flanked by a couple of military tunics worn by the prince when visiting front-line troops in the Serb–Bulgarian war of 1885.

From here it's a brief stroll north to **Sofia University**, the country's most prestigious educational establishment. Founded a decade after the Liberation, it was named after Kliment Ohridski, a pupil of saints Cyril and Methodius, who as ninth-century bishop of Ohrid in western Macedonia had an important impact on the flowering of Slav culture. The portals of the university building are framed by statues of Evlogi and Hristo Georgiev, the Odessa-based merchants who dug deep into their pockets to fund Bulgarian-language education in the years before the Liberation.

A block further north lies the **National Library**, a handsome colonnaded building with angular statues of the aforementioned saints Cyril and Methodius standing guard outside. Five minutes further on stands the weathered stone **Vasil Levski Monument** (*Levski pametnik*), marking the spot where the "Apostle of Freedom" (see p.286) was hanged by the Ottoman authorities in 1873.

The Soviet Army Memorial and Orlov Most

Immediately opposite the mausoleum stands the towering **Monument to the Soviet Army**, erected in honour of the "liberation" of Bulgaria in 1944. Although allied to Nazi Germany during World War II, the Bulgarians always shrank from declaring war on the Soviet Union, mindful of the long tradition of Russo–Bulgarian friendship. The Soviets, however, regarded Bulgaria as ripe for conquest, and despite the Bulgarian government's readiness to change sides as the war neared its end, the Red Army invaded anyway. The centrepiece of the monument is a Red Army soldier flanked by a worker and a peasant woman with a child, an archetypal symbol of Bulgaro–Soviet friendship which used to feature in monuments and propaganda billboards throughout the land. Nowadays it serves as the backdrop to the antics of skateboarders, who practise manoeuvres on the flagstoned area between the monument and the main road to the north.

Just east of the monument, the modest dribble of the River Perlovska is spanned by **Orlov most** or Eagle Bridge, crowned with four ferocious-looking birds of prey. Set amid weeping willows, the bridge marks the spot where Bulgarian prisoners of war – released from Ottoman prisons in Anatolia – were greeted by their compatriots just after the Liberation. The returning heroes were bestowed with the nickname of "the eagles" (*orlite*), and the bridge has borne their name ever since.

Borisova gradina (Freedom Park) and beyond

From here the main highway to Plovdiv heads southeast, flanked on one side by Sofia's largest park, **Borisova gradina** (literally "Boris's garden", although many locals still use its Communist-era name, *Park na svobodata* or "Freedom Park"). Partially influenced by St James's Park in London, it was laid out during the reign of Tsar Ferdinand and named in honour of the then prince Boris. With its lily ponds, bandstands, flowerbeds and thickets of trees, it's an ideal place for an aimless stroll. Marking the northwestern end of the park is the huge, doughnut-shaped Vasil Levski National Stadium, where the Bulgarian football team plays most of its matches. A bowl-shaped velodrome and another football ground (belonging to club side CSKA) lie further on among the trees.

Over towards the southeastern end of the park is the so-called **Bratska mogila** ("Mound of Brotherhood"), a Communist-era monument honouring those who fell in the struggle against fascism. Comprising a 42-metre-high obelisk surrounded by groups of sculpted Red Army officers and Bulgarian workers, it's a fine example of ideologically loaded socialist art.

The Military Museum

A short walk east of Borisova gradina (or a ride on tram #20 from the centre), occupying a compound on the corner of ul. Han Omurtag and Cherkovna, the **Military Museum** (Wed–Sun 9am–5pm; 10Lv), is an essential stop-off for anyone interested in military history. Four floors of exhibits bring together weaponry and uniforms from the history of the Bulgarian army, with particularly effective dioramas illustrating front-line life during the Balkan Wars (1912–13) and World War I. A fearsome array of hardware is ranged outside, including T34 tanks, MiG fighter jets, and one of the warhead-bearing SS23 missiles formerly stored in silos south of Sofia.

Ploshtad Balgariya and the NDK

On summer evenings city-centre office workers, shoppers and youngsters pour down bul. Vitosha to **ploshtad Balgariya**, a huge plaza featuring flowerbeds, lawns, shrubs and outdoor cafés. Dominating the park's southern end is the huge concrete hexagon of the **NDK** or National Palace of Culture (*Natsionalen Dvorets na Kulturata*), an eight-storey complex containing concert halls, congress facilities, office space and a subterranean arcade packed with clothes stalls. Completed in 1981, the building was originally intended to commemorate the 1300th anniversary of the founding of the Bulgarian State – a year-long celebration designed to add legitimacy to the increasingly nationalistic regime of Todor Zhivkov. The NDK was subsequently renamed in honour of Zhivkov's daughter Lyudmila, who had served as minister of culture before dying suddenly of a brain tumour at the age of 39. Initially earmarked as Zhivkov's successor, Lyudmila's enthusiasm for esoteric Eastern religions and decadent Western culture soon dismayed her father but made her correspondingly popular among Bulgarian intellectuals. The most telling aspect of the NDK was its colossal cost, and with this in mind, Sofians invented a sarcastic pun on its initials, which can also stand for "another hole in the belt". Nowadays, the NDK's main hall is still the best-equipped venue in the country for classical concerts and rock gigs – although the building as a whole displays an increasingly forlorn, uncared-for appearance.

Also intended to commemorate the 1300th anniversary of the Bulgarian state was the **Thirteen Hundred Years Monument**, which still looms over the northern end of the square. A modernist grey slab garnished with anguished-looking statues (one of whom, it's rumoured, bears the features of Todor Zhivkov), it was never popular with Sofians, who soon dubbed it the *sedmoagalen petohui*, or "seven-angled thing with five pricks". Speedily erected from cheap materials, the monument began to disintegrate over a decade ago, and is now a likely candidate for outright demolition.

Boyana

Seven kilometres southwest of central Sofia, **BOYANA** (БОЯНА) is an affluent village suburb lying in the shadow of Mount Vitosha (see p.100). For decades it has been the favoured retreat for Sofia's elite, and since the 1990s a new class of nouveaux riches has moved in to build villas and flats. Most of Boyana's luxury dwellings are hidden away behind high fences in the narrow lanes on the western side of the village, and the centre of the settlement isn't particularly attractive. The village's importance to sightseers, however, is guaranteed by the presence of the **Boyana Church**, whose unique medieval frescoes are once again accessible to the public after many years of restoration; and the **National History Museum**, which was moved to Boyana from its previous home (the Palace of Justice; see p.84) in 2000.

The National History Museum

Occupying a former government palace beside the Okolovrashten pat, a dusty highway which marks the northern boundary of Boyana, the **National History Museum** (Ⓦ www.historymuseum.org; daily April–Oct 9.30am–6pm, Nov–March 9am–5.30pm; 10Lv, combined ticket with Boyana Church 12Lv) presents a colourful and entertaining pageant of the nation's past. That said, the dubious nature of much that is on display (some of the exhibits are replicas rather than originals) casts doubt on its status as a serious institution. The archeological and ethnographic sections do, however, contain much that is unique, and the building itself – an opulent residence once used by Todor Zhivkov and his cronies – helps make the trip worthwhile.

Getting to the museum is straightforward: catch trolleybus #2 (either from opposite Sofia University or from the junction of bul. Vitosha and bul. Patriarh Evtimiy) to the final stop, walk straight ahead and cross Okolovrashten pat, then walk left for 200m to find the access road. There's a simple café inside the museum, but no other facilities within reasonable walking distance, so it's best to catch bus #63 or taxi onwards to the Boyana church once you've looked around.

Ancient artefacts

Stairs lead up from the main entrance to Hall 1, which contains artefacts from various Neolithic cultures between the seventh and third millennia BC – including stone **goddess figures** inscribed with rams, birds, chevrons and labyrinths, and some of the oldest gold jewellery ever unearthed, found near Varna. Hall 2 contains the great gold and silver hoards associated with the **Thracians**, who inhabited the eastern Balkans during the pre-Christian era. It's hard to predict what will be on show here at any given time: many of the museum's most valuable Thracian exhibits are frequently starring in touring exhibitions abroad, and their place is often taken by empty display cases or (inadequately labelled) replicas. Occupying centre stage if you're lucky will be the **golden treasure of Panagyurishte**, a collection of eight *rhyta* (drinking vessels) and one *phiale* (a kind of plate) made by Greek artisans of the Dardanelles area and imported into Thrace by a wealthy chieftain. Each *rhyton* is designed in the shape of an animal's head, with mythological scenes shown in relief around the side.

Bulgarian treasures

Hall 3 is probably the most disappointing part of the museum: the bas-reliefs, ceramics, silverware and frescoes illustrating the artistic heights attained during the medieval era are mostly replicas of items kept elsewhere in Bulgaria. Things pick up in Hall 4, designed to show how the Bulgarian Church kept national culture alive during five centuries of Ottoman rule, which whisks you through the various schools of **icon painting** that flourished in rural Bulgaria throughout the Ottoman period, and contains several examples of the **frescoes** that decorated Bulgarian monasteries. An early example is the sixteenth-century *Last Judgement* from the Church of the Nativity in Arbanasi, in which true believers are transported to a paradise stocked with exotic beasts while the ungodly are suspended over fires or have spikes inserted in their backsides.

Heading upstairs, Hall 5 covers Bulgarian history from the establishment of an independent Bulgarian state in 1878 to the end of World War II, with a non-chronological jumble of photographs and artefacts. Most people will find something enjoyable here – whether it's the generous collection of military uniforms, or the theatre posters and opera costumes from interwar Sofia. The rest of the upper floor is occupied by the museum's **ethnographic collection**, featuring richly coloured costumes from all over Bulgaria and some bright hand-woven rugs.

Boyana Church

Two kilometres south of the National History Museum, just above Boyana's village square, a small garden surrounds the ivy-covered **Boyana Church** (daily April–Oct 9am–5.30pm; Nov–March 9am–4.30pm; 10Lv, combined ticket with National History Museum 12Lv, English-language guided tour an extra 5Lv), home to a justly famed set of medieval frescoes, largely drawn in 1259 and included on the UNESCO World Heritage list. Visitors are only admitted to the church in small groups (so be prepared to wait) and are only allowed to spend ten minutes inside – a measure designed to protect the frescoes from sudden changes in temperature and humidity.

▲ Frescoes, Boyana Church

The church began life as a tenth-century chapel attached to Boyana fortress and dedicated to St Nicholas. It was expanded in the mid-thirteenth century by local ruler (and cousin of Bulgarian Tsar Konstantin Asen) Sebastocrator Kaloyan, who added a two-storey annexe intended to serve both as family burial vault and a shrine to his patron Saint Panteleimon. Kaloyan employed Constantinople-trained artists to cover the interior of the church with uniquely vivid frescoes. The degree of realism present represents a radical departure from the Byzantine style, and many art historians place them on a par with the early works of the Italian Renaissance.

Visitors enter via a nineteenth-century annexe before passing through a barrel-vaulted porch into the oldest part of the church. Eighteen scenes from the Life of St Nicholas range across the walls, beside lifelike portraits of Sebastocrator Kaloyan with his wife Desislava – faced on the opposite wall by Tsar Konstantin Asen and Tsaritsa Irina – all clad in sumptuous robes. Portrayals of the Virgin and Child, Christ in the Temple, and Bulgaria's national Saint John of Rila possess a degree of psychological depth which seems highly advanced for the time. The floor-to-ceiling frescoes continue into the newer (thirteenth-century) part of the church, dominated by a dome-filling rendition of Christ the Pantokrator. As well as biblical themes, the artist drew on contemporary life for inspiration: the Last Supper scene filling the northern wall shows the disciples tucking into the typical Bulgarian peasant's staples of garlic, radishes and bread; while many of the saints portrayed in frieze form in the horizontal bands above are clad in medieval Bulgarian dress.

Mount Vitosha

A wooded mass of granite 19km long by 17km wide, **MOUNT VITOSHA** (ВИТОША), whose foothills begin some 7km from the city centre, is very much a part of the capital and is the source of its pure water and fresh breezes. *Sofiantsi* come here to picnic, gather wild herbs and berries, savour magnificent views or ski. Vitosha's highest point, the 2290-metre **Cherni vrah**, is an easily bagged peak well within range of the moderately fit rambler. Vitosha's two main recreation centres, connected to the city by asphalt road, are **Aleko**, just above the treeline and within easy reach of the summit, and **Zlatni mostove**, on the wooded western flanks of the mountain. Both give access to Cherni vrah; Aleko is the closer, but the longer ascent from Zlatni mostove takes you through more varied terrain.

Routes from central Sofia to Vitosha pass through the villages (suburbs, really) nestling beneath its foothills: **Dragalevtsi**, with an attractive wood-shrouded monastery just above it, and **Simeonovo** are the starting points for the ski lifts to Aleko. Neither of the above villages, however, are worthy stop-offs in their own right: despite their status as exclusive suburbs for Sofia's post-Communist nouveaux riches, they remain drab, uninspiring little places overshadowed by the mountain above.

Skiing is possible on Vitosha from late December through to mid-March, with Aleko providing access to the principal pistes. There's a small winter resort here with three hotels, where you can enquire about equipment rental and sign up for ski schools.

Hiking is an all-year-round activity. The green-jacketed 1:50,000 map of Vitosha published by Cartographia and available from Sofia bookshops or the Zig-Zag travel agency (see p.75) is the best guide for hikers.

Dragalevtsi and Simeonovo

Arriving in **DRAGALEVTSI** (ДРАГАЛЕВЦИ), 3km south of the Hladilnika terminus, you'll either be dropped in the centre of the village or at the **Dragalevtsi chairlift** (1.50Lv each way to Aleko), some thirty minutes' walk above the village square. Ascending to Aleko via the **Bai Krastyo** middle station in about twenty minutes, the lift offers excellent views of Sofia stretched out on the plain to the north. An asphalt path winds up from the Dragalevtsi lift station to **Dragalevtsi Monastery**, a peaceful spot enshrouded by beech woods which serves as the summer residence of the Bulgarian patriarch. There's a fourteenth-century church – the only part of the original monastery that remains – and cells around its leafy courtyard, which during the nineteenth century sheltered the revolutionary Vasil Levski (see p.286). The monastery comes alive on August 15, the **Feast of the Assumption** (*Uspenie Bogorodichno* or more colloquially *Golyama Bogoroditsa*), when families from far and wide spend the day picnicking in the grounds or praying to the Virgin, the monastery's patron.

From Dragalevtsi, you can catch bus #98 to **SIMEONOVO** (СИМЕОНОВО), the next village-suburb to the east, and terminus of the **Simeonovo gondola** (3Lv each way to Aleko), which gives great views of the Sofia plain.

Aleko

Some twenty minutes beyond Dragalevtsi, bus #66 arrives at **ALEKO** (АЛЕКО), an expanding **winter sports centre** with three hotels (the *Prostor*, *Moreni* and *Shtastlivetsa*), and a range of pistes to suit all grades of skiers. During

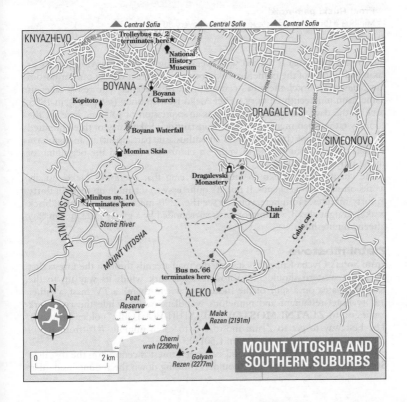

MOUNT VITOSHA AND SOUTHERN SUBURBS

Getting to Vitosha

Public transport to Mount Vitosha is fairly straightforward, with **buses for Dragalevtsi, Simeonovo and Aleko** starting from the Hladilnika terminus on Sofia's southern outskirts, at the end of tram route #9. After disembarking from the tram, head through a small bazaar area and turn left: buses for Vitosha destinations depart from stands 300m away at the end of the street. **Zlatni Mostove** can be reached via minibus from Ruski Pametnik in the city centre.

As a rule, there are more buses to Vitosha on Sundays than on other days of the week, especially if you're aiming for Zlatni Mostove. **Journey times** from Sofia to any of the Mount Vitosha destinations take between thirty minutes and an hour, depending on the traffic and weather conditions. Sofia public transport tickets and travelcards are valid for all the above services except for buses #61, #62 and #66, for which separate tickets must be bought from kiosks at the relevant terminals.

From Hladilnika
Bus #64: to Dragalevtsi, Boyana, and Ovcha kupel (every 20–30min)

Bus #66: to Aleko (Mon–Fri 5 daily; Sat & Sun hourly)

Bus #93: to Dragalevtsi chairlift (only on days when the chairlift is running; every 30min)

Bus #98: to Dragalevtsi and Simeonovo (every 30–40min)

Bus #122: to Simeonovo gondola (only on days when the chairlift is running; every 30–40min)

From Ruski pametnik
Minibus #10: to Zlatni mostove (Sat & Sun; every 30 min)

the summer, the area is packed with weekending *Sofiantsi* enjoying picnics or taking advantage of the numerous hiking possibilities that radiate outwards from the *Shtastlivetsa* hotel, the area's central point of reference. The resort takes its name from nineteenth-century writer Aleko Konstantinov (see p.194): in 1895, back in the days when hill-walking was an expression of patriotic love for the country rather than mere recreation, Konstantinov led a party of three hundred idealistic Bulgarians (Ivan Vazov was an enthusiastic participant) in an assault on Vitosha's highest point, Cherni vrah – a climb that marked the beginning of alpine pursuits in Bulgaria.

The chairlift from Aleko to Stenata, the crag that overlooks Aleko, usually works on summer weekends. If not, it's quite easy to scramble up there in thirty to forty minutes. From here, you can see the 2290-metre **Cherni vrah** ("black peak") straight ahead, a clump of rocks surrounded by a grassy plateau – an easy fifteen-minute hike.

Zlatni mostove

From Sofia's Ovcha Kupel bus station, the road ascends through the forests that cloak the western shoulder of Vitosha. A left fork winds its way up to the **Kopitoto** area on a spur of the mountain, where there's a TV mast, a rather snooty hotel-restaurant and numerous woodland walks, while the right fork carries on to **ZLATNI MOSTOVE** (ЗЛАТНИ МОСТОВЕ; "golden bridges"). The best way to get to Zlatni mostove is to catch minibus #10 from Ruski Pametnik (Sat & Sun every 30min; 1.50Lv).

This area of mixed deciduous and evergreen forest is centred on the so-called **Stone River**, a ribbon of huge boulders running down the mountainside that was once the moraine of an ancient glacier. Beneath the boulders burbles a rivulet that used to attract gold-panners, hence the locality's name. Tracks lead from the bus stop in all directions, past trade union-owned rest homes and small shacks selling drinks and snacks. The most popular walking route is a well-signed, medium-difficulty ascent of Cherni vrah, taking two to three hours. The path leads up the side of the Stone River, passing the *Kumata* and *Konyarnika* huts before emerging above the treeline onto a boggy plateau. From here the path runs alongside a protected area known as the **Peat Reserve** (*Torfen rezervat*) – a squelchy wilderness area covered with wildflowers in spring – before climbing up towards Cherni vrah.

Zlatni mostove is also a good starting point for **walks down the mountain**, with well-signed paths heading north towards the *Momina skala* hut, from where there's a choice of onward routes: a leftward path leads through meadows towards Kopitoto (see opposite), while the rightward alternative crosses the Boyana stream and then veers into woodland (follow the sign to Boyansko ezero). A left fork after five minutes takes you onto a green-marked trail that zig-zags its way down towards the foot of the **Boyana Waterfall** (*Boyanski vodopad*), a cascade that empties into a steep-sided ravine. From here you can follow the path downstream past smaller falls and rapids, eventually emerging into the village of Boyana, just above the Boyana Church (see p.99) – from where you can catch bus #64 back to Hladilnika.

Kremikovtsi

Twenty kilometres northeast of Sofia, nestling in a crook of the Balkan mountains, the village of **KREMIKOVTSI** (КРЕМИКОВЦИ) is home to one of the biggest steelworks on the Balkan peninsula. It's also famous for the fourteenth-century **Monastery of St George,** which occupies a fir-shrouded hillside overlooking the village. Lurking inside a flower-filled courtyard, the monastery church is filled with vibrant frescoes dating from the 1500s, evidence that wealthy Bulgarian nobles were spending considerable sums of money on religious art even at the height of the Ottoman occupation. A picture of St George, seated on a throne and using a dragon as a footrest, straddles the archway leading through to the naos, the inner sanctum of the church. The naos itself is dominated by a rendition of the Virgin Mary behind the altar, arms outstretched in a protective gesture. Look out, too, for a niche on the right bearing another portrayal of St George, this time riding his horse and planting a spear in the dragon's throat.

The best time **to visit** the monastery is at the weekend or on one of the big feast days, as the nun who unlocks the church for visitors can be difficult to track down at other times. The monastery attracts most visitors on St George's Day (*Gyergyovden*, May 6), although it also gets pretty busy on other big holidays, notably Assumption (*Golyama Bogoroditsa*, August 15) and the Birth of the Virgin (*Malka Bogoroditsa*, September 8). Note that there's nowhere to eat or drink in the village, save for a couple of rudimentary cafés, so bring your own supplies.

Getting to Kremikovtsi
Tram #22 runs from Knyaz Dondukov to the Avtogara Iztok in the northeastern suburbs (on some signs Avtogara Iztok is called "Avtostantsia Iztok", to differentiate it from Avtogara Poduyane, which is sometimes also misleadingly referred to as Avtogara Iztok by locals), where you change to **bus** #117. The bus passes the

sprawling steelworks before entering Kremikovtsi village: get off at the village library (*chitalishte*), a two-storey concrete building where the bus veers off to the right. Instead of following the route of the bus, bear left uphill through the village, and the monastery is about thirty minutes' walk; you should be able to pick out the church's cupola and bell tower on the hillside ahead.

If you're **driving**, head out of Sofia along Botevgradsko shose for about 10km, then turn left to Kremikovtsi at the KAT (traffic police) checkpoint.

Eating

While none of Sofia's restaurants could be classed as truly outstanding, you'll at least find a greater choice here than anywhere else in the country. Mainstream restaurants aiming at modern European cuisine tend to be disappointing, and you would be better off sticking to the increasing number of establishments rediscovering the virtues of **traditional Bulgarian cooking**. Many of these restaurants feature live music – usually an inoffensive mixture of folk and international easy-listening. Decent, inexpensive Chinese restaurants are thick on the ground, especially in the streets just west of the centre around the Zhenski pazar. Summer brings out the best in the city, when places with outdoor seating remain packed well into the evening.

As far as **fast food** is concerned, pizza slices, salad bars and basic Bulgarian grilled snacks can be found at the food courts in the central shopping centres: the Halite covered market on the corner of bul. Knyaginya Mariya Luiza and ul. Ekzarh Yosif (see p.86) is conveniently central; and the food halls in Mall of Sofia, at bul. Aleksandar Stamboliyski 101, and City Center Sofia, at bul. Arsenalski 2, are only a short walk away.

The **market** on ul. Graf Ignatiev, alongside the Sveti Sedmochislentsi church, is the handiest place to pick up fresh fruit and veg. Well-stocked **supermarkets** include Piccadilly, in the basement of the Mall of Sofia and City Center Sofia shopping malls (both daily 10am–10pm); and Billa, slightly further afield at ul. Sofiiski Geroi 4 and bul. Balgariya 55 (both Mon–Sat 8am–10pm, Sun 9am–9pm).

Fast food and pizzerias

Baalbek ul. Dyakon Ignatiy 4. Lebanese-run takeaway serving up kebabs, spicy *sudzhuk* sausages, falafel, and dainty spinach-and-feta pies. Mon–Sat 10.30am–10pm, Sun 11am–8pm.

Mimas bul. Vasil Levski 68. Long-established burger joint catering for daytime office workers and night-time clubbers. Regular burgers are so stuffed with chips and mayonnaise that they're impossible to eat without spilling half the contents on the street, but this has always been part of the Mimas ritual. Open 24hr.

O! Shipka ul. Shipka 11 ☏ 02/449288 (see map, p.78). Moderate pizza place just east of the centre, popular largely because it is cheap, lively and has a big summer garden. Open 24hr.

Piccola Venezia ul. Georgi Benkovski 12A. Just downhill from the Aleksandar Nevski Memorial Church, this rather plain pizzeria is dependable for reasonably authentic thin-crust pies, and also serves good-quality, heavy-duty steaks. Open noon–midnight.

Pizzeria Victoria bul. Tsar Osvoboditel 7. One of the better high-street pizzerias, with a good choice of both Italian-inspired and Bulgarian-based toppings, a big menu of salads, and comfortable, restaurant-style surroundings. Large open-air terrace at the back of the building, just behind the pl. Aleksandar Nevski flea market. Open 24hr.

Ugo corner of bul. Vitosha and ul. Gladston. Satisfying pizzas from one of the more reliable central outlets. Matt black interior and arty lounge-bar lighting add a touch of style. Open 24hr.

Cafés

Art Museum Café corner of ul. Saborna and ul. Lege. Lunch here amid the Thracian tombstones in a very pleasant patio café at the back of the Archeological Museum. Salads, pasta and other light meals. Open 24hr.

Before & After ul. Hristo Belchev 12. Quality coffee and cakes in a restored Art Nouveau building. Daily 10am–midnight.

Dani's ul. Angel Kanchev 16. Deli-style café just off bul. Vitosha serving up generous soups, salads and sandwiches washed down with home-made lemonade. Pricier than average but worth it. Daily 10am–10pm.

Dvete Fukli ul. Karnigradska 14. Small daytime café and cake shop just off bul. Vitosha. It's one of the best of the central cafés, with great cakes and good service. Daily 10am–9pm.

Jimmy's Sladoledena kashta ul. Angel Kanchev 9. Mecca for ice cream (both eat-in and take-out), as well as the usual coffee and cakes. Mon–Sat 8am–midnight, Sun 10am–midnight.

Laguna ul. Hristo Belchev 13. Great place for pancakes and ice cream, served up in one of central Sofia's weirdest interiors – think of a lounge bar crossed with a science-fiction movie set. Open 9am–midnight.

Restaurants

For most visitors, eating in a restaurant is relatively cheap, especially if you stay out of deluxe hotels and avoid imported drinks; even in the topnotch establishments, a three-course meal with drink rarely exceeds 30-45Lv per person. Most restaurants open from about 11am until 11pm, with some closing one day a week, often Sunday. Telephone numbers are included below for those restaurants where reservations are a good idea at weekends.

Central Sofia

All the restaurants listed below are marked on the Central Sofia map (pp.82–83).

Brasserie ul. Solunska. Lounge bar-cum-restaurant with a small but well-executed menu of modern European dishes, with pastas, steaks and salads figuring prominently. Main courses hover around the 20Lv mark. Chill-out music and a big list of cocktails add to the atmosphere. Daily noon–1am.

Checkpoint Charly ul. Ivan Vazov 12 ☎02/988 0370. Chic diner featuring matt-black surfaces and a Cold-War theme (note the grainy pictures of East Germany on the walls and the Communist-era Bulgarian newspapers on the tables), serving international food of the highest quality – with plenty of vegetarian dishes. International wine list, good service and live jazz several nights a week. Mains 20Lv and upwards. Daily noon–midnight.

Da Vidi ul. Han Asparuh 36 ☎02/980 6746. Upscale but not-too-formal restaurant featuring floor-to-ceiling windows, minimalist décor and an eclectic choice of Mediterranean dishes, including some exquisitely prepared fish. Expect to pay over 40Lv for a full meal with drinks. Mon–Sat 11am–11pm, Sun 6–11pm.

Divaka ul. 6 Septemvri 41a ☎02/986 6971. Lively place serving up superb Bulgarian meat-dominated dishes, excellent salads and decent sweets – all at very reasonable prices. You can get away with a slap-up meal for under 20Lv a head. Unsurprisingly it is always full. There's another branch at ul. Gladston 54 (☎02/989 9543) and at ul. Hristo Belchev. Open 24hr.

Dream House ul. Alabin 50A. First-floor vegetarian café-restaurant perched above a certain burger franchise, offering a satisfying range of soups, tofu-based dishes and Bulgarian standards such as fried aubergines with yoghurt and peppers stuffed with cheese. Inexpensive.

Egur Egur ul. Dobrudzha 10 ☎02/989 3383. Popular Armenian restaurant with plush seats, formal service but only slightly higher-than-average prices. The English-language menu guides you through the exotically flavoured lamb stews and wonderfully tasty vegetarian side dishes. Mains in the region of 15–20Lv. Big international wine list. Daily noon–midnight.

Gioia ul. Lavele 11 ☎02/986 0854. Snug, six-table restaurant offering some of the most delicious Italian food in Sofia. The fresh pasta is first class, and the meat and seafood main courses are a cut above those offered by most other international restaurants in the capital. Italian wines and desserts complete the picture. With mains in the 20–40Lv range, it's pricier than average, but well worth it. Daily 11.30am–11pm.

Happy Bar & Grill corner of bul. Stamboliyski and pl. Sveta Nedelya. Home-grown chain decked out in colourful style, with a jumble of pictures, neon signs and musical instruments on the walls making it a popular place for family outings and parties. The menu is dominated by chicken-and-chips options, plus some traditional Bulgarian dishes, all at below average prices. There's another branch at ul. G. S. Rakovski 145. Open 24hr.

Manastirska Magernitsa ul. Han Asparuh 67 ☏ 02/980 3883, ⓦ www.magernitsa.com. Plushly decorated townhouse with a large outdoor terrace, a few steps east of the main bul. Vitosha. Huge range of traditional Bulgarian dishes in all price ranges including all the grilled-meat favourites, and a host of vegetarian side orders that could be grouped together to provide a sumptuous beast-free feast. Daily 11am–1am.

Mahaloto bul. Vasil Levski 47 ☏ 0887 617 972. Imaginative mix of traditional Bulgarian grilled meats and modern European cuisine, served up in an atmospheric brick cellar decked out in illustrations from Parisian magazines of the 1930s. With mains hovering around the 12Lv mark it is eminently affordable. Outdoor tables in summer. Open noon–midnight.

Niky ul. Neofit Rilski 16. Grill restaurant set in a fancy garden (complete with water features) behind the hotel of the same name. A simple but effective menu of pork and chicken standards, none of which wll break the bank. Daily noon–midnight.

Otvad aleyata, zad shkafa ("Beyond the alley, behind the cupboard") ul. Budapeshta 31 ☏ 02/983 5545. Upmarket place hidden away in a residential street northeast of the centre, with pleasant garden seating and Art Nouveau touches inside. The food is a mixture of modern European and traditional Bulgarian, with excellent sweets. A full meal with drinks will set you back 40–50Lv per head. Daily noon–midnight.

Pri Yafata ul. Solunska 28 ☏ 02/980 1727. Authentic Bulgarian food in rooms decorated with traditional textiles and nineteenth-century knick-knacks (including the odd musket). One of the few places in Sofia where you can get *patatnik*, a vegetarian potato-and-cheese dish from the Rhodope mountains. Popular with tourists and prone to overcrowding at the weekend, but a reliable place for quality food, and prices are still reasonable with main courses falling in the 8–14Lv bracket. Daily 10am–midnight.

Zhadnata lamiya ul. 13-ti Mart 2 ☏ 02/964 0640. Homely restaurant-cum-pub with wooden-beamed interior, featuring a semi-circular bar at one end and a handful of dining tables squeezed into the other. Although there are some adventurous-looking international dishes on the menu, it's probably best to stick to the inexpensive Bulgarian staples. Daily noon–midnight.

Out of the centre

All restaurants listed below are marked on the map of Sofia (pp.78–79).

Captain Cook bul. Pencho Slaveykov 12–14 ⓦ www.captaincook.bg. Big, modern, bright and ever-so-slightly upmarket, *Captain Cook* is one of the best places in Sofia to tuck into top-quality grilled fish. It's priced per 100g but you can examine what's on offer in the chilled cabinet and have it weighed before placing your order. Shellfish, lobster and an international wine list are also on offer. On the expensive side, but well worth the splash. Daily noon–midnight.

Chevermeto bul. Cherni vrah 31 ☏ 02/963 0308, ⓦ www.chevermeto-bg.com. Folk-styled restaurant in the basement of the *Hotel Hemus*, 2km south of the centre, offering traditional food amid colourful rural furnishings. Live performances by folklore groups constitute the main attraction, however. Daily noon–1am.

Hadzhidraganovite kashti ul. Kozloduy 75 ☏ 02/931 3148, ⓦ www.kashtite.com. Themed restaurant in the backstreets between the centre and the Central Station, with an ensemble of traditionally furnished rooms representing different areas of Bulgaria. Pretty much everything from the Bulgarian culinary repertoire is on the menu, and the list of *rakiyas* is long and appetizing. Folk music most nights. Daily noon–2am.

Pod lipite ul. Elin Pelin 1 ☏ 02/866 5053. Traditional Bulgaria fare in a suite of rustic-styled rooms, a few steps away from the Borisova gradina park. Sword-skewered pork kebabs, oven-baked lamb dishes and an unusually broad choice of fried or grilled vegetable dishes, all accompanied by an impressive range of *rakiyas* and wines. Live music most nights. Daily noon–1am.

Pri Latsi ul. Oborishte 18 ☏ 02/846 8687. Small and intimate restaurant with a Hungarian theme, serving up several mouthwatering variations on the goulash theme and some enticing desserts. Daily 11am–11pm.

Pri Miro ul. Marfi ("Murphy") 34 ☏ 02/943 7127, ⓦ www.restaurantmiro.com. Popular Serbian restaurant 3km east of the centre in the Oborishte district (take a taxi). The repertoire of mincemeat rissoles and *pljeskavice* (Serbian burgers) is expertly done and goes down a treat with traditional garnishes such as *ajvar* (pepper and aubergine purée). There's sometimes live music in the large garden at weekends. Daily noon–midnight.

Drinking

Drinking in Sofia is a round-the-clock activity, with numerous cafés and kiosks doling out coffee, juice and alcohol during the day, and bars and pubs pulling in punters by night. Many of the smaller bars close at around 11pm or midnight, although there are plenty of city-centre establishments catering for those who want to continue until the early hours. Spring and summer bring out the best in the drinking scene, when café life moves out onto the pavements, and alfresco bars and beer pavilions (some of which are open 24hr) emerge – the City Garden and pl. Balgariya are good places to look.

All of the places listed below are marked on the Central Sofia map on p.82 unless otherwise stated.

Bars and Cafés

The Apartment ul. Neofit Rilski 68. Probably one of the strangest apartments you're likely to visit, with five sitting rooms decorated in a range of Bohemian-to-lounge-bar styles, art exhibitions in the hallways, a room set aside for film shows, and a bar area that consists of a fridge filled with beers, spirits and home-made chocolate desserts. Totally unique. Daily noon–2am.

Babbles ul. Tsar Shishman 22. Groovily furnished drinkery that looks like a 1960s science fiction movie. Great cocktails, with DJs at weekends. Tucked in a courtyard behind *Bilkovata* (see below). Daily 5pm–3am.

Bilkovata ul. Tsar Shishman 22. A buzzing, smoky cellar with decent music and a young crowd, *Bilkovata* is something of a legend in Sofia, fondly remembered by successive generations of students, arty types and young professionals, and still going strong. Packed beer garden in summer. The name refers to the *bilkovata apteka* ("herbal pharmacy") that used to stand here. Daily 10am–2am.

Blaze ul. Slavyanska 36. Snazzy bar in the streets behind the university with cutting-edge dance music on the sound system and a trendsetting clientele. Equally as legendary as *Bilkovata* (see above). Daily 9am–3am.

By the Way ul. G. S. Rakovski 166. Big, brash, busy café-bar that pulls a regular after-work crowd and keeps on going till the early hours. Daily 10am–1am.

Flannagan's *Radisson Hotel*, pl. Narodno Sabranie 4. Roomy Celtic-themed pub that doubles as a dining venue, on the ground floor of the *Radisson* hotel. Popular with movers and shakers due to its position immediately opposite the Bulgarian parliament, it frequently packs out with busily networking expats. Daily noon–1am.

Hambara ul. 6-ti septemvri 22. Hidden behind an unmarked doorway just off the street, this dark, candle-lit, stone-floored bar is one of the most atmospheric places in the centre for a long night of drink-fuelled conversation. Live jazz several nights a week. Daily 7pm–2am.

J.J. Murphy's ul. Karnigradska 6. The best of Sofia's "Irish" pubs by far, with laid-back but lively atmosphere, decent bar food, and European football games on the big screen. Daily noon–midnight.

Kyubcheto ul. Tsar Asen. A tiny space lurking behind a multicoloured, mosaic-decorated portal, this is one of the most charming of the neighbourhood bars that cram the streets west of bul. Vitosha. Daily 11am–11pm.

Lodkite southwestern side of Borisova gradina, near bul. Dragan Tsankov (see map, p.78. Wonderful outdoor bar set in a former children's playground, favoured by students and young professionals. DJs spin either mainstream dance music or something totally weird. Usually open 24hr from May to October.

Motto ul. Aksakov 18 ⓦ www.motto-bg.com. Chic bar and diner combining exposed brickwork with comfy leather sofas, subdued lighting and clubby DJ sounds. Mediterranean-leaning menu, good cocktails, and courtyard seating in the summer. Daily 10am–1am.

Tea House (*Chay vav fabrikata*) ul. Georgi Benkovski 11. Relaxing café-bar-cum-art gallery which radiates a slightly alternative vibe but remains elegant with it. The bar is well stocked with speciality teas as well as the usual beers and spirits, and there's often something in the cakes and biscuits line as well. Live jazz or world music at least once a week. Daily 10am–11pm.

Toba&co ul. Moskovska 6. Relaxing bar occupying a semicircular summer pavilion built onto the back of the former royal palace, with a large area of parkside outdoor seating in the summer. Nice place to linger over speciality teas or coffees during the daytime, although the decibel level moves up a notch in the evenings, when there may well be DJs. Daily 9am–5am.

Sofia's gay scene

Sofia now has a number of dedicated gay and lesbian drinking venues and a useful website (ⓦ www.bulgayria.com) that tells you where the currently fashionable spots are. Well-established places include *Vital*, at ul. Alabin 5, which functions as a relaxing café-bar during the daytime and a DJ-driven party venue at night; and *Exit*, at ul. Lavele 16 (ⓦ www.exit-club.com), a popular venue for club nights that also serves food in the daytime and early evening.

Entertainment

Sofia's real forte is **drama**, **ballet** and **classical music**, all of which are of a high standard and inexpensive. The theatre and music seasons tend to run from late September to mid-June, since most of Sofia's cultural institutions take a long summer break. Live **rock and pop** music is slightly harder to find than the high-brow stuff, although a vibrant and hedonistic club scene ensures that

▲ Bilkovata bar

DJ culture is well established. The most popular form of entertainment for many locals is the **cinema** – and the flood of (subtitled) Hollywood movies sweeping the country means that you won't have any problems understanding the dialogue.

The *Sofia Echo* newspaper carries weekly cinema **listings** alongside fragmentary information on other cultural events. Quarterly guide *Sofia In Your Pocket* has a useful round-up of the main cultural happenings of the season. The best source of day-to-day listings, however, is the website of Bulgarian magazine *Programata* (Ⓦ www.programata.bg), which comes with an English-language version.

Tickets for most events can be purchased at the box office of the relevant venue or from web-based agents such as Ticketstream (Ⓦ www.ticketstream.bg; counter service inside the Plesio electronics shop at ul. Angel Kanchev 5) or Ticketpro (Ⓦ www.ticketpro.bg; counter service in the Orange multimedia shop; see p.112).

Cinema

Central Sofia has a good choice of both modern multiplexes showing the latest blockbusters and single-screen cinemas offering a more art-based programme.

Cinema City bul. Aleksandar Stamboliyski 101 ℡ 02/929 2929, Ⓦ www.cinemacity.bg. Multiplex on the top floor of the Mall of Sofia shopping centre, surrounded by fast-food outlets and cafés. **Cineplex** bul. Arsenalski 2 ℡ 02/964 3007, Ⓦ www.cineplex.bg. Multi-screen cinema in the City Center Sofia shopping mall, with numerous drinking, snacking and popcorn-buying possibilities in the vicinity.

Dom na kinoto ("House of Cinema") ul. Ekzarh Yosif 37 ℡ 02/980 3911. Art-house films in an old-style single-screen cinema with few facilities (so bring your own popcorn). **Odeon** bul. Patriarh Evtimiy 1 ℡ 02/969 2469. Independent cinema showing oldies and prize-winning art films past and present. Small café in the lobby.

Theatre

Plays are, naturally, performed in Bulgarian, so not knowing the language is a distinct drawback, but the general standard of performances can make a visit to the theatre rewarding.

Dramatichen Teatar Sofia bul. Yanko Sakazov 23A. Big productions and musicals, as well as some edgy contemporary stuff. **Kuklen Teatar** ul. General Gurko 14. Stunningly designed shows by a highly regarded puppet theatre, with daytime performances for children and occasional evening shows of adult-oriented drama. **Malak Gradski Teatar "zad kanala"** bul. Madrid 1 ℡ 02/846 2020, Ⓦ www.theatreoffthechannel .com. One of the best places to see modern works in a small, intimate auditorium, next door to the Dramatichen Teatar Sofia. **Naroden Teatar Ivan Vazov** ul. Dyakon Ignatiy 1A ℡ 02/811 9219, Ⓦ www.nationaltheatre.bg. Works by eminent Bulgarians and classical writers performed by the national theatre company. **Salza i Smyah** ul. Rakovski 127 ℡ 02/987 1952, Ⓦ www.salzaismiah.com. The oldest professional

theatre company in Sofia, dating from 1892, with a reputation for challenging drama. **Satirichen Teatar Aleko Konstantinov** ul. Stefan Karadzha 26 ℡ 02/987 6606. The place to go for comedy and cabaret. **Teatar 199** ul. Slavyanska 8 (entrance from ul. Rakovski) ℡ 02/987 8533. Originally named after its 199 seats (recent renovations have left it with slightly fewer), this is a comfy and reasonably intimate space in which to enjoy contemporary international drama in Bulgarian translation. **Teatralna Rabotilnitsa Sfumato** ul. Dimitar Grekov 2 ℡ 02/944 0127, Ⓦ www.sfumato .info. Award-winning experimental theatre group with a reputation for producing challenging, unmissable pieces. Based 2km east of the centre on the fringes of Oborishte Park.

Music

The National Palace of Culture, or **NDK** (☎02/916 2368), is the venue for many of the bigger symphonic concerts or operatic productions; otherwise **symphonic music** can be heard at the Zala Balgariya, at Aksakov 1 (☎02/987 7656), which hosts performances by the Sofia Philharmonic in the main auditorium, chamber concerts and solo recitals in the chamber hall. The traditional home of **opera and ballet** is the Narodna Opera, at ul.Vrabcha 1 (☎02/987 1366, ⓦwww.operasofia .com). The Stefan Makedonski State Musical Theatre, at ul. Panayot Volov 2 (☎02/944 5085, ⓦwww.musictheatre.bg), is the place to go for operetta and musicals. The main festival to look out for is the **Sofia Music Weeks** (late May to late June), featuring international soloists and ensembles.

Clubs and live music

There's a growing club scene in Sofia, offering a wide range of DJ-driven music, although venues go in and out of fashion from one year to the next. Regular gig venues devoted to new music are a rarity in Sofia, although plenty of bars and clubs feature cover bands. Clubs can fill up on Fridays and Saturdays, when you may be kept waiting outside. Entrance fees range from 5Lv to 20Lv depending on the venue, more if a major western DJ is manning the decks.

Bulgarian pop stars, and the occasional Western act who can be bothered to make the trip, play in the NDK or in the large multipurpose halls such as Zala Universiada, at ul. Shipchenski prohod 2.

Alcohol ul Rakovski 127. Underground nightspot that looks like a huge subterranean barn and has an eclectic something-for-everybody music policy. An Oriental-style chill-out room boasts cushions and hubble-bubble pipes.

B29 Piano Bar ul. Vladayska 29, ⓦwww .b29pianobar.com (see map, p.78). Classy drinking venue offering nightly live music with a piano, naturally, taking centre stage. Musical styles range from crooner-accompanied piano tinkling to jazz and dancefloor-filling boogie-woogie.

Backstage bul. Vasil Levski 100. Roomy disco–bar, with live bands playing jazz, pop/rock covers or indie rock. There's a billiard room at the back.

Brilyantin ul. Moskovska 3. Stylish modern pop/retro-dance sounds and a cool matt-black interior have ensured the popularity of Brilyantin ("Grease") with a sophisticated twenty-something crowd.

Chervilo bul. Tsar Osvoboditel 8. Stylish city-centre club offering the latest in house, techno, Latin and lounge music on two floors. The action spreads out onto the terrace in summer, when it's more like an elite, pay-to-enter pavement café than a club.

Escape ul. Angel Kanchev 1. Centrally located home-from-home for techno-heads.

My Mojito ul. Ivan Vazov 12. Dark, cosy and rather stylish corner in which to while away a lengthy evening. DJs playing different styles of music on different nights draw a wide range of discerning drinkers and dancers.

Sin City pl. Vazrazhdane (see map, p.78). Mega-club on three floors with a glitzy, hip-shaking hall dedicated to *chalga* (oriental folk-pop) in the ground floor, and international dance-pop sounds in both the lobby and the upstairs bar.

Swingin' Hall bul. Dragan Tsankov 8 (see map, p.78). Buzzing suburban bar housed in a sequence of cosy cellar-like chambers. Clientele ranges from arty students to business types. With live performances six nights a week – ranging from pop/rock cover bands to jazz and alternative rock – this is one of the best music venues in the city.

Yalta bul. Tsar Osvoboditel 20. At the forefront of Bulgarian dance culture for nearly two decades, Yalta is something of a nightlife institution, attracting international DJs and a glamorous local crowd.

Football

Sofia has two **football teams** with a mass following. Levski have been the most successful in recent years, winning a string of first division championships and qualifying for the UEFA Champions' League in 2006. Their home is the Stadion Georgi Asparuhov, northeast of the city centre on Todorini kukli (trolleybus #1 from bul. Levski). Levski's bitter rivals are CSKA (originally a military team, CSKA means "Central Army Sports Club"), who play at Stadion CSKA in the middle of the Borisova gradina park. The capital's two other clubs are Slaviya, who are based at Sporten Kompleks Slaviya just behind the Ovcha Kupel bus station (tram #5 from behind the Palace of Justice), and Lokomotiv, whose ground is on bul. Rozhen in the northwestern suburb of Nadezhda (tram #12 from the train station). Matches involving the national side, as well as derby matches between Levski and CSKA, take place at the Vasil Levski National Stadium at the western end of Borisova gradina. **Tickets** for regular league games (rarely costing more than 3Lv or so) are usually sold at turnstiles on the day of the match. For international fixtures, buy tickets from the national stadium box office as far in advance as possible.

Shopping

The best of Sofia's **high-street fashion stores** are located around bul. Vitosha and ul. Graf Ignatiev. Otherwise the best places to find clothes, electronic goods and domestic hardware are in modern **malls** such as City Center Sofia, on the corner of bul. Arsenalski and bul. Cherni vrah, and Mall of Sofia, at bul. Aleksandar Stamboliiski 101. Both offer the added attractions of well-stocked supermarkets, trendy cafés, fast-food outlets and multiplex cinemas. Luxury goods, clothes and accessories are also on display at Tzum, a three-storey shopping centre on the corner of bul. Mariya Luiza and pl. Nezavisimost. Tzum served as the city's main department store during the Communist period, and still radiates a modicum of Stalin-era grandeur.

The main fruit, vegetable and cheap clothes **market** is Zhenski pazar on ul. Stefan Stambolov. There are also good fruit and veg markets on ul. Graf Ignatiev; at Rimska stena, just south of the city centre on ul. Hristo Smirnenski; and, best of all, Sitnyakovo, 2km southeast of the centre on ul. Shipchenski prohod (tram #20 from Knyaz Dondukov).

Souvenirs and gifts

There's a long line of open-air stalls just in front of the Aleksandar Nevski Memorial Church selling paintings, reproduction icons, Russian-style fur hats, antiques, lace and embroidery. All prices are negotiable.

Carpet House/Tchu kilim ul. G.S. Rakovski 38 ⓦ www.tchukilim.com. Small shop selling high-quality carpets from the weaving town of Chiprovtsi (see p.182). Will take orders if you're going to be around in Bulgaria for the one to two months required to make a bespoke carpet.
Ethnographic Museum pl. Aleksandar Batenberg. The museum's ground-floor shop has the city's biggest choice of woodcarving, embroidery, ceramics, woollen kilims and folk CDs.
Todoroff bul. Vasil Levski 83 ⓦ www .todoroff-wines.com. Sofia outlet for quality wines

(mostly merlots and mavruds) from the Todoroff boutique winery just south of Plovdiv.
Traditzia bul. Vasil Levski 36 ⓦ www.traditzia .bg. Ceramics, kilims, handmade greetings cards, jewellery and other handiwork. Items on sale are made by village artisans, handicapped artists and disadvantaged children – and the profits are ploughed back into development projects. Higher-than-average prices, but worth it for the quality of craftsmanship on offer and the ethical incentive.

Books

The huge outdoor **book market** on pl. Slaveykov is an enjoyable place to browse for Bulgarian-English dictionaries, large-format art books and tourist-oriented coffee-table books with plenty of pictures. Not all of the stallholders know a great deal about books, however, and it's best to head for a mainstream bookstore if you're after something specific.

Booktrading ul. Graf Ignatiev 15. High-street store with plenty of English-language art books, Rough Guides, maps and other tourist publications.
Knigomania Top floor, Mall of Sofia ⓦwww .knigomania.bg. Big store selling international magazines, guide books, maps and a selection of English-language novels.
Nissim bul. Vasil Levski 69. Tiny shop about the size of a large cupboard, run by book enthusiasts

who will do their best to find what you're looking for if you give them a couple of days. Small range of English-language paperbacks in stock.
Orange ul. Graf Ignatiev. Three-storey multimedia store offering stationery, CDs, DVDs and lots of books – including a smattering of English-language paperbacks.

Music

Balgarski kompozitor (Bulgarian Composers' Union) ul. Ivan Vazov 2. Big choice of classical, folk and jazz CDs, as well as sheet music and some traditional musical instruments.
Dukyan Meloman ul. 6 Septemvri 7A. A basement-bound treasure trove of jazz and world

music CDs (including plenty of Bulgarian folk), plus boxes of secondhand vinyl.
Gega ul. Solunska 49. Retail outlet of the Gega record company. Stocks many contemporary Bulgarian folk CDs.

Hiking and camping equipment

Stenata ul. Bratya Miladinovi 5 ⓦwww.stenata .com. Footwear, fleeces, tents, rucksacks and

pretty much everything else you need for an outdoor trip.

Listings

Airlines For a list of low-cost airlines which fly in and out of Sofia airport but which don't have offices in the city, see p.32. Aeroflot, ul. Oborishte 23 ⓣ02/943 4489, ⓦwww.aeroflot.ru; Air France, ul. Saborna 5 ⓣ02/939 7010, ⓦwww.airfrance .com; Alitalia, ul. Angel Kanchev 5 ⓣ02/981 6702, ⓦwww.alitalia.com; Austrian Airlines, bul. Vitosha 41 ⓣ02/980 2323, ⓦwww.aua.com; British Airways, bul. Patriarh Eftimiy 49 ⓣ02/954 7000, ⓦwww.ba.com; Bulgaria Air, call centre ⓣ02/402 0400, counter service at the Transport Service Centre underneath the NDK ⓣ02/402 0405, ⓦwww.air.bg; Czech Airlines, ul. Saborna 9 ⓣ02/981 5408, ⓦwww.czechairlines.com; LOT, bul. Stamboliiski 27A ⓣ02/987 4562, ⓦwww.lot .com; Lufthansa, ul. Bacho Kiro 26-30 ⓣ02/930 4242, ⓦwww.lufthansa.com; Olympic, bul. Stamboliiski 55 ⓣ02/981 4545, ⓦwww .olympicairlines.com; Turkish Airlines, ul. Saborna 11A ⓣ02/988 3596, ⓦwww.thy.com.

Airport information ⓣ02/937 2211.
Car rental Avis, ul. Orion 84 ⓣ02/826 1100, at the airport ⓣ02/945 9224, ⓦwww.avis.bg; Drenikov, Oborishte 55 ⓣ02/944 9532, ⓦwww .drenikov.com; Europcar, ul. Kozloduy 4 ⓣ02/931 6000, and at the airport ⓣ0887 503 030; Hertz, ul. Rakovski 135A ⓣ02/980 2467, and at the airport ⓣ02/945 9217; Penguin Travel, ul. Orfey 9 ⓣ02/400 1050, ⓦwww.penguin.bg; Sixt, Hilton Hotel, bul. Balgariya 1 ⓣ02/963 3002, and at the airport ⓣ02/945 9276 ; Zig Zag, ul. Stamboliiski 20-B, ⓣ02/980 5102, ⓦwww.zigzagbg.com.
Currency exchange There's no shortage of cash-only exchange bureaux in central Sofia, although be warned that those on the main strip (bul. Knyaginya Mariya Luiza and bul. Vitosha) tend to offer rip-off rates, and you'll get a better deal in the side-streets on either side. For travellers' cheques and credit card advances, Bulbank, on pl. Sveta Nedelya, is the most reliable bank.

Moving on from Sofia

Sofia **airport** (℡02/937 2211, @www.sofia-airport.bg) is located 10km east of the city centre and has two terminals about 2km apart – so check which one you're flying from before setting out. From the Orlov most, bus #84 runs to Terminal One, bus #284 to Terminal Two. A full list of airline addresses and telephone numbers appears opposite.

When leaving Sofia **by train**, remember that tickets for lines covering the northern half of Bulgaria (including the routes to Vidin, Ruse and Varna) are sold on the ground floor of the station; all others in the basement. The system of platform numbering is incredibly confusing (each platform is also divided into *iztok* – eastern – and *zapad* – western – sections, referred to as *i* or И and *z* or З respectively on the departures board), so allow plenty of time to catch your train. Beware, also, of pickpockets, beggars and con men who offer to help you onto your train, then make aggressive demands for money. To beat the queues, you can make advance bookings at the **Transport Service Centre**, or TsKTON, in the basement shopping arcade below the NDK (Mon–Sat 7am–7.30pm; domestic ℡02/658402, international ℡02/657186). The same office handles bookings for sleeper services and also sells tickets for international trains. International tickets can also be bought from a counter in the Central Station or from the Rila Bureau, at ul. General Gurko 5 (Mon–Fri 7am–7.30pm, Sat 7am–6.30pm; ℡02/987 0777, @www.bdz-rila.com).

The majority of **inter-city buses** depart from the **Tsentralna Avtogara** on bul. Knyaginya Mariya Luiza (℡0900 21 000, @www.centralbusstation-sofia.com), where a confusing array of private companies sell tickets from booths in the main departure hall – fortunately there's an English-speaking information desk near the entrance. A few services still use bus stations in suburban Sofia – Avtogara Poduyane, Avtogara Ovcha Kupel and Avtogara Yug – which serve different out-of-town regions: see "Travel Details" on p.114 for an idea of which one to head for. To get to **Avtogara Poduyane** (destinations to the north and northeast) on ul. Todorini Kukli, take bus #75 from Orlov most, or trolleybus #1 from bul. Levski. For **Avtogara Ovcha Kupel** (destinations to the southwest) take tram #5 from behind the Palace of Justice, and get off at the eleventh stop, or take tram #19 from the train station. For **Avtogara Yug** (destinations to the southeast), on bul. Dragan Tsankov, catch tram #18 from ul. Graf Ignatiev to the *Park-Hotel Moskva*, and continue on foot for a further 500m in the same direction – the bus station is concealed beneath an underpass on the main road.

International buses use either the **Tsentralna Avtogara** or the adjacent **Trafik-Market bus park**, where numerous international bus firms keep their offices.

Embassies and consulates Albania, ul. Krakra 10 ℡02/943 3857; Australia, ul. Trakiya 37 ℡02/946 1334; Canada, ul. Moskovska 9 ℡02/969 9710, @www.canada-bg.org; Denmark, bul. Knyaz Dondukov 54 ℡02/917 0100, @www.ambsofia.um.dk; Greece, ul. San Stefano 33 ℡02/946 1027, @www.greekembassy-sofia.org; Ireland, ul. Bacho Kiro 26-28 ℡02/985 3425, @www.embassyofireland.bg; Macedonia, ul. Frederik Zholiyo Kyuri 17 ℡02/870 1560; Netherlands, ul. Oborishte 15 ℡02/816 0300, @www.netherlandsembassy.bg; Norway, bul. Knyaz Dondukov 54B ℡02/981 1106, @www.norvegia.bg; Romania, bul. Sitnyakovo 4 ℡02/973 3081; Russia, bul. Dragan Tsankov 28 ℡02/963 0914; South Africa, ul. Bacho Kiro 26 ℡02/981 6682; Sweden, ul. Alfred Nobel 4 ℡02/930 1960, @www.swedenabroad.com/sofia;

Turkey, bul. Vasil Levski 80 ℡02/935 5500; UK, ul. Moskovska 9 ℡02/933 9222, @www.british-embassy.bg; USA, ul. Kozyak 16 ℡02/937 5100, @www.usembassy.bg; Serbia, ul. Veliko Tarnovo 3 ℡02/946 1633.

Hospitals The city's main casualty department is at Pirogov Emergency Hospital, opposite the *Rodina* hotel, at bul. General Totleben 21 (℡02/915 4411). For an ambulance call ℡150.

Internet Garibaldi, ul. Graf Ignatiev 6, @www.garibaldicafe.net; Site, bul. Vitosha 45, @www.siteout.net. Expect to pay around 2Lv/hr.

Left luggage Central train station (daily 6am–11pm); central bus station (24hr).

Libraries British Council, ul. Krakra 7 (Mon–Fri 9am–noon & 2–5pm; @www.britishcouncil.org /Bulgaria.htm); French Cultural Institute, pl.

Slaveykov (Mon–Fri 11am–6pm, Sat 11am–1pm); Goethe Institut, ul. Budapeshta 1 (Mon & Fri 10am–2pm, Tues–Thurs 2–7pm; ⓦ www.goethe.de/sofia).
Newspapers Foreign newspapers and magazines can be bought from the newsstands in the City Center Sofia shopping mall, on the corner of boulevards Arsenalsi and Cherni vrah.
Pharmacies 24hr service at Apteka Sveta Nedelya, corner of pl. Sveta Nedelya and bul. Stamboliiski; and Saldzhi, bul. Vitosha 35.
Photographic supplies Kodak Express, pl. Slaveykov 11.
Post office ul. General Gurko 6 (Mon–Sat 7am–8.30pm, Sun 8am–1pm).
Radio BBC World Service (91.0 VHF); Radio France Internationale (103.0 VHF).
Swimming Banya Mariya Luiza outdoor pool in the southeastern reaches of Borisova gradina is the place to head for in summer, and is the nearest thing to a beach you'll find this far inland. Otherwise, try the Spartak indoor and outdoor pools, bul. Arsenalski 4 (tram #6 from pl. Vazrazhdane to the end).

Taxis OK Supertrans ⓣ 02/973 2121; Taxi S Express ⓣ 91280.
Telephones BTC Centre (next to the post office), ul. General Gurko 4 (open 24hr).
Train information ⓣ 02/931 1111 and ⓣ 932 3333, ⓦ www.bdz.bg.
Travel agents Zig-Zag, at bul. Stamboliiski 20B (ⓣ 02/980 5102, ⓦ www.zigzagbg.com) are the longest-established independent travel specialists, organizing accommodation bookings, hiking itineraries, snow-shoeing and all manner of other activity-based trips. Lyuba Tours, at ul. Tsanko Tserkovski 22 (ⓣ 02/963 3343, ⓦ www.lyubatours .com) arranges tailor-made itineraries and special-interest weekend trips to Bulgarian towns and villages. Penguin Travel, at ul. Orfey 9 ⓣ 02/400 0150, ⓦ www.penguin.bg, can organize trekking tours and tailor-made arrangements. Usit Colours, at bul. Vasil Levsi 35 ⓣ 02/981 1900, ⓦ www.usitcolours.bg, specializes in youth and student travel.
Visa extensions Available at the Immigration Office at bul. Knyaginya Mariya Luiza 48 (ⓣ 02/982 3764; Mon–Fri 9am–5pm).

Travel details

Trains

Sofia to: Burgas (3 daily; 6hr 30min); Kazanlak (3 daily; 3–4hr); Koprivshtitsa (5 daily; 1hr 40min); Pleven (10 daily; 3hr); Plovdiv (12 daily; 2hr 45min); Ruse (4 daily; 7hr); Sandanski (4 daily; 3hr); Varna (6 daily; 8hr 30min); Vidin (3 daily; 5hr); Vratsa (4 daily; 2hr).

Buses

Tsentralna Avtogara to: Ahtopol (summer only 1 daily; 8hr 30min); Blagoevgrad (4 daily; 2hr); Burgas (8 daily; 7hr); Dobrich (4 daily; 7hr); Gabrovo (2 daily; 3hr 30min); Haskovo (3 daily; 4hr); Kardzhali (3 daily; 5hr); Kazanlak (5–7 daily; 5–6hr); Kiten (summer only 1 daily; 8hr); Lovech (1 daily; 3hr); Melnik (1 daily; 5hr); Nesebar (summer only 1 daily; 7hr 30min); Plovdiv (hourly; 2hr); Razgrad (2 daily; 6hr); Ruse (12 daily; 5hr); Sandanski (8 daily; 3hr); Shumen (6 daily; 6hr); Silistra (1 daily; 7hr); Sozopol (summer only 1 daily; 7hr 30min); Stara Zagora (4 daily; 4hr); Svilengrad (1 daily; 5hr); Svishtov (1 daily; 4hr 30min); Varna (5 daily; 7hr); Veliko Tarnovo (8 daily; 4hr); Vidin (hourly; 4hr).
Trafik-Market to: Koprivshtitsa (2 daily; 2hr).
Avtogara Ovcha Kupel to: Bansko (8 daily; 3hr); Dupnitsa (hourly; 1hr 30min); Gotse Delchev

(8 daily; 4hr); Kyustendil (hourly; 2hr); Pernik (hourly; 40min); Rila Village (2 daily; 2hr).
Avtogara Poduyane to: Etropole (Mon–Sat 5 daily; Sun 3 daily; 1hr 30min); Koprivshtitsa (2 daily; 2hr); Pravets (4 daily; 1hr); Teteven (3 daily; 2hr 20min); Troyan (1 daily; 3hr).
Avtogara Yug to: Panagyurishte (4 daily; 2hr); Pazardzhik (3 daily; 1hr 30min); Samokov (every 30min; 1hr 15min); Velingrad (Mon–Thurs 4 daily, Fri & Sun 5 daily; Sat 3 daily; 3hr).

Flights

Sofia to: Burgas (1 daily; 1hr); Varna (3 daily; 1hr).

International trains

Sofia to: Belgrade (2 daily; 10hr); Budapest (1 daily; 16hr); Bucharest (2 daily; 11hr); Istanbul (1 daily; 15hr); Moscow (connection in Bucharest; 1 daily; 45hr); Thessaloniki (3 daily; 10hr).

International buses

Tsentralna Avtogara to: Athens (2 daily; 15hr); Istanbul (4 daily; 10hr).
Trafik-Market to: Belgrade Niš; (2 daily; 8hr); Istanbul (2 daily; 10hr); Ohrid (1 daily; 9hr); Skopje (3 daily; 5hr); Thessaloniki (1 daily; 6hr).

2

The southwest

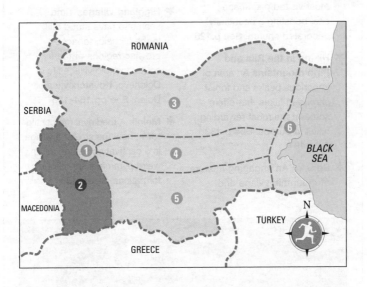

CHAPTER 2 # Highlights

* **Kukeri** Nowhere in Bulgaria is the tradition of Shrovetide masked revels as well preserved as it is in the southwest: Pernik, Razlog and especially Eleshnitsa are the best places to catch them. See p.119

* **Rila Monastery** Bulgaria's most visited pilgrimage site, boasting a beautifully decorated church. See p.126

* **Hiking in the Rila and Pirin mountains** An area of imperious peaks and forest-shrouded lakes that offers some of the most rewarding hikes in Europe. See p.133 & p.149

* **Bansko** An engaging mixture of mountain village and modern holiday resort. See p.142

* **The train ride from to Bansko Septemvri** It may be painfully slow, but this narrow-gauge railway provides access to some of the most wonderful mountain scenery in the Balkans. See p.151

* **Highland villages** Time seems to have stood still in the archaic, tobacco-growing regions of the far south: sample village life in Delchevo, Kovatchevitsa or Dolen. See pp.154–156

* **Melnik** A medieval mercantile town, now the size of a village, in a captivating setting among weird pyramidal sandstone formations. See p.158

▲ Narrow-gauge train from Bansko to Septemvri

2

The southwest

The landscape of Bulgaria south of the capital is dominated by the River Struma, which rises on the southern slopes of Mount Vitosha before sweeping west then south through a series of arid gorges and fertile flood plains. Both the main southbound train route and the E79 highway to Greece follow the Struma Valley for much of its length, skirting some of the country's most grandiose scenery on the way. Although the major towns along the route are pleasant enough, most of the area's real attractions lie in the mountains to the east.

The **Rila and Pirin ranges** contain Bulgaria's highest, stormiest peaks: swathed in forests and dotted with alpine lakes, they reward exploration by anyone prepared to hike or risk their car's suspension on the back roads. In the Rila range, the modern resort of **Borovets** is a major **winter sports** centre, while the much smaller **Malyovitsa**, nearby, is the starting point for some classic summer hikes. On the way to Borovets you pass through the historic crafts town of **Samokov**, whose artists adorned **Rila Monastery**, the most revered of Bulgarian holy places. The Pirin range offers an even more dramatic cluster of rugged, granite-topped peaks. The tallest of them, **Mount Vihren**, is accessible from the fast-growing ski resort of **Bansko**, whose nest of old stone houses makes it among the most attractive of the mountain towns. On the southern fringes of the Pirin range near the Greek border, the monastery of **Rozhen** lies at the end of a great hike from the village of **Melnik**, known both for its wine and its vernacular architecture.

Slightly nearer to Sofia, the route leading west towards the Republic of Macedonia takes you past the ancient **monastery of Zemen** and the spa town of **Kyustendil**, which retains a smattering of Ottoman-period remains. Destinations like these – along with many others in the southwest – are possible day-trips from the capital.

Southwest of the capital

Aside from its rugged yet fertile landscape and lack of tourists, the chief attractions of the region to the southwest of the capital are the small, reclusive **Zemen Monastery** and the mellow spa town of **Kyustendil**. Three or four

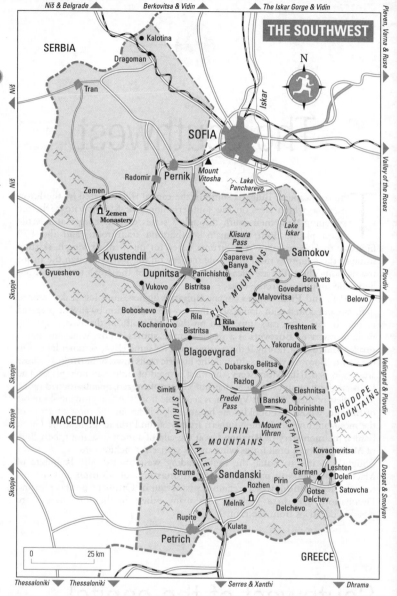

THE SOUTHWEST

N

SERBIA

Kalotina

Dragoman

Tran

SOFIA

Iskar

Radomir   Pernik   *Mount Vitosha*   Lake Pancharevo

Zemen

⌂ Zemen Monastery

Klisura Pass   Lake Iskar

Kyustendil   Dupnitsa   Sapareva Banya   Samokov
Panichishte

Gyueshevo   Vukovo   Bistritsa   RILA MOUNTAINS   Borovets

Boboshevo   Govedartsi
Malyovitsa

Rila   ⌂ Rila Monastery   Belovo

Kocherinovo   Treshtenik

Bistritsa   Yakoruda

Blagoevgrad

Dobarsko   Belitsa   RHODOPE MOUNTAINS

Simitli   Razlog   Eleshnitsa

STRUMA   Predel Pass   Bansko   Dobrinishte

MACEDONIA   PIRIN MOUNTAINS   *Mount Vihren*   MESTA VALLEY

VALLEY   Kovachevitsa

Struma   Sandanski   Leshten
Rozhen   Pirin   Garmen   Dolen
Melnik   ⌂   Gotse   Satovcha
Delchev
Rupite   Delchevo

Kulata

Petrich

GREECE

0   25 km

◀ Niš   ◀ Niš   ◀ Niš   ◀ Skopje   ◀ Skopje   ◀ Skopje   ◀ Skopje

trains a day between Sofia and Kyustendil stop at Zemen, making it possible to visit the monastery before catching a later train on to Kyustendil; unfortunately, buses between Kyustendil and Sofia take a more direct route, bypassing Zemen. Both road and rail routes pass initially by the coal-mining town of **PERNIK (ПЕРНИК)**, famous for its January *kukeri* rites (see box, p.120) but otherwise of marginal interest to tourists.

Zemen Monastery

Forty-five kilometres southwest of Pernik, the sleepy village of **ZEMEN** (ЗЕМЕН) owes its place on the tourist trail to the small but spectacularly decorated **Zemen Monastery** (*Zemenski manastir*; Mon, Wed, Fri & Sat 9am–5.30pm, Tues & Sun 11am–3pm; 10Lv), which clings to a wooded hillside 3km to the southwest.

The monastery lacks the high walls and decorative facades that characterize Bulgaria's other religious foundations, and its small twelfth-century cruciform **Church of St Ivan the Theologian** appears similarly modest from the outside. Inside, however, are some of Bulgaria's finest surviving **medieval frescoes**, sensitively restored between 1970 and 1974. The frescoes – produced by anonymous artists during the 1350s for local noble Konstantin Deyan – are examples of the Macedonian School of painting, which was somewhat cruder and less formalized than the predominant style of Tarnovo. Against a background of cool blues and greys, the saints with their golden halos and finery are depicted in hierarchies, including Deyan and his wife Doya, who appear on the wall of the right-hand apse as you enter. Further along the same wall, there's an unusual rendition of Christ giving Holy Communion to the disciples, in which he's portrayed as two separate people – one giving bread, the other pouring out the wine. Elsewhere, dark blues and reds are employed to highlight the gravity of episodes like the *Treason of Judas*, the *Judgement of Pilate* and, most famously, the depiction of blacksmiths forging nails in readiness for the Crucifixion (in the second archway to the left as you enter).

The monastery is easy to find: simply proceed along the village's main street (ul. Zemenski Manastir) in a southwesterly direction and keep going as it begins to wind its way uphill.

▲ Church of St Ivan the Theologian, Zemen Monastery

Kyustendil

Thirty kilometres southwest of Zemen, the town of **KYUSTENDIL** (КЮСТЕНДИЛ), with its fertile plain and thermal springs, has attracted conquerors since Thracian times. The Romans developed this into a popular spa, and the Turks who settled here in large numbers after the fourteenth century constructed the *hammams* and mosques that gave Kyustendil its Oriental character. Some of this atmosphere lingers on in the old backstreets, although the centre of town has undergone considerable modernization, most of it tasteful. The town's wide, tree-shaded avenues lined with cafés are as agreeable as any in Bulgaria but specific sights are limited, so you could easily see all it has to offer in an afternoon.

The Town

Both the bus and train stations are near the northern end of **bulevard Balgariya**, just beyond the high-rise landmark *Hotel Velbazhd*. Diagonally opposite the hotel looms the future home of the **History Museum**, a large warehouse currently undergoing major renovation. For the time being a small pavilion behind the warehouse (Tues–Sun 9am–noon & 1–5pm; 2Lv) holds the museum's absorbing collection of Neolithic figurines, Thracian burial finds (including a reconstructed ceremonial chariot) and Roman votive tablets.

Continuing along bul. Balgariya for another five minutes and detouring left onto ul. Patriarh Evtimiy brings you to the Kyustendil **art gallery** (Tues–Sun 9am–noon & 2–5pm; 5Lv), largely devoted to the works of Bulgaria's greatest

---

Pernik and the kukeri

The Pernik region has retained many of the midwinter folk festivals that have all but died out in other parts of Bulgaria. Most important of the seasonal revels are those involving grotesquely masked mummers known as **kukeri**, who mark the new year by processing noisily through the village, rhythmically jumping around to shake the cowbells strapped to their waists. It is believed that the long nights of winter provide the ideal cover for malevolent spirits, and the *kukeri* rites are necessary to scare them off. Many villages in the Pernik region have their own troupe of *kukeri* made up of local menfolk, who enact their rites every year on January 14 (New Year's Day according to the old-style Orthodox Calendar). After gathering in the centre of the village and making as much noise as possible, the *kukeri* then proceed to visit each household of the village, where they're treated to a slice of *banitsa* and a glass of *rakiya*.

Yardzhilovtsi, a small town 10km west of Pernik, is the scene of particularly lively celebrations, when *kukeri* from surrounding suburbs and villages converge on the schoolyard in the centre of the village. Other villages with strong *kukeri* traditions include Kosharevo and Banishte, pressed up against the hills to the west. Travellers driving through the area on January 14 should be aware that each village exerts a symbolic "tax" on passing motorists (a small sum should suffice) before inviting them to join the revels.

Pernik itself marks the *kukeri* season with a biennial **Festival of the Kukeri** (officially entitled the "International Festival of Masquerade Games"; ⓦ www.surva .org), held every even-numbered year on the first or second weekend after January 14. All the *kukeri* from surrounding villages participate, as well as guest folklore groups from other parts of Europe where similar rituals are practised.

Other parts of southwest Bulgaria where *kukeri* rites are still observed include Razlog (see p.141) and Eleshnitsa (p.151).

Tradition and ritual

Folk practices still form part of contemporary life in Bulgaria, with saints' days, seasonal rites and other celebrations providing the ideal excuse to don kaleidoscopically colourful costumes and show off a rich repertoire of traditional song and dance. Religious festivals form the backbone of the calendar, although some of the zaniest celebrations are those associated with archaic, pre-Christian fertility rites, like the extravagantly costumed *kukeri* (mummers), who stomp and shake their way through village streets. Music fans should visit the set-piece folk festivals, most of which occur around August.

Folk festivals

The biggest traditional music events are the **Koprivshtitsa** festival, which attracts performers from all over Bulgaria, and **Pirin Sings** (*Pirin Pee*), which concentrates on the rich folkloric traditions of the southwest. Both feature an organized programme on a series of stages, as well as a host of unofficial performances by village musicians, making these occasions seem more like medieval fairs. Traditionally, each takes place only every four or five years, but such is their popularity that smaller, scaled-down versions of the main events are now run annually. There's also a host of local festivals in villages around the country, often using traditional feast days such as St Elijah's Day (*Ilinden*) or the Assumption (*Golyama Bogoroditsa*) as an excuse for a day or two of dancing and drinking.

Baba Marta

National Festival of Bulgarian Folk Art, Koprivshtitsa ▲
Martenitsas tied to trees ▼

Bulgarians mark the imminent arrival of spring on the first of March, greeting each other with the words "Chestita Baba Marta", or "Happy Granny March". Baba Marta symbolizes the unpredictability of the weather at this time of year – a capricious old woman serving up wind, rain or sunshine according to whim. Bulgarians also celebrate March 1 by presenting each other with a **martenitsa**, a good-luck charm made of entwined red and white thread. Intended to bring health and good fortune (the white symbolizes long life, the red symbolizes strength and health), the *martenitsa* is worn around the wrist until the first storks of spring are sighted – a sign that summer is near and the bracelet's protection is no longer required.

Easter

The period around Easter has always had enormous ritual significance in Bulgaria, combining Christian beliefs about the Resurrection with much older pagan celebrations connected with the return of springtime fertility after the barren winter. On the Saturday prior to Easter week (Lazarovden or St Lazar's Day), groups of teenage girls travel from house to house performing songs intended to bring fertility both to themselves and the people they're visiting. According to folk wisdom, girls who don't take part in Lazarovden will fail to attract the right kind of suitors. Although you won't see Lazarovden celebrated in the big cities, it's still carried out in small towns and villages. One occasion that involves pretty much everyone is Varbnitsa or Palm Sunday, when Bulgarians flock to the flower stalls to buy willow branches or floral bouquets, in symbolic celebration of Christ's palm-paved entry into Jerusalem.

▲ Patriarch at Easter Service, Sofia
▼ Women during Easter, Koprivshtitsa

Easter itself, or Velikden in Bulgarian, is the most important holiday in the Orthodox Church, and for many Bulgarians represents an even more important family get-together than Christmas. The main event of Easter weekend is the church service late on Saturday, when priests emerge from behind the iconostasis at midnight bearing candles symbolizing the Resurrection. Members of the congregation light their own candles from those borne by the priests, before moving outside to process around the church three times. Hand-painted eggs are also produced and knocked together with those of a near-neighbour – bringing luck to those whose eggs don't crack.

Kukeri rites

One favourite ritual in Bulgarian towns and villages is the annual parade of **kukeri** or mummers – men dressed in grotesque animal masks and with cowbells hung from their belts, leaping and gyrating rhythmically to create as raucous a din as possible. This is partly a mid-winter cleansing ritual, intended to drive away malevolent spirits. It is also a fertility rite that anticipates spring: in some areas, *kukeri* lightly strike women with phallic wooden swords.

Kukeri rituals usually take place at Shrovetide, although they are enacted at New Year in the Razlog and Pernik regions, in early spring in Shiroka Laka (see p.350), and on Easter Sunday in the village of Eleshnitsa (see p.151). Wherever they take place, *kukeri* rites are usually a day-long affair, with participants visiting each house of the village to guarantee the inhabitants good luck in the coming year – and receiving *banitsa* (cheese pie) and *rakiya* (brandy) in return.

Kukeri performance ▲
Fire dancing ▼

Fire-dancing

Many of Bulgaria's seasonal rites date back to pre-Christian times, and may have evolved from the ecstatic, Dionysian religion of the ancient Thracians. Nowhere is this more apparent than in the practice of *nestinarstvo* or **fire-dancing**, in which villagers fall into a trance and dance on hot coals to strident bagpipe-and-drum accompaniment. A frequent ingredient in tourist-oriented folklore shows, authentic fire-dancing still takes place on the feast day of Saints Konstantin and Elena in the village of Balgari in the Strandzha (see p.429). It's both a solemn and riotously enjoyable occasion for the locals, with icons of saints paraded around the village, and sheep sacrificed prior to communal feasting.

twentieth-century painter, **Vladimir Dimitrov-Maistora** (1882–1960). Smitten by Eastern philosophy, and seeing parallels in it with the values of Bulgaria's peasantry, Dimitrov reacted against the art of the West, decrying Modernism as a destructive force innately hostile to the ideal of beauty. It's an attitude which had a profound effect on Bulgarian art throughout the twentieth century, effectively isolating it from avant-garde developments elsewhere. A recurring image in Dimitrov-Maistor's paintings is that of the idealized peasant maiden surrounded by fruit and flowers – his contemporary interpretation of the Madonnas produced by medieval Bulgarian icon painters – and there are examples aplenty on display here. A bearded, guru-like figure who preferred the simplicity of village life to that of the city, Dimitrov-Maistor was viewed as both a saintly figure and an eccentric misanthrope – a rumour that he had an incestuous relationship with his sister Yordana (whose portrait hangs upstairs beside his) has recently enjoyed popular credence, although plenty of his admirers deny it.

Just behind the gallery, occupying a whitewashed two-storey house at ul. Tsar Simeon I 11, the **Dimitar Peshev House-Museum** (Tues–Sun 9am–noon & 2–5pm; 2Lv) celebrates one of Bulgaria's most unlikely heroes, the Kyustendil-born MP (1894–1973) who, contrary to the policy of the right-wing government in which he served, protested against the deportation of the Bulgarian Jews in 1943. Peshev – supported by other MPs, lawyers and local bigwigs – kicked up such a fuss over the planned deportations that the Bulgarian government resisted German demands for shipments of Jews to the death camps, opting to intern them locally instead (see box on pp.88–89 for a fuller version of the story). English-language texts, alongside pictures of Peshev and fellow protestors, tell the tale, while relics such as Peshev's backgammon board and hiking rucksack help to round out the personality of this relatively little-known politician.

A couple of blocks southeast of the Peshev museum is the **Chifte Bathhouse** (Mon & Thurs–Sat 5.30am–8.30pm, Wed & Sun 5.30am–12.50pm), a shabby postwar conversion of another, larger Ottoman bath, which in turn was built on top of a Roman spa centre. Divided into men's and women's sections, the warren-like, elaborately tiled interior contains a series of pools filled with 41°C, sulphate-rich water, which is also used in several local sanatoria for the treatment of gynaecological and nervous disorders. Behind the baths stands the sixteenth-century **Ahmed Bey Dzhamiya**, an impressive mosque with a tie-beamed porch, overlooking the excavated foundations of a Roman bath. There's no longer a significant Muslim population in Kyustendil, and the mosque now serves as display space for the town **history musem** (Tues–Sun 9am–noon & 1–5pm; 2Lv). There's usually a different archeology-related exhibition here every year, but no permanent collection.

From the mosque, you can turn right to reach **ploshtad Velbazhd**, a modernized square featuring a **memorial to Todor Aleksandrov**, the Macedonian revolutionary assassinated by a group of his own colleagues in 1924. Though not in the historical territory of Macedonia itself, Kyustendil occupied a special role in the struggles for Macedonian liberation at the start of the twentieth century, with groups of heavily armed guerrillas regularly descending on the town before crossing the border into Ottoman territory. Beneath the chestnut trees at the southwest corner of the square, and nestling amid beautiful gardens, the **Church of Sveta Bogoroditsa** (the Holy Virgin) sports a trio of hexagonal domes and contains a rich collection of nineteenth-century icons in the porch. The church was built slightly below ground level and partially covered with earth during the Ottoman period in order to comply with restrictions governing the height and visibility of Christian places of worship. Dug out after the Liberation, the church still exudes a semi-secret, subterranean atmosphere.

Backtracking along bul. Demokratsiya, you'll pass the tumbledown, overgrown **Fetih Mehmed Dzhamiya**, its minaret etched with hexagonal patterns, an effect achieved by inserting red tiles into the darker brown brickwork.

Hisarlak hill

Just to the east of the mosque, traders and shoppers crowd the daily **market**, south of which pathways begin the ascent of **Hisarlak hill**, shrouded in wooded parkland. Allow about twenty minutes to hike up the path, although in summer you can take the "tourist train", which makes its way up the hill from Kyustendil's main square whenever enough people assemble. Near the summit you can see the **ruins** of what was originally an extensive Roman settlement around the Asclepion, the sacred baths where Emperor Trajan cured his skin complaint and renamed the town Ulpia Pautalia (Ulpius being the name of his father; Pautalia a local Thracian word meaning "place of springs") to mark the occasion. Intermingled are the remains of a medieval fortress once occupied by the boyar Konstantin Deyan. The Ottomans, who supplanted his rule over the region during the mid-fourteenth century, designated their new acquisition "Konstantin's land" – *Kostandinili* in Turkish – which eventually gave rise to the name of the town.

Practicalities

If you want to stay in some comfort and make use of state-of-the-art spa facilities then you can't do any better than the *Hotel Strimon*, a much-renovated former sanatorium at ul. Tsar Simeon I 24 (☎078/559 000 and 551 355; ⓦstrimon-spaclub.com; rooms ❼ suites ❽). It has deep-carpeted en suites with reproduction-antique furnishings, some lovely fifth-floor rooms with skylight windows, and two highly desirable split-level suites with Jacuzzi. The basement-level spa centre features a swimming pool, a Roman-style bath fed by Kyustendil's natural mineral water, and numerous massage and beauty treatments. A cheaper option is the *Hotel Balgariya*, just off the central pl. Velbazhd at ul. Konstantinova Banya 3 (☎078/51200, ⓦwww.bgglobe.net /bulgaria.html; ❹), whose simple en suites range from the bright and spacious to the cramped and gloomy. There's also the smaller *Lazur*, in between the stations and the centre at ul. Kiri i Metodii 15A (☎078/26368; ❸), which offers a handful of loudly decorated but comfortable rooms, some with shower, some with bathtub. An enticing option if you've got your own transport and twenty minutes' driving time to spare is the *Tri Buki*, in the hills 20km southwest of town (head out along ul. Tsar Osvoboditel, take the road to the village of Bogoslov and keep going; ☎078/522 332, ⓦwww.tribuki.com; ❹), a contemporary conversion of an old trade-union resort offering chic, comfy rooms with shower and TV. There's a decent restaurant, an outdoor pool in summer and a short downhill skiing piste in winter.

As far as **eating** and **drinking** in Kyustendil are concerned, the pavement cafés and pizzerias along bul. Balgariya will suffice for refuelling purposes. For something more substantial, the back-garden restaurant attached to the *Lazur* offers dependable Bulgarian fare, although the *Hotel Strimon*'s restaurant offers more in the way of international dishes and quality wines. Up on Hisarlak hill, there's a pleasant al-fresco restaurant next to the former Hisarlaka hotel, serving up grilled meats on an attractive terrace.

Moving on from Kyustendil

Bulgaria's main **border crossing** into Macedonia is 22km southwest of town, just above the village of **Gyueshevo** (ГЮЕШЕВО). There are no local buses to the frontier (taxis cost about 25Lv), so if you're travelling this way it makes sense to catch one of the three daily services to Skopje (one of which continues to the lakeside resort of Ohrid), which originate in Sofia but pass through Kyustendil bus station en route. Twenty kilometres northwest of Kyustendil there's also a crossing point into **Serbia** – with no buses of any description travelling this route, you'll have to rely on taxis on both sides of the border.

If you're **heading southwards**, it's a toss-up between catching a bus to Blagoevgrad, a good base for trips to the Pirin, or the nearer town of Dupnitsa, which offers two daily connections to Rila Monastery (see p.126), but is no place to get stranded. The only other thing in Dupnitsa's favour is that the road there passes the dreamily graceful **Kadin most**, a famous old bridge over the Struma in the middle of **Nevestino** (НЕВЕСТИНО), a one-horse town 15km east of Kyustendil. This five-arched seventeen-metre span was constructed after 1463 to guarantee the Ottoman lines of communication between the Danube and Salonika, although local legends advance different explanations. According to one, Vizier Isak Pasha took pity on a maiden separated from her betrothed by the river, and had it built as a wedding present – hence its original name, the Bride's Bridge. Another tale has it that the builder, Manuil, suggested to his brothers that they appease the river god by offering one of their wives as a sacrifice, the victim being whichever one arrived first with her husband's lunch. Manuil's wife turned up and was promptly immured, weeping and begging that they leave holes so that she might see daylight and continue to suckle her child.

The Rila Mountains

South of Sofia, Mount Vitosha gives way with barely a pause to the **Rila Mountains**, an area of wild highlands enclosing fertile valleys. Much of the massif falls under the protection of the Rila National Park (Ⓦ www.rilanationalpark.org), and the range's hiking trails are among the best maintained, best marked and most popular in Bulgaria. On the western fringes of the range, the dull lowland town of **Dupnitsa** is the obvious stepping stone from which to approach **Rila Monastery**, the finest in Bulgaria. Over on the range's northeastern side, the town of **Samokov** provides access to the ski resort of **Borovets** and the hiking base of **Malyovitsa**.

Dupnitsa

Heading south from Sofia, the first town in the Struma Valley of any significance is **DUPNITSA** (ДУПНИЦА), which is still known to some locals by its Communist-era name Stanke Dimitrov (Stanketo for short). Its only real claim

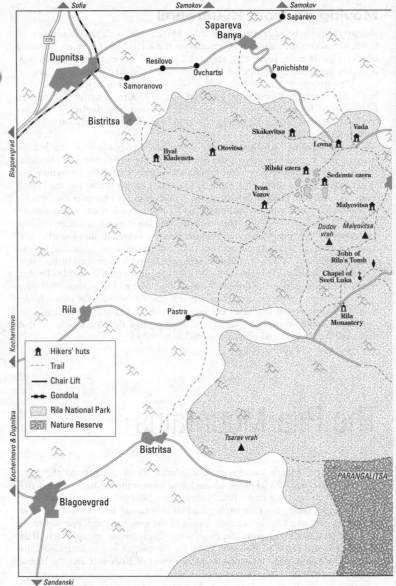

to fame is its **tobacco industry**: every year some eight million kilos of the stuff passes through Dupnitsa's warehouses and processing plants, the river is tinted a nicotine yellow, and you can see huge quantities of tobacco growing, or spread out to dry, throughout the surrounding countryside. However, the only reason for travellers to come here is to catch a bus to more appealing destinations in the Rila mountains.

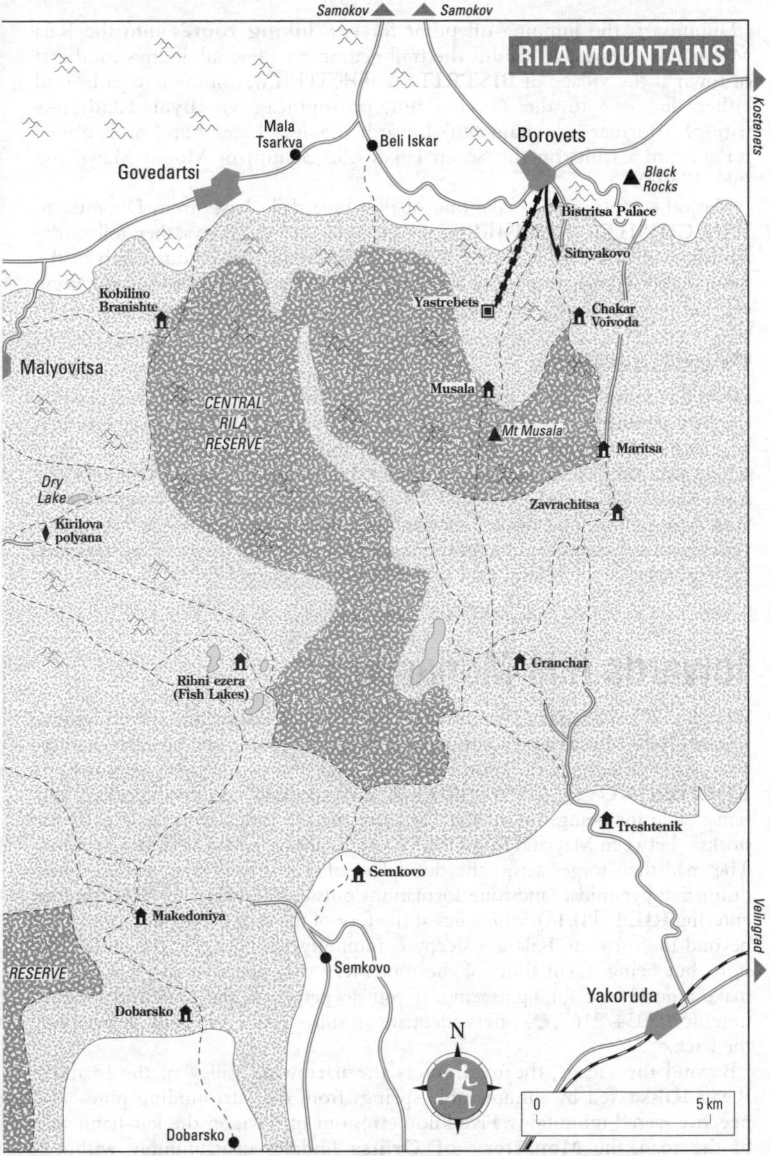
RILA MOUNTAINS
Samokov
Samokov
Kostenets
Mala Tsarkva
Beli Iskar
Borovets
Govedartsi
Black Rocks
Bistritsa Palace
Sitnyakovo
Kobilino Branishte
Yastrebets
Chakar Voivoda
Malyovitsa
Musala
CENTRAL RILA RESERVE
Mt Musala
Maritsa
Dry Lake
Zavrachitsa
Kirilova polyana
Granchar
Ribni ezera (Fish Lakes)
Treshtenik
Semkovo
Velingrad
Makedoniya
Semkovo
RESERVE
Yakoruda
Dobarsko
N
0
5 km
Dobarsko
Razlog
Belitsa, Razlog & Bansko
Razlog & Bansko

If you have an hour to kill, there are a couple of monuments worth a look. Just off the modernized main square is a sixteenth-century **mosque**, whose simple domed structure has an elegance that displays Ottoman architecture's debt to Byzantine church building; it currently houses a bookshop. Behind it is the **Okoliiskata kashta**, a house of the same period that once served as the *konak* of the Ottoman governor, and is now a small art gallery.

Dupnitsa is the jumping-off point for two **hiking routes** into the Rila Mountains. Nearest at hand is the trail beginning a few kilometres southeast of town at the village of **BISTRITSA** (БИСТРИЦА), from where paths lead either due east to the *Otovitsa* hut, or southeast via **Byal Kladenets** (site of a former mountain hut) towards the *Ivan Vazov* hut – well placed for onward assaults on the Seven Lakes (2hr 30min) or Mount Malyovitsa (6hr 30min).

The other option is to take one of the three daily buses from Dupnitsa to **PANICHISHTE** (ПАНИЧИЩЕ), just south of Sapareva Banya, then follow the asphalt road to the *Lovna* hut – the start of a popular four-hour climb to the Seven Lakes. Remember to ask about current weather conditions before setting off, and travel with proper walking boots and waterproof clothing.

Practicalities

Dupnitsa's **train station** is about fifteen minutes' walk from the centre, while the **bus station** is a block or so off the main square. There are currently two buses a day directly to Rila Monastery and another one or two to Rila village, where you can pick up an onward service. If you need to stay in Dupnitsa, the town-centre *Rila* **hotel** (☎0701/59610 & 59630; ❸), with its plain en suites, is your only option. The usual smattering of cafés adds a vivacity of sorts to the pedestrianized streets leading off the main square, and there's a nice **restaurant**, the *Panorama*, in the hilltop park overlooking the square.

Towards Rila Monastery

Roughly 20km south of Dupnitsa, a road branches east off the main highway towards **Rila Monastery**, southwestern Bulgaria's most visited tourist destination. After a couple of kilometres the road passes through the town of **KOCHERINOVO** (КОЧЕРИНОВО), architecturally undistinguished but remarkable for being one of the favourite nesting grounds in these parts for storks – between May and August the rooftops are swarming with the creatures. The road then forges across the floodplain of the Struma river, passing some distinctive pyramidal sandstone formations outside the village of **Stobi** before entering **RILA** (РИЛА), which lies at the foot of the Rila mountains some 8km beyond the turn-off. Rila is a sleepy community with a few cafés and a food store, but being 27km short of the monastery that shares its name, it doesn't make a good base for sightseeing. If you do get stuck, the four-storey *Orbita* hotel (☎07054/2167; ❸) offers adequate en suites and a tiny outdoor pool out the back.

Beyond the village, the road enters the narrowing valley of the foaming River Rilska, fed by innumerable springs from the surrounding pine- and beech-covered mountains. Five kilometres out of Rila, on the left-hand side of the road, the **Monastery of Orlitsa** huddles unassumingly within a plain-looking walled enclosure. Built as a staging post for monks and pilgrims en route for the much more important foundation upstream, it's a relaxing little place, consisting of a grassy courtyard and dainty seventeenth-century church. The porch of the church, decorated by Samokov painter Nikola Obrazopisov, contains a lively portrayal of a procession bearing the bones of St John of Rila – which were brought back to Bulgaria for reburial in 1469.

Rila Monastery

As the best known of Bulgaria's monasteries – justly famed for both its architecture and its mountainous setting – **Rila Monastery** (*Rilski manastir*) receives a stream of visitors, who now arrive by bus or car rather than on foot or by mule, as did pilgrims in the old days. Despite its popularity with tourists, the forest-girdled site still exudes the air of a wilderness, and it's easy to see why ninth-century holy man **John of Rila** (*Ivan Rilski*; see box, p.128) chose this valley as his retreat. What began as a hermitage became an important spiritual centre after his death, and the monastery forged links with others in the Balkans and played a major role in Orthodox Christianity throughout the Middle Ages.

Although most visitors come on packaged day-trips, it is perfectly possible to get here independently, and the abundance of trails leading off into the densely forested hills make an extended stay more than worthwhile. Though the monastery gates are open daily to visitors from dawn until dusk, some of the sights within the complex keep more restricted hours. If you want to see (or take part in) a **service**, morning prayers start at 7 or 8am, evening prayers at 4 or 5pm. Services are preceded by monks hammering on wooden panels in the monastery courtyard, a ritual designed to remind the congregation of Christ's nailing to the cross. The start of the Saturday evening service is usually announced by a monk ringing a carillon of bells from Hrelyo's tower (see p.130), while the Thursday morning service is traditionally dedicated to St John himself, and features sacral chanting thought to date from the fifteenth century. Apart from Easter, the two main religious **festivals** celebrated here are the birthday (Aug 18) and feast day (Oct 19) of St John of Rila.

Getting to the monastery

Getting to Rila Monastery **from Sofia** comes down to how much money or time you're willing to spend. The easiest option is to take one of the **day-trips**

▲ Rila Monastery

advertised at hotel reception desks or by agents like Zig-Zag (see p.75). Usually these involve renting a car and driver with the latter doubling up as guide. Prices fall within the 160–220Lv margin: reasonable if there are three or four of you but a bit steep if you're on your own.

Travelling **by public transport**, it's possible to treat the monastery as a day-trip from Sofia providing you catch the morning service (currently departing at 10.20am) from the Ovcha Kupel terminal to Rila village, where you pick up a connection to Rila Monastery itself. This leaves you with a couple of hours to look around before catching the return service. If you're not too pressured by time there are a number of other ways of getting to the monastery: half-hourly buses leave Ovcha Kupel in Sofia for **Dupnitsa**, from where there are two daily services to the monastery (if you miss these, take one of the four daily buses from Dupnitsa to Rila village, and try to pick up a connecting service there). If you're approaching the area from the south, you might be able to save time by catching one of the hourly buses to Rila village from **Blagoevgrad** – although bear in mind that you might have a long wait in the village before a bus to the monastery shows up. Whichever direction you're travelling from, it pays to check timetables carefully at each stage of the journey in order to plan your return trip.

Accommodation

Staying in the monastery's sparsely furnished guest "cells" (head for the lodgings office in the southeast corner of the yard; ❷) has some appeal if you don't mind the lack of hot water, or that the gates close at 8pm in summer, 5pm in winter (the porter can in theory be roused until midnight but don't bank on it). Two hundred metres outside the monastery's eastern gate, the *Tsarev vrah* (☎07054/2280; ❹) offers acceptable en suites with

St John of Rila (880–946)

John of Rila, known to his compatriots as **Ivan Rilski**, was one of many ninth-century hermits and mystics who took to the wilds of Bulgaria and Macedonia in search of solitude and enlightenment. Having acquired a reputation as a wise man and healer, he finally yielded to his followers and established a monastery high in the Rila Valley, where he could combine the virtues of a religious community with ascetic solitude. It's said that he took steps to embalm himself by consuming herbs and potions, and his corpse was believed to possess curative powers. As a result, Rila became famous throughout the Balkans as a pilgrimage site.

In the Middle Ages, the bones of saints were important symbols that added legitimacy to the rule of whoever could establish control over them, so Tsar Petar had John of Rila's **remains** moved to Sofia in the mid-900s, where they were kept in the Rotunda of St George (see p.84). In 1183 they were stolen from here by the Hungarian King Béla III, who carted them off to the Catholic city of Esztergom, whose bishop reputedly went blind after denying that the bones were those of a saint and only regained his sight after publicly recanting. Their return to Sofia in 1187 was secured by the Byzantine emperor Isaac Angelus, to win support against the rebellion of the Bulgarian nobles Petar and Asen, though this didn't prevent Asen from capturing the city and bearing the bones off to his new capital, Veliko Tarnovo, in 1194. They finally returned to Rila in 1469 – though St John's right hand toured Russia in the sixteenth century to raise funds for the restoration of Bulgarian monasteries. The left hand is still kept in the monastery church – although it's not always on display.

bland furnishings and Bulgarian-style open showers. About 1500m further on, the *Rilets* hotel (☎07054/2106; ❹), on the opposite bank of the river, is an uninspiring building with adequate, functional en suites, but has the advantage of an enchanting woodland setting. A left turn on the access road to the *Rilets* brings you to *Bor* **camping**, a primitive but beautiful site on the riverbank. Back on the other side of the river, the *Zodiak* campsite (☎048/772657) offers bungalows (❶), a restaurant and a field for tents at the back, but can get noisy at weekends.

Assuming you have your own transport, there is a better choice of accommodation west of the monastery on the road back to Rila village: *Pchelina*, 5km away (☎0888 393 058; ❹) offers comfortable en suites with TV in a modern building incorporating traditional folksy elements, and has an attractive garden-restaurant. A kilometre further downhill, the *Gorski kut* (☎07054/2170 and 0888 710 348, ⓦwww.gorski-kut.com; ❸) is a modern three-storey affair with en-suite rooms, some of which have small balconies; there's also a good restaurant overlooking the River Rilets.

The monastery

Refounded in 1335, 4km west of St John's original hermitage, Rila Monastery was plundered during the eighteenth century, and repairs had hardly begun when the whole structure burned down in 1833. Its rebuilding was presented as a religious and patriotic duty: urged on by opinion-forming educationalist Neofit Rilski (see p.146), public donations were plentiful and master craftsmen such as Aleksiy Rilets and Pavel Milenkov gave their services for free. Work continued in stages throughout the nineteenth century, and the east wing was built as recently as 1961 to display the monastery's treasures, recognized by UNESCO as a World Heritage Site. The whole ensemble is ringed by mighty walls, giving it the outward appearance of a fortress.

Once you get through the west gate, however, this impression is dispelled by the beauty of the interior, which even the milling crowds don't seriously mar. Graceful arches surrounding the flagstoned courtyard support tiers of monastic cells, and stairways ascend to top-floor balconies which – viewed from below – resemble the outstretched petals of flowers. Bold red stripes and black-and-white check patterns enliven the facade, contrasting with the sombre mountains behind, and creating a visual harmony between the cloisters and the church within.

The monastery church

The monastery church has undulating lines, combining red and black designs with arches and a diversity of cupolas. Richly coloured **frescoes** shelter beneath the porch and within the interior – a mixture of scenes from rural life and Orthodox iconography, executed by muralists from Razlog, Bansko and Samokov, including nineteenth-century Bulgaria's greatest artist, Zahari Zograf. The murals on the church's exterior include archetypal images of cataclysm: the fall of Constantinople, apocalypses and visions of hell, complete with the bat-winged demons that seemingly loomed large in the Bulgarian imagination. On the left-hand side of the porch as you face the main entrance, the wrongdoings of sinners are portrayed with a love of grotesque detail; one picture shows rich men quaffing wine around a table, ignoring the pleas of St Lazarus, whose wounds are being licked clean by a posse of compassionate street dogs.

Inside the church, the **iconostasis** is particularly splendid: almost 10m wide and covered by a mass of intricate carvings and gold leaf, it's one of the finest achievements of the Samokov woodcarvers (see p.132). In front of the iconostasis, a wooden box hidden behind a curtain holds the holiest of the monastery's relics; a silver case containing the **left hand of St John of Rila**. The box is only opened up for the benefit of genuine pilgrims (monks are unlikely to be impressed by appeals from foreign tourists), who gaze upon the hand and cross themselves before taking away a wad of cotton wool which, by virtue of having spent time in proximity to the relic, is capable of sending those who sniff it into a heightened state of spiritual grace.

Halfway down the nave, on the left-hand side as you face the iconostasis, a wooden drawer (often closed, so ask a monk to pull it out) holds a miraculous **icon of the Virgin**, a remarkably serene example of twelfth-century Byzantine icon painting, presented to the monastery by the then Emperor Theodore Comnenus (c.1185–c.1253). Mounted in an elaborate frame containing other saintly relics, the icon is paraded around the monastery courtyard on the occasion of the Feast of the Assumption (*Golyama Bogoroditsa*) on August 15.

A chapel on the opposite side of the nave contains the **heart of Tsar Boris III**, buried beneath a simple wooden cross. Boris died of a mystery illness after a visit to Berlin in 1944, prompting many to speculate that he'd been poisoned by his Nazi hosts. After 1945, the Bulgarian Communists scattered his remains in the Iskar gorge in order to prevent his grave from becoming the focus of anti-Communist sentiment, but the former monarch's principal organ survived, to be ceremonially interred here in 1993.

Beside the church rises **Hrelyo's Tower**, the sole remaining building from the fourteenth century, which you can sometimes ascend in order to visit the top-floor chapel. Its founder – a local noble – apocryphally took refuge as a monk here and was supposedly strangled in the tower; hence the inscription upon it: "Thy wife sobs and grieves, weeping bitterly, consumed by sorrow".

Other parts of the monastery

Huge cauldrons that were once used to feed pilgrims occupy the old **kitchen** (*magernitsa*) on the ground floor of the north wing, where the soot-encrusted ceiling has the shape and texture of a gigantic termites' nest. Beneath the modern east wing there's a wealth of objects in the **treasury** (daily 8.15am–4.15pm; 8Lv), including icons and medieval gospels, Rila's charter from Tsar Ivan Shishman, written on leather and sealed with gold in 1378, and the door of the original monastery church. Pride of place goes to the fourteen-inch-high wooden cross made by the monk Rafail during the 1790s. Composed of 140 biblical tableaux containing more than 1500 human figures (some no larger than a grain of rice), this took twelve years for Rafail to carve with a needle, and cost him his eyesight.

A doorway under the arch of the east gate leads to an **ethnographic collection** (same times; 5Lv) housed in an atmospheric sequence of stone-clad chambers. Judging by the profusion of stewpots, dairy churns, wooden bowls and cooking utensils on display here, monastic life clearly revolved around the hearty consumption of food.

Around the monastery

Just above the car park outside the monastery's western gate, beside the main hiking trail heading up into the Rila mountains, a handsome slab of dark stone marks the final resting place of J.D. Bourchier (pronounced "*Bow*-cher"), the *London Times* journalist whose support for the Bulgarian cause in the years before World War I was rewarded with this grave-plot. Outside the monastery's eastern gate, a path descends towards the river and the **Church of the Presentation of the Virgin**, a decrepit late eighteenth-century structure surrounded by the graves of several generations of monks. The chapel on the church's upper storey is richly decorated with scenes from the life of the Virgin. A painting in the porch shows the Archangel Michael stomping on the body of a bearded wrongdoer. Look out for the *kostnitsa* or **ossuary** on the ground floor, housing the skulls of former monks.

Rila Monastery is the starting point for numerous short **hikes** (see box, p.133), the most agreeable of which is the short stroll to **St John of Rila's cave** (2hr return trip). The trail begins by the road about 2km beyond the east gate: a fairly obvious path bears left about 100m past the *Bachkova cheshma* restaurant, leading up through the woods to the **Chapel of Sveti Luka** after twenty minutes. The chapel, named after a nephew of St John of Rila who acted as the ageing hermit's servant, contains frescoes depicting him with the three other hermit-superstars of the Bulgarian–Macedonian borderlands: Gavril of Leshnovo, Prohor of Pchinya and Ioakim of Osogovo. Twenty minutes further on, the **Chapel of St John of Rila** is built into the rock beside the cave or "**Miracle Hole**" where he spent his last twenty years. Having made it this far, most visitors plunge into the (admittedly rather dark) cave and work their way up through a fissure in the rock, emerging a few seconds later on the hillside just above – a reasonably unstrenuous task for the moderately fit. Traditionally, pilgrims were required to pass through this hole before proceeding to the monastery, and the conscience-smitten were regularly unable to do so. These people were judged to be sinners and forced to go home to repent for a year before coming back to Rila.

Eating and drinking

For **snacks**, pick up delicious bread, *mekitsi* (Bulgarian doughnuts) and yoghurt from the bakery run by monks that's just outside the east gate. Otherwise, the **restaurants** outside the monastery are a bit of a rip-off and it's best to go further afield if you can. *Chicho Kiro*, 7km east of the monastery (and accessible via the eastbound asphalt road) at Kirilova polyana, is a good place to enjoy traditional Bulgarian food in an idyllic foot-of-the-mountain location. West of the monastery, both the *Pchelina* and *Gorski kut* hotels have good restaurants, while the *Magiyata na Rila* restaurant, 7km west of the monastery just above the village of Pastra, does good pan-fried trout and has outdoor seating beside the river.

Samokov, Borovets and around

Access to the northern slopes of the Rila Mountains is provided by the burgeoning package resort of **Borovets**, and its smaller, less developed neighbour **Malyovitsa**. Occasional buses run direct to both places from Sofia, although it's easier to pick up one of the half-hourly services from Sofia's Yug terminal to the provincial town of **Samokov**, from where there are numerous onward services. Samokov itself has sufficient historic interest to merit a stopoff of an hour or two, but is hardly the kind of place that you'd want to plan your holiday around. Of the numerous hiking possibilities in the region, there are a couple of classic walking routes over the mountains from Malyovitsa to Rila Monastery; those heading to the monastery by public transport from Borovets or Malyovitsa will have to head back to Samokov, catch a bus to Dupnitsa (see p.123) and change there.

The one-hour journey **from Sofia to Samokov** follows a scenic, forest-shrouded road up the narrow valley of the River Iskar, passing the rather down-at-heel watersports centre of **Lake Pancharevo** after about 10km. Entering the defile between the Lozhen and Plana massifs, you should be able to glimpse the ruined fortress of **Urvich**, where Tsar Shishman allegedly withstood the Turks for seven years. There's a scattering of **restaurants** along the road catering for Sofia folk out for a weekend drive: the *Zlatna Ribka*, about 10km beyond Lake Pancharevo, just before the village of **Pasarel**, is renowned for offering excellent local carp and trout. Beyond Pasarel lies the massive **Iskar Dam** and **Lake Iskar** – a man-made body of water 16km long, sometimes known as the "Sea of Sofia".

Samokov

Founded as a mining community in the fourteenth century, **SAMOKOV** (САМОКОВ) soon became one of the busiest manufacturing centres in the Turkish empire (its name derives from the Bulgarian verb "to forge"), where all kinds of crafts guilds flourished, particularly weavers and tailors, who turned flax (still a major product) into uniforms for the Ottoman army. From the seventeenth century until the end of Turkish rule, Samokov's stature eclipsed that of Sofia and Kyustendil, thanks partly to the artistry of its woodworkers and painters, who decorated Bulgaria's finest monasteries. Nowadays it's a rather drab grey town, known primarily as the centre of Bulgaria's most prolific **potato-growing** area – and you'll see sacks of them sold by roadside hawkers on your journey into town. Though foreign tourists from nearby Borovets are sometimes bussed in to wander around during the day, the place isn't really geared up for tourism, so it's best to digest what there is and move on.

The Town

There's plenty of evidence of Samokov's past in and around the **centre**, although modern urban planning has left its monuments marooned in a sea of crumbling paving stones. The ornate **fountain** or *cheshma* on the main square is a legacy of the Turks, who considered running water an essential part of civilized living. Close by stands the only surviving example of Samokov's once numerous mosques, the **Bairakli dzhamiya** (Mon–Fri 8am–noon & 1–5pm; 3Lv), preserved as a monument to the skills of local builders rather than as a place of worship. Commissioned by the pasha in 1840, its design betrays Bulgarian influences: the roof-line mimics the shape of a *kobilitsa*, or yoke, while the interior decoration relies upon plant motifs rather than arabesques.

Just off the square to the east, the **History Museum** (Mon–Fri 8am–noon & 1–5pm; 2Lv) traces Samokov's evolution up to the present day. The town's industrial past is remembered in a sequence of models illustrating the mining and smelting of iron ore: one shows a gargantuan, waterwheel-powered set of bellows used to force air into the furnaces. There's a wonderful upstairs gallery devoted to the **Samokov school of icon painters**, who decorated churches and monasteries throughout Bulgaria in the nineteenth century, and a display cabinet containing the personal effects of **Zahari Zograf**, the greatest of their number.

Continue east for 400m and you'll stumble upon the impressive shell of a derelict **synagogue**, built to serve Samokov's prosperous Jewish community in the nineteenth century. Next door, a walled garden filled with fruit trees wraps itself around the dazzling, blue and white **Sarafina House** (*Sarafskata kashta*; Mon–Fri 8am–noon & 1–5pm; 3Lv), home to a rich Jewish trading family in the 1860s, and fully restored in the 1970s. Inside, chambers lead off from the main reception room, each sumptuously kitted out with traditional carpets, floral wall paintings and intricately carved wooden ceilings.

Hiking in the Rila Mountains

The **Rila National Park**, established in 1992, covers almost half the Rila mountain range (including its fourteen highest peaks), with a network of **hiking trails** and huts built in Communist times. These are slowly being refurbished with an eye to ecotourism, though most are still rudimentary, and information on vacancies or the weather remains scarce. For any of the hikes below, **food** supplies and a **map** of the mountains are essential, and it's prudent to pack a **tent** in case the huts are full or you need to take shelter. It's strictly forbidden to pick flowers or light fires (except at designated spots).

Starting from Rila Monastery, a noticeboard in the car park maps out the options for hikers. From here, two trails (which later converge at Dodov vrah) lead to the *Ivan Vazov* hut – about six hours' hard slog. This is a good base from which to press on to the *Sedemte ezera* or **Seven Lakes**, an ascending sequence of high-altitude pools surrounded by a curved line of rugged peaks. As one of the most visually stunning areas of the Rila massif, it's an enormously popular target for hikers. There are two huts here: the old *Sedemte ezera* hut (❶), on the shores of the lowest of the lakes, is pretty basic; while the new *Rilski ezera* hut (❷), 1km further west and at a slightly lower altitude, boasts almost hotel-like standards of accommodation. The lakes themselves, lying in an ascending succession of niches in the mountains, are eerily beautiful sights. It will take you a good two hours to walk from the *Sedemte ezera* hut to the seventh lake and back again.

One other popular ascent to the Seven Lakes is from the north, with the *Lovna* hut (reached by asphalt road from Panichishte; see p.126) or the *Vada* hut (reached from Govedartsi; p.136) acting as the most obvious trailheads. Tackling the Lakes from this direction makes them a feasible day-trip destination providing you make an early start.

The less well trodden paths of the Rila mountains lie over on the eastern side of the range. Trails leading northeast from Kirilova polyana, 5km east of Rila Monastery, take you up towards Suhoto ezero, or **Dry Lake**, before wheeling northwest over the range towards Malyovitsa – although there's no hut on this route, so you'll need to camp overnight at the lake.

East of Rila Monastery, the Ribnite ezera (**Fish Lakes**) are another feasible destination, with a hut nearby. You can reach them by following the Kirilova polyana road to its end, and then following the Rilska up to its source in the mountains, or by a trail bearing southeast about halfway along the road, which crosses the ridge and passes some smaller lakes en route. Both walks take six to seven hours.

Southeast of Rila Monastery is another hut, *Makedoniya*, accessible by several paths originating from the minor road forking off a few kilometres west of the monastery. From the hut it's a day's hike west down to **Bistritsa** (from where buses run to Blagoevgrad), or a few hours' walk east to the *Semkovo* hut, which can also be reached from the Fish Lakes and may serve as a way-station for walkers making longer hikes (2–3 days) towards the Pirin or Rhodope mountains. Semkovo lies on the way to Belitsa and Yakoruda, two villages linked by bus or train to Razlog, Bansko and Velingrad. Hikers can also descend from here to the village of **Dobarsko** (see p.150) via the hut of the same name. Alternatively, the *Granchar* hut (named "*Boris Hadzhisotirov*" on older maps), due east of the Fish Lakes, serves hikers bound for Mount Musala and Borovets, or those pursuing a more easterly path down to Yakoruda.

Ulitsa Tsar Boris III leads west from the main square towards the old residential quarter of town, and the *metoh*, or **Convent of Sveta Bogoroditsa**, at no. 77 (daily 6am–8pm). In the porch of the convent church there's a fine nineteenth-century painting of a winged Virgin Mary who extends her cloak to shelter the believers – the local priests and their flock – who gather beneath it. The church interior features colourful modern murals by local artists, imitating the folksy style of Zahari Zograf and his generation, while outside, a cobbled alley leads past a ramshackle collection of nunnery buildings and a beautifully maintained garden.

Practicalities

There's little point in staying in Samokov when both Borovets and Sofia are so close at hand. Should you get stuck, *Hotel Sonata*, at ul. Beron 4 (☎0722/27534; ➌) offers simple en-suite rooms in a residential street just west of the centre. Aside from a smattering of **cafés** on the main square, refreshment opportunities are scarce: the *Café Papillon*, opposite the History Museum, is probably your best bet.

Moving on from Samokov, there are buses roughly every hour to Borovets (the last one leaves at 7pm), six daily to Govedartsi, and two minibuses to Malyovitsa. For Rila Monastery you need to take the 10am bus to Dupnitsa and change there (see p.123). Dupnitsa-bound buses go by way of **Sapareva banya**, Bulgaria's most ferocious mineral baths, whose hottest spring is fed by a super-heated geyser (102°C) gushing 550 gallons of sulphurous water a minute.

Borovets

Towards the end of the nineteenth century, Prince Ferdinand of Bulgaria built three villas and a hunting lodge among the aromatic pine woods covering the northern slopes of Mount Musala, a mile above sea level. The Mamrikoff family – after whom a verb meaning "to steal from an exalted position" was coined – and other wealthy folk did likewise, founding an exclusive colony, Chamkoria, from which **BOROVETS** (БOPOBEЦ) has developed. Effectively nationalized for the benefit of union and Party members in 1949, Borovets became a major **winter sports** resort in the 1960s, and is now largely geared towards package tourism. Lifts to a number of beginner and intermediate slopes are stationed right in the middle of the resort, so in terms of convenience, Borovets has got a lot going for it. It is also a popular place for Bulgarians to escape the heat during July and August, but pretty quiet during the intermediate months before and after the skiing season.

Competitively priced **package holidays** ensure that you get lodgings, skiing equipment and tuition – none of which is assured if you just turn up on spec. Also, most package operators offer lift passes and "ski packs" (including equipment rental) for a lower cost than you pay on the spot, making package holidays even more worthwhile.

Modern Borovets is a rather artificial place, with the monstrous **Hotel Rila** acting as its main point of orientation. You'd be well advised to escape to the mountains as soon as possible unless asphalt walkways lined with souvenir stalls are your cup of tea. The one worthwhile sight in the resort is the **Bistritsa Palace** (Tues–Sun 10am–3.30pm; 2Lv), fifteen minutes' walk northwest from the *Hotel Rila* along the Malyovitsa road. A rambling whitewashed mansion with carved wooden balconies, it was built as a hunting lodge for Tsar Ferdinand (who entertained Kaiser Wilhelm of Germany here in 1913) and used by his son, Boris, before passing into the hands of Bulgaria's Communist elite, and back again to Ferdinand's grandson, Simeon of Saxe-Coburg-Gotha. The interior is decorated in a mix of High Victoriana and Samokov woodcarvings, and bristles with animal heads and pelts, while heraldic lions crown the lampposts outside. Just downhill, Tsar Ferdinand's still-functioning hydroelectric power station occupies a squat white building in the palace park – a door or window is usually open so you can admire the whirring machinery.

Skiing

The official **skiing** season lasts from mid-December to mid-April, though the snow cover is most reliable in late February and early March. Immediately in front of the *Hotel Rila*, the nursery slopes are served by ten drag lifts (daily in winter; 9.30am–4.50pm), and overlooked by a steep slope topped by the *Sitnyakovo* chalet, once one of Ferdinand's villas, that's accessible by chair lift (same hours; winter only) from behind the *Hotel Rila*. Experienced skiers favour the pistes on the western ridge of the mountain, which can be reached by a five-kilometre-long gondola (daily in winter, summer opening times depend on how full the resort is; 9am–4.30pm) running from near the *Hotel Samokov* up to the *Yastrebets* hut. Another chair lift serves the two ski jumps (55m & 75m long), while there are also shuttle-buses to the start of three cross-country runs at Shiroka Polyana, 2km away.

Hiking

The *Yastrebets* hut (4hr 30min walk or 35min by gondola) is the starting point for the ascent of **Mount Musala**, the highest peak in the Balkan peninsula (2925m). The first leg (1hr) brings you to the *Musala* hut at the foot of the mountain, from where it's an hour and forty minutes' walk to the summit. From Mount Musala it's six hours' trek southwards to the *Granchar* hut, where one path leads down to Yakoruda on the narrow-gauge railway line **to Bansko**; the other **to the Fish Lakes** (5hr) where, after sleeping at the *Ribnite Ezera* hut, hikers can push on to **Rila Monastery** (5–6hr).

If these sound too much effort, you could try an easy, ninety-minute walk to the **Black Rocks** (Cheverni skali), east of Borovets. A row of crags with sheer drops on both sides, they were used by the secret police in the late 1940s as a killing ground for "enemies of the people", who were simply pushed off to their deaths. The trail begins after the *Hotel St Ivan Rilski*, entering the woods beside a cross-braced fence. Bear right at the fork 100m later, then left downhill and left at the next fork; when you reach the farm buildings take the middle, gravelled route and turn left at the fork onto a sandy track that gets narrower and stonier en route to a picnic area near the Black Rocks.

Accommodation

Borovets has plenty of serviceable three- and four-star hotels in the centre of the resort, but finding **accommodation** from December through to early April can still be a problem if you're not on a package or haven't booked in advance. At any other time of year, there should be plenty of beds, although places may close for a while off-season.

Alpin ☎07128/2201, ⊛www.alpin-hotel.bg. Centrally placed, piste-side building with mock-gothic turrets and chintzy, well-equipped en suites. ❹

Flora ☎07128/2520, ℮flora_hotel@abv.bg. Reliable mid-range choice offering functional en suites, although the colour schemes are dowdier than elsewhere. ❸

Popangelov ☎07128/2666. Homely seven-room pension in the heart of the resort run by champion skier Petar Popangelov, with skiing memorabilia cluttering the hallways. The simple en-suite doubles, triples (**❸**) and quads (**❹**) have pleasant pine furnishings. **❷**

Rila ☎07128/2658, ⓦwww.balkantourist.bg. Enormous package-oriented four-star right in the middle of the resort, at the bottom of a popular ski run. **❻**

Samokov ☎07128/2581 or 2306, ⓦwww .samokov.com. Three-hundred-room vacation hutch providing everything you need for a lazy holiday: fully equipped if old-fashioned en-suite rooms, an indoor pool, ten-pin bowling and immediate access to the pistes. **❼**

Yastrebets ☎0750/32212, ⓦwww.hotelyastrebets .bg. Three kilometres out of town, near the ski pistes, this alpine-style hotel offers swish rooms, each featuring flat-screen TV and bathtub. Indoor pool, gym and massage facilities on site. **❻**

Eating and drinking

There are innumerable places to eat and drink in the vicinity of the *Hotel Rila*, mostly hastily erected huts serving up pizzas, burgers, grilled chicken and beer. There are also various places serving decent and inexpensive Bulgarian fare on the pedestrianized strip leading uphill from the *Hotel Rila* – the *Beliya Kon* is a family-run place with reliable standards, while *The Blue* has funkier décor and a more extensive menu including plenty of fish dishes.

Govedartsi, Malyovitsa and beyond

Thirty kilometres southwest of Samokov, Malyovitsa is everything that Borovets isn't: a tiny, secluded hiking base with limited but rewarding skiing in the winter, no package tourists, and a single, rather frugal, hotel. It's reached by a minor road which heads out of Samokov along the banks of the Cherni Iskar, a burbling rivulet whose banks used to be packed with people camping wild before 1990. A private minibus shuttles between Samokov and Malyovitsa twice daily in the summer and winter seasons: otherwise you're on your own.

You can also get to Malyovitsa via a little-frequented mountain road that leaves Borovets near the Bistritsa palace: this joins the Samokov–Malyovitsa route just short of **GOVEDARTSI** (ГОВЕДАРЦИ), a sleepy village worth mentioning as the location of the *Kalina* **hotel**, just off the main road (☎07125/2643 and 0888 883 847, ⓦwww.kalina-hotel.com; **❷**), a family-run B&B which serves as a good base for touring in the area if you've got your own transport. Continuing westwards you'll pass *Camping Bor* (☎071252/304; **❶**), 2km beyond Govedartsi, a secluded spot in the forest with simply furnished bungalows.

A couple of kilometres west of the campsite, a branch road snakes up through the forest for 8km to **MALYOVITSA** (МАЛЬОВИЦА) itself, 1750m above sea level. There's not much here apart from the *Malyovitsa* **hotel** (☎07125/2222; **❷**), a gloomy place which will appeal to those with a taste for solitude and very few frills. There's a new slalom track and chairlift a short walk from the hotel, and plenty of huts renting out ski gear in season. However the place comes into its own as a base-camp for summer hikes, with a well-trodden trail leading south up a narrow valley overlooked by several peaks, most imperious of which is the 2729-metre **Mount Malyovitsa**.

The one-hour ascent to the *Malyovitsa* hut at the head of the valley constitutes the first leg of several hikes: from here it's seven hours' walk to the beautiful **Seven Lakes** (*Sedemte ezera*) cabin, or six hours to the *Ivan Vazov* lodge. Heading east from the Malyovitsa hut, refuges to the north of the Dry Lake (*Suhoto ezero*), serve as way-stations along the route to the hut beside the **Fish Lakes**:

Every August, the Rila Mountains' Seven Lakes become a place of pilgrimage for the **Danovisti** (also known as the **Byaloto bratstvo** or "White Brotherhood"), members of a sect which formed around the teachings of Bulgarian mystic **Petar Danov** at the start of the twentieth century.

Combining Orthodox Christianity with meditation, sun worship, vegetarianism and yoga, the sect was widely popular in Bulgaria before World War II and tolerated by both Church and state until the Communist era, when it was obliged to go underground. Having re-emerged in the 1990s, Danovism is now regarded as yet another authentic manifestation of Bulgaria's rich spiritual culture, which also embraces Orthodoxy, paganism, faith-healing and clairvoyancy.

The son of an Orthodox priest from Varna, Danov studied theology in Boston, USA, returning to his homeland with a new-found enthusiasm for theosophy and spiritualism. He tried to weld the various religious and spiritual currents to which he had been exposed into a unified belief system, and after several years of solitary contemplation emerged with a book, *The Seven Conversations*, in 1900. In it he claimed that he had been appointed by God as His emissary on earth, entrusted with the task of building the "new culture of the sixth race". Precisely what Danov meant by the sixth race remains shrouded in verbose theorizing, but he essentially envisaged a higher level of human evolution in which man's spiritual nature would be more keenly developed – ushering in a new era of peace, love, justice and togetherness.

Danov immediately embarked on a speaking tour of Bulgaria, gathering followers who formed the White Brotherhood – an informal association bound together by Danov's personal charisma. Danov was already a national figure by World War I, when he was briefly interned by the Bulgarian government for his pacifist ideals. Bulgaria's defeat in the war, and the years of political instability that followed, created an urban intelligentsia disillusioned by political ideologies, and they increasingly gravitated towards Danov's simple message of peace, unity and nature worship. One of Danov's followers, Lyubomir Lalchev, was a close advisor to Tsar Boris III, leading to rumours that Danov himself exerted a Rasputin-like influence at court, though there's little evidence that he ever used this connection to do more than preach his message – indeed, throughout the interwar period, the only allies the Brotherhood cultivated were the Bulgarian Esperanto and Vegetarian societies.

Danov saw himself as a teacher rather than a leader, and thousands came to hear him deliver lectures at 10am every morning outside his house at ul. Opalchenska 66 in central Sofia (Georgi Dimitrov, the future Communist leader, lived next door). In the 1930s he established a Danovist commune on the southeastern fringes of the capital, calling it *Izgrev*, or "Sunrise". He died in 1944, three months after the Communist takeover of Bulgaria, and was buried at **Izgrev** (with special permission from former neighbour Georgi Dimitrov, despite the danger that his grave might become a focus for anti-Communist pilgrimages). The Brotherhood itself was gradually harrassed into nonexistence, and the commune was demolished in the 1980s to make room for the (then) Soviet Embassy, though the suburb that now occupies the site still bears its name.

The Brotherhood re-emerged after 1989 – although typically for post-Communist Bulgaria, two competing organizations claimed the Danovist mantle, leading to a protracted court battle that wasn't resolved until 1995. The tradition of holding annual meetings on and around August 19 (the date chosen by Danov as the divine world's New Year's Day) was soon re-established, and in the week surrounding this date the Danovisti gather to camp by the shores of Babreg, the fifth of the Seven Lakes, worshipping the sun with pan-rhythmic dances accompanied by violin music composed by Danov himself.

nine hours' hike in all. Another popular trail leads south to **Mount Malyovitsa** and **Rila Monastery**. Climbing the mountain from *Malyovitsa* hut takes about three hours, an easier ascent than by the steeper southern face. Afterwards, follow the path west along the ridge before taking the trail branching left, which leads to the monastery in the thickly wooded valley below (a further 3–4hr). For more information on hiking in the Rila range, see the map on pp.124–125 and the box on p.133.

The Pirin range and the far south

Protected by the Pirin National Park (ⓦwww.pirin-np.com), the **Pirin mountains** are arguably the most dramatic in Bulgaria, comprising a cluster of sharp-tipped, granite peaks surrounding the central summit of the 2914-metre

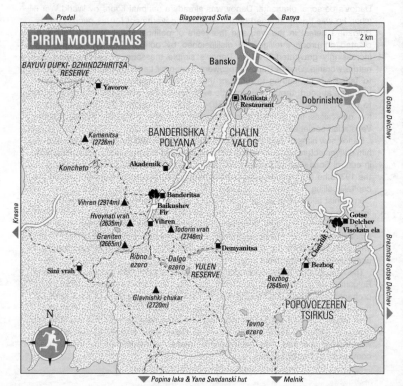

PIRIN MOUNTAINS

▲ Predel   Blagoevgrad Sofia ▲   ▲ Banya

0   2 km

Kresna ◀

Bansko

BAYUVI DUPKI- DZHINDZHIRITSA
RESERVE

■ Yavorov

■ Motikata
Restaurant

Dobrinishte

Gotse Delchev ▶

Kamenitsa
(2726m) ▲

Koncheto

BANDERISHKA
POLYANA

CHALIN
VALOG

Akademik ■

●●●■ Banderitsa
Baikushev
Fir

Vihren (2914m) ▲

Hvoynati vrah
(2635m) ▲

■ Vihren

▲Todorin vrah
(2746m)

Gotse
Delchev
■■
Visokata ela

Graniten
(2665m) ▲

Ribno
ezero

Dalgo
ezero

■Demyanitsa

YULEN
RESERVE

Chairtiri

■ Bezbog

Breznitsa Gotse Delchev ▶

Sini vrah ■

Glavnishki chukar
(2720m) ▲

Bezbog
(2645m) ▲

POPOVOEZEREN
TSIRKUS

N

Tevno
ezero

▼ Popina laka & Yane Sandanski hut   ▼ Melnik

Mount Vihren. Densely forested slopes and glacier-gouged highland lakes make for some spectacular hiking terrain, while the slopes above Bansko provide the best downhill skiing opportunities in the country. Indeed it is rapidly growing **Bansko** that offers most in the way of tourist facilities and routes into the mountains. From Bansko there's a scenic route down the Mesta Valley to **Gotse Delchev**, an attractive town surrounded by historic unspoiled villages. On the western side of the mountains, the spa resort of **Sandanski** is the jumping-off point for **Melnik**, **Rozhen** and **Rupite**. The region's main service centre is **Blagoevgrad**, a lively university town in the Struma valley and an important local transport hub.

Blagoevgrad

Administrative capital of the Pirin region, **BLAGOEVGRAD** (БЛАГОЕВГРАД)'s useful **transport** links with Rila, Melnik, Bansko and beyond make it the region's most important transit point, although it's too far from the national park to act as a touring base. It does have a few attractions of its own, however, boasting a reconstructed old quarter, a pedestrianized civic centre where most of southwest Bulgaria comes to shop, and a youthful buzz generated by approximately sixteen thousand **university students**.

Historically Blagoevgrad was an important crafts town, predominantly inhabited by Turks from the sixteenth century until their flight in 1912, after which it was settled by local peasants and displaced Bulgarians from Macedonia and the Aegean seaboard. In 1950 it was renamed Blagoevgrad in honour of **Dimitar Blagoev**, the founder of Bulgarian Marxism, and has chosen to stick with it in the post-Communist era because citizens either absolved Blagoev of any blame for Communism, or rejected restoring the former Turkish name, *Gorna Dzhumaya* – which was bestowed instead on a vile brand of cigarettes from one of the local **tobacco** factories.

The Town

Modern Blagoevgrad is centred on an extensive pedestrian zone focused on the spacious flagstoned expanse of pl. Georgi Izmirliev Makedoncheto. Most prominent of the public buildings grouped around it is the **American University in Bulgaria** (AUB), established in Blagoevgrad in 1991 because the council offered it free use of the former Communist Party headquarters. It currently has roughly a thousand students from across the Balkans and the ex-Soviet Union. East of the square, ul. Dimitar Talev leads to the social hub of town, **ploshtad Balgariya**, surrounded by scores of **cafés** on Todor Aleksandrov, Raiko Daskalov and other side-streets near the river.

At the eastern end of pl. Balgariya a footbridge leads towards the **Varosha**, an area of cobbled alleys and nineteenth-century-style houses intended to evoke the Blagoevgrad of old – although the overriding impression is that of a Balkan film set rather than a thriving quarter of town. The one authentic part of the Varosha is the **Church of the Annunciation of the Virgin** (*Vavedenie Bogorodichno*), a masterpiece of pre-Liberation architecture whose fluid roof-line mimics the shape of a carrying yoke, while the black, red and white pattern on its facade extends right around a three-sided arcade linking the church to a freestanding bell tower. Occupying a box-like modern building nearby, the **History Museum** (Mon–Sat 9am–noon & 1–6pm; 3Lv) exhibits some fine icons and carvings from churches in Melnik and Dobarsko,

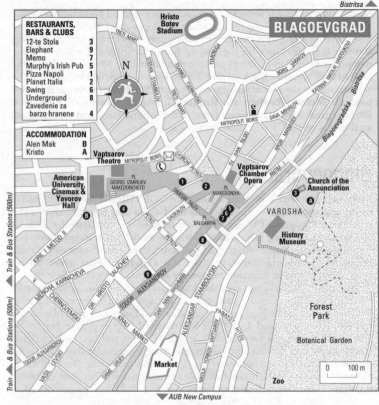

alongside Thracian, Roman and Greek relics, stuffed Pirin wildlife, and brightly coloured folk costumes.

Practicalities

Blagoevgrad's **train station** is about 1km southwest of the centre on ul. Sveti Dimitar Solunski; bus #2 or #3 will save you the walk into town. The majority of Sofia-Blagoevgrad **buses** pick up and drop off in the car park immediately in front of the train station; most other services use the terminal 200m south along the same street.

Blagoevgrad's two downtown **hotels** cost about the same, but are completely different: the allegedly three-star *Alen Mak* near the main square (☎073/884 076; ❹) is a large, soulless Communist-era establishment with notoriously bad service, while the *Kristo*, in the Varosha district, just uphill from the Church of the Annunciation (☎073/880 444; ❸), offers cosy en suites with TV and fridge in a traditional-style galleried building.

Good places **to eat** and watch the streetlife are *Pizza Napoli*, on the eastern side of pl. Georgi Izmirliev Makedoncheto, and *Planet Italia*, on the nearby pl. Makedoniya, both of which offer tolerable thin-crust pizzas and a decent choice of big salads. For a quick, functional and good-value feed, you can't beat the cafeteria-style *Zavedenie za barzo hranene*, round the side of an office block diagonally opposite the American University. For something a bit more substantial, *12-te stola* in the Varosha district has a reasonably priced range of grilled meats and fried fish, plus a pleasant courtyard, although the restaurant of the nearby *Hotel Kristo* has a broader menu and better views from its terrace. The coolest places to **drink** are in the trio of narrow pedestrianized streets linking pl. Balgariya and Makedonya: current student favourites include *Swing*, *Memo* and *Murphy's Irish Pub*, all on ul. Sandro i Petar Kitanevi, although there's a fairly rapid turnover of what's in and what's out. Recognizable by its London tube sign, *Underground*, at the junction of pl. Balgariya and ul. Todor Aleksandrov, is a split-level cellar club with three

Macedonia

Once you get beyond the Rila mountains, you're entering the Bulgarian corner of a vast historical territory which, during the dying days of the Ottoman Empire, went under the name of **Macedonia**. In the decades preceding World War I, the problem of what to do with this multi-ethnic region (dubbed the "Macedonian Question" by politicians of the time) drove the diplomats of Europe to despair. Now divided between Bulgaria, Greece and the Republic of Macedonia (formerly part of Yugoslavia), the heritage of historical Macedonia still exerts a powerful hold on the popular imaginations of all the region's inhabitants – not least because of the often heroic struggles waged by its constituent peoples to free themselves from the Ottoman yoke.

By far the greatest of the Macedonian freedom movements in the early twentieth century was the **Internal Macedonian Revolutionary Organization** or **IMRO** (VMRO in Bulgarian), members of which fought, depending on the political climate, either for the incorporation of Macedonia into Bulgaria, or for the establishment of Macedonia as a separate territory – a paradox which has turned historical discussion of the Macedonian Question into something of a minefield ever since.

To summarize a century of misunderstanding in a few words, Bulgarians (including those in the southwest) regard Macedonia and its people as a historical part of the Bulgarian nation, while citizens of the Republic of Macedonia tend to see themselves as a separate nation and the historical victims of Bulgarian arrogance and insensitivity. While disputing the latter assertion, most modern-day Bulgarians have become reconciled to the fact that the Republic of Macedonia is now an independent country with its own destiny, and are quite happy to concentrate on building good relations with their neighbours. However, arguments about history still mean a lot in these parts, so you'd be well advised to adopt a sensitive attitude when discussing the subject with locals.

Memories of Macedonian history in general, and the IMRO in particular, are strong in the southwest, with most Bulgarians – with some justification – regarding the IMRO fighters of yore as part and parcel of the Bulgarian national tradition. Since 1989 most towns in the southwest have named streets and squares after IMRO heroes, and a right-wing political party has adopted both the IMRO name and associations to become one of the most influential organizations in the region.

Despite modern-day political boundaries, the Macedonia of old still retains a certain **ethnographic unity**: the songs, dances and dialects of the Bulgarian southwest are often closer to those in the Republic of Macedonia than they are to the rest of Bulgaria. Grandiose folklore festivals like **Pirin Sings** (see p.148) are the best occasions at which to sample this unique culture, although you'll find Macedonian songs performed live or on the radio in restaurants and bars all over the region – especially in Bansko, where every tavern in town seems to offer folkloric entertainment of some sort at the weekends.

bars with pop, retro and house themes. Further up Todor Aleksandrov on the corner with ul. Pero Toshev, *Elephant* lounge bar and disco club is the best place for house and techno.

Bansko and the mountains

Bansko, a burgeoning tourist centre that mixes traditional Bulgarian architecture with holiday-resort flair, makes a good base for some amazing hikes in the **Pirin National Park**, and is a transport nexus, with buses to the Struma and Mesta valleys flanking the Pirin range, and trains to Velingrad in the western Rhodopes. It also gives easy access to the attractive, traditional village of **Dobarsko** and the mountain-bottom logging town of **Dobrinishte**, both of which are surrounded by stunning countryside.

The road from the Struma Valley follows the River Gradevska that separates the Rila and Pirin ranges, and crosses the **Predel Pass**, site of the **Pirin Sings folklore festival** (see p.148), where amateur musicians and dancers from towns and villages throughout the region perform on a series of small stages.

The route also passes through **RAZLOG** (РАЗЛОГ), 6km north of Bansko, which is a less attractive town, notable only for its *kukeri* **rites** on January 1, when large processions of costumed revellers take over the centre.

Bansko

Nestling on a green valley plain at the foot of the Pirin mountains, **BANSKO** (БАНСКО) is one of the fastest-growing highland resorts in the whole of Europe. A fairly low-key skiing centre until its fortunes were transformed by the construction of a new cable-car system in 2004, Bansko has been catapulted to the forefront of Bulgarian winter tourism, and has undergone frenzied development as a result. Hotels and apartment blocks – many hastily constructed in far from attractive shades of concrete – now occupy spaces where goats were happily grazing a few years ago.

Such dramatic growth has (so far) failed to destroy the atmosphere of Bansko's nineteenth-century centre, a maze of cobbled lanes where the timber-framed stone houses hide behind thick walls with stout double doors. A century and a half ago Bansko was an important trading post on the caravan

Skiing in Bansko

Bansko's main **skiing** activity takes place on the slopes of **Mount Todorka**, 4km southwest of town. Access is provided by the shiny new cable car which ascends from the southwestern end of ul. Pirin (about a thirty-minute walk from the centre) to the 1467-metre peak of **Chalin valog**, starting point of some short intermediate runs. From here you can take the second stage of the cable car to the 1635-metre **Bunderishka polyana**, where you'll find a couple of beginner runs, a snowboarding half-pipe, and chair lifts ferrying skiers further up the slopes of Mount Todorka. There's a big range of beginner and intermediate descents from here, and – for advanced skiers – the punishing Alberto Tomba run. Many of the pistes converge on **Shiligarnika**, halfway down the mountain, where further chair lifts will whisk you up onto the southern shoulder of the mountain, and a further choice of blue and red runs. You can rent gear from a gaggle of outfits near the cable-car terminal. Max Sport, in the same building as the *Strazhite* hotel, is the best-stocked ski shop.

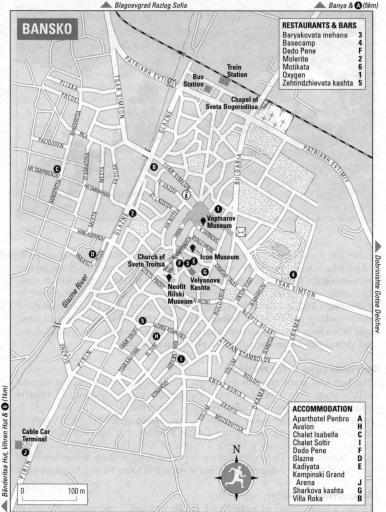

BANSKO

▲ *Blagoevgrad Razlog Sofia*   ▲ *Banya &* Ⓐ *(5km)*

RESTAURANTS & BARS
Baryakovata mehana	**3**
Basecamp	**4**
Dedo Pene	**F**
Molerite	**2**
Motikata	**6**
Oxygen	**1**
Zehtindzhievata kashta	**5**

Train Station
Bus Station
Chapel of Sveta Bogoroditsa

Vaptsarov Museum ❶

Icon Museum
Church of Sveta Troitsa
Velyanova Kashta
Neofit Rilski Museum

Glazne River

► *Dobrinishte Gotse Delchev*

◄ *Bänderitsa Hut, Vihren Hut &* Ⓖ *(1km)*

Cable Car Terminal Ⓙ

0   100 m

N

ACCOMMODATION
Aparthotel Penbro	**A**
Avalon	**H**
Chalet Isabella	**C**
Chalet Soltir	**I**
Dedo Pene	**F**
Glazne	**D**
Kadiyata	**E**
Kempinski Grand Arena	**J**
Sharkova kashta	**G**
Villa Roka	**B**

routes linking the Aegean port of Kavalla with the Balkan hinterland. Bansko's rich mercantile elite used their wealth to endow churches or restore Bulgarian monasteries, and the town became an important centre for house-builders, icon painters and other craftsmen. When the trade routes moved westward in the twentieth century, Bansko settled back into rusticity, and despite the recent move into tourism many of its inhabitants continue to be involved in agriculture, with goats and donkey-drawn carts sharing road space with the latest 4WDs.

Outside the skiing season, Bansko is a popular weekend resort, with visitors crowding into *mehanas* to be entertained by local folk groups singing traditional Macedonian songs about anti-Ottoman brigands. Whichever day of the week you

▲ Skier, Bansko

arrive, Bansko is a great base for **walking**, with many of the Pirin's highest peaks a day's hike from town. Most hotels (and a couple of high-street travel agents) rent out **mountain bikes** (25Lv per day), and although biking routes aren't properly signposted you should be able to improvise some interesting itineraries by purchasing a hiking map and following a few country lanes. One cultural event worth looking out for is the **Bansko Jazz Festival** (Ⓦ www.banskojazz.com), held over a long weekend in mid-August, when top jazz musicians from Bulgaria and abroad play on an open-air stage on the main square.

Arrival and information

The **bus and train stations** are on the northern fringes of town, ten minutes' walk from the central pl. Vaptsarov, where Bansko's **tourist information centre** (officially Mon–Fri 9am–1pm & 2–5pm, although be prepared for unannounced closure due to staff shortages; ☎0749/88580) lurks in an arcade below a concrete Cultural Centre. Whether they have any useful information or free brochures is largely a matter of luck. The winter-season listings guide *Bansko In Your Pocket* (Ⓦ www.inyourpocket.com), available free in hotels and restaurants, is pretty indispensable if you're staying in town for any length of time.

Accommodation

There's a huge choice of **hotels and B&Bs** in Bansko, and although many of them are block-booked by ski-package companies in the winter season, it's rarely difficult for independent travellers to find a bed. Note that the prices quoted below are for summer; expect to pay double in winter.

Avalon ul. El Tepe ☎0749/883 99, Ⓦ www.avalonhotel-bulgaria.com. Welcoming mid-sized hotel in a central, old-town location, featuring neat en-suite rooms – some of the top floor rooms have attic ceilings and gorgeous views of the mountains. There is a relaxing lobby-cum-lounge area with an open fire, and the enthusiastic Bulgarian-British hosts offer useful advice on local skiing, hiking and biking possibilities. ❹

Chalet Isabella ul. Banderitsa 32 ☎0885 060 095, Ⓦ www.chalet-bulgaria.com. Six-bedroom house on a quiet street, with bright en-suite rooms rented out individually on a B&B basis in summer, or all together as a ski chalet in winter. Warm colours, hardwood floors, fully equipped kitchen, big lounge and engaging hosts add to the feeling of domestic well-being. ❸

Chalet Soltir ul. Kiril i Metodii 19 ☎0895 330 349, Ⓦ www.boardingbansko.co.uk.

Attractively refurbished nineteenth-century house in the old part of town, mixing Bulgarian folksy elements with British-style B&B snugness. Cozy bedrooms, homely social areas and charming young hosts. You can rent the whole house as a ski chalet in winter, or individual rooms on a B&B basis in summer. ❸

🎿 **Dedo pene** ul. Aleksandar Buynov 1 ☎0749/85073, ⓦwww.dedopene.com. Traditional inn with en-suite rooms grouped around a galleried courtyard, each featuring traditional fabrics and furnishings (note the milk pails serving as bathroom sinks). Also the site of one of Bansko's best restaurants (see p.147). ❸

Glazne ul. Panayot Hitov 2 ☎0749/88022, ⓦwww.glazne.bansko.bg. Reliable 4-star with central location, pastel-coloured en-suite rooms, a small pool, sauna and gym on-site. ❻

Kadiyata ul. Yane Sandanski 8 ☎0749/88555 and 0899 969 370, ⓦwww.kadiata.bansko.bg. Family-run place in the heart of the old town offering smart en-suites with modern furnishings and TV. ❷

Kempinski Grand Arena ul. Pirin 96 ☎0749/88888, ⓦwww.kempinski-bansko.com. Five-star comforts right next to the cable car, complete with spacious rooms, wellness centre, outdoor pool and a huge lobby-cum-café with great views towards the mountains. ❽

Sharkova kashta ul. 5-ti Oktomvri 26 ☎07443/85024 and 0899 447 952. Seven neat and tidy en-suite doubles with TV, either on the second floor of a typical Bansko house (where you get wooden beams and traditional textiles), or in an adjoining bungalow in the garden. There's no breakfast and the ground-floor *mehana* doesn't open until noon, but it's comfy and central never-theless. ❶

Villa Roka ul. Glazne 37B ☎0749/883 37, ⓦwww.villaroka.com. If you've had enough of stripy Bulgarian rugs and other ethnic touches, then the *Villa Roka* is something of an antidote, featuring minimalist furnishings, matt surfaces, and a state-of-the-art wellness centre in the basement. ❻

Out of the centre

🎿 **Aparthotel Penbro** ul. Neofit Rilski 2, Banya ☎0889 859 902, ⓦwww.penbro.com. Five kilometres north of town in the rustic village of Banya, featuring six apartments (either studio or split-level), each with cooking facilities, TV, and a mixture of modern and traditional furnishings. ❸–❹

The Town

Bansko's modern, pedestrianized zone is centred on **ploshtad Nikola Vaptsarov**, named after the revolutionary poet. On the corner of the square, near a postwar statue of Vaptsarov in a declamatory pose, is the house where he was born, now the **Nikola Vaptsarov Museum** (Mon–Fri 8am–noon & 2–6pm; 3Lv), which recreates his childhood home and expounds on his life and poetry (in Bulgarian only). An engineer by training, he shared the Futurists' enthusiasm for the machine age and joined the wartime resistance with the courage of his Communist convictions. Vaptsarov's final poem was composed in a Sofia prison as he awaited execution in 1942:

The fight is hard and pitiless
The fight is epic, as they say:
I fell. Another takes my place –
Why single out a name!
After the firing squad – the worms.
Thus does the simple logic go.
But in the storm we'll be with you
My people, for we loved you so.

Attached to the museum is a **crafts exhibition** of textiles, woodcarvings and paintings by local artists, some of which are for sale. The carpets are simply patterned (with green and black stripes predominating) and nothing for serious collectors to get excited about, but as authentic handmade local crafts they make nice souvenirs, and cost less here than in Sofia.

Bansko's old town begins a short way uphill on **ploshtad Vazrazhdane**, dominated by a large monument to Otets (Father) Paisii, also known as Paisii of Hilendar (1722–73), author of the *Slav-Bulgarian History*. Begun in 1745, when Paisii became a monk at the Bulgarian monastery on Mount Athos, but not widely distributed until over fifty years later, this seminal work exalted the nation's past glories, kick-starting the upsurge in cultural and political consciousness that became known as the "National Revival".

The growing confidence of Bulgaria's nineteenth-century elite was often expressed in the building of new churches – although the local Ottoman authorities didn't always grant permission without a bribe. The **Church of Sveta Troitsa**, on the south side of pl. Vazrazhdane, got the go-ahead after Bansko merchants paid off a local official to declare that a miraculous icon had been discovered on the site (which qualified it as "holy ground" suitable for a Christian place of worship). A wall was then raised to conceal the townsfolks' enlargement of the church beyond the size set by Ottoman clerks – for which the mayor of Bansko was jailed for five years. The resulting structure is one of the largest in Bulgaria outside Sofia; a huge lump of grey-brown stone whose appearance is softened by the addition of a delicate wooden porch around the main doorway. Icons of local origin pack the spacious interior, where an intricately latticed screen partitions off the rear of the nave where women were once obliged to pray in segregation. Many of Bansko's elderly women still regard attendance at the 9am Sunday service, dressed in traditional striped aprons, as *de rigueur*, converging on the town centre as the church's belfry rings out an impressive peal of bells.

Approaching and leaving the church through the walled enclosure you'll pass a monument remembering Peyu Yavorov (see p.94), the poet guerrilla leader who celebrated Bansko's liberation from the Turks in October 1912 by proclaiming "Throw away your fezzes, brothers! From today you are free Bulgarians."

The Neofit Rilski House-Museum, the Icon Museum and the Velyanov House

Behind the church, a short distance along ul. Pirin, the **Neofit Rilski House-Museum** (Mon–Fri 9am–noon & 2–5pm; 5Lv) remembers another key figure in the nineteenth-century resurgence of Bulgarian education and church life. Born in Bansko in 1793, the son of the local priest, Rilski looked set to join one of the local icon-painting studios until a visit to Rila filled him with enthusiasm for the monastic life. He went on to become one of the great scholars of the age, translating the New Testament into Bulgarian and producing a mammoth Greek-Bulgarian dictionary that took a lifetime to compile. Despite his monastic vocation, he pioneered the development of secular education in Bulgaria, becoming the first head of the Aprilov School in Gabrovo (see p.251), before moving on to establish an equally renowned school in Koprivshtitsa (see p.273). The museum holds a dull didactic display of photographs and (Bulgarian-only) texts outlining Rilski's career, although the chance to pause in the lovely chestnut tree-shaded courtyard makes a visit here worthwhile.

Just off the northeast corner of pl. Vazrazhdane, on ul. Yane Sandanski, a former way-station for monks travelling towards Rila monastery now serves as an **Icon Museum** (Mon–Fri 9am–noon & 2–5pm; 5Lv) showing the achievements of Bansko's nineteenth-century icon painters. This was a school whose principal figure was the Vienna-educated Toma Vishanov (nicknamed

Molera), who, with sons Dimitar and Simeon Molerov, travelled from village to village decorating local churches. Vishanov's exposure to Western art filtered through into the style of the Bansko School, which generally features more realistic human faces than those of the highly stylized Samokov School (see p.132). There are photographic reproductions of the frescoes Vishanov and the Molerovs painted for Rila Monastery, and a good selection of icons produced by other local painters. One highlight is an anonymous *Wheel of Time*, in which everyday village scenes are encircled by portrayals of the different ages of man.

A couple of minutes' walk south of pl.Vazrazhdane, the **Velyanova kashta**, at ul.Velyan Ognev 5 (Mon–Fri 9am–noon & 2–5pm; 5Lv), is one of the best surviving examples of the nineteenth-century Bansko house, comprising a stone-clad storehouse on the first floor and elegant, balconied living quarters above. Local lore tells that the house was built for the craftsman Velyan Ognev of Debar, who worked on the iconostasis in Bansko's Church of Sveta Troitsa and decided to stay on in town; falling in love with the priest's daughter was an added inducement. Highlights include a nicely restored kitchen-cum-living room, in which the entire family slept on a single mattress on the floor, and the wonderfully decorated Blue Room, covered with frescoes of fanciful cityscapes, thought to have been painted by Ognev for his wife.

Last but not least, the **market** that enlivens ul.Tsar Simeon on Sunday mornings is worth a visit for its handwoven blankets, rugs and clothing, which are on sale alongside workaday objects such as cowbells, saddles and harnesses.

Eating, drinking and nightlife

Bansko is famous for its *mehanas*, offering standard Bulgarian fare in a folksy, checked-tablecloth environment. Menus are pretty much the same wherever you eat, with Bansko specialities such as *banski starets* (home-cured sausage), *chomlek* (mixed meats stewed with potatoes and vegetables), *kapama* (mixed meats stewed with sauerkraut and rice) and *katino meze* (spicy meat and onion fry-up). Such is the competition between Bansko *mehanas* that prices are reasonable pretty much everywhere you eat, with main courses rarely exceeding 12–15Lv. Most central *mehanas* feature live music – usually sentimental Bulgarian-Macedonian songs performed by a band featuring accordion, clarinet and *darbuka* drum.

Most drinking customarily takes place in the *mehanas* too, although there's a growing range of bars and clubs catering for the winter tourist trade.

Restaurants

Baryakovata mehana Velyan Ognev 3. Long-established *mehana* with reliable standards, plus a lovely galleried courtyard at the back. Pretty much everything in the Bulgarian culinary repertoire is on the menu somewhere, although specialities include oven-baked lamb, *dzholan* (shin of pork) and *sache* dishes served on a sizzling iron plate.

Dedo pene ul. Aleksandar Buynov 1. The whole range of traditional Bulgarian food and Bansko specialities, in a characterful dining room crammed with folksy decorations – and you can sit in the vine-shaded courtyard in summer.

Molerite ul. Glazne 41. Two floors of wooden benches and ethnic textiles, and superb local specialities such as roast lamb and sword-grilled shish kebabs. Turns into a folk-pop disco after about 11pm.

Motikata ul. Pirin. Just south of town on the road to the Banderitsa hut, *Motikata* ("the hoe") is away from the main *mehana* crawl and relies on good food and an unpretentious atmosphere to pull in an appreciative crowd of locals and tourists. Pretty much anything from the grill is excellent.

Zehtindzhievata kashta ul. Georgi Kovachev 11. Traditional *mehana* with a huge menu of Bulgarian fare and Bansko favourites.

Bars

Basecamp ul. Tsar Simeon ⓦwww
.basecamp-bansko.com. Cult bar on the edge of
town just beyond the sports stadium, with an
eclectic music policy and frequent live gigs. Popular
in both summer and winter.

Oxygen ul. Stefan Karadzha 27. Basement bar
in the town centre with mixed programme of
DJ-driven sounds, potent cocktails and
good vibes.

Around Bansko

Hemmed in by the Pirin Mountains to the west, the Rila massif to the north,
and the Rhodopes to the east, Bansko and its surrounding countryside boasts
some great walks. Bansko itself is the most convenient starting point for hikes,
although the nearby villages of **Dobarsko** and **Dobrinishte** are also important
trail-heads; the former has enough going for it to be worth a visit in its own
right. The only other place worth mentioning in this neck of the woods is
Eleshnitsa, site of a renowned folk festival on Easter Sunday.

The Pirin Mountains

Looming over Bansko to the west are the **Pirin Mountains**, Bulgaria's wildest
range, consisting of 45 peaks, all more than 2590m tall. Snowcapped for much of
the year, they're subject to such powerful winds and violent storms that the early
Slavs were convinced that this was the abode of the Thunder God, Perun. Pure
water tarns and short-lived wild flowers abound in the highland valleys, and
the slopes are a botanist's delight, with clumps of Scots, Corsican, Macedonian
and white pine. The **Pirin National Park** covers over four hundred square
kilometres of this terrain, including the Bayuvi dupki–Dzhindzhiritsa and Yulen
biosphere reserves. Its mountains are predominantly granite, with scores of
glacial cirques, at the bottom of which are 186 lakes. There is also a karst region
of limestone crags and caves. The highest peaks and most of the lakes are in the
northern Pirin, which is crisscrossed with hiking **trails** between *hizhi* – simple
huts connected to the outside world by radio telephone. Although, by law, they
are forbidden to turn anyone away, you could end up on a bed in the corridor
if all the rooms are occupied.

The Pirin Sings folk festival

One of the greatest of Bulgarian folklore festivals, second in importance only to that
in Koprivshtitsa (see p.274), **Pirin Sings** (*Pirin Pee*) is a two-day celebration of the
music of the Pirin region held at **Predel**, an area of meadows and woodland 15km
west of Bansko on the road to Blagoevgrad. The action takes place on a series of
outdoor stages, each devoted to a different part of southwestern Bulgaria, with
folklore societies from every conceivable town and village strutting their stuff to
appreciative crowds. Like most such events in Bulgaria, the festival combines serious
cultural interest with the laid-back atmosphere of a mass country picnic. Many locals
pay as much attention to the numerous stalls selling grilled meats and beer as they
do to the official programme, and there's usually plenty of impromptu singing and
dancing to get involved in. At dusk, gypsy bands gather around campfires to blast
out tunes on the *zurna*, an impressively raucous wind instrument of Turkish origin.

The festival was held every odd-numbered year until 2001, after which it was
decided to hold a smaller (but still highly worthwhile) festival every year, with the
full-scale bash occurring at four-year intervals (the next one is in 2009).

Both the small and full-scale festivals straddle the Saturday and Sunday nearest to
August 15, although it's a good idea to check precise dates with the Bansko tourist
information centre (see p.144) before you travel.

Hiking in the Pirin

If you're considering **hiking in the Pirin**, it's essential to get a good map, Cartographia's green-jacketed 1:55,000 map of the Pirin being your best bet. Besides this, stout boots, warm waterproof clothing, a sleeping bag and food are essential. You can camp at designated spots (not within nature reserves), but only during the summer; inexperienced hikers should avoid high peaks and snowy ground and, ideally, join a group familiar with the mountains, or hire a guide through the tourist office in Bansko.

The **trails** below cover only part of the northern Pirin; determined hikers could continue farther south towards Gotse Delchev or Melnik. Staying within the region of Bansko and Dobrinishte, you can still enjoy the Pirin at its best on a two- or three-day hike around Mount Vihren and the lakes, on a circuit beginning or ending at a hut that's accessible by road from Bansko or Dobrinishte. By taking a taxi instead of walking to the hut you'll be fit to start hiking immediately. As the road from Bansko to the *Vihren* hut is more direct than the journey from Dobrinishte to the *Bezbog* hut, it's easier to start from Bansko and end at Dobrinishte, although it's feasible to complete the circuit in either direction.

From Bansko, take the minor road heading south, which forks after 6km. The right-hand, better-surfaced fork leads to the *Banderitsa* hut 8km away, and on past the **Baikushevata mura** (Baikushev Fir) – a mighty tree that is 1300 years old – to the larger *Vihren* hut, 2km beyond. From here on the scenery is magnificent, whether you make the two-and-a-half hour ascent of **Mount Vihren** (2914m), Bulgaria's second highest peak – with the option of carrying on into the karst region (see below) – or trek westward past lakes and **Mount Todorin** (2746m) to the *Demyanitsa* hut (4hr). For those with more time, there's a trail (3hr) south to the *Tevno ezero* (Dark Lake) in the heart of the Pirin, and another to the *Yane Sandanski* hut, a base for weekend hikers from Sandanski. Otherwise, head eastwards to the *Bezbog* hut, on a trail (4hr 30min) that skirts the **Yulen Nature Reserve**, passing some unforgettable vistas.

Starting from Dobrinishte entails reaching the *Gotse Delchev* hut by a 12km mountain road that peters out into a track. In the vicinity of the hut is the 45-metre-high Visokata ela (Tall Fir), the tallest in the Pirin Mountains, and a chair lift to the *Bezbog* (Godforsaken) hut, 700m higher up, which is also accessible by footpath (2hr 30min). Beside the lakes near the hut there are signposted trails to the **Bezbog Peak** (1hr 30min) or a larger cluster of lakes at **Popovoezeren tsirkus** (1hr 30min), not to mention the *Demyanitsa* hut, if you're doing the circuit in the other direction.

Another possibility is to explore the **karst region** north of Mount Vihren, where the trail from Mount Vihren to the *Yavorov* hut (7hr) is the longest, hardest and most exciting in the Pirin, crossing spectacular cols, serpentines and other rock formations. The most memorable part is the Koncheto (Horse), a 1500-metre-long ridge less than a metre wide, above an abyss; a steel rope provides a handhold. From the *Yavorov* hut the trail continues past the **Bayuvi dupki–Dzhindzhiritsa Reserve**, a massif ringed by karst cirques and peaks over 2800m tall, down to the Predel Pass (see p.142).

Access to the range from Bansko is provided by the minor road which heads southwest from the town before winding tortuously up towards the *Vihren* hut, some 13km distant, which stands in the shadow of the 2914–metre **Vihren peak** – the Pirin's highest. From the hut, numerous marked paths lead across the alpine meadows or up onto the shoulder of the mountain – the box above contains more details of the routes available. During the summer there are three daily minibuses from Bansko bus station to the *Banderitsa* hut on the eastern shoulder of Mount Vihren, continuing on to the slightly higher *Vihren* hut if there are enough passengers.

▲ Hikers in the Pirin mountains

Dobarsko

Twenty-three kilometres north of Bansko, the village of **DOBARSKO** (ДОБЪРСКО) perches on a forested southern spur of the Rila mountains, surrounded by a patchwork of tobacco crops, corn fields and pasture. Its greatest historical asset is the seventeenth-century **Church of SS Teodor Tiron and Teodor Stratilat** (Mon–Fri 9am–noon & 2–5pm; 4Lv), a simple stone shed of a building which lurks unassumingly behind a wall in the centre of the village. Inside are some of the most spectacular frescoes of the period, including, above the arch on the left-hand side of the nave, a much-hyped picture of the Ascension, in which Jesus is enclosed in a multicoloured rhomboid shape intended to convey the concept of the Divine Light. Elsewhere in the nave, the New Testament is related in storyboard style, while pictures of the saints to which the church is dedicated hover watchfully over the main entrance. The *Dobarsko* hut in the hills north of Dobarsko is the starting point for **hikes in the Rila Mountains** to the *Makedoniya* hut, the Fish Lakes and beyond (see p.133).

To **get here** from Bansko, you need to change buses in Razlog, though a taxi all the way is an affordable alternative (expect to pay upwards of 40Lv to get there and back).

Dobrinishte

Heading southeast from Bansko on the main road to Gotse Delchev, **DOBRINISHTE** (ДОБРИНИЩЕ; served by all Bansko–Gotse Delchev buses) is the first place of any size, a frumpy village where lumbering is the main industry. Dobrinishte's proximity to Bansko – and the likelihood that the Bansko ski region will be extended eastwards in the future – suggests that Dobrinishte is ripe for tourist development. For the time being Dobrinishte serves as a useful staging post for hikers en route to the eastern limbs of the Pirin range, largely thanks to the **Gotse Delchev chair lift** (July–Aug Sat & Sun; 5Lv each way) located 12km up a side valley to the south. The lift hoists you up to the *Bezbog* mountain hut, immediately beyond which lies the Bezbog Lake – a beautifully desolate spot surrounded by grim peaks. For more on hiking routes from here, see the box on p.149.

The ☀ *Makedonska krachma* **inn**, at the centre of Dobrinishte at ul. Georgi Dimitrov 1, serves up some of the best traditional food in the region in an atmospheric interior crammed full of nineteenth-century k nick-k nacks; it also offers accommodation in a clutch of comfortable en-suite rooms above (℡0888 792 299; ❸).

Eleshnitsa

Nestling among hills 10km northeast of Dobrinishte, the former uranium-mining town of **ELESHNITSA** (ЕЛЕШНИЦА) is the venue for some of the most remarkable **kukeri celebrations** in the country, which take place here on Easter Sunday instead of January, the usual time for their enactment elsewhere. Each of the town's three *mahalas* or quarters organizes a team of mummers or *kukeri* who, dressed from head to toe in sheepskins, converge on the town square, accompanied by a deafening cacophony of drumbeats. They then parade around the square performing crazy, trance-like dances aimed at driving away evil spirits. In theory, the *mahala* producing the loudest, most frightening display is declared the winner, but few of the onlookers seem interested in the result, concentrating instead on the enthusiastic outbreak of mass folk-dancing which invariably follows the performance.

There are no buses to Eleshnitsa on Easter Sunday, so you'll need a car – or a taxi from Bansko – to get there (and back, as there's nowhere in town to stay).

Northeast of Bansko: Belitsa, Yakoruda and beyond

From Bansko, the main roads (and most buses) either head west via the Predel Pass to Blagoevgrad (see p.139), or south through the Mesta valley to the southern Pirin town of Gotse Delchev (see p.152).

Alternatively, you can take advantage of the **narrow-gauge railway** from Bansko to the mainline junction of Septemvri, which passes through the spa resort of Velingrad (see p.357). From Septemvri, there are trains to either Sofia or Plovdiv. Three trains go from Bansko to Septemvri each day, all of which are exceedingly slow, but it's a stupendously scenic journey, passing over a pasture- and forest-covered spur of the western Rhodope mountains. It's a route that you can follow by road, too, providing you have your own transport.

From Bansko the road heads northeast up the gradually narrowing Mesta valley, with the Rila Mountains looming up to the north and the Rhodopes to the southeast. About 20km out of Bansko a secondary road splits from the main road/rail route and heads north up a side valley towards the village of **BELITSA** (БЕЛИЦА). A former uranium-mining village now scarred by high unemployment, Belitsa has latterly become famous as the site of the **Belitsa Dancing Bear Park** (daily 9am–dusk; donation requested), located in a wooded valley 7km north of the village at the end of a badly surfaced road. Founded in 2000 by the Austria-based Vier Pfoten/Four Paws organization (and partly funded by the Brigitte Bardot Foundation), the park provides a refuge for beasts exploited as dancing bears – a practice which, despite being outlawed in 2002, still occurs in isolated cases. The sanctuary purchases bears from their (usually gypsy) owners and lets them loose in a twenty-acre enclosure of forested hillside. Almost all of the bears were taken from their natural habitat when they were cubs, and can never be released back into the wild. The bears are reasonably sociable and you stand a good chance of seeing them lounging around in the open, unless you arrive in winter – when some of the bears are relearning how to hibernate.

Returning to the main Mesta valley route, both road and railway pass through the logging town of **YAKORUDA** (ЯКОРУДА), 5km beyond the Belitsa turn-off, which is a predominantly Pomak (Bulgarian Muslim) settlement. As you approach you'll see the gleaming white minarets of newly renovated mosques spearing up from the valley floor, imitating the surrounding pines. After this there's a sudden ascent into real mountain territory, where the railway and road part company: the rail route twists and turns its way east, passing through the wayside halt of **Avramovi Kolibi** – at 1250m above sea level the highest "station" on the Balkan Peninsula – before descending towards Velingrad, and ultimately Septemvri. The road continues north, passing through Yundola (see p.358) before crossing a mountain pass where locals – mostly Pomaks – sell freshly picked wild berries by the roadside. The road then drops away to meet the Sofia-Plovdiv highway at **BELOVO** (БЕЛОВО), a rather drab town that rejoices in being the **toilet-paper capital** of the Balkans. A local factory churns out tons of the stuff, some of which is given to the workforce in part payment of wages, then sold at roadside stalls to passing motorists. If you're running a bit short, then this is definitely the place to stop off.

Gotse Delchev and around

Despite being named after Macedonia's greatest revolutionary (see box opposite), **GOTSE DELCHEV** (ГОЦЕ ДЕЛЧЕВ) is one of the Pirin's mellowest towns, set in a wide valley watered by the Mesta and suffused with a bucolic air, with chickens clucking in back gardens and tobacco leaves hanging out to dry in suburban streets. Though short on sights, Gotse boasts a vivacious café society and serves as a useful base for several attractive highland villages in the region, such as the beautiful **Delchevo** to the south, and **Leshten**, **Kovachevitsa** and **Dolen** to the east. With a new frontier post 20km south of town near the village of Ilinden, Gotse is also a good base for onward travel to **Greece**.

Gotse Delchev

From the bus station, ul. Vancharska leads past a red-brick synagogue (long since converted into apartments), to some nineteenth-century **crafts workshops** at the lower end of the main shopping street, ul. Targovska, a cobbled boulevard lined with trees and colourful nineteenth-century houses. On ul. Botev, which crosses it, the old Prokopov House contains a **History Museum** (Tues–Sat 10am–noon & 2–6pm; 2Lv) with a collection of folk costumes, plus artefacts from Nicopolis ad Nestrum (see p.154), but a better attraction is the **Rifat Bei kashta** (same hours; 2Lv), with displays on the lifestyle and crafts of the National Revival era. It's located beside the Delcheska River on the far side of the canal, near a 500-year-old, 24m-high plane tree called Chinarbei.

Practicalities

Gotse Delchev has two **bus stations** – the larger *darzhavna* (or "state") *avtogara* and the smaller *chastna* ("private") *avtogara* – both on different sides of the large market area at the southern end of town. As a rule, buses to and from Sofia use the *darzhavna*; services to the outlying villages depart from the *chastna*.

Gotse Delchev (1872–1903)

Born in Kukush (now Kilkis in northern Greece) and inspired by Balkan revolutionaries Vasil Levski and Hristo Botev (see p.286), **Gotse Delchev** dedicated himself to the cause of a free Macedonia, organizing a network of underground cells for the IMRO (see p.141 & p.164) while publicly leading the life of a teacher. An enlightened and unusually liberal revolutionary, he was similar to his idol Levski in refusing to target local Turks, declaring that they too were victims of Ottoman oppression. While undoubtedly in the Bulgarian revolutionary tradition, he stood for an **autonomous Macedonia** as part of some future Balkan federation, as opposed to the right-wing, Sofia-based *Varhovisti* or Supremists, who sought its union with Bulgaria.

Killed in a skirmish with Turkish troops three months before the long-awaited and abortive Ilinden uprising, Delchev neither witnessed nor was tarnished by the IMRO's decline into sectarian butchery, and is still honoured as a hero in both Bulgaria and the Republic of Macedonia, where his moustached portrait hangs in many a café. Initially buried in Rila Monastery, his bones were taken after World War II to the Macedonian capital Skopje, where his tomb lies in the courtyard of the Church of Sveti Spas.

The only biography of Delchev in the English language is Mercia Macdermott's *Freedom or Death* (see p.462 in Contexts). Researched in Bulgaria during the Communist period, it tends to exaggerate his role as an ardent socialist and Bulgarian nationalist, but is an inspiring account nonetheless.

Looming above the main square, the high-rise *Nevrokop*, at ul. Mihail Antonov 1 (℡0751/61240 or 61241, Ⓦwww.hotelnevrokop.com; ❸), contains functional but pleasing pastel-coloured rooms with TV, fridge and small bathroom. The *Malamovata kashta*, just off the square at ul. Hristo Botev 25 (℡0751/61231 and 61230; ❷) contains slightly more ramshackle en-suites with TV in a restored nineteenth-century mansion. The bright, modern *Valentino*, 3km southeast of the centre on ul. Dunav (℡0751/60750 or 60751, Ⓔvalentino_pgm@abv.bg; ❷), has browny-yellow rooms with TV and fridge, some with shower, others with bathtub, plus a handful of triples and roomy apartments (❸).

There's an attractive clutch of pavement **cafés** on the main square, in front of the Gotse Delchev statue. The *Malamovata kashta* contains a good **restaurant**, while the *Banita*, slightly downhill from the main square at Solunska 1, serves up well-prepared regional dishes in a pleasant garden.

Delchevo

You'd be foolish to visit Gotse Delchev without making the effort to visit **DELCHEVO** (ДЕЛЧЕВО), a wonderfully atmospheric village perched up in the mountains just south of town. Buses are infrequent (currently Mon & Fri only at 8am & 4pm), but a taxi there and back shouldn't cost more than 30Lv. If you're driving, head out of town along ul. Papalezov and keep going.

Almost immediately the road begins switchbacking up a steep hillside, passing lush orchards and vineyards, with occasional gaps revealing fine views of the town sprawled across the plain below. A few kilometres out of town you'll pass the **convent of Sveta Bogoroditsa**, a minor foundation which nevertheless boasts a tranquil garden and a large meadow for picnics – the latter pressed into service on major Orthodox feast days like Assumption (*Golyama bogoroditsa*; August 15). After 9km of twisting and turning you arrive at Delchevo itself, its streets ranged amphitheatre-style around the curving mountainside. Most of its houses are built in the frugal Rhodope style rather than mortared and multistoreyed in the Pirin fashion – the circle of houses around the church is especially fine. There's also a spectacular panorama of the Mesta valley from the village square. If you want to stay, *Etnografski kompleks Delchevo* (☎0898 414 141, ⓦwww.delchevo.info; ❹) offers comfortable en-suite rooms in two traditional houses, each with stone-built lower stories and wooden verandahs.

Highland villages east of Gotse

Although most easily reached from Gotse Delchev, the mountains on the eastern side of the Mesta valley technically represent a spur of the Rhodopes, not the Pirin. The feel of the place is different too: the land is dry and stony, with Muslim and Christian villages dotted among stunted oaks, acacias and wild thyme, with goats and tobacco forming the backbone of the local economy.

Village tourism is the new cottage industry and buzzword in the region, as wealthy Sofians pay to live in authentic highland hamlets, consume local food and wine, and revel in the scenery – yet still enjoy decent bathrooms and cable TV. In fact, amenities vary from village to village – or house to house in places – from tastefully modernized stone houses to spartan lodgings with a local *baba* (grandmother).

Unfortunately, this rural idyll is poorly served by **buses**. The daily service to Dospat follows the main road east out of Gotse Delchev, and although it's an exhilaratingly scenic ride, the route doesn't take you near enough to any of the key villages to make it worth your while stopping off. There is one bus on alternate days to Kovachevitsa via Leshten, and one daily service to Dolen. Local **taxis** are the only other option, with prices inflated by the state of the road – the one to Kovachevitsa is awful. If you have your own transport, then visiting Dolen, Leshten and Kovatchevitsa as a day-trip makes for a great excursion – although the rustic charms of the last may well make you want to stay.

Towards Leshten

East of Gotse the main road to Dospat (see p.355), Devin (p.353) and ultimately Smolyan (p.346) dives across the Mesta valley, while a secondary road heads northeast towards the village of **Ognyanovo** on the far side of the river. On the way it passes the **ruins of Nicopolis ad Nestrum**, once a staging point on the Roman road from Constantinople to the Adriatic. There's not a lot left to see save for lines of stones in the grass, but it's an evocative site, framed by the distant mountains which stand guard on either side of the valley. From Ognyanovo an unmarked road (ask for Kovatchevitsa if it's not immediately apparent) winds its way eastward into the hills, passing a dirt-poor gypsy village before leaving the Mesta valley behind. It's an impressively scenic route, providing views of distant peaks to the south and west as the road heads up the scrub-covered slopes of a narrow side valley.

After 10km of potholes, however, it's a relief to reach **LESHTEN** (ЛЕШЕН), a pretty, picture-postcard village whose 35 inhabitants can be outnumbered by guests in the fifteen **apartments** here (☎07527/552 or 0751/29107, Ⓔleshten@yahoo.com; 60Lv for two people, 100Lv for three or four). Converted from traditional homes by the owner of the **restaurant** beside the church, all the apartments have bare wooden floorboards, traditional textiles, simple pine furnishings and a functional WC/shower room. Some have self-catering facilities, although the quality of food at the restaurant is a convincing argument for giving up cooking altogether. Four kilometres beyond

Leshten, the road passes through **Gorno Dryanovo**, a Pomak (Bulgarian Muslim) village which ekes a living from nearby tobacco fields.

Kovachevitsa

Another 4km or so uphill from Leshten, **KOVACHEVITSA** (КОВАЧЕВИЦА; Ⓦwww.kovachevica.com) is far bigger and far less sanitized, its tumbledown stone houses leaning over narrow cobbled alleyways or mud tracks, with expansive vistas of the Pirin mountains to the southwest. It has long been the favoured end-of-the-world retreat for Sofia media types – indeed, numerous historical epics have used Kovachevitsa's old houses as a backdrop – but much of the local population has moved down the valley to Gotse Delchev, leaving the elderly to tend the fields and graze the goats. Roaming the steep, crooked alleyways and admiring the sturdy, many-storeyed houses is the main activity for visitors, while there are also plenty of rural walks to enjoy – albeit along unsigned goat-tracks.

Practicalities

There are plenty of places **to stay**, with several old houses transformed into B&Bs: ask at the *kmetstvo* (mayor's office) at the entrance to the village or enquire at the *Sinya Vir* bar opposite. The best place is ♨ *Kapsazovite kashti* at the downhill end of the village (Ⓣ0898 296 669 and 0899 403 089, Ⓔkapsazovs_houses@yahoo.com; ❹), a tastefully restored 200-year-old house with characterful rooms decorated with goat-hair rugs, iron bedsteads and quirky Surrealist paintings, and a wonderful garden. Rooms are rented on a half- or full-board basis – and as the lady of the house is a cookery writer, it's undeniably worth it. Occupying another lovingly renovated village house, *Byalata kashta* (Ⓣ07523/232 and 0899 886 342; Ⓦwww.ecotourbg.com; ❸) offers eight en-suite rooms with traditional rugs, modern furniture and TV. Simpler in style but equally welcoming is the home of *Maria Milcheva* (Ⓣ07527/445; B&B ❶, half-board ❷), with an owner who speaks French (but not English) and three cosy rooms furnished with traditional knick-knacks and textiles, shared WC/shower in the corridor, and another fine garden; advance notice is required. The *Bayateva kashta* in the middle of the village (Ⓣ07527/3044 and 0898 770 418; ❶) is a fine old balconied house with simply furnished rooms, a couple of which are doubles (the others sleep four or five), with shared facilities. There's a well-stocked *mehana* in the centre of the village, with a lively garden terrace, while the *Sinya Vir café-bar*, at the entrance to the village, also offers simple food.

Dolen

Back on the main eastbound Gotse Delchev-Dospat route, a fifteen-kilometre journey through the pine-covered foothills of the western Rhodopes brings you to the turn-off for **DOLEN** (ДОЛЕН), a mixed Christian-Pomak village nestling between pasture-covered hills a further 3km off the main road. It's another extraordinarily time-warped place, with barnyard smells hovering over a maze of ramshackle houses and unpaved streets. To get to the oldest part of the village, take the right fork just after the ugly-looking *Valentino* hotel. It's a great place for a wander, and the locals – who you'll see sitting outside their houses in summer sorting the tobacco crop – are by and large a friendly lot.

Dolen is served by a mere three buses a week from Gotse Delchev, but more buses (including Sofia-Vaklinovo services from Ovcha Kupel) pass the Dolen turn-off. Numerous people rent out rooms on an informal basis if you ask around. Established sources of **accommodation** include *Doganovata kashta*, the creamy-coloured house diagonally opposite the post office (☎0898 702 899; ❷), with small doubles leading off a central hall and shared WC/shower; and the *Dzhalovata kashta*, downhill near the church (☎0888 471 313 or 0888 543 440; ❷), a creaky old wooden house furnished with local rugs, where many of the rooms retain their traditional hooded fireplaces. Both of the above will offer half- or full-board arrangements; otherwise there's a quaintly uncommercialized village store-cum-café in the lower part of Dolen – just ask for the *kafene*.

Moving on from Gotse

There are regular buses from Gotse Delchev to Bansko and Blagoevgrad, and a handful of services heading east into the Rhodopes, but westbound public transport towards Sandanski and Melnik is meagre in the extreme. For those with their own transport, there's also a spectacular **road** though the mountains **to Rozhen and Melnik**, although with the road surface crumbling to bits in some places and covered with rock-fall debris in others, it shouldn't be attempted on bad-weather days. If you do take this route, then consider taking the detour to the village of **PIRIN** (ПИРИН), 2km down a side road about 30km out of Gotse. Spectacularly located at the bottom of a high-mountain ravine, it's another place that seems to have been totally bypassed by the modern world, with new-fangled innovations like shops and motorcars conspicuous by their absence. Ancient stone houses perch improbably on the hillsides, while their inhabitants use four-legged transport to travel to and fro between the thin patches of cultivable land.

Sandanski

On the other side of the Pirin Mountains from Gotse Delchev, **SANDANSKI** (САНДАНСКИ) enjoys the warmest, sunniest climate in Bulgaria, with alpine breezes mellowing its Mediterranean aridity. The curative effects of the town's hot mineral springs have been appreciated since Roman times, making it a **health resort** *par excellence*. You don't have to be ill to enjoy the baths and pampering at its spa hotels – great if you've just been hiking in the mountains – nor the town's evening promenade, which flows along ul. Makedoniya. Moreover, Sandanski offers the best public transport access to Melnik, Rozhen and Rupite – the chief attractions in the far south – plus another way into the Pirin range, via the mountain resort of Popina Laka and the *Yane Sandanski* hut.

Sandanski's modern appearance belies its origins as Desudava, a settlement of the Thracian Medi tribe and the likely birthplace of **Spartacus**, who led the great slave revolt against the Roman Empire in the first century BC. The revolt originated in Sicily, where Spartacus – like other Medi – had been deported to labour on the island's estates following the Roman conquest of Thrace. While a Spartacus monument is visible from the highway, vestiges of the past in the centre of town relate to the Orthodox **saints Kozma and Damyan**, local brothers whose healing skills earned them the accolade *Sveti vrach* (Blessed Doctor) – which was also the town's name prior to the Turkish conquest. A provincial *chiflik* under Ottoman rule, it rivalled Melnik as a market town in the nineteenth century and surpassed it after disaster befell Melnik in 1913 (see p.158). The town's present name, bestowed in 1949, pays tribute to the nineteenth-century Macedonian freedom fighter Yane Sandanski (see p.164).

The Town

The predominantly pedestrianized ul. Makedoniya runs from east to west through the centre of town, cutting through the main square, **ploshtad Balgariya**, on the way. It's a wonderfully leafy, café-lined boulevard, especially the section to the east of pl. Balgariya which leads towards the town's spa park. Before you reach the park, beside the ruins of an early Byzantine Episcopal Basilica, is the **Archeological Museum** (Mon–Fri 9am–12.30pm & 2.30–6pm, plus summer Sat & Sun 10am–12.30pm & 4–7.30pm; 3Lv). Built over a late Roman villa with a walk-round display of a mosaic floor found in situ, its upper floor is filled with funerary stoneware from the necropolis of Muletarovo, including a child's sarcophagus with bull- and ram-head reliefs. Votive tablets feature Zeus and Hera or a hunter figure presumed to be Artemis, carved in a vigorous, almost naive style suggesting that Desudava was a predominantly Thracian, rather than a Roman or Hellenic, town.

A hundred metres or so beyond the museum, on the other side of the road, lies the ziggurat-shaped *Hotel Sandanski* (see below), and beyond that a 192-acre **park** planted with more than two hundred exotic species including Japanese ginkgos and Californian sequoias. Its two mineral water-fed **pools** (May–Sept daily 9am–8pm), water-slides, boating lake and paths into the hills are all open to the public.

Arrival

Sandanski's **train station** is 4km west of town, and although trains are met by a bus into the centre, it's not the most convenient of places for speedy arrival and departure. Far better to travel to Sandanski by **bus**: the main terminal is a few blocks downhill from pl. Balgariya.

Accommodation

Aneli ul. Gotse Delchev 1 ☎0746/28952 and 31844. No-frills accommodation just uphill from pl. Balgariya, with smallish, simply decorated en-suite rooms with TV and Bulgarian-style open showers. No breakfast. ②

Medite Polenitsa ☎0746/33200, ⓦwww .hotelmedite.com. Three kilometres outside town, in a semi-suburban area of old village houses and modern apartment developments, *Medite* is the place to be if you're a connoisseur of modern design. The en-suite rooms feature TV, minibar and furnishings which look like they've dropped from the pages of an Italian design catalogue. There's a lovely swimming pool and "spa" area, although they are not fed by genuine Sandanski mineral water. ⑤

Panorama Okolovrastno shose 1 ☎0746/34500, ⓦwww.panoramahotelsandanski.com. Behind the spa park and slightly uphill, this angular modern structure looks a bit like a suburban apartment block, but offers comfortable en-suite rooms, outdoor pool and a wealth of wellness and massage treatments. ⑤

Sandanski at the end of ul. Makedoniya ☎0746/31165. Centrally located 300-room hotel right beside the park, with 1970s colour schemes and a full range of spa treatments, plus a large indoor pool. ④

Sveti Nikola ul. Makedoniya 1 ☎0746/33035, ⓦwww.hotel-sveti-nikola.ltd.bg. Seven-storey Communist-era lump which has been nicely refurbished, although many of the en-suite rooms still feature frumpy décor. On the main street, a 5min walk uphill from the bus station. Health centre with pool and hydro-massage facilities, fed by Sandanski spa water. ③

Sveti Vrach ☎0746/28626, ⓔspartakturs @infotel.bg. Former Politburo resort 5km out of town, occupying a wonderful hilltop setting, with a Henry Moore sculpture and a duck-filled lake in the grounds. For real opulence take the Presidential suite (350Lv) once enjoyed by Todor Zhivkov. Heated indoor pool. ⑤

Eating and drinking

Two *mehanas* on ul. Makedoniya, *Sveti vrach* and *Trima Musketari*, serve good, cheap Bulgarian meals. Of the innumerable grill restaurants springing up all over town, *Barbeque*, just off ul. Makedoniya on ul. Voden, is probably the best. Stylish **cafés** cluster around the eastern end of ul. Makedoniya, near the *Sandanski* hotel, offering plenty of opportunities for alfresco evening drinking.

Melnik and Rozhen Monastery

Deservedly the most popular destination in the southern Pirin, the tiny town of **Melnik**, 20km southeast of Sandanski, is known for its robust red wine, impressive houses and natural surroundings. An ideal place to relax, favoured by Sofians at weekends, it's readily accessible on one of the three public buses daily from Sandanski. Coming by car from the Sandanski direction, head south along the main E79 highway and take the Petrich/Rupite turn-off, taking care not to head in the Petrich/Rupite direction – double back under the highway and head east instead.

The route from Sandanski passes tobacco fields hugging the roadside above the fertile bed of the Struma, before snaking into hills that become arid and rocky, swelling into desolate mountains stretching towards Greece and the Aegean. Roads deteriorate and faded notices attest to the border zone that existed here in the Communist period, when Greece was regarded as a hostile Western state. If you're not in a hurry, stay at least one night in Melnik and walk over the hills to the Rozhen Monastery – one of Bulgaria's oldest, most picturesque foundations.

Melnik

Approaching **MELNIK** (МЕЛНИК) you'll catch glimpses of the wall of mountains that allowed the townsfolk to thumb their noses at the Byzantine Empire in the eleventh century. Melnik hides until the last moment, encircled by hard-edged crags, scree slopes and sandstone cones. Its straggling main street is lined with whitewashed stone houses on timber props festooned with flowers, and vines overhanging cobbled alleys and narrow courtyards. Rooms for rent and wine for sale make it plain that the locals are used to tourists, while the new hotels being built attest to the sums that outsiders are now investing. But it remains to be seen if this will reverse Melnik's extraordinary decline, from a town of twenty thousand people in 1880 to a village of around three hundred today. A century ago the population was largely Greek, making it a unique outpost of Hellenic civilization in a Slav sea, where mules departed laden with wine for foreign lands. But the economy waned towards the end of the century and the Second Balkan War of 1913 destroyed the town, sundered its trade routes and provoked a bout of ethnic cleansing.

Melnik's **layout** is simple, with a single main street running alongside a (usually dry) riverbed spanned by rickety footbridges. Due to the terrain, houses are small at ground level but expand outwards further up, with the living quarters on the upper floors jutting out above the lower barred and shuttered levels that function as barns or wine cellars. Tiny backstreets invite aimless wandering, while the hillsides abound in tortoises and lizards.

Arrival and accommodation

Buses stop on the western edge of Melnik, just short of the gulley-side streets that serve as a town centre. The nearest **banks** and ATMs are in Sandanski, so make sure you change enough money in advance.

Pretty much every other house in Melnik offers **private rooms** (look for signs reading *stayi za noshtuvki;* "rooms for rent"; ●) but with no tourist office

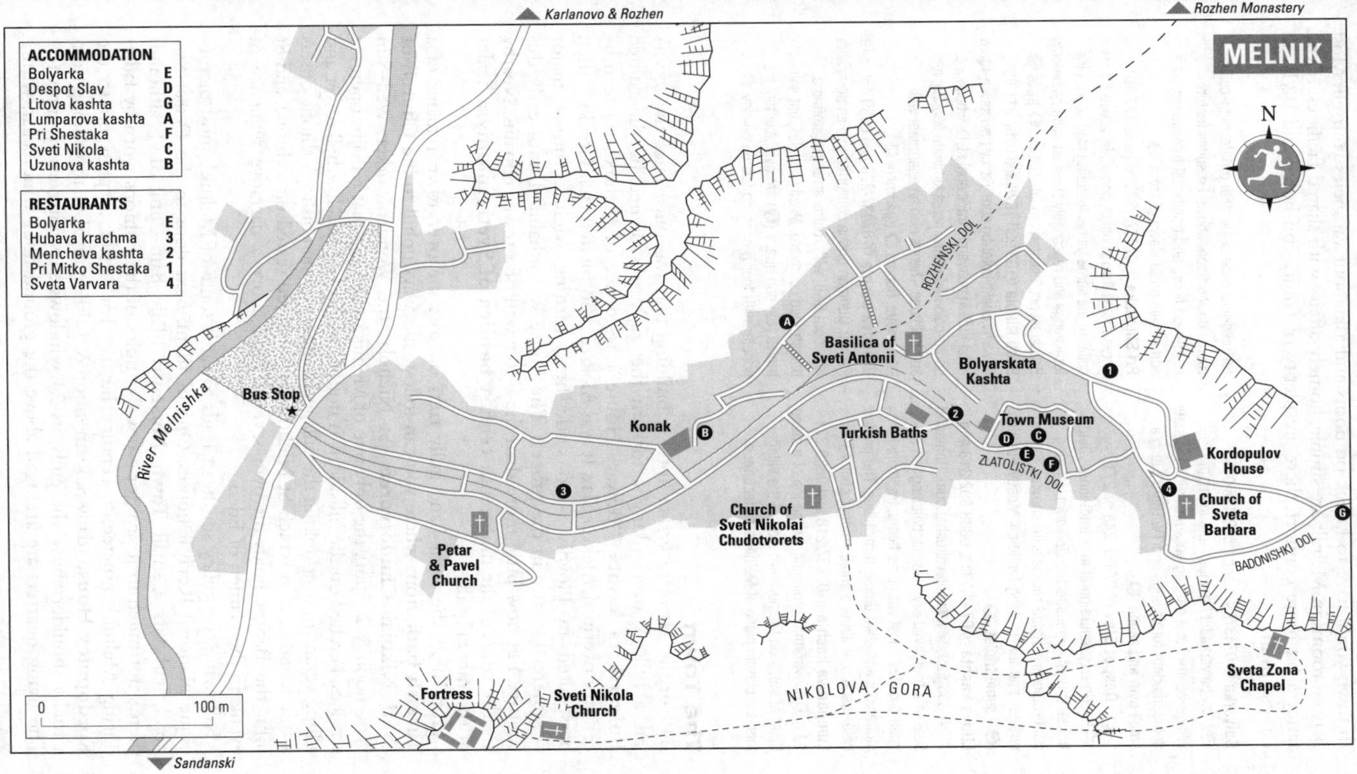

MELNIK

N

▲ *Rozhen Monastery*

◀ *Karlanovo & Rozhen*

◀ *Sandanski*

ACCOMMODATION
Bolyarka E
Despot Slav D
Litova kashta G
Lumparova kashta A
Pri Shestaka F
Sveti Nikola C
Uzunova kashta B

RESTAURANTS
Bolyarka E
Hubava krachma 3
Mencheva kashta 2
Pri Mitko Shestaka 1
Sveta Varvara 4

Kordopulov House
Church of Sveta Barbara
Town Museum
Bolyarskata Kashta
Basilica of Sveti Antonii
Turkish Baths
Church of Sveti Nikolai Chudotvorets
Konak
Petar & Pavel Church
Sveti Nikola Church
Fortress
Sveta Zona Chapel

BADINSKI DOL (KISININ) DOL

ZLATOLISTKI DOL

ROZHENSKI DOL

NIKOLOVA GORA

NIKOLOVA

Bus Stop

River Melnishka

0   100 m

in town you'll have to knock on doors and ask about vacancies yourself. Most private rooms in Melnik are simple, homely affairs with shared facilities. If you fancy a bit more comfort, there are plenty of family-run hotels and B&Bs to choose from.

Bolyarka ☎07437/383 and 0888 455 045, ⓦwww.bolyarka.hit.bg. Plush and intimate village-centre hotel offering en-suites with laminate floors, modern furnishings and TV. There's also a small gym and sauna. ❸

Despot Slav ☎07437/248 or 271. Snazzy, small hotel in a traditional village house roughly opposite the *Bolyarka*, offering contemporary-styled rooms with shower, TV and coffee- and tea-making facilities. Mostly doubles (❸), some triples (❹).

Litova kashta ☎07437/313, 0888 302 313 and 0888 635 529, ⓦwww.litovakushta.com. Upmarket B&B in a traditional-style house, boasting ten en-suite doubles, most with pine floors, traditional stonework and solid timber furnishings. The garden café-restaurant abuts a small outdoor pool. ❹

Lumparova kashta ☎07437/218 and 0889 231 933, ⓔdilova@mail.orbitel.bg. At the top of a steep flight of steps on the northern side of the village, this is a classic piece of Melnik architecture: a fortress-like wine cellar with ornate, high-ceilinged rooms on the floors above. En suites feature hardwood floors and traditional furnishings, plus some have great views of town. ❸

Pri Shestaka ☎07437/239 and 0886 177 401. Three rooms (two doubles, one triple) above the wine cellar of the same name, featuring tiled floors, pine furnishings and reasonably sized en-suite bathrooms. Breakfast not included though. Double ❶ triple ❷

Sveti Nikola ☎02/980 1628 and 0887 211 931, ⓦwww.qualityhotel-bg.com. Fancy new seven-room hotel built in outwardly traditional style, whose bright-coloured rooms boast laminate flooring, a/c and bathtubs. There's also an apartment with kitchenette. Rooms ❺ apartment ❻

Uzunova kashta ☎07437/270 and 0889 450 849. Former Ottoman prison converted into an agreeable ten-room B&B, with rooms arranged around a balustraded courtyard. Mostly doubles, but some triples (❸) and quads (❹) are available too. It's popular with tour groups, so fills up quickly. ❷

The Town

East of the *Uzunova kashta* hotel, a building that was once once the town's jail, a hillock overlooking a fork in the gully is crowned by the ruined **Bolyarskata kashta** ("Bolyar's House"), residence of Melnik's thirteenth-century overlord, Aleksei Slav. It was Aleksei who invited rich Greeks – then persecuted in Plovdiv – to settle here, turning Melnik into a major commercial centre in the process. The house was inhabited until early this century, but now little more than the outer wall of a tower remains. Nearby are the ruins of the nineteenth-century **basilica of Sveti Antoniy**, a healer of the mentally ill.

From here, the right-hand gully runs on past the overgrown remains of a **Turkish bath**, from where you can follow alleyways uphill to the **Church of Sveti Nikolai Chudotvorets** (St Nicholas the Wonder-worker; Wed–Sun 9am–noon & 2–5pm), the only one of Melnik's churches that remains open for services. Perched on the hillside, it is notable for its minaret-like bell tower and a long verandah overlooking the village. Inside, a wooden bishop's throne offsets a fine iconostasis in which St Nicholas is portrayed seated on a throne, and St John the Baptist holds his own severed head above a narrative sequence of events in the Garden of Eden.

Following the gulley southeast leads towards some of Melnik's most pictur-esque National Revival houses. One of them, next door to the *Despot Slav* hotel, harbours a small **Town Museum** (daily 8am–2pm; 3Lv), although there's not much in it save for a few examples of the fashions worn by ladies during Melnik's nineteenth-century heyday. Far better to press on to the **Kordopulov House** (daily 8.30am–noon & 1.30–6pm; 5Lv), protruding from a rocky shoulder above the gully, its 24 windows surveying every approach. The living quarters are arranged above the ground floor wine cellar, with a central reception room surrounded by bedrooms and guest rooms. Each room features painted panelling, rows of cushioned *minder* or bench-seats lining the walls, intricate latticework ceilings and numerous stained-glass windows. The Kordopulov (or Kordopoulos) who built the house in 1754 was a rich merchant of Greek extraction known for his anti-Ottoman sympathies, who prudently installed a secret room as a refuge for the family in emergencies. The Kordopulovs were key figures in the town's social and political life, and Macedonian revolutionary Yane Sandanski (see p.164), who ruled over the Melnik region like a gang boss, was a frequent guest here in the years before World War I. Below ground visitors can access the wine cellars, huge wooden barrels occupying caverns cut from the hillside, connected to the vineyards at the rear of the house by a network of tunnels.

Immediately below the Kordopulov House lies the shell of the medieval **Church of Sveta Barbara**.

Eating and drinking

A dozen places to eat offer similar dishes at similar prices, and all stop serving food by 10pm. All of the hotels listed on opposite have decent *mehanas*; otherwise the *Hubava krachma* just west of the Konak is a good place to enjoy quality local fare in a semi-folksy, semi-antique-shop interior. Similarly cosy is the *Mencheva kashta* near the *Bolyarka* and *Despot Slav* hotels, where you can feast on grilled meats and spicy traditional stews in an engaging trio of rooms stuffed with bric-à-brac. *Sveta Varvara*, just below the Kordopulov House, has a balustraded terrace looking across the valley and a workmanlike menu of grills and *gyuveche*-style stews.

Venues for **drinking** include all the above, plus a handful of signposted wine cellars (*izba*) higher uphill or in the ravines. The view from the terrace of the *Pri Mitko Shestaka* cellar, up behind the *Bolyarskata kashta*, makes the struggle uphill worthwhile.

Melnik wine and festivals

Justly famed throughout Bulgaria, full-bodied red **Melnik wine** once enjoyed an international reputation, enriching Aleksei Slav and remaining popular throughout the Ottoman era, when the wine trade was organized by merchants from Dubrovnik. Locals boast that Winston Churchill ordered the wine for his son's wedding.

Wine still plays a considerable role in the local economy. The vineyards are planted with small, dark grapes of the variety known as Melnik Broad Vine, introduced from Syria in the fourteenth century. After harvesting, the grapes are allowed to cool in basements before being pressed and left to ferment in the chilly cellars that riddle the hills around Melnik. The best of the harvest goes to commercial wineries such as Damyanitsa, located several kilometres west in the Struma valley (and whose products are visible on supermarket shelves throughout the country), although everyone in Melnik either makes wine or has a relative who does. The local *mehanas* slosh it around and locals are keen to flog tourists their home brew. There is no quality control however, and while everything you buy in the village will be drinkable, you shouldn't count on a Melnik trip as a reliable way of stocking up your cellar at home.

Wine is central to two of Melnik's **festivals**. On **Trifon Zarezan** (February 14) the vineyards are ritually pruned and sprinkled with wine to ensure a bumper crop, and families sample the young wine from last year's harvest. The **harvest** can fall any time from late September to mid-October, but is always celebrated on October 18. Another festival with *horo* dancing occurs on the last Sunday in August.

Around Nikolova Gora

To stretch your legs before hiking to Rozhen Monastery, explore the scattered ruins atop the **Nikolova Gora** plateau, south of Melnik, where the start of the trail is signposted (look for a perplexing blue sign reading "Melnik God Created Town from a Demolition to a Raise") near the Church of Sveti Nikolai Chudotvorets. The path curves its way up towards the plateau, forking after about ten minutes: taking the left (east) fork will bring you to the **Sveta Zona Chapel**, an isolated shack overlooking Melnik. On Zona's name-day (April 1) there is an overnight vigil here, and children are blessed during the day. The right fork turns west, passing the remains of a monastery en route to the eighteenth-century **Sveti Nikola Church**, its apses bearing traces of frescoes of Adam and Eve, and the dramatic ramparts of Aleksei Slav's **fortress**. With ravines overlooked by sand pyramids to the north and south, and the whole of the Struma valley laid out to the west, the views from here are spectacular.

The route to Rozhen Monastery

Rozhen Monastery makes a great excursion from Melnik, and although it's accessible by bus, anyone who's able would do better to walk and enjoy the scenery. The **trail over the hills** (6.5km; 1hr 30min) has suffered a good deal from soil erosion in recent years, and can no longer be recommended to people with heavy backpacks (or a fear of heights). It starts at the northeastern end of the village in the Rozhenski Dol ravine, just below the staircase to the *Lumparovata kashta* hotel. From here the route is marked with stripes of green paint – at those points where the paint has faded, hikers have left small piles of stones to guide you on your way. The track leads through a sequence of narrowing gulleys before ascending a steep, scrambly hillside and reaching the crest of a ridge, where your efforts will be rewarded by a stunning view of knife-edged crags and mushroom-like slabs of hard rock poised upon eroded columns. In Robert Littell's thriller *The October Circle*, it's here that the blind

▲ Rozhen Monastery

Witch of Melnik resides, foretelling the townsfolk's destiny for lumps of sugar in lieu of silver coins – a character based on the real-life oracle Baba Vanga (see p.164). The final downhill stretch towards the monastery winds its way along stark sandy hillsides and is perilously narrow in parts.

If you'd rather catch a **bus** (two daily; 15min) or walk the 7km (1hr 30min) along the **road from Melnik to Rozhen**, look out for the 100m-tall sandstone pyramids on either side of the road, and the ramshackle village of **KARLANOVO**, where tumbledown houses and subsistence agriculture seem a world away from touristy Melnik. Carrying on from Karlanovo towards Rozhen, the road (unlike the walking trails) brings you to Rozhen village first instead of the monastery.

One final word of warning: heavy rain causes subsidence in the sandy area around Melnik, so none of the above itineraries should be attempted (either on foot or by car) if there's any chance of a heavy downpour.

Rozhen Monastery

Sited on a plateau above the village, **Rozhen Monastery** (*Rozhenski manastir;* open dawn to dusk) is small and outwardly austere, having survived looting and burning many times since its foundation in the ninth century, on the site of an earlier monastery. Dedicated to the "Mother of God's Nativity", its name derives from the ancient form of the word *roden*, meaning "born". The irregular courtyard is intimate and unadorned, save for trestles supporting a canopy of vines whose root is as thick as a thigh. In the **bakery** the oven and walls consist of mud-and-straw bricks, giving the entire room the texture of a very coarse wholemeal loaf. Only at the far end, where cell is stacked upon cell, does the woodwork display the finesse found at Rila. The **cells** themselves are arranged to give some idea of monastic life through the ages. The accent is on asceticism, although the vivid colours of rugs and cushions counterpoint the simplicity of the furnishings, and it's clear that leading clerics led a somewhat softer life than their charges, enjoying the use of silver coffee sets and book-holders inlaid with mother of pearl.

Within the monastery, the **Church of the Birth of the Holy Virgin**'s cloister shelters a battered *Judgement Day* fresco, which shows the righteous assisted up one side of the ladder to heaven by angels, while sinners attempting to climb the other side are tossed by demons into the mouth of a large red serpent. The torments of hell are vividly depicted on the right, where the damned meet a gory end (prodded by toasting forks and suchlike). Inside the narthex, delicately restored murals include the varied sea-beasts of a *Miraculous Draught of Fishes*, and a splendid *Dormition of the Virgin*. Inside the church itself, the endless ranks of saints covering the walls are eclipsed by a magnificent iconostasis, the work of Debar artisans. Flowers, birds and fishes swirl about the richly coloured icons, and the whole screen – unusually wide in proportion to its height – is a triumph of the woodcarver's art.

A side chapel holds an apparently miracle-working **Icon of the Virgin,** which attracts a steady stream of pilgrims. Decked out in dark red robes, she's rather alluring, in a come-hither, early-Byzantine way. To see monastic ritual at its best, attend the **Rozhenski sabor** on the day of the Birth of the Virgin (*Malka bogoroditsa*; Sept 8), when the miraculous icon is paraded around the grounds and symbolic offerings are made.

Rozhen village

In the valley below the monastery, **ROZHEN** (РОЖЕН), a workaday village of whitewashed, vine-shrouded houses with rickety wooden balconies, is in

Yane Sandanski

Just downhill from Rozhen monastery, outside the nineteenth-century **Church of SS Kiril i Metodii**, lies the grave of the great Macedonian freedom fighter **Yane Sandanski** (1872–1915), inscribed with one of his favourite rallying cries: "To live is to struggle: the slave struggles for freedom; the free man, for perfection!" Of all the Macedonian revolutionaries to have stalked the mountains of southwestern Bulgaria, Sandanski was one of the most controversial. He was an early advocate of the creation of a Macedonia that would be separate from the influence of the Bulgarian state – and Bulgarian nationalists have viewed him as a traitor ever since. Sandanski first came to prominence by organizing the **kidnapping** of an American Protestant missionary, **Miss Ellen Stone**, outside Bansko in September 1901. The affair successfully catapulted the Macedonian Question into the pages of the world's press, and after a six-month period the Ottoman government agreed to pay the (then huge) ransom of US$63,000. Having made his reputation as a revolutionary, Sandanski became head of the IMRO in the Melnik region, which he proceeded to turn into a personal fiefdom from which rival IMRO leaders were excluded. He was gunned down near Rozhen by IMRO rivals (possibly with the encouragement of Tsar Ferdinand) in 1915.

many ways more authentic than neighbouring Melnik. You can enjoy traditional **food** and local wine on the terrace of the *Hanche Rozhen*, on the edge of the village towards Karlanovo. If you feel like staying, there are plush **apartments** at the *Complex Rozhena* (☎07437/211; ❸), uphill from the road out of the village, which also has a shaded café-restaurant and an outdoor swimming pool.

Petrich and around

Thirty kilometres southwest of Melnik, and lying just off the main southbound route to Greece, **PETRICH** (ПЕТРИЧ) is strictly for those interested in Balkan towns that have got rich quick by shady means. During the Communist period, Petrich's proximity to the Greek frontier ensured a steady trickle of illicit Western goods, and Sofia folk came down here to buy much sought-after goods, such as Levis jeans and Abba records, from local black-market traders. Throughout the 1990s, customs officials working at the nearby Kulata border crossing (most of whom live in Petrich) lined their pockets by demanding bribes from lorry drivers entering or leaving Bulgaria.

Other than its pavement cafés, Petrich offers few attractions to the traveller, but serves as a useful base from which to visit the modern-day cult site of Rupite.

Practicalities

Accommodation options in central Petrich begin with the gloomy but tolerable three-star *Hotel Balgariya*, directly opposite the bus station at ul. Dimo Hadzhidimov 5 (☎0745/22233, ℮ oofice@belatour.bg; ❸). Two kilometres east of the centre, the *Agata*, next to the Tsar Samuel sports complex (☎0745/24246; ❸), offers serviceable en suites and has a marvellous complex of outdoor swimming pools, complete with alfresco bars and cafés, right on the doorstep.

Rupite

Twelve kilometres northeast of Petrich, **RUPITE** (РУПИТЕ) is famed in Bulgaria as the home village and burial place of the blind oracle **Baba Vanga**. Legend has it that at the age of six, she saw an angel who offered her the choice between sight and clairvoyance, and she chose the latter. Vanga's subsequent prophecies and healing skills gained her a wide following (including Politburo members), and her vision of Varna engulfed by water was vindicated when it was discovered that the city stood upon an underground lake – from which day on, high-rise building was prohibited. In old age she had fewer VIP visitors but her predictions were still heeded – not least by people choosing their lottery numbers.

After her death in 1996, Vanga was buried in the **Sveta Petka Church**, a postmodern fusion of Slav and Byzantine design, decorated with Expressionist murals and icons by the contemporary artist Svetlin Rusev, and surrounded by an unusually well-watered and manicured park. Its location in the crater of an extinct volcano makes the place even more special for Bulgarian New Agers, who believe it's a powerful energy node – although the scruffy car park and grill-bars at the entrance to the site are unlikely to place you in a meditative frame of mind.

Getting to Rupite (and back) by **bus** from Petrich or Blagoevgrad is fraught with uncertainty, with only one or two services a day. A taxi here and back from Petrich shouldn't cost more than 20Lv.

Travel details

Trains

Bansko to: Dobrinishte (4 daily; 15min); Razlog (4 daily; 20min); Septemvri (4 daily; 5hr 20min); Velingrad (4 daily; 4hr 30min).
Blagoevgrad to: Dupnitsa (4 daily; 45min); Sandanski (4 daily; 1hr–2hr 15min); Sofia (4 daily; 2hr 30min–3hr 30min).
Dupnitsa to: Blagoevgrad (4 daily; 45min); Kulata (4 daily; 2hr–3hr 45min); Sofia (5–7 daily; 2hr–2hr 45min).
Kulata to: Dupnitsa (3 daily; 2hr–3hr 45min); Sandanski (4 daily; 30–45min); Sofia (3 daily; 4hr 30min).
Kyustendil to: Pernik (6 daily; 2hr–2hr 30min); Sofia (3 daily; 2–3hr); Zemen (3 daily; 30min–1hr).
Pernik to: Kyustendil (6 daily; 2hr–2hr 30min); Sofia (hourly; 45min).
Petrich to: Sandanski (3 daily; 50min).
Razlog to: Bansko (3 daily; 15min); Dobrinishte (3 daily; 25min); Septemvri (3 daily; 4hr 45min); Velingrad (3 daily; 4hr 15min).
Sandanski to: Blagoevgrad (4 daily; 1hr–2hr 15min); Dupnitsa (4 daily; 2–3hr); Kulata (4 daily; 30–45min); Petrich (3 daily; 50min); Sofia (4 daily; 3hr).
Sofia to: Blagoevgrad (4 daily; 2hr 30min–3hr 30min); Dupnitsa (5–7 daily; 2hr–2hr 45min); Kocherinovo (4 daily; 2hr 15min–3hr 15min); Kyustendil (3 daily; 2–3hr); Pernik (hourly; 45min); Sandanski (4 daily; 3hr); Zemen (3 daily; 1hr 30min–1hr 45min).

Zemen to: Kyustendil (3 daily; 30min–1hr); Sofia (3 daily; 1hr 30min–1hr 45min).

Buses

Bansko to: Blagoevgrad (12 daily; 1hr); Gotse Delchev (12 daily; 1hr); Plovdiv (2 daily; 4hr); Razlog (10 daily; 30min); Sofia (12 daily; 3hr).
Blagoevgrad to: Bansko (12 daily; 1hr); Dupnitsa (hourly; 45min); Gotse Delchev (12 daily; 2hr); Kyustendil (6 daily; 1hr 30min); Melnik (1 daily; 1hr 30min); Petrich (7 daily; 1hr 30min); Plovdiv (1 daily; 5hr); Rila village (hourly; 35min); Sandanski (7 daily; 1hr); Samokov (1 daily; 2hr); Sofia (hourly; 2hr); Velingrad (1 daily; 2hr 15min).
Dupnitsa to: Bistritsa (10 daily; 25min); Blagoevgrad (hourly; 45min); Kyustendil (8 daily; 50min); Panichishte (3 daily; 1hr); Rila Monastery (2 daily; 1hr); Rila village (5 daily; 30min); Samokov (4 daily; 1hr); Sapareva Banya (hourly; 35min); Sofia (every 30min; 1hr 30min).
Gotse Delchev *Avtogara darzhavna* to: Bansko (12 daily; 1hr); Blagoevgrad (8 daily; 2hr); Dolen (1 daily; 1hr); Dospat (1 daily; 2hr); Kovachevitsa (3–4 weekly; 45min); Petrich (1 daily except Tues & Thurs; 4hr); Razlog (2 daily; 1hr 15min); Sofia (8 daily; 4hr). *Avtogara chastna* to: Dolen (1 daily; 1hr); Kovachevitsa (2 daily; 45min); Leshten (2 daily; 30min).
Kyustendil to: Blagoevgrad (6 daily; 1hr 30min); Dupnitsa (8 daily; 50min); Sofia (hourly; 2hr).

Melnik to: Blagoevgrad (1 daily; 1hr 30min); Sandanski (3 daily; 30min).

Petrich to: Bansko (1 daily; 2hr 30min); Blagoevgrad (6 daily; 1hr 30min); Gotse Delchev (1 daily except Tues & Thurs; 4hr); Kulata (5 daily; 25min); Sandanski (4 daily; 30min).

Rila village to: Blagoevgrad (hourly; 35min); Dupnitsa (5 daily; 30min); Rila Monastery (2–3 daily; 30min).

Samokov to: Blagoevgrad (1 daily; 2hr); Borovets (hourly; 30min); Dupnitsa (4 daily; 1hr); Govedartsi (6 daily; 40min); Malyovitsa (minibuses; 2 daily; 1hr); Plovdiv (1 daily; 2hr 15min); Sandanski (1 daily; 3hr); Sofia (every 30min–1hr; 1hr).

Sandanski to: Blagoevgrad (7 daily; 1hr); Gotse Delchev (1 daily except Tues & Thurs; 3hr); Melnik (3 daily; 30min); Petrich (5 daily; 30min); Samokov (1 daily; 3hr); Sofia (8 daily; 3hr).

Sofia *Avtogara Yug* to: Samokov (hourly; 1hr 15min); *Avtogara Ovcha Kupel* to: Bansko (12 daily; 3hr); Dupnitsa (every 30min; 1hr 30min); Gotse Delchev (8 daily; 4hr); Kyustendil (hourly; 2hr); Pernik (every 30min; 40min); *Tsentralna Avtogara* to: Blagoevgrad (hourly; 2hr); Sandanski (8 daily; 3hr).

International trains

Blagoevgrad to: Thessaloniki (1 daily; 7hr 45min).
Dupnitsa to: Thessaloniki (1 daily; 8hr 30min).
Sandanski to: Thessaloniki (1 daily; 6hr 30min).

International buses

Blagoevgrad to: Athens (1 daily; 14–16hr); Prilep (1 daily; 5hr);Thessaloniki (2–3 daily; 11–12hr).
Gotse Delchev to: Dhrama (3 weekly; 2hr).
Kyustendil to: Ohrid (July & Aug 1 daily; 9hr 40min); Skopje (1 daily; 3hr).

3

The Balkan Range and the Danubian Plain

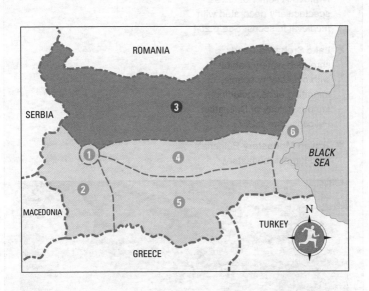

CHAPTER 3 # Highlights

✳ **Belogradchik** An amazing landscape of time-weathered limestone pillars and cliffs. See p.185

✳ **Ruse** The most central-European of Bulgaria's urban centres, combining Art Nouveau architecture and absorbing museums with an invigorating, big-city feel. See p.195

✳ **The Rock Churches of Ivanovo** A series of caves spectacularly decorated with medieval frescoes. See p.204

✳ **Lake Srebarna** Reed-shrouded watery habitat with over eighty species of migrating birds, including a famous colony of Dalmatian Pelicans. See p.207

✳ **Troyan Monastery** Bulgaria's third-largest monastery, famed for its vivid and often macabre frescoes by Zahari Zograf. See p.224

✳ **The Tsarevets, Veliko Tarnovo** The remains of this imposing fortress occupy a commanding spot above the River Yantra. See p.234

✳ **Church of the Nativity, Arbanasi** Though plain on the outside, this beautiful church is a riot of colour inside.

▲ Rock Church, Ivanovo

The Balkan Range and the Danubian Plain

The Balkan Range cuts right across the country, a forbidding swathe of rock known to the Bulgarians as the **Stara planina** – the "Old Mountains". In the seventh and eighth centuries, the Balkan Mountains were the birthplace of the Bulgarian nation-state. It was here, first at Pliska, and later at Preslav, that the Bulgar khans established and ruled over a feudal realm – known to historians as the "First Bulgarian Kingdom". Here too, after a period of Byzantine control, the Bulgarian nobility (the *bolyari*) proclaimed the "Second Kingdom" and established a new and magnificent capital at Veliko Tarnovo. During the Ottoman occupation, the villages and monasteries of the Stara planina helped to preserve Bulgarian traditions, preparing the ground for the re-emergence of native culture during the nineteenth-century National Revival.

Given the mountainous topography and the vagaries of the road and train network, **routes** through the Balkan Range are many and complex. The main northbound route from Sofia to the Danubian citadel town of **Vidin** provides access to a range of off-the-beaten-track destinations in the rural northwest, with settlements like **Vratsa**, **Berkovitsa**, **Chiprovtsi** and **Belogradchik** giving access to the stupendous – and very varied – mountainscapes of the western Balkan Range. Attractions are by no means limited to the great outdoors: Vratsa's historical museum contains the best collection of Thracian treasures in this part of Bulgaria, while Chiprovtsi is a carpet-weaving centre of long standing. For those heading for the central and eastern Balkan Range, east–west routes between Sofia and the sea skirt the highest peaks, and tend to be much quicker than north–south routes across the backbone of the Range. Hence many people approach the area by **train** from either the Sofia–Burgas line through the Valley of the Roses (see Chapter Four), or the Sofia–Varna line which arcs round the mountains to the north. The latter gives access to three potential urban bases from which to explore the area: **Pleven**, whose numerous museums commemorate a

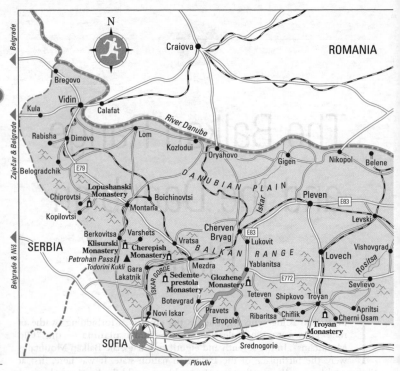

celebrated episode from the War of Liberation, when Bulgarian independence was wrested with the aid of Russian arms; the aforementioned medieval capital of **Veliko Tarnovo**, one of Bulgaria's most visually impressive cities and a convenient base for visiting a string of nearby medieval monasteries and an ensemble of craftworking towns; and **Shumen**, close to the First Kingdom capitals of Pliska and Preslav, as well as the enigmatic cliff-face sculpture of the **Madara Horseman**. However, it's in the countryside that the real rewards of travel in this region lie. There's an increasing range of accommodation in heritage villages like **Arbanasi** and in more traditional rural settlements such as **Cherni Osam** and **Apriltsi**, the latter two being important trailheads for hiking routes south into the mountains. A different kind of rural environment reigns in the rolling hills of the Ludogorie north of Shumen, an enticingly undeveloped area in which the **Thracian tomb at Sveshtari** and the Muslim holy site of **Demir Baba Tekke** – both near Isperih – are the most worthwhile destinations.

The Sofia–Varna route also skirts the **Danubian Plain** (*Dunavska ravnina*), stretching from the northern foothills of the Balkan Range down to the banks of the river, which forms a natural boundary with Romania. Despite the name, it's by no means uniformly flat, rather a rich and hilly agricultural area. The Central European ambience of **Ruse** and the nearby Rusenski Lom nature park – home to the **rock churches of Ivanovo** and medieval **citadel of Cherven** – are the likely highlights of any trip across the plain. Travelling from the Danube towards the Black Sea coast you'll pass through the relatively unknown

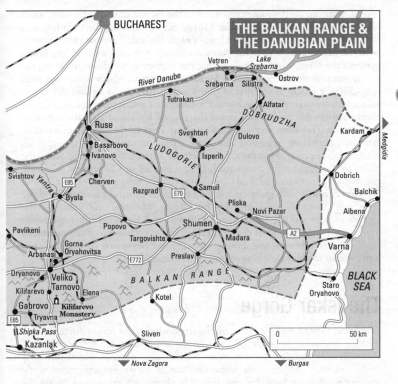

Dobrudzha, a rich, grain-producing plain which lies at the southernmost limits of the Eurasian Steppe. Although short on specific sights, its wide-open skies nevertheless exert a certain fascination.

The Western Balkan Range

Travelling between Sofia and Vidin takes you across the western spur of the **Balkan Mountains**, an area of forested highlands scattered with tortuous rock formations. Although not as high as the Rila or Pirin ranges to the south, the peaks of northwest Bulgaria present some of the country's most rewarding walking and rambling areas. Practical maps of the area are, however, thin on the ground, and serious hikers will have to pick up local knowledge from the Bulgarians staying at the region's mountain huts, or *hizhi*. The largely rural, undeveloped character of the northwest marks it out as an ideal destination for off-the-beaten-track travel, although tourist accommodation is limited to the odd hotel, a couple of monasteries, and the aforementioned *hizhi*. There are several routes across the mountains north of the capital: travelling by train, you'll pass through the magnificent **Iskar Gorge** before reaching the train junction at Mezdra, after which you'll head via **Vratsa** towards Vidin and the Danube, with the mountains to your left. Most road traffic from Sofia (including buses) bypasses the Iskar Gorge entirely, taking the motorway northeast to Botevgrad before turning northwest towards Mezdra. It's a route which is clogged with long-distance trucks at the best of times, so you may prefer to take the minor road north through the gorge instead: a slower, but much more scenic, ride. An alternative northbound route crosses the rugged terrain of Bulgaria's western borderlands. This takes you via the **Petrohan Pass** to the mountain resort of **Berkovitsa**, before rejoining the main road northwards at the region's administrative centre, **Montana**. From here it's a straightforward trip across the plains to Vidin, although minor roads head westward to **Chiprovtsi**, a historic rug-weaving centre backed by sumptuous mountain scenery, and **Belogradchik**, whose spectacular rock formations demand a detour. For those who want to explore the area **by bus**, Vratsa, Montana and Vidin are the gateway towns serving Berkovitsa, Chiprovtsi and Belogradchik respectively. You can also achieve a great deal **by train** if you're prepared to study timetables carefully, with a branch line serving Montana and Berkovitsa leaving the main Sofia–Vidin route at Boichinovtsi, north of Vratsa.

The Iskar Gorge

The **Iskar Gorge** is the most scenically impressive of the routes north. It's also within easy enough reach of Sofia to be a popular day-trip destination, although only the slow *patnicheski*, or "local" trains (most of which run early in the morning and late in the afternoon) stop at the smaller settlements along the gorge. Beware too that the gorge is almost totally devoid of tourist **accommodation** – Sofia and Vratsa are the most convenient places to stay. The most breathtaking stretches of the gorge, where the river is squeezed beneath soaring crags, lie between **Gara Lakatnik** and **Mezdra**; it's quite feasible to stop off at one of the halts between these places, indulge in a spot of walking, and pick up another train later in the day.

Things begin to get interesting just beyond the town of **Novi Iskar**, 10km north of the capital, where the gorge burrows northwards into the Balkan massif, gradually becoming narrower and deeper, the road and railway competing for space above the river. Strewn with boulders and scored by gullies, it's archetypal partisan country. There's a monument near **Batuliya** village commemorating the 24 partisans who clashed with local police in May 1944, and a train halt called *Tompsan* after **Major Frank Thompson** (brother of left-wing English historian and veteran CND campaigner E.P. Thompson) who fought and died with them. A member of the British mission sent to observe the effectiveness of Bulgaria's anti-fascist fighters (and evaluate their suitability to receive Allied aid), Thompson was fondly remembered by the postwar Bulgarian regime, and his uniform used to be exhibited in Sofia's long-defunct Museum of the Revolution.

Walks around Gara Lakatnik

GARA LAKATNIK (ГАРА ЛАКАТНИК; literally "Lakatnik Station") stands astride some promising Iskar Gorge walking trails, the most popular of which snake their way up the **Lakatnishki skali**, a precipitous knuckle of

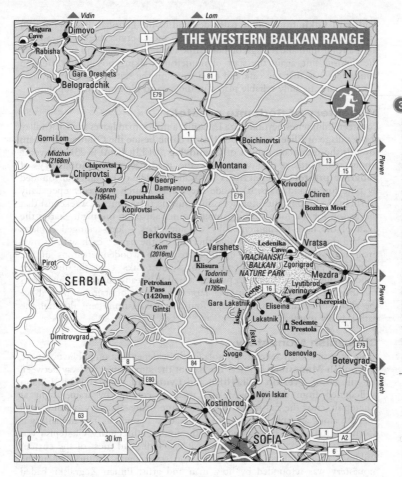

rock just north of the station on the west side of the valley. To get here, walk downhill from the station, cross the river, turn right onto the main road and walk straight on for about 1500m. Footpaths ascend the side of the cliff from beside a small (and sporadically open) roadside café-restaurant, working their way past two *dupki* or **caves** before emerging onto the grassy uplands at the top of the *skali*. **Temnata dupka** is the larger of the two caves here, extending for nearly 3km across four levels and including several lakes fed by a subterranean river. However, it's doubtful that anyone will be on hand to offer tours to casual visitors.

An alternative route into the hills is to head south along the main road from the station, turning right after about 1km onto a minor road which heads up beside the Proboinitsa stream. After about 1500m, beyond a small bridge, a path heads up the small side valley to the right, passing several waterfalls and pools before leading on to the meadowy plateau above the *skali*. Keeping to the main Proboinitsa valley road, on the other hand, will bring you after 10km to the *Proboinitsa hizha*, base camp for assaults on the 1785-metre-high

Todorini kukli, from where paths descend to the Petrohan Pass (see p.179) on the other side. South of Gara Lakatnik, a more serviceable road heads for the pastoral highland village of **Lakatnik** itself, 8km away, and beyond that, the *Trastena* hut, again the start of numerous walking possibilities. Bear in mind, however, that the café and food store on the station platform at Gara Lakatnik are the only reliable places in the area to pick up **food** supplies.

Monastery of Sedemte prestola

Fourteen kilometres beyond Gara Lakatnik, a minor road leaves the Iskar valley at the village of **Eliseina** (ЕЛИСЕИНА) to climb beside the Gabrovnitsa stream towards the mountain hamlet of **Osenovlag** (ОСЕНОВЛАГ), 23km beyond. About two-thirds of the way along, the road passes the **Monastery of Sedemte prestola** ("Seven Altars"), a walled huddle of buildings surrounded by pine forests and crags. It's inside the dainty church (officially open daily 10–11am & 3–4pm, but often accessible outside these times at weekends) that the reason for the monastery's name becomes apparent: the main altar at the head of the nave is augmented by six side altars – low-ceilinged cubicles reached through arched doors on either side of the nave – each with its own small iconostasis and candle-lighting area. The wooded environs of the monastery present the perfect place for a short hike: cross the footbridge opposite the monastery gate to pick up a trail that leads up into hay meadows and the pines beyond. In theory the *Tarstena hizha*, a mountain hut high above the village of Lakatnik to the west, is four hours' walk from here, although the path is badly marked.

Cherepish Monastery

More accessible than Sedemte prestola for those dependent on public transport, **Cherepish Monastery** lies near the halt of the same name, midway between the villages of **Zverino** (ЗВЕРИНО) and **Lyutibrod** (ЛЮТИБРОД). It's also well-signed from the Sofia–Mezdra road. If coming by train, alight at Cherepish, cross the rail tracks towards a large ochre seminary building, and bear left along an asphalt track until you reach a T-junction. The monastery is down the hill to the left. Founded in the fourteenth century, Cherepish was sacked by the Turks almost as soon as it was built, and most of the current buildings date (at least in part) from the seventeenth century, when the monastery was refounded by holy man and artist Pimen Zografski. Faded fragments of Pimen's work, notably his *Tree of Jesse*, can still be seen in the monastery **church**, although much better preserved are the **frescoes** completed by Tryavna master Papa Vitan in 1836. His frieze of early Christian warrior saints (including George, Demetrius and other martyrdom-hungry Roman soldiers) reveal the nineteenth-century Bulgarian Orthodox Church's taste for images of steely-eyed resistance and suffering. The intricate woodcarving of the iconostasis – with griffins and ears of corn exquisitely rendered by Debar masters – also stands out. There's a small **museum** outside the church displaying a few monastic vestments and icons, although opening times are unpredictable. Thousands of pilgrims descend on Cherepish for the Feast of the Assumption (*Golyama Bogoroditsa*) on August 15, when the monastery grounds are full of picnicking families.

Immediately northeast of Cherepish, the Iskar Gorge ends with a final geological flourish nicknamed *Ritlite* or the "Cart Rails": three parallel ribs of fissured rock up to 198m high which you'll see a few miles before the road and rail track enter **Mezdra** (МЕЗДРА). A useful transport hub at the junction of the Sofia–Vidin and Sofia–Pleven–Varna lines, Mezdra has little else to offer.

Vratsa

Twenty kilometres northwest of Mezdra, **VRATSA** (ВРАЦА) is one of Bulgaria's most dramatically situated towns, sprawling at the base of a grizzled wall of grey mountains known as the **Vrachanski balkan**. It's this stunning rocky hinterland, starting with the **Vratsata Gorge** cutting through the mountains just west of the town centre, which constitutes the main attraction for visitors, although good **ethnographic** and **historical museums** (the latter worth visiting for the Rogozen treasure alone; see p.176) provide a pair of worthwhile urban sights. Just south of Vratsa is **Mount Okolchitsa**, where **Hristo Botev**, one of the more romantic figures in Bulgaria's struggle for liberation (see p.286), met his death.

The Town

Vratsa's **train and bus stations** stand together just east of the centre, from where the pedestrianized ribbon of bul. Nikolai Voivodov curves its way northwest, passing a vast open-air market, to meet the main thoroughfare, **bulevard Hristo Botev**. Turn left here to reach a plaza built around the **Kula na meschiite**, a seventeenth-century fortified tower commissioned by local lords as much for reasons of prestige as defensibility. Shortly after this, ul. Targovska breaks off to the left, a sidestreet blessed with a picturesque collection of pastel-coloured nineteenth-century townhouses. At the end of the street stands a monument to **Sofronii Vrachanski**, local church leader and key figure in Bulgaria's nineteenth-century National Revival.

The Ethnographic Museum and complex

Immediately behind the Vrachanski statue is the **Ethnographic Museum** (Tues–Sun 9am–noon & 2–5pm; 5Lv, ticket also valid for Historical Museum), housed in a National Revival-period former girls' school, a fine half-timbered structure vaguely reminiscent of Tudor architecture. Inside is one of provincial Bulgaria's best collections of folk costumes and crafts, particularly strong on local marriage customs: exhibits include the enigmatic *svatbeni bardeta* or "wedding pitchers", twelve earthenware jugs hanging from a two-metre-long wooden pole. One entire floor is devoted to brass-band instruments, imported from central Europe by village ensembles at the beginning of the twentieth century, while outside, a pavilion displays nineteenth-century carriages and carts (and a particularly ornate bright-blue ceremonial sled) built by the local Orazov factory, Bulgaria's leading coachmakers.

Next door to the museum is an **ethnographic complex**: a clutch of National Revival-style houses grouped around the **Vaznesenska Church**, which itself contains a display of icons from the Vratsa area.

The Historical Museum and around

Back on bul. Hristo Botev, it's a short stroll south to another seventeenth-century tower, the **Kula na Kurt Pashovtsi**, and another modern plaza, pl. Hristo Botev, home to the **Historical Museum** (Tues–Sun 9am–noon & 3–7pm; 5Lv, ticket also valid for Ethnographic Museum), a gloomy concrete building which nevertheless holds an outstanding collection. Predictably, it harbours a "Botev Room" full of reminders of the warrior-poet's fateful march into Ottoman territory, but the real delights lie in the archeological section, which begins in the basement with stylish zig-zag-patterned Stone Age pots, and continues with Neolithic and Bronze Age idols, including a crowd of well-endowed fertility figures.

The display of **Thracian artefacts** upstairs kicks off with finds from *Mogilan-skata mogila*, a large tumulus unearthed in the town centre in 1965. Three tombs were found here, dating from the fourth century BC, the largest of which contained a chieftain accompanied by two young women, both of whom appear to have suffered violent deaths at the time of the burial – possibly consorts of the deceased who were required to accompany him into the afterlife (see box, "The Thracian Way of Death", p.295). Three horses, two of them harnessed to a ceremonial chariot, completed the burial party. The more elaborately dressed of the women sported a pair of exquisitely filigreed earrings and a **golden laurel wreath** of great delicacy, featuring eighty finely sculpted leaves grouped around little berries. An adjacent cabinet displays one of the chieftain's **shin-guards**, engraved with the portrait of a tattooed Thracian warrior, flanked by fantastical-looking birds holding serpents in their beaks.

Housed in a climate-controlled gallery on the top floor is the **Rogozen treasure** (*Rogozenskoto sakrovishte*), a hoard of more than a hundred silver vessels unearthed by a farmer in the village of Rogozen, near Vratsa, in 1983. This was in all probability a family treasure, accumulated by wealthy nobles of the Triballi tribe sometime between 500 and 350 BC. The scenes that decorate many of the vessels portray typically Thracian concerns: hunting trips involving a variety of wild beasts, and archetypal goddess figures – one in a chariot drawn by winged horses, another riding a golden-headed lioness.

For great views of the town centre, take the flight of steps at the southeastern end of the main square, which ascends to a statue of a cossack trumpeter, honouring the Tsarist army's liberation of Vratsa in the 1877–78 war. The yellow building next to the statue, known locally as the **Hizha** ("mountain hut"), holds a café and a small museum (daily 9am–5pm; free) with a words-and-pictures display documenting the history of tourism in the area.

▲ Part of the Rogozen treasure, Vratsa Historical Museum

Practicalities

The combined **tourist office and souvenir shop** near the ethnographic museum at ul. Dimitri Hadzhitoshin 6 (daily 9am–7pm; ☎0888 502 027, Ⓦwww.visit.vratza.com) sells maps and provides advice on local sights. As with most towns in this corner of Bulgaria, the choice of **accommodation** on offer is pretty modest. The hundred-room *Hemus*, on pl. Botev (☎092/661 649, Ⓦwww.hotelhemus.com; ❸), offers rather utilitarian en suites with TV, although its central-square location is a major plus. A step up in the comfort stakes is provided by the *Chaika*, 1km further west of the centre on the road through the Vratsata Gorge (☎092/622367, Ⓔchaika_hotel@avb.bg; ❸), where you can treat yourself to deep-carpeted en suites with modern furnishings, air conditioning and minibar – but there are only five rooms, so ring ahead.

Nicest of the town–centre **restaurants** is the *Pintata*, hidden away in a quiet garden courtyard just north of the main square on ul. Sofroniy Vrachanski 17 (closed Sun), offering a broad menu of Bulgarian meat staples alongside fresh-water fish. First-class food is also on offer at the restaurant of the *Chaika* hotel, which has a big outdoor terrace on the edge of an artificial boating lake, within sight of the Vratsata Gorge.

The numerous pavement **cafés** make central Vratsa an invigorating place to be on a warm summer's day. *Trakiiska Printsesa*, halfway down ul. Nikola Voyvodov, the pedestrianized street linking the town centre with the station, is the place to go for coffee, ice cream, cakes and pancakes; while *Caramel* on the main square gets its fair share of youthful drinkers at night. *Jazz Club*, a tightly packed basement bar just north of the pedestrianized area at Mito Orozov 4, is a cosy place for a drink and has live music once or twice a week.

The Vrachanski Balkan

Known as the Vrachanski Balkan or "Vratsa Balkans", the dramatic karst mountainscape west of Vratsa offers some of the most rewarding and accessible hiking in northwestern Bulgaria. The sheer limestone walls of the Vratsata Gorge are within easy walking distance of the town's main square, while other attractions – such as the Vratsa Ecotrail or the Ledenika Cave – are a long day's hike (or short car-ride) from town. Much of the region comes under the aegis of the Vrachanski Balkan Nature Park (Priroden Park Vrachanski balkan), which has signposted a handful of local trails and published a Vrachanski Balkan hiking map, which you can probably get from the tourist office in Vratsa (see above).

The Vratsata Gorge

The most easily accessible part of the Vrachanski Balkan is the **Vratsata Gorge**. To get here, walk west from Vratsa's town centre to pick up the asphalt road which heads between the stupendous limestone teeth that form the gorge. You only have to venture about 2km out of town to savour the gorge at its awesome best: sheer, ragged cliffs plunging towards grassy riverbanks where locals come to sunbathe, graze their goats or wash carpets. There are a couple of café-restaurants in the gorge bottom, one of which is attached to the *Alpiiski Dom*, a training base used by rock climbers who regard the Vratsata Gorge as the most challenging cliffscape in Bulgaria.

Vratsa Eco-trail

A little way beyond the *Alpiiski Dom*, the left-hand fork of the road heads for the timelessly rustic village of **Zgorigrad.** Continuing through Zgorigrad and following the road up the valley for 3km brings you to a plaque

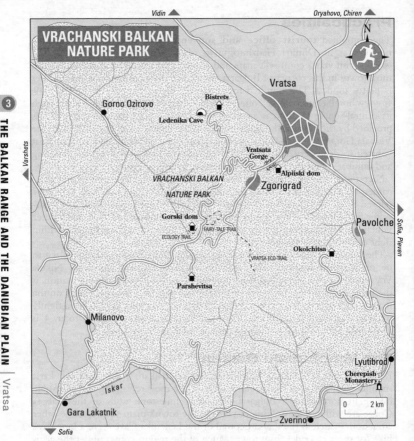

VRACHANSKI BALKAN
NATURE PARK

Vidin

Oryahovo, Chiren

N

Vratsa

Gorno Ozirovo

Bistrets

Ledenika Cave

Varshets

Vratsata
Gorge

Alpiiski dom

VRACHANSKI BALKAN
NATURE PARK

Zgorigrad

Gorski dom

FAIRY-TALE-TRAIL

Pavolche

ECOLOGY TRAIL

Okolchitsa

Sofia, Pleven

VRATSA ECO-TRAIL

Parshevitsa

Milanovo

Lyutibrod

Cherepish
Monastery

Iskar

0   2 km

Gara Lakatnik

Zverino

Sofia

commemorating those killed by a mudslide in 1966, when basins holding slurry from the local zinc mines burst their banks. From here a path heads uphill through a mixed forest of beech, walnut and conifers to the start of the **Vratsa Eco-trail**, a well-signed hiking route that ascends a gradually narrowing ravine. Involving steep stretches and rickety wooden bridges, it's an invigorating scramble, emerging after about two hours at the foot of the Borov kamak waterfall.

Ledenika Cave and around

Returning to the junction east of Zgorigrad and taking the right-hand fork takes you up a winding road that emerges onto a goat- and sheep-nibbled alpine plateau rich in wild flowers and herbs. It's an area of inestimable tranquillity and beauty, offering great views towards Mount Okolchitsa to the south. If you follow all the road's twists and turns from the valley bottom to the plateau, it's about 10km to the top – hikers are better off opting for the various paths and short cuts which dive through fields and forests on the way up. However you reach the top, you'll soon pick up an asphalt track heading north across the gently undulating plateau towards the **Ledenika cave**

(*Ledenichkata peshtera*; daily 9am–5pm; 2Lv if you arrive at the same time as a group and can tag along; 15Lv if you're on your own), 4km from the edge of the plateau and 16km from central Vratsa by road. Formed over a period of two million years by seeping rainwater, the cave gets its name from the icicles that form here during the winter (*leden* means icy). The 40-minute guided trek through the cave is icy underfoot and involves a tight squeeze through narrow passageways here and there, but takes you through a fascinating environment of stalagtites and strange rock formations. You may also catch sight of the **bat population** for which the cave is famed.

Returning from the cave and heading south instead of back towards Vratsa takes you along a ridge-top road, which brings you after 3km to the *Gorski dom* mountain hut. On either side of the hut are well-signalled starting points for two interlocking trails, the Fairy-Tale Path (*Pateka na prikazkite*) and the Ecology Path (*pateka na ekologiyata*). Both are easy-walking 2hr circuits which range across pine-covered hillsides before looping back towards the *Gorski dom*. The Fairy-Tale Path comes with the added attraction of wood-carved goblins and witches positioned along the route.

Bozhiya most

Located in rolling countryside some 15km northwest of Vratsa is one of northwestern Bulgaria's most captivating geological curiosities, **Bozhiya most** ("God's Bridge"). The "bridge" in question is basically a tunnel-like sequence of limestone arches about 25m wide and 20m high, which S-bends its way above a winding stream for about 100m. Although locals come to picnic or light fires by the waterside, the site is little visited by tourists and may not even be properly signposted.

To get there from Vratsa, take the main road to Oryahovo (ОРЯХОВО), turning left towards **Chiren** (ЧИРЕН) after 6km. Another 6km further on, an unmarked left fork leads out onto an open hillside, petering out just before a ruined medieval fortress. Just behind one of the fortress's corner towers, a balustraded path leads down to Bozhiya most.

The Petrohan Pass and Berkovitsa

The road that heads northwest from Sofia, route 81, skirts round the western edges of the Balkan Range on the way to the mountain health resort of **Berkovitsa**, passing over the 1446-metre **Petrohan Pass** on the way. Most Sofia–Berkovitsa buses travel this road – Berkovitsa itself is also well-served by bus from Montana (see p.182) in the northeast; and by train from Boichinovtsi, a junction on the Sofia–Vidin line.

After about 65km the road from Sofia begins to ascend the Petrohanski prohod or **PETROHAN** (ПЕТРОХАН) **PASS**, a wooded defile that sits between Mount Zelena Glava (literally "green-head") and the jagged **Todorini Kukli**. About 7km short of the summit you'll pass through the straggling village of **GINTSI** (ГИНЦИ), where locals line the roadside to sell the best **sheeps' milk yoghurt** (*ovche mlyako*) in Bulgaria, as well as local honey. The summit itself is marked by a scattering of truck-stop cafés and grill stalls, and a couple of signed trails leading east onto the slopes of Todorini Kukli. Deer, rabbits and roe deer reportedly abound here, and for the hardy souls who wish to stay, **accommodation** can be found at the *Motel Petrohan*, at the summit (☎07192/230 and 0888 325 172; ❷), with a mixture of primly decorated doubles, triples and quads, some with en-suite facilities. From the pass the road zigzags down into the valley of the northward-flowing Barziya, from where it's a short twenty-kilometre drive to Berkovitsa.

Berkovitsa and around

Surrounded by orchards, rest-homes and hills, **BERKOVITSA** (БЕРКОВИЦА) is a drab, dozy place that nowadays betrays little of its former status as a high-altitude health resort and favoured training camp of Bulgaria's wrestlers and weightlifters. Yet it's an important gateway to the highland area around Mount Kom, and contains a couple of worthwhile historic sights. In addition, Klisurski Monastery (not one of the major foundations, but charmingly situated nevertheless) is easily visited from here.

Berkovitsa's few remaining nineteenth-century attractions lie between the modern town square and the River Berkovska. Hidden in a lush rose garden on ul. Cherkovna, the sunken **Church of Sveta Bogoroditsa** (the Holy Virgin) features icons by Dimitar and Zahari Zograf, plus a carved wooden iconostasis on which angels blow trumpets and dragons attack lions. Three blocks east on ul. Berkovska reka is the **Ivan Vazov House-Museum** (officially Mon–Fri 8am–noon & 2–5pm; enquire at the Ethnographic Museum if shut; 2Lv), occupying the house where Bulgaria's "national writer" spent two years as the local magistrate. While the lower floor is taken up with the usual pictures and quotes, the upper floor features a fabulous Tryavna ceiling and the sitting rooms where Vazov and his landlord, Ivan Stoyanov, held court. Both are furnished in traditional Ottoman style, with comfy *minderi* (low bench-seats padded with cushions) surrounding a central *mangal* (lidded charcoal brazier). The **Ethnographic Museum**, just around the corner on ul. Poruchnik Grozhdanov (Mon–Fri 8am–noon & 2–5pm; 2Lv), harbours a

Vazov in Berkovitsa

In 1878 the infant state of Bulgaria was desperately short of trained personnel, and a reasonable level of secondary education was often enough to secure a top government job. Thus it was that the 27-year-old poet **Ivan Vazov** (see p.287) was appointed magistrate in Berkovitsa, despite his complete lack of legal experience. Faced by a local populace accustomed to the partial justice of the Ottoman courts, Vazov was soon out of his depth. On one occasion he had to sentence a dog to death for savaging a chicken – an attempt to appease townsfolk who would have otherwise taken the law into their own hands. As a result, Vazov's reputation was rubbished by a gleeful Sofia press, and the government was forced to offer him an inferior post in Vidin. Seething with humiliation, Vazov resigned and left the Principality of Bulgaria for Eastern Rumelia – where he made his name as a journalist and writer.

What's remembered most about Vazov's stay in Berkovitsa is his mildly scandalous affair with a 19-year-old Turkish girl called **Zihra**. Local legends maintain that Zihra entered Vazov's house rolled up in a carpet, or was lowered over the wall in a basket, in order to avoid the prying eyes of gossip-mongers, although the reality is more prosaic. Zihra was initially married to a local Turkish *bey* and drunkard who fell into a river and drowned during the Russo-Turkish War of 1877. The wife of Vazov's landlord and colleague, Ivan Stoyanov, took pity on Zihra, engaging her as Vazov's housekeeper, and she tended the tubercular young writer through frequent bouts of ill health. He fell for her in a big way, referring to her as his first and greatest love, but unfortunately Zihra – who clearly had a thing about men in uniform – left him for the dashing Bulgarian officer Hristo Chavov.

display of local arts and crafts, including a room devoted to the yellow- and green-splashed pottery that used to be a Berkovitsa trademark, but is nowadays made by just a few craftspeople.

Practicalities

Berkovitsa's **train station** is fifteen minutes' walk east of town at the end of ul. Atanas Kyorkchiev, while the **bus station** lies on the eastern fringe of the town centre on ul. Brezi. The **tourist information centre** on the main square (officially Mon–Fri 9am–5pm but don't count on it; ℡0953/88682) is an enthusiastic source of local information. The town's cosiest **accommodation** is at the *Starata kashta*, near the museums at ul.Vladimir Zaimov 6 (℡0888 986 158, ⓦwww.viptour-bg.com; ❸), a traditional-style house within a walled enclosure offering bright, simply furnished en suites. Well worth trying if you have your own transport are the *Old Bistrilitza Houses* (*Stari bistrilishki kashti*; ℡09528/559 and 0887 428 108, ⓦwww.bistrilitza.com; 3- or 4-bed house ❺–❻), 15km north of Berkovitsa in the village of Bistrilitsa, where you can rent self-catering apartments in a group of three restored nineteenth-century houses.

For **restaurants**, try the *Adashite*, which offers good grilled food and plenty of outdoor seating directly opposite the church; or the slightly superior *Krasteva kashta*, an atmospheric nineteenth-century house with walled garden on ul. Sheinovo.

There's a big Saturday-morning **market** next to the bus station, selling clothes, bric-à-brac and crafts.

The hills around Berkovitsa

You can explore the hilly terrain surrounding Berkovitsa by following any of the farm tracks leading out of town, although the most rewarding itineraries take you west towards the glowering ridge of the western Balkan Range. To get started, follow ul. Kiril i Metodii west from the main square, past the sports grounds to the end of town, until it splits into right and left forks. The right fork winds its way round the near side of the *Mramor* marble factory before heading into the wooded valley of the Berkovska Reka, finishing up at the popular picnic spot of **Haidushki vodopadi** ("*haidut* waterfalls"; 1hr 30min), a series of cataracts where the young river tumbles down a boulder-strewn valley floor. The left fork zigzags steeply up towards two **mountain huts** 12km away (confusingly, both are known as *Hizha Kom*), useful starting points for assaults on the 2016-metre summit of **Mount Kom** itself (about 2hr from either *hizha*). Attempting to walk from Berkovitsa to Kom summit and back in one day is somewhat ambitious (unless you drive as far as the *hizhi*), and most people stay at least one night in one of the *hizhi* – the northernmost one of the pair (℡0953/804026; ❷), nearest to Berkovitsa, is the newer and better equipped – where you can pick up advice on upward routes onto the mountain.

Downhill **skiing** on Mt Kom looks set to develop over the next few years. There is already one 1400m-long downhill run serviced by chairlift, and the construction of further lifts and pistes is on the cards.

Klisurski Monastery

Ten kilometres southeast of Berkovitsa, just off the road to the dowdy spa town of Varshets, **Klisurski Monastery** crouches beneath the pine-laden eastern slopes of Mount Todorini Kukli. Completely renovated in the 1990s, the monastery's whitewashed buildings surround a courtyard and a small church, but it's the atmosphere of rural peace – rather than any architectural or historical pedigree – that's the real attraction here. The woods outside the monastery walls are worthy of exploration, although the numerous new tracks bulldozed by forestry workers have made it difficult to pick out the hiking route to Todorini Kukli (and onwards to the *Hizha Petrohan* on the other side) that once existed here.

Three daily **buses** from Berkovitsa to Varshets go past the access road to the monastery, from where it's a pleasant 2.5km walk (bearing left after 200m) to the monastery itself. Catching a bus back can be more problematic: you'll have to enquire at Berkovitsa bus station about return services from Varshets and make your own calculations as to when you need to be back on the main road ready to flag one down. Walking back to Berkovitsa along the road (2hr) is always an option if you can avoid the summer heat.

Montana, Chiprovtsi and around

MONTANA (МОНТАНА) – largely rebuilt in concrete – is a brazenly modern town with a revolutionary tradition. Originally called Kutlovitsa, the town was known as Mihailovgrad for much of the postwar period in memory of local revolutionary Hristo Mihailov, a leader of the Communist uprising of **September 1923**. Socialist historians always overestimated the importance of the revolt – a short-lived farce that never enjoyed popular support – but the way in which the right-wing Tsankov regime put the uprising down, massacring thirty thousand Bulgarians within a couple of weeks, ensured that it was remembered as one of the most bloodily heroic episodes in Bulgarian history. After a local referendum in 1993 the town was renamed, ostensibly because a Roman settlement called Montana existed here in the first century AD.

Montana merits little more than a fleeting visit, to use its onward transport connections to more appealing destinations in the shadow of the mountains, such as Chiprovtsi and Lopushanski Monastery. If you've time to kill between buses – the terminal is diagonally opposite the train station – head through the fruit and veg market next to the bus station to reach a park where you'll find a small **History Museum** (Mon & Wed–Sat 8am–noon & 2–6pm), housing a Roman tombstone or two and sepia photographs of nineteenth-century town life. There are plenty of **cafés** a block south of the train and bus stations on Montana's flowerbedded, fountain-splashed main square, where you'll also find two **hotels**: the high-rise *Zhitomir*, at pl. Zheravitsa 1 (☎096/306176 and 305 582; ❷), which has comfortable but characterless en-suite rooms, some with TVs; and the slightly snazzier *Ogosta*, at ul. Peyu Yavorov 1 (☎096/306310 and 306309; ❹), which has the edge in terms of comfort and service.

Chiprovtsi

Regular buses make the 25-kilometre journey west from Montana to the carpet-making village of **CHIPROVTSI** (ЧИПРОВЦИ), nestling beneath the highest mountains of the northeast, their jagged peaks marking the frontier between Bulgaria and Serbia. Chiprovtsi was an important gold and silver mining centre in the late Middle Ages, and Saxon miners were encouraged to settle here, bringing new technology, Catholicism and blond-haired, blue-eyed bloodlines in their wake. Despite the Ottoman conquest, the village went on to become an important centre of Catholic learning, with local children sent to Italy for training in the priesthood. Seventeenth-century statesmen **Peter Bogdan Bakshev** (Catholic Archbishop of Sofia) and **Peter Parchevich** (Archbishop of Marcianopolis – modern-day Devnya) were born in Chiprovtsi and spent most of their lives trying to persuade the rulers of Europe to give the oppressed Balkan Slavs a helping hand. Neither lived to see the glorious failure that was the **Chiprovtsi Uprising of 1688**, when the Austrian army's successes against the Turks persuaded many in the Bulgarian northwest that the hour of their liberation was nigh. Unfortunately the advancing Austrians were slow in reaching Chiprovtsi, by which time the Ottomans had razed the village to the ground and scattered its inhabitants. It wasn't until 1737 that their descendants were allowed back.

Iron-ore mining was a mainstay of the local economy right up until the late 1990s, giving the place a gruff, working-class feel, and the village's proximity to what was until 1989 a closed border zone means that tourism is still very much in its infancy. However, Chiprovtsi is surrounded by some of the best scenery in the northwest, and for those prepared to rough it a bit, a short stay here has its rewards.

The Village

Chiprovtsi lacks the historic buildings that would put it firmly on the tourist route, and it's really the surrounding bowl of pastured hills that give the village its visual appeal. Buses stop beside a modern flagstoned square, from where a lane ascends to the right to the National Revival-era **Church of Vasnesenie Hristovo** ("the Resurrection"), a sunken structure that harbours valuable icons but is rarely open. The ruins of a Catholic basilica can be traced in the grass outside. The next-door **museum** (Mon–Fri 9am–5pm, Sat–Sun 10am–4pm; if closed, call at the museum administration office on the opposite side of the road; 2Lv) tells the story of the village in familiar words-and-pictures style. There are some delicately filigreed buckles, clasps and necklaces made by seventeenth-century silversmiths, and a

Chiprovtsi carpets

When the Ottoman authorities finally allowed Bulgarians to resettle in Chiprovtsi after the 1688 Uprising, carpet-weaving quickly became a key factor in the village's regeneration. Most Chiprovtsi carpets are **kilims** – double-sided woollen carpets hand-woven on a compact vertical loom known as a *stan*. They're famous for their colourful, stylized geometric designs, resembling more the paintings of Paul Klee than the products of some age-old peasant craft. Most characteristic of the Chiprovtsi designs is the *karakachka* ("black-eyed bride"), a geometrical form (usually red-on-black or black-on-red) that resembles a woman carrying two buckets of water. Although of eighteenth-century origin, it clearly harks back to pagan depictions of the earth mother. Other stylized forms favoured by successive generations of Chiprovtsi weavers include *lozite* ("vines"), *piletata* ("chickens"), and *saksiite* ("flowerpots") – each serving as a symbol of nature's bounty.

The craft has changed little over the last three and a half centuries, although the quality of the wool – nowadays coloured with chemical rather than vegetable dyes – may not be what it was. Certain kilim-related **customs** still prevail: it's common, for example, for a daughter or granddaughter to be swung hammock-style in a newly completed kilim, to ensure that she, too, will grow up to be a skilled weaver.

There are few official **retail outlets** in Chiprovtsi (most of the village's production goes straight to shops in Sofia), although staff at the museum or the tourist information office will be happy to tell you where the best local workshops are. Whether they have any surplus kilims for sale is really a matter of pot luck. The Chushkarcheto workshop in Chiprovtsi makes kilims for the Tchu kilim carpet shop in Sofia (ⓦwww .tchukilim.com; see p.111), which is probably the best place to go if your heart is set on an authentic souvenir.

whole room devoted to Chiprovtsi **carpets**, where museum staff are usually on hand to demonstrate the workings of a traditional *stan* or vertical loom. The museum has an **ethnographic section** (same times) just downhill behind the tourist information centre (see below), where brightly embroidered local costumes are on display.

Practicalities

The **tourist information centre** (Mon–Fri 9am–5pm, ⊜tic.chiprovci @gmail.com) on ul. Pavleto can help with accommodation and local hiking opportunities. Good-quality B&B **accommodation** is on offer at *Torlatsite*, at ul. Pavleto 31 (⊕0887 892 790 and 0885 358 592, ⊛www.torlacite.com; ❷), which has three en-suite doubles with pine floors and folksy furnishings, and one triple. The family makes and sells carpets, and can demonstrate weaving and dyeing techniques if you're interested. Just down the street, *Pavlova kashta* at ul. Pavleto 17 (⊕09554/2242, ⊜office_gl@videx.bg; ❷) has two doubles and a four-person apartment, all furnished with TV, laminated floors and locally produced carpets.

Both *Pavlova kashta* and *Torlatsite* serve hearty local **food**. In addition, *Gostopriemnitsa Kipro*, slightly uphill at Balkanska 46, offers good home-cooking in a wooden-benched interior hung with textiles; while the *Kiprovets* café-restaurant just below the museum serves up the full range of Bulgarian food and has an outdoor courtyard overlooking the river.

Chiprovski Monastery

Having destroyed Chiprovtsi in the wake of the 1688 Uprising, the Ottomans also burned down the nearby **Monastery of St John of Rila** as a token of their disapproval. About 6km east of town just off the Montana road (Montana–Chiprovtsi buses may drop you off here, but seem to have an aversion to picking passengers up), the most recent incarnation of the monastery dates mostly from the early nineteenth century, although a honey-brown tower at the rear of the walled compound still retains its medieval brickwork. The dainty monastery church is rich in vividly coloured icons, most the work of an itinerant master from Koprivshtitsa. The healing energies of the place are widely respected: prayers requesting cures for visitors' ailments are incanted daily at 10am, and the iconostasis is littered with votive offerings left by grateful believers – mostly cellophane-wrapped shirts and socks.

Lopushanski Monastery and around

Ten kilometres due east of Chiprovtsi is **Lopushanski Monastery**, situated in one of the area's prettiest valleys, the Dalgodelska ogosta. Lurking in a grove of pine trees just beyond the village of **Georgi–Damyanovo**, the monastery church is particularly noted for two icons by Samokov master Stanislav Dospevski, the *Virgin and Child* and *Christ Pantokrator* – both works showing an almost photographic realism. It's an easy place to get to on public transport, with four daily Montana–Kopilovtsi **buses** passing the monastery entrance.

For a taste of the mountains, it's worth continuing west of the monastery to the village of **Kopilovtsi** (КОПИЛОВЦИ), 17km upstream at the head of a northern branch of the valley. From here an asphalt road continues a further 5km to **Kopren** (КОПРЕН), site of a few privately owned holiday villas and a rest-home known as the Prophylactorium. Round the back of the Prophylactorium, a track leads to the start of one of the nicest short walks in Bulgaria, the **Kopren ecotrail** (ekopateka "Kopren"; 1hr 30min one way). The trail – steep, boulder-strewn and badly marked in parts – works its way up a wooded ravine, passing a waterfall and several smaller cataracts, before emerging onto a highland meadow ringed by looming peaks. The imposing 1964-metre **Mount Kopren**, marking the border with Serbia, is straight ahead.

Belogradchik and around

Lying in a bowl beneath the hills just east of the Serbian border, **BELOGRADCHIK** (БЕЛОГРАДЧИК; literally "small white town") gives its name to Bulgaria's most spectacular rock formations, the **Belogradchishkite skali**, which cover an area of ninety square kilometres to the west. The limestone rocks greatly impressed French traveller Adolph

▲ Rock formations at Belogradchik

Blanqui in 1841, who described them as an "undreamt landscape" rising in shades of scarlet, buff and grey, with shapes suggestive of "animals, ships or houses, Egyptian obelisks" and "enormous stalagmites".

The towering rocks nearest the town form a natural fortress whose defensive potential has been exploited since ancient times. Begun by the Romans, continued by the Bulgars during the eighth century, and completed by the Turks a millennium later, the castle at Belogradchik used to command the eastern approaches to the Belogradchik Pass. Although no longer in use, the pass was for centuries the main trade route linking the lower Danube with the settlements of Serbia's Morava Valley. In Ottoman times the citadel and its garrison served to intimidate and control the local populace, and hundreds of Bulgarian insurgents were held here after the failed uprising of 1850. One particularly unsavoury tale relates that many of the prisoners were slaughtered when the Ottomans forced them to pass through a low doorway, only to have their heads lopped off by swordsmen lurking on the other side.

The town and the citadel

Ruddy pinnacles of rock are immediately visible on arrival, glowering over the town from the hilltop around which Belogradchik is draped. The town's main street, lined with early-twentieth-century houses with spindly cast-iron balconies, winds up towards the summit, passing a small **art gallery** (Mon–Fri 9am–noon & 2–5pm) with modest exhibitions of local work. There's also a **museum** (same times; 2Lv), strong on local folklore, and the almost derelict **Huseyn Pasha mosque**, its former glory recalled in the delicate green-and-purple abstract swirls adorning the main entrance. Before long you'll reach the entrance of the **citadel** (*kaleto*; daily: June–Sept 9am–8pm; Oct–May 9am–5pm; 2Lv), with three levels of fortifications representing different periods of occupation. The lowest two levels are Ottoman: solid, utilitarian blocks of stone enlivened here and there by the occasional floral-patterned relief. A steep climb between two enormous pillars of rock leads to the highest and oldest level, occupied by the medieval Bulgarian stronghold. The rocks themselves provided the perfect fortified enclosure, and apart from the tumbledown wall of a medieval reservoir there's little man-made to see. Enjoy instead the marvellous panorama of surrounding hills.

The rocks and the Natural History Museum

The best way of approaching the rocks is to head downhill from Belogradchik's main T-junction (overlooked by the multi-storey *Hotel Belogradchishkite Skali*), where concrete steps descend into a dry valley overlooked by some of the more spectacular formations. A path continues along the valley floor for several kilometres, providing views of a whole series of extravagantly weathered pillars, most of which are associated with unlikely **stories**: the *Nun*, who was supposedly turned into stone for becoming pregnant by a knight; and the *Schoolgirl*, who was likewise afflicted after she was trapped between a hungry bear and a lusty dervish.

The number of rock eagles and other hunting birds frequenting the Belogradchik area is said to be on the increase, although the only ones you're likely to catch sight of are the stuffed versions housed in the village's small **Natural History Museum** (Mon–Fri 8am–noon & 2–5pm; ring the bell; 2Lv). To find it, take the road leading downhill from the *Hotel Belogradchishkite Skali* and look for a left turning into the woods.

Practicalities

Lying a good 12km west of the main E79 between Montana and Vidin, Belogradchik is easily reached by **bus** from the latter. The town's **bus station** lies immediately below the main street. Trains on the Sofia–Vidin line stop at Oreshets station 10km to the east, from where there are regular buses.

The **tourist information centre**, on the main street at pl. Vazrazhdane 1 (June–Sept: daily 9am–5pm, Oct–May: Mon–Fri 9am–5pm; ☎0936/3291, ⓦ www.tic.belogradchik.info), is a mine of information on regional attractions and can advise on accommodation. There's plenty of **B&B** accommodation in town, and the *Belogradchishkite Skali* **hotel** (currently undergoing renovation) will one day reopen as a comfy 4-star. The road heading downhill from the *Belogradchishkite Skali* leads after 1km to the *Madona* **campsite** (no relation to the *Madona* hotel; see below), a friendly, partly wooded place which also has a couple of bungalows (❶), but only one WC/shower on site.

The *mehana* of the *Madona* guesthouse (see below) is Belogradchik's one must-eat destination, offering local specialities such as *chorba ot kopriva* (nettle soup), *grohchano* (diced pork with garlic) and stuffed peppers, alongside mainstream Bulgarian fare – either in the cosy indoor dining room or on an outdoor terrace with views of the fortress. The **café-restaurant** of the *Turisticheski Dom*, a down-at-heel hotel behind the sports stadium, is rather basic in comparison, although the terrace has spectacular views looking out towards the rocks.

Guesthouses and B&Bs

Kashta na gosti Genchevi ul. Vasil Levski 8 ☎0936/5024 and 0899 529 265, ⓔmariusa_todorova@abv.bg. Simply decorated en-suite doubles and a four-person apartment, in a family house. Breakfast available on request. ❷

Madona ul. Hristo Botev 26 ☎0936/5546 and 0898 457 198, ⓦwww .madonainn-bg.com. Hidden away in residential streets uphill to the south, this is another family-run concern with minuscule but cosy en suites in the main building, and slightly bigger en suites in

an adjoining annexe. Breakfast on an attractive garden terrace. ❸

Pri Sasho ul. Poruchnik Dvoryanov 27 ☎0936/3558 and 0888 842 897, ⓔsacho@dir.bg. Simple doubles above a food shop at the citadel end of town, with use of a kitchen. ❶

Skalite ul. Hadzhi Dimitar 1 ☎0936/4002 and 0898 733 818. ⓦwww.valentine.bat-bel.com. Smart, medium-sized guesthouse above the bus station, offering doubles and a couple of triples, each boasting pine furnishings and small TVs. ❷

The Magura Cave

Twenty-five kilometres northwest of Belogradchik lies the village of **RABISHA** (РАБИША), a couple of kilometres short of the spectacular **Magura Cave** (ⓦwww.magura.hit.bg; daily tours usually at 11am, 1pm and 3pm but call Belogradchik tourist information office to confirm; 4Lv per person if you join a group; 35Lv if you're on your own). As early as 2700 BC, the cave was occupied by hunters, traces of whom are now displayed in a small museum (entry included in the cave ticket) near the entrance. The cave is a popular nesting ground for bats – although theoretically inactive during the winter, they are often disturbed by the cave's lighting system and can be seen fluttering around.

The cave itself is accessed by a steep (and sometimes slippery) staircase, and explorable along a 2km trail through the chambers. The whole tour takes just over one hour, beginning with the so-called Triumphal Hall, thought to have been occupied from 3200 to 1800 BC. The cavern is so large that Neolithic inhabitants actually built individual wicker huts on the cave floor. Off to the left is the Gallery of Drawings, decorated with 4500-year-old rock paintings executed in bat-droppings, which depict giraffe-like animals, hunting scenes and fertility rites. The female figures tend to be bigger than the male figures, suggesting that women enjoyed superior status in the cave society of the time. Other chambers include the Oriental Town, where a forest of slender stalagmites resemble minarets; and the Hall of the Fallen Pine, named after a stalagmite 11m long and 6m wide, which is said to be the largest example ever discovered in Bulgaria.

The Danubian Plain

Stretching from the northern slopes of the Balkan Range to the Danube, the **Danubian Plain** (*Dunavska ravnina*) is a more undulating region than its name would suggest, an agriculturally rich area crowded with maize fields, sunflowers and vineyards. The river itself forms Bulgaria's frontier with its northern neighbour Romania, before wheeling away beyond Silistra to join the Black Sea far to the north. The shorelines possess different characters: the Bulgarian side is buttressed by steep bluffs and tabletop plateaus, while the opposite bank is low-lying and riven by shallow lakes called *baltas*, which merge first with marshes, then the Wallachian plain. Between the two lies a shoal of wooded islands that provide a haven for local birdlife, a population sustained by the river's rich stocks of fish.

In ancient times the Danube was one of Europe's most important **frontiers**, a natural barrier separating the riches of southern Europe from the barbarian tribes to the north. The Macedonian kings tried to make the Danube the northern boundary of their domains – Alexander the Great campaigned against the Getae here in 335 BC – but their hold on the area was always superficial. The **Romans** were the first to turn the Danube into a permanent, fortified line of defence, building a series of garrison towns and administrative centres along its length. By the second century AD, thriving civilian towns such as Ratiaria, Oescus, Novae and Durostorum were beginning to emerge alongside the armed camps.

The Danube regained its strategic importance in the Middle Ages, when Bulgarian Tsars built stout fortresses at **Vidin** and Nikopol to defend their realm against Russians, Tatars, Hungarians and other interlopers. Their Ottoman successors were great fortress builders, erecting the eighteenth-century citadels of Ruse and **Silistra** in an attempt to strengthen the Danube frontier against the advance of Russian power.

During the nineteenth century, increased river transport brought the goods and culture of Central Europe down the valley, turning the towns along its banks into cosmopolitan outposts. European fashions and styles often arrived here first before being transmitted to the rest of Bulgaria, turning towns such as Svishtov and Ruse into unlikely centres of elegance and sophistication. With the development of the railways, however, the river trade went into decline, and nowadays most of Bulgaria's Danubian towns are quiet, provincial places, focusing their attention not on the river itself, but on the bigger cities inland. The only real exception is **Ruse** – an important business and cultural centre that commands the major road and train route to Bucharest and the north. Ruse is a good base from which to visit the valley of the **Rusenski Lom**, a hauntingly beautiful spot which harbours important medieval ruins – the most famous being the **rock churches of Ivanovo** – and several lesser sights along the river, such as the small port of **Svishtov** to the west. Elsewhere along the river, however, public transport is meagre, and tourist attractions few and far between. Heading along the riverbank from Vidin to Ruse is only practical if you have a car: most bus links connect the Danubian towns with places inland rather than with each other, and reliable accommodation is practically nonexistent.

Public transport is much better if you're travelling eastwards from Ruse into the **Dobrudzha**, a vast expanse of grain-producing land that extends all the way from the Danube to the Black Sea. The main attractions here are the bird-rich **Srebarna nature reserve** and the laid-back riverside town of Silistra.

Vidin

"One of those marvellous cities of eastern fairytale which, secure behind their fortress walls, is decorated with spires and cupolas and minarets piled one upon another in a fantastic medley of creeds, ages and styles." So **VIDIN** (ВИДИН) was rather fancifully described by Lovett Edwards in his book *Danube Stream* in 1941. Nowadays you'll find that the truth is more prosaic: although the great sweep of the fortress walls still dominates much of the riverfront, the spires and minarets characteristic of Edwards' day have largely gone, to be replaced by utilitarian housing projects. Ample reason for visiting is, however, still provided by the showpiece medieval **citadel of Baba Vida**, presiding over luscious riverside parklands on the northern edge of town.

Some history

Vidin's potential as a fortress was exploited by successive waves of Celts, Romans and Byzantines, but it was under the Bulgarian tsars and their Ottoman conquerors that the most frenzied castle building took place. Vidin's relative isolation from major power centres like Tarnovo and Constantinople made the place a breeding ground for semi-independent local kinglets, and the citadel they built was much coveted by neighbouring powers. In the fourteenth century it was the power base of **Mihail Shishman**, whom the nobles elected tsar rather than see Vidin secede from Bulgaria, and after 1371 it was the capital of an independent kingdom ruled by Mihail's grand-nephew, **Ivan Stratsimir**. Vidin fought a rearguard action against Ottoman expansion in the Balkans, grudgingly accepting Turkish suzerainty in the 1390s – only to throw it off again as soon as help emerged from the West in the shape of the Crusade of 1396. The city was recaptured by Sultan Bayezid's army two years later.

In the late eighteenth century Vidin was the capital of **Osman Pazvantoglu**, a local ruler who rebelled against Sultan Selim III in 1794. Energetic, despotic and fond of inventing tortures, Pazvantoglu pillaged as far afield as Sofia in defiance of the Sultan, and strengthened Vidin's fortifications with the assistance of French engineers sent by Napoleon, who envisaged him as a potential lever for toppling the Ottoman Empire.

These days Vidin is comparatively quiet, but with the Romanian town of Calafat just across the river, and the Serbian border 30km northwest, the town

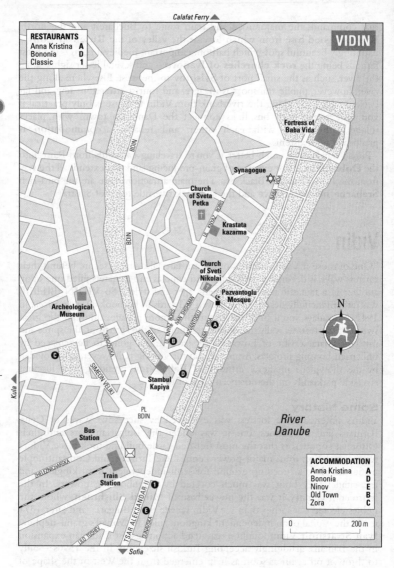

Calafat Ferry ▲

RESTAURANTS
Anna Kristina   **A**
Bononia   **D**
Classic   **1**

VIDIN

Fortress of Baba Vida

Synagogue

Church of Sveta Petka

Krastata kazarma

Church of Sveti Nikolai

Pazvantoglu Mosque

Archeological Museum

Stambul Kapiya

PL. BDIN

River Danube

Bus Station

Train Station

ACCOMMODATION
Anna Kristina   **A**
Bononia   **D**
Ninov   **E**
Old Town   **B**
Zora   **C**

0   200 m

▼ Sofia

◄ Kula

still retains a little of its former cosmopolitan feel. A planned road bridge over the Danube to Calafat (to be completed in 2010–11) promises to bring more vibrancy to Vidin in the future.

Arrival and accommodation

Most of the town's amenities lie in the modern centre a short distance from the main square: both **bus** and **train** stations are a couple of blocks to the west. There's a good choice of centrally located accommodation, although rooms fill up fast at weekends, so it's wise to reserve.

Hotels

Anna Kristina ul. Baba Vida 2 ☏ 094/606 038, ⓦ www.annakristinahotel.com. Newish four-star occupying a nineteenth-century villa right by the riverside park, offering business-class en suites with TV, minibar and a/c. Choose the attic-ceilinged top-floor rooms if you want a bit of atmosphere. The outdoor pool (open to the public) is a lively place in summer. ❹

Bononia ul. Bdin 2 ☏ 094/606031, ⓦ www .hotelbononia.net. Servicable two-star dating from the Communist period, offering plainly decorated rooms with TV and a few rough edges. The city-centre, riverside location is the major selling point. ❸

Ninov ul. Dunavska 28 ☏ 094/600402 and 600475, ⓦ hotel-ninov.vidin.net. Medium-sized hotel near the riverfront with comfortable en-suite doubles with TV and a/c, and a handful of two- to three-person apartments with workdesk, lounge and bathtubs. ❹

Old Town ul. Knyaz Boris I 2 ☏ 094/600 023, ⓦ www.oldtownhotel.dir.bg. Family-run hotel in a superbly central position, with eight cosy en suites (each with TV and desk), and a snug breakfast room. ❹

Zora ul. Naicho Tsanov 3A ☏ 094/600290 and 606330, ⓦ www.hotelzora.hit.bg. Upmarket B&B offering soothingly furnished rooms with reasonably sized bathrooms; it also has a couple of bright, tiled-floor apartments sleeping three or four. ❸

The Town

Vidin's modern heart stands at the southern end of the fortified old town, based around the flagstoned central square, **ploshtad Bdin**. The square is dominated by customary examples of socialist urban planning, from the high-rise-style former headquarters of the Communist Party to the equally brutal modernism of the *obshtinski savet*, or town council building, next door. Somewhat less imposing are the structures lining the main downtown streets, which radiate outwards from here – drab lumps of ochre and grey that reveal little of the town's former glory.

The only real interest in modern Vidin is the **Archeological Museum** (Tues–Sat 9am–noon & 1.30–5.30pm; 3Lv), housed in a much-rebuilt Ottoman *konak* west of the main square at the end of ul. Targovska. The display begins with prehistoric bone and stone tools found in the Mirizlivka cave near the village of Oreshets, but most space is devoted to Roman-period finds from the regional centre of Ratiaria, founded by Trajan in about 107 AD near the modern village of Archar, 25km southeast of Vidin. A floor mosaic on which a stag is chased by a wild cat, and a fine collection of small-scale sculpture, reveal something of the sophistication and comfort of life in this otherwise rather provincial outpost. An adjoining section of the museum deals with the National Revival period, with particular reference to the local peasant uprising of 1850, centred on the towns of Gradets and Belogradchik.

The old town

On the northern side of the main square, the borders of old Vidin are marked by the Stambul Kapiya or Istanbul Gate, a stocky portal in the Turkish style. Beyond it lies a pleasant early-twentieth-century residential district with an extensive riverside park to the east. On the edge of the park stands the early nineteenth-century **Osman Pazvantoglu mosque**, the only surviving mosque in the city – most of the others were knocked down in the 1970s and 1980s. Extensively renovated in 2003, it's a graceful and alluring building, and is frequently open to visitors during the day (Friday is usually the best time to visit). Instead of the customary Islamic crescent, both the portal and the minaret bear the heart-shaped personal emblem of Osman Pazvantoglu – a sign of his rejection of Ottoman symbols. If asked, attendants will open up Pazvantoglu's *kitabhane* or Koranic library, a squat building just outside the

Osman Pazvantoglu and the Kardzhali

By the early 1790s Ottoman-ruled northern Bulgaria was sliding slowly into chaos, with provincial Ottoman governors increasingly in revolt against a reforming sultan – Selim III – whom they saw as a threat to their traditional powers. The provincial governors had begun to staff their private armies with a new class of dispossessed freebooters, mostly former imperial soldiers, known as **Kardzhali**, who roamed the countryside in search of food and plunder, terrorizing Christian villages.

Foremost among the provincial power barons was **Osman Pazvantoglu**, born in Vidin in around 1758, the son of a local janissary executed in 1788 for leading a revolt. Osman himself was also sentenced to death for participating in the revolt, but managed to escape, re-emerging in the 1790s to harness the discontent whipped up by his father. Ruler of Vidin from 1794 onwards, Pazvantoglu attracted *Kardzhali* from all over northern Bulgaria, not least because the town was seen as a safe zone where they could store their booty and sell it – with Pazvantoglu taking a percentage of the proceeds. The Ottoman sultan laid **siege** to Vidin in 1795 and again in the winter of 1797–8, only to see the bulk of his troops melt away and join Pazvantoglu's rebels. Pazvantoglu was popular with Islamic traditionalists who saw him as a bulwark against a Westernizing sultan, but he also took care to win the support of local Christians, cutting taxes and feudal impositions, and promising to treat all subjects as equals whatever their faith. For a time Pazvantoglu seemed capable of overthrowing the sultan and installing himself as ruler in Constantinople, but somehow failed to press home the advantage. Ultimately he was kept in check by the Russians, who feared that the autocratic structure of society in Eastern Europe might suffer general collapse if truculent upstarts like Pazvantoglu were seen to get their way.

The **Serbian Uprising of 1804** spelled the end for Pazvantoglu. Many of his Bulgarian subjects were tempted to join their Serb neighbours, thus destroying the Muslim–Christian alliance that had thus far prevailed in Pazvantoglu's territory. January 1806 saw Pazvantoglu launch a vicious **pogrom** against Bulgarian priests and civil leaders in Vidin, fearful that they were about to launch a revolt of their own. Frequent outbreaks of plague gnawed away at the city's self-confidence, and Vidin was in steep decline by the time of Pazvantoglu's own death in February 1807. His uncharismatic successor, Idris Molla, was unable to prevent the gradual reimposition of Ottoman control.

mosque – nowadays devoid of books, it is nevertheless a wonderfully intimate and graceful domed space.

Immediately opposite the mosque stands the modern **Church of Sveti Nikolai**, inside which Cyril, Methodius and other saints are rendered in colourful realist frescoes, rather like illustrations in a children's encyclopedia. Hidden around the back is the much smaller – and easily missed – **Church of Sveti Panteleimon**, an austere twelfth-century basilica made from heavy stone.

From Sveti Nikolai, ul. Baba Vida hugs the park's western flank, leading towards the shell of a derelict **synagogue**. Vidin was an important centre of Jewish culture until the late 1940s, when most local Jews emigrated to Palestine. The synagogue was used as a warehouse before ambitious planners began turning it into a concert venue in the 1980s. Unfortunately the money ran out, leaving the synagogue in the skeletal form that greets visitors today. Parallel to Baba Vida to the west is ul. Knyaz Boris I, site of Pazvantoglu's **Krastata Kazarma** (the "cross-shaped barracks"), now an ethnographic **museum** (usually Mon–Fri 9–11.30am & 2–5pm; ring the bell and hope that a curator is around; 2Lv). It's an enormously colourful collection, comprising local costumes, pottery and carnival masks. Across the road, stranded behind railings in a patch of wasteland between two school playgrounds, is the seventeenth-century **Church of Sveta Petka**, an unassuming, sunken structure, traces of bright blue on the exterior giving some idea of its former appearance.

From the northern end of the riverside park, stone ramparts run alongside the shoreline for over a kilometre, largely overgrown and deserted, eventually curving inland to protect the **Fortress of Baba Vida** (Mon–Fri 8.30am–5pm, Sat & Sun 10am–5pm; 3Lv). Surrounded by huge walls and a deep, dried-out moat, the fortress dates from the thirteenth century, although the brutal, blockhouse appearance of its turrets and towers owes more to the continuous improvements carried out by the Turks and the Habsburgs, who briefly occupied the town in the sixteenth century. Once inside, you can scramble around an extensive network of courtyards and ramparts, and survey the Danube from gun positions overlooking the river. Further stretches of wall extend well to the west of the citadel, and crumbling gates stand surreally amid the modern housing estates.

Eating and drinking

Daytime drinking and snacking is best in the **cafés** along ul. Targovska, or in the riverside park, where there are several open-air establishments. The **restaurant** of the *Ana Kristina* hotel serves up quality meat and freshwater fish (augmented by a huge menu of *rakiyas*) on an outdoor terrace squeezed between the hotel swimming pool and the riverside gardens. The *Hotel Bononia*'s restaurant is a good place for Balkan grilled food and frequently has live music, while *Classic*, on Dunavska, is a brash pizzeria with a river-facing terrace and a satisfying range of big salads.

Svishtov

East of Vidin, a succession of bland and disappointing provincial towns line the banks of the Danube, and it's only at **SVISHTOV** (СВИЩОВ; 260km east of Vidin and 90km west of Ruse) that there's any reason to stop. A long-established port and crafts town that grew up just west of the former Roman city of Novae, Svishtov today preserves a smattering of nineteenth-century architecture and a couple of worthwhile museums. The town controlled an important Danube ferry crossing point before the building of the bridge at Ruse downstream, and witnessed both the arrival of the Russian liberators in 1877 and the invasion of Romania by German and Bulgarian forces in 1916.

Served by bus from Ruse and Veliko Tarnovo (but not from Vidin), Svishtov is also at the northern end of a little-used rail line that starts in Troyan (see p.223)

Crossing into Romania

Roughly every hour a **car ferry service** (*feribot*; winter 6am–midnight; summer 24hr) shuttles between Vidin's grandiosely named International Dock, 5km north of town, and the port of Calafat on the Romanian side of the River Danube. Fares are around 7Lv for pedestrians, 25Lv per car. Bus #1 runs from outside Vidin train station to the ferry dock, but timings are irregular. A taxi from the station to the dock will set you back about 10Lv, more if coming in the opposite direction.

EU, US and Canadian citizens can enter Romania without a **visa**; other nationals should contact the Romanian embassy in their home country before setting out. Trains run from Calafat on to Craiova and Bucharest.

in the central Balkan Range, before passing through Lovech (see p.220), and Levski, a junction on the main Sofia–Varna line.

The Town

Svishtov's **bus** and **train** terminals both lie in a drab riverside area just below the bluff upon which the town is built. Roads from here curl up and converge on a main square which marks the midpoint of the principal downtown thoroughfare, ul. Tsar Osvoboditel. A short distance downhill from the square you'll come across a small plaza grouped around the nineteenth-century **Preobrazhenie** (Transfiguration) **Church**, which harbours a fine Tryavna iconostasis, topped with the customary bestiary of dragons and mythical birds.

Just beyond lies the attention-grabbing, pink-painted former **house of Aleko Konstantinov** (Mon–Fri 8am–noon & 1–5pm; 2Lv), a satirist remembered for creating *Bay Ganyu*, an itinerant pedlar of rose oil and rugs who remains one of the most popular characters in Bulgarian fiction. The house itself, built by Konstantinov's merchant father in 1861 (and used as a stopover by the invading Tsar Alexander II in 1877), was one of the first Western-style houses built in Svishtov, and is crammed with imported Viennese furniture alongside brightly coloured Bulgarian rugs. The most striking exhibit is a jar containing Aleko Konstantinov's pickled heart – the writer was killed by mistake in 1897 by assassins aiming for the lawyer with whom he was travelling.

The backstreets on either side of Konstantinov's house hold a couple more museum attractions, starting with the musty **Ethnographic Museum** (same times; 2Lv) at ul. Georgi Vladikin 14, with some wonderful folk costumes and an extensive collection of *pafti*, the metal waist buckles which form an essential part of traditional Bulgarian dress. Round the corner on ul. Dimitar Shishmanov, a half-timbered nineteenth-century house is the site of a modest **Archeological Exhibition** (same times; ask at the Aleko Konstantinov house for access; 2Lv), designed to showcase the finds excavated at nearby Novae (see below). There's not much here, to be honest, although it's worth pausing to admire the collection of third-century-AD clay and bone statuettes depicting human beings in a variety of erotic poses, and an impressive marble head of Caracalla – a rare portrait of the little-sculpted Roman emperor (211–217 AD).

Returning to the main square and heading up ul. Tsar Osvoboditel for about 500m brings you to the **Church of Sveta Troitsa** (Holy Trinity), arguably the crowning achievement of National Revival architect Kolyo Ficheto (see p.245). The curving lines of the roof, said to be a conscious imitation of the waves of the River Danube, were designed to offset the angular, almost neo-Gothic charms of a pinnacled octagonal bell tower, which was sadly destroyed by an earthquake in 1977, and is currently being rebuilt.

Novae

Starting from the Church of Sveta Troitsa, it's a four-kilometre walk (or taxi ride) east along the main Ruse road to the site of **Novae**, a first-century Roman military camp which subsequently became an important civilian centre and later the capital of the Goths – until it was abandoned some time in the seventh century. Housed in a modern pavilion beside the road, the **Novae Tourist Centre** (Mon–Fri 11am–6pm; 2Lv) displays ceramics and weaponry found at the site, alongside travelling exhibitions on more general historical themes. The site itself straddles both sides of the main road, with the main legionary headquarters and barrack buildings lying over to the south side – where you can also see the remains of a fifth-century basilica. Over on the north side, where the ruins lead right down to the banks of the Danube, you can look out across the remains of the Roman legionary hospital. You can clearly make out the central courtyard, and the separate wards, each designed to hold three patients, grouped around it.

Practicalities

Should you decide **to stay** in Svishtov, the comfiest place in town is the central *Hotel Voenen Klub*, at ul. Aleko Konstantinov 2 (☏0631/64274; ❸), which offers smart en suites with laminated floors, warm furnishings and air conditioning. *Kaleto*, on a bluff overlooking the Danube at ul. Toma Panteleev 2 (☏0631/25417 and 23247; ❷), has a mixed bag of en suites, some with modern furnishings, others slightly careworn – but the hotel's café terrace has a great view of the river. Just south of the centre on the Veliko Tarnovo road, *Stopanska Akademiya Korpus Yug*, at ul. Patriarh Evtimiy 105 (☏0631/60882, ✉korpus_iug@uni-svishtov.bg; ❷), is a student dormitory which also functions as a hotel, with neat, bright en suites with TV. Two good **restaurants** serving traditional Bulgarian food at moderate prices are the *Svishtov*, housed in the same building as the Archeological Exhibition (see opposite) and boasting an attractively shaded courtyard; and the *Bay Ganyu*, just off the main street at ul. Dragan Tsankov 12, which is decorated with traditional textiles and has an attractive walled garden.

Ruse and around

"Everything I experienced later in life had already happened in **RUSE**" (РУСЕ), wrote Elias Canetti in the autobiographical *Tongue Set Free*, remembering his childhood home as an invigorating city of different races and creeds, whose cosmopolitan culture placed it firmly in the orbit of Central Europe. Although the ethnic mix of Canetti's day has long since disappeared, travellers continue to be surprised by Ruse's Austrianate elegance. Despite being blighted by the customary concrete-and-steel overlay provided by Bulgaria's postwar urban planners, it's still a city of peaceful residential streets, where Art Nouveau-inspired ornamentation drips from delicate houses. Ruse bears a similarity to Bulgaria's other Danubian towns in lacking a riverfront of any great beauty, but a scattering of historic sights and the relaxed feel of its downtown streets more than compensate. An important cultural centre with an animated café life, the city also plays host to one of the liveliest evening *korsos* in Bulgaria. In addition, Ruse makes a good base for exploring the nearby **Rusenski Lom** national park, home to the dramatic **Rock Churches of Ivanovo** and the ruined city of **Cherven**.

Some history

Ruse was an important naval base under both the Romans and Byzantines, and subsequently served as the headquarters of the Ottoman army's Danube fleet. The town took off as a trade and business centre under the enlightened governorship of **Midhat Pasha** (see box, p.198), who provided the town with schools, hospitals, factories and, most importantly, the British-financed Ruse–Varna rail line. Until the construction of the more direct Belgrade–Sofia–Istanbul line in the 1880s, travellers flooded through Ruse on their way from Central Europe to Constantinople.

Trade received a further boost after the Liberation, and for many years Ruse had more inhabitants, consulates, factories, hotels and banks than Sofia. The city's economic and cultural wealth owed a lot to the merchant families – including Germans, Greeks and Armenians – who settled here. Most numerous,

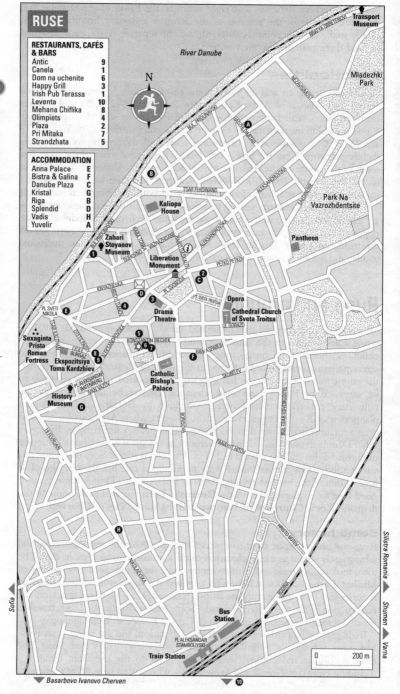

RUSE

RESTAURANTS, CAFÉS & BARS

Antic	9
Canela	1
Dom na uchenite	6
Happy Grill	3
Irish Pub Terassa	1
Leventa	10
Mehana Chiflika	8
Olimpiets	4
Plaza	2
Pri Mitaka	7
Strandzhata	5

ACCOMMODATION

Anna Palace	E
Bistra & Galina	F
Danube Plaza	C
Kristal	G
Riga	B
Splendid	D
Vadis	H
Yuvelir	A

however, were the **Sephardic Jews** (of whom Elias Canetti was one, born here in 1905), descendants of those Jews given refuge in the Ottoman Empire after their expulsion from Spain in 1492.

Ruse lost much of its cosmopolitan character during the Communist period, but its citizens played an important part in the democratizing tide of the late 1980s, when locals began to protest against the ecological damage caused by the **chemical plant** just across the river in Romanian Giurgiu. Chlorine gas emissions wafting over the river caused an upsurge in respiratory complaints – something that Bulgaria's Communist rulers were keen to keep quiet. The Committee for the Protection of Ruse, formed in 1988, was one of the first non-Party organizations to be created in Bulgaria, and provided the spur for reformist campaigners elsewhere. With the Giurgiu plant now closed, Ruse's air is relatively clean once more.

Ruse's post-Communist fate has mirrored that of the country as a whole, with economic decline and social decay coexisting alongside an upsurge of private enterprise, and renewed cultural contacts with the outside world. Most positively, the EU-funded renovation of many key buildings has restored to the city much of its *belle-époque* sheen.

Arrival, information and accommodation

Ruse's **train** and **bus** stations stand at the head of ul. Borisova, 2km south of the centre. The train station is a particularly gloomy and unwelcoming place, patrolled by crooked cab drivers and other over-friendly parasites. **Trolleybuses** #1, #11, #12 and #18 head up ul. Borisova to the main square, **ploshtad Svoboda**. Just off the square, the Ruse **tourist information centre** at ul. Aleksandrovska 61 (Mon–Fri 9am–5pm; ☎082/824704, ⑩www.tic.rousse.bg) can advise on accommodation and sightseeing in Ruse and the surrounding region.

There's a reasonable choice of centrally located **hotels**, with enough variety to suit most tastes and budgets.

Hotels

Anna Palace ul. Knyazheska 4 ☎082/825 005, ⑩www.annapalace.com. Plush establishment guarded by liveried bellhops and with repro furniture packing out the lobby areas. Standard doubles have thick carpets, neutral modern furnishings and showers; apartments come with nineteenth-century ceramic ovens and bathtubs. Rooms ❻, apartments ❽

Bistra & Galina ul. Asparuh 8 ☎082/828 233, ⑩www.bghotel.bg. Stylish modern interiors in a convenient downtown setting. Roomy en suites with TV and minibar, all done out in pastel colours. ❻

Danube Plaza pl. Svoboda 5 ☎082/822 950, ⑩www.danubeplaza.com. A much-improved grey lump from the Communist era, superbly located on the main square. Comfortable en suites with TV, and some plusher business-class rooms on each floor. ❻–❽

Kristal ul. Nikolaevska 1 ☎082/824 333, ⑥hotel_kristal@abv.bg. Recently refurbished modern block in a reasonably central location. Rooms feature thin carpets, budget-superstore furniture and small

bathrooms, but everything is clean and tidy. ❹

Riga bul. Pridunavski 22 ☎082/822 042. ⑩www.hotel-riga.com. Once-swish high-rise hotel with far more rooms than potential guests, but offering improving standards of service after several years in the doldrums. Acceptable business-standard rooms, and an enviable riverside position. ❺–❽

Splendid ul. Aleksandrovska 51 ☎082/825 972, ⑩www.splendid.rousse.bg. Comfortable hotel right behind the main square, offering en suites with TV. ❹

Vadis ul. Nikolaevska 73 ☎082/818 910, ⑩www.vadisbg.com. Seven spacious rooms featuring thick carpets, deep armchairs and big desks. High standards of service. The 15min walk to the centre is the only potential drawback. ❼

Yuvelir ul. Hadzhi Dimitar 26 ☎082/823 536 or 823532. Twelve odd-shaped rooms squeezed into a suburban house just east of the centre. Choose between prim, tile-floored en suites with pine furnishings and TV, or snazzy studio apartments with bathtubs. Rooms ❹, apartments ❻

Ploshtad Svoboda and around

A spacious mixture of concrete and greenery bordered by flower sellers and open-air cafés, the central **ploshtad Svoboda** (Freedom Square) is watched over by one of Ruse's trademarks, the 1908 **Liberation Monument**, a classical pillar surmounted by an allegorical figure of Liberty. Occupying the southwest side of the square is Ruse's **Drama Theatre**, a once-magnificent neo-Renaissance pile that was the centre of social life in pre-Communist Ruse. It was popularly known as the *Dohodnoto zdanie* ("cash cow" would be a very free translation) due to the profits the city council raked in by renting out of its floor space to shops, restaurants and a public library. Used for purely theatrical purposes after 1945, it was closed entirely in the 1980s prior to its reconstruction as a state-of-the-art drama venue. Adequate funding for the project never materialized, however, and after a quarter century of false starts the building's makeover is only now nearing completion.

Midhat Pasha (1822–1884)

Born in the village of Zavet between Ruse and Isperih, **Midhat Pasha** enjoys an ambiguous reputation in modern-day Bulgaria. As an ethnic Turk and loyal Ottoman bureaucrat, he was on the wrong side during Bulgaria's nineteenth-century struggle for liberation, and his achievements as a statesman have been largely omitted from the history books as a result.

Educated in France, and rising rapidly through the Ottoman civil service, Midhat Pasha was a man of enlightened, Westernizing tastes, who saw economic development, social reform and moderate constitutionalism as the best way to keep the empire's disparate peoples together. He put this blueprint into effect in 1864, when he was made governor of the **Tuna Vilayet** ("Danube province"), a territory that stretched over much of northern Bulgaria and eastern Serbia, and had its capital at Ruse. The region was already one of the more affluent parts of the Empire, and Midhat set about turning it into the showcase province of the Ottoman world, using state money to build roads, railways and factories. Ruse's port was modernized, and town-planning regulations stipulated that only two-storey, European-style houses were to be built in the town centre. Midhat also established cooperative banks that would extend credit to local farmers – an attempt to win the loyalty of the Christian peasantry. Midhat Pasha believed that the empire of the sultans could be saved from decay by the creation of a genuinely "Ottoman" civic identity that would transcend national and religious divisions. Few Bulgarians shared his dream, however, preferring the struggle for national self-determination to Midhat's vague promises of a democratizing multinational state.

After four years in Ruse, Midhat was recalled to Constantinople, where he occupied a series of influential posts in the imperial administration. Rising to the position of Grand Vizier, Midhat drew up plans for a **democratic constitution** in December 1876 – a constitution which was quietly abandoned after Russia's declaration of war on Turkey in April 1877. Considered too liberal by authoritarian Sultan Abdulhamid, Midhat left office, subsequently serving as governor in Syria, then Smyrna before being exiled to Yemen in 1881. Midhat was murdered by Abdulhamid's agents three years later.

Modern-day Ruse folk feel rather ambivalent about Midhat Pasha. On the one hand he put their city on the map, turning it into a major trade centre endowed with imposing, European-style public buildings; on the other he was a typical agent of Ottoman power, hunting down Bulgarian rebels (like Stefan Karadzha; see p.304) and signing their execution warrants. Hardly surprising, then, that Midhat Pasha is one local-boy-made-good who has never been honoured with a statue.

▲ Lyuben Karavelov Library, Ruse

Ulitsa Aleksandrovska, the Historical Museum and around

Skirting the northern side of the square is the city's main commercial and social artery, **ulitsa Aleksandrovska** – a great venue for shopping, drinking and aimless strolling. There's a food **market** and diverse street traders along the road's eastern stretches. Aleksandrovska's western end opens out into **ploshtad Aleksandar Batenberg**, another refined, flowerbed-filled space with more outdoor cafés, and a monument to those who fell for the motherland in the Serbo-Bulgarian War of 1885.

On the northwestern corner of pl. Batenberg stands a stately nineteenth-century villa built to serve as the regional residence of Prince Aleksandar Batenberg, and now serving as a suitably elegant home to the **Ruse Historical Museum** (Mon–Fri 9am–noon & 1–5pm; 2Lv). A well-designed display tells the story of Roman, Byzantine and Bulgarian settlement of the area, although pride of place is given to the Borovo Treasure, a fifth-century-BC hoard of silver Thracian drinking horns, decorated with horses' heads and other animal shapes.

Much of the rest of central Ruse is made up of a patchwork of residential streets lined with nineteenth-century bourgeois residences, nowadays divided up into apartments. A particularly beautiful example is **ulitsa Ivan Vazov**, which runs east from pl. Aleksandar Batenberg to join up with ul. Borisova. Among the numerous stately pieds-à-terre along its length is the **Palace of the Catholic Bishop of Ruse**, a wonderfully unrestrained architectural jumble in which Gothic, Neoclassical and Baroque elements jostle for attention. Hidden away behind a fruit-and-veg market on the adjoining pl. Dr Mustakov is one further reminder of Ruse's cosmopolitan past, the former **synagogue**, which spent most of the postwar period as regional headquarters for Bulgaria's equivalent of the football pools, before being returned to the Jewish community.

Along the riverfront

Ulitsa Knyazheska leads downhill from pl. Svoboda towards the riverfront pl. Sveti Nikola and the former merchants' quarter of town, an area of dust-laden stuccoed buildings where Elias Canetti's family used to have a warehouse, a few steps southeast at ul. Slavyanska 12. Heading southwards from pl. Sveti Nikola up ul. Tsar Kaloyan, a pathway on the right leads to a gated archeological park marking the site of the **Sexaginta Prista Roman fortress** (Rimska krepost "Seksaginta Prista"; Mon–Fri 9am–noon & 1–5pm; 2Lv), where a surviving section of third-century defensive wall runs along a bluff overlooking the Danube. A Roman garrison was established here during the reign of first-century-AD emperor Vespasian and survived for six centuries, its name (Sexaginta Prista meaning "sixty ships" in Latin) reflecting its importance as a harbour. There's a selection of richly decorated tombstones and a good view of the river.

Northeast of pl. Sveti Nikola, the cobbled bul. Pridunavski runs along the **waterfront** – a relatively bland area save for a few townhouses, the odd stretch of riverside parkland and a couple of worthwhile museums. The first of these is the **Zahari Stoyanov Museum**, at bul. Pridunavski 15 (Mon–Fri 9am–noon & 2–5pm; 3Lv), which commemorates the journalist, politician and author best known for his *Notes on the Bulgarian Uprisings*, a record of the author's experiences during the 1870s. By the time of the April Rising of 1876 Stoyanov was attached to the rebel group commanded by Georgi Benkovski, a leader of the Rising in the Koprivshtitsa area (see p.280). Stoyanov's subsequent account served to immortalize Benkovski and other personalities behind the revolt, and helped enshrine the Rising as the crucial event in the nation's liberation. He married the youngest daughter of Baba ("Granny") Tonka Obretenova, a formidable matriarch who was at the forefront of revolutionary activity in nineteenth-century Ruse. Her five sons all took part in the April Rising, and their portraits fill one of the rooms here (the Obretonov House-Museum, 100m away on the corner of bul. Pridunavski and ul. Baba Tonka, is currently under reconstruction).

As well as books and manuscripts recalling Stoyanov's work, the museum displays one of the suitcases Stoyanov was travelling with when he dropped dead in Paris in 1889. Much attention is also lavished on another revolutionary, Panayot Hitov, who retired to Ruse as a national hero after spending most of the 1860s and 1870s leading warrior bands in the mountains. Guerrilla life is remembered with items such as Hitov's embroidered tobacco pouch, his secret money belt, and numerous antiquated pistols and shotguns.

Further along the riverbank, opposite the *Hotel Riga*, lies a museum of nineteenth-century urban life which is popularly known as the **Kaliopa House** (Mon–Fri 9am–noon & 2–5pm; 3Lv) after one of its former inhabitants, Maria Kalich, who was nicknamed Kaliopa on account of her supposed resemblance to an ancient Greek demigoddess. After Kaliopa moved out, the house was bought by Bulgarian merchant Stefan Kalburov, who commissioned the wonderfully opulent Neoclassical interior that visitors can see today. A wall painting of Cupid and Psyche presides over the stairs leading to the upstairs salons, where walls and ceilings decorated with Grecian urns awaited guests invited to the music recitals and literary evenings once held here.

The Cathedral Church and the Pantheon

A couple of blocks east of pl. Svoboda on ul. Gorazd is the **Cathedral Church of Sveta Troitsa** (Holy Trinity), dating from 1632 and twice rebuilt in successive centuries. The resulting building borrows liberally from Russian models, sporting a curious Baroque facade and a medieval Muscovite spire. Steps descend into an icon-rich subterranean nave, its stuccoed ceiling supported by trompe-l'oeil marble-effect pillars crowned with Corinthian capitals.

Further east across bul. Tsar Osvoboditel, you'll find the **Park na Vazrozhdentsite** (Park of the Men of the Revival), where the **Ruse Pantheon** (Mon–Fri 9am–noon & 2–5pm; 3Lv), a mausoleum devoted to nineteenth-century revolutionary heroes, squats on a flagstoned plaza. It's a grossly overstated building: a kind of high-tech Maya temple surmounted by a giant golden ping-pong ball. Despite its patriotic intent, the pantheon has never been wholly popular with Ruse folk, not least because a cemetery and a church were razed in order to make way for its construction in 1975. In a symbolic attempt to re-Christianize the site, a large cross was placed on top of the pantheon in 2001. Inside lie the bones of hundreds of Bulgarians who served the national cause, the most prominent of them being honoured with marble grave slabs on either side of the chamber. The central dome is flanked by four female statues – allegories, respectively, of slavery under the Ottoman yoke, the cultural awakening of the nineteenth century, the mourning of Bulgarian mothers for fallen freedom fighters, and the Liberation of 1877. The whole lacks the delicacy of the smaller, more tasteful nineteenth-century chapels – honouring, among others, Zahari Stoyanov (see opposite) – which lie under the trees of the surrounding park.

Mladezhki Park and the Transport Museum

North of the Pantheon, Park na Vazrozhdentsite fades imperceptibly into **Mladezhki park** or "Youth Park", where tree- and shrub-lined avenues provide a popular strolling area. Steps at the northern end of the park descend to the riverfront and the **Transport Museum** at ul. Bratya Obretenovi 1 (Mon–Fri 8am–noon & 2–5pm; 2Lv; 2Lv extra for the outdoor section; 4Lv extra for a guided tour of the rolling stock). The museum celebrates Ruse's role as the starting point of Bulgaria's first-ever railway with sepia photographs and models of steam engines throughout the ages. Vintage steam engines are lined up outside, include locomotive no. 148, built for the railway by a Manchester firm in 1866. Among the luxury rolling stock parked behind the museum are the ornate *Sultaniye* carriage built for Sultan Abdul Aziz, and the leather-upholstered state carriage in which Tsar Ferdinand trundled across the country. Ferdinand's son Boris III was so enamoured of trains that he insisted on driving them himself whenever possible; the tiny locomotive he regularly piloted from Kocherinovo to Rila monastery (a narrow-gauge line which, sadly, was pulled up long ago) is proudly parked outside the museum building.

Eating, drinking and entertainment

Most of Ruse's eating venues are found on and around **ploshtad Svoboda** and the adjoining **ulitsa Aleksandrovska**, and there's not much point in straying beyond this area unless you're seeking out one of the more chic restaurants. Wherever you eat, the price of a three-course meal with drinks will rarely exceed 30–40Lv per person. For **picnic food**, head to the fresh fruit and veg stalls at the market on pl. Ivan Vazov. The best places for **drinking** are the pavement cafés scattered throughout the central area, although the trendy ones go in and out of fashion very quickly.

Restaurants

Antic ul. Otets Paisii 2 ☎082/877 887. A modern European menu of salads, risottos, pastas and steaks, in a snazzy white-furnished interior with a sprinkling of houseplants. Popular at lunchtimes, when daily specials are chalked up on a board outside.

Dom na Uchenite ul. Konstantin Irechek 16. Basement restaurant with a refined but not over-formal atmosphere, and a Bulgarian–European menu. Good for fish.

Happy Grill pl. Svoboda. Bulgaria-wide franchise serving up grills and chicken-and-chips dishes in a central location. The large square-side terrace is always busy.

Leventa Located in an eighteenth-century Ottoman powder magazine right under Ruse TV tower, this restaurant's series of barrel-vaulted chambers are each painted with scenes from Bulgarian history. Quality food (Bulgarian and international dishes) and excellent service. Mains around 20Lv.

Mehana Chiflika ul. Otets Paisii 2. Traditional Bulgarian food at reasonable prices, with seating on two levels and traditional rustic-style furnishings. Live folk-pop in the evening.

Olimpiets ul. Hristo Danov 4. Top-quality Bulgarian fare served up in a restaurant that mixes starched-napkin stylishness with folksy décor. Very popular on summer nights, when the big outdoor terrace is open.

Plaza ul. Petko Petkov. Popular open-air restaurant in a garden behind the *Danube Plaza* hotel, packed with locals in summer. Indifferent food, but live music and dancing most nights.

Strandzhata ul. Konstantin Irechek 5 ☎082/828 977. Roomy basement restaurant with a head-scratchingly long menu of Balkan specialities, including charcoal-grilled meats and tasty *menche* dishes (stewed in a clay pot), and *sache* meals (sizzled on an iron metal plate). Gets lively after about 10.30pm when pop-folk singers hit the stage.

Drinking

There's a strip of flashy café-bars along the northern side of pl. Svoboda, which stretches eastwards to cover the first hundred metres or so of ul. Aleksandrovska. There's little point in giving specific recommendations – places open up, close down or change name with frightening regularity – but if you want cheap beer, cheery pop music and dressed-up local youth for company, then this is the area to head for. Drinking venues with more clearly defined character include the nameless bar at the corner of ul. Duhovno Vazrazhdane and Baba Tonka, which eschews techno music and attracts a discerning studenty crowd as a result; and *Pri Mitaka*, at pl. Ivan Vazov 2, which squeezes a similarly Bohemian clientele into a boisterous beer garden, and has a basement bar where DJs spin after midnight. *Irish Pub Terassa*, on the riverfront at bul. Pridunavski 6, is a brash modern drinking hole playing mainstream music to a fun-seeking crowd. Immediately beneath it, *Canela* is a late-opening bar and disco offering cocktails, mirror balls, and stools that look like kettle drums.

Music venues

Ruse's **Opera House**, on pl. Sveta Troitsa, is one of the finest in Bulgaria. Other types of classical music are showcased in the annual **March Music Weeks**, which attract some of the best ensembles, soloists and conductors in Europe. Tickets for all musical events can be bought from the **concert bureau**, at ul. Aleksandrovska 61 (Mon–Fri 10am–1pm & 3–6pm).

Listings

Airline ticket agent Balkan luxair, ul. Konstantin Velichkov 3 ☎082/821212.

Bus ticket agent Plaza Tours, ul. Petko Petkov (behind the *Danube Plaza* hotel).

Car rental Eurokontakt, bul. Gotse Delchev ☎082/626241.

Hospital Bratya Obretenovi on the edge of Park na Mladezhta ☎887.

Pharmacy Apteka Kalinovi, ul. Aleksandrovska 69 (daily 7am–11pm).

Post office pl. Svoboda (Mon–Fri 7.30am–6.30pm, Sat 7.30am–6pm).

Taxis Head for the taxi ranks at the northern end of ul. Borisova or the western end of ul. Petko Petkov (round the side of the *Danube Palace* hotel). Alternatively ring ☎8112, 8113 or 8141.

Telephones at the post office (daily 7am–10pm).

Train ticket agent Rila/BDZh, ul. Knyazheska 39 ☎082/834860.

Moving on from Ruse

If you're **entering or leaving Bulgaria** via Ruse you'll first cross the three-kilometre-long *Dunav Most* or "Danube Bridge" (known as "Friendship Bridge" back in the days of socialist brotherhood), which spans the river on the outskirts of Ruse and Giurgiu. This ugly yet technically impressive structure was built by both Romania and Bulgaria (with Soviet assistance) between 1952 and 1954. Citizens of the EU, USA and Canada can enter Romania without a visa; other nationals should contact the Romanian Embassy in their home country before leaving home.

Travellers **leaving Ruse by train** have a choice of services and destinations. There are direct trains to **Sofia** and **Varna**, although those travelling south into the **Balkan Range** will probably have to change at Gorna Oryahovitsa. International connections are good, with three daily trains to **Giurgiu** on the Romanian side of the bridge, and a further two daily express trains (three in summer) that continue on to **Bucharest**; one of these continues onwards to **Budapest**.

International **tickets** can be bought in advance from the Rila bureau at ul. Knyazheska 39 (Mon–Fri 9am–noon & 12.30–5pm; ℡082/834860) or from the Rila counter at Ruse train station (opening times usually coordinated with train departures). You can also get tickets on the train itself, although prices are about fifty percent higher and payment can only be made in Bulgarian currency.

Privately run **Ruse-Sofia** buses pick up and drop off outside the train station.

The Rusenski Lom

Ruse is the obvious base from which to venture southwards into the **Rusenski Lom** (РУСЕНСКИ ЛОМ), a steep-sided, canyon-like valley through which the River Rusenski Lom winds its way towards the Danube. The valley forms a picturesque setting for a trio of worthwhile attractions, beginning with the (still functioning) rock-hewn **Monastery of the Blessed Dimitar Basarbovski** just outside Ruse, and continuing with the much older and considerably more spectacular **rock churches of Ivanovo**, famed for their medieval frescoes. Beyond Ivanovo lies the evocatively windswept hilltop **citadel of Cherven**. Both Ivanovo and Cherven fall within the boundaries of the **Rusenski Lom Nature Park** (*Priroden park Rusenski Lom*), formed to protect the diverse flora and fauna of the valley. The riverside cliffs provide nesting grounds for hawks, eagles, griffon vultures and black storks; while on the valley floor a variety of tortoises, lizards and snakes roam among exotic ferns and orchids. There are paths in the valley floor between Ivanovo and Cherven, and although there are as yet no signs or hiking maps, you should not be discouraged from exploring.

The Rock Monastery of Dimitar Basarbovski

Located halfway up a cliff on the banks of the Rusenski Lom, the **Rock Monastery of the Blessed Dimitar Basarbovski** (*Skalen manastir na Prepodobni Dimitar Basarbovski*) lies just beyond the village of **BASARBOVO** (БАСАРБОВО), about 7km south of Ruse. To get here, head out of Ruse on the Sofia road and take the Basarbovo exit just outside the city limits. Once you get to Basarbovo, pass right through the village and keep following the riverbank for 2km until you get to the monastery car park. A taxi from central Ruse shouldn't set you back much more than 12Lv each way.

Although a monastery has existed here since at least the fifteenth century, it takes its name from a seventeenth-century local monk who led a life so spiritually pure that his body miraculously failed to decompose after his death.

Initially kept in a local church, his corpse was presented to the Cathedral of SS Constantine and Elena in Bucharest in 1774 in recognition of Romanian help in the Russo-Turkish wars, while the rock monastery here became an important local focus for followers of his cult. Nowadays it consists of a few uninhabited rock-hewn cells (the trio of monks still attached to the monastery reside in a pavilion down below) and a small cave-like church, reached via a cliff-hugging stairway. Inside, the main altar bears a nineteenth-century icon of Dimitar in the company of the Virgin; while over to the left is a much older, miracle-working icon showing scenes from his life.

The Rock Churches of Ivanovo

The most famous of the ruins in the Rusenski Lom valley belong to the so-called **Rock Churches of Ivanovo** near Ivanovo village, 18km south of Ruse. Among the rocks on both banks of the river, several monasteries were hewn into the craggy gorge whose caves provided shelter for Stone Age tribes and medieval hermits alike. Monks first arrived at the gorge in the thirteenth century, a royal donation enabling one Yoakim of Tarnovo to establish an extensive monastery complex, its churches, cells and galleries cut from natural caves in the sheer cliff. At the time the main road linking Tarnovo to the Danube ran through the gorge, providing the monasteries with a steady stream of pilgrims.

The churches are reached by following the village's main street northwards from Ivanovo train station for 1.5km, then turning right into a minor road which leads over the fields and down into the valley of the Rusenski Lom (4km). The road peters out at a car park-cum-picnic spot, above which lies the one church which is regularly open to tourists, the fourteenth-century **Tsarkvata or "church" cave** (Wed–Sun 9am–noon & 2–5pm; 5Lv). Inside are two chambers, the walls and ceilings of which are covered with vivid New Testament scenes. In the first chamber, the ceiling is dominated by a depiction of Christ enveloped by a star-like form, a typical representation of the Divine Light as envisaged by the hesychast monks of the time. Just beyond, the *Mocking of Christ* sees the Saviour surrounded by snarling, cudgel-wielding tormentors. In the second chamber, Christ's betrayal by Judas is followed by a grisly portrayal of the latter's suicide. *The Beheading of John the Baptist* at the far end of the room betrays a similar lack of squeamishness.

Heading back to the car park, you can pick up **trails** leading upstream along the valley floor. You can in theory walk all the way to Cherven (see opposite) from here in four to five hours, passing the confluence of the Beli and Cherni Lom rivers (take the right fork to follow the Cherni Lom) on the way. An alternative is to head back along the road in the Ivanovo direction, turn right to find a bridge across the river, and explore the riverbank path on the other side. There's a line of rock churches in the cliffs above, and although their interiors are unlikely to be open to visitors, they provide a useful excuse to wander this far. First up, the so-called **Buried Church** (Zatrupanata tsarkva) cave features a damaged mural of Tsar Asen presenting a model of the church to the Archangel Michael, with a depiction of his miracles on the ceiling. Nearby is another, more derelict **baptismal church** (krashtelnata tsarkva) decorated with a scene of the visions of St Peter of Alexandria. Along the same bank, the **Chapel of Gospodev dol**, or "The Lord's Valley" (with portraits of its patron saints, Vlassius, Spiridon and Modestus), and the accurately named **Demolished Church** (Saborenata tsarkva), both contain murals, variously faded by time.

Practicalities

The main entry point to the region is the village of **IVANOVO** (ИВАНОВО) itself, 4km west of the caves and on the main Ruse–Sofia rail line – it's served by five daily *patnicheski* trains from Ruse. Diagonally opposite the train station, the large concrete town council building contains an enthusiastic information office (Tsentar po ekologiya, kultura i turizam; Mon–Fri 9am–5pm; ☎08116/2715 and 2253), where you can pick up leaflets about the nature park and book rooms in local houses that offer B&B arrangements. The number of guesthouses in and around Ivanovo is growing (see below). There's a **restaurant**, the *Kladenets*, serving grilled Bulgarian standards in the courtyard of the *Chervenata kashta* guesthouse next to the train station, and a rough-and-ready **café** right beside the train-station platforms.

Guesthouses

Chervenata kushta (Red House) next to the train station ☎082/846 783 and 0899 773 288. A broad mixture of en-suite rooms, most featuring colour-clash interiors and homely furnishings – scattered among which are some genuine antiques. **②**

Polomie Lodge ☎0899 478 531, ⓦwww .polomie.eu. Quality B&B accommodation in a swish house that combines traditional and modern elements. Rooms come with wood floors and furniture, and there is a small outdoor pool in the walled garden. Extra meals are available on request, and the hosts can also organize biking and bird-watching trips. **③**

Villa Angel 7km south of Ivanovo in the village of Koshov ☎08159/479 and 0889 899 254. Family-run guesthouse on a hillside above the river Cherni Lom, with simple rooms with shared facilities in the main building, and small but tidy en-suite rooms in a bungalow-like annexe. **②–③**

Cherven

Fifteen kilometres south of Ivanovo, a fork in the gorge provides a niche for the **ruined citadel of Cherven** (ЧЕРВЕН), clinging to the rock. Formerly known as the "City of churches" or "City of bishops", Cherven was founded in the sixth or seventh century when recurrent barbarian invasions compelled the inhabitants of Ruse to seek a more defensible site inland. The citadel was devastated by the Turks, but Cherven survived as the region's administrative centre for some time, with Ottoman governors and Orthodox bishops coexisting until the seventeenth century, when they both relocated to Ruse. Nowadays Cherven resembles a desolate and brutish version of Machu Picchu (albeit at a considerably lower altitude), with its meagre remains standing high above the valley on a rocky table flanked on three sides by unscalable cliffs. There are good views of the Cherni Lom gorge, with the red-roofed houses of **Cherven village** clinging to the limestone ridges above it. You can still make out the ground plans of Cherven's many churches, although the biggest of the town's structures was the fortified complex of the local *bolyarin*, Cherven's feudal lord. A still-discernible main street runs past his palace and on towards the rude dwellings of his underlings.

It can be difficult **getting to Cherven** without a private car. Sporadic buses to the village of Cherven may be running from Ruse's bus terminal; otherwise you'll have to take a *patnicheski* train to the Koshov stop, walk south for 1km, turn left, then walk the remaining 7km into Cherven village. The road winds its way through the village before arriving at a car park at the base of the citadel, 1km beyond. There's a rudimentary **café** about 400m short of the citadel car park.

Patrolled by a motley collection of sheep, pigs, horses and farmyard cats, Cherven itself is the kind of village you might want to spend some time in before moving on. The *Petrova kashta* **guesthouse**, at ul. Hristo Botev 8

(☎08156/410 and 0898 235 065, ✉ginka2006@mail.bg; ❷), offers three rooms featuring pine furnishings and house plants, plus a single shared WC/bathroom. Meals are available for a few extra leva if you ask in advance.

The Dobrudzha

Beyond Ruse, routes head into an extension of the Danubian plain known as the **Dobrudzha**, Bulgaria's main grain-producing region. Numerous buses follow the main eastbound road along the Danube, calling in at the sleepy riverside town of Tutrakan before arriving at the much larger port of **Silistra** – site of some rewarding Roman remains and the main jumping-off point for the birdwatcher's paradise of **Lake Srebarna**. Beyond here the river swings north into Romania, leaving travellers with the choice of heading south across the Ludogorie hills towards Shumen (see p.254), or continuing across the eastern part of the Dobrudzha towards the Black Sea coast.

Silistra

The last town on the Bulgarian stretches of the Danube, **SILISTRA** (СИЛИСТРА) may lack the vigour and sophistication of Ruse, but can boast an equally impressive historical pedigree. As the fortified Roman frontier town of Durostorum, it was the home of a legion during the reign of Emperor Trajan (98–117 AD), and went on to flourish as a military and civilian centre under the Byzantines, Bulgarians and Ottomans. Silistra is nowadays a laid-back provincial town with a river harbour exporting Bulgarian grain, and a little-used road frontier serving the Romanian half of the Dobrudzha. For the traveller, the nearby **nature reserve at Srebarna** provides the main reason to visit, but there's little to justify a stay of any length.

The Town

From the **train** and **bus** stations on the town's western outskirts, ul. Simeon Veliki winds its way eastwards through the town centre, arriving at a typically flagstoned and flowerbedded town square. Here, the **Silistra Art Museum** (Mon–Fri 8am–noon & 2–6pm; 1Lv) contains a comprehensive round-up of twentieth-century Bulgarian art, including canvases by Vladimir Dimitrov-Maistora and Zlatyu Boyadzhiev. A few steps beyond at ul. G. S. Rakovski 24 is the **Archeological Museum** (Tues–Sun 8am–noon & 2–6pm; 2Lv), where a rich fund of material on life in Durostorum includes the epigraph-laden tombstones of the soldiers stationed here with the XI Legion. In addition, there's a rather captivating first-century sundial, decorated with a relief of Orpheus twanging away on his lyre to an audience of attentive animals; and a hoard of Roman jewellery including some alluring golden earrings.

To the north of the Archeological Museum, nineteenth-century residential houses occupy a grid of tree-shaded streets that separate central Silistra from the river. It's among these modest early-twentieth-century mansions, many with Art Nouveau details such as caryatids peering from upper storeys, that you get some impression of the elegance once enjoyed by the Danubian towns.

Occupying a hill 3km south of town (best reached by walking along ul. Izvorite from the centre) are the remains of the Turkish fortress of **Medzhiditabiya**, another corner of the defensive quadrilateral built by the Ottomans, and one that was frequently attacked in the course of successive Russo-Turkish wars. The hilltop park also features a TV tower complete with revolving café, and there are expansive views of the Danube below, backed by the yellow and green hues of the Wallachian plain beyond.

Practicalities

The best of the central **hotels** is the *Drustar*, on the riverbank at ul. Kapitan Mamarchev 10 (☎086/812 200, ⓦwww.hoteldrustar.com; ❺), a smart modern building with mock-castle turrets and well-appointed en suites, some with Danube-facing balconies. The smaller and cheaper *Bartimex*, at ul. Kapitan Mamarchev 20 (☎086/820118, Ⓔbartimex@ccpro.com; ❸), has plain but snug en suites with TV.

Most characterful of the **restaurants** is the *Nikulden*, at ul. Pristanishna 2, a wood-panelled cabin by the riverfront serving up tasty pan-fried fillets of fresh-water fish. The restaurant of the *Drustar* hotel offers good food in a slightly more formal ambience, and there is a disco-bar in the hotel basement.

Lake Srebarna

Nineteenth-century Hungarian traveller Felix Kanitz called **Lake Srebarna**, 17km west of Silistra near the Danube shore, "the Eldorado of wading birds". The lake – and the expanse of reedy marshland that spreads around it – is now a protected nature reserve, providing ninety species of wildfowl (including seventy different types of heron) with a secure habitat. The lake is also frequented by around eighty migratory species: there are **egrets** in the summer, and as many as fifty thousand **geese** in the winter. Srebarna's most famous denizens are the **Dalmatian pelicans**, about seventy pairs of which nest here from April to July and return again briefly in the autumn.

Just off the main Silistra–Ruse road, the reserve is approached from the villages of Srebarna to the west, or Vetren to the northwest. Both are served by **bus** #222 which leaves from the main road outside Silistra bus station every two hours or so between 7am and 9pm (ask at the bus station about exact timings). You can also catch one of the frequent Silistra–Ruse buses, and ask to be set

▲ Red-breasted goose, Lake Srebarna

down at the Srebarna stop on the main road, which is a walkable 2km away from Srebarna village itself.

Your first stop should be the **Natural History Museum** (Prirodonauchen muzei; Mon–Fri 10am–4pm; 1Lv), tucked away at the northeastern end of Srebarna village but well-signed. The collection of stuffed fauna inside provides a useful introduction to the wildlife of the region, and the telescope on the top floor provides a good view of what's occurring on the water – and provides the best way of observing the pelicans if they're in residence. Starting behind the museum, a marked path leads round the lake, remaining at a respectful distance from nesting grounds on the water's edge.

The Dobrudzha in history

"A wintry land deficient in cultivated grains and fruit", inhabited by a people "who are barbarous and lead a bestial existence" was how the third-century BC Thracian chieftain Dromichaetes described the **Dobrudzha** to his Macedonian captive Lysimachus, berating him for bothering to invade such a barren region in the first place.

Windswept in winter and parched in summer, the Dobrudzha has always had a reputation for harshness and inhospitality. Geographically speaking, it stretches from the mouth of the Danube in the north to the Gulf of Varna in the south, marking the southwestern extremity of the great **Eurasian steppelands** that once swept uninterruptedly round the north coast of the Black Sea and eastwards towards Central Asia and Mongolia. Successive generations of horseriding invaders have used the steppe as a corridor leading to the riches of southeastern Europe, and faced by such recurring dangers, Western civilization's hold on the region was always tenuous. Successive Macedonian, Roman, Byzantine and Bulgarian empires always found the Dobrudzha to be the most difficult part of the northern frontier to defend, and by the thirteenth century, when **Tatar bands** were beginning to roam the region with impunity, the area was well on the way to becoming a lawless desert.

Arab chronicler Ibn Battuta, crossing the Dobrudzha in the fourteenth century, was struck by its desolate appearance, describing it as "eighteen days of uninhabited wasteland, for eight days of which there is no water". By the time the Ottoman Sultan Mehmet I conquered the Dobrudzha in 1416, the region was so depopulated that he had to colonize it with **Turkish settlers** in order to provide the newly won province with inhabitants capable of defending it – with the result that the local ethnic mix still includes a fair proportion of Turks. These are intermingled with the Turkish-speaking **Dobrudzha Tatars**, descendants of Crimean Tatars who were expelled from the Russian Empire in the wake of the Crimean War.

By the beginning of the twentieth century, migrant Bulgarian peasants began to outnumber the other national groups in the area, but the ethnic balance of the region was altered yet again during the interwar period, when the Dobrudzha became part of Romania. Eager to boost the Latin element among the population, the Romanian government encouraged the immigration of Romanian-speaking **Vlachs** from Macedonia. After regaining the territory in 1941, the Bulgarian authorities imported Slav colonists to redress the ethnic balance, but the existence of so many non-Bulgarian minorities in an area so crucial to the economy was a source of concern to the country's postwar Communist bosses. Special attention was paid to the Dobrudzha during the 1980s, when the controversial *Vazroditelniyat protses* or Regeneration Process tried to force local Muslims to speak only the Bulgarian language in public and to adopt Bulgarian names. Nowadays you'll find inter-ethnic relations more relaxed, and the babble of Bulgarian and Turkic tongues heard in the region reflects the meeting of cultures from the Dobrudzha's turbulent past.

There are a couple of restful places **to stay** in Srebarna, beginning with the Pelican Lake Guesthouse (℡08515/322 and 0885 671 058, Ⓦwww .srebarnabirding.com; ❸), a beautifully renovated village house near the museum, offering a pair of double rooms, an adjoining kitchen, and friendly hosts who are experts on the local fauna and are brimming with advice on how to explore the lake. Occupying a lakeside position on the eastern outskirts of the village, *Hotel Srebarna* (℡08515/462 and 0889 441 116, Ⓔlubabriz@ccpro.com; ❷) contains a handful of neat, pine-furnished rooms with shared facilities, with a lake-facing terrace and a nice garden.

The Central Balkan Range

For more than a thousand years, the **Balkan Range** (in Bulgarian, the **Stara planina** or "Old Mountains") has been the cradle of the Bulgarian nation. Sloping gently towards the Danubian Plain, the Balkan's fertile valleys supported the medieval capitals of Pliska and Preslav (mere ruins today) and Veliko Tarnovo (still a thriving city), while steep ranges with defensible passes shielded them to the south. Much was destroyed during the Ottoman conquest, but the thread of culture was preserved by monasteries and the crafts centres that re-established themselves under the Turkish yoke.

The range's gentler slopes lie just **east of Sofia**, where small towns like **Etropole** and **Teteven** provide a measure of rural tranquillity lacking in the more touristed Balkan centres further east. First of these is **Lovech**, a well-preserved nineteenth-century town which lies within striking distance of **Troyan Monastery**, and, to the north, at the foot of the mountains, **Pleven**, site of a crucial battle in the Russo-Turkish War.

However, the best touring base in the central part of the range is **Veliko Tarnovo**. A beautiful city in its own right, with a medieval citadel and several historic churches, Tarnovo has good transport links with such villages rich in vernacular architecture as **Arbanasi**, **Elena**, **Tryavna** and **Etara**. It also makes a good base to visit a whole cluster of monasteries: **Preobrazhenski**, **Dryanovo** and **Kilifarevo** are the big three, but numerous smaller foundations merit further exploration.

The main urban centre in the east is **Shumen**, site of a fine medieval fortress and close to Bulgaria's first two capitals, **Pliska** and **Preslav**, and the enigmatic rock sculpture of the **Madara Horseman**. From here, routes towards the Danube and the Dobrudzha pass through the Ludogorie hills, where the **Thracian tomb** and **Dervish Tekke** at **Sveshtari** provide the chief attractions.

Towns in the western part of the central Balkan Range can be easily reached **by bus** from Sofia. The **Sofia–Varna rail line**, skirting the mountains to the north, is the fastest way of accessing places further afield. It passes through Pleven, whence buses depart to Lovech and Troyan; Gornya Orahovitsa, with regular train and bus connections to Veliko Tarnovo, Tryavna and Gabrovo; and Shumen, before forging onwards to the coast. Once established in any of the above places, you can explore neighbouring attractions using local buses.

East of Sofia

Travelling east by train, you completely bypass the foothills of the central Balkan Range northeast of Sofia. However, the main Sofia–Veliko Tarnovo–Varna highway (a gorge-defying dual carriageway for the first 60km or so) heads straight across the westernmost shoulder of the range, passing a handful of worthwhile villages and monasteries along the way. The market town of **Teteven** and nearby village of **Ribaritsa** are the most attractive of the region's settlements if you need a base from which to explore. Otherwise, most of the area's sights are accessible by bus from Sofia, or Lovech to the east.

Pravets, Etropole and Yamna

About 10km beyond the turn-off to Botevgrad, another minor road forks east to **PRAVETS** (ПРАВЕЦ), a previously unremarkable village whose status as the birthplace of former dictator **Todor Zhivkov** (see box, p.212) made it into one of the most prosperous communities in Bulgaria. It's in places like Pravets that nostalgia for the certainties of the Communist era is at its strongest. However, his modest childhood home is no longer open to the public, and there's little to make a visit worthwhile.

Thirteen kilometres southeast of Pravets is **ETROPOLE** (ЕТРОПОЛЕ), a quiet agricultural town surrounded by subalpine pastures. The centre, a couple of blocks west of the bus station, harbours an eighteenth-century **clock tower** and a small **museum** (summer daily 8am–noon & 1–5pm, winter closed Sun; 2Lv), the latter housed in the old Turkish municipality offices and containing memorabilia of Etropole's past as a wealthy mining town in the Middle Ages. Today, most visitors come for the fresh mountain air and numerous walking possibilities, while the **monastery of Sveta Troitsa**, 4km to the east above the village of **Ribaritsa**, also offers an interesting diversion. Founded in 1158, the monastery complex centres on its church, with its four hexagonal towers, set in a grassy courtyard. Although the monastery was a well-known literary centre in the sixteenth and seventeenth centuries, when monks copied and distributed Bulgarian manuscripts, these days only a priest remains and its rooms are rented to tourists (℡0720/2042; ❶).

Getting to the monastery is fairly easy. About five daily **buses** run from Etropole to Ribaritsa, but these are usually early in the morning or late in the afternoon. Alternatively, it's an hour's **walk**: turn right out of Etropole bus station into ul. Partizanska, walk to the end of the street where the

---

The Stara Planina Tourist Association

The **Stara Planina Tourist Association** coordinates the work of eight tourist offices in towns bordering on the central Balkan Range. The tourist offices share information, and can book accommodation in any of the areas covered by the association, making it possible to structure your itinerary in advance around the towns where the offices are found. It's also worth noting that some of the offices rent **mountain bikes** (stocks permitting) for 5Lv per day, and you're allowed to return the bikes to any office within the scheme. You'll find details on addresses and opening times of the tourist offices – in **Teteven, Troyan, Apriltsi, Tryavna, Dryanovo, Sevlievo, Lovech** and **Gabrovo** – in the relevant sections of the guide.

If you want information and advice on the region before you travel, contact the Stara Planina Tourist Association, 3rd Floor, ul. Raicho Karolev 4, 5300 Gabrovo (Mon–Fri 9am–6pm) ℡066/807137, ⊛www.staraplanina.org.

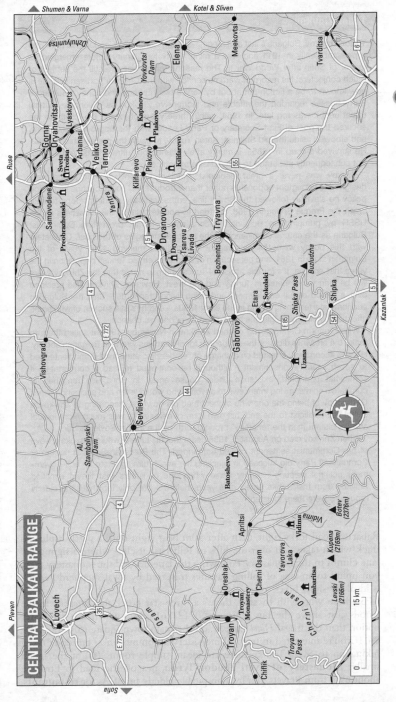

CENTRAL BALKAN RANGE

Todor Zhivkov, Bulgaria's last and longest-serving Communist leader, was born into a peasant family in 1911 and was a minor Party functionary before emerging as mayor of Sofia after World War II. The reasons for his rise are still the subject of much conjecture: his record of wartime service with the Chavdar partisan brigade is now known to be a fiction put about by servile biographers, and none of Bulgaria's Party bosses regarded the affable and inoffensive Zhivkov as a serious political threat until it was too late. In 1954, within three years of joining the Politburo, he secured the post of First Secretary or Party Leader with the approval of Moscow, and elbowed aside the old Stalinist, Anton Yugov, to claim the premiership in 1962. He survived a coup in 1965 – a murky affair blamed on "ultra-leftists" at the time, but subsequently attributed to nationalist army officers.

Zhivkov was never a great ideologist: most of his political innovations were designed to wrongfoot opponents rather than introduce real social change. In foreign policy he slavishly followed the Soviet line, enthusiastically sending troops to help crush the Prague Spring in 1968. He tried to counterbalance this closeness to the USSR by pumping up Bulgarian nationalism at home, presenting Communist Bulgaria as the natural culmination of the national struggles of the past. Consistent with this policy were the extravagant celebrations marking 1300 years of the Bulgarian state in 1981, and persecution of Bulgaria's ethnic Turkish population in the years that ensued. It's for this abuse of Turkish human rights that the Zhivkov years will be long remembered in Turkey and the West. However, Zhivkov also presided over a period of full employment and rising living standards – until the Bulgarian economy started going wrong in the early 1980s – and he's still spoken of with some affection by elderly Bulgarians bewildered by economic change.

When "reform Communists" ditched Zhivkov in November 1989, it suited them to make the erstwhile dictator the scapegoat for all that was wrong in Bulgarian society. He was accordingly arrested on a charge of "embezzling state funds" and sentenced to seven years' imprisonment – although he continued to lead a comfortable, if somewhat restricted, existence under house arrest in Sofia. He remained in combative spirits, giving interviews to anyone who would listen and accusing Mikhail Gorbachov of being the one who orchestrated his downfall. According to Zhivkov, a skilful self-publicist to the end, his own form of *perestroika* was much more logical and consistent than the "anarchy" brought forth by the former Soviet leader.

When Zhivkov died on August 5, 1998, fears that his funeral would provoke a wave of pro-Communist sentiment proved unfounded. The Bulgarian Socialist (ie former Communist) Party did succeed in hijacking the event, turning it into an anti-government political meeting – rather ironic when one considers that they'd expelled Zhivkov from their ranks barely nine years before – but only ten thousand elderly mourners were there to listen.

Ribaritsa road forks right, then after 50m bear right onto a partly asphalted track which takes you over the hills to Ribaritsa itself – where a signposted lane climbs to the monastery. Following the lane beyond the monastery takes you uphill to an area of rolling pastures traversed by local shepherds, which is ideal for short hikes.

For those who wish to **stay**, there's a three-star hotel, the *Etropole*, in the woods just above the bus station (℡0712/3616; ❷), which is a far better option than the frugal *Hotel Etropole*, on the main town square (℡0712/2018; ❶). If you're interested in tranquil monastery accommodation but don't fancy hiking up to Sveta Troitsa, there are clean, simple rooms (❶) at the much smaller **Monastery of Sveti Teodor Tyron**, just off the road to Etropole about 6km from Pravets, run by a hospitable elderly priest. As for **restaurants**, the *Oasis*, just off the market square, offers a decent range of local cuisine, as does the *Etropole*.

Four **buses** a day make the ten-kilometre journey from Etropole to **YAMNA** (ЯМНА), a tiny scenic village that stretches along the road into the mountains. There are plenty of picturesque walks in the region, most of them following unmarked trails, but the friendly owners of *Camping Vodenitsata* (☎07106/243 and 0887 521 875) can point you in the right direction. Situated at the start of the village their campsite offers a handful of small modern bungalows (❷) next to a rushing stream, and space for tents (❶). It's a rustic location complete with excellent home cooking, a hundred-year-old water mill, and an unusual natural washing machine. Further on, the *Perfect Komplex* (☎07106/212, ⓦwww.hotelperfect-bg.com; ❸) offers comfortable rooms with views of the valley.

Teteven and around

Back on the main highway, the next place of any importance is **Yablanitsa** (ЯБЛАНИЦА), renowned for its *halva* and *lokum* (Turkish Delight). It's a local bus hub and site of a turn-off for the Vit Valley, where the market town of Teteven and village of Ribaritsa provide access to some verdant pastures and craggy hills. Ten kilometres up the valley the road hits **GLOZHENE** (ГЛОЖЕНЕ), a drab industrialized village known chiefly for the nearby **monastery** (8am–9pm; donation), perched high above and practically invisible from the valley. It's a small monastery, housing a tiny nineteenth-century church enclosed by fortress-like living quarters with stone walls and overhanging timber upper storeys. Monks will show you round a museum containing the church silver, and you can enjoy views of the surrounding countryside from the monastery's cliff-top eyrie. A small *mehana* serves up simple food on site. Most vehicles will struggle on the gravelled roadway that winds up to the monastery from the village, so it's better to opt for the longer but more scenic route, which takes you back along the Yablanitsa road for 8km before turning southwards to the village of Malak Izvor, then eastwards to the monastery itself. If you fancy walking, a shorter route (allow 50min) takes you south from Glozhene's central bus stop along the Teteven road, across a footbridge spanning the Vit, around the Spartak sports field, up a cobbled hillside path, and then forks right up a wooded ravine. The monastery has a small **restaurant** and the nearest **accommodation** is available at the snug, welcoming and rustic ⚒ *Little Spring* guesthouse in Malak Izvor, whose affable English owner also runs guided **mountain bike** tours of the region (☎06990/272, ⓦwww.littlespring.eu; ❸).

Teteven

Surrounded by imposing mountains further up the valley, **TETEVEN** (ТЕТЕВЕН) once inspired writer Ivan Vazov to declare that had he not come here, "I should regard myself as a stranger to my native land … Nowhere have I found a place so enchanting as this." An endorsement a shade too fulsome for modern Teteven, but the town is certainly appealing in a laid-back way. Teteven comes to life on Saturday mornings, when the town **market** attracts a deluge of visitors from surrounding villages – most notably the local Pomaks, easily recognizable by their *shalvari*, the brightly coloured trousers worn by the women.

Despite the undoubted prettiness of the pastel-coloured houses ranged above the main square (a couple of blocks south of the bus station), there's little in the way of specific sights, other than an **art gallery** (Mon–Fri 9am–noon & 2–5.30pm;

2Lv) on the square itself, displaying work by local artists, and a small town **museum** (daily 9am–noon & 2–5pm; 2Lv), also on the square. The museum houses a colourful display of local costumes and crafts, notably the town's characteristic *chergi* – hand-woven carpets or runners. Several women still weave in Teteven, using local wool dyed with the extracts of indigenous plants, and the tourist office (see below) can arrange visits. Sadly, there's nowhere to buy *chergi* in town, although individual weavers are always happy to take orders if you're going to be staying in Bulgaria for some time.

Practicalities

The Teteven **tourist office**, just south of the square (Mon–Fri 8am–12.30pm & 1–5.30pm, weekends 9am–1pm & 2–6pm; ℡0678/4217, ⊛www.teteven .bg), offers local advice, sells maps, and can book accommodation in both Teteven and Ribaritsa further up the valley. Staff here can also arrange hiking guides if you give them a couple of days' notice, and will provide information on Saeva Dupka, a cave system 25km to the north of Teteven. The best of the town's hotels is the central *Vit* at ul. Michal Koychev 2 (℡0678/2034, ⊛hotelvit.googlepages.com; ❷), which has a small outdoor pool and live music at weekends. Another central option is the modern, brightly coloured *Maxim* at ul. Emil Markov 27 (℡0678/5552, ⊛www .balkania.org; ❸), while the *Zdravets*, up the road from the bus station at ul. Petrahilya 29 (℡0678/5551; ❷), is a large, somewhat dated option. The *Olymp* hotel (℡0678/2067; ❷) is conveniently located next to the bus station; don't be too put off by the latter's concrete-block exterior – it has been internally refurbished to modern standards. There's also an ample supply of **private rooms** (❶–❷), with prices a little cheaper than the hotels – enquire at the tourist office. There are **cafés** aplenty around the main square, *Vit* and *Maxim* have good **restaurants**, and the *Mehana Teteven* opposite the nineteenth-century **Church of Vsech Svyatich** (All Saints) on ul. Ivan Vazov serves traditional cuisine in an impressive building once inhabited by a pair of revolutionary brothers. **Nightlife** revolves around a few discos, the best of the bunch being an unnamed affair on the first floor of the shopping centre next to the main square.

Ribaritsa

Twelve kilometres beyond Teteven at the end of the valley lies **RIBARITSA** (РИБАРИЦА), a mountain village straddling the babbling river Vit and a popular location for bathing in summer. It is served by five daily buses from Teteven, and there's ample accommodation, mostly in the form of **private rooms** (❶–❷) bookable either through the small tourist office here (Tues–Sun 10am–1pm & 3–8pm; ℡06902/2588), the larger one in Teteven (see above), or directly from one of the many houses along the thoroughfare displaying signs offering *kvartiri*. **Hotels** include the *Ribaritsa* (℡06902/2302, ⊛www.hotel-ribaritsa-bg.com; ❶), up a steep track towards the end of the village and with a great view of the valley; and the centrally located *Pochiven Kompleks Ribaritsa* (℡06902/2301, ℻06902/2381; ❷) with a fitness centre, tennis courts, pool, disco and comfortable rooms. Further up the scale is the luxurious *Evergreen Palace* (℡06902/2066, ⊛www.evergreen-palace.com; ❼), which offers a similar range of facilities to the *Pochiven Kompleks Ribaritsa*. Way beyond that is one of Bulgaria's most expensive and exclusive hotels, *Casa Domini* (℡06902/2030, ⊛www.casadomini.com; ❾) which sports a colonnaded facade and Versace furniture throughout; this is the place where the country's elite spend their weekends. There are several decent **restaurants** in the village besides those in the hotels: the triangular *Alpinska*

Kushta has a garden and serves tasty local dishes, while for something a little different try the *Express* – a converted railway carriage with indoor and outdoor seating offering simple Bulgarian fare. The *Green Garden* is also a popular central option, with shaded outdoor seating and decent local cuisine.

The *Ribaritsa, Casa Domini* and the *Evergreen Palace* all offer **4WD safaris** in the surrounding mountains (100Lv per day per jeep); the latter also rents out bikes (15Lv per day) and can arrange basic **horse-riding trips** for 40Lv per hour. **Fishing** enthusiasts should head for the small but idyllic Varbaka lake next to the road as you enter Ribaritsa; a kiosk rents out rods and charges for what you catch; on-site bungalows are available (☎0897/897175; ❷). **Walks** from Ribaritsa head either southwest up the Kostina Valley (also cycleable if you rent a bike in Teteven), where, after 4km, you'll see a monument to **Georgi Benkovski**, the Koprivshtitsa-born revolutionary killed here in 1876; or south up the Zavodka Valley towards **Mount Vezhen**, which, at 2198m above sea level, is the highest point in the Tetevenska *planina*. There's a hiker's **chalet**, *Hizha Vezhen* (also accessible by asphalt road) some two hours short of the summit. If you are hiking in the area, the 1:65,000 *Teteven Balkan* **map** (on sale at the Teteven tourist office) will prove an invaluable aid.

East of Ribaritsa, the main road climbs out of the Vit valley and crosses the hills towards Troyan (see p.223), some 40km away. It's another scenic route by car or bike, taking in heath-covered moorland and deep forest, although no buses pass this way.

Pleven

Sited where the foothills of the Balkan Range descend to meet the Danubian Plain, the industrial city of **PLEVEN** (ПЛЕВЕН) is an important regional centre with an unusually high quotient of worthwhile urban sights. Many of these are monuments or museums honouring the **siege of Plevna**, probably the most decisive episode of the War of Liberation. When the Russians crossed the Danube at Svishtov in 1877, their flank was threatened by the Turkish forces entrenched at Plevna (as the town was then known), which resisted three assaults and cost the Russians thousands of casualties. In response to Grand Duke Nicholas's pleas, Romanian reinforcements came with King Carol I, who personally led his troops into battle (the last European sovereign to do so) crying, "This is the music that pleases me!" Russia's top generals, Skobelev and Totleben, then arrived to organize a professional siege, weakening the defenders by starvation and blasting each redoubt with artillery before the attackers made repeated bayonet charges, finally compelling the Turks to surrender on December 10. More than forty thousand Russians and Romanians and uncounted numbers of Turks and civilians died, but as a consequence of Plevna's fall northern Bulgaria was swiftly liberated. The defeat had a shattering effect on Ottoman morale, but garnered a great deal of public sympathy in the West, allowing the British and Austrian governments to adopt a much more openly anti-Russian line in the peace negotiations that followed. Pleven's other claim to fame is its extreme **climate**: Bulgaria's hottest summer temperatures are usually recorded here, and it's correspondingly cold in winter.

Easily reached from Sofia, Varna or Ruse by train, Pleven stands at the centre of an extensive local **bus network** that serves the smaller towns along the Danube to the north as well as Lovech and Troyan to the south.

Arrival and information

Pleven's **bus** and **train** stations are at the northern end of town; to get to the centre, follow ul. Danail Popov (or take any bus) south until you hit pl. Sveti Nikolai. From here, Osvobozhdenie continues a short way south to **ploshtad Svobodata**, which in turn opens onto the main square, **ploshtad Vuzrazhdane**.

The most useful of the local **travel agencies** is Mizia, just off pl. Svobodata at Ivan Vazov 3 (Mon–Fri 8am–6pm; ☎064/801215, ⍬www.miziatour.hit.bg), which organizes sightseeing trips of the city, runs excursions to places like Etara (see p.253), Veliko Tarnovo (see p.228) and Troyan monastery (see p.224), and can arrange car rental and hotel accommodation. The newly opened **tourist information centre** on pl. Vuzrazhdane (Mon–Fri 8.30am–5pm; ⍬www .pleven.bg) offers a less comprehensive service. If you're just passing through Pleven, there's a **left-luggage office** (*garderob*) in the train station (daily 6am–10pm, but with unpredictable lunch breaks), and another in the bus station (daily 7am–6pm). **Internet** access is available at the *Computer Club*, next door to the mausoleum on the city's main square.

Accommodation

Balkan 2km east of the centre at bul. Ruse 85 ☎064/822215, ⍬www.hotel-balkan.com. This socialist-era three-star high-rise looms over the town centre and has comfortably refurbished en-suite doubles. ❻

Face ul. Svoboda 12 ☎064/801613 A smart new hotel that's the most central and best value of those in the city. Also has a good restaurant and a popular café. ❹

🏃 **Orbita Palace** Kailaka Park, 6km south of Pleven ☎064/807937, ⍬www.orbitapalace .com. Modern place that offers acupuncture, mud

cures and massage, and can arrange hunting trips in the Byalka hunting reserve. ❺

Rostov just off pl. Svobodata at Slava Aleksiev 2 ☎064/801095, ⍬www.rostov.bg. This refurbished high-rise offers a reasonable standard of comfort, including a pleasant courtyard restaurant. ❼

Spartak Komplex Kailaka Park, 6km south of Pleven ☎064/804137. Surrounded by forest, this simple hotel has comfortable wood-panelled rooms, a small restaurant and helpful staff. ❷

The Town

At the southern end of Danail Popov, in a paved plaza, stands the sunken **Church of Sveti Nikolai**. A nineteenth-century portrait of the saint himself presides over the doorway of this simple structure, believed to date from the 1300s. Inside is a collection of icons, including works by the Samokov masters Stanislav Dospevski and Zahari Zograf, although many of the most attractive are by anonymous artists from villages in the Pleven region. Beyond the church lies **ulitsa Vasil Levski**, Pleven's busiest thoroughfare, lined with smart cafés and bars. Follow this south and you'll pass the **Museum of Liberation** in the park between Vasil Levski and bul. Osvobozhdenie (Mon–Sat 9am–noon & 1–5pm; free), occupying the small wooden house where the Turkish commander Osman Pasha formally surrendered to Tsar Aleksandar II in 1877. Inside you'll see weaponry, mementos and plans detailing each phase of the battle.

A little further on is pl.Vuzrazhdane, the city's **main square**, a fountain-splashed expanse of flagstones, flowers and shrubs dominated by a Russo-Byzantine-style **mausoleum** (daily 9am–noon & 1–6pm; free), built to commemorate the Russian soldiers who died at Pleven, although the number of Romanian names on the lists of the fallen makes it clear who saw the worst of the fighting. Garishly modernist grey-and-brown frescoes swirl around inside, while marble tombs and

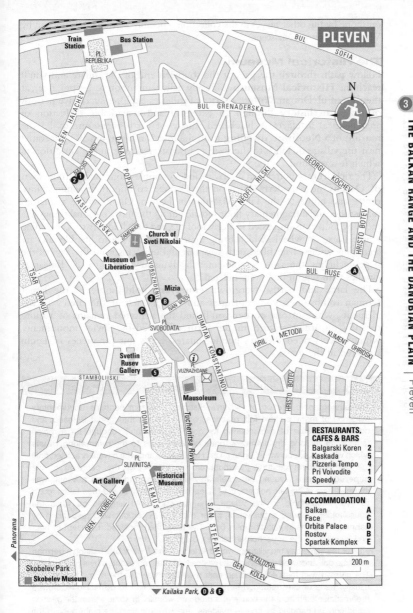

PLEVEN

Train Station

Bus Station

PL. REPUBLIKA

BUL SOFIA

BUL GRENADERSKA

N

ASEN HALACHEV

DANAIL POPOV

VASIL LEVSKI

TSAR SAMUIL

NIKOLA TSANOV

UL ZAMENHOF

NEOFIT RILSKI

GEORGI KOCHEV

HRISTO BOTEV

Church of Sveti Nikolai

Museum of Liberation

OSVOBOZHDENIE

Mizia

NAN VAZOV

PL SVOBODATA

DIMITAR KONSTANTINOV

BUL RUSE

KIRIL I. METODII

KLIMENT OHRIDSKI

Svetlin Rusev Gallery

STAMBOLIISKI

VUZRAZHDANE

HRISTO BOTEV

Mausoleum

UL DOIRAN

Tuchenitsa River

PL SLIVINITSA

Art Gallery

HEMUS

Historical Museum

GEN. SKOBELEV

SAN STEFANO

CHETALDZHA

GEN. KOLEV

Panorama

Skobelev Park
Skobelev Museum

Kailaka Park, **D** & **E**

RESTAURANTS, CAFES & BARS

Balgarski Koren	2
Kaskada	5
Pizzeria Tempo	4
Pri Voivodite	1
Speedy	3

ACCOMMODATION

Balkan	A
Face	C
Orbita Palace	D
Rostov	B
Spartak Komplex	E

0   200 m

plaques adorn the crypt. To the west of the square are the **old public baths**, a curious pseudo-Byzantine structure whose red-and-white striped facade could be easily mistaken for that of a church. It's now home to the **Svetlin Rusev Gallery** (Tues–Sun 9am–6pm; free), honouring the Pleven-born painter and former Politburo member (born 1933). His florid figurative works look strangely conservative when compared to the postwar art of the West, and are easily outshone by the other pieces in the collection – notably a striking self-portrait by Vladimir Dimitrov-Maistora.

The Historical Museum

Follow paths through the park at the southern end of the square and you'll reach the **Historical Museum** (officially daily 9am–noon & 1–5pm; free), at the foot of ul. Doiran. Within, a series of galleries explores successive periods of Bulgarian history through an extensive and remarkable collection of archeological artefacts. A blackened square of earth turns out to be the remains of a **Neolithic dwelling** from the fourth millennium BC, excavated near the village of Telish to the west and transferred here in the condition in which it was found.

The rich array of pottery on display includes examples from the **Roman town of Oescus**, near modern Gigen on the Danube, an important administrative centre and home to the Fifth Macedonian Legion. On show are numerous tombstones and a fragmentary floor mosaic but it's the more personal things like the baby footprints impressed in a clay roof tile, and the children's toys, including a little horse on wheels, which bring these ancient people to life. Upstairs are seemingly endless halls filled with weapons and uniforms from the days of the siege, including the samovars presented by Russian officers to the Bulgarian families with whom they were billeted.

The large and partly overgrown **courtyard** holds some of the larger Roman tombstones, votive plaques and statuary, left at the mercy of the elements, while in one corner you'll find the shattered remains of a more recently discarded culture, in the form of carved-up Soviet monuments, which once graced Pleven's public squares. Look out for pieces of Lenin scattered in the grass.

Bulgarian rainmaking rituals

The ethnographic section of Pleven's Historical Museum contains documentary evidence of many archaic folk practices once common throughout Bulgaria, and now on the verge of disappearing for good. Appropriately enough for a region famous for its long dry summers, pride of place goes to the **rainmaking rituals** which villagers hoped would bring an end to drought, and which were practised until the mid-twentieth century. Foremost among these was the parading of the **peperuda**, when a young girl (preferably an orphan, and always a virgin) was stripped bare by female helpers, clad in leaves and branches, and then taken round to every household in the village. The helpers would sing songs while the householder emptied a bucket of water over the *peperuda*, who responded by flapping her arms in imitation of a bird. The party then received a present of flour and beans from the householder before moving on.

Later the same day the villagers would emerge with a funeral bier bearing a **german** – a male doll endowed with an overlarge phallus (often represented by a red pepper). The *german* was then either buried near a well or thrown in the river. The doll was usually made of clay, although in the Pleven region it had to be fashioned from a broomstick stolen from the house of a pregnant woman. In some areas, the *german* could only be handled by chaste maidens, and had to spend the night prior to the ritual in the house of the girl chosen to play the *peperuda*.

The symbolic burial of the *german* seems to echo the fertility rites common to Indo-European peoples in ancient times, when, according to one branch of anthropological opinion, human sacrifices were made to mother earth in order to ensure good harvests.

▲ The Panorama, Pleven

Skobelev Park

Just to the southwest of the barracks, a lengthy processional stairway ascends towards **Skobelev Park**, passing the city **art gallery** (Mon–Fri 10am–5pm; free) on the way. Inside are several more examples of Svetlin Rusev's work, and the inevitable idealized-peasant-girl canvas courtesy of Dimitrov-Maistora. The park is laid out on a hill formerly occupied by the **Isa Aga Redoubt**, the object of fierce fighting in 1877, now restored and crowned with an obelisk commemorating the 405 troops who died capturing it. The **Skobelev Museum** (daily 9am–noon & 12.30–6pm; free) at the centre of the park holds a small display of photos and documents relating to the siege and the Russian general after whom the park is named. Numerous cannons are secreted within the greenery hereabouts, but the main focus of visitors' attention is the **Panorama** (same hours as museum; 5Lv), an enormous concrete funnel of a building housing a huge depiction of the early days of the siege, comprising three-dimensional figures set against a circular backdrop. Downstairs, a smaller diorama shows the Turkish commander Osman Pasha retreating over a bridge in the wake of the victorious Russian assault.

Kailaka Park

Leaving central Pleven by either of the main southbound boulevards, San Stefano or Vardar, it's 2km to the extensive **Kailaka Park**, laid out around the lush and rocky Tuchenitsa defile, and connected by regular buses to the town centre. The site of a Thracian settlement that the Romans took over and named Storgosia, it's here that the citizens of Pleven unwind at weekends, taking advantage of the park's swimming baths, watersports facilities and open-air theatre. There are also a couple of restaurants, including the *Peshtera*, in a cave at the foot of a limestone cliff – and below the baths a monument to the Jews who perished here in 1944 when the camp in which they were imprisoned was destroyed by fire. (Although anti-Semitism has never been prevalent in Bulgaria, the government jailed the Salonikan Jews during the latter stages of the war to appease its Nazi allies.) Three kilometres up the River Tuchenitsa, a bronze statue of General Totleben (Russian hero of the 1877 siege) surmounts the **Totleben rampart**, which separates two reservoirs: the lower reservoir is a popular bathing venue in summer. Not far from the entrance to the park on San Stefano is the castellated Basein sports complex (daily 9am–8pm; 3Lv), which has a small swimming pool, basketball court and snack bar. Trolleybuses #3 and #7 connect central Pleven with the northern entrance to the park.

Eating and drinking

Pleven's eating and drinking venues are mostly found around pl. Svobodata and ul. Vasil Levski. The best of the **restaurants** are in a small complex of National Revival-era houses just off the northern end of Vasil Levski, near the junction with Naicho Tsanov: *Pri Voivodite* is a traditional-style *mehana* in an atmospheric old building, while *Balgarski Koren*, just round the corner, has a lovely courtyard built around a pair of fountains. *Kaskada*, right behind the Svetlin Rusev Gallery, is a nice outdoor restaurant serving the usual grilled snacks and sandwiches, while *Pizzeria Tempo*, on ul. Dimitar Konstantinov, offers decent Italian-style fare, and *Speedy*, on pl. Svobodata, is a popular Bulgarian fast-food restaurant. The *Face*, *Balkan* and *Rostov* hotels all have good restaurants of their own.

Ulitsa Vasil Levski is the place to hang out in summertime, with a string of pavement cafés suitable for **drinking** day and night. For late-night entertainment try *Club Anaconda* next to *Face* hotel for mainstream techno, or *Club Faith* across the street from the Museum of Liberation for good dance music. As a last resort the *Rostov* hotel has a regular disco (10pm–5am), occasionally with live music.

South of Pleven: Lovech and Troyan

Lying just off the main road and train routes, the towns of **Lovech** and **Troyan** are often missed out by those travelling east to west. However, they do sit on one of the important trans-Balkan routes linking Pleven, on the margins of the Danubian Plain, with the Valley of the Roses to the south. In terms of scenery or sheer excitement, this route can't match crossing the more famous Shipka Pass (see p.296), but there are compensations. Lusher and less craggy than the mountains further east, the landscape has its own attractions, and **Troyan Monastery** certainly merits a visit. The small settlements around Troyan make good bases from which to explore the mountains, and the range of accommodation now available in the villages makes them infinitely preferable to the towns for an overnight stay; the tourist office in Troyan (see p.223) can make bookings.

Plenty of **buses** ply the Pleven–Lovech–Troyan route, and Lovech is also accessible by **train**, lying at the end of a branch line which leaves the main Sofia–Varna line at the otherwise unimportant town of Levski.

Lovech

LOVECH (ЛOBEЧ) lies an hour's drive to the south of Pleven, situated between the rolling foothills of the Balkan Mountains. It divides precisely into two sections, the flagstoned walkways and plazas of the modern centre contrasting with the grey stone roofs and protruding *chardaks* of the nineteenth-century **Varosh**, or **old town**, now an architectural preservation area. An important strategic point since Thracian times, standing guard over the northern approaches to the Troyan Pass, Lovech become famous as the headquarters of **Vasil Levski** (see p.286), whose statue and museum are now major attractions.

Nowadays Lovech is notorious for having been the site of one of Bulgaria's largest postwar concentration camps, which the inmates dubbed **Slanchev bryag** (Sunny Beach) in a grimly ironic reference to the well-known Black Sea holiday resort. On a happier note, the town is home to the Liteks **football team**, whose rise in recent years from obscurity to the upper reaches of the league (they were national champions in 2003) is one of the more positive stories to emerge from an otherwise stagnating sport.

The Town

Lovech's bustling centre is largely modern, an area of concrete and steel grouped around the pedestrianized **ulitsa Targovska**. Heading south along here, you'll soon reach the older parts of town, coming first to the **Pokritya most** or "Covered Bridge", the only one of its kind in the Balkans. Spanning the River Osam to link the new town with the old, it was originally designed by National Revival architect Kolyo Ficheto in 1874. The bridge burned down in 1925, and the present incarnation is the result of successive renovations; it now holds an arcade of boutiques, craft shops and cafés. At the eastern end of the bridge is **ploshtad Todor Kirkov**, named after the local revolutionary executed on this spot by the Turks in 1876 after taking part in the April Rising in Tryavna. Just behind the square is the town **Art Gallery** (Mon–Sat 9am–noon & 1–6pm; free), which houses a display of rustic scenes, many by local artists, and rotating exhibitions. One block south, the National Revival-style facade of a kindergarten announces the boundary of the Varosh, which stretches up the flanks of the hill from here.

The Ethnographic Museum

Most of the buildings in the Varosh are in fact modern constructions executed in traditional style, but the narrow cobbled lanes that run up the hillside are more authentically atmospheric. One of them, ul. Marin Pop Lukanov, leads to a couple of buildings occupied by the **Ethnographic Museum** (daily: 8am–noon & 1–5pm; 3Lv). Both of the wooden houses that make up the complex were built in the first half of the nineteenth century, on seventeenth-century foundations, although they have been furnished to represent two distinct, later periods. The first house has been kitted out in the style of the late nineteenth century, when even wealthy Bulgarians seemingly spent much of their lives close to the floor, eating their food from low wooden tables and sleeping on low beds. The more affluent lifestyles of the early twentieth century are shown by the imported Viennese furniture that fills a couple of set-piece rooms, along with an enormous British iron bedstead. Below in the cellar are a wine press, vats and huge barrels, as well as a *rakiya* still and a soap-making vessel in which fats were squeezed together and blended with natural perfumes. The second house has been restored to its 1930s appearance, and has a markedly more "Western" feel, with a modern kitchen range and a cosy little study lined with books. The furnished salon is inhabited by a family of costumed mannequins, a fashion of the day.

The Vasil Levski Museum

Just up the hill from here, a modern concrete structure houses the **Vasil Levski Museum** (daily: 8am–noon & 1–5pm; 3Lv). Between 1869 and 1872, Levski (see box, p.286) was chiefly responsible for establishing a network of revolutionary cells in Bulgaria. The organization's largest base was in Lovech, where Levski usually stayed at the home of Nikola Sirkov, arriving and leaving in disguise. In 1872 he was betrayed to the Turks and arrested in the neighbouring village of Kakrina, and following interrogation and torture, he was hanged on a winter's morning in Sofia in 1873.

Despite the lack of captions in any language other than Bulgarian, several of the museum's exhibits are self-explanatory. There are copies of Levski's letters bearing the lion seal of the revolutionary committee, as well as the Lovech committee's original printing press – a wooden tray no bigger than a hand into which tiny lines of type were set – accompanied by the amazingly professional-looking documents thus produced. Levski's sabre and dagger lie downstairs, perched atop a shrine-like lump of stone.

Uspenska church and around

Right next door to the museum is the **Uspenska church** (Mon–Fri 8am–5pm; free). The interior is a fresh and colourful showcase of contemporary artistry, the walls covered in a mixture of restored and new murals, while the ceiling and patches elsewhere still need work. Further up the hill, steps ascend to the tall and heroic **Levski statue** on Stratesh hill, where townsfolk come to admire the view. Higher again, up a badly pot-holed path, are the partly reconstructed walls of a medieval Bulgarian **fortress**, occupying a commanding position on the summit. Byzantine attempts to strangle the Second Bulgarian Kingdom at birth ended here in 1187, when they were forced to sign a peace treaty in Lovech castle recognizing Bulgarian independence.

Practicalities

Lovech's **train and bus stations** are next door to each other on high ground west of the town centre (tickets for express buses to Sofia are sold from booths in the train station forecourt); from here a five-minute walk down ul. Zacho Shishkov will bring you towards the main street, ul. Targovska. There's a **tourist office** at ul. Vasil Karakanovski 2 (Mon–Fri 9am–1pm & 2–5pm; ☎068/604218, ⓦwww.staraplanina.org/engl/lovech.php) next to the art gallery, which has maps and brochures, as well as details of local excursions. The best of these is to the **Devetazhkata cave**, 18km northeast of town, where a rich assortment of archeological artefacts has been found, indicating human occupation as far back as the Paleolithic era.

Accommodation

Bilyana ul. Vasil Karakanovski ☎068/604347. Situated in the tranquil streets of the old town, this family-run hotel offers clean, modern rooms in a cosy old-style house with a shaded courtyard. ❷
Lovech ul. Turgovska ☎068/685126. This once proud hotel is now a rather gloomy affair that has been eclipsed by the splendid new *Presidivm*. Three-star standards and comfortable rooms mean that it's still an agreeable choice for business travellers on a budget. ❸

Oasis ul. Ivan Drasov 17 ☎068/600612. Tucked away in a quiet part of town next to the river, the hotel has clean modern rooms with balconies and a/c. Polite staff provide a professional service. ❷
Presidivm ul. Turgovska ☎068/687513, ⓦwww .presidivm.com. Superb new central hotel featuring smart boutiques, a glass lift, stylish design and a high-class restaurant. ❺

Eating and drinking

The *Varosha mehana* and the *Pri Voivodite mehana* on ul. Poplukanov both have lovely courtyard gardens surrounded by wooden balconies, and are the most pleasant places to **eat and drink** in old Lovech, with regular performances of traditional music in the evenings and a wide range of traditional Bulgarian dishes. One of Lovech's best restaurants, which also specialises in local cusine, is the *Drakata*, on pl. Todor Kirkov, whose balcony affords a splendid view of the river and the covered bridge. Those after a more international menu should head for the *Presidivm*'s excellent *Apollo* restaurant. Cafés and snack bars are in plentiful supply around pl. Todor Kirkov, or along ul. Targovska in the new town. *Café Versailles*, at ul. Targovska 85, is the best place in town for cocktails, with a riverside terrace.

Troyan and around

The journey south from Lovech takes you through wooded hills to **TROYAN** (ТРОЯН), a ramshackle town ranged along the banks of the River Osam. Though no great attraction in itself, Troyan has a relaxing, semi-rural feel, and provides transport connections to a host of places sheltering in the folds of the Balkan mountains. **Troyan Monastery** and the hiker-friendly villages of **Cherni Osam** and **Apriltsi** are the main places to aim for southeast of town, while subalpine settlements like **Shipkovo** and **Chiflik** lurk in side valleys to the west. All offer excellent walking opportunities and make good bases for exploring the Central Balkan National Park, which lies to the south, and for which the 1:65,000 *Troyan Balkan* **map** (available from the Troyan tourist office; see below) is indispensable.

The Town

Troyan's **bus station** lies a couple of blocks east of the town centre, where the flagstoned main square contains the **Museum of Folk Crafts and Applied Arts** (daily 9am–5pm; 3Lv), a superbly organized display with English-language texts. Here you'll find comprehensive displays of local ceramics, woodcarvings, musical instruments and folk costumes, as well as reconstructions of a wood-turner's workroom and a nineteenth-century house. Troyan became a major centre of **ceramic** production in the nineteenth century, and most of the souvenir pottery you'll see for sale around Bulgaria is still made here. Troyan wares are instantly recognizable from the *Troyanska kapka* ("Troyan droplet") design, achieved by allowing successive layers of colour to drip down the side of the vessel before glazing. A few items are on sale in the museum, and visits to local ceramicists, which usually involve an opportunity to purchase, can be organized through the tourist office. Next door to the Museum of Folk Crafts is the **Historical Museum** (daily 9am–5pm; 3Lv), holding the usual patriotic exhibition chronicling the Uprising and Liberation, and occupying a building once used as a Turkish police station.

Practicalities

Ulitsa Vasil Levski, the main street, heads north from the main square passing the very helpful **municipal tourist office** at no. 133 (summer daily 10am–7pm, winter daily 10am–5pm; ℡0670/60964, ⓦ www.troyan-bg.com). The office sells maps, rents **bikes** (1Lv per hour), gives advice on **walking** in the Central Balkan National Park, hires out English-speaking hiking guides, organizes **pony-trekking** trips (from one hour to one week), and even offers **microlite** flights over the region (2Lv per minute). It also arranges **accommodation** in small hotels and private rooms, although most of these are in the surrounding villages of Oreshak, Cherni Osam, Chiflik and Shipkovo rather than in Troyan itself. The town suffers from a dire lack of accommodation: at present visitors must choose between the lavish four-star *Hotel Plaza Troyan* at ul. Slaveikov 54 in the centre (℡0670/64399, 🌐www.troyanplaza.com; ⑥) and the recently refurbished *Park Hotel Troyan*, occupying an enviable perch on the Kapina hill above town to the east and offering a spa centre, indoor pool and fitness facilities (℡0670/60964; ④).

The *Plaza Troyan's* Bulgarian style **restaurant** is the best in town; the *Fenerite mehana* on ul. Dimitar Ikonomov is a more modest alternative. The *One* bar next door is a good place to down a beer or two. There are numerous **bars** and **cafés** along ul. Vasil Levski: *Dreams*, a swish, modern establishment right opposite the tourist office, is one of the best places for coffee and cakes. For **Internet** access, try the Internet Game Centre at ul. Vasil Levski 63. If you're in town on the last Saturday of September, you'll coincide with the annual **Rakiya Festival**, which takes place in various locations across town, with music, dancing, parades, and, of course, the opportunity to sample the local spirit from which the festival takes its name.

Troyan Monastery

Nine daily buses head east from Troyan up the Cherni Osam valley, through the straggling village of **Oreshak** (ОРЕШАК) to Bulgaria's third-largest monastery. Perched on the west bank of the Cherni Osam River and shaded by trees, the **Troyan Monastery** (Troyanski manastir; daily dawn–dusk; free) was founded in the early fifteenth century, though its church, Sveta Bogoroditsa, wasn't built until four hundred years later. It is the church, however, that is of most interest, principally because of its **frescoes** by **Zahari Zograf**, Bulgaria's most outstanding exponent of nineteenth-century religious art.

The highlight of Zograf's work is outside the church porch, a vivid series of scenes depicting the *Last Judgement*, including a suitably macabre figure of Death bundling unfortunates into the gaping mouth of hell. The theme is continued in slightly faded scenes along the west side of the church's outer wall, with St Peter admitting the virtuous to the walled garden of paradise, and a wonderfully vulgar scene revealing what the Orthodox Church really thought of rural Bulgaria's *vrachka* (wise woman), whose herbal remedies are being deposited in her hand by a demon, squatting on her head. More of Zahari's work appears in the vestibule, where the artist even took the liberty of including a self-portrait (visible in a window niche on the north side of the nave), next to a picture of Hadzhi Filotei, the abbot who commissioned the work. Zahari's brother Dimitar painted the icons which feature in the exquisite, Tryavna-produced **iconostasis**, with its intricately wrought walnut pillars topped by exotic birds of prey, each holding a snake in its beak.

Outside the church, on the third floor of the monastery living quarters, is a small "**hiding-place museum**" (daily 9am–6pm; 2Lv), set up when Vasil Levski encouraged the monks to start a branch of the revolutionary underground at Troyan. The table and food bowl used by the itinerant patriot stand beside the wooden cupboard in which he supposedly hid whenever agents of the sultan came calling. An adjacent room displays icons, archiepiscopal robes and church regalia, including the surviving doors of an eighteenth-century iconostasis from the previous monastery church.

A popular side-trip from the monastery is to walk to the much smaller (and rarely manned) **Monastery of Sveti Nikolai**, thirty minutes' walk uphill on the other side of the valley. Cross the footbridge opposite Troyan Monastery's gate and bear right, picking up a track to the left when you see a small graveyard. From here a stony path zigzags uphill, offering a challengingly steep but well-shaded climb. There's nothing to see at the tumbledown monastery itself, but its fragrant woodland setting makes the walk worthwhile.

Shipkovo, Chiflik and the Troyan Pass

The main road heading south out of Troyan takes the high-mountain route over the Troyan Pass, but just after the end of town, two turn-offs give access to a couple of attractive side valleys. The northern turning heads up the Razhdavets valley, at the top of which sits the village of **SHIPKOVO** (ШИПКОВО), sandwiched between steep wooded slopes with a small spa resort at its western end. Served by five buses a day from Troyan, it's an unassuming, family-oriented destination where people flock to use the open-air swimming pool in summer. The family-run *Bakhus* hotel (☎06966/385, ⓦwww.bgglobe.net/bakhus.html; ❹) stands beside the road 1km before the centre; newly built in traditional style with wide wooden balconies and a hot pool, it's popular with both Bulgarian and foreign tourists. There's a cluster of trade-union rest-homes and hotels on the opposite side of town, all of which can be booked through the Troyan tourist office: the *Planinska Rai* (☎06966/531; ❷) has a superb position with great views and an outdoor pool, the *Victoria Hotel* (☎06966/661, ⓕ262; ❷) is a two-star place with en-suite rooms and satellite TV, while a notch lower in terms of comfort, the *Villa Borovets* (☎06966/251, ⓕ625; ❶), is a cosy place, but with shared facilities. Beyond Shipkovo, the road winds its picturesque way over the hills towards Ribaritsa and Teteven (see p.213).

The middle turning follows the river towards the village of **Beli Osam**, an unspectacular place with a decent **hotel**, the *Bile* (☎0695/333; ❸), and plenty of **private rooms**, such as at the *Haik* house (☎06965/734, ⓔhaik @mail.bg; ❷) whose owner can arrange hiking trips in the locality. The village stretches lazily along the roadside for several kilometres before fading imperceptibly into the attractive settlement of **CHIFLIK** (ЧИФЛИК; two daily buses from Troyan), squeezed between narrowing valley walls. There are some very comfortable **private rooms** (❶) here; look out for roadside signs advertising the *Ilian* house (☎0670/25190; ❷), or contact the Troyan tourist office for other addresses and advance bookings. At the far end of Chiflik the road peters out beside another, more spectacularly located, open-air swimming pool, fed by mineral water that arrives warmed from local springs. Overlooking the pool is the *Chiflik* hotel (☎0670/22038; ❹); set back in the forest, the luxury spa *Komplex Diva* (☎0670/60935, ⓦwww.pmk-bg.com; ❹) has its own 35°C mineral pool and offers massage, sauna and physiotherapy. Nearby, the brand-new *Venika Palace* spa complex (☎0670/60000, ⓦwww .venika.net; ❺) overlooks the river and provides a high standard of facilities. From the road end, a steadily worsening asphalt track continues for 4km to the *Haidushka Pesen* hut, which is the starting point for the two-hour hike to the **Kozya stena ridge** and, a little way beyond, the *Kozya Stena* chalet.

Continuing south along the main road, you'll begin to climb slowly through dense forests towards the **Troyan Pass**, past the fledgling ski-centre of **Beklemeto** just below the summit. A wonderful panorama appears as the road crosses the 1450m-high pass, with the Stryama valley receding towards the Sredna Gora, and its highest peak Mount Bogdan (1714m), and the Plain of Thrace beyond leading to the bluish silhouette of the distant Rhodopes. At the foot of the mountains lies **Karnare**, a nondescript town where you can catch regular buses or trains into the neighbouring **Valley of the Roses** (see Chapter Four). The pass is accessible via two daily Troyan–Plovdiv **buses** that currently leave Troyan at 7am, returning from Plovdiv at 1.30pm (mid-April to mid-Oct depending on snow).

Practicalities

Accommodation is available in the Troyan monastery from an office just inside the main gate, which offers double rooms for 40Lv – but note there's a

10pm curfew. Things get busy during the days leading up to the monastery's main holy day, the Feast of the Assumption (*Golyama Bogoroditsa*) on August 15, but outside of this time you should have no problem getting a bed, though you can always phone ahead (☎06952/2866). There are numerous **guest houses** (❷–❸) in Oreshak, the southern end of which begins just outside the monastery gates, which are best booked through the tourist office in Troyan, and a couple of **hotels** – the three-star *Sveta Gora* (☎06952/3160; ❸), in the hills above the village, and the quiet *Edelweiss* (☎0670/35452; ❶), signposted off the main street.

Food and drink is available from the stalls in the parking lot outside the monastery, or the *Manastirska Bara* restaurant opposite, which has a wooden verandah overlooking the river. Alternatively, Oreshak has a couple of restaurants on or near its main street: the *Kaiser*, roughly halfway through the village, does a good barbecue in its courtyard, and the well-known *Dobrudzhanska Sreshta*, signed off to the left if coming from the Troyan direction, offers good Bulgarian food in traditionally furnished rooms; next door is the equally popular *Oresheka mehana*. It's also worth noting that Oreshak's **Fair of Arts and Crafts** (daily 9am–5pm; craft exhibition 3Lv), just before the monastery, sells pottery, textiles and woodcarvings from all over Bulgaria of much better quality than those on sale at the touristy souvenir stalls outside the monastery itself.

Cherni Osam and around

A couple of kilometres beyond the monastery, buses from Troyan come to rest in the village of **CHERNI OSAM** (ЧЕРНИ ОСЪМ), an unspoilt logging community which provides an excellent base to explore the upper reaches of the Cherni Osam Valley and the Central Balkan National Park, an extensive nature reserve which lies just south of the village. It's also home to a small **Natural History Museum**, located at the southern end of the village (daily 8am–noon & 1–5pm; 3Lv). Stuffed examples of the local wildlife are on show, including stags, bears and wolves, some mounted on revolving pedestals, with background tapes playing the appropriate howls and growls.

There are a few friendly, family-run **hotels** just off the main street, the most comfortable of which is the *Spomen* (☎06962/575; ❷), with five comfortable en-suite rooms grouped around a central courtyard; the price includes breakfast, and lunch or dinner can be arranged for an extra fee. The *Otdich* hotel (☎06962/528; ❷) offers rooms with self-catering facilities; and the more basic *Sherpa* (☎06962/269; ❶ with breakfast) is a converted house with a shared bathroom inside and another outside in the courtyard. The owner, Radyu Minkov, is an experienced hiker who can advise on the best of the local trails or organize guided walks and picnics, though only if you speak Bulgarian, French or German. A wonderful home-cooked dinner, with wine, is available for an extra charge. If you've got your own transport, you could consider staying in the hamlet of **Stoynovsko** (turn right over a bridge 3.5km south of Cherni Osam) at the *Rodan kashta* (☎06962/329; ❷), which offers traditional-style rooms, and a fabulous back garden with an outdoor kitchen that guests can use. For **eating and drinking**, the *Spomen* has a small bar and restaurant, and the *Kolibito* restaurant on the square adjacent to the *Sherpa* serves good food.

The most convenient starting point for forays into the mountains is **Yavorova Laka**, 9km south of Cherni Osam, where a fairly obvious trail ascends southwest beside the Malka Krayovitsa stream to the *Ambaritsa* **chalet** (2hr). From here, a path climbs steadily southwards to join the ridge of the main Balkan Range (1hr), just below the 2166-metre summit of **Mount Ambaritsa**. Another option is the hike up to **Zelenikovski Monastery**: drive or walk the

5km south from Cherni Osam to the tiny village of Vets, from where a well-marked path leads first to the isolated hamlet of Glushka (50min) and then to the monastery (1hr 10min), where you can sleep for a small fee; take food and a torch as facilities are basic.

Apriltsi

Five buses a day run east from Troyan to **APRILTSI** (АПРИЛЦИ), a large village nestling in the Vidima valley. It covers a wide area, with the suburbs of **Vidima** and **Ostrets** spreading many kilometres into the side valleys which fork away from the centre of the village. Buses from Troyan terminate in Ostrets, 3km southeast of the centre, so it's best to ask the driver for "Apriltsi", ensuring that you'll be put down somewhere on the main street, ul. Vasil Levski, where you'll find the **tourist office** at no. 102 (Tues–Sat 11am–7pm; ☎06958/3249). Helpful staff provide hiking advice and maps, rent bicycles, organize horse-riding trips and book **accommodation** in a number of guest houses and hotels (❶–❸), most of which offer half- or full-board for a little extra. The family-run *Tihiya Kat* hotel in the suburb of Ostrets (☎06958/2102 and 3363; ❷) is probably the smartest option, featuring a stylish open-air swimming pool and stunning mountain views; the *Apriltsi* hotel (☎06958/2191; ❸) overlooking the village is a larger, dated complex with a pool, tennis court, sauna and great views. In the centre of Apriltsi, the *Dr. Tsurov* (☎06958/2436; ❷) has its own restaurant and a pleasant garden courtyard as well as an outdoor pool. For more atmospheric accommodation try the *Skandaloto* (☎06964/243, ⓦwww .balkania.org/en/hotels_apr.html; ❷) in the sleepy village of **Skandalo**, six kilometres before Apriltsi.

The main trail-heads for **hikers** start 5km out from the centre, at the southern end of Vidima, where a right fork in the road leads to the head of the Starna valley 6.5km away, while a left fork heads up the Lyava Vidima valley, passing the *Vidima* chalet (9Lv per person) after another 3km, then petering out 4km further on. Either spot serves as the jumping-off point for paths to the *Pleven* chalet, a steep one-hour climb further south. The forbidding terrain of the main Balkan Range lies immediately beyond, although you'll need a **guide** hired through the Apriltsi tourist office to make full use of it.

East towards Veliko Tarnovo

If you have a car, it's relatively easy to cut northeast across country from the Troyan region to join the main E772 highway towards Veliko Tarnovo. Relying on public transport makes things more complicated, and you may have to double back to Lovech or Pleven in order to pick up eastbound buses and trains. Most eastward road routes come together at **SEVLIEVO** (СЕВЛИЕВО), 40km from Lovech, a small rural centre renowned for its world-class motocross track and unblemished nineteenth-century buildings. Ulitsa Skobelevska, the main street, bears a decrepit-looking **Church of the Prophet Elijah**, with icons by Tryavna masters; next door, the **Historical Museum** at no. 10 (Mon–Sat 8.30am–noon & 3.30–5pm; 2Lv), housed in the former village schoolhouse, details the various craft industries that characterized town life before the Liberation. One of the more important trades was leatherworking, memories of which are preserved in the **Tabahana**, at Tabashka 3 (Tues–Sun 8am–noon & 2–6pm; 2Lv), a nineteenth-century tannery decked out with original tools and animal skins. For local information try the **tourist office** on the main square (Mon–Fri 9am–noon & 1–5pm; ☎0675/30960). There's no reason **to stay** in Sevlievo, but if you have to, try either the luxurious central *Sevlievo Plaza Hotel*, at pl. Svoboda 6 (☎0675/30743, ⓦwww.sevlievo-plaza.com; ❼) or the smaller *Odessa Hotel* at ul. Dunov 1 (☎0675/30077; ❷).

Emen

Northeast of Sevlievo lies one of the major white-wine-producing areas of Bulgaria, with low vineyard-cloaked hills feeding the wineries of towns like **Suhindol** and **Pavlikeni**. There are no real tourist centres here yet, save for the village of **EMEN** (ЕМЕН) lying 8km north of the main Tarnovo-bound E772 on a minor road which cuts across country to Pavlikeni. If you're travelling by public transport, you'll have to catch a bus from Veliko Tarnovo in the direction of Sevlievo, getting off at Balyan and then walking or hitching the eight kilometres to the village. Emen offers rural peace, and the chance to walk through the **Emen Gorge**, where a wooden walkway leads past rushing waters to a small lake and a waterfall. Back in the village, the *Imenieto* **hotel** (☎062/550055, ⓦwww.imenieto .com; ❸) offers stylish air-conditioned accommodation in several small houses with neatly mown lawns. There's also a heated outdoor pool and the owners can arrange mountain biking and horse riding.

Veliko Tarnovo

The precipitously perched houses of **VELIKO TARNOVO** (ВЕЛИКО ТЪРНОВО) seem poised to leap into the chasms that divide the city into its separate quarters. Medieval fortifications girdling the Tsarevets massif add melodrama to the scene, yet even more transfixing are the huddles of antique houses that the writer Ivan Vazov likened to frightened sheep, bound to the rocks by wild lilac and vines, forming picturesque reefs veined by steps and narrow streets. Le Corbusier raved about Tarnovo's "organic" architecture, and even the dour Prussian Field Marshal Helmut Von Moltke was moved to remark that he had "never seen a town of more romantic location".

But for Bulgarians the city has a deeper significance. When the National Assembly met here to draft Bulgaria's first constitution in 1879, it consciously did so in the former capital of the Second Kingdom (1185–1396) whose medieval civilization was snuffed out by the Turks. Reclaiming this heritage was an integral part of the National Revival, and since independence (especially during the socialist era) archeologists have been keenly uncovering the past of Tarnovo "the Great" – not only the medieval citadel of **Tsarevets** but also the churches of **Sveta Gora** and **Trapezitsa**. Nor is the city an isolated case, for in the hills and valleys around Tarnovo are several monasteries and small towns founded during the Second Kingdom or in the aftermath of its collapse, which make great excursions from town. An added sense of vibrancy stems from its twenty thousand-strong student population who throng the streets by day and fill the town's bars and clubs by night.

Tarnovo's convenience as a touring base is backed up by the city's **train and bus links** with towns like Dryanovo, Tryavna and Gabrovo to the south, which all easy day-trips from here. In addition, the Bucharest–Istanbul express train travels through once a day in each direction – useful if you're travelling further afield, but note that tickets must be purchased in advance from the Rila/BDZh office (see listings, p.239).

Arrival and information

All **trains** between Sofia and Varna stop at Gorna Oryahovitsa (ГОРНА ОРЯХОВИЦА) to the north, from where ten local trains a day cover the remaining 13km to Veliko Tarnovo. In the middle of the day there's a large gap between services, so you can save time by hopping on the shuttle bus to Gorna Oryahovitsa's bus terminal, from where there's a connection every fifteen minutes (#10 or #14) to Veliko Tarnovo.

Tarnovo's **train station**, on the Stara Zagora–Ruse line, is 2km south of the centre – buses #4 and #13 (from the bus stop nearest to the station building) run to the main thoroughfare, bul. Levski. If you don't mind a fifteen-minute uphill walk, turn left out of the station yard and keep bearing left until you reach the centre. The main **bus terminal** (*Avtogara Zapad*) is southwest of town at the end of Nikola Gabrovski: take bus #10 or trolleybuses #1 and #21 to reach the centre. Privately operated bus services from Sofia and the coast pick up and drop off outside the *Hotel Etar*.

The excellent **tourist information centre** at ul. Hristo Botev 5 (summer daily, winter Mon–Fri 9am–noon & 1–6pm; ☏062/622148, ⓦwww .velikoturnovo.info) books hotels and arranges excursions and car rental, while the **Bulgarian Tourist Union** (Turistichesko Druzhestvo Trapezitsa 1902; ⓦwww.trapezitca1902.com), located in an office next to the Turistichni Dom *Trapezitsa* (see p.230), organizes walking, mountain-biking and climbing trips. Mountain bikes and a wide variety of outdoor equipment can be rented from Gorgona Shop (☏062/601400, ⓦwww.gorgona-shop.com) at ul. Zelenka 2.

Accommodation

Hotels are plentiful enough, with a growing number of small, family-run places and modern luxury concerns competing with the larger and older establishments. More are to be found out of town in Arbanasi, which makes an appealing rural alternative to staying in the city (see p.239). There are also a number of **hostels** offering comfortable dorm accommodation.

Hostels

Hikers Hostel ul. Rezervoarska 91 ☏062/604019 or 0887 098279, ⓦwww.hikers-hostel.org. Relaxed place with rustic furniture offering dorm beds, one double room, self-catering facilities and superb views of Tsarevets. Guests can pitch tents in the yard. Tents 12Lv; dorm beds 20Lv; rooms ②

Tarnovo's uprisings

The Ottoman-ruled city of Tarnovo played host to three proudly remembered **uprisings**. The first came in 1598, when locals aided by Dubrovnik merchant Pavel Džordžic rose up in the mistaken belief that the Austrian emperor Rudolf II had promised to send military help. The second, in 1688, came about when Polish victories against the Turks once again persuaded Tarnovo's *charshiya* that foreign armies were preparing to ride to their aid. Local noble Rostislav Stratsimirovich, a direct descendant of Tsar Ivan Stratsimir, was declared prince of Bulgaria, then forced to flee by the Ottomans, who set fire to the town in retribution. The third, known as **Velchova Zavera** or "Velcho's plot", was in 1835, when glass merchant Velcho Atanasov Dzhamdzhiyata hatched the hare-brained scheme of laying siege to the fortress of Varna in the hope of encouraging Russian intervention. Unsurprisingly, the conspirators were captured and hanged.

Hostel Mostel ul. Yordan Indzheto 10 ☎0897 859359, ⓦwww.hostelmostel.com. Spacious, comfortable place in a restored 200-year-old house with dorms, en-suite doubles and camping in the garden. Breakfast and an evening meal are included. Tents 14Lv; dorm beds 20Lv; rooms ❸

Loft Hostel ul. Kapitan Dyado Nikola 2A ☎0877 323255, ⓦwww.thelofthostel.com. Small, friendly hostel hidden away in the back streets with great views of the old town. Guests have use of a kitchen, laundry service and Internet access. Dorm beds 16Lv.

Nomads Hostel ul. Gurko 27 ☎062/603092, ⓦwww.nomadshostel.com. Well-located hostel with sweeping views of the Yantra valley. Hospitable staff organize local excursions and ensure that guests are well looked after. Dorm beds 18Lv.

Phoenix Hostel ul. Hristo Daskalov 12 ☎062/603112 and 0885 973532, ⓦwww .phoenixhostel.com. Pleasantly furnished hostel run by a pair of English bikers. It offers homely kitchen facilities, garage space, and a balcony with views of the town. Dorm beds 20Lv.

Hotels

Beyskata Kushta ul. Chitalishtna 4 ☎062/602480, ⓦwww.beiskata.com. Charming accommodation in a renovated old house surrounding quiet gardens. Nineteenth-century-style furnishings are tastefully combined with flat-screen TVs and Wi-Fi. ❹

Comfort Paneyot Tipografov 5 ☎062/628728, ⒺHotel_komfortvt@abv.bg. Friendly, basic but spotless pension with large en suites and stunning views of Tsarevets. ❸

Etar ul. Ivailo 2 ☎062/621838, ⓦwww.hoteletar .com. Imposing and slightly unkempt high-rise with good views of the old town, but slightly overpriced for what it offers. Rooms with shared facilities or en suites. ❸

Gurko ul. General Gurko 33 ☎062/627838, ⓦwww.hotel-gurko.com. Family-run hotel overlooking the river, offering large comfortable en suites with TV, minibar and a/c. ❺

Pink Bakery ul. Rezervoarska 5 ☎062/633339, ⓦwww.the-pink-bakery.com. Unmissable pink building in the old town offering comfortably furnished rooms, kitchen facilities and a large terrace. ❹

Premier Hotel ul. Sava Penev 1 ☎062/615555, ⓦwww.hotelpremier-bg.com. Luxurious modern place tucked away down a backstreet. Facilities include solarium, steam room, sauna and pool. ❺

Stambolov Guest House ul. Stefan Stambolov 27 ☎0888 835048, ⓦwww.stambolovhouse.hit.bg.

Hefty metal doors lead into this tall, narrow building perched high above the Yantra River. Quirky, spacious rooms are individually designed and feature exposed brick and timber as well as fantastic views. ❷

Tsarevets Hotel ul. Chitalistna 23 ☎062/601885, ⓦwww.tsarevetshotel.com. Plush sister hotel of the *Premier*. Housed in a refurbished nineteenth-century building just before Tsarevets with spacious well-appointed rooms and excellent service. ❺

Turistichni Dom Trapezitsa Stambolov 79 ☎062/622061. Unassuming but friendly hotel run by the Bulgarian Tourist Union on the old town's central thoroughfare. The rooms are clean with en-suite bathrooms, but they fill up quickly with holidaying Bulgarians. ❷

Veliko Tarnovo Emil Popov 2 ☎062/601000. Elegant concrete palace aspiring to an international business standard. Rooms come with the usual comforts, satellite TV and sweeping views of the old town. There's also an indoor pool, sauna and gym. Breakfast included. ❹

Voenen Club ul. Mayka Balgaria 1 ☎062/601521. Centrally located, clean, modern place behind Mustang Food. ❷

🏃 **Yantra** ul. Opalchenska 2 ☎062/600607, ⓦwww.yantrabg.com. One of the town's best central hotels, with superb views of Tsarevets to the rear. Facilities include fitness centre, indoor pool and Wi-Fi. ❺

The Town

Lying on an incline, the city's drab **modern centre** holds most of Tarnovo's downtown shopping area along bul. Levski and bul. Nezavisimost. From here you can proceed eastwards on foot and let yourself be drawn gradually into the **old town**. This is fascinating, not so much for its specific sights, of which there are relatively few, but for the feel of the place generally: there's always a fresh view of the city poised above the gorges or some new, unexpected detail.

Heading east along ul. Nezavisimost, you'll arrive at the small **ploshtad Pobornicheski** or "Combatants' Square", which has a monument to local rebel Bacho Kiro and other revolutionaries of 1876, whom the Turks hanged from gallows erected on what was then a rubbish tip. The "**House of the Little Monkey**" overlooking pl. Slaveikov at Vastanicheska 14 gets its nickname from the small grimacing statuette over the balcony, although the bay windows and deeply pointed brickwork are what make it so characteristic of Tarnovo architecture. It was designed in 1849 by Bulgaria's leading nineteenth-century architect Nikolai Fichev or "Kolyo Ficheto" (see p.245), the first of many Tarnovo buildings to bear his imprint. Like many of the town's old houses, it sits precariously above a limited ground space, with orieled living quarters above what used to be a shop or warehouse.

The bazaar and the Varosh quarter

Various restored workshops and the facade of an old *caravanserai* make up the Samovodska charshiya or **bazaar** at the junction of ul. Rakovski and pl. Georgi Kirkov. Aside from one surviving coppersmith and a weaver selling handmade *chergi* (rugs), most of the craftspeople who once had ateliers here have moved out to be replaced by clothes boutiques. It's still highly photogenic though, with its wrought-iron garnished facades and cobbled slopes. Starting from the square at the end of the bazaar, you can follow ul. Vastanicheska up into the narrow streets of the peaceful old **Varosh quarter**, whose two nineteenth-century churches are verging on the decrepit. The **Church of Sveti Nikolai** has a carving on the bishop's throne which shows a lion (representing Bulgaria) in the coils of a snake (the Greek Church) being devoured by a dragon (Turkey), and up the hill from here on ul. Kiril i Metodii the **Church of SS Kiril i Metodii** – with its belfry and dome by Kolyo Ficheto – still serves worshippers.

▲ Veliko Tarnovo

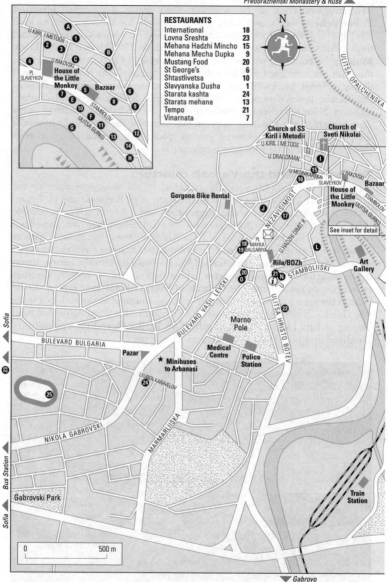

Preobrazhenski Monastery & Ruse ▲

RESTAURANTS

International	18
Lovna Sreshta	23
Mehana Hadzhi Mincho	15
Mehana Mecha Dupka	9
Mustang Food	20
St George's	6
Shtastlivetsa	10
Slavyanska Dusha	1
Starata kashta	24
Starata mehana	13
Tempo	21
Vinarnata	7

▼ Gabrovo

The Sarafkina House

Continuing from pl. Velchova Zavera along ul. Ivan Vazov, you'll catch sight of the **Church of SS Konstantin i Elena** on the right, skulking behind foliage at the bottom of a steep flight of steps. From here you can descend to what is perhaps the most characteristic of Tarnovo's streets, **ulitsa General Gurko**, where the houses – mainly dating from Ottoman times – look stunningly

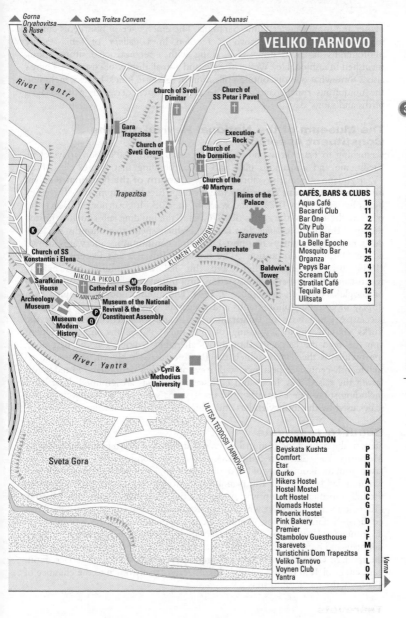

VELIKO TARNOVO

Gorna Oryahovitsa & Ruse — Sveta Troitsa Convent — Arbanasi

River Yantra

Church of Sveti Dimitar
Church of SS Petar i Pavel
Gara Trapezitsa
Church of Sveti Georgi
Execution Rock
Church of the Dormition
Church of the 40 Martyrs
Trapezitsa
Ruins of the Palace
Tsarevets
Patriarchate
Baldwin's Tower
Church of SS Konstantin i Elena
NIKOLA PIKOLO
KLIMENT OHRIDSKI
Sarafkina House
Cathedral of Sveta Bogoroditsa
Archeology Museum
U/VAN VAZOV
Museum of Modern History
Museum of the National Revival & the Constituent Assembly
River Yantra
Cyril & Methodius University
ULITSA TEODOSI TARNOVSKI
Sveta Gora
Varna

CAFÉS, BARS & CLUBS	
Aqua Café	16
Bacardi Club	11
Bar One	2
City Pub	22
Dublin Bar	19
La Belle Epoche	8
Mosquito Bar	14
Organza	25
Pepys Bar	4
Scream Club	17
Stratilat Café	3
Tequila Bar	12
Ulitsata	5

ACCOMMODATION	
Beyskata Kushta	P
Comfort	B
Etar	N
Gurko	H
Hikers Hostel	A
Hostel Mostel	Q
Loft Hostel	C
Nomads Hostel	G
Phoenix Hostel	I
Pink Bakery	D
Premier	J
Stambolov Guesthouse	F
Tsarevets	M
Turistichini Dom Trapezitsa	E
Veliko Tarnovo	L
Voynen Club	O
Yantra	K

picturesque, perched along the curve of the gorge. Don't miss the Sarafkinova kashta or **Sarafkina House** at no. 88 (Mon–Fri 9am–5.30pm; 4Lv), which is so contrived that only two floors are visible from General Gurko but a further three overhang the river. The interior is notable for the splendid octagonal vestibule with wrought-iron fixtures and a panelled rosette ceiling which, like the elegantly furnished rooms upstairs, reflects the taste of the architect and owner, the moneylender Dimo Sarafkina. The emergence of bourgeois culture in nineteenth-century Tarnovo is recalled in a gallery of sepia family photographs displayed downstairs, along with a reconstructed sitting room, furnished in fashionable "Western" style, and a small display of costumes. There's also a somewhat out-of-context collection of folkloric knick-knacks, including the ubiquitous ritual loaves, baked to celebrate such occasions as marriages, births and saints' days.

The Museum of the National Revival and the Constituent Assembly

Returning to Ivan Vazov and continuing southwards, you'll soon arrive at pl. Saedinenie and a spacious blue and white building that houses the *Muzei* "Vazrazhdane i Ureditelno sabranie" – the **Museum of the National Revival and the Constituent Assembly** (daily except Tues 9am–6pm; 4Lv). Designed by Kolyo Ficheto in 1872 as the *konak* of the Turkish governor, Ali Bey (who oversaw the trials of the rebels of 1876 here), the building subsequently hosted the first Bulgarian *sabranie* (parliament), which spent two months in 1879 deliberating the country's first post-Liberation constitution – afterwards known as the "Tarnovo Constitution". The union of Bulgaria and Eastern Rumelia (1885) was also signed here, and this hallowed building was exactly reconstructed (after being devastated by fire) in time to allow the proclamation of People's Power on September 9, 1944. The ground floor is occupied by a display of countless photographs and Bulgarian-only texts, paying homage to successive generations of Bulgarian patriots and their rebellions against the Turks – notably the local uprisings of 1598 and 1688 (see box on p.229). Unless you can read the language, though, it's all rather tedious. On the first floor, meanwhile, is the hall in which the Provisional Assembly sat, restored to its nineteenth-century appearance, with rows of benches upholstered in red velvet facing the raised daïs. Icons and ecclesiastical objects are grouped downstairs, including some fine examples from the Tryavna school, as well as weights and scales used by the moneylenders and a big still for *rakiya* brewing.

South to Tsarevets

Steps to the right of the National Revival Museum lead down to the **Archeology Museum** (Tues–Sun 9am–5pm; 4Lv), whose collection includes various artefacts taken from the Roman city of Nicopolis ad Istrum, 17km north of Tarnovo, which was founded by Emperor Trajan in 107AD. Around the corner and lower down the hill, a former Turkish prison now holds the **Museum of Modern History** (Tues–Sun 9am–5pm; 4Lv), which contains a few personal effects of Tarnovo-born politician Stefan Stambolov, an autocratic prime minister who was assassinated by disgruntled Macedonians in 1895, alongside photographs, drawings, military uniforms and firearms recalling the Balkan Wars and World War I. Above the square, the modern **Cathedral of Sveta Bogoroditsa** stands aloof on a terrace. From here, either ul. Ivan Vazov or Nikola Pikolo leads directly down to the entrance of Tsarevets, the medieval fortress.

Tsarevets

Approaching **Tsarevets** (daily: summer 8am–7pm, winter 9am–6pm; 4Lv) along the stone causeway that was erected after the original drawbridge collapsed beneath the *bey*'s harem, you can appreciate how the *boyars* Petar and Asen were emboldened enough by possession of this seemingly impregnable citadel to lead a rebellion against Byzantium in 1185. Petar's proclamation of the Second Kingdom and his coronation occurred when Constantinople was already preoccupied by the Magyar and Seljuk Turk menace, and when a punitive Byzantine army was eventually sent in 1190 it was utterly defeated at the Tryavna Pass. Now restored, the ramparts and the Patriarchate (plus the ruins of the palace and various churches) convey something of Tsarevets's grandeur during the Second Kingdom, when travellers deemed Tarnovo "second after Constantinople".

Gates and towers

Artisans and clerics serving the palace and the Patriarchate lived in the Asenova quarter below the hill, and entered Tsarevets via the **Asenova Gate** halfway along the western ramparts; foreign merchants, invited to settle here by Tsar Asen II, had their own entrance, the "Frankish" or **Frenkhisar Gate** near the southern end of the massif. The Second Kingdom attacked and defeated the first Latin emperor of the East, Baldwin of Flanders, in 1205, and the former emperor ended his days as a prisoner in the bastion overlooking the Frenkhisar Gate, thereafter known as **Baldwin's Tower**. No one knows exactly how Baldwin met his death. According to one fanciful legend, he resisted the advances of the Bulgarian queen, who promptly accused him of attempted rape and had him executed. Twenty years after Baldwin's capture, however, a hermit emerged in Flanders claiming to be the former emperor. Despite attracting a coterie of followers, the pretender was declared an imposter and put to death.

The old palace and the patriarchate

The **ruins of the palace** seem insignificant compared to the ramparts, but contemporary chronicles and modern excavations suggest that the royal complex was once splendid and opulent. Delicate columns divided the 35-metre-long throne room into aisles, which were adorned with green serpentine, Egyptian porphyry and pink marble, and mosaics and murals depicting the rulers of three dynasties. The church of the Blessed Saviour or **Patriarchate**, built early in the thirteenth century and now unconvincingly restored, was, significantly, the only structure permitted to surpass the palace in height. Ribbed with red brick and inset with green-and-orange ceramics, the church contains florid modern frescoes, which the visitor is invited to contemplate while curators switch on a backing tape of Orthodox choral music.

Execution Rock

The **Lobna skala** ("Execution Rock") at the sheer northern end of Tsarevets is associated with the dynasty that followed the brief reign of the swineherd **Ivailo** (1277–80). Proclaimed tsar after a popular anti-feudal revolt, Ivailo successfully organized resistance against invading Tatar hordes but neglected to guard against a coup by the *bolyari* (nobles), who had him flung off the rock. The **Terterid** dynasty which followed was chiefly concerned with its own survival and willing to suspect anyone of collusion

The son et lumière

Frequently on summer nights the entire Tsarevets massif is lit up by huge spotlights, and accompanied by a stirring musical soundtrack. Designed to tell the history of Tsarevets through the ages, the **son et lumière** is a stunning sight, especially when viewed from the terrace of open-air seating opposite the entrance to the fortress. Unfortunately, the shows are not guaranteed as they depend on tourist groups forking out for the electricity, but if you do hear of one taking place, don't miss it.

with the Tatars – even the patriarch, Yoakim III, who was also executed; it was only during the later, fourteenth-century reign of Todor Svetoslav that there was much progress or security.

Nonetheless, by the late fourteenth century the Second Kingdom had fragmented into several semi-autonomous states, and the hegemony of the kingdom had dissipated: individually, the states were no match for the expansionist Ottoman Turks, who besieged Tarnovo for three months before capturing, plundering and burning the city in July 1393.

The Asenova quarter

To the west of Tsarevets on both banks of the Yantra lies the **Asenova quarter**, where chickens strut and children fish beside the river. During the Middle Ages this was the artisans' quarter, which it remained until 1913, when it was struck by an earthquake which levelled most of the medieval buildings and did great damage to the (much-reconstructed) churches.

The **Church of the Forty Martyrs** (Tsarkva na chetirideset machenitsi; daily 9.30am–6pm; 4Lv), near the bridge, is a barn-like edifice founded by Tsar Ivan Asen II to commemorate his victory over the Byzantines on Forty Martyrs' Day in 1230. Subsequently much altered, to the extent that it has, apparently, baffled restorers, the church was the burial place of St Sava, founder of the Serbian Orthodox Church, and several Bulgarian tsars. Among the pillars within stands Khan Omurtag's Column, filched from another site, whose Greek inscription reads in part: "Man dies, even though he lives nobly, and another is

The Bogomils

Tarnovo was the venue for a famous synod of the Bulgarian Church in 1211, which tried (unsuccessfully) to curb the growth of a notorious medieval heresy that plagued the Second Kingdom – **Bogomilism**. The movement is thought to have emerged from the teachings of a tenth-century priest named Bogomil (literally "beloved of God"), who inherited the concept of dualism from the earlier Manichaean and Paulician heresies. This held that the entire material world was the creation of the devil, and only the human soul was the province of God. Jesus was sent to earth to defeat Satan's reign on earth, but his mission failed; the fight with Satan's power therefore continued to be a daily war of attrition for all believers. The growth of the Bogomils coincided with the fall of the First Bulgarian Kingdom to the Byzantines, and the movement was strongly critical of the Bulgarian establishment, especially the clergy. Left-wing historians have been quick to emphasize Bogomilism's social impact, especially its appeal to the poor.

Our only real knowledge of the Bogomils, however, comes from the movement's enemies – critics like the monk Cosmas, who described them as "lamblike and gentle, and pale from hypocritical fasting", but really "ravening wolves" who "sowed the tares of their preaching" among "simple and uneducated men".

Cosmas was not the only person worried by the spread of the heresy throughout the Balkan peninsula. Byzantine chronicler Anna Comnena relates how her father Emperor Alexius I had the Bogomil leader Basil publicly burned in the Constantinople hippodrome somewhere around 1100. Despite repeated efforts to stamp it out, Bogomilism remained a powerful force throughout the Balkans, although once-fashionable theories that Bogomilism became the state religion of fifteenth-century Bosnia are nowadays questioned. Byzantine propaganda accused the Bogomils of all manner of unnatural practices, most common among which was sodomy – the adoption of the word "bugger" by the English language derives from confusion over the terms "Bogomil" and "Bulgar".

born. Let the latest born, when he examines these records, remember him who made them. The name of the Prince is Omurtag, the Sublime Khan." Not to be outdone, Asen had another column inscribed with a list of his conquests from Adrianople to Durazzo (Durrës in Albania), whose inhabitants were spared "by my benevolence".

Further north, the early twentieth-century **Church of the Dormition** isn't intrinsically interesting, but stands on the site of the monastery of the Virgin of the Prisoners, where Tsar Ivan Aleksandar confined his wife as a nun so that he could marry the Jewess Sara. The **Church of SS Petar i Pavel** (Easter–Sept, unpredictable hours; free), 200m beyond, is more remarkable: it contains several capitals in the old Bulgarian style (carved with vine leaves in openwork) and some well-preserved frescoes of which the oldest – dating back to the fourteenth century – is the *Pietà* opposite the altar. The church was the site of the massacre of the *bolyari* in 1393 (only Patriarch Evtimii's intervention dissuaded the Turks from killing the entire population) and, much later, the place where the Ottoman-appointed Greek patriarch of Bulgaria was evicted by the citizenry.

On the other side of the river are two more restored churches. With its red-brick stripes and trefoil windows inlaid with orange plaques, the **Church of Sveti Dimitar** is the best-looking of the surviving medieval churches, although most of its original frescoes were painted over during the sixteenth and seventeenth centuries. It was during the consecration of the church that the *bolyari* Petar and Asen announced their rebellion against Byzantium, and St Demetrius (who, legend has it, came from Salonika to help the oppressed Bulgarians) became the patron saint of the Second Kingdom. The **Church of Sveti Georgi**, further to the south, is smaller but has better-preserved frescoes of Orthodox saints.

Overhead rises the massif known as **Trapezitsa**, where the *bolyari* and leading clergy of the Second Kingdom built their mansions and some forty private churches, sixteen of which are currently being excavated. It's an area of great archeological importance, and although tracks onto the hilltop do exist, visitors are discouraged.

Sveta gora

Sveta gora (Holy Hill), on the south bank of the Yantra, used to be a centre of monastic scholasticism, and nowadays provides the site for the **Cyril and Methodius University**, which is reached via a bridge to the south of Tsarevets, or on bus #15. The rocky spur, linked by footbridge to the *Hotel Veliko Tarnovo*, is adorned with an obelisk commemorating the 800th anniversary of the foundation of the Asenid dynasty, but visitors are generally more interested in the contents of the large, copper-roofed **art gallery** nearby (Tues–Sun 10am–6pm; 3Lv), whose theme is "Tarnovo through the eyes of diverse painters". A jumble of unchallenging townscapes and lionizations of medieval tsars for the most part, the collection is enlivened by a couple of naive exercises in mid-nineteenth-century portraiture by local artists Nikolai Pavlovich and Georgi Danchov.

Eating and drinking

Restaurants, cafés and **bars** line the main strip – ul. Nezavisimost, Stambolov and Vazov – that leads through the centre towards Tsarevets, from where the town's vibrant nightlife kicks off after dark. The main **food market** is the open-air *pazar*, on the corner of Vasil Levski and Nikola Gabrovski, and there's a 24-hour food shop with a good snack bar open until midnight at ul. Ilarion Dragostinov 11A, just behind the tourist information centre.

Restaurants

International pl. Mayka Balgariya. Oddly kitsch basement restaurant complete with Grecian statues and a fountain. Serves Bulgarian, Serbian, Greek and Chinese food.

Lovna Sreshta ul. Todor Balina 16. Another place offering (seasonally available) game dishes as well as a wide range of Bulgarian standards, just beyond the sports stadium. Big outdoor garden and live folk/pop music.

Mehana Hadzhi Mincho ul. Kyokotinitsa 2. Breezy, folk-style place just off ul. Stambolov. Good, cheap food in a small open courtyard.

Mehana Mecha Dupka ul. Rakovski. Cellar restaurant serving traditional Bulgarian cuisine, accompanied by nightly music and dancing.

Mustang Food pl. Mayka Balgariya. Neon-lit chain restaurant offering meaty dishes and salads.

Saint George's ul. Georgi Marmarkev 14. An atmospheric tavern-style eatery offering beans on toast, fish and chips, and chicken tikka masala for homesick Brits.

Shtastlivetsa ul. Stefan Stambolov 79. Laid-back place with a wide range of pizza and pasta dishes, plus fantastic views over the valley.

Slavyanska Dusha ul. Nikola Zlatarski 21. Hidden away in the old town, an unpretentious *mehana* with excellent Bulgarian cuisine.

Starata kashta ul. Ljuben Karavelov 63. One of the best restaurants in the new part of town, just off the eastern end of ul. Nikola Gabrovski, offering the usual range of Bulgarian dishes.

Starata mehana ul. Kolyo Ficheto 3. Cosy place with good home cooking and a verandah perched above the Yantra valley.

Tempo ul. Ivailo 3. Immensely popular pizza and pasta restaurant. Reservations often needed.

Vinarnata ul. Stefan Stambolov 79. Traditional style *mehana* with an open fire in winter and great views.

Cafés, bars and clubs

Aqua Cafe ul. Nezavisimost 3. Relaxed café serving alcoholic drinks and snacks, with a stylish interior including a number of fish tanks. Open until 11pm.

Bacardi Club ul. Stefan Stambolov 29. Dark and loud inside, plays techno until late most nights.

Bar One ul. Rakovska 1. Mediterranean-style bar that serves food and has live music.

City Pub ul. Hristo Botev 15. Bustling modern gastropub that stays open late.

Dublin Bar ul. Mayka Balgariya 26. Smoky, dimly lit bar serving bottled Guinness and Murphy's as well as dark Bulgarian beer.

La Belle Epoche ul. Samovodska Charshia. Smart Art Nouveau-style café and restaurant squeezed into an alley between ul. Rakovska and Stefan Stambolov.

Mosquito Bar ul. Stefan Stambolov 21. One of the coolest bars in town, with a small terrace overlooking the valley and weekend DJs playing dance music until late.

Organza Sportnata zala (ul. Maria Gabrovska). The town's largest club has three floors that play techno, disco and pop folk music.

Pepys Bar pl. Slaveykov 1. Sophisticated and subdued, decorated with sepia photographs and various oddments.

Scream Club ul. Nezavisimost 17. Bustling club that plays commercial dance music all night long.

Stratilat Café ul. Rakovski 11. Viennese-style café serving delicious cakes and coffee inside and outdoors.

Tequila Bar ul. Stefan Stambolov 30. Well-established and fashionable, playing mainstream dance music on two floors.

Ulitsata ul. Stefan Stambolov 79. Popular rock and heavy metal bar squeezed between two restaurants.

Listings

Bus companies Express buses to Sofia and the coast are operated by Etap Adres (office open daily 24hr; ☎062/630564) just round the side of the *Hotel Etar*.

Car rental Can be arranged by the Tourist Information Centre at ul. Hristo Botev 5 (Mon–Fri 9am–noon & 1–6pm; ☎062/622148).

Internet Navigator Internet, located in the dingy basement of the Evropa shopping complex at ul. Nezavisimost 3, is packed with computers and open 24hr.

Medical centre ul. Marno Pole 2 ☎062/621992.

Pharmacy There is a 24hr pharmacy at Vasil Levski 29.

Police ul. Bacho Kiro 7 ☎ 062/620001
Post office ul. Hristo Botev 1 (Mon–Fri
7.30am–7pm, Sat 8.30am–6pm).
Taxis Aleks OK Taxi ☎ 062/61616; Toptaxi
☎ 062/631111.

Train tickets Advance bookings and international
tickets from Rila/BDZh just behind the tourist
Information centre at ul. Kaloyan 2 (Mon–Fri
8am–noon & 1–4.30pm, Sat 8am-noon;
☎ 062/622042).

North of Veliko Tarnovo

The terrain **north of Tarnovo** is a wild confusion of massifs sundered by the River Yantra and its tributaries, abounding in rocky shelves rendered almost inaccessible by forests and torrents. Nearly twenty monasteries were established here during the Second Kingdom, and several survived the Turkish invasion. These formed a symbiotic relationship with the later towns and villages founded by refugees after the sack of Tarnovo. With a car it's feasible to visit the main sites within a day, but relying on public transport (or hiking), one expedition a day seems more realistic.

Arbanasi

Hiding high on a plateau 4km northeast of Tarnovo, and overlooking Tsarevets and Trapezitsa to the south, **ARBANASI** (АРБАНАСИ) is one of Bulgaria's most picturesque villages, resembling a cross between a *kasbah* and the kind of *pueblo* that Clint Eastwood rids of bandits. People vanish into their family strongholds for the siesta, and at high noon only chickens stalk the rutted streets.

The origins of Arbanasi have presented scholars with a characteristically Balkan ethnological puzzle. The village's name led most historians to assume that it was founded by Albanian refugees fleeing Turkish reprisals after a failed fifteenth-century uprising, although this is disputed by modern Bulgarian historians eager to establish the continuity of Slav settlement in the area. What's beyond doubt is that the people who lived here in the village's eighteenth-century heyday belonged to the Greek cultural orbit, speaking Greek and giving their children Greek names. The inhabitants grew rich on the proceeds of cattle-droving, drying meat for their own consumption and selling the fat to the local Muslims, who considered it a delicacy. Leather was loaded onto caravans and taken east, where it was exchanged for Asiatic luxury goods like silk and spices.

Arbanasi's merchants invested their wealth in the big, fortress-like stone houses for which the village is famed, but they also built churches, chapels and public drinking fountains, turning the village into a lively urban centre for the local Christian population, hidden from the eyes of Ottoman-dominated Tarnovo below. The town was sacked three times in the nineteenth century by the *kardzhali*, Turkish outlaws who menaced the townsfolk of the Balkans, and commerce became increasingly centred on Tarnovo and other lowland towns, forcing Arbanasi's merchants to relocate their businesses. Mass emigration during the war-ravaged winter of 1877 further confirmed Arbanasi's decline. Nowadays a traditional rural population coexists with tourists and city types staying at their holiday villas.

Accommodation

Arbanassi kashta ☎ 062/630074,
✉ arbanassi_resort@mail.bg. Located up the track
to the left of the *Arbanassi Palace*, this hotel has a
quiet garden and offers stylish rooms with views of
Veliko Tarnovo. ❸

Arbanassi Palace ☎ 062/630176, ⊛ www
.arbanassipalace.bg. The most luxurious of all the
hotels in Arbanasi, in a former Zhivkov family
residence on the southern edge of the village
commanding splendid views of the Tsarevets

massif immediately below. A brief visit to the timber-ceilinged hotel bar will be sufficient to give you an idea of the former dictator's taste for opulence. ❹

Bolyarska kashta Just off the main square ☏062/620484, ⓦwww.boliarihotel.com. Has en-suite doubles (❸) and roomy four-person apartments with bath (❺), all swankily furnished. Breakfast is included in the price.

Faklite Opposite the Kostantsaliev House ☏062/604496. Surrounded by high stone walls and lovely gardens, this renovated 270-year-old house has traditionally furnished rooms and a small *mehana* in its old wine cellar. ❷

Izvora Komplex Just along from the main square ☏062/601205, ⓦwww.izvora.com. At the high end of the scale, this stylish place offers four-poster beds and leather furniture. ❺

Kashtata s Raloto Off the main square ☏062/620370. A small hotel run by a friendly family. Offers five a/c rooms in a modern house. ❷

The Village

Squatting on high ground just above Arbanasi's main square is the **Church of the Archangels Michael and Gabriel** (ask staff at the Church of the Nativity to open it) – the pair are depicted in a mural above the western portal. Dating from 1600, the church is a solid brick structure adorned with irregular lines of blind arcading, its gloomy interior illuminated by tiny, iron-grilled windows. Local schoolmaster Hristo was called on in the early eighteenth century to execute most of the frescoes, including a panoramic Nativity scene in the apse, but look out also for the *Virgin Horanta* in the narthex (porch), painted jointly by itinerant masters Georgi of Bucharest and Mihail of Salonika.

The main road west of the village square brings you to the finest of Arbanasi's mansions, the **Kostantsaliev House** (daily 9am–6pm; 4Lv). Like other houses built after the fire that gutted Arbanasi in 1798, the ground floor (with servants' quarters and store-rooms) is built of stone, while the upper floor is made of wood. Many of the rooms have beautiful panelled ceilings and ornate plaster cornices bearing geometric or tulip motifs. However, the luxury didn't extend to any form of plumbing – the two toilets (his and hers) are simply holes in the wooden floor, directly above the garden. It's not hard to imagine the former owner, the Kokona Sultana (a relation of the *bey*), greeting her guests on the

▲ Traditional houses, Arbanasi

wooden staircase that ascends to the reception hall, from which one door leads to the "winter room" or communal bedroom. The other opens onto a corridor leading to the dining room and the office of her merchant husband, furnished with a low table or *sofra*.

Beyond the house lies the **Kokona fountain**, built in 1786 on the orders of Mehmed Said Ali, author of its Arabic inscription: "He who looks upon me and drinks my water shall possess the light of the eyes and of the soul". Turn left at the fountain to reach the village's most beautifully decorated church, the **Church of the Nativity** (Rozhdestvo Hristovo) (daily 9am–6pm; 4Lv). It's outwardly plain, but inside you'll find richly coloured frescoes dating from the seventeenth century. The main entrance leads into a long gallery, at the far end of which is the chapel of St John the Baptist, richly decorated with images of martyred saints, and divided into separate areas for men and women to pray. The main body of the church, to the right of the gallery, is again divided into male and female sections. The latter is the smaller of the two, notable for a frieze of Greek philosophers along one wall, while the screen dividing the male and female portions bears an extravagantly imagined rendering of the *Last Judgement*. At the far end of the men's chamber, the gilded iconostasis contains scenes from the Book of Genesis (in which Eden contains a dream-like menagerie of exotic animals), and a boldly colourful *pietà*.

Petropavlovski Monastery

From Arbanasi, it's a five-kilometre walk or drive northeast to the tenth-century **Petropavlovski Monastery** (Monastery of Peter and Paul), a foundation built on the site of a Roman fort. The monastery occupies a hilltop site overlooking the town of Lyaskovets, with the gently undulating arable land of the Danubian Plain stretching out beyond. The church and outbuildings are largely unremarkable nineteenth-century affairs, with the restful courtyard garden and great views being the real attractions.

To get here, you can either walk or drive along the asphalt road heading uphill to the southeast from Arbanasi's main square, which takes you along a ridge providing views of Tsarevets; turn left after 3km, then right after another 2km, and the monastery is 200m downhill from here. Alternatively, you could catch the #14 Lyaskovets bus from opposite Veliko Tarnovo's *Pazar*, alighting at Lyaskovets town park (recognizable by a big white Communist-era memorial on your left). An asphalt track leads uphill to the monastery from here (50min).

Practicalities

Despite Arbanasi's proximity to Tarnovo, both the gradient and the amount of traffic on the road make it an unappetizing, if not downright dangerous, walk – it's easier to take one of the minibuses that depart approximately every two hours from opposite Veliko Tarnovo's *pazar,* or to take a taxi, which shouldn't cost more than 5Lv. There's a small and very helpful **tourist office**, Val Turs, in the centre just behind an antiques shop (Mon–Sat 8.30am–5.30pm; ☏062/602575, ⓦwww.valturs.com) which can provide maps and arrange private rooms (❷–❸) and discounted hotel accommodation; it also offers horse riding for 30Lv per hour.

There are plenty of places to **eat and drink** in the village, especially around the main square. Most of the hotels have good restaurants, while the *Piyaka* just before the square, and the *Lyulaka* just down from it, are also worth trying for a traditional Bulgarian meal. For evening entertainment try the folky *Cheshmata* on the main square, which puts on Bulgarian music and dancing shows every weekend.

Preobrazhenski Monastery and Sveta Troitsa Convent

Four kilometres north of Tarnovo, high in the crags above the main E85 road to Ruse, sits **Preobrazhenski Monastery** (daily dawn–dusk). Founded in 1360 by Tsar Ivan Aleksandar's Jewish wife who converted to Christianity, the monastery was abandoned during the Ottoman period, then refounded in the 1820s by Tarnovo guilds, who had to bribe the city's Greek bishop to get a Bulgarian abbot installed here. Dimitar Sofyaliyata was commisssioned as architect, but after being implicated in Velcho's Plot of 1835 and hanged from the monastery gate, he was replaced by master-builder Kolyo Ficheto (see p.245). Zahari Zograf was brought in to do the frescoes, until he discovered that the monks were strict vegetarians and refused to work unless he was given meat. The monks relented, issuing him a contract which euphemistically promised the artist food "suited to his delicate stomach".

Finished in the 1860s, the monastery almost looks old enough to be medieval, with a canopy of vines strung between the spartan cells. However, Ficheto's elegantly proportioned, enclosed courtyard is sadly no more. Over the last decade repeated rock falls from the cliffs above have destroyed many of the monastery buildings (with more being demolished for safety reasons), although the central **Transfiguration church** still stands. Its south wall bears a remarkable painting of the *Wheel of Life* by Zograf, in which the stages of human existence correspond with allegorical representations of the four seasons. Rose- and green-hued **frescoes** predominate in the porch, with an eye in a circle (traditional symbol of the Holy Ghost) as a recurrent motif, and evil-doers being thrust across a river of fire and strangled by demons in the *Last Judgement*.

Getting to the monastery is relatively easy: regular buses from Veliko Tarnovo to Gorna Oryahovitsa pass by the turn-off, 4km north of town, from where a minor road zigzags 3km uphill through a lime forest.

Sveta Troitsa convent

More or less opposite Preobrazhenski on the other side of the valley, the **Sveta Troitsa convent** (daily dawn–dusk) sits on a narrow shelf of rock, at the end of a partially asphalted road which begins in Veliko Tarnovo's Trapezitsa quarter. The road is just about passable by car, although most people opt to walk – a journey of about ninety minutes. Founded as early as the eleventh century, Sveta Troitsa was a monastery rather than a nunnery during the Second Kingdom, when Patriarch Evtimii established a school of translators here. The convent's delicate red-brick church (also built during the nineteenth century by Kolyo Ficheto) is difficult to get access to, but the charming, flower-bedecked courtyard overlooked by sheer cliffs, and the impressive surroundings, make the trip worthwhile.

To **get to the convent**, leave Veliko Tarnovo on the Arbanasi road and take a left turn soon after passing the Church of Sveti Dimitar. Ignore roads leading left towards Trapezitsa train station, but bear left after this, and carry straight on past several decaying factories. Pay no heed to the multicoloured hiking waymarks that tempt you uphill to the right. You could also walk to Sveta Troitsa from Arbanasi, although you'll probably need local knowledge and plenty of time to spare – markings are inadequate, and paths confusing.

South of Veliko Tarnovo

The mill town of **Gabrovo** is the main urban centre south of Tarnovo, although it's in the smaller towns and villages, where rural architecture and crafts have been best preserved – notably **Tryavna**, **Bozhentsi** and the museum-village of **Etara** – that the main attractions lie. Several historic **monasteries**, such as Kilifarevo, Dryanovo and Sokolski, are within easy striking distance of these places. Veliko Tarnovo, Gabrovo and Tryavna are equally convenient as bases from which to explore the region, and even if you're reliant on **public transport** you'll find that you can reach several destinations in the space of one day-trip. Both Dryanovo and Tryavna are linked directly to Veliko Tarnovo by train, although continuing to Gabrovo involves a change at Tsareva Livada. Buses, too, are plentiful, with hourly services linking the area's major towns. Less well-served by public transport are the little-visited monasteries near the historic town of **Elena** to the southeast, although together they form an easily manageable cluster of rustic sights for those with access to a car.

Travelling onwards to the Valley of the Roses (see Chapter Four) from here involves two of Bulgaria's most scenic mountain routes. The Veliko Tarnovo–Tryavna rail line winds its way southwards through the densely wooded **Tryavna Pass** (where Petar and Asen defeated the Byzantine army in 1190, preserving the independence of the Second Kingdom), before joining the Sofia–Burgas line at Dabovo. By road, the E85 heads towards the impressive **Shipka Pass** just above Gabrovo (the place to catch buses over the pass), then drops down towards Bulgaria's "rose capital", Kazanlak (see Chapter Four).

Kilifarevo Monastery and around

Twenty kilometres south of Veliko Tarnovo lies **Kilifarevo Monastery**, once a favourite retreat for the tsars of the Second Kingdom. It was also the site of the famous college established by Teodosii Tarnovski in 1350, which translated literary works from Greek and Hebrew into Slavonic script, making them legible to scholars far beyond Bulgaria. As many as eight hundred monks and novices from all over the Slav world were based here at any one time, and the School of Kilifarevo might have achieved parity with the great European universities had it not been burned by the Turks in 1393.

Now a nunnery, Kilifarevo was rebuilt during the nineteenth century around a principal church – dedicated to St Demetrius of Salonika – designed by Kolyo Ficheto. The main body of the church contains an iconostasis by Tryavna craftsmen, and a mesmerizing icon (on the opposite wall as you enter) of St John of Rila, painted by Ficheto's contemporary Krastyu Zahariev. Outside, look out for a small but delicate relief of the Archangels Michael and Gabriel over the south portal. Ficheto's church is tacked on to two older sixteenth-century structures that lie to the rear, the chapels of Sveti Teodosii and Sveto Rozhdestvo Bogorodichno (Birth of the Virgin). Both contain valuable frescoes from the period.

The monastery lies just off the main Veliko Tarnovo–Stara Zagora road, about 5km south of the village of Kilifarevo. The access road to the monastery is badly signed – look out for the truck stop used by TIR drivers just opposite. Some of the six daily Veliko Tarnovo–Kilifarevo **buses** serve isolated villages south of Kilifarevo, and may take you near the monastery; otherwise, you'll have to walk from Kilifarevo village. It's best to save yourself a dull and potentially hazardous trudge along the main road by turning left into the village of Natsovtsi after

3km, and follow the river upstream to the monastery. Basic accommodation is available (☎06114/2480; ❶).

The monasteries of Plakovo and Kapinovo

Seven kilometres to the east of Kilifarevo, in a wooded valley near the commune of Plakovo, lies another monastery, whose superior, Father Sergius, was involved in "Velcho's plot" (see p.229) and tortured to death by the Turks after its discovery. A plaque on the stone fountain in the courtyard of **Plakovo Monastery** commemorates him and his fellow conspirators. Some of the Tarnovo–Kilifarevo buses continue on to Plakovo; check in Kilifarevo which ones.

Tracks continue 2km beyond Plakovo Monastery to the more impressive **Kapinovo Monastery**, where the timber verandahs of the monks' cells overlook a courtyard shaded by vines. Sofronii Vrachanski was head monk here before being elevated to the bishopric of Vratsa in 1794, putting the monastery at the forefront of the revival of Bulgarian language and scholarship. The monastery church contains an unmissable *Day of Judgement* painted by Razgrad master Yovan Popovich in 1845, with lurid scenes of the dead emerging from their graves.

Elena and around

Like nearby Kotel and Koprivshtitsa, the nineteenth-century National Revival-crafts town of **ELENA** (ЕЛЕНА), 40km southeast of Tarnovo and served by five daily buses, lay far enough away from the centres of Ottoman power for Bulgarian crafts and culture to flourish. The Turks used the town's population to guard the local mountain passes, giving them a measure of autonomy in return, so painters and woodcarvers of nineteenth-century Elena were able to decorate the churches of the surrounding countryside, and patriotic local merchants could finance the restoration of nearby monasteries like Kapinovo. Although Elena has not been renovated to the same extent as other National Revival towns, the core of nineteenth-century structures grouped around the hilltop church make a visit here worthwhile.

Beyond Elena, roads (but no public transport) head east through lonely highland villages towards the wooded **Kotel Pass**, on the far side of which lie the historic settlements of Kotel and Zheravna (see Chapter Four).

The Town

Heading downhill from the bus station then turning left into the main street, the first building of interest you come across is the **House-museum of Ilarion Makariopolski** (daily 9am–noon & 1–5pm; 2Lv), located in a walled garden off to the right. Born Stoyan Mihailov in 1812, and later elevated to the Bulgarian bishopric of Constantinople (a post which brought him the honorific title *Makariopolski*), Ilarion was the leader of the Bulgarian Church's battle against Greek control, and eventually persuaded the sultan to sanction an autonomous Bulgarian exarchate in 1870. The house is a lovely timber structure from the late eighteenth century, with vast verandahs overlooking the river on the first floor, where family and guests would sleep on warm summer nights. Chunky local carpets and a child's *lyulka* (hammock-like bed hung from the ceiling) provide a sense of period domesticity.

Beyond lies a bland town square, behind which the cobbled ul. Stoyan Mihailovski leads uphill to the **National Revival complex** (daily 9am–noon & 1–5pm; 2Lv), grouped around the mid-nineteenth-century church of the Assumption. However, the real star of the complex is the much smaller **Church** of **Sveti Nikola** downhill, a sixteenth-century structure rebuilt in 1804 after being burned by marauding *Kardzhali*, which has blindingly colourful icons and frescoes crowding the barrel-vaulted space inside. More devotional paintings are on display in the nearby **old school** (*Daskalolivnitsa*), including an 1873 *Last Judgement* displaying the hellish tortures beloved of Bulgarian artists of the period. At the bottom of the hill lies the **Ethnographic Museum**, also known as *Kamburov han*, a former inn now taken up with displays of local trades and crafts. Characteristic of Elena are the fluffy *guberi* (fleecy rugs) in bright reds and greens, often featuring a tree-like central symbol topped by a star. In the basement loom vast wine vats and a *korab* – a long wooden trough in which grapes were trodden.

Practicalities

The **tourist information centre** at ul. Ilarion Makariopolski 13 (Wed–Sun 9am–6pm; ☎06151/3430, ⓦwww.elena.bg) provides local maps and can book **accommodation** in hotels and private rooms (❶). The town's smartest hotels are the *Central* at ul. Syoyan Mihaylovski 4 (☎06151/2348, Ⓔhotel_central @elena.vali.bg; ❷), and the nearby *Tara* (☎06151/2148; ❷), which both offer functional modern rooms. The rather drab *Hotel Elena* on the main square (☎06151/3632, Ⓔelena_hotel@abv.bg; ❷) has simple en-suite doubles and a small restaurant, while the nearby *Turisticheska Spalnya Dr Momchilov* at Stoyan Mihailovski 7 (☎06151/4081 and 06151/3004; dorms 7Lv per person) is a traditional-style house offering rickety beds in spartan dorms; it also provides hiking guides and rents out mountain bikes. For food and drink try any of the cafés around the main square; the *Mehana Rai* **restaurant** just above, or the pleasant *Trukcheva Kashta* next to the river, both offer the usual range of grills and traditional dishes.

Mikovtsi

The cluster of tumbledown houses that makes up the tiny village of **MIKOVTSI** (МИКОВЦИ) lies 13km south of Elena, surrounded by wooded hills and barely touched by tourism. Visitors can stay at the *Kandaferi* guesthouse (☎0887 342 635 and 0887 976606, ⓦwww.kandaferi.com; ❶), a cosy family-run pension with its own *mehana* and unique wooden furniture carved by the owners' son. Marked paths of varying length meander through the hills and guests can use them for walking, cycling or pony trekking. Buses only stop at the village on Fridays and Sundays, so you'll need to take a taxi or phone the *Kandaferi* to collect you from Elena.

Dryanovo and Dryanovski Monastery

Thirty kilometres southwest of Tarnovo on the main road to Gabrovo, the drab town of **DRYANOVO** (ДРЯНОВО) is only really of note for its proximity to Dryanovski Monastery, another 4km south. The town's only sights are down to local boy Nikolai Fichev, popularly known as **Kolyo Ficheto** (1800–1881), who is honoured with his own **Historical Museum** at ul. Shipka 82 (daily 8am–noon & 1–5pm; 3Lv), which occupies a modern pavilion in the town centre. The most versatile of nineteenth-century Bulgaria's builders, he was responsible for townhouses in Tarnovo, bridges at Lovech and Byala, and numerous churches. Famous for the *Fichevska kobilitsa* (Fichev yoke), the wavy line which characterizes the roof-lines and pediments on all his best works, he often put double-headed eagles and lions on the eastern facade of his buildings, to symbolize the direction from which Bulgaria's liberation – in the shape of

Russian power – was expected to come. The museum contains superb scale models of all Ficheto's key works, including the **church of Sveti Nikola**, the original of which lies 200m away on the road to Gabrovo.

Dryanovo's **train and bus stations** are both a couple of blocks east of the main thoroughfare, ul. Shipka, although most buses on the Tarnovo–Dryanovo–Gabrovo route only stop on the main street.

Dryanovski Monastery

Set in a gorge beneath high crags, **Dryanovski Monastery** was chosen as the place from which to launch a local uprising in May 1876, while the fires of rebellion were still smouldering elsewhere after the suppression of the April Rising. Under the leadership of Bacho Kiro and the monk Hariton, several hundred rebels defended the monastery for almost a week against ten thousand Turkish troops rushed from Shumen, whose commander Pasha Fasla offered to spare Kiro if he publicly repented – and hanged him when he refused.

The monastery was pretty much destroyed in 1876 and rebuilt with public donations soon after the Liberation. A fine ensemble of timbered buildings was the result, although it's the restful ambience rather than any single architectural feature that makes the place a worthwhile visit. A small **museum** (daily 9am–5pm; 2Lv), just off the monastery courtyard, displays old photographs of Bacho Kiro and company, as well as an ossuary containing rebel skulls. The museum basement concentrates on Stone-Age pottery and arrowheads discovered in the **Bacho Kiro cave** (daily 9am–6pm; 3Lv), 500m beyond the monastery at the end of an asphalt path. A small part of the cave interior is floodlit, and there are some interesting curtain-like stalactite formations to admire, but nothing that justifies a special trip.

You can **walk** from Dryanovo to the monastery in about 45 minutes, or take one of the regular Dryanovo–Gabrovo **buses** which stop beside the monastery access road (marked by a big monument to the heroes of the April Rising), from where the monastery lies 1500m downhill. You can also get to the monastery by **train**, alighting at the first stop beyond Dryanovo, the Bacho Kiro halt, and walking the remaining 100m downhill (note that only *patnicheski* trains stop at the halt, which amounts to little more than a shed in the middle of the forest and is very easy to miss). The **tourist office** located in an old house above a *mehana* at ul. Stefan Stambolov 7 (Mon–Fri 8am–noon & 2–6pm; ℡0676/2332, Ⓦwww.dryanovo.com) provides maps and leaflets, and can arrange private rooms in the region. **Hotel** accommodation in the town is limited to the comfortable *Olymp* (℡0676/5395; ❷) and the more upmarket *Park Hotel Dryanovo* (℡0676/2245, Ⓦwww.parkhoteldryanovo.com; ❺), while the monastery itself offers simple double and triple rooms (℡0676/5253; ❷). One kilometre down the road, the *Strinava* campsite has small bungalows (❶), and a little further on the well-positioned *Bacho Kiro turisticheska dom* (℡0676/2106) has dorm beds only (8Lv per person) and a great view of the valley.

Tryavna

The old crafts centre of **TRYAVNA** (ТРЯВНА) may be a byword for icon painting and woodcarving, and features no fewer than 140 listed buildings, but it fortunately lacks the feel of a museum-town. For carless travellers, trains from Tarnovo or regular buses from Gabrovo provide the best means of **getting here** (travelling by train from Gabrovo entails a change at Tsareva Livada, which makes it quicker to go by bus).

The town's narrow streets are evocative of the nineteenth century: although Tryavna was founded by refugees from Tarnovo four hundred years ago, the oldest buildings all postdate the establishment of an official Guild of Master Builders and Woodcarvers in 1804. Often carved with birds and flowers, the wooden houses in the **old quarter** have an asymmetrical structure that disguises the essential similarity of their interiors. Traditionally, the large room containing the hooded *kamina* (hearth) was the centre of domestic life and led directly to the *chardak* or covered terrace; guests were received in a separate room and household goods stored in the ground-floor *odaya*.

Arrival and information

Tryavna is pretty easy to find your way around: turn right out of either the **train** or **bus station**, both north of the centre, and by walking straight on you'll pass most of the town's sights along the way. Tryavna's **tourist office**, just off the main square at ul. Angel Kanchev 33 (Mon–Fri 9am–noon & 2–5pm; ☎0677/2247, ⓦwww.tryavna.bg), sells maps, rents out bikes and organizes accommodation in **private rooms** (❶) and local hotels; otherwise try *Kia-Tours*, a few doors along at ul. Angel Kanchev 12 (Mon–Fri 9.30am–6pm; ☎0677/2303), which offers much the same service.

Accommodation

Familia ul. Angel Kanchev 40 ☎0677/4691, ⓦwww.tryavna.bg/web/family. A clean six-room family-run guest house in a quiet suburb. Pleasant garden to the rear. ❸
Ralitsa ul. Kaleto ☎0677/2262, ⓦwww.tryavna.bg/ralitsa. Superior and huge three-star place up a steep hill, commanding a splendid view over the town. ❸
Sezoni ul. Kancho Skorchev ☎0677/4937, ⓦseasons.tryavna.biz. A newly built luxury place with an open-air pool surrounded by forest. ❸

Tigara ul. Gorov 7A ☎0677/2469. A decent budget option, this is a clean family-run guesthouse with en-suite rooms and breakfast. ❷
Trevnenski kat ul. Angel Kanchev 8 ☎0677/2033. Located on the hillside opposite the *Ralitza* and *Sezoni*, this hotel has a great garden and comfortable rooms. ❷
Zograf ul. Slaveikov 1 ☎0677/4970, ⓦwww.tryavna.bg/zograf. Offers smart modern accommodation in a large old house with a cosy basement *mehana* and outdoor seating next to the river. ❸

The birthplace of Angel Kanchev

Most of the northern end of town is modern, although the **birthplace of Angel Kanchev** at ul. Angel Kanchev 39 is a prime example of the nineteenth-century Tryavna housebuilder's art. Disappointingly, though, only a couple of sparsely furnished upstairs rooms are on show, together with a tiny words-and-photos exhibition on the ground floor. Born in 1850, Kanchev's patriotism led him to join Belgrade's Artillery School at the age of 17, and later to spurn a lucrative job offer so that he could fight for Bulgaria's liberation. Sent to assist Levski in constructing the revolutionary underground, Kanchev had completed two clandestine "tours" by 1872, when he was caught boarding a steamer at Ruse without a passport. Fearful of betraying secrets under torture, he shot himself, crying "Long live Bulgaria!" – in Levski's words, "the most honourable death for justice that should be considered sweetest for every proud Bulgarian of today".

Around the main square

Before long ul. Angel Kanchev hits **ploshtad Kapetan Dyado Nikola**, a set-piece square which retains most of its nineteenth-century character. Dominating the scene is the **clock tower**, a solid stone pillar topped by a half-timbered octagonal structure that supports a dainty wooden bell tower. The **Church of Archangel Michael** (daily 7am–6pm) stands to one side, a

Bulgarian house-building rituals

As late as the nineteenth century, there were a number of unusual **customs and rituals surrounding house building** in Bulgaria. It was considered unlucky to build a house near an empty well, an old watermill or a graveyard, and when doubts arose about a prospective site a bowl of water would be left there for bad omens (impurities or clouding) to appear overnight. Before the foundations were laid, an animal was slaughtered on the site of the hearth or threshold, and the outlines of the walls were marked by dripping blood as an additional magical precaution. When the house was complete, blessings were shouted and the owners presented the builders with gifts before moving in themselves, preferably on a Monday, Thursday or Sunday at the time of a new moon. By custom, the eldest man would pour water over the threshold and scatter coins and wheat around the hearth in the hope of a future life "as smooth as water", prosperity and full barns. Once he had kindled the first fire with embers from the old family hearth, the woman of the family completed the occupation by breaking a loaf over the flames and hanging up a copper vessel.

low-lying edifice sheltering under the shallow overhang of its slate roof, from which a slender minaret-like tower emerges. Inside, the iconostasis is wonderfully rich and dark, with twelve intricate tableaux surrounding the crucifix and a carved pulpit wound around one of the columns. At the rear of the church, memorial photographs of the recently deceased are stuck into candelabras, part of the Orthodox forty-day mourning rite which Bulgarians also observe by putting up posters in the streets.

Immediately next door is the **Shkoloto** or old school (daily 9am–5pm; 2Lv), its heavy wooden doors leading to a cobbled courtyard surrounded by a timber gallery draped with ivy. On the first floor a gallery devotes itself to sentimental images of Bulgarian womanhood by contemporary Veliko Tarnovo painter and sculptor Nikola Kazakov, as well as ceramics, sculptures and paintings by his brother, Dimitar. Also on show is part of the personal collection of Buddhist art belonging to wealthy ex-pat Zlatko Paunov, including sixth-century bronze statues and silver jewellery from Tibet. In another gallery, there's an exhibition of the timepieces imported by middle-class Tryavna families of the nineteenth century.

Between the school and the church, an alley leads to **Raikova kashta** at ul. Prof. Raikov 1 (Wed–Sun 9am–1pm & 2–6pm; 2Lv). Originally the home of scientist Pencho Raikov, the "father of Bulgarian chemistry", the house features exhibits on the domestic life of Tryavna's late nineteenth-century middle class, displaying the mass-produced furniture and crockery that had begun to penetrate Bulgaria from the West.

Along ulitsa Slaveykov

A bridge leads from the square to the cobbled **ulitsa Slaveykov**, possibly the best-preserved National Revival-period street in all Bulgaria. Unusually for a Tryavna building, the **Daskalov House** at no. 27 (daily 9am–7pm; 2Lv) has a symmetrical plan with two wings joined by a curved verandah. The rooms inside are brightly carpeted, with arched windows and inbuilt *minderi*, and also contain superb panelled ceilings – sun motifs made from walnut wood, with fretted rays inlaid within a frame decorated with floral and bird shapes. The two ceilings in the first-floor bedrooms are the result of an art contest, arranged by the silk and rose-oil merchant Daskalov in 1808, pitting a master woodcarver, Dimitar Zlatev Oshanetsa, against his apprentice, Ivan Bochukovetsa. The apprentice, who produced the ceiling known as the "Burgas sun", was reckoned by Daskalov to be the winner, although the Guild of Carvers, who oversaw the proceedings, decided in favour of Oshanetsa. However, they too were impressed with the apprentice's work, which took six months to complete, and declared him a master. The ground floor holds a small museum of woodcarving, displaying the products of the State Woodcarving School, established in Tryavna in the 1920s to ensure the craft's survival, and including a reconstruction of a nineteenth-century woodworker's shop.

▲ Tryavna

Further along ul. Slaveykov are a couple more exhibitions of works donated by local artists: the **Totyu Gabenski Picture Gallery** at no. 45, and the **Ivan Kolev Exhibition House** at no. 47 (both closed for renovation at the time of writing). By heading west from ul. Slaveykov, across the rail line and up ul. Breza, you'll reach a stairway which climbs to a church-like edifice housing the **Museum of Icon-painting and Woodcarving** (daily 10am–6pm; 2Lv). Inside are numerous sumptuous products of the nineteenth-century **Trevnenska shkola** or "Tryavna School" – a guild with a distinctive style of cutting the wood back until acanthus leaves, birds and other favourite motifs were rendered in openwork like lace covering the surface.

Eating and drinking

There are numerous small **restaurants, cafés and bars** along pl. Kapitan Dyado Nikola and along ul. Angel Kanchev. The *Stranopriemnitza*, next to the Kolev house, the *Starata Losa*, opposite the Daskalov house, and the *Zograf mehana* are worth trying for good Bulgarian food in folksy surroundings. The well-signposted *Maestorat*, just off the main square at ul. Kaleto 7, is an excellent traditional restaurant, regarded by locals as Tryavna's best. For reasonable pizza try *Domino*, at ul. Angel Kanchev 36. **Nightlife** in town is limited to occasional live music performances in a few restaurants, while the **Slaveikov Days** festival, held on May 26 and 27 in odd-numbered years, brings together a range of cultural events and festivities.

Bozhentsi

Lying roughly between Gabrovo and Tryavna, **BOZHENTSI**'s (БОЖЕНЦИ) cluster of two-storey houses with stone roofs and wooden verandahs gives some idea of the museum-village Tryavna could so easily have become. According to legend, Bozhentsi was founded by survivors of the fall of Tarnovo, led by the noblewoman Bozhena and her nine sons. During the second half of the nineteenth century, Bozhentsi grew prosperous through the enterprise of its smiths, potters and weavers, and local merchants who traded as far afield as Hungary and Russia.

There are well over a hundred listed buildings in the village, but the main highlights are the **Kashtata na Doncho Popa**, the early nineteenth-century home of a wool merchant; the **Baba Kostadinitsa House**, a much more humble dwelling which showcases the frugal lifestyle of the rural majority; and the various **workshops** used by village artisans (daily 9am–6pm; 10Lv for a guided tour in English).

Practicalities

Bozhentsi is an easy **day-trip** from Veliko Tarnovo or Gabrovo. Privately owned minibuses run from Gabrovo's bus station during the summer, leaving when they have enough passengers. More regular are the Gabrovo–Tryavna buses that call at the Torbalbuzh stop about 2km downhill from Bozhentsi. If you're driving, you can approach Bozhentsi from the Dryanovo–Gabrovo road by turning south in the village of Kmetovtsi.

The **rooms** in Bozhentsi's old houses (❶) fill up quickly, so it's wise to book in advance through the **information centre** (☎066/804462) at the start of the village; alternatively, there are several private hotels in renovated old houses, the largest of them the *Hadjiliev han* (☎067193/424; ❸). Just before the village is the new *Bozhena Spa Hotel* (☎066/802096, ⓦwww.bogena .bg; ❹), a luxury complex with tennis courts, spa centre, and indoor and outdoor pools. Five kilometres north of Bozhentsi in **Kmetovtsi**, the *Fenerite Hotel* (℡067193/267, ⓦ www.fenerite.bg; ❸), a restored nineteenth-century inn with galleried courtyard, offers en-suite rooms, and has a **restaurant** serving traditional Bulgarian fare. There are also several traditional-style *mehanas* in Bozhentsi itself.

Gabrovo and around

Long known for producing leatherwork and textiles that earned the town the sobriquet of the "Manchester of Bulgaria", **GABROVO** (ГАБРОВО) is the focal point for trips to Bozhentsi, or south to the ethnographic complex at **Etara** and the nearby **Sokolski Monastery**. The town itself doesn't have a great range of things to do or places to stay, but it's a charmingly laid-back provincial place, and its efficient municipal tourist office is a good place to pick up information on the surrounding region. To the Bulgarians, Gabrovo is primarily known as the home of the **Dom na Humora i Satirata**, the House of Humour and Satire, opened on April Fool's Day 1972 in recognition of the position traditionally occupied by the town in Bulgarian humour. People in every country tell jokes about the supposed miserliness of a particular community, and in Bulgaria the butt of the gags has always been Gabrovo. A **Festival of Humour and Satire** takes place each May, comprising masked carnivals, folk music, animated cartoons, prize-giving and the ritual "cutting-off of the Gabrovnian cat's tail" (see box below).

The Town

The more interesting parts of Gabrovo are the older quarters, lying beyond the **Igoto Bridge** on both sides of the River Yantra which carves through the long, straggling town centre. A statue of Gabrovo's legendary sixteenth-century founder, Racho the Blacksmith, stands on a rock in midstream.

Your first port of call if arriving at the nearby bus or train stations, however, will probably be **Dom na Humora i Satirata** (daily 9am–6pm; 4Lv), standing on the west bank at the northern end of the centre. Inside is an extensive collection of cartoons, paintings, humorous writings and photos, plus carnival masks and costumes drawn from scores of countries across the world. Exhibits are changed regularly, but cartoons involving ironic observations of human nature or worthy allusions to global political concerns – such as pollution – seem to be the order of the day. More intriguing, though, are the surreal paintings by

Typical Gabrovo jokes

The tight-fisted nature of the citizens of Gabrovo has long been a subject of mirth. According to such **jokes**, *gabrovtsi* invented the one-stotinka coin, gliding, short skirts, narrow trousers, and matchboxes with only one side for striking; they stop their clocks at night and carry their shoes to reduce wear and tear; let a cat down the chimney rather than hire a sweep; and dock the tails of these luckless creatures so they can shut the door a fraction sooner, conserving warmth. Some typical jokes: one *gabrovets* says to another, "Where's your wedding ring?" "My wife's wearing it this week." Another approaches a taxi driver, asking "How much to the city centre?", to which the driver replies: "Two leva – jump in." "No thanks, I just want to know how much I'm saving by walking." Two *gabrovtsi* have a wager on who can give least when the collection plate comes around; the first donates one stotinka, whereupon the other crosses himself piously and tells the sexton, "That was for both of us." And so on …

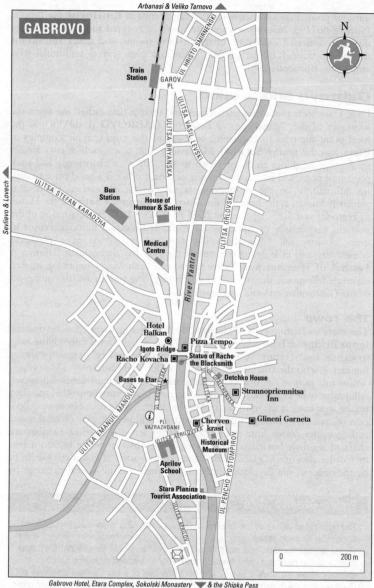

GABROVO

N

Arbanasi & Veliko Tarnovo ▲

Sevlievo & Lovech ◄

Train Station

GAROV PL

UL HRISTO SMIRNENSKI

ULITSA VASIL LEVSKI

ULITSA BRYANSKA

ULITSA STEFAN KARADZHA

Bus Station

House of Humour & Satire

Medical Centre

ULITSA ORLOVSKA

River Yantra

Hotel Balkan

Igoto Bridge

Racho Kovacha

Pizza Tempo

Statue of Racho the Blacksmith

Detchko House

Buses to Etar

UL SKOBELEVSKA

UL RADETSKA

UL OPALCHENSKA

Strannopriemnitsa Inn

Glineni Garneta

ULITSA EMANUIL MANOLOV

PL VAZRAZHDANE

ULITSA APRILOVSKA

Cherven krast

Historical Museum

Aprilov School

Stara Planina Tourist Association

UL PENCHO POSTOMPIROV

ULITSA KRAIDUN

0   200 m

Gabrovo Hotel, Etara Complex, Sokolski Monastery ▼ *& the Shipka Pass*

Bulgarian and foreign artists; look out for for striking images by Bulgarian artist Rosen Krustev, such as his *Hunting Scene*, showing miniature jockeys on rocking horses in pursuit of a butterfly.

Gabrovo's central area is on the east bank around ul. Radetska. The main sight of interest nearby is the **Detchko House**, at pl. 10 Yuli 2 (also, confusingly, referred to as the "Historical Museum"; officially daily 9am–5pm; 2Lv), a remarkable example of a restored nineteenth-century townhouse. Originally built for local businessman Hadzhi Detchko in 1835, the house was later used as a school and as a temporary hospital for Russian soldiers during the Russo-Turkish war of 1877. Today, you can traipse through a suite of elegantly furnished rooms that host occasional concerts and temporary exhibitions. The recently opened **Historical Museum** at ul. Nikolayevska 10 (Mon–Fri 9am–noon & 1–5pm; 2Lv) has a limited range of exhibits that chart the town's 700-year history; upstairs is an **art gallery** featuring twentieth-century works by local artists.

Practicalities

Gabrovo's **tourist office**, on pl. Vazrazhdane (Mon–Fri 8.30am–7.30pm; ☎066/818406), offers a whole range of advice on surrounding attractions and can book **rooms** in Bozhentsi, Etara and other nearby villages – including Uzana, a small mountain resort 23km southwest. Staff do not speak English, however. Further south, at ul. Raicho Karolev 4, is the Stara Planina Tourist Association (Mon–Fri 9am–5.30pm; ☎066/807137, ⓦwww.staraplanina.org), which can provide information (in English) on the wider area. Accommodation in central Gabrovo is limited to the high-rise, three-star *Hotel Balkan*, at ul. Emanil Manolov 14 (☎066/801054, ⓔhemustourist@dir.bg; ❹), which has prim doubles with bath and cable TV, with breakfast included. Alternatively, you could try the more modern *Gabrovo*, located around 4km south, on the way to Etara (☎066/801715; ❹), which also has roomy double apartments (❺).

For **eating**, the *Stranopriemnitsa Inn*, on ul. Opalchenska, serves traditional Bulgarian food in an attractive galleried courtyard, and sometimes has live folk music; not far beyond, at ul. Radion Umnikov 5, is the popular and modern *Glineni Garneta* café and restaurant. The *Cherven krast*, located behind a big white building with a red cross on it just over the bridge from the Aprilov School, has excellent food and service and a big summer garden complete with children's play area. At the eastern end of the Igoto Bridge, *Pizza Tempo* is a fairly standard Italian restaurant, while on the opposite side is *Racho Kovacha*, a small restaurant with a terrace overlooking the river serving sandwiches and other snacks. Numerous pavement **cafés** bring Gabrovo to life during the summer months, especially in the tree-shaded environs of pl. Vazrazhdane.

The Etara complex

Since Racho the Blacksmith set up his smithy beneath a large hornbeam (*gabar*, hence the town's name), Gabrovo has been a **crafts** centre, and gained fresh impetus at the beginning of the nineteenth century when waterwheels were introduced from Transylvania. By 1870 the town had more than eight hundred workshops powered by water, making iron and wooden implements, clothing, wool and blankets that were sold beyond the frontiers of the Ottoman empire; today it produces textiles in quantities exceeded only by Sliven, as well as half the leather goods in Bulgaria. To preserve traditional skills, Gabrovo has established the museum-village of **ETARA** (ЕТЬРА; daily: 9am–7pm; 4Lv entrance, an extra 7Lv for a guided tour), 9km from town on the banks of the Sivek, a tributary of the Yantra.

Strung out along a charming valley, with its clear bubbling stream and rich birdlife, the Etara complex has the look and feel of a film set, and even though it's artificial, it's nonetheless convincing, and a joy to explore. Traditionally, crafts were inseparable from the *charshiya*, and a **reconstructed bazaar** of the type once common in Bulgarian towns forms the heart of the complex. Throughout much of the day artisans are at work here, hammering blades, throwing pots, carving bowls and the like, and everything they make is for sale, although note that many of the artisans leave an hour or so before the complex officially closes. Even if your interest in crafts is minimal, it's difficult not to admire the interiors of the old houses, which achieve great beauty through the skilful use of simple materials. Besides dwellings and workshops, the bazaar includes a couple of places for grabbing a quick drink, including a traditional coffee house, and a bakery selling *lokum* (Turkish Delight), *halva* and other sweet treats. Another section contains a **watermill** (*karadzheyka*) and **hydro-powered workshops** for cutting timber, fulling cloth, and making braid (*gaitan*), wine flagons (*baklitsi*) and *gavanki* (round wooden boxes).

Etara is an easy **day-trip** from Gabrovo, or even Veliko Tarnovo. Take trolleybus #36 from central Gabrovo to the end of the line (the Instrument engineering works), where you change to buses #7 or #8. Should you want to **stay** longer, the *Hotel Perla*, near the eastern entrance to the complex (☎066/801984; ❷), has small en-suite doubles, while right opposite is the much larger *Stranopriemnitsa* hotel (☎066/801831; ❸), which has some great views and includes breakfast in the price. The *Stranopriemnitsa* **café-restaurant** is a standard *mehana*, while there's a traditional-style restaurant at the opposite end of the complex, the *Vuzrozhdeiska*, although it's only open the same times as the complex.

Sokolski Monastery

An hour or so's walk southwest of Etara (there's no public transport, although with a car you can drive there along the track that heads east from the complex), **Sokolski Monastery** perches on a crag above the village of Voditsi. During Ottoman times the monks offered succour to Bulgarian outlaws, putting up the band of local *haidut* Dyado Nikola in the 1850s, and providing the local rebels with an assembly point during the Rising of 1876. Nowadays it's a discreet, little-visited place, with rose bushes and privet shrubs laid out in a courtyard dominated by an octagonal stone fountain. The small church, dating from the monastery's foundation in 1832, lies at the bottom of a flight of steps to the right. The dome is supported by an unusually large drum of bright blue – also the dominant colour of the frescoes inside (primitively painted by the original pastor, Pop Pavel, and his son Nikolai), which include a vivid *Dormition of the Virgin* above the main entrance. Simple accommodation is available (❶).

Shumen

Lying midway between Veliko Tarnovo and Varna, **SHUMEN** (ШУМЕН) is the obvious base from which to explore the historical sites at Madara, Pliska and Preslav. The city itself has a fair share of ancient monuments and memorial houses, not least a spectacular **medieval fortress** that once guarded the road to Preslav. Called Shumla under Turkish rule, Shumen was one of the four heavily garrisoned citadel towns that formed the defensive quadrilateral protecting the northern frontier. Although the imposing Ottoman fortifications are no more, the thriving market town that existed within is still present in the shape of one surviving mosque, the **Tombul Dzhamiya**. Modern Shumen presents a good example of what state socialism brought to urban Bulgaria. Well-built, prestigious civic buildings line a showcase main boulevard, just seconds away from neglected, pot-holed side streets, where single-storey shacks rub shoulders with grey high-rises.

Arrival, information and accommodation

Both the **train** and **bus stations** are at the eastern end of central Shumen, a 20-minute walk (or short ride on bus #1, #10 or #12) from the civic buildings at the western end of bul. Slavyanski. Here the **tourist information centre** next to the town hall at bul. Slavyanski 17 (Mon–Fri 8.30am–5pm; ℡054/857 773, ©tic@shumen.bg) can advise on accommodation, sights and local transport although they may not have much available in the way of brochures or maps.

Accommodation in Shumen is improving, and there's now a handful of decent hotel options in or near the centre.

Hotels

Kyoshkove in the eastern reaches of Kyoshkove park, beside the road to Shumen fortress ℡054/801 301, ⓦwww.kyoshkove.com. If you don't mind being a 30min walk (or short taxi ride) from the centre, the park-side *Kyoshkove* contains soothing en-suite rooms with TV and minibar, surrounded by squirrel-infested fir trees. ❸

Minaliyat Vek ul. Tsar Osvoboditel 142 ℡054/801 615, ©milaliatvek@abv.bg. Intimate place in the heart of historical Shumen whose en suites come with thick carpets, rich colours, desk space and TVs. Eager-to-help staff, and Wi-Fi throughout. Breakfast costs a few extra leva in the hotel's traditional-style restaurant. ❸

Shumen pl. Oborishte 1 ℡054/800 003, ⓦwww.hotelsh.ro-ni.net. Socialist-era concrete mammoth featuring renovated rooms with plush carpets and Scandinavian-style furnishings, together with slightly dowdier, unrenovated but perfectly habitable en suites. Indoor pool and sauna on site. ❹–❺

Soho ul. P. Volov 2 ℡054/981 571, ⓦwww.hotelsolo-bg.com. Friendly small hotel in a very central street. The en-suite rooms are a bit on the small side but everything is neat and comfy, and breakfast is brought to your door on a tray. Wi-Fi throughout. ❸

The Town

Walking down **bulevard Slavyanski**, with its blend of stately Central European and smart modern architecture, you'll see a modern red-brick building housing the **History Museum** (Mon–Fri 9am–5pm; 3Lv), housing the pick of the region's archeological finds. A Bronze Age site at nearby Smyadovo yielded bone-carved idols from the fourth millennium BC, while the Thracian period is represented by silverware from two local burial sites, at Varbitsa and Branichevo, and a reconstructed war chariot. Also here are many of the best medieval artefacts from Pliska and Preslav, the cultural achievements of the latter revealed in the abstract floral patterns adorning the capitals of stone pillars, and in the delicacy of a tenth-century gold necklace.

Along ulitsa Tsar Osvoboditel

A hundred metres beyond the History Museum, ul. Layosh Koshut leads down to **ulitsa Tsar Osvoboditel**, and what's left of Shumen's old quarter. Standing at no. 115 is the rarely open **Kossuth House-Museum** (officially Mon–Fri 9am–5pm; 3Lv), a warren of panelled rooms linked by creaking corridors, where the Magyar revolutionary Lajos Kossuth stayed for three months after fleeing Hungary in 1849, before the Turks interned him in Asia Minor. Ten minutes' walk to the east, at Enyu Markovski 42, is the **Panaiot Volov Memorial House** (officially Mon–Fri 9am–5pm; 3Lv), home of one of the leaders of the April Uprising who drowned while swimming across the River Yantra to escape Ottoman troops. The house preserves the humble shoemaker's quarters where Volov grew up, while an adjoining pavilion holds the obligatory words-and-pictures display detailing his revolutionary career.

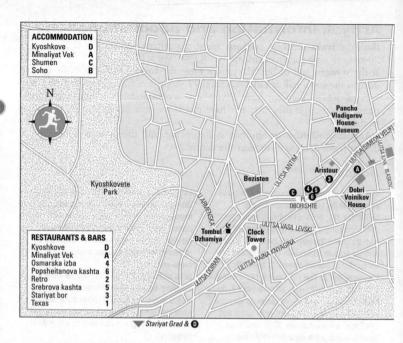

ACCOMMODATION
Kyoshkove   D
Minaliyat Vek   A
Shumen   C
Soho   B

N

Pancho
Vladigerov
House-
Museum

Kyoshkovete
Park

Bezisten   Aristour

Dobri
Voinikov
House

PL.
OBORISHTE

RESTAURANTS & BARS
Kyoshkove   D
Minaliyat Vek   A
Osmarska izba   4
Popsheitanova kashta   6
Retro   2
Srebrova kashta   5
Stariyat bor   3
Texas   1

Tombul
Dzhamiya

Clock
Tower

ULITSA ANTIM
ULITSA SIMEON VELIKI
ULITSA IVA BLASKOV
U. ARMENSKA
ULITSA VASIL LEVSKI
ULITSA DOIRAN
ULITSA RAINA KNYAGINA

Stariyat Grad &

A ten-minute walk west along Tsar Osvoboditel, the **Pancho Vladigerov House-Museum** (Mon–Fri 9am–5pm; 3Lv), honours the Shumen-born pianist (1899–1978) who made his reputation as Bulgaria's leading composer with stirring patriotic works such as the opera *Tsar Kaloyan* (1936), and the little-performed tribute to the socialist takeover *September 9* (1949). The staff will play a tape of his music as you examine the memorabilia on show, which include Vladigerov's raffish beret and suit, and some fine Chiprovtsi carpets.

The Bezisten and the Tombul Dzhamiya

West of ul. Tsar Osvoboditel, the broad asphalt sweep of ul. Rakovski – subsequently ul. Doiran – cuts past two impressive relics of Ottoman Shumla. Sheltering beneath chestnut trees is the **Bezisten**, or covered market, built to cater for the needs of Dubrovnik merchants who established a trading post here in the sixteenth century. Constructed from heavy blocks of stone retrieved from the ruins of Pliska and Preslav, it's now closed, and in need of repair.

Dominating the skyline to the west are the proud minaret and bulbous domes of Shumen's main sight, the **Tombul Dzhamiya** (daily 9am–6pm; 2Lv). Built in 1744 on the initiative of Sherif Halil Pasha, a native of Shumen who rose to become deputy grand vizier in Constantinople, the complex aimed to meet both the spiritual and educational needs of the community. A *mektep*, or "primary school", occupied the east wing, while a *medrese* (Koranic school) and *kitaphane* (library) surrounded the cloistered courtyard to the east. This is dominated by the *shadirvan* or "fountain", an eclectic structure mixing Moorish arches with classical, Corinthian pillars. Inside the prayer hall, carpets cover the floor beneath a dome decorated with floral swirls and paintings of the great mosques of the Middle East. Upstairs, a balustraded balcony provides segregated accommodation for female members of the congregation. The mosque was

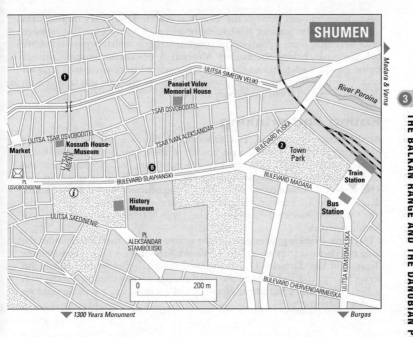

Madara & Varna

Burgas

1300 Years Monument

converted into a museum during the Communist era, but has now reverted to its original role, for the benefit of Shumen's considerable Islamic community. The city is once more an important religious centre for the Muslims of northeast Bulgaria, with believers from far and wide annually descending on the Tombul Dzhamiya to celebrate *Kurban bayram*, one of the major festivals of the Islamic calendar (see Basics, p.51).

The medieval fortress and the 1300 Years monument

Shumen is surrounded to the south and west by the **Shumensko plato national park**, a tableland of dense woodland. The most accessible part of it is the **Kyoshkove Park** at the western end of town (a 15-minute walk beyond the Tombul Dzhamiya, or buses #1, #10 or #11 from the train station), where tracks lead up into the hills past the sites of World War II partisan bunkers.

Immediately above Kyoshkove (and reached by walking 2km uphill from the Shumensko pivo brewery at the entrance to the park) is the **Stariyat grad** or "medieval fortress" (daily: summer 8.30am–6pm; winter 8.30am–5pm; 3Lv), whose monumental, part-reconstructed walls are reminiscent of Tsarevets in Veliko Tarnovo. The Thracians were the first to fortify the site, followed swiftly by the Romans, Byzantines and Bulgars, but it was during the Second Kingdom that the fortress developed its current monumental shape. Ruins of medieval houses outside the fortress walls show that the slopes of the hill harboured a sizeable civilian population during the thirteenth and fourteenth centuries; these people were subsequently driven from their homes and sent to live in the valley by the Ottomans. A small pavilion displaying finds from the fortress stands by the entrance, with an abundant collection of Thracian ceramics and brightly decorated tableware from the Second Kingdom.

Roadways lead east through the forest towards the **1300 Years of Bulgaria** monument (daily: summer 8.30am–6pm; winter 8.30am–5pm; 2Lv) – more easily accessible from a processional concrete stairway which begins just above bul. Slavyanski, behind the History Museum. A bewildering juxtaposition of khans, monks, *haiduti* and mother heroines rendered in concrete by a sculptor with Cubist inclinations, this extraordinary hilltop structure was unveiled on the nation-state's 1300th anniversary in 1981.

Eating and drinking

At the western end of ul. Tsar Osvoboditel, there's a row of **restaurants** occupying National Revival-style houses: of these, the *Popsheitanovata kashta* excels in grilled meats, traditional *gyveche* pot-roasts, and also has rabbit and lamb dishes that don't always crop up elsewhere; while the nearby *Minaliyat Vek*, at ul. Tsar Osvoboditel 142, offers top-quality traditional cooking in a shaded courtyard. Further afield, the restaurant of the *Kyoshkove* hotel is the place to tuck into steaks and fish dishes, with a terrace facing the trees of Kyoshkove park.

Daytime drinking takes place in the numerous cafés that shelter under the lime and chestnut trees along bul. Slavyanski. Enjoyable evening venues include *Texas*, at ul. Vasil Drumev 17, a brick-lined American-themed pub which also serves hearty food; and *Retro*, in the park between the town centre and the train station, which has a full menu of spirits and cocktails and a sizeable outdoor terrace under the trees.

Around Shumen

The northeastern fringe of the Balkan Range is distinguished by three archeological sites, all easily accessible from Shumen. The ruins of **Pliska** are less interesting to look at than to read about, but enough remains of **Preslav** to justify a visit if your taste inclines towards hunky masonry. As for the so-called **Madara Horseman**, the rockscapes all around make up for the eroded face of this unique and ancient bas-relief.

Fifteen kilometres northeast of the city, just beyond the village of Tsarev Brod, is the **Kabiyuk horse-breeding and riding centre**, founded by Ottoman governor Midhat Pasha in the 1860s to provide mounts for the Turkish army. Arabian, English thoroughbred and East Bulgarian (a cross-breed of domestic stock and both the former) horses are raised here, although if you want to view the stables and go on a short ride you'll have to arrange a visit through either the *Hotel Shumen*.

Preslav

Founded by Khan Omurtag in 821 AD, **VELIKI PRESLAV** (ВЕЛИКИ ПРЕСЛАВ) became the capital of the First Kingdom during the reign of Tsar Simeon (893–927) – although it began to eclipse the original capital, Pliska, at an earlier date. According to contemporary accounts, tenth-century Preslav was the most populous town in the Balkans, with extensive suburbs surrounding a walled inner town containing "large buildings of stone on both sides, decorated with wood". It also held a palace, a Royal School of Translators, the Patriarchate and other "churches ornamented with stones, wood and paintings, marble and copper, silver and gold". Preslav's downfall began when it was captured by the

Kievan prince Svetoslav, causing the Byzantine Empire to respond by razing the town in 972, and although it later revived, Preslav never regained its former size and was subsequently surpassed by Tarnovo. Eventually it was burned down by the Turks, who used the remains to construct their own buildings, including the Tombul Mosque in Shumen.

Despite its venerable history, modern Preslav is a grim place, offering few inducements to spend longer than an afternoon, and regular bus services to Shumen happily mean that you don't need to.

The Archeological Museum and the ruins

The **ruins of Preslav** are scattered over farmland signposted to the south of the modern town. Head north from Preslav's main square towards the site, which lies beyond the scruffy town park. Beyond the crest of a hill lurks a modern concrete bunker holding an **Archeological Museum** (daily: summer 9am–6pm; winter 9am–5pm; 3Lv), where plans and diagrams can be consulted before venturing out into the relic-strewn fields. The museum displays numerous examples of the ceramic tiles used to decorate the medieval town's buildings, showing the swirling abstract patterns which characterized decorative arts during the First Kingdom. Prime pieces from Tsar Simeon's golden age include a unique ceramic icon of St Theodore, and the exceptional gold treasure of Preslav, which is kept locked away in a strong room (a member of staff will open it up for you). Choice pieces among the treasure include a necklace adorned with enamel plaques showing peacocks and floral designs, and a gold and emerald brooch.

Approaching the ruins from here you'll pass through the northern gate, the first sign of the sturdy **walls** that envelop the medieval city – reconstructed with modern stone to something approximating their original height. To the west are the bare ruins of the **palace** where the tsar held court. Further west, the traces of a vast monastery complex lie raked across the hillside. About 300m beyond Preslav's south portal is the **Zlatna tsarkva** or "Golden Church", so called because the dome was said to be covered in gold leaf. Originally an arcaded rotunda with twelve apses (symbolizing the apostles), fragments of its walls and twelve marble columns still remain, although you'll have to study the model in the Archeological Museum to appreciate its true grandeur.

The Madara Horseman

The most popular destination for excursions from Shumen is the village of **MADARA** (МАДАРА), 10km to the east and served by frequent trains, where a range of cliffs show signs of human occupation dating back to the third century BC. The main road through the village leads up to Madara's most famous sight, the mysterious bas-relief known as the **Madara Horseman** (daily: summer 8am–7pm; winter 8am–5pm; 3Lv). Carved into the rockface at a height of 95m, it's so eroded that details are only apparent by the light of a setting sun, but the carving is said to represent a horseman whose mount is trampling a lion with the assistance of a greyhound, while he holds the reins in one hand and a wine cup in the other. Various Greek inscriptions next to the carving provide ambiguous clues to its age: the oldest inscription, recording a debt owed by the Byzantine emperor Justinian II to Khan Tervel, suggests that the Bulgars carved the horseman in the eighth century AD. However, some scholars believe it is far older than that. The figure, they argue, represents the nameless rider-god of the Thracians, and is of Thracian or Getae origin, the inscriptions merely evidencing that it was later appropriated by Bulgarian rulers.

▲ The Madara Horseman

Around the Horseman

To the right of the relief, a path winds off towards the **Large Cave** (Golyamata peshtera) beneath a giant overhang of rock. Beyond is a smaller cave, where flints, bones and pottery were discovered. Just above, you'll catch sight of the remnants of a fourteenth-century **rock monastery**, its crudely dug cells pitting the cliff face.

Not far away you'll find the source of the River Madara, where Thracian period plaques and statues honouring Dionysus, Cybele, the rider-god and three water nymphs have been discovered. There are also remains of an early medieval **grain store**, where enormous clay vessels were sunk into the ground to keep cool.

Early Bulgarian remains and the fortress

Most of the early Bulgarian finds are located to the left of the Horseman, where the barest outlines of eighth- and ninth-century churches and monastic complexes lie scattered at the foot of the cliff. Many of the churches were adapted from or built on top of earlier pagan structures – a sign that Madara was an important religious site from the earliest times. Paganism remained ingrained among the Bulgars long after Christianity became the official religion in 865 AD, and although the precise nature of their beliefs remains shrouded in mystery, the discovery of the eighth-century **Old Bulgarian baths** points to the existence of water-based purification rituals.

A rough-hewn pathway works its way up the cliff face to the plateau above. Roughly 500m to the west lies a **ruined fortress** of fifth-century origin, although the remaining walls mostly date from the Second Kingdom. There are also two **tumuli** left by the Getae – who buried their dead in ceramic urns – 300m north of the fortress, but the real attraction is the **view from the plateau**. Roman ruins are scattered about at the foot of the massif, while the surrounding plain is cut off by the Balkans to the south and the Ludogorie hills to the north – where sharp eyes might be able to discern the ruins of Pliska (see p.261) amid the acacia groves.

It's pretty easy to see the site and return to Shumen in the space of a morning or afternoon, though there is **accommodation** near the Horseman, should you wish to stay. The *Madara turisticheski dom* (☎0531/32091; ❶, dorms 11Lv per person) a few metres up the road from the Horseman, is dilapidated but offers superb balcony views of the rocks and the valley; much more comfortable is the *Madarski Konik* hotel (☎0531/32063; ❷–❸) just below, which also has a restaurant. Bungalows are available for rent at the *Madara* **campsite** (May–Sept; ❶), about 200m to the south, where you can also pitch tents. As for **eating** and **drinking**, light snacks are offered in Madara village at the *Mundaga* bar on the right before the railway crossing, as well as at the café and restaurant just outside the complex.

The Protobulgarians

Known to English-speaking historians as the **Bulgars**, and to the Bulgarians themselves as the *prabalgari* or "**Protobulgarians**", the rulers who founded Pliska and Preslav, and who may have been responsible for commissioning the Madara Horseman, started out as Turkic nomads from the Eurasian steppe.

Originating in western Siberia, the Bulgars coalesced into three warlike tribes in the sixth century: the **Onogurs**, **Utigurs** and **Kutrigurs**. The latter were the first to descend on the Balkans, reaching the walls of Constantinople twice in the mid-500s AD before being pushed back by the armies of Emperor Justinian. For the next half-century Byzantine diplomacy concentrated on keeping these three tribes at each other's throats, in an attempt to preserve the balance of power in the territories north and east of the Black Sea. Eventually, however, they began to cultivate the friendship of the Onogurs, who by this time ruled a swathe of steppe north of the Caucasus mountains – subsequently called **Old Great Bulgaria** by Byzantine chroniclers. The alliance was cemented in 619 with the baptism of the Onogur Khan Organa, together with his son Kubrat in Constantinople.

Nevertheless, things went awry when the Onogurs were driven from their lands by another Turkic tribe, the rapidly expanding Khazars. Kubrat's successor **Asparuh** led his people southwest to the Danube expecting hospitality from his Byzantine ally Emperor Constantine IV, who instead sent an army to prevent Asparuh from crossing the river. The Byzantine attempt failed, and by 681 Constantine was forced to recognize the existence of an **independent Bulgar state** ruled by Asparuh from his capital at Pliska.

The new kingdom was initially limited to the flatlands either side of the Danube, stretching from the Balkan Range in the south to the Carpathians in the north. However, the Bulgars began to expand beyond the Balkan Mountains and put down urban roots under Asparuh's successor, **Khan Tervel**, and the centuries-old culture of these Turkic-speaking steppe dwellers began to die out. An aristocratic elite ruling over a population of Thracians and Slavs (the latter, valued by the Bulgars as frontier settlers), became increasingly numerous, the Bulgars gradually lost their separate ethnic identity and became assimilated by their subjects. The process was confirmed by Tsar Boris's conversion to Christianity in 865 and the suppression of paganism that followed – many of the old Bulgar families, unwilling to break with the old faith, were simply wiped out.

Little is known about the beliefs and customs of the Bulgars. Byzantine chroniclers have provided us with a few scraps, telling us that they worshipped their ancestors, practised shamanism, sacrificed steppe wolves in times of trouble, and probably indulged in polygamy. Some Turkic-speaking Bulgars still exist, the so-called **Volga Bulgars** who survive in isolated pockets south of Kazan in Russia. They converted to Islam in the tenth century and enjoyed independent statehood until the thirteenth, when they were submerged beneath the advance of their fellow Muslims, the Tatars.

Pliska

Ten kilometres north of Madara, **Pliska** was a sophisticated and important settlement during its early medieval heyday, covering 23 square kilometres and protected by citadels on neighbouring hills. Pliska served as Bulgaria's capital from the seventh century, and it was here that the disciples of Cyril and Methodius, Naum and Kliment, came in 885 AD to help spread the Slav alphabet and the Christian religion. Pliska's days of glory were over by 900, after Tsar Boris I had come out of monastic retirement to stamp out a return to paganism sponsored by his son Vladimir – one of Boris's acts was to move the capital to Preslav in order to make a fresh start.

The ruins

Entered by a minor road running 3km eastwards from the village of Pliska, **the ruins** (daily 8.30am–5pm; 4Lv) still occupy a considerable area – as at Preslav, much of the outer walls have been partially rebuilt to give visitors an idea of how formidable a place Pliska once was. Rather than building a compact citadel on the western model, the early Bulgarians built a huge fortified compound protected by a stone wall with four gates, within which they could exercise their horses and pitch their tents. At the centre of the compound was a royal enclosure defended by an inner ring of ramparts – it was here, according to tradition, that Han Krum had his palace. A **museum** (same times and ticket) in the southeastern corner of the site boasts a beautifully arranged display of bronze jewellery, decorated pottery and weapons found at the site, together with diagrams and models of the Bulgarian capital as it once was.

What remains of the **Royal Basilica** (a few reconstructed walls and column fragments), built outside the city walls, lies 2km southeast of the entrance at the end of an asphalt track. Stranded among corn fields, it's an impressive but poignant sight.

Practicalities

Unless you have a car, **getting to Pliska** from Shumen is time-consuming, and only really worth the effort if you have a strong enthusiasm for First-Kingdom remains. Regular buses travel from Shumen to the industrial town of Novi Pazar (НОВИ ПАЗАР), 8km southeast of Pliska, from where four daily buses make their way to the village itself; from here it's still a thirty- or forty-minute walk to the ruins. There's a food shop and a café on Pliska's main square.

The Ludogorie

North of Shumen, the low-lying **Ludogorie hills** separate the Balkan Range proper from the flatter terrain of the Danubian Plain and the Dobrudzha beyond. The region harbours a large Muslim population of Turkish and Tatar descent, although it's a predominantly rural area with few worthwhile urban centres. The main town, **Razgrad**, is of limited appeal, although quieter **Isperih**, further northeast, is the gateway to one of Bulgaria's most compelling off-the-beaten-track destinations, **Sveshtari**, which is famous for its **Thracian tombs** and the Muslim holy site of **Demir Baba Tekke**.

Razgrad is served by plenty of intercity **buses** from Shumen and Ruse, as well as Ruse–Varna **trains**. Isperih is more tricky to get to, with less frequent buses departing from Ruse, Razgrad, Shumen, Dobrich and Varna. It also lies on a branch line which leaves the Ruse–Varna rail route at Samuil. Services along this route are sparse, but there is at least one through train from Sofia to Isperih a day.

Razgrad

Situated midway between Shumen and Ruse, **RAZGRAD** (РАЗГРАД) sprawls messily around the banks of the Beli Lom. Since the Liberation in March 1878, the narrow lanes and artisans' stalls that characterized the town during Ottoman times have gradually succumbed to modern urban planning. Apart from a restored *Varosh* quarter north of the river, where a succession of whitewashed National Revival-style houses provide homes for various artists' and writers' unions, Razgrad remains fairly lacklustre, largely because its one great attraction – the seventeenth-century **Ibrahim Pasha mosque** – looks set to remain closed for renovation for many years to come. An imposing block of heavy masonry topped by a graceful dome and tapering minaret, it's a lasting tribute to the skills of its Albanian and Bulgarian builders – and to the Turkish governor Ibrahim, who commissioned it in 1614.

Razgrad's only other sight, lying east of town on the Shumen road, just beyond a large pharmaceutical factory, is the remains of **Abritus**, the fortified Roman town that guarded the road between the Danube and Odessos (now Varna) on the Black Sea. Part of the walls that once surrounded the town (originally standing 12–15m high) can be seen by the roadside, while near the site of the town's eastern gate stand the foundations of the so-called **Peristyle building**, a 23-room complex grouped around a columned courtyard, once used by shopkeepers and artisans. Signs in English describe the outdoor artefacts, while a small, irregularly open **museum** at the site displays pottery fragments and grave inscriptions, plus a collection of bronze tablets depicting the variety of deities worshipped by the cosmopolitan bunch of troops used to garrison the area. The museum's most valuable treasure – a gold drinking cup in the form of a winged horse – is too valuable to be on display to visitors, and remains locked in a strongroom.

Practicalities

Razgrad's **train station** lies 5km north of town: although all trains are met by buses into the centre, it's not the most convenient point of arrival. The **bus terminal** is on the eastern edge of town, within walking distance of both the Ibrahim Pasha mosque (about 15min west) and the ruins of Abritus (about 15min east). Razgrad has a couple of acceptable **hotels** if you get stranded: the basic two-star *Central*, at ul. Beli Lom 40 (℡084/660919; ❸), and the towering, ziggurat-like, three-star *Razgrad* on ul. Zheravna, above the main square (℡084/660801; ❹). The hotel has a restaurant, and a sixteenth-floor bar and nightclub (daily 6pm–4am) that's well worth a visit for the stunning panoramic views from its terrace. Plenty of **cafés** and a couple more clubs cluster around Razgrad's main square.

Isperih

Forty kilometres northeast of Razgrad, **ISPERIH** (ИСПЕРИХ) is a sleepy market town lying between gently undulating pastures. It has a pleasant town centre splashed with the usual pavement cafés, and an animated Friday-morning **market** which attracts villagers from all over the Ludogorie. However, the town's importance to travellers is really as a jumping-off point for the historical sites around Sveshtari, 7km northwest (see p.264).

Head downhill from Isperih's **bus station** to reach the town centre, where you turn left then bear left again past a small park to find the administrative building of the **town museum** (Mon–Fri 9am–5pm; ✆08331/5619), which can book **private rooms** in nearby village houses (●). Most of these are in Malak Porovets (served by infrequent buses), a rustic spot 8km northwest of town on the Ruse road. Clean and basic **hotel** accommodation can be found at the *Alen Mak*, on the main street at ul. Vasil Levski 79 (✆08331/2359; ●), offering en suites in pastel colours.

Sveshtari

North of Isperih, in the **Sboryanovo** district just outside the village of **SVESHTARI** (СВЕЩАРИ), lies what is arguably the finest **Thracian tomb** yet discovered in Bulgaria. Unearthed in 1982, and included on the UNESCO World Heritage List in 1985, the so-called Royal Tomb dates from the third century BC and is the largest of a group of 26 *mogili* (tumuli) lying beyond the western fringes of the village. The tomb's interior decoration indicates a melding of Thracian and Hellenistic religious elements. Sboryanovo remains an active archeological site: two more tombs (known simply as tomb #12 and tomb #13) have been opened to the public, and excavation of other mounds in the vicinity is ongoing.

Archeologists believe that as many as five necropolises were in use around Sveshtari, comprising more than a hundred *mogili* in total. Some theories suggest that the configuration of the tombs either mirrors the constellations, or symbolizes the holy trinity of the Thracians, while ruins elsewhere in the vicinity have led many scholars to identify the Sveshtari neighbourhood with **Hellis**, capital of the **Getae** (see opposite). Cracks in some of the tombs suggest that an earthquake hit the area some time in the second century BC, probably causing the abandonment of the city.

The Sveshtari area retained its spiritual importance even after the Thracians – early-medieval Bulgarians honoured their chieftains with burial mounds at Sboryanovo, while the sixteenth-century Muslim shrine of **Demir Baba Tekke**, just north of Sboryanovo, still serves as one of the region's most important pilgrimage sites.

Visting the tombs

The **Sboryanovo visitors' centre** 1km north of Sveshtari village (*Priemen* tsentar Sboryanovo; March–Nov: Wed–Sun 9.30am–noon & 12.30–5pm; Dec–Feb: ring the museum administration in Isperih to arrange a visit; ✆08332/2579) runs regular tours of the three main tombs in Bulgarian, English or German for 10Lv per person.

Driving from Isperih, take the Tutrakan road and then follow the "Sveshtari" or "Sboryanovo" signs. Otherwise, there's an Isperih–Sveshtari bus that runs every couple of hours.

The tombs

Thought to have been built in the late fourth or early third century BC, the **Royal tomb** (Tsarskata grobnitsa) has been cleared of much of the earth that once covered it and is now encased in a climate-controlled protective shell. Only nine people are allowed in at a time for a period of fifteen minutes per group – be warned that individual travellers may have to wait while pre-booked tour-groups are given preferential treatment. Once inside, the tour of what is a surprisingly small space can be an intense and intimate experience. Above the doorway is a wonderful frieze of bull's heads and rosettes, after which a corridor leads to three chambers united by a semi-cylindrical vault; the central one is occupied by two stone couches on which a Thracian king and his wife were once laid (five horses were buried in the antechamber to ensure them a mount in the afterlife). The ten stone caryatids and Doric semi-columns that line the tomb's walls show obvious Hellenistic influences, though their sturdy upraised arms and full skirts suggest aspects of the Thracian mother goddess. At one end of the chamber, you can discern faint traces of a wall painting depicting a mounted horseman – presumably the deceased – being offered a wreath by a female deity, another possible representation of the mother goddess.

Compared to the Royal Tomb, **tombs #12 and #13** aren't nearly as dramatic – the former is a simple, single chamber whose roof collapsed centuries ago; while the latter preserves intact its barrel-vaulted burial chamber.

Hellis and Demir Baba Tekke

Beyond Sboryanovo, the road continues through a wooded valley and up onto a plateau, where the meagre remains of an ancient city can be seen beside the road. Archeologists believe this to be the site of **Hellis**, the fourth-century capital of the Getae tribe, who abandoned the area after an earthquake in around 250 BC.

Soon afterwards the road arrives at a small parking and picnic area, where a path leads downhill towards **Demir Baba Tekke**, a sixteenth-century Muslim shrine built on the grave of semi-legendary holy man Demir Baba. The *tekke* itself is a simple structure, a seven-sided tomb-cum-temple topped by a dome,

The Getae

Intense archeological activity in the Sveshtari region is shedding new light on the civilization of **the Getae**, an important Thracian tribe who inhabited both banks of the lower Danube in classical times. Ancient authors disagreed on whether to classify the Getae as Thracians or as Dacians (who lived north of the Danube in what is now Romania), although it's safe to assume that all these groups came from the same ethnic roots.

Thucydides alluded to their skill as horsemen, and they proved more than a handful for successive invaders – from Darius's Persians in the fifth century BC to the Romans in the first. In 335 BC **Alexander the Great** chased the Getae north of the Danube and destroyed some of their settlements, but failed to subdue them. His successor, Lysimachus, was captured by Getae ruler Dromichaetes in 292 BC, only to be lectured on the value of peace and sent home. However, their period of greatest glory came in the first century BC, when King **Burebista** presided over a short-lived Danubian empire which exercised control of the whole western seaboard of the Black Sea – from what is now the Ukraine in the north to Apollonia (present-day Sozopol) in the south.

Evidence suggests that the Getae honoured a trinity of deities comprising mother earth, sun and moon, and, indeed, items of treasure recovered from the Sveshtari tombs were often found positioned in symbolic groups of three. A sceptical Herodotus relates how the Getae believed they were immortal, and worshipped a certain **Zalmoxis** (thought to be a north Balkan version of Orpheus; see p.356), who hid himself in an underground chamber for several years before re-emerging, much to the surprise of his contemporaries, to proclaim that he had died and come back to life again. Herodotus also tells of how the Getae sent "messengers" to Zalmoxis every five years by choosing a suitable courier, then tossing him onto a forest of upturned spear-points.

The Aliani

Many of the Muslim communities of the Ludogorie are **Aliani** (known to the Turks as *Kizilbazi* or "red-heads"), a heterodox group who, like the Shiites, claim spiritual descent from Ali, the Prophet's son-in-law. Originally from Iran and Azerbaijan, the Aliani were distrusted by orthodox Sunni sultans, who had them forcibly resettled in the Balkans in order to serve the Ottoman empire as frontier troops. Mixing traditional Islamic beliefs with elements of Sufi mysticism and pre-Islamic Iranian sun worship, the Aliani exerted a strong influence over dervish orders, notably the powerful Bektashi, a connection which helped protect the Aliani from outright persecution. The Aliani of northeastern Bulgaria shunned links with Sunni Muslims, but entered into a symbiotic relationship with their Christian Bulgarian neighbours, sharing customs, superstitions, and rites. In the early fifteenth century, an Aliani leader from Silistra, Sheikh Bedredin Simavi, began preaching the equality of all the sultan's subjects, and led a combined Muslim-Christian revolt against the Ottoman feudal order. It took four years before the rebellion was stamped out.

Today the Aliani live in Sveshtari and several other villages between Isperih and the Danube. They don't have mosques in the traditional sense, preferring to meet for prayers in the house of a leading community member, and Aliani women don't wear the veil. They also have relaxed attitudes towards alcohol, and *rakiya* plays an important part in the rites conducted at Demir Baba.

but is accorded an otherworldly grandeur by the limestone cliffs which rear up immediately behind. A Neolithic settlement has been discovered by the **Pette Parsta spring** at the foot of the cliffs, and the site was subsequently home to a Thracian sanctuary, so the place's importance as a spiritual centre predates the arrival of Islam in the fourteenth century.

The *tekke* is sacred to the **Aliani** (see box opposite), a Muslim group whose rituals are open to the influence of the neighbouring Christian community, and both Aliani and Christian families visit the *tekke* on key holy days to picnic and dance to folk music. The most important dates are March 22 (*Chetirideset machenitsi* or Forty Martyrs' Day), May 6 (*Gergyovden* or St George's Day to the Christians; the spring festival of *Hidrelez* to the Aliani), August 2 (*Ilinden* or St Elijah's Day, adopted by the Aliani as a midsummer festival), and a hastily improvised autumnal date to mark the end of the harvest. People come here all year round to perform certain **rituals**: strips of cloth are tied to trees or the bars of the *tekke* windows to ward off evil, and items of female underwear are passed through a hole in a stone in the courtyard to ensure fertility. Inside the *tekke*, pilgrims lay presents (socks, handkerchiefs or small pieces of embroidery) on the tomb of Demir Baba, chant prayers and light candles.

Behind the *tekke*, a path leads up the side of the cliff to emerge on the plateau above, where the scant remains of Thracian stone circles and walled sanctuaries present further evidence that the territory around Sveshtari has been of great religious significance to successive civilizations.

Practicalities

The nearest **accommodation** to the tombs is either back in Isperih or in private rooms in the village of Malak Porovets (booked through the museum in Isperih; see p.264), or at the basic *Ahinora* chalet, just up the road from the picnic area near Demir Baba (☎08331/4750), with dorm beds for 10Lv a night. Although there are a couple of **food stores** (*hranitelni stoki*) and cafés in Sveshtari village, the only **restaurant** in the vicinity is the *Ahinora's* ground-floor *mehana*.

Travel details

Trains

Berkovitsa to: Boichinovtsi (4 daily; 1hr); Montana (4 daily; 45min).

Boichinovtsi to: Berkovitsa (4 daily; 1hr); Vidin (4 daily; 2hr 30min).

Dimovo to: Boichinovtsi (5 daily; 2hr).

Gabrovo to: Tsareva Livada (6 daily; 30min).

Gorna Oryahovitsa to: Pleven (12 daily; 1hr 30min); Ruse (10 daily; 2hr 30min); Shumen (9 daily; 1hr 30min); Sofia (9 daily; 4hr 30min); Targovishte (1 daily; 2hr); Veliko Tarnovo (10 daily; 30min).

Isperih to: Samuil (3 daily; 45min); Silistra (3 daily; 1hr 30min); Sofia (1 daily; 12hr).

Kardam to: Dobrich (3 daily; 1hr 15min).

Levski to: Lovech (6 daily; 1hr 30min); Pleven (7 daily; 30min).

Lovech to: Levski (4 daily; 1hr 30min); Troyan (2 daily; 1hr 10min).

Montana to: Berkovitsa (4 daily; 45min).

Pleven to: Gorna Oryahovitsa (14 daily; 1hr 30min); Levski (hourly; 30min); Ruse (4 daily; 3hr 30min); Shumen (8 daily; 4hr 30min); Sofia (10 daily; 3hr); Varna (5 daily; 5–6hr).

Ruse to: Gorna Oryahovitsa (6 daily; 2hr 30min); Ivanovo (5 daily; 30min); Pleven (4 daily; 3hr 30min); Sofia (4 daily; 7hr); Varna (3 daily; 4hr).

Shumen to: Gorna Oryahovitsa (9 daily; 2hr); Kaspichan (8 daily; 40min); Pleven (5 daily; 3hr 30min); Plovdiv (1 daily; 4hr 30min); Sofia (5 daily; 7hr); Varna (9 daily; 1hr 30min).

Silistra to: Isperih (3 daily; 1hr 30min).

Sofia to: Cherepish (6 daily; 2hr); Eliseina (6 daily; 1hr 30min); Gorna Oryahovitsa (6 daily; 4hr 30min); Lakatnik (7 daily; 1hr); Lyutibrod (6 daily; 2hr); Pleven (hourly; 3hr); Ruse (4 daily; 7hr); Vidin (3 daily; 5hr); Zverino (7 daily; 1hr 30min).

Svishtov to: Levski (4 daily; 1hr 30min); Troyan (3 daily; 5hr).

Tryavna to: Tsareva Livada (9 daily; 15min).

Tsareva Livada to: Gabrovo (6 daily; 30min); Gorna Oryahovitsa (3 daily; 1hr); Plovdiv (1 daily; 3hr); Ruse (4 daily; 1hr); Stara Zagora (4 daily; 2hr); Tryavna (6 daily; 15min); Tulovo (6 daily; 1hr 30min); Veliko Tarnovo (9 daily; 50min).

Veliko Tarnovo to: Dryanovo (6 daily; 30min); Gorna Oryahovitsa (6 daily; 30min); Tsareva Livada (8 daily; 50min).

Vidin to: Boichinovtsi (4 daily; 2hr 30min); Sofia (3 daily; 5hr).

Buses

Belogradchik to: Montana (1 daily; 1hr 15min); Oreshets (4 daily; 30min); Rabisha (2 daily; 30min); Vidin (4 daily; 1hr 45min).

Berkovitsa to: Montana (13 daily; 30min); Varshets (3 daily; 40min); Vratsa (1 daily; 1hr 30min); Sofia (10 daily; 2hr 20min).

Elena to: Veliko Tarnovo (4 daily; 1hr 15min).

Gabrovo to: Bozhentsi (4 daily; 20min); Burgas (2 daily; 5hr); Dryanovo (hourly; 50min); Lovech (9 daily; 1hr 30min); Kazanlak (9 daily; 2hr); Pleven (7 daily; 2hr); Plovdiv (3 daily; 3–4hr); Sevlievo (hourly; 30min); Sofia (11 daily; 4hr); Stara Zagora (6 daily; 2hr 40min); Troyan (1 daily; 2hr); Tryavna (hourly; 50min); Varna (2 daily; 4hr); Veliko Tarnovo (hourly; 1hr).

Isperih to: Dobrich (2 daily; 2hr); Gorna Oryahovitsa (1 daily; 2hr 30min); Ruse (2 daily; 2hr); Shumen (2 daily; 1hr 30min).

Lovech to: Kazanlak (1 daily, 3hr); Pleven (hourly; 40min); Sevlievo (7 daily; 30min); Sofia (10 daily; 3hr); Teteven (4 daily; 2hr); Troyan (hourly; 1hr); Veliko Tarnovo (1 daily; 2hr); Vratsa (1 daily; 2hr 30min).

Montana to: Belogradchik (1 daily; 1hr 15min); Berkovitsa (13 daily; 30min); Chiprovtsi (7 daily; 50min); Kopilovtsi (4 daily; 1hr 15min); Lopushanski Monastery (4 daily; 45min); Varshets (1 daily; 1hr); Vidin (1 daily; 3hr); Vratsa (5 daily; 40min).

Novi Pazar to: Shumen (6 daily; 1hr).

Pleven to: Belene (4 daily; 1hr 30min); Gabrovo (5 daily; 3hr); Lovech (hourly; 40min); Oryahovo (3 daily; 2hr 30min); Nikopol (4 daily; 1hr 15min); Svishtov (hourly; 1hr 15min); Teteven (2 daily; 2hr 30min); Troyan (1 daily; 1hr 30min); Veliko Tarnovo (3 daily; 3hr 30min); Vidin (1 daily; 4hr); Vratsa (2 daily; 2hr 15min).

Rabisha to: Belogradchik (2 daily; 30min).

Ruse to: Dobrich (2 daily; 4hr); Isperih (2 daily; 2hr); Pleven (1 daily; 2hr 30min); Razgrad (4 daily; 1hr 15min); Shumen (2 daily; 2hr 15min); Silistra (10 daily; 2hr 45min); Sofia (12 daily; 5hr); Svishtov (hourly; 1hr 30min); Varna (4 daily; 3hr 45min).

Sevlievo to: Lovech (5 daily; 30min).

Shumen to: Burgas (5 daily; 3hr); Dobrich (2 daily; 2hr 15min); Novi Pazar (6 daily; 1hr); Preslav (8 daily; 30min); Razgrad (5 daily; 1hr); Ruse (6 daily; 2hr 15min); Sofia (2 daily; 5hr 30min); Silistra (3 daily; 3hr); Varna (4 daily; 2hr).

Silistra to: Dobrich (7 daily; 2hr 15min); Ruse (10 daily; 2hr 45min); Shumen (3 daily; 3hr); Sofia (4 daily; 7hr); Tutrakan (12 daily; 1hr 20min); Varna (4 daily; 3hr 30min).

Sofia *Avtogara Poduyane* to: Botevgrad (hourly; 1hr); Etropole (Mon–Sat 7 daily; Sun 4 daily; 1hr 30min); Pravets (4 daily; 1hr); Teteven (3 daily; 2hr 20min); Troyan (Mon–Sat 2 daily; Sun 3 daily; 3hr).*Avtogara Sofia* to: Dobrich (4 daily; 7hr); Gabrovo (2 daily; 3hr 30min); Lovech (1 daily; 3hr); Ruse (12 daily; 5hr); Shumen (6 daily; 6hr); Silistra (4 daily; 7hr); Svishtov (1 daily; 4hr 30min); Veliko Tarnovo (8 daily; 4hr); Vidin (7 daily; 4hr); Vratsa (hourly; 2hr).

Svishtov to: Ruse (hourly; 1hr 30min); Veliko Tarnovo (3 daily; 2hr 45min).

Teteven to: Lovech (4 daily; 2hr); Pleven (1 daily; 2hr 30min); Ribaritsa (5 daily; 30min); Sofia (4 daily; 2hr).

Troyan to: Apriltsi (4 daily; 1hr); Cherni Osam (hourly; 40min); Chiflik (2 daily; 45min); Lovech (hourly; 1hr); Plovdiv (April-October 2 daily; 3hr 30min); Shipkovo (5 daily; 45min); Sofia (4 daily; 3hr).

Tryavna to: Gabrovo (every 30min; 50min).

Veliko Tarnovo to: Burgas (3 daily; 4hr 30min); Elena (4 daily; 1hr 15min); Gabrovo (11 daily; 1hr); Kazanlak (1 daily; 2hr 30min); Kilifarevo (6 daily; 50min); Lovech (5 daily; 2hr); Plovdiv (3 daily; 4hr 30 min); Ruse (7 daily; 1hr 30min); Sevlievo (4 daily; 1hr); Sofia (hourly; 4hr); Svishtov (7 daily; 2hr 45min); Varna (hourly; 5hr).

Vidin to: Belogradchik (4 daily; 1hr 45min); Montana (1 daily; 3hr); Pleven (1 daily; 4hr); Sofia (10 daily; 4hr 30min).

Vratsa to: Berkovitsa (1 daily; 1hr 30min); Mezdra (every 40min; 20min); Montana (6 daily; 40min); Pleven (2 daily; 2hr 15min); Sofia (hourly; 2hr); Zgorigrad (Mon–Sat 12 daily; Sun 7 daily; 20min).

International trains

Gorna Oryahovitsa to: Bucharest (3 daily; 5–6hr); Budapest (1 daily; 18hr); Istanbul (1 daily; 13hr); Moscow (connection in Bucharest, 1 daily; 48hr); Thessaloniki (1 daily; 13hr).

4

The Sredna Gora and the Valley of the Roses

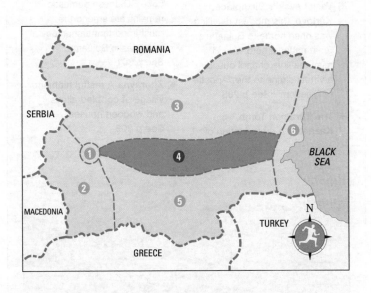

CHAPTER 4 # Highlights

* **Koprivshtitsa** A beautifully preserved museum town, famous as the site of the April Rising of 1876, and home to the finest National Revival architecture in Bulgaria. See p.273

* **Starosel** Enigmatic burial mounds from the fifth century BC, excavated in 2000 and now one of the most-visited archeological sites in the country. See p.283

* **Vasil Levski's Birthplace, Karlovo** This modest dwelling was once home to Bulgaria's great national hero – don't miss the little chapel outside, a virtual shrine to the "Apostle of Freedom". See p.288

* **The Thracian Tomb, Kazanlak** A reproduction of the nearby burial chamber, with its colourful and detailed murals illustrating a Thracian funeral feast. See p.293

* **The Shipka Pass** Famous as the scene of truly heroic resistance by Bulgarian and Russian forces against a much larger Turkish army in 1877. See p.296

* **The Neolithic Dwellings, Stara Zagora** Dating from 5500 BC, these domestic remains are among the most important archeological treasures in Bulgaria. See p.301

* **Zheravna** A restful highland village of cobbled alleys and wooden houses. See p.308

▲ Cannon at Shipka Pass

4

The Sredna Gora and the Valley of the Roses

The most direct route between Sofia and the Black Sea coast cuts straight across central Bulgaria, between the mountains of the Balkan Range to the north, and the **Sredna Gora** to the south. Lining the valleys of the latter are some of Bulgaria's most historic villages, renowned for their folkloric and revolutionary traditions – above all, **Koprivshtitsa**, the starting point of the ill-fated April Rising of 1876, and the site of some of Bulgaria's finest nineteenth-century architecture. Nearby are the museums and memorials of **Panagyurishte**, another centre of the Rising, and the ancient Roman spa town of **Hisar**. The eastern stretches of the Sredna Gora are gentler and less dramatic, but the city of **Stara Zagora**, site of one of Bulgaria's greatest archeological treasures, the 7500-year-old Neolithic dwellings, provides an excuse to break your eastward journey.

Between the Sredna Gora and Balkan ranges lies the **Valley of the Roses** (really two valleys: the upper reaches of the Stryama and the upper reaches of the Tundzha), named after the rose plantations to which the area owes its wealth. Though the valley is at its best when the rose crop is harvested in May, interest is provided throughout the year by the historic settlements lining the valley floor. Those most deserving of attention are **Karlovo**, the birthplace of the freedom fighter Vasil Levski and the best preserved of the valley's market towns, and the region's most convenient touring base **Kazanlak**. Known for the Rose Festival, a folkloric bash which attracts visitors in early June, Kazanlak is also home to a unique collection of Thracian tombs, earning this part of the valley the title of Bulgaria's "Valley of the Kings". To the north of Kazanlak lies the **Shipka Pass**, amid some of the highest peaks of the Balkan Range, the site of a crucial battle during the Russo-Turkish War of 1877–78.

Midway between the valley and the Black Sea, **Sliven** is the starting point for excursions to the highland craft towns of **Kotel**, a carpet-weaving centre, and **Zheravna**, with its unique nineteenth-century rural architecture.

Strictly speaking, both these places belong to the Balkan Range, but are included in this chapter because they're more easily visited by those travelling the Sofia–Black Sea route.

The Sredna Gora

... So, proudly you may gaze
Unto the Sredna Gora, the forest's single queen,
And hear the ring of swords, and all this song can mean ...

Pencho Slaveykov, *The Song of the Blood*

The **Sredna Gora** or "Central Highlands" stretch from the Pancharevo defile outside Sofia almost as far as Yambol on the Thracian plain. Thanks to its forests of oak and beech, and numerous caves and hot springs, the region has been inhabited by humans as early as the fifth millennium BC. The Thracians left a hoard of gold treasure at **Panagyurishte** (since moved to the National History Museum in Sofia, see p.98), and burial mounds outside the village of **Starosel**; while their Roman conquerors built a walled spa-city at **Hisar**. For many Bulgarians, however, the Sredna Gora is equally famous as the "land of the April Rising", the nineteenth-century rebellion against Ottoman rule that started in **Koprivshtitsa**. For tourists, too, this town is the region's highlight, its peerless National Revival architecture and pastoral beauty making it a must-see.

Lying roughly midway between Sofia and Plovdiv, the Sredna Gora is a popular excursion from both towns. Koprivshtitsa is served by minibus from Sofia, and by trains travelling the Sofia–Burgas route, although be aware that Koprivshtitsa's train station is over 8km north of the village itself (a connecting

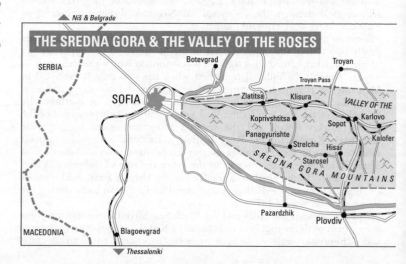

bus meets services). Panagyurishte is served by buses from Sofia and trains from Plovdiv, while Hisar can be reached by bus from either Karlovo, in the Valley of the Roses, or Plovdiv. However, **buses** running across the Sredna Gora range are few and far between, making travelling from Koprivshtitsa to Panagyurishte hugely inconvenient.

Koprivshtitsa

The small town of **KOPRIVSHTITSA** (КОПРИВЩИЦА; pronounced "Koprivshtitsa"), in the upper reaches of the Topolnitsa valley, is a lovely ensemble of half-timbered houses nestling amid wooded hills which, thanks to its elevated position 1060m above sea level, escapes the soaring summer heat experienced by much of lowland Bulgaria. It would be an oasis of pastoral calm were it not for the annual influx of summer visitors, drawn by the superb architecture and the desire to pay homage to a landmark in the nation's history. From the Place of the Scimitar Charge to the Street of the Counter Attack, there's hardly a part of town that isn't named after an episode or participant in the **April Rising of 1876**, when Bulgaria's yearnings for freedom from the Ottoman yoke finally boiled over (see p.276). It was Koprivshtitsa's role as a centre of commerce that provided the material basis for such an upsurge in national consciousness. Sheep and goat farming formed the backbone of the village's wealth, and the resulting wool and dairy products (including carpets, socks and cheese) were traded throughout the Levant. By the time of the Rising, Koprivshtitsa had a population of twelve thousand. After the Liberation, however, commercial life began to shift to the lowland towns, and places like Koprivshtitsa stagnated, leaving it as a kind of fossil. These days, its much reduced population of around 2600 relies heavily on tourism, yet, despite its museum-town status, it also remains a working agricultural community, with horsepower still a vital and visible part of everyday life. Horse-drawn carts loaded with hay, farm workers or shop goods trundle along the cobbled lanes, and if you're in town on a Friday morning, you can take a wander round the

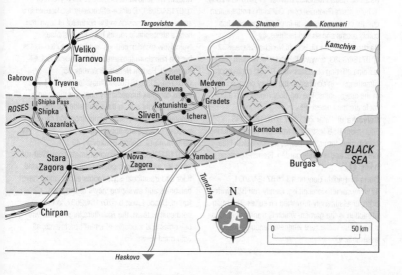

market on the main square, where horseshoes, harnesses, farm tools and other rustic neccessities are put out for sale.

Koprivshtitsa also occupies an important place in the Bulgarian folk music calendar. The **Koprivshtitsa national music festival**, a huge gathering of musicians from all over the country, takes place on a hill outside the town every five years (the next one is due in August 2010). A smaller **regional festival** involving local folk groups is held annually (except when the big event takes place), usually on the weekend nearest to the Feast of the Assumption (*Sveta Bogoroditsa*), on August 15. Other traditional celebrations to look out for are **Iordanovden** (6 Jan), when the priest throws a wooden cross in the river and local lads dive in to retrieve it, and the feast of **Todorovden** (St Theodore's day, the first Saturday of Lent), which is celebrated with horse races on the meadow at the northern end of the village.

Arrival and information

Most of the **train** services stopping at the Koprivshtitsa stop are met by a bus that ferries you the 8km south to the town itself (ticket 1Lv). There are no taxis. The times of buses back to the train stop are posted in the rarely staffed **bus station**, 200m south of the main square. There are four daily Sofia–Koprivsh-titsa minibuses: at the time of writing, two depart from the Trafik-Market bus park just outside Sofia's central train station, while the other two start out from Avtogara Poduyane. The **tourist information centre**, tucked away in the northwestern corner of the main square (daily 10am–7pm; ☎07184/2191, ⓦwww.koprivshtitsa.info) provides maps and general information.

Accommodation

Finding somewhere to stay in Koprivshtitsa is only likely to be difficult during the big five-yearly festival, when it's wise to reserve weeks ahead. At other times, **private rooms** (❶) can be arranged by the **tourist information centre** (see above). There are plenty of small **hotels** and pensions scattered throughout the village, most of them welcoming, family-run affairs.

Astra ul. Hadzhi Nencho Palaveev 11 ☎07184/2364, ⓔhotel_astra@hotmail.com. Out in the northeastern quarter of town, this small family-run pension has comfy rooms and shared facilities. ❷

Bashtina kashta ul. Hadzhi Nencho Palaveev 32 ☎07184/3033, ⓦwww.fhhotel.info. Modern building offering en suites with TV and contemporary furnishings – in contrast to the folksy décor on offer in the other rooms. The top-floor rooms with attic roofs are the cosiest. ❸

Bolyarka ul. Petar Zhilkov 7 ☎07184/2043. Four-room B&B just uphill from the centre, offering bright, pine-furnished rooms, a couple with little balconies, and a lovely garden. French-speaking hosts. ❷

Dona ul. Hadzhi Gencho 13 ☎07184/3031, ⓦwww.cometodona.hit.bg. Family-run B&B with prim, unassumingly furnished en suites. The main attraction is the garden, which is transformed into a barbecue restaurant whenever enough guests assemble. ❷

Hadzhi Ivanchova ul. Doncho Vatah Voyvoda 37 ☎07184/3080, ⓔoffice-s@rholiday.net. Housed in a stately yellow mansion to the northeast of town, the hotel's atmospheric rooms have Koprivshtitsa's typical low wooden ceilings and hand-painted motifs, but the humdrum furniture is a disappointment. ❷

Kalina ul. Hadzhi Nencho Palaveev 35 ☎07184/2032, ⓔHotelkalina@fog-bg.net. Large, gated complex immediately opposite the main square. Rooms are on the small side but nineteenth-century-style furnishings and carved wooden ceilings are appealing. ❸

Panorama ul. Georgi Benkovski 40 ☎07184/2035, ⓦwww.panoramata.com. Well-run complex with smart modern rooms on the ground floor and traditional-style rooms above; most have balconies and sweeping views of the town. ❷

Rai ul. Dyado Liben 8 ☎07184/2637. In the northeast of town, the *Rai* offers large rooms with balconies and a couple of smart apartments, all with great views. ❷

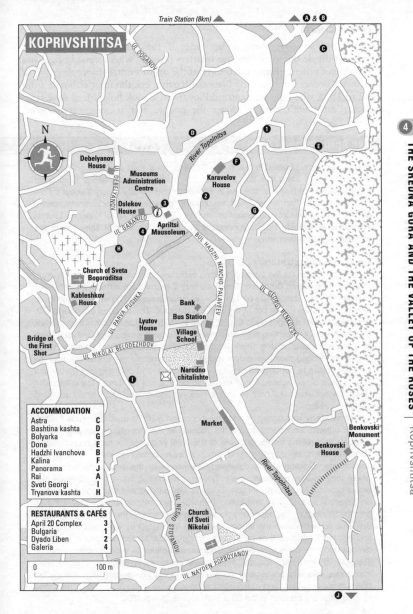

KOPRIVSHTITSA

Train Station (8km) ▲   ▲ Ⓐ & Ⓑ

Ⓒ

UL DOGANOV

River Topolnitsa

Ⓓ   Ⓘ

Ⓔ

Debelyanov
House

Museums
Administration   Ⓕ
Centre   Karavelov
House

UL DEBELYANOV

Oslekov   ③   Ⓖ
House   ⓘ
Apriltsi
UL GARANILO   Mausoleum
④

BUL HADZHI NENCHO PALAVEEV

Ⓗ

Church of Sveta
Bogoroditsa

Kableshkov
House   Bank

UL GEORGI BENKOVSKI

Lyutov   Bus Station
House
UL PARVA PUSHKA   Village
School

Bridge of
the First   UL NIKOLAI BELODEZHDOV
Shot
Narodno
chitalishte

Ⓘ

ACCOMMODATION   Market   Benkovski
Astra   C   Monument
Bashtina kashta   D
Bolyarka   G   Benkovski
Dona   E   House
Hadzhi Ivanchova   B
Kalina   F   River Topolnitsa
Panorama   J
Rai   A
Sveti Georgi   I
Tryanova kashta   H

RESTAURANTS & CAFÉS   UL NESHO STOYANOV
April 20 Complex   3
Bulgaria   1   Church
Dyado Liben   2   of Sveti
Galeria   4   Nikolai

0   100 m   UL NAYDEN POPBOYANOV

Ⓙ ▼

Sveti Georgi ul. Tomangelova 18 ☎07184/2393,
ⓦwww.eurotourism-bg.com. Pleasant traditional
hotel with simply furnished en-suite rooms. The
basement *mehana* is particularly snug in winter
and the restaurant serves a good standard of
Bulgarian cuisine. ②

Tryanova kashta ul. Gereniloto 5
☎07184/3057. Old house just up from the
main square, with delightful low-ceilinged en suites
in the National Revival style (although the TVs look
somewhat more contemporary), and a communal
chardak (porch) overlooking a grassy courtyard. ②

The Town

Koprivshtitsa straggles along either side of the River Topolnitsa, whose tributaries divide the town into five quarters (*mahala*) where stone bridges and the burble of water enhance the beauty of the **architecture**. More than 380 of the town's houses date from the National Revival era, the most elaborate from 1842 to 1870, when the symmetrical Plovdiv style took hold. Many have large wooden gates with separate doors for people and wagons; carved stone

The April Rising of 1876

The **1870s** were troubled times in the Balkans, as a tired and corrupt **Ottoman empire** tried to stem the tide of protest from subject nationalities longing for independence. In Bulgaria, the rise in education and literacy brought about by the National Revival had engendered an upsurge of national consciousness, and a generation of idealistic revolutionaries, such as Vasil Levski, Angel Kanchev, Lyuben Karavelov and Hristo Botev, succeeded in placing the idea of liberation in the forefront of Bulgarian minds.

Revolutionary strategy

In order to coordinate the struggle, various nationalist groups came together to form the Bucharest-based **Bulgarian Revolutionary Central Committee**, or **BRCK**. The network already established by Levski – who had travelled the country setting up revolutionary cells – was put at the BRCK's disposal. The death of Levski in 1873, and the failure of an uprising in Stara Zagora in 1875, persuaded many in the BRCK that the policy of fomenting armed insurrection had been a mistake. However several of the participants in the Stara Zagora uprising (future prime minister Stefan Stambolov among them) were determined to have another go. Encouraged by the Ottoman failure to put down a major revolt in Bosnia, and believing that Serbia and Russia were simply waiting for an excuse to declare war on Turkey, the veterans of Stara Zagora assumed control of the national movement and started planning another uprising.

Their **strategy** was based on the time-honoured guerrilla methods of the *haiduti*, Balkan outlaws who could survive for months in the mountains, harrying Turkish outposts and relying on the goodwill of the local populace for food and shelter. A series of *cheti*, or mobile armed groups, were formed to move through the countryside, avoiding heavily defended Ottoman positions, and gathering support where they could – eventually, it was hoped, snowballing into a popular revolt that would provoke foreign intervention. Bulgaria was divided into four regions (centred on Sliven, Vratsa, Plovdiv and Veliko Tarnovo), each responsible for organizing its own military action. The organizers placed their emphasis on the mountain regions of Bulgaria, firstly because the ethnic makeup of the highlands was solidly Bulgarian, and secondly because they calculated (wrongly, as it turned out) that it would be difficult and time-consuming for the Ottoman authorities to send in reinforcements. The idea of the Rising caught the popular imagination, and preparations were impressive: village tailors secretly made uniforms for the insurgents, lead was melted down to make bullets, and rudimentary cannons were made from cherry trees, one of which can still be seen in the Benkovski House (see p.280).

The Rising begins

The Rising was scheduled for May 1, and on April 14 insurgent leaders were summoned to the Oborishte clearing, 25km southwest of Koprivshtitsa, to receive their final instructions. Unfortunately one of those present at the meeting, Nenko Terziiski, was a spy for the Ottoman authorities, who responded by sending a small unit to Koprivshtitsa to arrest local rebel leader **Todor Kableshkov**. Kableshkov had fountains and troughs adorn the cobbled lanes that wend between them. The total effect is both delicate and rugged, as red, blue and ochre-painted stucco counterpoints the natural tones of wood and stone.

The six house-museums open to the public can be visited in any order, but the most obvious starting point is from the **main square**, dominated by the stone **Apriltsi Mausoleum**, inscribed "Let us guard the national liberty for which the heroes of the rising of 1876 fell." A combined **ticket** valid for all the

no choice but to launch the Rising ahead of schedule on April 20, capturing the Ottoman *konak* (see glossary, p.483) and dispatching the famous **Bloody Letter**, written in the blood of the first dead Turk, informing the Panagyurishte leaders that fighting had already broken out.

A Bulgarian **provisional government** was declared in Panagyurishte, but the authorities reacted swiftly, and the Ottoman governor of Plovdiv dispatched irregular troops to suppress the Rising. These were made up of Pomaks, Bulgarian Muslims eager to settle private scores with their Christian neighbours, and *bashibazouks*, rapacious freebooters drawn from the Tatar and Circassian populations, only recently expelled from Russia and therefore hostile to Slavs in general. As the *bashibazouks* burned the neighbouring towns of Panagyurishte and Klisura, refugees flooded into Koprivshtitsa spreading panic, and the local *chorbadzhii* (rural middle class) attempted to disarm the insurgents. The rebels took to the hills, where rain played havoc with their home-made gunpowder, and eventually they were hunted down. Koprivshtitsa's *chorbadzhii* bribed the *bashibazouks* not to burn the village, which survived unscathed to be admired by subsequent generations as a symbol of heroism.

Elsewhere in Bulgaria, the premature launching of the Rising took most insurgents by surprise. The **Batak** area rose up on April 21, but was soon mercilessly crushed (see p.355). By the time the central Tarnovo region began its action on April 28 it was already too late, and most of the leaders were arrested before any serious fighting took place. In a bizarre coda to the Rising, poet and revolutionary **Hristo Botev** (see p.286) collected emigrés living in Serbia and Romania, crossed the Danube in a hijacked Austrian steamboat on May 17, and tried to lend support to his (already defeated) countrymen by marching on Vratsa. They were wiped out on nearby Mount Okolchitsa.

The aftermath

Despite many individual acts of bravery, the Rising failed to win mass support, largely because local civilians were too afraid of Turkish reprisals. The expected intervention of Serbia and Russia took too long to materialize: although the Serbs later fought a short war with Turkey in the summer of 1876 (in which many Bulgarian exiles participated), they were quickly routed. However, the savagery of **Ottoman reprisals** against civilians (see p.355) in the aftermath of the Rising convinced the great powers of Europe that the Ottoman Empire could no longer be allowed a free hand to discipline its Balkan subjects. As news of the so-called "Bulgarian atrocities" spread, traditional allies like France and Britain lost the political will to shore up the empire against its critics. This suited Russia, which was angling for the creation of a Bulgarian state to serve its own interests in the region.

Ordinary Russians were in any case outraged by the treatment of their fellow Slavs by the Ottomans, and pressed for war. The government of Sultan Abdulhamid spoke vaguely of introducing reforms, then drew back from real action, giving Russia the excuse it needed to attack. Tsar Aleksandr II finally declared war on April 12, 1877, almost a year after the outbreak of the Rising. By the following January, the Ottomans were suing for peace, and Bulgarian independence was at last on the agenda.

houses (5Lv) is available at the museum administration office (Wed–Sun 9.30am–5.30pm) just behind the tourist information centre, or at any of the museum houses. Tickets for individual houses are priced at 2Lv each. On Mondays the Karavelov, Benkovski, and Lyutov houses are open; on Tuesdays the Oslekov, Kableshkov, and Debelyanov houses are open; and all six houses are open from Wednesday to Sunday (9.30am–5.30pm).

The Oslekov House

One of the finest houses in Koprivshtitsa stands just uphill from the main square, on ul. Garanilo. The **Oslekov House** was built in 1856 for local tax collector and much-travelled merchant, Nincho Oslekov. Its facade is upheld by pillars of cedarwood imported from Lebanon, and adorned with views of Padua, Rome and Venice – just some of the foreign cities visited by its proud owner – painted by the Samokov craftsman Kosta Zograf. The upstairs rooms have lovely fretted wooden ceilings and panelled walls, especially in the summer guest room, where one of the murals shows the original, symmetrical plan of the house, never realized since Oslekov's neighbours refused to sell him the necessary land. It was here that the uniforms for the revolutionaries of 1876 were made, and a spinning wheel and some of the shears, thimbles and suchlike employed in that furtive endeavour are on display.

The Debelyanov House and the Church of Sveta Bogoroditsa

On a sidestreet leading north from ul. Garanilo stands the small **Debelyanov House**, where the symbolist poet Dimcho Debelyanov was born in 1887. Painted

▲ The Oslekov House, Koprivshtitsa

royal blue with a white trim, its timbered upper floor contains a humdrum exposition of his tragically short career, with such personal items as his childhood cradle, and the suitcase of books that accompanied him to war. Amongst the many sepia photographs are **portraits** of two of his lovers, Ivanka, to whom he dedicated his poems, and the doomed Elena, whose father disapproved of the relationship so strongly that he finally killed both her and himself. There's also an intimate oil portrait of Debelyanov, painted by his friend, Georgi Mashev. In the garden is a poignant statue of Dimcho's mother, vainly awaiting his return from the battlefields of Greece, where he was killed in 1916.

An identical statue broods over his **grave** in the local cemetery, at the top of ul. Garanilo, whose inscription is from one of his own poems: "Delaying in a gentle dream she becomes her own child." Also in the cemetery stands the **Church of Sveta Bogoroditsa**, whose tolling bell proclaimed the beginning of the 1876 Rising. Built in 1817 on the site of an older church burnt down by the Turks, it is partly sunken into the ground to comply with the Ottoman edict that no Christian building should be taller than the local mosque. The interior is rustic in its simplicity, aside from an elaborate iconostasis by Teteven craftsmen, containing several icons by Zahari Zograf.

The Kableshkov House

Leaving the churchyard by a gate on the far side and turning left, you'll come to the **Kableshkov House**. Built by a local master-craftsman in 1845, its square plan and the combination of one curved and two square oriels on each side reflect the influence of the Plovdiv style. The ground floor preserves the simple living quarters of a reasonably prosperous *chorbadzhii* family, including a "women's work room" with a spinning wheel, and the room where Todor Kableshkov (see box, p.276) was born in 1851. Weapons used in the Rising are displayed on the top floor, whose circular vestibule has a wonderful ceiling with an abstract pattern based on the reflection of sunlight on rippling water. Kableshkov's decision to start the Rising ahead of schedule, after Turkish soldiers came to arrest him, was made at the "House of the Conspiracy" on a nearby street.

Kableshkov was later captured near Troyan, but managed to kill himself with a police revolver in Gabrovo, and is commemorated by a statue close to the **Bridge of the First Shot**, where the Rising began.

The Lyutov House and beyond

Cross the bridge and head up ul. Nikola Belodezhdov and you'll come to the white **Lyutov House**, distinguished by its double staircase and yoke-shaped porch, which is decorated on one side with a small lion breaking free of its chains, signifying Bulgarian aspirations of freedom. Built for a prosperous yoghurt merchant by Plovdiv craftsmen in 1854, the house, boasting one of Koprivshtitsa's most sumptuous interiors, is famed for its wealth of murals: palaces, temples and world cities splashed across the walls and *alafranga* wreaths, blossoms and nosegays in the Blue Room; and oval medallions adorning the ceilings. The house also holds a fine collection of Viennese furniture, while a splendid rosewater fountain forms the centrepiece of the extravagant parlour. The basement houses an exhibition of *plasti*, the locally made felt rugs which traditionally feature bold, sun-symbol designs.

Nearer the river stands a handsome pair of civic buildings, financed by local patriots. The former **Village School**, built in 1837 – the school where the great educational reformer Neofit Rilski (see p.129) taught and to which rich merchant families from all over Bulgaria sent their children – is now a conference and exhibition centre, while the nearby **Narodno chitalishte**, founded in 1869 as public reading rooms, played a big part in the National Revival, spreading literacy and nurturing a sense of national identity in towns and villages.

From Sredna mahala to Byalo kamane

To see more of life in Koprivshtitsa, take a ramble through the **Sredna mahala** (Central) and **Byalo kamane** (White Rocks) quarters. Sredna withdraws from an outdoor market into a *kasbah*-like maze of reclusive houses and lanes where elders gossip and goats forage. With luck, you'll emerge at the **Church of Sveti Nikolai**, behind a high wall with a bell tower above the gateway. Despite the church's dedication, its iconostasis dwells on St Spiridion, whose life is told in ten medallions surrounding a figure of the saint. On the corner of the lane is a fountain donated by the Moravenovs, a leading family in the early eighteenth century.

Walk downstream and cross the river to reach Byalo kamane, a *mahala* of stolid timber buildings on a steep slope, where the **Benkovski House** recalls another revolutionary. Georgi Benkovski (1844–76) helped to rebuild the clandestine networks set up by Levski, after the latter's execution. A tailor by profession, he made the rebels' white uniforms and silk banner – embroidered with the Bulgarian Lion and the words *svoboda ili smart* ("Liberty or Death"). During the Rising his *cheta* wheeled south via Panagyurishte, trying to rally the locals, but he was chased northwards and wiped out near Teteven. His career is covered in usual didactic style; among the texts is a quote from the Rising's chronicler, Stoyanov: "Koprivshtitsa was a republic for centuries, without senators, ministers or presidents; ten times more liberal than France, and a hundred times more democratic than America".

On the hillside above the house looms a striking **monument to Benkovski**, in the form of a socialist superhero astride a leaping horse.

The Karavelov House

Returning towards the main square along the east bank of the Topolnitsa, you'll find, near the Freedom Bridge, the **Karavelov House**, where Lyuben Karavelov was born in 1834. The son of a sausage merchant, his itinerant career was typical of the many patriots who spent years in exile trying to win support for the Bulgarian cause. Educated in Moscow, he was a strong believer in the need to attract Russian and Serbian help, and based himself in Belgrade, where he met Vasil Levski. His enthusiasm for the idea of a Balkan Federation proved too radical for his hosts, who forced him to flee into Habsburg territory, where he was promptly jailed. Karavelov later found refuge in Bucharest, where he organized the BRCK and for ten years advocated armed struggle in the columns of the émigré newspapers *Svoboda* and *Nezavisimost*. After Levski's execution, however, he repudiated direct action in favour of change through reform and education, and was ousted from the leadership of the committee by Hristo Botev.

The house itself contains the usual items of nineteenth-century domestic life, while in the little courtyard stands the rough wooden bench where Karavelov Senior made his sausages. Also on show is the printing press on which Karavelov's newspapers were produced, brought to Bulgaria after the Liberation. An adjacent summer house contains the personal effects of his younger brother, Petko, a prominent liberal politician after the Liberation, and twice premier.

Eating and drinking

There's no shortage of places to **eat and drink** in Koprivshtitsa, with little to choose between the numerous establishments offering good, traditional Bulgarian food. The *Dyado Liben Inn*, across the river from the main square, occupies a lovely old house, with a restaurant upstairs and tables outside in the courtyard. The *Bulgaria* to the northeast of town is a similar affair; its pretty garden is dotted with water features and replica cannons, while the *Bashtina Kushta's* smart restaurant offers a modern, but comparatively clinical alternative with a similar menu. The uninspiring *April 20 Complex* on the main square harbours a café, restaurant, and the occasional lacklustre disco; on the opposite side of the square is the garish neon-lit *Galeria* restaurant which boasts a **nightclub** open until 4am. For picnics, there's a fair range of fresh produce on sale at the **market** south of the bus station (daily except Sun).

Panagyurishte

After Koprivshtitsa, other towns in the Sredna Gora are an anticlimax, particularly **PANAGYURISHTE** (ПАНАГЮРИЩЕ), 39km southwest, whose memorials to the Rising hardly compare with Koprivshtitsa's magnificent houses. With a car, you could consider driving south across the mountains simply for the pleasure of the scenery en route – but if you're relying on meagre public transport (a few **buses** a day from Sofia's Avtogara Yug and three **trains** daily from Plovdiv), it hardly seems worth it.

The Town

Despite its antiquity as a settlement, the existing town is predominantly modern, as Panagyurishte was set ablaze by the Turks for its participation in the April Rising (the town was the base for Georgi Benkovski's cavalry division). The most obvious starting point is the austerely laid-out main square, **pl. Pavel Bobekov** – named after a local insurgent and overlooked from a hillside to the east by the **Memorial to the April Rising**, a towering structure typical of the part-modernist, part-Socialist Realist style that characterized Bulgaria's public monuments in the 1970s and 1980s. The memorial is reached by a processional stairway that runs past the **Church of Sveta Bogoroditsa**, partially burnt in the aftermath of the Rising. Patches of charred murals (immediately on the left as you enter) have been left *in situ* as a reminder of the conflagration. The rest of the interior was colourfully decorated by Samokov painters in the 1890s, who covered the walls with a pictorial history of the life of the Virgin consisting of more than a hundred individual scenes – each inscribed with the name of the local benefactor who paid for it.

West of the main square, ul. Raina Knyaginya heads uphill into what remains of the old town. The two towers of the colonnaded, turquoise-coloured **Church of Sveti Georgi** precede the **Shtarbanova House** at no. 26, home to a prominent member of the local rebel government during the Rising. The house forms one part of a complex of buildings containing the **town museum** (daily 9am–5pm; 2Lv), which is full of antique militaria, including a cherry-tree cannon. Opposite the church, across a small square, ul. Oborishte leads to the **Raina Knyaginya House-Museum** at no. 5 (daily 9am–5pm; 2Lv). As a girl, Knyaginya was the rebels' flag-bearer, mockingly nicknamed *knyaginya* (princess) by her Turkish captors. Tortured in Plovdiv and then exiled to Russia, she returned to Bulgaria after the Liberation to become a schoolteacher in Veliko Tarnovo. The house contains sepia family portraits alongside a "Liberty or Death" flag woven by Knyaginya herself in 1901, in memory of the one she had carried during the Rising. She is buried in the garden with her mother and father – the latter a casualty of the rebellion.

Practicalities

Arriving in town by **bus**, head up the road beside the stream past a hospital to find the main square, on the right. The **train station** is a bit further southeast of the centre down ul. Shiskov. Accommodation is provided by the *Kamengrad* **hotel**, an unmissable four-storey structure centrally located at ul. Bobekov 2 (☎0357/6113; ❷). It boasts tidy twin rooms with shower, TV and air conditioning, and a reasonable **restaurant**. Just beyond the Raina Knyaginya museum at ul. Oborishte 21, the *Kaba* hotel (☎0357/4005; ❶) has simple accommodation with shared bathrooms.

Hisar

Situated in the verdant foothills of the Sredna Gora, **HISAR** (ХИСАР; sometimes written as "Hisarya"), 55km east of Panagyurishte, was one of the great watering holes of antiquity, and the local bottled mineral water is still sold across the country. It was the Romans who founded the **spa**, building marble baths, aqueducts, temples and – after raids by the Goths in 251 AD – fortifications to protect the town, which they called Augusta. Subsequently an episcopal seat, it was devastated by Crusaders despite their appreciation of this "fair town", 150 years before its conquest by the Turks, who restored the baths in the sixteenth century and renamed the place Hisar ("the fortress"). Developed as a health resort for factory workers in Communist times, Hisar fell on hard times following the democratic changes of the early 1990s, though recent investment in its spa hotels combined with efforts to tidy the overgrown parks within the formidable ruins have given the place a long overdue revival.

The Town

A couple of blocks south of the bus and train stations, a sizeable chunk of Hisar's history confronts visitors in the form of the damaged but still imposing **fortress walls**, originally 2–3m thick and defended by 43 towers. The Roman builders employed the technique of *opus mixtum*, bonding stone and brick with red mortar – hence the sobriquet Kizil Kale ("red fortress") which the Turks coined when they besieged the town in 1364.

The northern wall that runs along bul. Botev is bisected by a promenade, leading towards the massive **Kamilite Gate** in the south wall of the fortress, so called after the camels that once passed through it. En route to this you'll see a pseudo-Grecian colonnade and **fountain**, where visitors fill bottles with mineral water and have their portraits taken against a backdrop of crumbling *fin-de-siècle* buildings. A right turn at the Kamilite Gate, followed by a left turn up a flight of steps at the bottom of a hill, will bring you to a fourth-century **Roman tomb** (opening times vary) with frescoed walls and a mosaic floor. Stonework, coins and other finds are displayed in a small **History Museum**, at ul. Stamboliiski 8 (daily 8am–noon & 1–4.30pm; 2Lv), one block east of the main drag.

Practicalities

Hisar is best reached by bus from Karlovo or Plovdiv, although there are occasional trains from the latter too: the stations are on the northern side of the centre, just outside the town walls. Hisar's best **hotels** are about 1km east

of here: the recently refurbished *Hissar* (☎0337/62781, ⓦwww.hotelhissar
.com; ❹) has high standards and offers a wide range of spa treatments, as does
the *Augusta* (☎0337/63821, ⓦwww.augustaspa.com; ❺). Its rooms have
en-suite bathrooms fed by mineral water, and there are both indoor and
outdoor pools. A slightly cheaper option is the newly opened *Galeri*
(☎0337/2085, ⓦgaleri.hisar.info; ❸), a bright orange hotel with comfortable
rooms at ul. Gurko 15. The *Augusta* rents bikes for 5Lv an hour, and organizes
trips to Starosel for about 30–50Lv per person depending on numbers. The
Hisar's Panorama **restaurant** has great views and serves Turkish as well as
Bulgarian cuisine. At the southern end of town, the *Izbora* restaurant, just
beyond the Kamilite gate, serves a wide range of Bulgarian meat-based dishes
in a large open-air courtyard with frequent live music; the *Sound Factory*
nightclub at the rear of the restaurant plays dance music till late.

Starosel

Twenty kilometres southwest of Hisar (take the Plovdiv road then turn onto the
westbound Strelcha road after 8km), **STAROSEL** (СТАРОСЕЛ) is a dusty
village typical of the southern Sredna Gora, its one-storey houses sheltering
secretively behind mud-brick walls. The place shot to prominence in 2000 with
the discovery of two grave barrows dating from the fifth century BC, leading
to speculation that the capital of the once-powerful Thracian Odrysae tribe may
well have been in the valley below. Starosel is served by five daily buses from
Karlovo via Hisar, although the tombs are quite a walk from the village, and it's
much more convenient to come by car.

The **tombs** (both daily: 9am–5pm; 3Lv) are reached by following a minor
road north out of the village; signs reading *Trakiiskite hramove* ("Thracian
Temples") guide the way. After 3km the first of the tombs, covered in a
protective wooden shell, hoves into view on the left. Consisting of a simple
quadrangular chamber fronted by an impressive six-pillar colonnade,
it probably had a combined role as aristocratic mausoleum and
ancestor-worshipping temple.

A similar purpose was served by the larger of the two tombs, a conical
mound nestling amid low hills some 3km further on. The biggest tumulus yet
discovered in Bulgaria, it's thought to be the last resting place of a powerful
Odrysae king. The stepped entrance to the tomb, made from huge blocks of
tufa brought from Zlatitsa 40km to the north, leads through to a circular inner
chamber, where a conical ceiling – intricately fashioned from overlapping
stone plates – is just about visible behind modern protective scaffolding.
Round the back of the mound, look out for a huge stone trough presumably
used for preparing ritual wine.

Nearby **accommodation** is available at the vast traditional-style *Starosel*
hotel (☎0897/870908, ⓦwww.starosel.net; ❸) and winery (*vinarna*) complex
outside the village on the road to the tombs. Built around a cavernous
underground wine cellar designed to resemble a Thracian tomb, the hotel has
a great **restaurant**, a pool, and wonderful chunky wooden furniture
throughout. Staff can arrange jeep safaris in the locality (50Lv per person),
treasure hunting (20Lv per person) and fishing trips on the nearby lakes
(20–40Lv per person depending on equipment required).

The Valley of the Roses

Lying midway between Sofia and the coast, the **Valley of the Roses** (*Rozovata dolina*) is perhaps the most over-hyped region of Bulgaria. A sunbaked and dusty place for most of the summer, from mid-May to early June it's partially transformed by the blooms that give it its name. Even then, however, much of the rose-growing activity takes place around the villages on the margins of the valley, and if you're speeding through the region by road or rail you won't see a thing. Whatever the time of year its towns can seem unexciting – "ramshackle collections of unplastered cottages which might have dropped off a lorry", thought Leslie Gardiner, and he wasn't far wrong. One compensation of travelling through the valley is the bewitching views of the imposing ridge of mountains to the north, which forms the backbone of the Balkan Range, or Stara planina ("old mountain"). Access to the mountains is via the towns of **Klisura**, **Sopot**, **Karlovo** and **Kalofer**, all with honoured niches in Bulgarian history as the scene of heroic events or the birthplace of writers or national heroes, but possessing little that's worth seeing beyond memorial museums to local sons, captioned in Bulgarian only. The region's main town, **Kazanlak**, is similarly bland, although it does feature some remarkable **Thracian tombs**, and hosts the Festival of Roses in early June. Within easy reach of the town to the north is the rugged **Shipka Pass**, heroically defended by Russian and Bulgarian troops during the 1878 War of Liberation.

Regular **trains** from Sofia to Karlovo or Burgas make it easy enough to travel through the valley (although express services don't stop at the smaller places en route, and there are few trains of any description between late morning and early evening). Coming down from the Balkan Range via the Troyan or Shipka

Roses: Bulgaria's gold

The **rose-growing area** between Klisura and Kazanlak produces seventy percent of the world's attar – or extract – of roses. Considering that perfumiers pay more than US$45 million a year for this, it's not surprising that roses are known as "Bulgaria's gold". Rose-growing began as a small cottage industry during the 1830s (supposedly started by a Turkish merchant impressed by the fragrance of the wild Shipka rose), and initially involved small domestic stills comprising a copper cauldron from which water-cooled pipes dripped the greenish-yellow rose oil. It became big business early in the twentieth century, but virtually ceased during World War II when Nazi Germany discouraged the industry in order to sell its own ersatz scents. Since then, however, Bulgaria's rose-growers have vastly expanded their operations.

Each acre planted with red *rosa damascena* or white *rosa alba* yields up to 1400 kilograms of blossom, or roughly three million rosebuds; between three thousand and six thousand kilos are required to make one litre of attar, leaving a residue of rosewater and pulp used to make medicaments, flavourings, *sladko* jam and *rosaliika* liqueur. The rose bushes (covering over fourteen thousand acres) are allowed to grow to head height, and are harvested during May between 3am and 8am before the sun rises and evaporates up to half of the oil. Nimble-fingered women and girls do most of the picking, while donkeys are employed to carry the petals away to the modern distilleries around Rozino, Karnare and Kazanlak. Kazanlak also has a research institute where pesticides are tested and different breeds of rose developed; according to the director, its gardens contain every variety in the world.

passes, you can pick up the valley route at Karnare or Kazanlak; Srednogorie and Karlovo are linked by buses or branch-rail lines to both the Sredna Gora and Plovdiv.

Towards Kazanlak

Immediately beyond the halt for Koprivshtitsa, trains enter a long tunnel beneath the Koznitsa spur, emerging into the Stryama Valley, the upper part of the Valley of the Roses. Bleached and arid from the end of the rose harvest until the autumn, the valley looks surprisingly lush the rest of the year, when groves of fruit trees give way to pastures dotted with wild flowers, and the surrounding hills are covered by deep forests.

Despite its dramatic situation at the head of the valley, there's little reason to stop at **KLISURA** (КЛИСУРА), although this small town "of tiles and flowers" is lauded for having been burned down during the April Rising, as described in Vazov's epic *Under the Yoke*. From here onwards it's roses all the way – at least during May. The next small town, **KARNARE** (КЪРНАРЕ), is the point of departure for Bulgaria's highest road, which winds north across the scenic Troyan Pass (see p.225).

Sopot

Further east along the valley is the sleepy little town of **SOPOT** (СОПОТ), which in recent years has become known as the **paragliding** capital of Bulgaria; in 2005 a round of the World Paragliding Championships was held here. Sopot's historical claim to fame is as the **birthplace of Ivan Vazov** (see p.287), Bulgaria's "national" writer, a bronze statue of whom stands on the main square. Immediately to the west lies Vazov's birthplace, now preserved as a **museum** (Tues–Sun 8.30am–noon & 1–5.30pm; 2Lv). The buildings, grouped around a peaceful vine-shaded courtyard, suggest the comfortable home of a middle-class merchant, with some choice pieces of furniture in the guest room, and good-quality imported porcelain. One room, which once served as a study, is today populated by a glassy-eyed company of costumed dummies, dressed in period clothing and grasping musical instruments of various kinds, illustrating the kind of gatherings that once took place in the Vazov household. A separate building houses an exhibition of photographs, documents and copies of Vazov's works in various languages (but not English, unfortunately).

Another of Sopot's attractions is the boulder-strewn **pine forest** that stretches up the lower slopes of the Balkan Range immediately north of town. Criss-crossed by paths, it's an excellent place for tranquil woodland walks, and a welcome escape from the often heat-hazed valley below. To get there, head uphill from the Vazov museum as far as the church tower, behind which a flight of steps leads to the edge of the woods.

The mountain ridge (1396m) above Sopot is the most popular **paragliding** venue in Bulgaria and can be reached by **chairlift** (daily 9am–6.30pm; 4Lv one way) from the Shambhala lift station northwest of town. Local outfit Skynomad, at ul. Vasil Levski 15 (☏03134/4251 or 0899/982566, ⓦwww.skynomad.com), organizes everything from one-off tandem flights (from 80Lv) to week-long courses (from 660Lv) between March and November (book in advance), and will arrange accommodation locally for its customers. The lift station is the site of an **aerial obstacle course** run by the Shambhala Extreme Sport Centre, at ul. Vasil Levski 5 (☏03134/3077 or 0885/132514, ⓦwww.shambhala-center.com),

Of all the patriots produced by nineteenth-century Kotel (see p.306), **Georgi Sava Rakovski** (1821–67) is the most fondly remembered; in many ways, he was the father of the national liberation movement. In 1860 he formed the Bulgarian Legion in Belgrade, which enabled young exiles to gain battle experience by fighting alongside Serbia in the latter's struggle against the Turks.

Increasingly influential in émigré circles, Rakovski's big idea was to send compact groups of armed men into Ottoman territory to gather support from the local populace, and instigate a mass uprising. In 1867 a trial run of Rakovski's theory took place, with *cheti* or armed groups led by Panaiot Hitov and Filip Totyu heading into occupied Bulgarian territory. The action achieved little, however, and Rakovski died a broken man in October of the same year. Only Ottoman over-reaction to the April Rising of 1876 saw the fulfillment of the final part of Rakovski's plan – intervention by Russia and defeat for the Turks.

Vasil Levski (1837–73), from Karlovo (see below, opposite), joined Rakovski's Bulgarian Legion in Belgrade, and after its disbandment sought refuge in Romania. He took part in Panaiot Hitov's notorious cross-border guerrilla raid of 1867, and was given the name Levski (from the word *lav*, meaning lion) because of the courage he showed in battle. But the failure of such raids – infuriating the Turks but winning little sympathy from the local population – convinced Levski that Ottoman rule could only be overthrown by a revolutionary organization based within Bulgaria itself. He developed the idea that an elite group of committed activists, or "apostles", should travel the length and breadth of the country establishing a secret revolutionary network. Levski set out on the first of his clandestine trips around Bulgaria in 1868, and over the next few years succeeded in establishing a virtual state-within-a-state dedicated to armed insurrection. In 1872, he was effectively appointed leader of the coming revolution by the newly formed Bulgarian Revolutionary Central Committe (BRCK) in Bucharest.

Towards the end of 1872, the revolutionary leader Dimitar Obshti led an ill-advised attack on a postal wagon to raise funds for arms purchases. Ambushed by gendarmes, Obshti told the Ottoman authorities everything. Mass arrests followed, and Levski was captured near Lovech. He was executed the following February in Sofia, on the spot now marked by the Levski monument. The traitor Obshti preceded him to the gallows.

Professional revolutionary, poet and idealist, **Hristo Botev** (1848–1876), born in Kalofer (see p.289), is perhaps the most romantic figure in Bulgaria's pantheon of

which also offers downhill mountain biking, mountain-boarding, hang gliding and horse riding.

Practicalities

Sopot is easily reached from Karlovo, just 5km down the road. **Bus** #4 from outside Karlovo's Vasil Levski museum (every 20–30min) drops you on the main square. The most laid-back place **to stay** is the *Skyview Hostel* at ul. Stara Planina 49 (℡0897/899328, ⓦwww.skyviewsopot.com; 16Lv per person) with wireless Internet, kitchen facilities and a free minibus to the lift station. On the main square is the *Hotel Shterev* (℡03134/2233, ⓦwww.shterev .com; ❹), whose dull concrete facade belies its reasonably comfortable interior. The *Motel Shterev* (℡03134/6161, ⓦwww.shterev.com; ❹), just west of Sopot in the village of Anevo, has higher standards; its ten tile-floored en-suites have TV and air conditioning, and there's a restaurant, gym, sauna and a tiny pool in the grounds. Places to **eat and drink** are limited to the mundane cafés round the main square. *Rodeo*, at the back of the square, is the best of the bunch, serving the usual grilled snacks. It also has some rooms (℡0889/358636, ⓦwww.sopot_rodeo.hit.bg; ❷).

heroes. After imbibing patriotism from his schoolteacher father, he developed an enduring faith in republicanism, socialism, and the revolutionary potential of the masses. Exiled for ten years in Romania after making a provocative speech on the Feast Day of Saints Cyril and Methodius, Botev contributed poetry and prose to a succession of revolutionary papers. In 1875 he became editor of the Bulgarian Revolutionary Central Committee (BRCK)'s official organ, *Zname* ("The Banner"). Plans to launch another new paper, *Nova Balgariya*, were cut short by the April Rising of 1876, when Botev – a man with no military experience whatsoever – agreed to lead a *cheta* across the Danube in support of the rebels. The expedition soon degenerated into farce; launched several weeks after the Rising itself had been put down, it was doomed before it even started. Having hijacked the Austrian steamship *Radetsky* in order to cross the Danube on May 17), Botev landed at Kozlodui with two hundred men disguised as market gardeners. Ironically his first speech on liberated "Bulgarian" soil had to be delivered in Romanian, as the local inhabitants were all Vlachs. Botev's stirring oratory succeeded in recruiting a grand total of two people to the cause. The Ottoman authorities, who had followed Botev's progress all the way from the Danube, had no trouble in neutralizing the *cheta*, killing most of its members and scattering the rest. Botev himself was cut down on Mount Okolchitsa near Vratsa on May 20.

Born into a merchant family in Sopot (see p.285), **Ivan Vazov**'s (1850–1922) youthful patriotism took him into exile in Romania as a teenager, where he met other Bulgarian revolutionaries, and began writing for émigré journals. On returning to Sopot he threw himself into revolutionary politics, but was forced to flee on the eve of the April Rising because of the threat of imminent arrest. Perhaps because he was unable to participate himself, the events of April 1876 inspired Vazov to write his best poetry.

He spent the following decade in liberated Bulgaria before moving to Odessa, where he began work on *Under the Yoke* (*Pod Igoto*), his classic tale of small-town life before and during the April Rising. Vazov returned to Bulgaria in 1889, and settled in Sofia, where episodes of *Under the Yoke* were published in the journal of the Ministry of Education. An immediate success, it made Vazov a national institution. After serving as Minister of Education (1897–99), he continued to write a stream of novels, articles and poems until his death in Sofia in 1922.

Karlovo and around

Set against a backdrop of lofty, arid crags and hollows descending to slopes partly covered with cypresses and fig trees, **KARLOVO** (КАРЛОВО) is one of the most attractive towns in the Valley of the Roses, despite its dreary suburbs and the presence of a large army garrison. Hidden uphill, the charming old quarter, birthplace of the great revolutionary, Vasil Levski (see above), is a pleasant place to wander.

Halfway between the train station and the centre of town, ul. Vasil Levski meets pl. Vasil Levski, an ensemble of nineteenth-century houses around a statue of Levski, who brandishes a pistol and has a small lion representing Bulgaria at his side. Off to the south is the colonnaded basilica of the **Church of Sveti Nikola**, with its separate and once elegant bell tower, both, sadly, in a state of disrepair. Just uphill from here, cobbled alleys lead into a quarter full of nineteenth-century houses and spruced-up mansions. The bright blue bell tower of the **Church of Sveta Bogoroditsa**, on ul. Vasil Levski, is the most eye-catching feature of this part of town; the church itself is also worthy of closer attention, not least for the colourful modern fresco on the porch, showing a saintly looking Vasil Levski, clad in ecclesiastical vestments and accompanied by a gathering of venerable churchmen. The dark interior is rather sombre in comparison, though it's enlivened by a splendid, and very high, wooden pulpit, and an ornate iconostasis adorned with double-headed eagles. A little further up and on the opposite side of the street, the **Centre for Crafts and Cultural Traditions** at no. 31A (*Tsentar za zanayati i kultirni traditsii*; daily 9am–5pm; free) occupies an attractively restored nineteenth-century house, and displays local woodcarving, embroidery and carpet weaving inside. At the top of the street is the disused **Kurshum Dzhamiya** ("Lead-roofed Mosque") dating from 1485, which has a spacious porch with cedarwood pillars, and a minaret shorn off just above roof level.

Further uphill lies pl. 20 Yuli, a split-level mix of *fin-de-siècle* and concrete postwar edifices enlivened by fountains and water features, which forms the centre of the new town. Heading west from here, you'll find the **Vasil Levski House-Museum** (daily 9am–1pm & 2–5pm; 2Lv), behind a low wall at ul. Gen. Kartsov 57. A simple quadrangle with a verandah, its living quarters are austere, furnished with the usual low wooden table and stools, while a single shelf arranged with pewter dishes provides the nearest thing to ornamentation. Levski's mother worked at the *boyadzhiinitsa* (dyeing shed), which is today filled with earthenware pots. Behind the house, a gallery holds a collection of paintings of Levski, in a variety of Christ-like attitudes, as well as photographs of his comrades in the First and Second Bulgarian Legions, and a few documents and weapons. The semi-divine treatment continues just outside the enclosure, in a tiny chapel where you can view a clump of Levski's hair, reverently housed in a glass reliquary beside the altar, while a recording of solemn chanting plays in the background.

Practicalities

From Karlovo's **train station** it's about 1km uphill to the centre; head straight across the park outside and up ul. Vasil Levski to reach the sights, or through the park and bear left to find the **bus station** – although some bus services, notably those to and from Kalofer, stop outside the train station itself. There's a small **tourist information centre** at the end of ul. Vodopad (Mon–Fri 9–11.30am & 1–6pm; ☎0335/95373, ⓦwww.karlovotur.hit.bg). You should be able to see all of Karlovo's sights (and make a short trip to Sopot) in the space of a day, but if you wish **to stay** the night, there are several options. The budget *Touristicheska Spalnya* (☎0335/93436 or 0896/688523; 6Lv per bed) has simple dorm accommodation and is a good place to meet Bulgarian hikers, while the *Hanut* (☎0898/940404, ⓦwww.hotelhanut.com; ❷), opposite the mosque at ul. General Kartsov 27, has pleasant air-conditioned en suites around a central courtyard restaurant. The equally comfortable two-star *Hotel Shterev*, on the main square in the upper part of town (☎0335/93380, ⓦwww.shterev.com; ❷) has pristine modern en suites with minibar and TV.

Several **cafés** are clustered around the main square, with the terrace of the *Hotel Shterev* providing the best venue for people-watching. *Edno Vreme*, east of the square at ul. Rakovska 9, is the best of the **restaurants**, offering everything from trout to roast beef and located in a nineteenth-century house surrounded by a well-kept garden. Nightlife revolves around the neighbouring **clubs** *Dream* and *Classico* on ul. Gurko just off the main square, and **Internet** access is available at *Cyber Warrior*, opposite the mosque at ul. Tarkovska 15.

The Stara reka and the Balkan Range

Karlovo makes an excellent base from which to explore the imperious peaks of the **Balkan Range** to the north. The main route to the uplands, along the gorge of the **Stara reka** ("old river"), begins immediately north of Karlovo town centre. The dramatic, steep-sided limestone defile has been declared a nature reserve, which means that the usual restrictions (don't pick plants and don't stray from marked paths) apply. The area is detailed on the excellent 1:100,000 *Central Balkan National Park* tourist map, which should be available at Karlovo and Kalofer's tourist information centres, though to be on the safe side try to pick one up from Zig-Zag/Odysseia-In in Sofia (see p.75).

To get to the **gorge**, follow ul. Vodopad north from Karlovo's main square, passing an area of riverside parkland where locals have barbecues and splash around on hot summer days. At the top of ul. Vodopad you'll find a hydro-electric plant overlooked by a small waterfall; just before the plant, a waymarked path heads left up the hillside. It's a steep, winding track, but after about an hour a marvellous panorama rewards your effort. From here, the path charts a course along the rocky walls of the gorge before arriving at the *Hizha Hubavets* hut after another hour or so. Here the gorge splits from the main path; following the right fork, you'll ascend to the *Hizha Balkanski Rozi* hut (1hr 30min) then the *Hizha Vasil Levski* hut (1hr more), which lies just beneath the main ridge of the Balkan mountains. With a good map, walking experience and plenty of time to spare, you can ascend the ridge: dog-legging your way up to the 2035m **Kostenurkata** ("the tortoise") just above *Hizha Levski* takes around 1hr 30min; otherwise the main routes lead to the 2376m **Vrah Botev** to the east (3hr), and the 2166m **Ambaritsa** to the west (2hr 30min). From **Vrah Botev** you can descend to *Hizha Rai* (2hr) in the Dzhendema Reserve, where Bulgaria's highest waterfall, Raiskoto Praskalo (124m), cascades down sheer cliffs below **Vrah Botev**. All these peaks provide access to lateral hikes along the ridge of the Balkan Range, or lengthy descents to the trailhead villages on the northern side of the Range, notably Apriltsi (see p.227) from the Vrah Botev direction, or Cherni Osam (see p.226) from Ambaritsa. Vrah Botev is also accessible by car from Kalofer (see below).

Kalofer

Whether travellers heading east from Karlovo see vineyards, tobacco plants or roses depends on the season, but whatever the time of year you'll pass some of the grandest peaks in the Balkans. Crossing the Staga ridge, which joins the Sredna Gora to the Balkan range, the road enters the small town of **KALOFER** (КАЛОФЕР), nestled in a lovely valley, and cut through by the River Tundzha. Like Karlovo, it has an attractive old quarter, and is indelibly associated with another revolutionary, **Hristo Botev** (see p.286), whose ubiquitous portrait has become an icon.

A heroic-modernist **statue** of Botev overlooks the main square from the foothills of the highest peak in the Balkan Range (2376m), which now bears his name, while Botev's exploits are detailed in a large modern **museum**, off to the right of the main square among the trees (daily 8am–5.30pm; 2Lv). Inside is a didactic, Bulgarian-only words-and-pictures chronicle of Botev's life, centred on the printing press on which he published the nationalist newspaper *Zname*. Outside is the tiny cottage where Botev was born, an even simpler dwelling than Levski's childhood home. If asked, the curator will open up the school museum (same times) on the opposite side of the square, where you can peer at a couple of recreated nineteenth-century schoolrooms and ponder the conditions in which Botev and his father once taught.

If you have a car, you can also use Kalofer as a jumping-off point for excursions to **Vrah Botev**, the Balkan Range's highest peak, which looms over the town from the northwest. An asphalt road (open May–Oct) winds tortuously to the summit; it's a signed left turn as you enter Kalofer from the west.

Practicalities

As Kalofer's station is several kilometres outside town, all **trains** are met by a bus. There's also a direct **bus** service to Kalofer from central Karlovo every hour or so. The **tourist office**, occupying a white house on the western side of the main square (daily 9am–12.30pm & 1.30–6pm; ☏03133/2988, ⊛www.kalofer .com & ⊛www.centralbalkannationalpark.org), offers advice on the whole of the central Balkan region. It also sells hiking maps and local crafts, and can arrange horse riding, rose picking, and visits to a woodcarving workshop. It can also book you into **B&B accommodation** in one of the village's twenty guest houses (12–15Lv per person) all of which are listed on the website. Best of the B&Bs is *Tsutsova kashta*, a pleasant National Revival-era house at ul. Blaskova 7 (☏03133/2483, ⊛www.cucovata.com; ❷), though bathrooms are shared. Back in central Kalofer, the *Kalofer Mehana*, on the eastern side of the square, does good grilled **food** and is also the handiest place for a drink.

Kazanlak

Forty kilometres beyond Kalofer, **KAZANLAK** (КАЗАНЛЬК) is the capital of the rose-growing region, although you wouldn't necessarily realize that unless you pass through town during the first weekend of June, when the long-standing but fairly lacklustre **Festival of Roses** (*Praznik na rozata*) takes place. A mix of folk music, dancing, and the appointment of a carnival queen, this is basically a tourist event – the rose harvest itself takes place in villages far from town at unsociably early hours of the morning. Nowadays Kazanlak is enjoying a new lease of life as the centre of the *Dolinata na trakiiskite tsare* – the **Valley of the Thracian Kings**. Once an important area of Thracian settlement, the vicinity of Kazanlak is dotted with countless burial mounds, many of which are still to be excavated. Enough of them have been opened to the public, however, to make the town an essential stop for anyone remotely interested in the Bulgarians' ancient predecessors. The most famous of the tombs is the UNESCO-listed **Kazanlak Tomb**, which lies just outside the town centre and contains unique paintings, although only a replica of the tomb is accessible to the public. Further groups of tombs lie in the surrounding countryside, and can be visited by arrangement with the local history museum providing you give a few hours' notice (see p.294 for details).

While there's a reasonable selection of accommodation in Kazanlak, the town's location at the centre of both north-south and east-west routes makes it a feasible day-trip destination from Plovdiv, Gabrovo, Veliko Tarnovo, or – at a pinch – Sofia. It also lies at the southern end of the **Shipka Pass** road, one of Bulgaria's most spectacular cross-mountain routes.

Some history

The area around Kazanlak has attracted successive waves of settlers and invaders, not least because of its strategic importance in controlling approaches to the Shipka Pass. In ancient times, the Tundzha Valley was the domain of the Thracian **Odrysae**, who exploited the vacuum left by the retreat of the Persians in the fifth century BC to forge a powerful tribal state on the southern slopes of the Balkan Range. Their power was temporarily broken by Philip II of Macedon in 342 BC, but they re-emerged a generation later under **King Seuthes III**, an

KAZANLAK

Tomb Replica

Kazanlak Tomb

Tyulbeto Park

Turbe of Lale Shahin Pasha

Kulata Ethnographic Complex

Iskra Museum

Church of the Assumption

N

RESTAURANTS

Chiflika	F
Hadzhieminova kashta	E
Kazanlak	G
New York Pub	1
Teres	C

ACCOMMODATION

Chiflika Complex	F
Hadzhieminova kashta	E
Kazanlak	G
Kransko hanche	A
Palas	H
Teres	C
Vesta	D
Zornitsa	B

Bus Station

Train Station

0   100 m

Karlovo

Sliven

unruly vassal of Alexander the Great's successor Lysimachus, who built a new capital, Seuthopolis, 7km west of present-day Kazanlak – it's now submerged beneath a reservoir. The River Tundzha is thought to have been navigable as far as Seuthopolis in ancient times, bringing trade, profits and Hellenistic culture to the Odrysae, who expressed their wealth in the solid but exquisitely decorated **tombs** in the region. Seuthopolis soon fell into decline however, and a deluge of **Celts** arrived around 280 BC, many of whom settled in the plain just east of Kazanlak. There was a fortified medieval Bulgarian settlement at Kran, just to the northwest (where a village of the same name still exists), but the town of Kazanlak itself is relatively modern, dating from the Ottoman occupation. Its name loosely translates as the "place of the copper cauldrons", a probable reference to the giant stills in which rose oil was prepared. By the beginning of the twentieth century Kazanlak's streets were filled with the shops and store-houses of the rose merchants – a breed of Balkan trader that has long since disappeared, squeezed out by social ownership and state control.

Arrival and accommodation

Kazanlak's **train** and **bus stations** are just south of the centre on ul. Sofronii Vrachanski, from where a five-minute walk up bul. Rozova Dolina will bring you to the town's main square, pl. Sevtopolis.

Just off the main square at ul. Iskra 4 is the **tourist information centre** (Mon–Fri 9am–5pm; ☎0431/62817, ⊚www.tourism.kazanluk.bg), which provides maps and arranges excursions. There's a good choice of **accommodation** in the centre, and a couple of out-of-town places which are easily accessible if you have your own transport. Campers can pitch tents in the grounds of the *Kransko hanche* motel (see below).

Hotels

Chiflika Complex ul. Knyazh Mirski 38 ☎0431/21411, ⊚www.chiflika-bg.com. Part of the Ethnographic Complex and next door to Hadzhieminova kashta, its spacious traditional-style rooms with a/c overlook a pretty walled garden. ❷

Hadzhieminova kashta ul. Nikola Petkov 22 ☎0431/62595. Four-room hotel in the Ethnographic Complex offering traditionally furnished rooms with carved wooden ceilings and sheepskin bedspreads. Apartments have bathtubs, regular rooms have basic showers. Apartments ❸, rooms ❷

Kazanlak pl. Sevtopolis ☎0431/63210 or 63666, ✉hotelkazanlak@abv.bg. Standard high-rise three-star on the main square offering neat pastel-hued rooms, although you'll have to shell out a bit extra if you want a proper bathtub. There's an indoor swimming pool on site. ❸

Kransko hanche 4km north of town on the Shipka road ☎0431/63123. Roadside motel with a couple of nondescript accommodation blocks and a grassy camping ground out the back. Doubles come with dated brownish colour schemes, simple showers, TV and sagging beds. There are also some simple double bungalows (❶), and a restaurant. Buses #5 or #6 pass by. ❷

Palas ul. Petko Staynov 9 ☎0431/62311 or 64411, ⊚www.hotel-palas.com. Medium-sized hotel on a quiet central side-street boasting rooms with reproduction nineteenth-century furniture, cable TV and proper bathtubs. There's also a sauna, solarium and swimming pool. ❸

Teres ul. Lyubomir Kabakchiev 16 ☎0431/64272, ⊚www.hotelteres.com. Just north of the Ethnographic Complex, the *Teres* offers modern standards in a traditional-style building. Rooms have a/c, Wi-Fi and minibar. ❸

Vesta ul. Chavdar Voyvoda 3 ☎0431/20350 or 40039, ⊚www.hotel-vesta.com. Family-run place 5min north of the centre offering neat, tiled-floor rooms with Wi-Fi, a/c, TV and fridge. Breakfast is served in a shady courtyard. ❸

Zornitsa Tyulbeto Park ☎0431/63939, ⊚www.zornica.bg.com. Modern building on the brow of the hill behind the Thracian tomb, with spacious, creamy-coloured rooms with modern toilet/shower and TV, an outdoor pool that's popular with the locals in summer, and great views across town from the terrace. ❺

The Town

The hotel and civic buildings on Kazanlak's main square – **pl. Sevtopolis** – present an uncompromisingly modern contrast to the remnants of the prewar town that straggle untidily westwards. The nineteenth-century **Church of the Assumption**, just off the square to the east, contains an exquisite iconostasis carved by Debar craftsmen, while a host of finds from ancient Seuthopolis are displayed in the basement of the **Iskra Museum**, to the north of the square (daily 9am–5pm; 2Lv). Weapons, pottery and coins minted by Seuthes III help to illustrate life in his capital, while the reconstructed floor plans of domestic houses reveal the bowl-like depressions that served as cult hearths, for appeals to tribal deities. More recent discoveries on display include a golden wreath of acorns and oak leaves, a hinged silver shell and an elaborate golden wine cup. Upstairs is a display devoted to nineteenth-century life, with huge copper stills impressively illustrating the rose-oil business, and a picture gallery with a reasonable cross-section of twentieth-century Bulgarian art and a smattering of saintly icons.

Ten minutes' walk northeast of the museum is the **Kulata Ethnographic Complex**. Along here, several nineteenth-century houses have been restored to their former splendour, one of which serves as a **museum** (daily 9am–5pm; 2Lv), where period furnishings and an elegant walled garden recall the lifestyles of Kazanlak's rose merchants. Visitors can have a free taste of rose-flavoured jam or rose *rakia* if they wish. If the rose industry fires your imagination, you might want to trek out to the **Museum of the Rose Industry** (*Muzei na rozite*; May 1 to Oct 31: daily 9am–5pm; 2Lv), 2km from the centre along the Shipka road – bus #6 passes by. Though there's relatively little information given in English, the museum successfully conveys an idea of how rose jam, toothpaste, eau-de-cologne, jelly and, of course, attar of roses are produced. There's also a small shop selling rose-based products. The rose fields out the back may only be of interest to those with a genuine interest in rose cultivation, though, as they are not laid out as an attractive garden.

Tyulbeto Park and the Kazanlak Tomb

On a hillside immediately north of the Ethnographic Complex, **Tyulbeto Park** is the site of two renowned funerary monuments. A stairway beyond the park gates ascends to the skeletal remains of the **Turbe of Lala Shahin Pasha**, conqueror of much of Bulgaria and first Ottoman governor of Rumelia He fell in battle here, and it's thought that his entrails were interred on the spot before the rest of him was carried back to Bursa (probably embalmed in honey) to be buried in a much finer *turbe* closer to home.

Immediately behind the *turbe* is a protective structure built over the so-called **Kazanlak Tomb** (*Kazanlashkata grobnitsa*), the first of the many **Thracian tombs** in the area to be excavated. Originating in the late fourth or early third century BC, the burial chamber was unearthed by chance in 1944 during the construction of an air-raid post, and is now a listed UNESCO monument. Its frescoes are so delicate that only scholars with authorization from the Ministry of Culture may enter (and only then with a good reason), but the replica (daily 9am–5pm; 5Lv), built 50m east along the path, is an atmospheric enough re-creation. Once inside, the domed burial chamber is approached through a low-roofed, narrow antechamber decorated by two bands of murals – one ornamented with plant and architectural motifs, the other displaying battle scenes. The floor and walls are stained a deep red, while in the cupola are the **paintings** for which the tomb is famed. They depict a procession of horses and servants approaching the chieftain for whom the tomb was built, who sits behind a low table laden with food. His wife, face downcast in mourning, reposes on an elaborate throne beside him, and the couple touch hands in a tender gesture of farewell. A bowl of pomegranates – a fruit associated with immortality – is offered to the deceased by a female figure to the right, who has been linked with both the Great Mother Goddess common to Thracian tribes, and Persephone, the queen of the underworld in the Greek pantheon. Racing chariots wheel around the apex of the dome, a possible reference to the games that often accompanied a Thracian funeral (see p.295). With its graceful composition and naturalistic details, the painting is a masterpiece of Hellenistic art, although opinions differ as to whether the frescoes are the work of an itinerant Greek master or an inspired local.

The Valley of the Thracian Kings

The area northwest of Kazanlak was a sacred place for the inhabitants of Seuthopolis, and they left a string of necropolises on either side of the road that runs along the Shipka Pass. Not all the 1500 **burial mounds** (*mogili*) in the vicinity contain the stone-built tombs of the wealthy, and it's not known which classes of Thracian society actually qualified for one: kings, priests, or noble

▲ Detail of the Kazanlak Tomb

families in general. It is clear, however, that the prevalence of tombs reflects the growing wealth and self-confidence of Odrysian society from the fifth century BC onwards. After years of intense archeological activity, a group of six tombs has now been opened to the public. However the Ministry of Culture looks set to limit further excavations, as the number of open tombs is outstripping the ability of the authorities to look after them adequately. **Mogila Oshtrusha** on the road to Shipka is open from Wednesday to Sunday and **Mogila Gulamata Kosmatka**, opposite Shipka, is open daily. Visits to the other tombs must be arranged through the **Iskra Museum** – arrive early in the morning or try calling ☎0431/63762. The cost of 8Lv per person per tomb (most people visit three or four to make the trip worthwhile) includes an English-speaking guide, but you'll need to pay extra for a driver if you don't have your own transport.

The nearest of the tombs to Kazanlak on the south side of Shipka village is **Mogila Ostrusha**, which dates from the fifth century BC and contains a remarkable granite burial chamber in the form of a miniature Greek temple; it may have served as a place of worship before being used as a tomb. The ceiling of the chamber was painted with a grid of small scenes, of which only one survives in recognizable form – a faded and tiny portrait of a red-haired girl, unique for the period. The curator of Ostrusha can also open **Mogila Griffon**, which features circular seating around a central chamber thought to have been used as a temple.

The remaining tombs date from at least a century later than Ostrusha and, like the Kazanlak tomb, are built in the form of a domed burial chamber approached through a narrow, corridor-like antechamber. Two are in the Shushmanets complex, an ensemble of six mounds on the eastern fringes of Shipka village. The burial chamber of the **Mogila Shushmanets** itself is characterized by a single Doric column which supports the ceiling, while the nearby **Mogila Helvetsia**, named in honour of Switzerland, whose government paid for its excavation, boasts an elegant pointed-arch entrance. **Mogila Gulamata Kosmatka** lies opposite Shipka and conceals the immense tomb of King Seuthes III, which is carved from a single block of granite; golden treasures from his burial chamber are on display at the Iskra museum. Finally, just beyond Shipka village on the road to Gabarevo, the **Mogila Arsenalka** (so named because of its proximity to the Arsenal Kalashnikov factory) features an outer facade fashioned from blocks of porphyry granite quarried on the south side of the valley. Inside, the chamber is simple and undecorated but exudes harmony, with a stone bed for the deceased and a circular hearth on the floor for lighting sacrificial fires.

Eating and drinking

Central Kazanlak doesn't have a great deal going for it as far as dining is concerned. The *Hotel Kazanlak* has a good-quality restaurant and there's also the

The Thracian way of death

The Bulgarian countryside is dotted with **Thracian burial mounds** or *mogili*, the majority of which remain unexcavated. They were erected by a society which set great emphasis on the role of the tomb, both in providing the deceased with a lasting memorial and in creating a focus for the ancestor-worship cult which flourished in this culture. Some tombs served as family mausoleums, containing the bones of several generations. Principal tombs that are open to the public can be found near Kazanlak and Sveshtari (see p.264); otherwise, most Bulgarian museums house Thracian burial finds of one sort or another.

According to **Herodotus**, deceased Thracian nobles were laid out for three days, during which time a short period of mourning was held, followed by a great communal feast. The body was then either buried or cremated, with a tumulus raised over it, and a series of athletic games and contests were begun, the biggest prizes being awarded for single combat. Herodotus also notes that amongst those tribes where polygamy was practised, the wives of a dead warrior would compete vigorously for the honour of being declared his favourite, and so be slaughtered and buried alongside him. This is partly borne out by the evidence of some of the excavated tumuili, where the bones of young females have been found lying next to those of the chieftain. In many cases, however, the deceased made do with the company of his favourite horse.

Modern archeological evidence points to a rich **funerary culture**, full of symbolic actions whose meanings can only be guessed at. Many tombs were regularly reopened so that sacrifices and other rituals could be carried out, suggesting that burial places served as cultic centres for the surrounding settlement. In some areas, the body was disinterred and moved to another location, either within the tomb or elsewhere, pointing to ritual reburial as an important part of funerary practice.

Each season of excavation reveals yet stranger rites: one of the Sveshtari tombs was found to contain half the skeleton of a large dog – the other half had been buried outside, possibly a ritual means whereby the spirit dog would guard the approaches to his master's tomb, as well as keeping by his side. Indeed, hunting dogs may well have accompanied tribal chieftains into the afterlife, the existence of which the Thracians took for granted, although it's unclear if life beyond the grave was enjoyed by all, or merely the elite group of nobles and priest-kings. Herodotus relates how certain tribes mourned the birth of children, thinking of the sufferings they would endure through life, and would celebrate "with merriment and rejoicing" the death of one of their number, who could no longer by touched by pain or sorrow. Thracian beliefs about the immortality of the soul undoubtedly spread southwards to Greece, where they contributed to the development of mystery cults such as Orphism (see p.356).

New York Pub on the ground floor with a long square-side terrace that serves pizza and baked potatoes. Next to the Ethnographic Complex, the restaurant of the *Hadzhieminova kashta* hotel serves Bulgarian dishes and has a decent range of freshwater fish, all served up in a courtyard shaded by figs and other trees. The restaurants in the *Teres* and *Chiflika* hotels also have a decent range of Bulgarian dishes. The streets to the west of the main square are lined with **cafés** and **bars**.

The Shipka Pass

For drama and majestic vistas, few routes in Bulgaria match crossing the **SHIPKA PASS** (ШИПЧЕНСКИЯ ПРОХОД). Rising sharply from the valley floor, the mountains present a seemingly impenetrable barrier; at sunset, when the sky darkens and a chill wind disperses the tourists, you get a tangible sense of the pass's potent historical significance. Ever since Alexander the Great drove back a force of Triballi here in 335 BC, control of Shipka has been an important strategic imperative.

When present-day Bulgarians think of Shipka, however, they recall the Russo–Turkish War, when six thousand Russians and Bulgarians resisted a 27,000-strong Ottoman force that was dispatched northwards to break the **siege of Plevna** (modern-day Pleven) in August 1877. Snow exacerbated the hardships of Radetsky's ill-equipped Bulgarian volunteers (many of whom had been civilians in Gabrovo just days before), and despite the local women who brought supplies, the defenders' ammunition was exhausted by the third day of the battle and they resorted to throwing rocks, tree trunks and finally corpses at the Turks. The pass held, however, and in due time Plevna surrendered, whereupon the Russians reinforced Radetsky's army and ordered it to fight its way down the snowy mountainside to defeat the remaining 22,000 Ottoman troops outside Kazanlak – which it did.

The journey across the mountains between Kazanlak and Gabrovo takes about ninety minutes **by bus**, and it's wise to book seats when leaving either town – even if you're planning to stop halfway and then continue on or return by a later service (there are usually some empty seats by the time buses reach the pass). Most visitors head for three major destinations around Shipka: the scenery and war memorials of the **summit** itself; the neighbouring **Mount Buzludzha**, where renowned *haidut* Hadzhi Dimitar bit the dust (see opposite); and the **Shipka Memorial Church**, just 12km north of Kazanlak.

The Shipka Memorial Church

From a stop near the corner of Sofronii Vrachanski and Rozova Dolina in Kazanlak, you can catch bus #6 out to **Shipka** village, a rustic huddle of buildings a little way off the main road to the pass. From the wooded hillside rise the gold onion domes of the **Shipka Memorial Church** (daily 8am–5pm), built by the Czech architect Tomisko after the Liberation as a monument to both Russian and Bulgarian dead, and finally consecrated in 1902. Conceived by philanthropic Russian aristocrats and financed by public donations, the edifice was modelled on Muscovite churches of the seventeenth century.

The church is a vibrantly coloured confection of pinks and greens, topped off with a fifty-metre-high spire on the bell tower. Its **interior**, the work of Bulgarian artists under the direction of the Russian painter Pomerantsev, is perhaps the best example of the academic realist style that flourished in Bulgaria around the beginning of the twentieth century. Folk-influenced floral and geometric patterns rich in primary colours weave their way around naturalistic depictions of Bulgarian saints and tsars. Many of them are dressed in Byzantine costume, a reminder of the pre-World War I days when Bulgaria's desire to extend its frontiers towards the former imperial capital was reflected in a passion for all things Byzantine. At the western end of the church, murals portray great figures from Russian history, including the fourteenth-century ruler Dmitri Donskoi being blessed before going off to smite the Tatars, and an allegorical scene of Cyril and Methodius bringing literacy to the Slavs.

The nearest **accommodation** is the *Shipka IT* in Shipka, at ul. Kolyo Adzharo 12 (℡04324/2112, ⓦwww.shipkaithotel.com; ❸), a pleasant new family-run hotel with English-speaking owners who can arrange guided walks in the region. Rooms have Wi-Fi and views of the nearby Mogila Gulamata Kosmatka.

The summit

Though the car park at the summit of the **pass** itself has degenerated into a truck-stop, it's impossible not to be awed – and exhausted – by the final ascent of the nearby **Mount Stoletov**, whose summit the Bulgarians held during the battle, and which overlooks the pass. Visitors struggle up five hundred steps, past heroic bas-reliefs, to reach the towering stone **Freedom Monument**, erected in the 1890s, which commands a glorious panorama of the Sredna Gora and the Valley of the Roses (the monument itself can be seen from Kazanlak). The tower contains a symbolic sarcophagus and a **museum** (daily 9am–7pm; 2Lv) with weapons and paintings detailing each phase of the battle, but the real lure is the observation platform on the roof, affording superb views of the mountains. From here you can see the **Russian cemetery**, 300m to the northwest, which is the largest of the many concentrations of cannon and gravestones planted on the slopes of the surrounding hills.

Accommodation at the Shipka Pass is pretty limited but does at least offer a wonderful sense of isolation. Right by the summit, the humdrum *Hotel Shipka* (℡04324/2730; ❷) is a large gloomy building offering poorly furnished rooms and shared facilities, but it does at least have a decent **restaurant**; while the *Opalchenets*, on the opposite side of the road (℡0899/420248; ❶), has slightly comfier rooms with 1970s decor and simple showers. There's also a rather forlorn **campsite** (mid-May to Sept) with chalets, 1km down the road towards Gabrovo. Don't miss sampling the buffalo-milk yoghurt, a local speciality sold at the pass.

Mount Buzludzha

From the pass a side road runs 12km east to **Mount Buzludzha**, topped by a bizarre structure resembling a spaceship come to earth, that counterpoints the monument at Shipka. It was on Mount Buzludzha that Hadzhi Dimitar and his rebels died fighting the Turks on August 2, 1868, while the Bulgarian Socialist Party was founded on the same day in 1891, following a clandestine congress, also on the mountain. The "spaceship" was built to house a museum covering both events, although it's now in a semi-derelict state. This gem of Communist kitsch can in any case only be reached by car, as there are no longer any buses from Kazanlak. Just below the summit the recently refurbished *Vuzludzha* **hotel** (℡04324/2198 or 0886/022171) has a superb location with sweeping views and offers doubles (❶), apartments (❷) and dorm beds (12Lv per person). It also has **ski hire** for use of the three mid-range ski runs nearby.

Beyond the Valley of the Roses

East of Kazanlak the Tundzha Valley broadens out, although it continues to be flanked by the wall of the Balkan Range and the lower, wooded hills of the Sredna Gora. Lurking on the far side of the latter is **Stara Zagora**, Bulgaria's sixth-largest city, with a population of 150,000. Home to one of the most important Neolithic sites in Europe, Stara Zagora warrants at least a brief detour, especially for those travelling southwards from the Valley of the Roses towards Plovdiv, Haskovo, Kardzhali or Turkey – all are easily accessible by train or bus from here.

Another obvious stop on the way to the coast is **Sliven**, the most important town between the Valley of the Roses and the sea. Lying snugly beneath the craggy Balkan Range, it is a good base from which to explore the **Blue Rocks** nearby or the historic craft villages in the mountains to the north; **Kotel**, with its array of intriguing museums; or **Zheravna**, a captivating huddle of rustic architecture which is worth the effort required to get there.

Stara Zagora and around

STARA ZAGORA (СТАРА ЗАГОРА) means "Old Town behind the Mountain", an apt name for this settlement on the far flanks of the eastern Sredna Gora, with a history of occupation stretching back some seven thousand years. Neolithic farmers were the first on the scene, bequeathing the town a fascinating snapshot of their humble dwellings (see p.301), while it was the Thracians, in the fifth century BC, who established the first significant town. Reconstructed and refounded by the Romans in the second century AD, it stood at the crossroads of two important trade routes, and commanded a fertile area still noted for its wheat fields and fruit orchards. This attractive location had its downside, though; the town was repeatedly attacked, destroyed and rebuilt by a succession of native and foreign conquerors throughout the Middle Ages, and each time acquired a new name. Under Ottoman rule, Stara Zagora was one of the centres of the Bulgarian renaissance, but was burned down by the Turks in 1877 for welcoming the Russian army of General Gurko. Rebuilt on a strict grid plan, today it's a thriving city dotted with carefully tended parks and centred on leafy boulevards strewn with cafés.

Arrival, information and accommodation

Stara Zagora's **train station** lies about five blocks south of the central City Garden, near the bottom of bul. Ruski, while the **bus station** is further northeast on bul. Slavyanski; both are just ten minutes' walk from the centre. The **tourist information office** beneath the art gallery at bul. Ruski 27 (Mon–Fri 9am–6pm; ☎042/627098, ⓦwww.tour.starazagora.net) can arrange hotel accommodation, car rental, and excursions to the Stara Zagora mineral baths (*Starazagorski mineralni bani*; see p.302). There's a good choice of

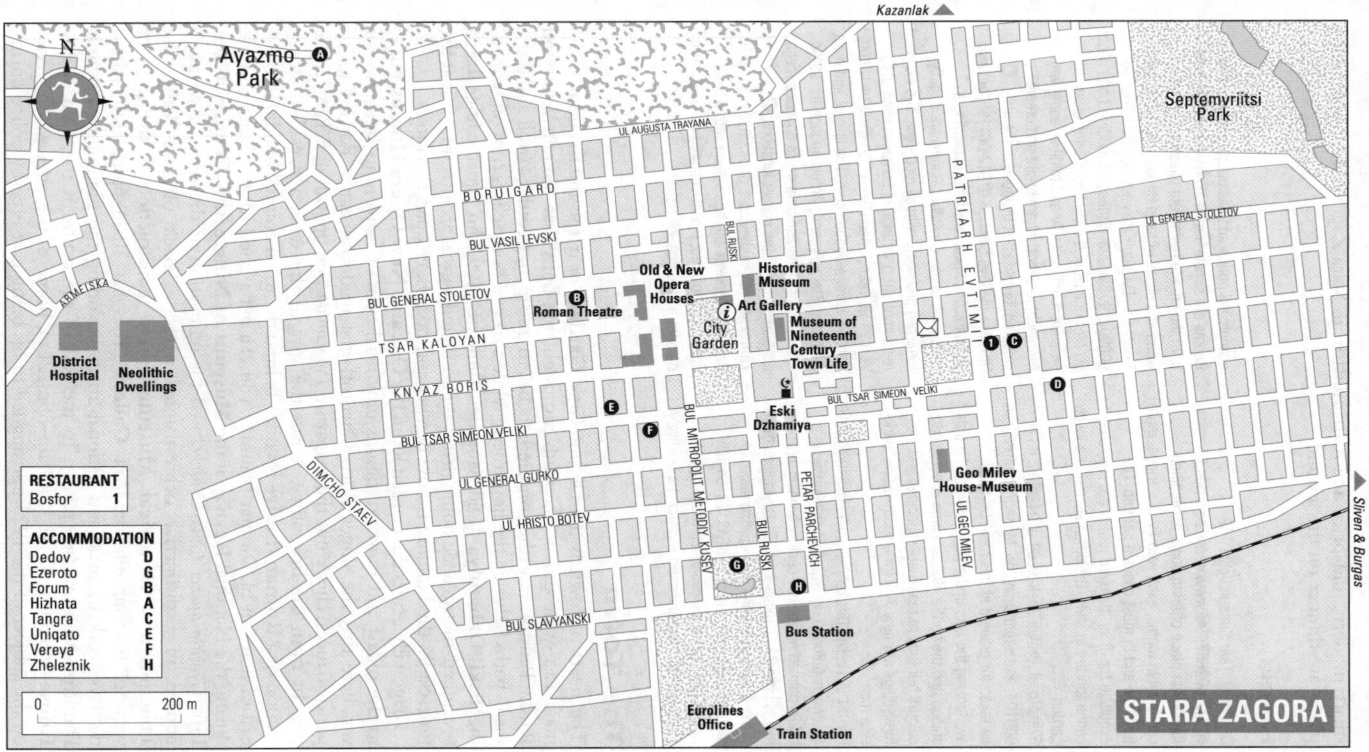

STARA ZAGORA

▲ Sliven & Burgas

◄ Kazanlak

Septemvriitsi Park

UL GENERAL STOLETOV

PATRIARH EVTIMII

Ayazmo Park ⒶA

District Hospital

Neolithic Dwellings

UL AUGUSTA TRAYANA

BUL GENERAL STOLETOV

BOR UI GARD

BUL VASIL LEVSKI

TSAR KALOYAN

KNYAZ BORIS

BUL TSAR SIMEON VELIKI

UL GENERAL GURKO

UL HRISTO BOTEV

DIMCHO STAEV

BUL SLAVYANSK

Old & New Opera Houses

Roman Theatre ⒷB

Historical Museum

Art Gallery

City Garden

Museum of Nineteenth Century Town Life

Eski Dzhamiya

BUL RUSKI

BUL MITROPOLIT METODIY KUSEV

BUL TSAR SIMEON VELIKI

UL GEO MILEV

Geo Milev House-Museum ⒹD

ⒿⒸ

ⒻF

ⒺE

PETAR PARCHEVICH

ⒼG

ⒽH

BUL RUSKI

Bus Station

Eurolines Office

Train Station

PENEVETSKA

N

0   200 m

RESTAURANT
Bosfor   1

ACCOMMODATION
Dedov   D
Ezeroto   G
Forum   B
Hizhata   A
Tangra   C
Uniqato   E
Vereya   F
Zheleznik   H

299

smart, modern, mid-price **accommodation** in Stara Zagora, although budget places are thinner on the ground.

Hotels

Dedov ul. Tsar Simeon Veliki 162 ☏ 042/602667, ⓦ www.dedov.bg. Friendly, family-run place offering some exceedingly comfortable rooms, each with TV, a/c, fridge, repro furniture and in most cases a bathtub. The exquisite top-floor mansard rooms are resolutely contemporary in style. Breakfast served in a lovely garden. **❺**

Ezeroto ul. Bratya Zhekovi 60 ☏ 042/600103 or 600104, ⓔ ezeroto@mail.bg. Modern comforts can be taken for granted at this four-star hotel, overlooking the lake in the park between the train station and the centre. Rooms come in some odd colours but they're reasonably spacious and the furnishings are new. Ask for a south-facing, park-side room. **❸**

Forum ul. Hadzhi Dimitur Asenov 94 ☏ 042/631616, ⓦ www.hotelforum.bg. Swanky hotel housed in a boldly painted nineteenth-century building. A/c rooms have Wi-Fi, minibar and TV. Downstairs there is a cosy restaurant and wine-tasting room. **❹**

Hizhata Ayazmo Park ☏ 042/643128. Slightly further afield, in the pleasant surroundings of Ayazmo Park, the renovated *Hizhata* is a relatively

economical option and fills up quickly as a result. Rooms are simple but have shower and TV, while from the on-site restaurant diners can glimpse wonderful views of town through the trees. **❷**

Tangra ul. Lyuben Karavelov 80 ☏ 042/600901 or 600902, ⓕ 600903. A pleasant modern hotel about six blocks east of the centre, offering clean, tiled en-suite rooms with TV and minibar, some with frumpy blue décor, others bright and cream-coloured. Breakfast is included in the price. **❸**

Uniqato ul. Sava Silov 36 ☏ 042/661155, ⓦ www.uniqato.com. Plush new hotel occupying a nineteenth-century building. Rooms are brightly furnished and come with all mod-cons. The excellent restaurant offers a range of European cuisine. **❺**

Vereya ul. Tsar Simeon Veliki 100 ☏ 042/618600, ⓔ hotel_vereya@yahoo.com. The largest and most central of Stara Zagora's hotels, though the string of late-night cafés and bars on its doorstep means it's also in one of the noisier locations. **❸**

Zheleznik ul. Parchevich 1 ☏ 042/622158. High-rise opposite the bus station with a large stock of renovated, pastel-coloured en suites with modern bathrooms. **❷**

The Town

The heart of town is the elegant **City Garden**, near the intersection of the main east–west and north–south thoroughfares, bul.s Tsar Simeon Veliki and Ruski. Pensioners gather on the benches to gossip and couples stroll along the shady paths between the flowerbeds, while a row of booksellers runs off towards the **Eski Dzhamiya** (Old Mosque). Built in 1409, this squat edifice has a seventeen-metre-wide dome that was considered a great architectural feat at the time. Sadly, the building is now derelict and no longer open to visitors.

Diagonally across the Garden loom the **Old and New Opera Houses**, home to the oldest and most prestigious provincial opera company in Bulgaria – it was here that the singer Boris Christoff first made his name. For listings of performances, check out the magazine *Programata* (see opposite); tickets can be bought from the box office. Across the way to the west, a sizeable restored section of a **Roman theatre** is visible behind the town council building. To the east of here, on ul. Dimitar Naumov, you can get a good idea of bourgeois life during the National Revival, at the **Museum of Nineteenth-Century Town Life** (*Kashta-muzei Gradski bit*; closed for renovation at the time of writing), housed in a distinctive ochre-painted mansion. Back on bul. Ruski, the ambitious new **Historical Museum** (under construction at the time of writing) lies opposite the **Art Gallery** (Tues–Sat 10am–6pm; 2Lv), which displays work by local and national artists including the ubiquitous Vladimir Dimitrov-Maistora (see p.121). To the east of the centre is the **Geo Milev House-Museum** (Mon–Sat 9am–5pm; 2Lv), home of the poet whose verses on the subject of the 1923 uprising led to his being garrotted by police during his interrogation. The museum contains several rooms recreating his abode, a section on other local poets such as Ivan Hadzhihristov, and a nice café.

The Neolithic dwellings

Stara Zagora's chief attraction, the **Neolithic dwellings** (*Neolitni zhilishta*) were unearthed in 1969 during the construction of a hospital. Of the several dwellings excavated – the remains of a settlement destroyed by fire around 5500 BC – two houses were preserved in the state in which the archeologists found them and covered by a custom-built pavilion, which is now a **museum** (Tues– Sat 9am–1pm & 1.30–5.30pm; 5Lv; guided tour in English or French depending on which members of staff are on duty; 5Lv). Inside, first impressions are of a moonscape of crumbling walls and pottery, but familiar domestic details become recognizable on closer inspection.

Each family occupied a single-roomed dwelling, usually detached – although the two preserved here were built back-to-back, possibly the sign of an extended family. In one corner of the house stood a basic stove, in which bread was baked from flour ground on a nearby millstone. Amazingly, the floor is still scattered, in places, with burnt grains. Another corner of the room was a cult area, used to keep idols of the household gods. A **gallery** in the basement holds the artefacts unearthed by the excavation, covering several millennia – the earliest ones include household implements such as sickles and spoons made out of bone – although most objects date from the sixth and fourth millennia BC. Some of the day-to-day pottery used by the Neolithic inhabitants of the houses preserved upstairs shows a surprising degree of sophistication, decorated with geometric patterns and chequerboard designs, while pots adorned with human stick figures, classic maze patterns and primitive animals have been identified as cultic vessels. One of the more intriguing pot fragments shows a shaman performing a rain-dance. The collection of marble and clay female fertility goddesses also gives a fascinating insight into the religious beliefs of these ancient people; the strictly symbolic older figures, with their outsized hips and posteriors, being replaced in later periods by more naturalistic forms. Pottery animals, including a headless hedgehog, may have had some ritual significance, while the poignant models of tiny houses, furniture and sheep appear to have been used as children's toys. A delicate child's bracelet from the fifth millennium BC is one of the oldest pieces of gold jewellery ever found.

To **get here**, walk west along bul. General Stoletov for fifteen minutes until you reach the district hospital (*okrazhna bolnitsa*), then bear left into Armeiska, where steps between the residential blocks on the left descend towards the museum, in a drab, squat building behind the basketball court.

Eating and entertainment

For **eating**, the *Tangra, Dedov, Forum, Uniqato* and *Ezeroto* hotels (see "Accommoda-tion", opposite) all have good restaurants, while *Bosfor*, not far from the *Tangra* hotel, at ul. Kiril i Metodi 64, serves good-quality Bulgarian and Turkish cuisine in an intimate little courtyard, and is regarded as one of the best in town. Cafés and *sladkarnitsi* on Mitropolit Kusev and Tsar Simeon are the best places to linger over a **drink** or an ice cream. *Cosmopolitan* **club** just north of the *Vereya* hotel on bul. Tsar Simeon Veliki plays mainstream dance music until late. Up-to-date listings can be found (in Cyrillic) in the free weekly *Programata* guide (ⓦ www.programata.bg) for Plovdiv and Stara Zagora, distributed at bars, restaurants and hotels.

Folkloric events worth catching include the **Trakia Pee** ("Thrace Sings") festival, which involves folk groups from throughout Thrace performing in outdoor venues in early June, and the national **festival of Gypsy music**, which takes place in Ayazmo Park, north of the centre of Stara Zagora, in August. Other civic events worth catching include the **festival of the opera and ballet** in May and the **beer festival**, held every September – a good opportunity to sample the famous local brew, Zagorka.

Stara Zagora mineral baths

The Stara Zagora mineral baths (*Starazagorski mineralni bani*) nestle in a peaceful wooded valley of the Sredna Gora mountains, 15km west of town and served by hourly buses. Until recently they were the site of a dilapidated jumble of Socialist-era rest homes and spa centres, but fresh investment has given the resort a much-needed facelift. Of the nine renovated hotels, the *Armira* (T04111/2223, Wwww.armirahotel.com; ❾) and the *Izvor* (T0411/2214, Wwww.izvor-hotel.com; ❺) offer the highest standards and a wide range of facilities; the *Grodi* (T04111/2338; ❸) is a mid-range option with a pleasant tree-shaded pool, and the *Zagore* (T04111/2319; ❷) is similar and has a comprehensive range of spa treatments but lacks a pool.

Sliven and the Blue Rocks

SLIVEN (СЛИВЕН) lies at the feet of craggy mountains that once sheltered so many bands of *haiduti* that Bulgarians called it the "town of the hundred *voivods*" after the number of their chieftains. The heyday of famous *haiduti* such as Hadzhi Dimitar and Panayot Hitov coincided with the industrialization of Sliven, where Bulgaria's first textile factory was established in 1834 – its founder, Dobri Zhelyazkov (known as *Fabrikadzhiyata*, "the gaffer"), acquired parts and plans of looms by smuggling them back from Russia in bags of wool. The industry grew rapidly, and Sliven was soon likened to a Bulgarian Manchester. Nowadays, Sliven makes a convenient stop-off between Sofia and Burgas on the coast – not so much for the town itself as for the nearby **Blue Rocks** (*Sinite kamani*), an alluring outcrop of grey-purple stone that lies on the eastern outskirts of town. The cable-car ride to the summit of the rocks, site of the mountain resort of **Karandila** (КАРАНДИЛА), is a popular local outing.

Arrival and accommodation

Sliven's **train station** is about 3.5km southeast of the centre, at the end of Sliven's main artery, bul. Hadzhi Dimitar: trolleybus #13 will take you as far as the market on ul. Tsar Simeon, a few steps west of the main square. The **bus station**, also on bul. Hadzhi Dimitar, is roughly halfway between the city centre and the train station. A central **tourist information office** at bul. Tsar Osvoboditel 1 (Mon–Fri 9am–5pm; T044/611148, Wwww.infotourism.sliven.bg or Wwww.sliven.bg) has maps and can arrange **accommodation**. There's a reasonable choice of hotel accommodation in Sliven, although some of the better options occupy out-of-town locations in the Blue Rocks and Karandila area.

Hotels

Byala Mechka Karandila T044/667150. Small family-run hotel on top of the Blue Rocks, about 1km southeast of the chair-lift terminus. Two simple but tidy en-suite doubles and a couple of lounge-style apartments with TV. Great away-from-it-all location with mountain walks on the doorstep. ❷

Chateau Alpia ul. Veliko Knyazhevska 13, 4km northeast of town next to the Karandila chairlift T044/622432, Wwww.alpia-tur.com. Boldly

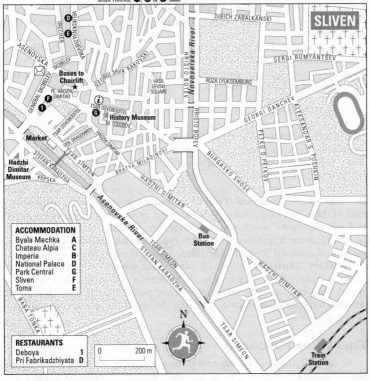

SLIVEN

Blue Rocks, **A**, **B** & **C**

DIBICH ZABALKANSKI

SERGI RUMYANTSEV

NovoselskaRiver

ASENOVSKA

VELIKOKNYAZHEVSKA

IRECHEK

SKOBELEV

GEORGI SAVA RAKOVSKI

VASIL LEVSKI SQUARE

ROZA LYUKSEMBURG

GENERAL SKOBELEV

Buses to Chairlift

PL. HADZHI DIMITAR

TSAR OSVOBODITEL

History Museum

M. TODOROV

HRISTO BOTEV

GEORGI DANCHEV

ALEKSANDAR S. PUSHKIN

PETKO D. PETKO

TSAR OSVOBODITEL

GEN. DRAGOMIROV

HADZHI DIMITAR

BURGASKO SHOSE

Market

Hadzhi Dimitar Museum

STEFAN KARADZHA

POPSKA

BRATYA MILADINOVI

HADZHI DIMITAR

Asenovska River

TSAR SIMEON

STEFAN KARADZHA

ACCOMMODATION

Byala Mechka	A
Chateau Alpia	C
Imperia	B
National Palace	D
Park Central	G
Sliven	F
Toma	E

Bus Station

HADZHI DIMITAR

BABA TONKA

RESTAURANTS

Deboya	1
Pri Fabrikadzhiyata	D

N

0   200 m

TSAR SIMEON

Train Station

imaginative building that looks like a cross between a mountain chalet and a Romanesque cathedral. Rooms (some with shower, some with bathtub) are decked out in weird browns and greys, but are still eminently comfortable. ❹

National Palace ul. Veliko Knyazhevska 29 ☎044/662929, ⓦwww.nationalpalace.bg. Incredibly plush new hotel complex built around a 300-year-old house that contains the excellent *Pri Fabrikadzhiyata* restaurant. Immaculate rooms with Wi-Fi and a/c are complemented by high standards of service. ❹

Park Central ul. Tsar Osvoboditel 6 ☎044/501700, ⓦwww.hotel-park-central.bg. Large central hotel

with excellent facilities. It's good, but doesn't quite meet the *National Palace's* standards. ❹

Sliven pl. Hadzhi Dimitar 2 ☎044/627056 or 624056. Standard Communist-era high-rise with functional doubles with shower and TV, and slightly smarter "lux" rooms. The main selling point is the ultra-central location. ❸

Toma ul. Veliko Knyazhevska 27 ☎042/623333, ⓦwww.hoteltoma.com. Next door to the *National Palace*, the *Toma* is housed in a renovated nineteenth-century house. Carved wooden beds and hairy Rhodopean rugs emphasise the traditional Bulgarian style while a/c and Wi-Fi add a modern touch. ❸

The Town

A sprawl of crumbling apartments and red-roofed houses, Sliven converges on a leafy plaza where the high-rise *Hotel Sliven* and an ugly concrete theatre complex fail to provide the focal point that the planners have evidently been groping for. The square is named **pl. Hadzhi Dimitar** after Sliven's most famous son (1840–68), a statue of whom stands to the northeast of the plaza.

To learn more about Dimitar, head off past the **Deboya** or "Depot" – once an arsenal and then a *caravanserai* – through the covered **market** beside the River Asenovska.

Down a side road, at the corner of ul. Asenova, the **Hadzhi Dimitar House-Museum** (daily 9am–noon & 2–5pm; 3Lv) honours the man who became Panaiot Hitov's standard-bearer by the age of 20, later teaming up with Stefan Karadzha in Romania to form a *cheta* that made guerrilla raids into Bulgaria. Eventually Turkish troops caught up with them at Mount Buzludzha, where Dimitar fell in battle, and Karadzha was clapped in irons and taken to be hanged in Ruse. The building itself used to be an inn, run by Dimitar's father; today you can see everything set up as it was when he lived here. Frugal bedding on the floor denotes the guests' sleeping quarters: the family lived in the more comfortable rooms to the rear, dining on a balcony carpeted with rush mats.

Sliven's other sights can be found along two streets running eastwards from the main square. **Bulevard Tsar Osvoboditel** is an attractive pedestrian zone of shops and cafés, ending in a very busy crossroads, though you'll need to keep your wits about you to dodge the speeding skateboarders and cyclists. Note the impressive **thousand-year-old oak tree** that survived the burning of medieval Sliven by the Turks. Among the best of the collection at the **History Museum** at no. 18 (daily 9am–noon & 1–5pm; 3Lv) are funerary relics from Kaloyanovo – where a Thracian chieftain was buried with his favourite horse and Greek pottery – and a collection of superbly intricate *shishane* rifles, showing the artistry of nineteenth-century local gunsmiths.

The Blue Rocks

In the early morning and late afternoon, the porphyry massif to the northeast of Sliven assumes a smoky blue hue in the translucent light. A welcome respite from the town, the appropriately named **Blue Rocks** (СИНИТЕ КАМЬНИ; *Sinite kamani*) feature scree slopes swathed in wiry trees and shrubs, with a profusion of streams and butterflies; the crags above are eyries for birds of prey, while animals such as boars, foxes and deer roam this rocky terrain. Just beyond the summit of the rocks lies the area known as **Karandila**, a plateau of pastureland and forest crisscrossed by hiking trails.

You can drive to the Karandila area by a circuitous but scenic route, following the Kotel road from Sliven and taking a signed left turn 15km out of town. A more popular excursion, though, is to ascend the rocks by the **chairlift** 4km northeast of central Sliven (near the end of bus route #12 from the corner of pl. Hadzhi Dimitar and ul. Rakovski), a clearly visible left turn off the Kotel road. Located just beyond the *Chateau Alpian* hotel (see p.302), the **chairlift** (*lifta*; 8Lv one way; 12Lv return) in theory operates between 8.30am and 5pm (except on Mon when it doesn't start up until noon), with shorter hours in winter and breaks for maintenance in spring and autumn. However, there are often long breaks for lunch, and staff may wait for enough customers to turn up before switching it on.

The best-known feature of the Blue Rocks can actually be reached on foot, by slogging uphill to the fifth pylon of the chairlift and then bearing left. A jagged arch nearly 8m tall, the **Ring** (*Halkata*) is associated with several legends. Ancient mariners supposedly moored their boats here during the Biblical Flood while fairytales have it that a girl passing through will turn into a boy (or vice versa), and a couple doing so will fall in love forever.

The Karakachani festival

The Karandila area becomes especially animated on the third weekend of August, when there's a festival celebrating the music and culture of the **Karakachani**, a minority community who live scattered throughout the Sliven and Kotel area. Although today's Karakachani no longer lead the nomadic pastoral lives of their forefathers, they retain a distinct identity, speaking a dialect of Greek and bringing out their dazzling white-smocked costumes on feast days.

The chairlift gets you to the summit in twenty minutes, giving wonderful views only slightly marred by the TV tower on **Mount Tyulbeto** (if you miss the chairlift back down, it takes an hour to scramble down the mountainside, following a path below the lift). Once at the top, head right up the steps from the terminal and across the road into the woods, where a trail soon emerges at the *Pobeda* **hut**, which has dorm beds and a café. One kilometre east of the chair lift, the *Karandila* hotel, though a concrete eyesore and eclipsed by the nearby *Byala Mechka* (see p.302) and other privately run places along the same road, is a popular refreshment stop for day-trippers.

Eating and drinking

There are plenty of snack bars, pizzerias and simple grills along bul. Tsar Osvoboditel, though for a more leisurely dining experience try the *Deboya*, diagonally opposite *Hotel Sliven*, where you can feast on meat and fish in an atmospherically arched, low-ceilinged interior or a glass pavilion at the front. Alternatively head to the *Pri Fabrikadzhiyata* restaurant in the *National Palace* hotel (see "Hotels"; p.302), where just about every dish in the traditional Bulgarian repertoire is served up in a 300-year-old house with a lovely garden.

Café-hopping along bul. Tsar Osvoboditel on a warm summer evening before moving on to the *Energy* **club** opposite *Hotel Sliven* is about the limit of the town's **nightlife**.

Around Sliven

Like Koprivshtitsa in the Sredna Gora or Elena in the Balkan Range, **Kotel** and **Zheravna** were important centres of Bulgarian culture during the nineteenth century, and made a contribution to the National Revival way out of proportion to their small size. Located in the hilly sheep-rearing terrain northeast of Sliven, they're both picturesque highland settlements with their fair share of traditional wooden architecture. Nearby, the villages of **Katunishte**, **Medven** and **Ichera** are well known for their nineteenth-century houses. If an off-beat village holiday is what you're after, Zheravna in particular is as good as they get.

It's worth making the effort for the scenery alone, with the road from Sliven zigzagging over the Blue Rocks massif and down into pine-clad valleys where gypsies camp among the wildflowers and herds of sheep block the roads. It's an enchanting, almost time-warped corner of Europe which still follows a pastoral way of life, with many of the villages along the route preserving rickety examples of nineteenth-century village architecture, although rural poverty and depopulation have given the whole region a careworn feel.

Getting around the region by **public transport** isn't difficult providing you start from Sliven, from where there are hourly buses to Kotel, three a day to Zheravna, and two daily buses to Katunishte, Medven, and Ichera. Despite their proximity to each other, Kotel and Zheravna are connected by just two buses a day, currently leaving Kotel at 7.45am and 11.30am.

Kotel

Founded by sixteenth-century migrants from the Ottoman-dominated plains, **KOTEL** (КОТЕЛ) was one of those remote towns where Bulgarian customs and crafts survived centuries of Turkish rule, to re-emerge with new vigour during the National Revival. This was in part due to the special privileges awarded the town by the Ottoman authorities, who employed *Kotlentsi* to defend the nearby mountain passes against brigands and allowed them to carry arms in return. Uniquely in Ottoman-occupied Bulgaria, the locals were allowed to build fortifications around the town in 1800 to deter attacks by the *kardzhali*, outlaws who sacked nearby Zheravna instead. Such was the extent of Kotel's autonomy that not only were Turks forbidden from settling here, they weren't even allowed to enter the town on horseback. Kotel's main source of income was from **sheep- and goat-breeding**, with local herdsmen crisscrossing the eastern Balkan Range seeking pastures. Herders often spent up to three years away from home at a stretch, and were engaged to local girls *in absentia* to prevent them from settling down elsewhere.

Though much of old Kotel was destroyed by fire in 1894, one quarter, containing around a hundred houses from the National Revival period, survived

Kotel carpets

Alongside Chiprovtsi (see p.182), Kotel is Bulgaria's major carpet-weaving centre. Manufactured here since the seventeenth century on vertical looms, Kotel carpets come in the form of either **kilims** (carpets with a complex design and a distinct border round the edges) or **chergi** (carpets with simpler designs, often just stripes of different colours). *Chergi* are often long, thin affairs used as runners, although they may be stitched together to form a larger floor covering. They're made from sheep's wool nowadays, although rough goat's wool carpets were popular in the past. Also made here are the tufted woollen **rugs** known variously as *guberi*, *kitenitsi* or *postelki*, which are traditionally used as blankets.

Kotel **designs** are very distinctive, and always feature four colours: black, red, blue and green. Kilims usually have lozenge- or diamond-shaped geometric patterns, many of which symbolize the stars, sun, moon, or more abstract ideas like the struggle between good and evil – shown by juxtaposing triangles of different colours. Kilims featuring the design known as *tablite* (literally "the trays") were traditionally made for the weaver's first-born granddaughter; those featuring *krasti* ("crosses") were made for a grandchild's christening.

There's very little in the way of a retail **market** for carpets in Kotel itself. The Carpet Exhibition (see opposite) has a small range of pieces for sale, and can arrange visits to see weavers at work. If you're staying in Bulgaria for more than a month or two, you can order a rug from a weaver, pay a deposit, and pick it up later. When buying from individuals, however, all prices are subject to negotiation, so it pays to check prices at the Carpet Exhibition first to get an idea of the going rate per square metre. As a general rule, anything bought in Kotel is about half the price of carpets bought in Sofia or the Black Sea coast (you can expect to pay roughly 200Lv per square metre in Kotel).

to become the subject of modern-day preservation orders. The local industry is **carpetmaking**, with weavers still producing handmade kilims and *chergi*, either at home or in the factory just outside town. Kotel is also the site of Bulgaria's foremost **folk music school** (*muzikalno uchilishte*), where talented youngsters from all over the country come to study traditional instruments – you may get to see a performance if you visit the town as part of a tour group.

The Town
From Kotel's bus station, flights of steps ascend to a plaza dominated by the **Pantheon of Georgi Sava Rakovski** (daily: summer Mon–Fri 9am–6pm, winter 8am–noon & 1–5pm; 5Lv). A gigantic stone cube with glass panels, it supposedly holds the bones of Rakovski, a Kotel-born revolutionary (see box, p.286), and there is a **museum** devoted to him and other local patriots, notably church leaders Sofronii Vrachanski and Neofit Bozveli, as well as educationalist Petar Beron, who wrote the first Bulgarian-language school primer in 1824. Arranged in a series of gloomy subterranean halls, the museum is more like the sepulchral vault of an ancestor-worshipping cult than a tourist attraction, with the shrivelled, embalmed heart of Petar Beron on display, along with some of Rakovski's letters and personal effects, and an extensive collection of weaponry. The alleged tomb of Rakovski lies in a sombre marble hall down a further flight of stairs, where suitably solemn taped music is played when visitors enter.

Follow ul. Izvorska from the plaza down past the **Church of the Trinity**, and you'll enter the Galata quarter of squat, vine-covered wooden houses and steep, cobbled alleys. Here you'll find the **Carpet Exhibition** (*Izlozhba na kotlenski takani*; daily: summer Mon–Fri 9am–6pm, winter 8am–noon & 1–5pm; 5Lv), housed in an old schoolhouse, which displays a colourful collection of antique and modern kilims, alongside some rather ill-advised contemporary tapestries based on medieval frescoes. From the fountain opposite, ul. Shipka runs uphill to an **Ethnographic Museum** (daily: summer Mon–Fri 9am–6pm, winter daily 8am–noon & 1–5pm; 5Lv), which occupies the house of a nineteenth-century seed merchant. Although well-off by Kotel standards, the family of eight all slept in the same room (on a floor softened with layered carpets), as was the custom, with the baby slung from the ceiling in a hammock-like cot. The kitchen was housed in a small, separate building in the courtyard, now restored to its original appearance and stocked with the usual array of period culinary implements. The opening times of both these museums tend to be regulated by the arrival of coach parties, so you may have to knock to gain access. Carrying straight on along ul. Izvorska from the Carpet Exhibition, you'll come to the bosky **Izvorite Park**, named after nearby springs. There are so many that settlers likened them to a bubbling cauldron (*kotel*) – hence the name of the town. These days the park is looking a little overgrown and neglected, though it's still a wonderful place for woodland walks.

At the western end of Izvorite Park, the **Natural History Museum** (daily 9am–6pm; 2Lv) is popular with Bulgarian school parties, housing the biggest and best-presented collection of stuffed fauna in the country. Although labelled exclusively in Bulgarian, it's an enjoyable display, and may constitute your only real chance of getting up close to the local wolves and bears.

Practicalities
The most central **hotel** is the smart new *Kristal* (℡0453/2298, ⓦwww .staratavodenica.hit.bg; ❸) just off the main plaza at ul. Izvorska 2. The

owners of *Kristal* also run *Starata Vodenitsa*, west of the bus station at ul. Luda Kamchiya 1 (☎0453/2360, ⓦwww.staratavodenica.hit.bg; ❸), a traditional-style building incorporating wooden panelling, stuffed hunting trophies and Kotel carpets. Two kilometres south of town on a partly wooded hillside, the *Chukarite* (☎0453/2475, ⓔtvkotel@mail.bg; ❷) is a small hotel boasting neat and tidy en-suite rooms with TV; it's accessible by a signed road across a bridge just after the bus station. Below the *Chukarite* is *Mirage*, a development of comfortable two-bedroom bungalows, spaced well apart and offering accommodation and kitchen facilities for up to seven people (☎0453/2457 or 0896/662868, ⓦwww.miragekotel.com; ❶).

The best place **to eat** is the restaurant of the *Starata Vodenitsa*, where meat-heavy Bulgarian standards are served by costumed waiting staff in an attractive courtyard. *Pizzeria Prima* opposite the Church of the Trinity serves a decent range of food in a shaded courtyard.

Zheravna

ZHERAVNA (ЖЕРАВНА) huddles on a ridge 6km off the main road between Sliven and Kotel, surrounded by steep pastures and maize fields. Its spacious and elegant wooden houses date from as early as the seventeenth century, when the village earned its living from sheep-breeding and diverse crafts, and the cobbled alleys still reverberate to the tinkle of goat bells and the rumble of donkey-drawn carts. With an array of **house-museums** open to visitors (all daily 9am–6pm; 4Lv), and a population of less than seven hundred, it offers a good mix of day-tripper-oriented tourism and rural peace.

The main road into Zheravna terminates at a car park at the bottom of the village where there's a bus stop and a small market. Heading uphill from here you'll soon come upon the village's main street, which ascends gently past the best of the houses. Built by itinerant Tryavna craftsmen in the mid-1700s, the **Sava Filaretov House**, home of a local educationalist, is a triumph of the woodcarver's art, squatting beneath a vast overhanging roof supported by spindly pillars decorated with zigzags and sun symbols. Inside, the main living and sleeping room is a picture of domestic harmony with ornate fitted cupboards stuffed with rugs, while the *minsofa*, or guest room, has a strange domed ceiling. A little further up the road is the **Rusi Chorbadzhii House**, a typical example of a nineteenth-century merchant's home, with more kilim-rich wooden interiors. There's a dazzling display of local carpets in the basement. Signposted high up on the northwestern side of the village is the **Yovkov House**, where writer Yordan Yovkov (1880–1937) spent the first years of his life before moving to the Dobrudzha. Yovkov remained a regular visitor to his native village, and tales of nineteenth-century Zheravna life form the core of his best-known short story collection, *Legends of the Stara Planina*. Also in the upper part of the village, you'll find the **church of Sveti Nikolai**, whose frivolous birthday-cake interior features a painted icon screen and leafy-capitalled columns. Lining the porch outside are stacks of eighteenth-century gravestones, carved with crosses, sun symbols and vividly depicted dragons.

An accommodation bureau (*byuro na nastanyavane*; irregular hours) opposite the bus stop offers traditionally furnished **private rooms** in village houses from 16–20Lv per person. There are also several reliable **B&Bs**, including *Ekohotel Zheravna*, just uphill from the bus stop (☎04585/359, ⓦwww.ekohotel-jeravna .hit.bg; ❷), a wonderfully antiquated wooden house with an assortment of

▲ Traditional house, Zheravna

en-suite doubles and triples sporting traditional textiles. *Filyovata kashta*, just uphill from the main street in the northern part of the village (℡04585/389 or 0898 698 566; ❷) also has a handful of comfy doubles and triples, all en suite. A couple come in true Zheravna style with wood-panelled interiors and traditional textiles, while the others have tiled floors and modern fittings. *Hadzhigergevata kashta*, at the western end of the village (℡0887/719/964 or 0887/718/709; ❷), is a 250-year-old house with carved wooden ceilings and a few other restored period touches. Rooms are simply furnished and facilities are shared, but you do get to sleep under traditional goat-hair rugs instead of a duvet.

As far as **eating and drinking** goes, both the *Ekotel Zheravna* and the *Filyovata kashta* have their own restaurants, each offering a range of traditional dishes in a pleasant outdoor setting. The *Mehana Starya* next to the church of Sveti Nikolai serves similar food and also has rooms (℡04585/200; ❷).

Katunishte, Medven and Ichera

Six kilometres southeast of Zheravna, and accessible by an asphalt road which arcs towards Gradets on the main Sliven to Kotel road, **KATUNISHTE** (КАТУНИЩЕ) is another village that harbours a rich ensemble of century-old wooden houses. It's an evocative spot, stretched along a babbling stream amid woodland and wheatfields. There are no museum-houses to visit, but **accommodation** is available at the *Eko Complex* (℡0899/971261 or 0899/886286; ❶), which has comfortable rooms in a renovated house and rents out bikes (5Lv per day).

MEDVEN (МЕДВЕН) lies slightly further afield in a lovely hill-encircled bowl, some 8km northeast of Gradets. Central Medven looks like a typical post-Communist village, but the outer *mahali* (quarters or suburbs), where geese and turkeys stalk the cobbled alleys, seem to have come straight out of the nineteenth century. It's reached by turning off the Sliven-Kotel road just north of Gradets. Two daily buses from both Sliven and Kotel serve the village.

After turning left in the centre a road brings you to the most atmospheric of the old quarters, about 500m from the main village, where there's a small **museum-house** honouring local boy-made-good **Zahari Stoyanov** (Wed–Sun 9am–noon & 1–6pm; 5Lv), whose eyewitness account of the 1876 insurrection, *Notes on the Bulgarian Uprisings*, became a classic piece of reportage. There's not much to see save for the author's coat, favourite ashtray (a curious affair in the form of a partridge), and the suitcase he was using when he suddenly dropped dead in a Paris hotel in 1889.

On no account leave Medven before embarking on the forty-minute walk to **Siniya Vir** ("Blue Whirlpool"), a popular local beauty spot which is reached by following the asphalt road beyond the Stoyanov House down to the river, crossing the bridge and following the path along the opposite bank. After crossing a weir you arrive at the pool, a wonderful cliff-enclosed stretch of turquoise fed by a slender waterfall issuing from a cleft in the rocks.

Should you wish to **stay**, the small family-run *Hotel Medven*, at ul.Vasil Lolov 10 (℡04582/2458, ⊛www.infotour.org/tarnovo/medven.html; ❷), to the right of the village's main crossroads and down a narrow cobbled street as you enter from the Sliven direction, offers cosy low-ceilinged rooms (a couple of doubles plus a triple and a quad) decked out with striped rugs. Just opposite the post office is *Orlitsa Kushta* (℡0888/808073 or 0887/454 7263; ❷), which offers similar accommodation, as does the *Chorbadzhi Petr* hotel (℡0888/616155 or 0888/334124, ⊛www.chorbadjipetar.hit.bg; ❷), a slightly larger affair at the other end of the village at ul. Kapitan Mamarchev 30. The lovely garden restaurants of the *Medven* and the *Chorbadzhi Petr* are the best places in the village **to eat**.

Midway along the road between Sliven and Gradets is **Ichera**, a quiet working village seemingly populated by itinerant farm animals. Its mixture of old and new buildings has been renovated in recent years by Bulgarians from Burgas in search of tranquil second homes and although there's little to do here it's certainly a great place to relax. The only **accommodation** is provided by the *Ichera* hotel (℡04517/268 or 0888/564791, ⓦwww.ichera.com; ❹), housed in a superbly restored old building with low wood-panelled ceilings, a swimming pool, and air-conditioned ensuite rooms. Bike hire is available for 5Lv per day.

Travel details

Trains

Hisar to: Plovdiv (6 daily; 1hr).

Kalofer to: Burgas (1 daily; 4–6hr); Sofia (2 daily; 2–3hr); Varna (1 daily; 6–7hr).

Karlovo to: Burgas (3 daily; 4–6hr); Kalofer 1 daily; 20min); Kazanlak (6 daily; 45min–1hr 15min); Koprivshtitsa (5 daily; 1hr); Plovdiv (5 daily; 1hr 45min); Sliven (4 daily; 2–3hr); Sofia (6 daily; 2–3hr).

Kazanlak to: Burgas (5 daily; 3hr); Karlovo (6 daily; 1hr); Plovdiv (2 daily; 3hr); Sliven (5 daily; 1hr 30min); Sofia (3 daily; 3–4hr); Varna (2 daily; 6–7hr); Veliko Tarnovo (1 daily; 2hr).

Koprivshtitsa to: Burgas (1 daily; 5hr); Karlovo (5 daily; 1hr); Sofia (4 daily; 1hr 30min–2hr 30min).

Panagyurishte to: Plovdiv (3 daily; 2hr).

Sliven to: Burgas (3 daily; 1hr 45min); Karlovo (5 daily; 2hr 30min); Kazanlak (6 daily; 1hr 30min); Plovdiv (4 daily; 5hr); Sofia (3 daily; 5hr); Stara Zagora (4 daily; 2hr); Varna (3 daily; 4hr).

Sofia to: Karlovo (6 daily; 2hr 30min–3hr 30min); Kazanlak (3 daily; 3–4hr); Koprivshtitsa (5 daily; 1hr 40min).

Stara Zagora to: Burgas (5 daily; 2hr 30min–3hr 30min); Plovdiv (12 daily; 1hr 30min–2hr); Sofia (6 daily; 5hr); Varna (3 daily; 4hr).

Buses

Hisar to: Karlovo (7 daily; 35min); Panagyurishte (1 daily Fri–Sun only; 1hr 30min); Plovdiv (hourly; 1hr); Sofia (1 daily; 2hr); Starosel (4 daily; 40min).

Kalofer to: Karlovo (every 30min; 30min); Plovdiv (1 daily; 1hr 30min); Sofia (2 daily; 3hr).

Karlovo to: Hisar (5 daily; 35min); Kalofer (every 30 min; 30min); Klisura (5 daily; 50min); Plovdiv (hourly; 1hr 15min); Sofia (2 daily; 2hr 30min);

Sopot (every 15–30min; 15min); Starosel (5 daily; 1hr 25min); Troyan (1 daily April–Oct; 2hr 30min).

Kazanlak to: Burgas (6 daily; 4hr); Gabrovo (10 daily; 2hr 15min); Lovech (5 daily; 2hr 30min); Plovdiv (5 daily; 2hr); Sofia (6 daily; 3hr 30min); Stara Zagora (9 daily; 45min); Veliko Tarnovo (4 daily; 3hr).

Koprivshtitsa to: Plovdiv (1 daily; 2hr 30min); Sofia (4 daily; 2hr).

Kotel to: Burgas (3 daily; 4hr); Plovdiv (4 daily; 3hr); Shumen (3 daily; 2hr 30min); Sliven (8 daily; 1hr 30min); Sofia (2 daily; 4hr 30min); Zheravna (2 daily; 30min).

Panagyurishte to: Hisar (1 daily; 1hr 30min); Pazardzhik (hourly; 45min); Plovdiv (3 daily; 2hr); Sofia (2 daily; 2hr).

Sliven to: Burgas (hourly; 3hr); Haskovo (1 daily Fri–Sun only; 4hr); Ichera (2 daily; 40min); Katunishte (2 daily; 1hr 15min); Kotel (hourly; 1hr 30min); Medven (2 daily; 1hr 30min); Shumen (2 daily; 3hr); Stara Zagora (hourly; 1hr 45min); Veliko Tarnovo (7 daily; 4hr); Zheravna (3 daily; 1hr 15min).

Sofia *Avtogara Poduyane* to: Koprivshtitsa (2 daily; 2hr). *Avtogara Yug* to: Panagyurishte (4 daily; 2hr). *Tsentralna Avtogara* to: Kazanlak (5–7 daily; 5–6hr); Stara Zagora (4 daily; 4hr). *Trafik-Market* to: Koprivshtitsa (2 daily; 2hr).

Stara Zagora to: Ahtopol (6 daily; 3hr 30min); Burgas (6 daily; 3hr); Gabrovo (6 daily; 3hr); Harmanli (1 daily; 2hr); Haskovo (11 daily; 1hr 15min); Kardzhali (5 daily; 2 hr); Kazanlak (every 30min; 45min); Plovdiv (hourly; 2hr); Sliven (every 30min; 1hr); Sofia (hourly; 5hr); Varna (hourly; 4hr); Veliko Tarnovo (1 daily; 4hr).

Zheravna to: Kotel (2 daily; 30min); Sliven (3 daily; 1hr 45min).

5

The Rhodopes and the Plain of Thrace

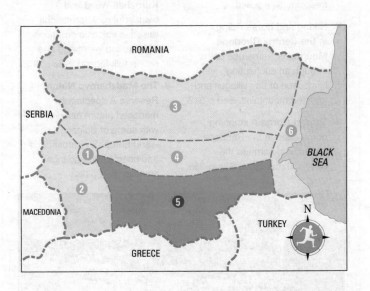

CHAPTER 5

Highlights

✳ **The Old Town, Plovdiv**
A superb assemblage of
National Revival architecture
with several beautiful houses
open to the public. See p.326

✳ **The Roman Theatre, Plovdiv**
One of the best-preserved
Roman monuments in
Bulgaria, still used for concerts
and plays today. See p.330

✳ **Bachkovo Monastery**
Bulgaria's second – largest
monastery is famed for its
frescoes. See p.340

✳ **Hiking and horse riding
in the Central Rhodope
Mountains** Numerous paths
through an enchanting
landscape of tiny villages and
forested mountains. See p.342

✳ **Trigrad Gorge** A stunning
gorge deep in the Rhodope
mountains, home to the
Devil's Throat cave. See p.353

✳ **The Historical Museum,
Kardzhali** One of the best
collections of its kind,
showcasing local trades,
crafts and folklore, and
an impressive display of
archeological finds. See p.360

✳ **Perperikon** A breathtaking
hilltop temple and fortress
hewn from rock and linked to
the worship of Dionysus and
the cult of Orpheus. See p.362

✳ **The Rock Formations,
Kardzhali** Weird and
wonderful rock formations,
raised in volcanic eruptions
forty million years ago and
rich in folk legend. See p.362

✳ **The Madzharovo Nature
Reserve** A spectacular
managed nature reserve,
with some of Bulgaria's
– and Europe's – rarest birds
and scarce and endangered
animals. See p.363

▲ Perperikon

5

The Rhodopes and the Plain of Thrace

ew parts of Bulgaria are as closely associated with antiquity as **the Rhodopes and the Plain of Thrace**. If the Balkan Range was the cradle of the Bulgar state, then the fertile plain between the Sredna Gora and the Rhodope Mountains was the heartland of the Thracian community and the magnet that drew conquerors like Philip of Macedon and the Romans, whose legacy still remains in the graceful ruins of **Plovdiv**. Bulgaria's second city, and a fair rival to the capital in most respects, Plovdiv never fails to charm with its old quarter – a wonderful melange of Renaissance mansions, mosques and classical remains, spread over three hills. The whole region is full of memories of the Turks, whose descendants still inhabit the area around **Kardzhali**, while the mosques and bridges built by their forebears constitute the chief sights of **Pazardzhik**, **Haskovo**, **Harmanli** and **Svilengrad**, strung out along the route between Sofia and Istanbul.

The Rhodope Mountains to the south of the plain harbour **Bachkovo Monastery** and small towns such as **Shiroka Laka** and **Batak**, whose fortified houses testify to the insecurity of life in the old days, when bandits and Muslim zealots marauded through the hills. While **Pamporovo**, one of Bulgaria's major ski resorts, attracts thousands of winter tourists, the Rhodopes have become a key summer destination for hikers and those in search of rural tranquillity. The scenery in Bulgaria's southern margins can be truly stupendous, ranging from rugged gorges to dense pine forests and alpine pasturelands. The stunning caves around the **Trigrad Gorge**, and the wonderful hikes around the pilgrimage site of **Krastova Gora**, are two of the highlights.

The website Ⓦwww.rodopi-bg.com is a useful source of information about the region.

The Plain of Thrace

Watered by the Maritsa and numerous tributaries descending from the
Balkans and the Rhodopes, the **Plain of Thrace** (*Trakiiskata nizina*) has been
a fertile, productive land since antiquity. The ancient Greeks called it Upper
or Northern Thrace, to distinguish it from the lush plains on the far side of
the Rhodopes in Greece and Turkey, collectively known as Thrace after the
tribes who lived there. A Bulgarian legend has it that God, dividing the world
among different peoples, forgot the Bulgars until they mentioned the
oversight. God replied: "There is nothing left, but since you are hard-working
folk I will give you a portion of Paradise." And so the Bulgars received part
of Thrace.

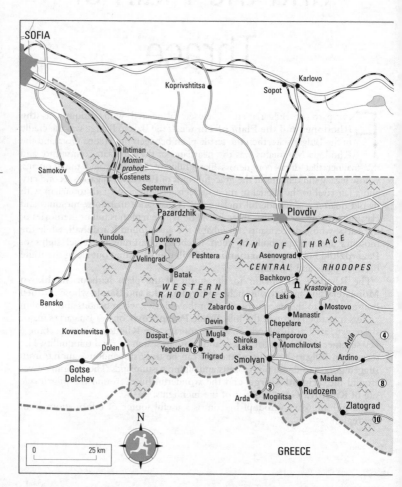

The E80, which now links Istanbul and Sofia, essentially follows the course of the Roman Serdica–Constantinople road, past towns ruled by the Ottomans for so long that foreigners used to call this "European Turkey". The most important town, of course, is **Plovdiv**, which quite simply overshadows all the others. The provincial centres of **Pazardzhik**, **Haskovo**, **Harmanli** and **Svilengrad** have their points of interest, but hardly warrant extensive investigation.

Travelling this route is fairly straightforward. Roughly every hour, trains depart **from Sofia** bound for Plovdiv – a journey of two and a half hours by express (*barz*) or intercity services. If you'd rather travel by road, take one of the hourly departures from the bus station, which do the journey in around the same time. **From other parts of Bulgaria**, there is at least one direct train a day from both Burgas and Varna on the coast; while travellers coming from Ruse and Veliko Tarnovo will probably need to change trains at Stara Zagora. Numerous buses and at least one train a day link Plovdiv with

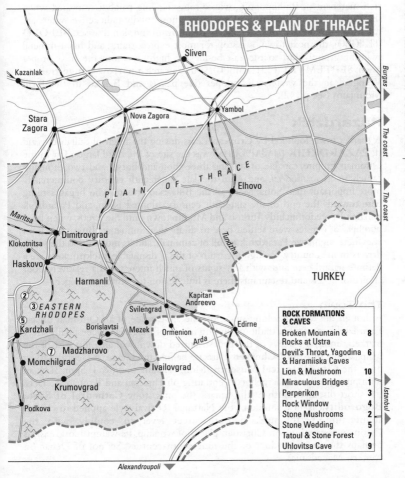

RHODOPES & PLAIN OF THRACE

ROCK FORMATIONS & CAVES

Broken Mountain & Rocks at Ustra	8
Devil's Throat, Yagodina & Haramiiska Caves	6
Lion & Mushroom	10
Miraculous Bridges	1
Perperikon	3
Rock Window	4
Stone Mushrooms	2
Stone Wedding	5
Tatoul & Stone Forest	7
Uhlovitsa Cave	9

Istanbul: travelling by road you'll cross the border at Kapitan Andreevo (see p.337); by train at Svilengrad (p.337).

Sofia to Plovdiv

Travelling west to east along the E80, the first town you come across after leaving Sofia is **IHTIMAN** (ИХТИМАН), set amid beautiful subalpine scenery. There's a central **hotel**, *Air Sofia* (☎0724/2065, ⓦ www.airsofia.com; ❸), and a smart eighteen-hole *Air Sofia Golf Club* and horse-riding centre (☎0724/3530; 60Lv per game) on the outskirts. If you're on a direct bus, you'll follow the dual carriageway as far as Plovdiv, bypassing the towns below, but if you're taking the Sofia–Plovdiv rail line, or driving along the old Sofia-Plovdiv road, you'll wind your way in a leisurely fashion through the hills that precede the Maritsa Valley, before entering **KOSTENETS** (КОСТЕНЕЦ), a small town encroaching on **Momin prohod** ("Maiden's Pass"). This gets its name from the daughter of a rich merchant of Philippopolis, whose long-standing paralysis vanished when she bathed here in the **mineral springs**, whose mildly radioactive waters are still used today to treat diabetes, ulcers, rheumatism and skin diseases. **BELOVO** (БЕЛОВО), the next town, is a stop for most express trains, and has a mineral swimming pool 5km to the east beside the highway. From the next proper town, **SEPTEMVRI** (СЕПТЕМВРИ), you can catch a **narrow-gauge train** to Velingrad in the western Rhodopes (see p.357) and Bansko in the Pirin Mountains (see p.142).

Pazardzhik

A market town founded by Crimean Tatars during the reign of Sultan Bayezid II, **PAZARDZHIK** (ПАЗАРДЖИК) was the site of the third largest fair in the Ottoman Empire, capable of stabling three thousand horses and two thousand camels in its *caravanserai*, and until the late nineteenth century commercially more important than Sofia. Many of the Bulgarian artisans who began settling here towards the end of the sixteenth century adopted Islam, and Pazardzhik remained a predominantly Turkish and Muslim town until the 1960s, when large numbers of gypsies were settled here to dilute their influence. Bulgarians from elsewhere stigmatize Pazardzhik as full of criminals, and its motorists as the worst drivers in the country. Though the truth of this is disputable, **pickpockets** are a definite hazard here and, with few sights of much interest and a relatively poor choice of hotels and restaurants there is little reason for visitors to linger.

The Town

Although the town has long since lost the appearance of an Ottoman bazaar, Pazardzhik's mercantile traditions live on in one of Bulgaria's liveliest daily street markets, lining the alleys of the pedestrianized downtown area just east of the main square, **ploshtad Cherven**. Directly behind the square, at Georgi Kirkov 34, is the **City Historical Museum** (Mon–Fri 9am–noon & 1–5pm; 3Lv), an uninspiring collection largely concentrating on Thracian and Roman artefacts.

A short distance south of the square, the pink stone **Cathedral of Sveta Bogoroditsa** is an example of the National Revival style applied to church architecture, partly sunk beneath street level to comply with the Ottoman restrictions on Christian places of worship. Its walnut iconostasis is perhaps the finest product of the nineteenth-century School of Debar (in western Macedonia).

Zahari Zograf aside, Bulgaria's most famous nineteenth-century painter was probably **Stanislav Dospevski** (1826–76), whose former house and studio opposite the cathedral is now a **museum** (officially Mon–Fri 9am–noon & 1–5pm; 3Lv). Born in Pazardzhik and educated at the Academy of Fine Art in St Petersburg, Dospevski drew extensively during visits to Odessa and Constantinople, but is best remembered for his icons, portraits and murals, several of which decorate the walls of the house. A participant in the April Rising, he was flung into the dungeons of Constantinople and died before Bulgaria's Liberation.

Most of Pazardzhik's surviving nineteenth-century houses lie near the Dospevski museum, where squat pastel-coloured structures huddle along either side of a stream, or among the tree-lined residential streets just west of the cathedral. On the far side of the park north of the centre is the **Kurshum dzhamiya**, or "Bullet Mosque", so-called because of its pointed dome. Built in 1667, it is larger and grander than the mosques in Plovdiv and Haskovo, but sadly derelict.

Practicalities

Pazardzhik's **train station** lies about 5km south of the centre, and all arrivals are met by buses into town. The **bus terminal**, a couple of blocks north of the town centre, is a more convenient point of entry.

With regular **buses** to Plovdiv, Batak in the Rhodopes and Panagyurishte in the Sredna Gora, Pazardzhik is the kind of place to spend an afternoon before moving on. If you do wish **to stay**, however, your best bet is the small, family-run *Riva*, at ul. Tsar Asen 23 (☎034/444734; ❶), a quiet pension in the backstreets near the bus station. Otherwise, options are limited to the uninspiring *Hotel Trakiya*, on the main square (☎034/446008; ❸), or the *Elbrus*, at pl. Olimpiiski 2 (☎034/445530; ❸), which has air-conditioned rooms and features a late-night **bar** and **disco**.

Beyond Pazardzhik

The road between Pazardzhik and Plovdiv runs straight as an arrow across the widening plain beside the River Maritsa, flanked by acres of trees bearing apples, plums and pears. Bulgarians say that, traditionally, passers-by may pick fruit from roadside orchards providing they eat it on the spot, but removing any constitutes theft in the eyes of the law. The road finally enters Plovdiv through the city's northern suburbs.

Plovdiv

PLOVDIV (ПЛОВДИВ), Bulgaria's second–largest city (with a population of 360,000), is one of its most attractive and vibrant centres, with arguably more to recommend it than Sofia, a city that the proud locals of Plovdiv tend to regard with some disdain. Certainly there's plenty to see: the old town embodies Plovdiv's long and varied history. Thracian fortifications subsequently used by Macedonian masons, overlaid with Byzantine walls, and by great timber-framed mansions erected during the Bulgarian renaissance, look down on the Ottoman mosques and artisans' dwellings of the town that Lucian the Greek once called "the biggest and most beautiful of all" in Thrace. But Plovdiv isn't merely a parade of antiquities: the city's arts festivals and trade fairs rival Sofia's in number, and its restaurants and promenade compare very favourably with those of the capital.

Some history

An ancient Thracian site, rebuilt and renamed by Philip II of Macedon in 342 BC, classical **Philippopolis** was initially little more than a military outpost designed to keep a watchful eye over the troublesome natives. It was a rough frontier town that the Macedonians deliberately colonized with criminals and outcasts; the Roman writer Pliny later identified it with Poneropolis, the semi-legendary "City of Thieves". Under Roman rule urban culture developed apace, with the town's position on the Belgrade–Constantinople highway bringing both economic wealth and a strategic role in the defence of Thrace.

Plovdiv was sacked by the Huns in 447 AD, and by the seventh century, with the Danube frontier increasingly breached by barbarians, the city was in decline. With the arrival of the Bulgars, Byzantine control over the area became increasingly tenuous. "Once upon a time", lamented Byzantine chronicler Anna Comnena in the twelfth century, "Philippopolis must have been a large and beautiful city, but after the Tauri and Scyths [Slavs] enslaved the inhabitants ... it was reduced to the condition in which we saw it." In Comnena's time Philippopolis was a notorious hotbed of heretics, a situation usually blamed on local Armenians, who migrated to Thrace en masse in the eighth and tenth centuries, bringing with them the dualistic doctrines of Manichaeanism and Paulicianism. Although these heresies eventually fizzled out, Plovdiv's Armenian population has endured to this day.

The Byzantine town was further damaged by the Bulgarian Tsar Kaloyan in 1206, and it was a rather run-down place that the Turks inherited in the fourteenth century, renaming it Filibe. It soon recovered as a commercial centre, with a thriving Muslim quarter, complete with bazaars and mosques, growing up at the base of the hill where Plovdiv's Christian communities continued to live. Many of the latter were members of a rich mercantile class by the mid-nineteenth century, and they expressed their affluence in the construction of opulent townhouses that showcased the best of native arts and crafts. Plovdiv's urban elite also patronized Bulgarian culture, and had the Great Powers of Europe not broken up the infant state of Bulgaria at the Congress of Berlin in 1878, Plovdiv would probably have been designated as its capital. In the event, it became instead the main city of **Eastern Rumelia**, an Ottoman province administered by a Christian governor-general. Much of the Christian population naturally wanted union with the rest of Bulgaria, which was finally attained in 1885.

Plovdiv has continued to rival Sofia as a cultural and business centre ever since, not least because of the **international trade fairs** held here in May and September (see box below). With its longstanding liberal-bourgeois

---

The Plovdiv fair

A trade centre of long standing, **Plovdiv** became Bulgaria's principal marketplace during the 1870s, when the railway between Europe and Istanbul was completed and the great annual fair held at Uzundzhovo since the sixteenth century was moved here. Plovdiv's first international trade fair (1892) was a rather homespun affair – a man from Aitos proposed to show his hunting dogs, while Bohemia exhibited beehives – but since 1933 the event has gone from strength to strength, and nowadays claims to be the largest of its kind in the Balkans. There are actually two annual **fairs**: the spring event, devoted to consumer goods, in early May, and the larger autumn industrial fair, during the second half of September. Both are held at the complex on the north bank of the river. Members of the public are free to come along, and there's a special bus service laid on between the train station and the fairground.

tradition, Plovdiv is politically the "bluest" city in Bulgaria, a stronghold of the conservative SDS since the demise of Communism. Plovdiv's proximity to Turkey and Greece has ensured that private enterprise has flourished here more than anywhere else in the country.

Arrival, orientation and information

Trains arrive at the central train station (*Tsentralna gara*) to the south of central Plovdiv, near two of the city's three **bus terminals**: Rodopi, serving the mountain resorts of the south, is just on the other side of the train tracks (accessible via the underground walkway from the station), while Yug bus station, serving the southeast, is one block east of the train station. Sever bus station, which runs services to northern towns such as Panagyurishte, Ruse, Pleven and Koprivshtitsa, is several kilometres north of the river – reached by bus #12 from the train station, or minibuses #4, #17 and #19 from the centre. A brisk ten-minute walk north of Yug bus station, along ul. Ivan Vazov – or three stops on buses #2 or #102 – brings you to **ploshtad Tsentralen**, immediately north of which is the modern town centre.

Though most of Plovdiv's sights are near enough to be explored on foot, the city is divided into two distinct parts, quite different from each other in atmosphere: the nineteenth-century **Stariyat grad** or Old Town, covering the easternmost of Plovdiv's three hills; and the **lower town** – predominantly modern with a scattering of Turkish and Roman relics – which spreads across the plain below.

The **tourist information office** (☎032/656794, ⊛www.plovdiv.bg) at pl. Tsentralen 1, behind the post office, is a good starting point and can organise excursions, book hotels and arrange car rental. Private agencies such as Astral Holidays at Otets Paisi 24 (Mon–Fri 9am–7pm & Sat 10am–3pm; ☎032/626608, ⊛www.astralholidays.bg) and the Esperansa agency (see below) offer similar services. All the agencies dispense free brochures and should stock up-to-date **maps** such as the *Plovdiv City Guide*. Look out for the free weekly cultural guide *Programata* (⊛www.programata.bg), distributed at hotels, bars and restaurants. **Walking tours** of the old and new town (2hrs; 70Lv per group) are provided by City Tour Guides, which is based in an upstairs office at ul. Knyaz Aleksandar 39 (☎032/262784 or 0896/680846, ⊜rustt@mail.bg).

Accommodation

The only time you might have trouble finding somewhere to stay is during the trade fairs in May and September, when all the better hotels and private rooms are taken; if you're particular about where you stay, reserve a month ahead. The most convenient source of **private rooms** is Esperansa, at ul. Ivan Vazov 14 (daily 24hr; ☎032/265127, ⊛www.esperansa.hit.bg), which charges 25Lv for a single and 40Lv for a double room in the centre. For motorists coming from Sofia or Turkey it's easier to use the Traikov Agency, on the north side of the river at ul. Ibar 31 (Mon–Fri 9am–5pm; ☎032/963014, ⊜et_traykov@yahoo.com), which charges similar rates and also rents apartments with kitchens (40Lv a night). Plovdiv's **hotels** are almost as expensive as Sofia's and hike their prices by up to 100 percent during the fairs. The influx of backpackers has generated a surge of decent new **hostels** offering sociable dorm accommodation in line with the prices of private rooms. Unless otherwise stated, all the hotels below are marked on the Plovdiv map on pp.322–323. The city's three **campsites** are some way from town along the Sofia–Plovdiv–Istanbul E80 highway – too far away for those who want to be at the centre of things.

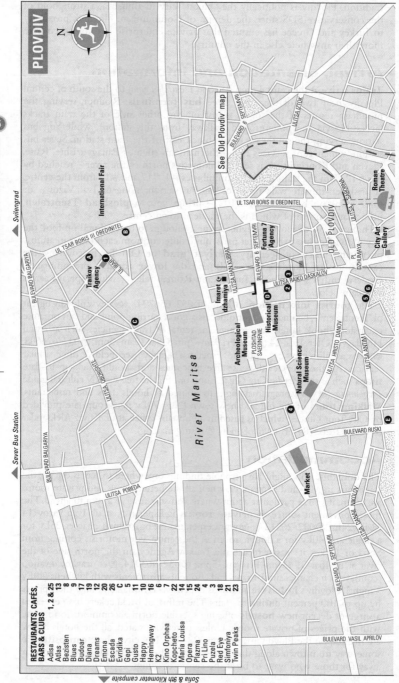

PLOVDIV

N

See 'Old Plovdiv' map

International Fair

Traikov Agency

Imaret dzhamiya

Fortuna Agency

Archeological Museum

Historical Museum

PLOSHTAD SAEDINENIE

Natural Science Museum

River Maritsa

Market

OLD PLOVDIV

Roman Theatre

City Art Gallery

PL. DZHUMAYA

ULITSA HAN KUBRAT

ULITSA RAIKO DASKALOV

UL TSAR BORIS III OBEDINITEL

BULEVARD 6 SEPTEMVRI

ULITSA IZTOK

ULITSA HRISTO DANOV

ULITSA ANTIM I

ULITSA IVAN VAZOV

ULITSA DANAIL NIKOLOV

BULEVARD 6 SEPTEMVRI

BULEVARD RUSKI

BULEVARD VASIL APRILOV

ULITSA OSBORNE

ULITSA HASHOVE

BULEVARD BALGARIYA

BULEVARD BALGARIYA

UL IBAR

ULITSA POBEDA

▲ Svilengrad

▲ Sever Bus Station

▲ Sofia & 9th Kilometer campsite

RESTAURANTS, CAFÉS, BARS & CLUBS	
Adisa	1, 2 & 25
Atlas	13
Bezisten	8
Blues	9
Budoar	17
Diana	19
Dreams	12
Emona	20
Escada	26
Evridika	C
Gepi	5
Gusto	11
Happy	10
Hemingway	16
K2	6
Kino Orphea	7
Kopcheto	22
Maria Louisa	14
Opera	15
Plazma	24
Pri Lino	3
Puzela	4
Red Eye	18
Simfoniya	21
Twin Peaks	23

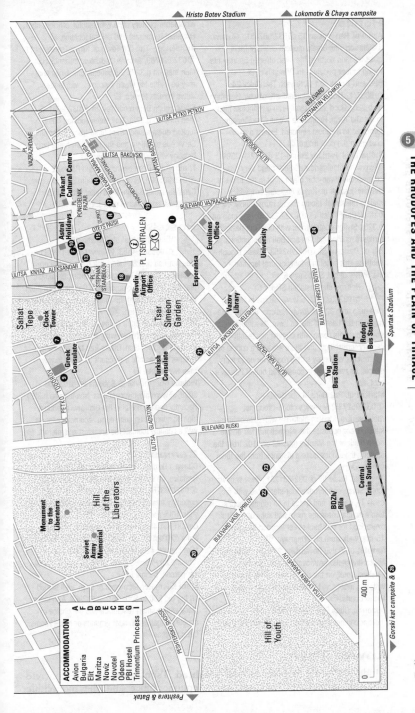

▲ Hristo Botev Stadium   ▲ Lokomotiv & Chaya campsite

ULITSA PETKO PETKOV

PL VAZRAZHDANE

ULITSA RAKOVSKI

BULEVARD KONSTANTIN VELCHKOV

ULITSA BOGOMIL

Trakart Cultural Centre

Astral Holidays

PL PONEDELNIK PAZAR

OTETS PAISII

BULEVARD VAZRAZHDANE

Eurolines Office

University

ULITSA KNYAZ ALEKSANDÅR

PL STEFAN STAMBOLOV

Plovdiv Airport Office

Esperansa

BULEVARD HRISTO BOTEV

PL TSENTRALEN

SAHAT TEPE

Clock Tower

Tsar Simeon Garden

Vazov Library

Rodopi Bus Station

▲ Spartak Stadium

Greek Consulate

UL PETKO D ODOROV

Turkish Consulate

ULITSA AVKSENTII VELESHKI

Yug Bus Station

GLADSTON

ULITSA IVAN VAZOV

BULEVARD RUSKI

ULITSA

BDZh Rila

Central Train Station

Monument to the Liberators

Hill of the Liberators

Soviet Army Memorial

BULEVARD VASIL APRILOV

ULITSA LYUBEN KARAVELOV

▲ Gorski kat campsite &

PESHERSKO SHOSSE

Hill of Youth

▲ Peshtera & Batak

ACCOMMODATION

Avion	A
Bulgaria	F
Elit	D
Maritza	B
Noviz	E
Novotel	C
Odeon	H
PBI Hostel	G
Trimontium Princess	I

0   400 m

Hotels

Avion ul. Han Presian 15 ☎032/967451, ⓦwww
.hotelavion.info. Small, modern establishment in a
quiet location north of the river, offering apartments
for up to four people with TV and a/c. ❻

Bed and Breakfast ul. Knyazh Tseretelev 24
☎0887/420185, ⓔbedbreakfast@abv.bg. (see map
on p.328). Good-value family-run guesthouse high
in the Old Town. Rooms are a/c and traditionally
furnished to a decent standard. Expect a name
change in the near future. ❹

Bulgaria ul. Patriarh Evtimii 13 ☎032/633599,
ⓦwww.hotelbulgaria.net. Smart and very
comfortable three-star place right in the heart of
the city, just off ul. Knyaz Aleksandar I, which
makes the street-facing rooms rather noisy. ❻

Dali ul. Otets Paisii 11 ☎032/621530. (see map on
p.328). Stylish central hotel with plenty of designer
furniture, quirky features and Dali reproductions. ❻

Elit ul. Daskalov 53 ☎032/624537. Basic though
spotless little hotel in a fairly central location, on
the corner of bul. Septemvri 6. ❸

🏃 **Hebros** ul. Konstantin Stoilov 51
☎032/260180, ⓦwww.hebros-hotel.com
(see map on p.328). A lovely National Revival-style
house in the heart of the old town. Its atmospheric
en-suite rooms come with original nineteenth-
century furnishings, and there are also a couple of
apartments with cosy sitting rooms for up to four
people. Its restaurant is considered one of Plovdiv's
best. ❼

Maritza ul. Tsar Boris III Obedinitel 42
☎032/952735, ⓦwww.victoria-group.net
/hotelmaritza. Modern high-rise with extraordinarily
kitsch décor opposite the international fair on the
north bank of the Maritsa (bus #2 or #102 from the
station), though it's quite a distance from the town
centre. ❼

Noviz bul. Ruski 55 ☎032/631281, ⓦwww.noviz
.com. Small, comfortable four-star hotel, with a/c,
cable TV, minibar and fridge in all rooms; there's
also a sauna, massage room and solarium. A little
overpriced for this backstreet location though. A
15-min walk from pl. Dzhumaya. ❻

Novotel ul. Zlatyu Boyadzhiev 2 ☎032/934444,
ⓦplovdivhotels.com/novotel.shtml. Plovdiv's
plushest hotel, on the north bank of the Maritsa,
with a/c, indoor and outdoor pools, sauna and
tennis courts. ❽

Odeon ul. Otets Paisii 40 ☎032/622065, ⓦwww
.hotelodeon.net. Renovated to a high standard in
nineteenth-century style with helpful, efficient staff.
Excellent restaurant and central location. ❼

Residence – The Old Town ul. Knyaz Tseretelev 11
☎032/620789, ⓦwww.theoldtownresidence.com.
(see map on p.328). Sumptuous furnishings (that
may be a little too kitsch for some), with fantastic
views from its terrace. ❼

SN ul. Hristo Dyukmedzhiev 28 ☎032/260135.
(see map on p.328). Tiny, three-roomed hotel
tucked down a side street 5min from pl. Dzhumaya.
Service is excellent and the top room has a large
balcony with views of the town. ❸

Trimontium Princess ul. Kapitan Raicho 2
☎032/605000, ⓦwww.trimontium-princess.com.
Centrally located high-class hotel with lavishly
furnished, comfortable rooms. ❽

Hostels

🏃 **Hiker's Hostel** ul. Saborna 53
☎0885/194553, ⓦwww.hikers-hostel.org.
(see map on p.328). Laid-back place with a great
position in the Old Town. Free Internet, breakfast,
tea, coffee, and pick-up service. Campers can pitch
tents in the yard and the manager runs day-trips
throughout the region. ❶

PBI Hostel ul. Naiden Gerov 13 ☎032/638467.
Centrally located hostel with dorm beds and one
en-suite double room. Offers free tea and coffee,
Internet access and a discount for stays longer
than two nights. ❶

Plovdiv Guesthouse ul. Saborna 20 ☎02/400
3098, ⓦwww.plovdivguest.com. (see map on p.328).
Recently opened hostel in the Old Town offering a
high standard of en-suite dorm accommodation as
well as double rooms. Free breakfast and Internet. ❶

Campsites

Chaya 11km east of Plovdiv just off the old E80 to
Haskovo, on the banks of the River Chepelarska
☎032/263763. A pleasant site let down by its
proximity to a truck stop and a busy road. Open all
year. 10Lv per tent, bungalows ❶

Gorski kat 4km west of town on the old E80 to
Sofia ☎032/951360. Most convenient of the sites;
take bus #4, #20, or #44 from opposite the
Trimontium Princess hotel. Open all year. Tents 3Lv
per person, bungalows ❷

Ninth Kilometer 9km west of town, well signed
off the old E80 to Sofia ☎032/632992. A modern
place with a smart restaurant and the choice of
double bungalows in neat grounds or motel rooms.
Open all year. ❷

Lower Town

Modern Plovdiv revolves around **ploshtad Tsentralen**, an arid concrete
plaza dominated by the post and telephone office and the monolithic

Trimontium Princess hotel. Remnants of a **Roman forum** were discovered during the development of the area – you can explore a section of this marble-paved, once-colonnaded square by descending into a sunken area in front of the hotel. Further remains can be seen on the other side of the post office. Just east of here is ul. Kapitan Raicho, a leafy residential street enlivened by a daily open-air clothes market.

To the west of pl. Tsentralen, the **Tsar Simeon Garden** – a lovely patch of greenery with an unusual musical fountain at its heart – marks the tail end of the evening *korso*, an animated promenade in which hundreds of people stroll down Plovdiv's main street, **ulitsa Knyaz Aleksandar I**. Pedestrianized and lined with shops and café-bars with outdoor tables, the street was named after the ideologue Vasil Kolarov in Communist times, but now has its prewar title again. The **City Art Gallery** at no.15 (Mon–Sat 9am–5.30pm; 2Lv, free on Thurs) houses a fine collection of nineteenth-century portraits, including one deeply reverent, almost iconic *Portrait of Bishop Sofronii of Vratsa*, painted in 1812 by an unknown artist. Also look out for Tsanko Lavrenov's pictures of nineteenth-century Plovdiv, painted in the 1930s and 1940s and suffused with a dreamlike nostalgia. The ground floor is given over to regularly changing exhibitions of modern works, including many by local artists.

The massive stone slabs paving **the Archeological Underpass** (*Podlez Arheologicheski*), east of ul. Knyaz Aleksandar I and beneath ul. Tsar Boris Obedinitel, date back to Roman times. The **Trakart Cultural Centre** (daily 9am–7pm; 4Lv) preserves in situ the foundations and mosaic floors of a fourth-century AD Roman residence that once stood beside the street; the centre hosts regular art exhibitions and sells ceramic replicas of ancient finds.

Ploshtad Dzhumaya and beyond

Further north, ul. Knyaz Aleksandar I leads onto **ploshtad Dzhumaya**, where Plovdiv's history and social life coexist in an amiable confusion of monuments, cafés and stalls, around a concrete pit exposing the **ruins of a Roman stadium**. This is but a meagre section of the original, horseshoe-shaped arena where the Alexandrine Games were held during the second and third centuries: as many as thirty thousand spectators watched chariot races, wrestling, athletics and other events from the marble stands that once lined the slopes of the neighbouring heights.

A more impressive structure is the **Dzhumaya dzhamiya** or "Friday mosque", with its diamond-patterned minaret and lead-sheathed domes. Its thick walls – badly cracked in places – and the configuration of the prayer hall (divided by four columns into nine squares) are typical of the so-called "popular mosques" of the fourteenth and fifteenth centuries, although it's believed that the Dzhumaya might actually date back to the reign of Sultan Murad I (1362–89). It is open most days, and visitors are welcome to inspect the pale blue interior, with its fountain and floral-patterned walls.

Northeast of the mosque lies the old *charshiya*, or **bazaar quarter**, where narrow streets still bear the names of the trades that used to operate from here: ul. Zhelezarska was the preserve of the ironmongers, and Abadzhiiska, that of the weavers and cloth merchants. The name *abadzhiya* derives from *abas*, the coarse woollen cloth that the Plovdiv merchants bought from Rhodopi shepherds before exporting it throughout the Levant. In Ottoman times Plovdiv's commercial district stretched from here northwards to the River Maritsa, and in the sixteenth century the Arab traveller Chelebi counted 880 shops raised "storey above storey". There is little trace of the old crafts and trades today, but the modern ul. Raiko Daskalov is nevertheless lined with shops, banks and cafés, with stalls selling books as far north as the pedestrian subway beneath bul. 6 Septemvri, and clothes stalls right across the footbridge to the north bank of the Maritsa, making it almost as lively as it must have been in Chelebi's day.

Imaret dzhamiya and the Historical and Archeological museums

Just south of the river stand two further relics of Turkish rule. The **Turkish baths** near pl. Hebros were allowed to rot for decades but have recently been restored and now host exhibitions and performances (officially Tues–Sun 1–6pm; 2Lv), while Plovdiv's Muslim community has repaired and reopened the **Imaret dzhamiya**, on ul. Han Krubat (daily from noon for prayers), whose prayer hall contains honeycomb squinches, traces of Arabesque frescoes, and the tomb of Gazi Shahabedin Pasha. The mosque was built on Sultan Bajazet's orders in 1444, and got its name from the pilgrims' hostel (*imaret*) that once stood nearby. Zigzag brickwork gives the minaret a corkscrew twist, jazzing up the ponderous, red-brick bulk of the building, which a frieze of "sawtoothed" bricks and a row of keel arches with tie beams fail to do.

Further west, on pl. Saedinenie, the **Historical Museum** (summer Mon–Sat 9am–5pm, winter Mon–Fri 8am–4pm; 3Lv) houses photographs and documents chronicling the unification of north and south Bulgaria in 1885. Next door, the brand-new **Archeological Museum** (not open at the time of writing) promises to be a treasure trove of Thracian and Roman antiquities from the region including a replica of the gold Panagyurishte treasure contained in the National History Museum in Sofia (see p.98). To the southwest, at ul. Hristo Danov 34 is the **Natural Science Museum** (Tues–Sun 8.30am–noon & 1–5pm; 1Lv), which houses a collection of stuffed wildlife, fossils and minerals (all labelled in Bulgarian).

Old Town

With its cobbled, hilly streets and orieled mansions, Plovdiv's old quarter (most of which is designated an "Architectural-Historical Reserve") is a painter's dream and a cartographer's nightmare. Attempting to follow – let alone describe – an itinerary is impractical given the topography and the numerous **approaches**, each leading to a different point in the quarter. Glimpses of ornate

Old Plovdiv's National Revival architecture

Blackened **fortress walls** dating from Byzantine times can be seen lurking beyond several streets, sometimes incorporated into the dozens of **National Revival-style houses** that are Plovdiv's speciality. Typically, these rest upon an incline and expand with each storey by means of timber-framed oriels – cleverly resolving the problem posed by the scarcity of ground space and the nineteenth-century merchants who demanded roomy interiors. The most prominent oriel on the facade usually denotes the grand reception room inside, while the sides of the upper storeys sometimes feature blind oriels containing kitchen niches or cupboards. Outside and inside, the walls are frequently decorated with niches and *trompe l'oeil* floral motifs and columns painted in the style known as *alafranga*, executed by itinerant artists. The rich merchants who lived here also sponsored many of the artistic developments that made up the Bulgarian National Revival, and much of Plovdiv's cultural role is reflected in the numerous small art galleries and concert venues that crowd into the houses.

facades or interiors tempt visitors to stray down the occasional alleyway or into a courtyard – and generally speaking, that's by far the best way to see the area.

Along ulitsa Saborna

Most people approach the old town from pl. Dzhumaya, from which ul. Saborna gently draws you upward into Old Plovdiv past a succession of well-stocked antique shops. Perched high above the new town and accessible by a flight of steep steps to the right is the **Danov House** (Mon–Fri 9am–noon & 2–5pm; 3Lv), the former home of Bulgaria's first large-scale publisher and now home to a museum of printing. Among the exhibits are rare books from the National Revival period, Danov's personal belongings, and an uninspiring mock-up of a nineteenth-century classroom. Danov was one of those who regarded distribution of the printed word as a patriotic duty, a crucial step in the people's struggle against five centuries of Ottoman rule. He was the founder of Plovdiv's first daily newspaper, *Maritsa*, in 1878 – a title resurrected after the changes of November 1989.

Perched on a bluff just beyond, the imposing **Church of Sveta Bogoroditsa**, with its pink and blue bell tower, is decorated with frescoes of Orthodox saints, and one traumatic scene of chained peasants being threatened by a sword-wielding Turk. It also contains some icons by the Samokov master Stanislav Dospevski. Opposite, in a smartly renovated old trader's house, is the **Philippopolis Art Gallery** (daily 10am–7pm; 2Lv) whose impressive domestic collection includes seascapes by Alexander Mutafov, landscapes by Georgi Kovachev and Tsanko Lavrenov, and works by Svetlin Rusev. Also worth seeing are the furnishings and medallions in the nineteenth-century **Apteka Hipokrat** (Mon–Fri 9am–5pm; free) which has been preserved as a pharmacy museum. It's uphill just past a branch of the **State Gallery of Fine Arts** (Mon–Sat 9am–5.30pm; 3Lv, free on Thurs). The absorbing collection of nineteenth- and twentieth-century Bulgarian paintings includes several portraits by Dospevski and some garish examples of Vladimir Dimitrov-Maistor's work. Ivan Angelov's studies of peasant women and Georgi Mashev's nightmarish, fable-like visions are among the other highlights.

Up some steps to the right after Apteka Hipokrat is the private **Georgi Bozhilov-Slona Gallery** at ul. Knyaz Tseretelev 1 (daily 10am–6pm; 3Lv), which houses a permanent exhibition of the artist's boldly abstract works. Further along ul. Saborna, the spacious **Zlatyu Boyadzhiev House** (daily 9am–noon & 1–6pm; 3Lv) is now a gallery devoted to one of postwar Bulgaria's best-loved painters. Works like *Pernik Miners*, and numerous others romanticizing rural peasant life, show a genuine sympathy for the struggles of working people and won Boyadzhiev the favour of the Party. After a stroke paralysed his right hand, he turned to painting with his left and produced earthier, more mystical pictures like *Dve svadbi* ("Two Weddings") and *Orfei* ("Orpheus").

Just beyond here, at no. 22, the **Museum of Icons** (Mon–Sat 9am–5.30pm; 3Lv) is rich in fifteenth- and sixteenth-century specimens rescued from the region's churches, while next door is the walled **Church of SS Konstantin i Elena** (daily 8am–6pm). The frivolous floral patterns adorning its porch give way to a riotously colourful interior, with the brightly painted geometric designs of the ceiling held aloft by pillars topped with Corinthian capitals. Scenes from the Gospels cover the surrounding walls, and there's a fine gilt iconostasis by Debar master Ivan Pashkula, partly decorated by Zahari Zograf.

Upon leaving the church you can turn left at the **crossroads** to reach the Balabanov and Hindlian houses; go straight uphill past the Ethnographic

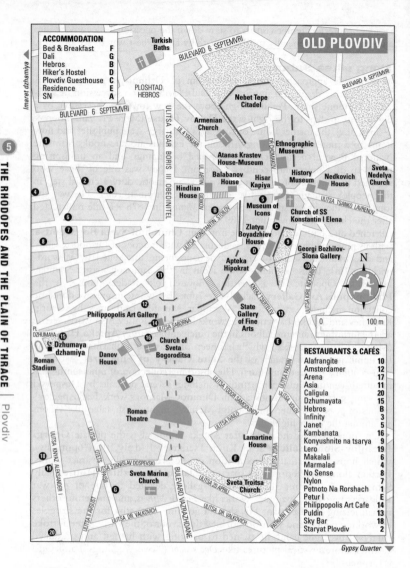

ACCOMMODATION
Bed & Breakfast   F
Dali   G
Hebros   B
Hiker's Hostel   D
Plovdiv Guesthouse   C
Residence   E
SN   A

OLD PLOVDIV

Turkish Baths

BULEVARD 6 SEPTEMVRI

BULEVARD 6 SEPTEMVRI

Imaret dzhamiya

PLOSHTAD HEBROS

BULEVARD 6 SEPTEMVRI

Nebet Tepe Citadel

Armenian Church

Ethnographic Museum

Atanas Krastev House-Museum

Balabanov House

Hisar Kapiya

History Museum

Nedkovich House

Sveta Nedelya Church

Hindlian House

Museum of Icons

Church of SS Konstantin I Elena

Zlatyu Boyadzhiev House

Georgi Bozhilov-Slona Gallery

Apteka Hipokrat

State Gallery of Fine Arts

Philippopolis Art Gallery

N

0   100 m

PL DZHUMAYA

Dzhumaya dzhamiya

Church of Sveta Bogoroditsa

Roman Stadium

Danov House

Roman Theatre

Lamartine House

Sveta Marina Church

Sveta Troitsa Church

RESTAURANTS & CAFÉS
Alafrangite   10
Amsterdamer   12
Arena   17
Asia   11
Caligula   20
Dzhumayata   15
Hebros   B
Infinity   3
Janet   5
Kambanata   16
Konyushnite na tsarya   9
Lero   19
Makalali   6
Marmalad   4
No Sense   8
Nylon   7
Petnoto Na Rorshach   1
Petur I   E
Philippopolis Art Cafe   14
Puldin   13
Sky Bar   18
Staryat Plovdiv   2

Gypsy Quarter ▼

Museum towards the Nebet Tepe Citadel; or turn right and pass under the Hisar Kapiya – as described in the following sections.

Around Nebet Tepe

Turn left at the crossroads then head downhill and you'll come to the maroon-coloured **Balabanov House**, on the corner of Konstantin Stoilov and 4 Yanuari (daily 9am–5.30pm; 3Lv). Once the home of merchant Luka Balabanov, it's now a venue for modern art shows and contains some fine ceilings and a large-scale model of Old Plovdiv. More impressive, however, is the pale blue **Hindlian House** (Mon–Fri 9am–5pm; 3Lv), further downhill at ul. Artin

Gidikov 4. The Hindlians were Armenian merchants who travelled as far as Alexandria, St Petersburg and Venice, hence the cityscapes painted in niches upstairs, where the salon contains a wall fountain that once gushed rosewater. An eclectic collection of furniture from other homes fills much of the house, including two Biedermeier-period sitting rooms packed with trinkets from Vienna. Downstairs, the family bathroom resembles a miniature *hammam*, with a marble floor and fountain. Many of Plovdiv's surviving Armenian families still live nearby, sustaining their identity through an **Armenian church** (Mon–Fri 10am–5.30pm & Sat–Sun 10am–1pm), school and cultural centre, with a monument in the yard recalling the Plovdiv Armenians who died for "Mother Bulgaria" in the Balkan Wars and World War I.

Back at the crossroads, take ul. Dr Chomakov northwards to the summit of the hill on which the Old Town is built, and you'll pass Plovdiv's most photographed building, the **Kuyumdzhioglu House**, named after the Greek merchant who commissioned it in 1847. It was built by Hadzhi Georgi of Constantinople, who combined Baroque and native folk motifs in the richly decorated facade, painted black with a yellow trim, its undulating pediment copying the line of the *kobilitsa* or carrying yoke. Now an **Ethnographic Museum** (Tues–Sun 9am–noon & 2–5pm; 4Lv), the mansion's lower rooms display fine paste jewellery and traditional Rhodopi folk costumes and crafts, a rose-still and a splendid oil painting of Plovdiv streetlife during the nineteenth century. Upstairs is a grand reception hall with a rosette-and-sunburst ceiling, and two rooms furnished with objects reflecting the *chorbadzhii's* taste for Viennese and French Baroque. During the summer, the building plays host to regular **concerts** of classical and traditional folk music.

Further up the street and signposted to the left, the **Atanas Krastev House–Museum** (daily except Wed 10am–7pm; 2Lv) is home to the Red Pony (*Chervenoto Poni*) gallery, which contains modern paintings and sculpture collected by Atanas Krastev (1910–2003). A popular intellectual nicknamed the "mayor of Old Plovdiv", Krastev initiated the renovation of 130 buildings in the Old Town between 1954 and 1986. Old Plovdiv received UNESCO's gold medal for exceptional services to protect European culture in 1974, and Krastev was given the title of Honoured Cultural Worker, and Honorary Citizen of Plovdiv. Also on show here are portraits of Krastev by various Bulgarian modernists.

At the top of ul. Dr. Chomakov, beyond some derelict nineteenth-century houses, lie the overgrown ruins of the **Nebet Tepe Citadel**, marred by graffiti and rubbish. Although it's difficult to discern precise features among the pits and rubble, the site is archeologically rich. Fortified by the Thracian Odrysae tribe as early as the fifth century BC, the hilltop and the settlement of **Eumolpios**, below, were the beginnings of modern Plovdiv, captured by Philip II of Macedon in 342 BC. Philip ordered the former to be rebuilt in tandem with the new town – modestly named Philippopolis – which his son, Alexander the Great, abandoned in search of new conquests in Asia. Over the following centuries, the inhabitants must have often resorted to the secret **tunnel** linking Nebet Tepe with the riverbank, as the town and citadel were sacked by Romans, Slavs, Bulgars, Byzantines and the Ottomans, to name but a few.

From Hisar Kapiya to the Roman theatre

Turn east at the crossroads, around the corner from the Church of Sveti Konstantin i Elena, and you'll pass under the gloomy-looking **Hisar Kapiya** or "fortress gate", which has been rebuilt countless times since Philip II of Macedon built it to form the citadel's eastern portal. Beyond the gate, it's the structure rather than ornamentation that makes the the **Georgiadi House** on ul. Tsanko Lavrenov, home to the **Museum of History** (closed for renovation at the time of writing), so remarkable: the architect has combined "box" oriels with bay windows on a monumental scale. Built for a rich Turk in 1846–48, the mansion contains a gallery where musicians once played, plus various salons dedicated to Bulgaria's liberation from the Turks. Pride of place is given to replicas of the bell that tolled and a cannon that fired during the April Rising, when the *bashibazouks* (see p.482) hung Plovdiv's streets with corpses that the Turks forbade people to bury, so that locals would be reminded of the penalties for rebellion. The next-door **Nedkovich House** (Mon–Fri 9am–5.30pm; 3Lv) contains an impressive collection of nineteenth-century furnishings.

The alleys running downhill behind the Georgiadi and Nedkovich houses lead to several **craft workshops** and many humbler dwellings that have yet to be renovated despite their obvious architectural merits. The only exception is the recently restored **Church of Sveta Nedelya** on the left, a three-aisled basilica that contains a delicately carved wooden iconostasis and bishop's throne. Walk further down Lavrenov and at the end of the road you'll come across yet more sadly neglected and rubbish-strewn **Roman remains**. It's difficult to make out much, although the recumbent columns, Corinthian capitals and large, ornate fragments of shattered entablature indicate a civic building of some size and importance.

Just beyond, the dusty roads and shabby houses mark the beginning of Plovdiv's Gypsy quarter. Most visitors, however, head south from here along ul. Kiril Nektariev, one of old Plovdiv's best roads: few facades can match that of the house at no. 15, embellished with swags, medallions and intricate tracery in a vivid shade of blue. Follow Nektariev to the end (the far end of the road is known as ul. Paldin), and you'll arrive at the Mavrudi House, popularly referred to as the **Lamartine House** after the French poet who stayed here in 1833. A large buff-coloured mansion with dozens of windows and sturdy ribs supporting the oriels, it's at the corner of Knyaz Tseretelov and Todor Samodumov.

Ulitsa Tsar Ivailo continues west from here to the **Roman theatre** (daily 9am–5pm; 3Lv), whose stands provide a wonderful view of the distant

▲ Roman Theatre, Plovdiv Old Town

Rhodopes, and a splendid venue for **concerts and plays**. Unearthed during the 1970s, it once seated six thousand spectators. Only twenty of the amphitheatre's original 28 rows of carved marble seats have survived, though it still holds up to three thousand for major events such as the International Folk Festival (see p.334). These imposing ruins are practically the only remains of an acropolis that the Romans built when they raised Trimontium from the position of a vassal town to that of provincial capital during the second century AD. The acropolis, like the residential districts below, was devastated by Kiva's Goths in 251, and later used as building material when the town revived. From here, paths descend to bul. Vazrazhdane, at the point where it enters the tunnel beneath the hill, beside which stands the walled **Church of Sveta Marina** (entered from ul.s Dospevski or Dr Valkovich). The church has boldly coloured murals beneath its porch and beguiling devils, storks and other creatures peeping out from the wooden foliage of its intricate iconostasis.

Southwest of Old Plovdiv

As well as the three hills covered by the old town, there are three more heights ranged across the southwestern quarter of Plovdiv. The one nearest to the centre, **Sahat Tepe**, provides a great view of the city, and the site for what some believe is the oldest **clock tower** in eastern Europe, restored by the Turks in 1809, with an inscription enjoining visitors to "look upon" it "and admire!" From here one can gaze across to the giant **Soviet Army Memorial** nicknamed "Alyosha" (which Plovdiv's SDS Mayor wanted to remove but couldn't afford to) on the **Hill of the Liberators**, which also has a pyramidal monument to the liberators of 1878 on a lower peak, where a Thracian temple dedicated to Apollo once stood. Further to the southwest lies the **Hill of Youth**, the largest and most park-like of the three.

Eating

Plovdiv is full of kiosks and cafés selling coffee, *hamburgeri*, sandwiches and other **snack food**, especially along Otets Paisii and Knyaz Aleksandar I, where you'll also find a McDonald's (the first to open in Bulgaria) at no. 42. For fresh fruit and veg, there's an outdoor **market** known as the Polnedelnik pazar on pl. Vazrazhdane, to the east of Otets Paisii, and a larger one near the junction of bul.s Ruski and 6 Septemvri, west of pl. Saedinenie.

The choice for evening **meals** is equally wide. Some of the most stylish places are in the National Revival-style houses of Old Plovdiv. They are expensive by native standards, but still affordable to most visitors, if you don't mind splashing out 20–40Lv a head for a first-class meal. Restaurants tend to open between 10am and noon and close around midnight.

Lower Town

Adisa A popular, three-outlet chain serving an excellent selection of cheap, ready-prepared Bulgarian dishes at ul. Opalchenska 4 in the centre, ul. Ivan Vazov 98 opposite the train station, and ul. Ibar 31 opposite the Plovdiv Fair.

Amsterdamer ul. Konstantin Stoilov 10. Atmospheric reproduction of a Dutch restaurant serving dishes from a reasonably priced international and Bulgarian menu.

Asia bul. Tsar Boris 58. Plovdiv's best Chinese restaurant serves a good standard of cuisine in a large oriental-themed building at mid-range prices.

Diana bul. Vazrazhdane. This lively restaurant, on several levels of a nineteenth-century house with a palm-filled garden, serves good mixed grills and fish at moderate prices and is one of the town's only 24hr eateries.

Evridika ul. Zlatyu Boyadzhiev 2. One of the *Novotel's* restaurants, this is a truly stylish affair with curved ceilings and floors creating a pod-like environment. Expect high standards and high prices; pheasant, rabbit and paella feature on the menu.

Gusto ul. Otets Paisii 26. Smart Italian restaurant serving a wide range of quality pasta, pizza and fish dishes at reasonable prices.

Happy ul. Patriarh Evtimii 13. Part of a national chain that serves a reliable and affordable variety of Bulgarian and international dishes from a pictorial menu.

Hemingway ul. Gurko 10. Classy and pricey restaurant and bar with Serbian meat specialities, plenty of Black Sea fish, and live acoustic music after 8pm.

K2 ul. Tsaribrod 6. Free Wi-Fi Internet attracts lunching professionals to this modern central restaurant where diners choose dishes such as lasagne and steak from an international and reasonably priced menu.

Kopcheto bul. Vasil Aprilov 7. *Kopcheto*, which translates as "the button", is a popular, above average spot that aspires to French gourmet standards and offers a vast array of wines to complement a menu offering duck and rabbit among many other dishes.

Lero ul. Knyaz Alexandur 32. Fashionable place on the top floor of a shopping centre with a great roof terrace. Modern interior design by a local artist, polite service and delicious food make it worth the price.

Odeon ul. Otets Paisii 40. Part of the *Odeon* hotel, this restaurant is an expensive high-class affair popular with business diners. International and Bulgarian cuisine.

Opera General Gurko 19. An inexpensive garden restaurant serving a limited range of quality Bulgarian and Turkish dishes. Daily noon–midnight.

Pri Lino bul. 6 Septemvri 135. A lavishly decorated place situated in a converted mosque with a good standard of moderately priced Bulgarian and international cuisine.

Staryat Plovdiv ul. Yulio Curi 6A. Inexpensive eatery with outdoor terrace, good service and excellent Bulgarian food.

Twin Peaks bul. Vasil Aprilov 18. A local favourite. Affordable traditional-style restaurant serving some good Rhodopean specialities.

Old Town

Alafrangite ul. Kiril Nektari 17. Superb National Revival-style restaurant in an atmospheric nineteenth-century mansion. Live music takes place every night in the fig-shaded courtyard. Mid-range prices.

Hebros ul. Konstantin Stoilov 51. Considered one of Plovdiv's finest restaurants. The above-average prices charged for the limited menu (20–40Lv per main dish) are justified by high standards of cuisine and service.

Janet ul. 4 Yanuari. Located in an atmospheric old house with indoor and outdoor seating and a good range of slightly pricey Bulgarian and international dishes.

Kambanata ul. Saborna. Modern a/c restaurant built into a cellar beneath the Church of Sveta Bogoroditsa. The affordable menu features snails and other oddities, besides all the usual native dishes. Daily noon–midnight.

Konyushnite na tsarya ul. Suborna. Cheap outdoor eatery with a simple menu and a pleasant location just behind Zlatyu Boyadzhiev House. Bands play fairly frequently on the outdoor stage.

Petur 1 ul. Knyaz Tseretelev 11. Extravagant and expensive Russian-style restaurant in the lavish *Old Town Residence* hotel with sweeping views from its terrace.

Philippopolis Art Cafe ul. Saborna 29. Smart outdoor café next to the art gallery overlooking the town and offering a mid-range menu of light dishes.

Puldin ul. Knyaz Tseretelev 3. Located on the site of a Christian monastery that was later converted to Dervism, the building oozes history. A wonderful traditional-style restaurant complete with water features, rustic furniture and subdued lighting is hidden away far below the entrance. Above average prices.

Drinking

As elsewhere in Bulgaria, you can snatch a quick **coffee** or **fruit juice** almost anywhere in the downtown area from breakfast time until after midnight – and the same goes for drinking alcohol, whether you're talking beer, vodka or cocktails.

Cafés and bars

Arena Pleasant outdoor café in Old Plovdiv next to the Music Academy and overlooking the amphitheatre.

Atlas ul. Knyaz Alexandur 41. Great spot for coffee or cocktails. Outdoor seating and three indoor floors with wonderful high ceilings.

Bezisten ul. Naiden Gerov 5. Small, busy bar just off ul. Knyaz Alexandur I. Bare brick walls and a few decorative objects provide a backdrop for rock and retro tunes. Open until 11pm.

Blues ul. Preslav 29. A smoky basement bar just around the corner from the *Blue Heaven Inn*. Stays open late and has an English-language snack menu.

Dreams Knyaz Aleksandar I 42. Trendy and continually busy place serving up coffee, cakes and ice cream, with extensive outdoor seating on the edge of pl. Stephan Stambolov.

🏃 **Dzumayata** ground floor of the Dzumaya mosque. Excellent modern café serving traditional Turkish coffee and sweets right by the mosque entrance.

Kino Orphea ul. Todor Kableshkov. Laid-back outdoor café serving coffee and cocktails. During summer the neighbouring open-air cinema shows films daily at 8pm.

Maria Louisa bul. Maria Louisa 15. Stylish arty bar on two floors, with basement DJ at weekends.

🏃 **Nylon** ul. Benkovski 8. Unsigned bar opposite *Makalali*. The most underground of Plovdiv's venues, its rock music, murky interior and live bands attract a lively crowd.

Red Eye ul. Gladston 8. Tiny but incredibly popular bar with a staple diet of rock and retro crammed into the first floor of a rickety old building.

Simfoniya Tsar Simeon Garden. Very popular 24-hour terrace restaurant and bar beside the "musical fountain", offering light meals and an extensive drinks menu. Also has a children's play area.

Sky Bar ul. Knyaz Alexandur 32. Sleek outdoor cocktail bar with white leather sofas and plasma video screens overlooking ul. Knyaz Alexandur I. An accompanying nightclub is due to open in the near future.

Entertainment

Although much of the city's nightlife revolves around well-advertised *chalga* or commercial folk music clubs such as *Budoar, Maritsa* and *Escada*, there's also a thriving rock, retro, and dance scene to be found in a number of small clubs and bars; check the weekly *Programata* guide (see p.321) for the latest events. Over the summer also try the outdoor disco next to the rowing lake (*grebnata baza*) in Loven Park, 5km west of the centre, which is a popular hangout. You can get there on bus #5 or #15 but will need to take a taxi back.

Clubs and live music

Budoar bul. Maria Louisa 3. Expensive *chalga* club with lavish furnishings. DJs most nights with occasional live performances.

Caligula Knyaz Aleksandar I 30. Gay nightclub which puts on regular transvestite shows and stays open until 6am.

Emona ul. bul. Vasil Aprilov 52. Funky spot with leather sofas, a dance floor, and plenty of retro hits with a bit of mainstream techno.

Escada ul. Tsarevets 1A. Kitsch *chalga* club with three floors pumping out Balkan and Western commercial pop.

🏃 **Gepi** ul. Lady Strangford 5. Vibrant bar-cum-club with frequent live music as well as retro, dance, jazz, and Latino nights.

Infinity ul. Bratya Pulevi 4. Medium-sized dance club that fills up quickly at weekends.

Makalali ul. Benkovski 7. African tribal-style club with requisite zebra-striped stools and bamboo structures. Plays house music until late for a lively crowd.

Maritsa ul. Tsar Boris III 42 (*Maritsa* hotel). Massive and well-established *chalga* club that plays the cheesiest of Bulgarian commercial folk music till 6am.

Marmalad ul. Bratya Pulevi 3. A well-established bar-cum-club with bare brick walls and stylish furnishings. Features live bands, karaoke and dance nights.

No sense ul. Evlogi Georgiev 5. Immensely popular club that's full most nights thanks to the DJ policy of playing something for everyone.

🏃 **Petnoto na Rorshach** ul. Yoachim Gruev 36. Regular DJ nights and live local bands in a suitably underground setting.

Plazma ul. Hristo Botev 82. Large dance club playing commercial house and techno until 2am.

Puzela ul. Bratya Pulevi 1. Legendary basement club that hosts regular gigs by local rock outfits.

Music

Plovdiv takes its culture seriously, and hosts a comprehensive programme of music all year round. Unfortunately, there's no centralized office where you can find out what's on and events are simply publicized by banners or posters – invariably in Bulgarian only. **Classical concerts** take place at the Plovdiv Philharmonic Orchestra's concert hall on the south side of pl. Tsentralen, while the Mesalitinov Theatre at Aleksandrovska 36 is the best venue for **drama**.

There's a busy schedule of festivals too. During the first half of January, the **Winter Festival of Symphony Music** allows the Philharmonic Orchestra to flex its muscles, while international virtuosi participate in the prestigious **Festival of Chamber Music**, held in the courtyard of the Ethnographic Museum in June every odd-numbered year (native ensembles play on until Sept, and during even-numbered years). **Trakiisko lyato** ("Thracian summer") in August features pop and classical music, as well as **folk dancing** ensembles from as far away as Egypt, performing in the spectacular surroundings of the Roman theatre – which is also used for staging **opera** and **drama** in May and September (coinciding with the fairs). A particularly lively event is the annual **Night of the Galleries and Museums** on the last Friday of September, when the town's galleries and museums open their doors to the public from 7pm until 3am and street performances and outdoor concerts provide entertainment for the curious crowds.

Listings

Airlines Tickets for all airlines serving Bulgaria are available at the Plovdiv Airport office at ul. Gladstone 8 (☎032/631537), Fortuna 7 at ul. Benkovski 1 (Mon–Fri 9am–6pm; ☎032/622595 or 628929, ⊛www.fortuna7.visa. bg), and Astral Holidays' offices at ul. Otets Paisi 24 (☎032/626608, ⊛www.astralholidays.com).

Books and newspapers There's a foreign-language bookshop at ul. Tsaribrod 1 opposite the mosque. A stall on the pl. Tsentralen sells foreign newspapers.

Buses Eurolines has an office (⊛www.hebrosbus .com) immediately behind the *Hotel Trimontium Princess* at ul. Krali Marko 4 (Mon–Sat 9am–6pm; ☎032/269652). At the Yug bus station, Hebros Bus (daily 5.30am–midnight; ☎032/626916) is an agent for Eurolines, and sells tickets for western European destinations as well as Greece and Turkey; Metro (daily 8am–midnight; ☎032/267879)

books seats on daily services from Yug bus station to various Turkish cities.

Car rental Rent-a-car, at ul. Vasil Levski 14 ☎032/969666; Drenikov, at bul. Maritsa 98 ☎032/650042. The tourist information centre also arranges car rental.

Car repairs Opel, north of the river at bul. Vasil Aprilov 158 ☎032/940898.

Consulates Greece, at Preslav 10 ☎032/632003, ⓔgrconsfil@evrocom.net; Turkey, at Filip Makedonski 10 ☎032/632309, ⓔtcbk_filibe @plovdiv.ttm.bg.

Dentist Odesay Dentist at bul. Ruski 102 ☎032/643543.

Hospital Sonel Farma Medical Centre, at bul. Hristo Botev 47A ☎032/632094.

Football Plovdiv has two first-division teams: Botev and Lokomotiv. Botev, currently the city's premier outfit, play at the Hristo Botev stadium east

Moving on from Plovdiv

From Plovdiv there are frequent trains to **Sofia** plus two daily expresses to **Burgas** and one to **Varna**. Reaching **central or northern Bulgaria** often entails a change of trains at Stara Zagora, but direct services run to Karlovo, Asenovgrad and Hisar.

Travelling to **Turkey** from Plovdiv, the Balkan Express runs daily trains to Istanbul throughout the year (8hr 30min), while an additional service, the Istanbul Express, operates between May and September. If travelling to **Greece**, there's a connecting service to Thessaloniki at Svilengrad (12hr). You can buy tickets at the railway bookings office on bul. Hristo Botev (see "Listings", above).

Hebros Bus (see "Listings", above) offers daily **buses** to Thessaloniki (14hr), and Athens (23–26hr), and daily services to Istanbul (6hr). Metro (see "Listings", above) also runs daily services to Istanbul as well as less frequent services to Izmir (8–10hr), Bursa (7–8hr) and other destinations in Turkey.

of the centre on bul. Iztochen (trolleybus #3 from the station), and have a hard core of supporters, known as the "Canaries Ultras", with a reputation for violence. Some of them are linked to far-right groups. The Lokomotiv stadium is farther south off bul. Sankt Peterburg, and best reached by taxi.

Internet Zeon next to the Roman Stadium below pl. Dzhumaya; open 24hr.

Pharmacies Kamea, next to Union Bank at bul. 6 Septemvri 76, is open 24hr.

Police ul. Knyaz Bogoridi 7 ☎032/932239.

Post office pl. Tsentralen 1 (Mon–Sat 7am–7pm & Sun 7–11am).

Telephones At the post office on pl. Tsentralen 1 (daily 7am–10pm)

Train tickets Domestic and international bookings from Rila/BDZh, opposite the train station at bul. Hristo Botev 31A (Mon–Fri 8am–6pm, Sat 8am–2pm; ☎032/643120).

Websites ⊛www.plovdivcityguide.com and ⊛www.plovdiv.org are two of the more useful sites.

Plovdiv to the Turkish border

There are good reasons why so many visitors travel between Plovdiv and Turkey nonstop. The settlements along the way are mainly workaday places lacking in specific attractions, and there are more facilities for travellers along the E80 than there are off the highway.

Travelling **by road** you'll pass **Klokotnitsa** village, just west of Dimitrovgrad, the site of Ivan Asen II's victory (1230) over Theodor Comnenus, the usurper of Byzantium, that forced the empire to recognize Ivan as "Tsar of the Bulgarians and Greeks" and accept the betrothal of his daughter to Baldwin, the teenage emperor of Byzantium. Approaching the border **by train** means a brief encounter with Dimitrovgrad – full of power stations and reeking chemical factories – before speeding on to Svilengrad and the Turkish border or catching a bus or train south to Haskovo and Kardzhali.

Haskovo

Little visited by tourists except as a stopover en route to Turkey, **HASKOVO** (ХАСКОВО), 78km southeast of Plovdiv, has the dubious honour of being home to the country's largest cigarette factory, although textile production is gradually replacing the town's declining tobacco industry. The place has slightly more to offer than first meets the eye, hosting festivals throughout the year and serving as a springboard for visiting the **nature reserve** at Madzharovo (see p.363). Aside from that, its appeal lies in the faintly raffish mixture of Turkish and Bulgarian culture, symbolized by the oldest mosque in the Balkans and a smattering of National Revival buildings. The town was founded in around 1395 and named Haskoy by the Turks, who predominated here for the next five hundred years until the development of the tobacco industry and the Balkan War of 1912 swelled the number of Bulgarians, who now form the majority. Relations between the two are good, however, with both communities represented in local politics.

The Town

Civic and social life revolves around **ploshtad Svoboda**, a T-shaped junction of flagstones, flowerbeds and fountains centred on a memorial to the dead of successive wars. The **History Museum**, on the junction's southern arm (Tues–Sun 9am–noon & 2–5pm), contains a fine collection of pre-Ottoman artefacts – especially Roman, Byzantine and medieval **coins** – but passes over five centuries of Turkish rule in relative silence; the tobacco workers' strike of 1927 gets more attention.

A block or so south towards the river, a graceful minaret rises above the **Eski dzhamiya** (Old Mosque), whose facade has been replastered so that it's hard to believe that this was the first mosque erected on the Balkan peninsula, immediately after the Ottoman conquest. Even during the 1980s, when mosques elsewhere in Bulgaria were locked and derelict, Haskovo's remained in use, its prayer hall covered in carpets and its imam unfazed by foreign visitors, who are nowadays more welcome than ever.

Follow bul. Balgariya beside the River Haskovska (or take bus #1, #12 or #102) to find the **Church of Sveta Bogoroditsa**, a simple basilica of heavy brick filled with fussy woodcarving. By crossing over the road bridge and heading back towards the centre just off Tsar Osvoboditel you can also visit the fairly uninspiring range of nineteenth- and twentieth-century works on display in the **art gallery** housed in the Paskalevata kashta, at ul. Episkop Sofroni 3 (officially Mon–Fri 9am–noon & 2–5pm; free). This period-furnished house was the birthplace of Aleksandar Paskaliev, a pioneer of Bulgarian publishing.

The wooded **Park Kenana** to the north of town is a favourite place for recreation, with tennis courts, restaurants and cafés; catch bus #2 or #102 from pl. Spartak, on the north bank of the bend in the river. Just south of the river on the edge of Mladezhki Halm Park is the towering marble **Virgin Mary Monument** (*Monument Sveta Bogoroditsa*), erected in 2005 as a symbol of Haskovo. On the last weekend in May special buses are laid on to take people to the **Gathering of Beautiful Trakiya** (*Sabor Krasiva Trakiya*), a festival of folk groups from the southeastern Rhodopes and Aegean Thrace. Two other events for music lovers are the three-day **Jazz Festival** in late September or early October, and the **Festival of Symphonic Music** at the end of October. During the first week of June the town hosts a **Theatre Festival** with street entertainers and performances from the country's best theatre groups. Lastly, the festival of **Young Poets** (late April) celebrates new poetic talent, while the **Haskovo Fair** (around Sept 8) is a week-long festival with a variety of cultural events. The website Ⓦwww.haskovo.net is a useful source of information.

Practicalities

From the **bus station** on bul. Saedinenie, ten minutes east of the centre along ul. San Stefano, there are hourly buses to Kardzhali, Svilengrad, Plovdiv and Sofia, but the most useful are the two daily buses to Madzharovo – enabling one to reach the nature reserve there (see p.363). There are also six daily buses to Istanbul. The **train station**, 1.5km further out along bul. Saedinenie (bus #5, #12 or #13), is of less use.

The best-value **hotels** in town are the smart *Rodopi* at bul. Balgariya 39 (℡038/609660; ❷) or the stylish *Central* at ul. Varna 1 (℡038/660333; Ⓦwww.geocities.com/hotel_central_haskovo; ❷). The three-star *Haskovo* at ul. Vasil Drutenel 20 (℡038/602525, Ⓦwww.hotel-haskovo.com; ❸) offers higher standards for half the price of the glass-fronted *Diamond Plaza* at bul. Bulgaria 83 (℡038/605500, Ⓦwww.hotel-diamond-plaza.com; ❻). If you've got your own transport, the modern *Bulgaria* (℡03722/2404; ❸) in the small spa resort of Haskovski Mineralni Bani, 20km from town (also accessible by bus every two hours from Haskovo), has comfortable accommodation, hot pools, a sauna and fitness facilities; it's just by the crossroads as you enter the resort.

There's no shortage of places **to eat and drink** around pl. Svoboda. One that's highly rated is the *Gurkovata kashta*, in an old house in the Bulgarian quarter with a garden, which can be reached from the Church of Sveta Bogoroditsa by heading up ul. Berkovski and turning right into General Gurko. It charges around 20Lv for a three-course meal, and stays open until midnight. In the centre at ul. Otors Paisi 23, the *Orient* serves decent Turkish cuisine on the second floor. Late-night entertainment is provided by *Club Exclusive* on pl. Svoboda.

Svilengrad and the borders

Despite its proximity to two busy border crossings, **SVILENGRAD** (СВИЛЕН-ГРАД) is a pretty dozy place. There's little specific to see save the sixteenth-century **Mustafa Pasha Bridge** – known to the locals as *Stariya Most* – which links the town with village-like suburbs on the far bank of the River Maritsa. This 295-metre-long structure of Karabag stone supported by thirteen arches is an even finer achievement than the Gurbav Bridge in nearby Harmanli. There's a surprising range of **accommodation** in the town, of which the best are the comfortable *Central* on the main square (☎0379/70320; ❸), which boasts an English-themed pub, and the Greco-Roman-style *George*, just off the square at ul. Septembritsi 2 (☎0379/71797; ❸).

Worth a visit if you have a car are a couple of antiquities near the village of **MEZEK** (МЕЗЕК), 10km southwest of town, reached by turning off near the truck park for the Greek border crossing. Just before the village, a road to the left leads past an abandoned army base to a **Thracian tomb**, 21m long and corbel-roofed, like the stairway in the Great Pyramid, with a circular funerary chamber (where bronze artefacts were found, from the fourth century BC). If you find the tomb locked, ask staff at the municipality office in Mezek (Mon–Fri 8.30am–noon & 1–5.30pm) to open it. About 1km beyond Mezek, the ruined **Neutzikon fortress** (or *Kaleto*) is the best-preserved of the many fortresses raised to guard against Byzantine incursions during the eleventh and twelfth centuries. Both languish in a so-called *granichna zona*, or **border zone**, which used to be strictly off-limits in Communist times and is still patrolled by border police, nowadays engaged in keeping refugees out rather than Bulgarians in. You'll be expected to produce your passport if you're stopped. Comfortable **accommodation** is available at the *General Complex* (☎0889/566667 or 0888/201166; ❷) where several air-conditioned bungalows overlook a tennis court and the village below.

Crossing into Greece or Turkey

Svilengrad's **train station** is 5km west of town, with irregular buses to and from the centre, so travellers heading for Turkey should either stay aboard the train from Plovdiv and skip Svilengrad entirely, or be sure to leave plenty of time to get to the station to catch a train to Istanbul around 2am. Trains to Alexandroupoli in Greece run daily, while the 24-hour **road crossing into Greece**, 2km nearer town than the station, is used almost exclusively by truckers.

Far more traffic crosses the **Turkish border** at **KAPITAN ANDREEVO** (КАПИТАН АНДРЕЕВО), 15km east of Svilengrad (nine buses daily), where vehicles entering Bulgaria are liable to rigorous examinations. Inside Turkey (where motorists and train passengers undergo customs at Kapikule), it's pretty easy to catch a *dolmus* (shared taxi) to **Edirne**, 19km east, which should drop you in the centre near the town's splendid mosque; the bus station is 3km to the southeast and the train station 2km further out.

The Rhodopes

According to Thracian mythology, the mortal lovers Hem and Rhodopis dared call themselves after the divine Zeus and Hera, who duly punished the couple by turning them into mountains separated by the River Maritsa – him the Balkans and she **the Rhodopes**. Straddling Greece and Bulgaria, the Rhodopes are the land where panpipes, Orpheus and the Orphic Cult originated, a region rich in gems and ores, but otherwise not fit for much beyond raising sheep and growing tobacco. Unlike the rest of Bulgaria, whole communities converted to Islam after the conquest, and of the numerous Turks who settled here many outstayed the empire's collapse – their descendants now constitute Bulgaria's largest ethnic minority. While hydroelectric schemes and tourism have pushed the Rhodopes into the twenty-first century, the region is still, as Leslie Gardiner noted in the 1960s, a weird mixture of opposites: "donkeys and turbo-generators, Alpine flowers and tropical foliage, bikinis in winter and thick Turkish woollens in summer".

The legacy of history is far from abstract here, as Bulgarians recall five centuries of oppression epitomized by the massacre at **Batak** in 1876, while the Pomak (Slav Muslim) and ethnic Turkish inhabitants of the Rhodopes have living memories of the "name-changing campaign" and "Great Excursion" of the late 1980s, when more than 200,000 of them fled to Turkey (most later returned). Though it's partly due to the state's efforts to hide what was happening in the region that the Rhodopes remained *terra incognita* for so long, even in olden times road-builders were sometimes attacked by villagers, who preferred to be as remote as possible – as the Turks living between **Krumovgrad** and **Ivailovgrad** still do.

While the ski resort of **Pamporovo** and the **Bachkovo Monastery** are well known to foreigners, the region's scenic highlands and picturesque villages have only been "discovered" quite recently. Of all Bulgaria's mountain ranges, this is the best for **walking** (the central and western Rhodopes especially), **caving** (around Trigrad), **birdwatching** (near Madzharovo) and other special interests. The Rhodopes are also home to some fantastic folk music and **festivals** (mostly in August) at Shiroka Laka, Rozhen, Dorkovo and Madzharovo. Shiroka Laka is deservedly renowned for its traditional architecture, though the finest examples are at the Agushev Konak at **Mogilitsa**, near the regional capital, **Smolyan**. In the eastern Rhodopes, **Kardzhali** can serve as a base for exploring the recently discovered 4000-year-old temple and fortress at **Perperikon**, the lesser but equally fascinating ruins at **Tatul**, and the weird rock formations of the region; its museum has a fine collection of folk costumes, gemstones and historical artefacts.

Organized tours

Should you wish to join an **organized hiking tour** in the region, contact the Sofia-based adventure tourism agency ZigZag Odysseia-In (ⓦwww.zigzagbg.com; see p.75), whose Rhodopes itinerary includes Mostovo, Krastova Gora, Manastir, Rozhen, Progled and Trigrad, and can be extended into the Pirin and Rila mountains if desired. Tours booked abroad through a foreign operator are likely to be handled by **SunShine Tours** (ⓦwww.sunshinetours.net), also based in Sofia.

Tourist facilities and public transport vary from good to nonexistent, though the recent growth in **private hotels** is gradually reaching most areas. While a car provides greater flexibility, there's enough public transport and accommodation for you to be able to visit almost all of the region's attractions, given sufficient time. **Buses** from Plovdiv run to Bachkovo, Pamporovo and Smolyan in the central Rhodopes, Velingrad to the west, and Kardzhali to the east; while Madzharovo can be reached from Haskovo. With the exception of the scenic narrow-gauge line linking Septemvri on the plain with Bansko in the Pirin Mountains, the limited **train** service in the Rhodopes is of little use.

The central Rhodopes

The northernmost spurs of the Rhodopes rear up from the plain barely 10km south of Plovdiv, with numerous minor roads running up the narrow valleys of the streams that gush down to feed the Maritsa. The main route south into the **central Rhodopes**, however, starts beyond the town of **Asenovgrad**, and follows the ruggedly beautiful valley of the River Chepelarska past the historic **Bachkovo Monastery** up to the ski resorts of **Chepelare** and **Pamporovo**, before descending to **Smolyan**. This road is well served by bus, unlike those in other parts of the highlands, where you need a car to get around or enough time to go walking. The scenery in this region is magnificent and there are enough villages offering accommodation to support all kinds of hikes around **Mostovo**, **Manastir** and **Progled**.

Asenovgrad

Half-hourly buses speed across the dusty plain between Plovdiv and **ASENOVGRAD** (АСЕНОВГРАД) 20km south, a light and breezy town built around a large park. **Train and bus terminals** lie on the northern outskirts, from where it's a short walk through a park and across the river to a modern town square. Two church spires are visible on the hill immediately above: the resplendently ochre-coloured Sveti Dimitar on the left and the smaller Sveta Troitsa on the right. More interesting, however, is the town's main shopping thoroughfare running south from the square, where a small **Historical Museum** (Tues–Sun 8am–noon & 1–5pm; 1Lv) holds local Neolithic and Thracian finds, including a fine bronze helmet and the iron wheel rims of a Thracian chariot.

It was the Thracians who first fortified a crag overlooking the entrance to the Chepelarska gorge, which can be reached by a side road 2.5km south of town. If it seems a hard slog, remember that the thirteenth-century **Church of Sveta Bogoroditsa** just below the summit was rebuilt by a disabled man who walked every day to work on his self-appointed task. Higher uphill are the **remains of** a **medieval fortress** founded during the eleventh century and enlarged after Asen II's victory over the Byzantine Empire in 1230, half of which slid down the hill some years ago.

If you want **to stay**, you could try either the two-star *Hotel Asenovets* on the main square (☎0331/62127; ❷), or the comfortable *Cosmos* at ul. Saedinenie 18 (☎0331/22004; ❸), though you'd do better to take one of the regular buses up the valley towards Bachkovo, Chepelare or Smolyan and find accommodation there.

Bachkovo Monastery and around

Nine kilometres south of Asenovgrad, the village of **Bachkovo** (БАЧКОВО), with its stone houses overgrown with flowers, gives no indication of what to expect 1.5km further up the road at **BACHKOVO MONASTERY** (*Bachkovski manastir*; daily 7am–8pm; free). Gardiner's description of it as "a mixed bag of buildings – chapels, ossuaries, cloisters, cells – daubed with frescoes more naive than artistic" doesn't do justice to Bulgaria's second largest monastery, which is under consideration for UNESCO World Heritage Site status. It was founded in 1083 by two Georgians in the service of the Byzantine Empire, one of whom, Grigoriy Pakuryani, renounced the governorship of Smolyan and Adrianople to devote the remainder of his life to meditation.

You enter the monastery through a small iron-plated door which opens onto a cobbled courtyard surrounded by wooden galleries. There are also a couple of fountains, where locals and pilgrims fill up their plastic bottles. The wall of the refectory on the left is covered with **frescoes** providing a narrative of the monastery's history: they show Bachkovo roughly as it appears today, but watched by God's eye and a celestial Madonna and Child, with pilgrims proceeding to a hill in the vicinity to place icons. Other frescoes depict the slaying of the dragon: a powerful archetype in ancient European mythology, repeated in the image of the Thracian Rider. It can also be read as an allusion to the Turks who destroyed Bachkovo in the early sixteenth century, and the patient restoration of the monastery by the Bulgarians.

Though it's not immediately apparent, the monastery consists of two separate courtyards connected via the wing containing the seventeeth-century **refectory** (*trapeznitsa*; 6Lv entrance, guided tour 5Lv extra), whose vaulted hall is decorated with a *Tree of Isaiah* and a *Procession of the Miraculous Icon* executed by pupils of Zahari Zograf. If the gate into the second courtyard is open, you can view one of Bachkovo's churches, **Sveti Nikolai**, whose porch features a fine *Last Judgement*, which includes portraits of the artist Zograf and two colleagues in the upper left-hand corner.

The oldest building in the monastery is the principal church, **Sveta Bogoroditsa**, built in 1604. Frescoes in the porch of its bell tower depict the horrors in store for sinners: among the scenes of retribution, a *boyar* (a medieval nobleman) is tormented on his deathbed by a demon dangling a doll-like figure over him (presumably representing the man's ailing soul), while women watch in horror. The entrance is more cheerful, with the Holy Trinity painted on strips set at angles in a frame, so that one sees God or Christ flanking a dove, depending on which side you approach from, like a medieval hologram. On the right of the nave as you enter is a fourteenth-century Georgian **icon of the Virgin**, which legend claims to be an authentic portrait of Mary, painted by the Apostle Luke. The icon plays a central role in celebrations of the name-day of the Assumption of the Virgin (August 15), and a ritual procession to a chapel in the nearby hills 25 days after the Orthodox Easter (see p.50).

Walks around the monastery

If you want to make more of your visit, there's a pleasant thirty-minute walk to a shrine near the spot where Bachkovo's treasures were once hidden from the Turks – a deed commemorated by an annual procession of believers bearing an icon. The path begins opposite the monastery gates and passes by the **church of Sveta Troitsa**, which contains early medieval frescoes and life-size portraits of Tsar Ivan Aleksandar (1331–71) and his family who endowed the monastery, but is kept locked to protect them from looters. Don't be led astray by the red arrows near the picnic meadow, fifteen minutes or so further on. Instead take

▲ Bachkovo Monastery

the path straight ahead across the meadow, which leads shortly to a sign marking the **Chervenata Stena nature reserve** of Balkan plant species, and a chapel built beside a stream, on the far side of which rock-cut steps lead to a cave chapel and a stone-built one: the three are collectively known as **Ayazmoto**.

The **trail** continues upwards via dramatic waterfall basins (traversable only in summer on ladders made of branches) and punishing switchbacks (known as the "Forty Legs"), to the *Martsiganitsa* chalet with dorm beds for 14Lv per person – a strenuous but exhilarating three- to four-hour trek. From the chalet, an easier path leads back down to the road a few kilometres past the monastery in the direction of **Narechenski Bani** (НАРЕЧЕНСКИ БАНИ). This small resort with open-air mineral baths makes a good base for exploring some more delightful trails into the foothills, which abound in butterflies, insects, fungi and rare herbs; if you're lucky, you might even see a spotted eagle.

Practicalities

An easy day-trip from Plovdiv, the monastery can be reached by any of the hourly **buses** to Chepelare or Smolyan, as well as hourly services from Asenovgrad to Bachkovo, which run past the monastery drive. It's hard to find out the exact times of buses returning (there's usually one every hour until about 5pm), so you may be in for a wait, though minibuses between Smolyan and Plovdiv sometimes pick up passengers here.

In the vicinity of the monastery are three **restaurants**, the best of which is *Vodopada*, whose patio is centred on a little waterfall gushing out of the hillside. There are also a number of snack stalls selling drinks and ice cream. You can **stay** in the monastery's guest "cells" (☎03327/277; ❸) or in a dormitory (❶), but you must be back before the gates close at 8pm. Across the river the *Eco* hotel (℡03327/343; ❸) has clean doubles, while further on, the *Dzhambura* (℡03327/320, Ⓦwww.djamura.com; ❷) offers more comfortable and attractive rooms as well as a good restaurant. The next available accommodation is 14km farther on in **Narechenski Bani**, which also has two decent hiking chalets, plenty of private rooms (❶; ask around at the bus station), the friendly *Lyubina* hotel and restaurant (℡0334/2240; ❸) and two local tavernas serving delicious traditional food.

Three kilometres beyond Narechenski Bani is a turning to the tiny village of **Kosovo**, surrounded by forest and full of tumbledown houses that are gradually being renovated. The *Hadzhiskata kashta* (℡0334/2333 or 0888/150352, Ⓦwww.selokosovo.com; ❹) overlooks the village and has been lovingly restored. The owners organise hiking and horse riding and can collect guests from Narechenski Bani.

Hikes around Manastir

About 40km south of Bachkovo, **MANASTIR** (МАНАСТИР), 1500m above sea level, is the highest village in Bulgaria and (they say) the Balkan peninsula. With its steeply terraced houses, potato and tobacco plots, stacks of firewood and scampering goats, Manastir makes a good base for hiking and gives a feel of rural life in the Rhodopes. The easiest way to get here is on the daily **bus** (at 5pm) from **Laki** (ЛЪКИ), 20km north.

One of the best hikes from Manastir is to **Progled**, a trip which can be done in three to four hours, but is far nicer stretched out with an overnight stay at a hiking chalet; you'll need the Rhodopi map 1:100,000 published by Cartographia (Ⓦwww.cartographia-bg.net) available at bookshops and Zig Zag Odysseia-in (see p.75). The trail begins behind Manastir, with blue and white markers starting at a fountain five minutes' walk uphill, from where it's fifteen minutes to a flat, stony track where you bear right into the woods after 500m to find an old Roman road. Another twenty minutes brings you to a junction of trails, a blue one to the *Svoboda* and a red one to the *Prepsa* chalet. The latter passes a beautiful clearing of fallen pines and purple thistles and is easy-going all the way, so that you arrive at *Prepsa* two and a half hours after setting out, in the mood to press on to *Svoboda* (2hr) or westwards to Haidushki polyani (35min) and the *Momchil Yunak* chalet (1hr more).

Haidushki polyani ("Outlaws' Meadows") is a trade union resort where you can sink a beer before examining an obelisk in the woods, on the spot where leaders of the Macedonian revolutionary movement decided to launch the 1903 Ilinden uprising. The partisan figures on the obverse side typify the Communist Party's efforts to identify itself with past liberation movements. Sporadic red and white markers indicate the trail from here to *Momchil Yunak*, with dorm beds for 15Lv per person, a basic chalet near an ex-Party villa that's now the *Starata Kashta* hotel (℡03095/8765; ❷). From here it's twenty minutes' walk to the main road; if you're heading to **Progled**, simply stay on the main road, and follow it downhill for 11km.

Practicalities

There's no shortage of places **to stay** in any of the villages mentioned above. In **Manastir**, your best bet is with the Angelovi family (℡030528/289; ❶), the Petrovi family (℡030528/292; ❶), or the Kolevi family (℡030528/233; ❶), all of whom provide breakfast, and serve delicious home-cooked Rhodopean dishes. The bar-grill on the square can rustle up surprisingly good **meals** and sometimes has music and dancing.

South of Bachkovo, there are some superb **hikes** amidst stunning mountain scenery, which can be tackled by arranging for a driver to drop you at one location and pick you up elsewhere – a strategy which can also be applied to longer hikes involving an overnight stay at the *Svoboda* chalet or Manastir (see opposite). Such **buses** as exist in the region centre on the ugly mining village of **Laki**, 24km south of Bachkovo, with one a day from Plovdiv and four from Asenovgrad, plus local services to Belitsa (two daily) and Borovo (one daily). All the walks described below are covered by Cartographia's Rhodope maps (ⓦwww.cartographia-bg.net).

One of the most rewarding walks in the area is to the summit of **KRASTOVA GORA** (КРЪСТОВА ГОРА; "Hill of the Cross"), a place of pilgrimage for centuries until the Communists suppressed it, but now revived. Its holiness derives from a fragment of the True Cross that was sent for safekeeping to Bachkovo after the fall of Constantinople, and transferred to a monastery here after Bulgaria was invaded by the Turks. After the Ottoman yoke was lifted, a cross was erected on the summit weighing 99 kilos (three times the age of Christ when he was crucified) and the **Sveta troitsa** church was built with stones from the original monastery. Legend has it that if a pregnant woman enters the church she can choose the sex of her child. Traditionally, pilgrims spend the eve of *Krastovden* (September 14) camped out on the mountain, before greeting the sunrise with a special liturgy devoted to health. Spartan dorm beds are available for 10Lv per person.

Krastova Gora is accessible from the village of **BOROVO** (БОРОВО) off the road to Laki, which has a number of guest houses; the *Villa Princesa* (ⓣ0899/016186; ❶) has sweeping views of the valley and a communal kitchen, while the *Borikite* (ⓣ0331/28412, ⓦwww.borikite.bol.bg; ❷) has a pleasant garden and excellent home-cooked food. A nicer approach is to walk there from **MOSTOVO** (МОСТОВО), on the other side of the hills. The village's name derives from a natural rock bridge (*most*) in the gorge below, where the river vanishes underground – you can see it before entering Mostovo, then pick up the **trail to Krastova Gora** near the top of the village, on ul. Hristo Smirnenski. Initially a steep goat track that divides after 45 minutes, the path to Krastova Gora is clearly signposted and walkable in just over an hour – providing you turn right upon emerging from the woods. By turning left instead you'll be on the **trail to Velichki Vrah**, passing an ex-Party hunting lodge en route to the **Karadzhov Kamak** (1hr 30min) – colossal rocks dimpled with giant "fingerprints" and topped with the ruins of what's thought to be a Thracian temple. A further hour brings you to a clearing where the trail starts descending; an hour and forty minutes later you face a brief, taxing ascent of a ridge called the **Rodopskoto konche** ("Rhodope Horse"), before reaching a forestry road down to Perleza, a good place to be met if you're not up to carrying on to the *Svoboda* chalet (a further two hours). Also well worth a visit are the face-shaped rocks and Thracian remains above the tiny hamlet of **BELINTASH** (БЕЛИНТАШ), which lies 10km along the dirt track to Tri Mogili after Mostovo and is served by a daily bus from Asenovgrad. The hospitable owners of *Kashta Chotrovi* in Belintash (ⓣ0889/375 418) offer dorm accommodation for 8Lv per person, as well as good food and useful local information.

OREHOVO (ОРЕХОВО), a quiet village of ageing stone-roofed houses, lies 7km off the main road, midway between Bachkovo and Chepelare, and is famed for its male folk ensemble. *Kashta Rai* (ⓣ03053/2737; ❷) offers cosy wood-panelled rooms in an eco-house constructed from traditional building materials. The village hosts a folk music festival on the last weekend of July, and the bagpipe-playing owner of *Kashta Rai* can arrange impromptu performances for those interested.

Six kilometres after Chepelare is **PROGLED** (ПРОГЛЕД), a village perched on the side of a steep hill with pricier accommodation reflecting its proximity to Pamporovo. Of the small chalet-style family hotels (whose prices tend to halve in summer) try the *Priroda* (℡03095/8879; ❸), the equally comfortable and very friendly *Sarievi* (℡03095/8588; ❸), or *Kushta Milushevi* (℡03095/8809; ❸). All have satellite TV and rent ski equipment. The village also boasts a surprisingly classy restaurant, the *Progledski Hanche*, which is open 24 hours.

Chepelare, Progled and Zabardo

The small mountain town of **CHEPELARE** (ЧЕПЕЛАРЕ), 6km north of Progled, is popular with Bulgarians who want somewhere quiet to relax and enjoy the fresh air and scenery, and are unfazed by such blots on the landscape as a timber mill or the Orion ski factory – the only one in Bulgaria. Aside from its **ski run** – at over 5km, the longest in the Rhodopes – the only specific attraction is the well-signposted **Speleological Museum** (officially Tues–Sat 9am–5.30pm, but hours variable) that whets your appetite to visit the local caves. Some "cave pearls" from the Yagodina Cave (see p.354) are its most prized exhibit.

Chepelare has many new **hotels**. The *Rhodopski Dom* is a huge five-star affair (℡03051/3529, Ⓦwww.pmk-bg.com; ❺); the smart *Agarta* at ul. Bor 2 (℡03051/4408, Ⓦwww.hotelagarta.com; ❸) is smaller and better value, offering doubles, triples and maisonettes with luxury furnishings. ✸ *Shoky* at ul. 24 Mai 70 (℡03051/3343; Ⓦwww.hotelshoky.com; ❸) is a friendly family-run hotel whose English-speaking owners are qualified ski instructors and mountain guides. *Ivan*, at ul. Progres 6 (℡03051/3113; ❷), *Martin*, at ul. Kiril Madzharov 23 (℡03051/2194; ❸), and *Savov*, at ul. Devech 7 (℡03051/2036; ❷) are of a decent standard for the price, with satellite TV and en-suite bathrooms; all rent out ski equipment and can arrange bus transfers to Pamporovo. Although there's no tourist information office, a free telephone and map marked with hotels is positioned opposite the post office. The best **restaurants** in which to enjoy Rhodope specialities, and a roaring log fire, are the *Gergana* and *Gorski Kat*, both moderately priced; for pizza and cakes try the *Vienska Salon* on the main square. **Nightlife** revolves around the *Zdravets* disco, also on the main square, which plays a mix of commercial dance and folk music all night long.

In a valley off the main road, 28km northwest of Chepelare, **ZABARDO** (ЗАБЪРДО) is the best-known **weaving** village in the Rhodopes, and home to the colourful rugs and blankets that abound in the region. Here, you can buy a *kozek* (the local word for a rug) from individual weavers, and watch them at their work. Unusually for what is a predominantly Pomak (Slav Muslim) village, Zabardo has a **folk music festival** on the Day of the Assumption (August 15). With a car, you can also visit the so-called **Miraculous Bridges** (*Chudnite mostove*), rock formations that form a natural bridge over a narrow stream, created when an earthquake destroyed a cave. Near the second bridge is the entrance to the Icy Cave, which remains below freezing even in summer, while close by is the Big Cave, where pottery fragments dating from the sixth century BC have been discovered. The bridges are sited in another side valley, accessible by a fork in the road to Zabardo. Simple **accommodation** is available at the *Chudnite Mostove* chalet (℡03059/3261; ❶), which also has a small restaurant.

The great outdoors

Bulgaria boasts so much varied and unspoilt countryside that no single visit could fit it all in. The interior is dominated by the fir-clad peaks of the Balkan range, while the alpine scenery and glacial lakes of the Rila mountains, and the curious rock formations in the south, are major draws. Numerous uncultivated wilderness areas provide excellent wildlife habitat: white storks, deer and wild boar are among the creatures you're more likely to see, although wolves, lynx and brown bears also frequent the more inaccessible highland areas.

The mountains

Inland Bulgaria is dominated by a series of dramatic mountain chains that offer some of the most exciting hiking opportunities in Europe (see overleaf). The **Pirin mountains**, in the southwest, are the wildest and most picturesque, with 45 peaks over 2590m, deep valleys, karst massifs and glacial lakes. To the north, the **Rila mountains** are awash with magnificent coniferous forests and wild flowers; here Mount Musala (2925m) stands as the highest peak in southeastern Europe. Both these ranges abut the **Rhodopes**, with a mixture of pine forests, crags, highland meadows and villages of stone houses. All three ranges are crisscrossed by well-maintained, well-marked paths, with a network of mountain huts, or *hizhi*, providing basic but cosy accommodation.

Pirin National park ▲

Mushroom stone rock, Kardjali ▼

Rock formations

Bulgaria is scattered with some startling rock formations, with some of the most accessible at **Belogradchik** (see p.185 and cover image). Changing from red to grey to purple according to the light, the sandstone rocks have been carved by wind and rain into tortured shapes, many of which have names suggestive of the animated, organic forms they seem to have adopted ("the Nun" or "the Schoolgirl"). Equally captivating is the *pobiti kamani* or "Stone Forest" just west of **Varna** (see p.373), where pillars of chalky stone up to seven metres high were once considered evidence of some antique civilization. The most famous formations are the sand pyramids at **Melnik** (see p.158), where steep-sided tawny-coloured pinnacles of rock loom eerily above gulleys carved by seasonal floods.

Wetlands

Bulgaria is rich in wetland environments, especially along the banks of the Danube and in the lagoons and lakes neighbouring the Black Sea coast. Teeming with fish and insects, these are ideal feeding and nesting grounds for migrating birds – of which over four hundred species pass through Bulgaria in spring and autumn. The marsh-shrouded lakes Poda and Mandra are famous for their marsh harriers, nuthatches and herons; while the reed-shrouded lakes between Shabla and Durankulak attract cormorants and red-breasted geese. One of the richest habitats for wading birds in southeastern Europe, the UNESCO-listed Lake Srebarn (see p.207), offers ideal conditions for greylag geese, mute swans and Dalmatian Pelicans – who have a thriving breeding colony there.

▲ River Kamchiya meeting the Black Sea
▼ Yagodina Cave in the Rhodope Mountains

Caves

Bulgaria is something of a paradise for cavers, with innumerable caverns and potholes hollowed out of the porous limestone of the Balkan and Rhodope mountains. There's also a handful of spectacular show-caves fitted with walkways and modern lighting, including the popular Ledenika (see p.178), which takes you through a sequence of huge chambers and tight passageways, passing some awesome stalagmites and stalagtites – including the 4.5-metre-long "Mother In Law's Tongue". More enigmatic still are Magura's cave paintings (see p.187), executed in bat droppings some four millennia ago and showing Bulgaria's stone-age inhabitants hunting and dancing. Deep in the karst terrain of the southern Rhodopes is the Yagodina (see p.354), which also shows signs of prehistoric settlement in the shape of makeshift huts and kilns.

Vulture-watching at Madzharovo

Griffon vulture with Egyptian vulture in background ▲

Swans near Varna ▼

With its forests of pine and spruce, alpine meadows, crags and gorges, **Madzharovo** (see p.363) in the eastern Rhodopes is one of the wildest and most beautiful regions of Bulgaria. It is also home to 32 of all 34 species of birds of prey found in Europe, with the cliffs of the Arda Gorge just outside town providing the perfect breeding ground for three types of vulture – the Egyptian, Griffon and Black. Vulture-watching at the Madzharovo nature reserve isn't your standard ornithological experience, as vultures are ugly, vicious creatures that feed on carrion; their intestinal systems have evolved to handle any microbe nature can throw at them. Enjoying protected status as a nature reserve since 1994, the Arda gorge at Madzharovo also boasts eight kinds of falcons and nine kinds of woodpecker as well as black storks, bee-eaters, olive-tree warblers, and several species of bats.

Top five hikes

▸▸ **From Zlatni mostove to Boyana** Admire the weird and wonderful Stone River before returning to suburban Sofia via meadows, wooded ravines and waterfalls. See p.102

▸▸ **From Lovna Hut to the Seven Lakes**. Ascend the pine-covered slopes of the Rila Mountains to these extraordinary glacier-gouged lakes. See p.133

▸▸ **Melnik to Rozhen monastery**. Scramble your way up into the otherworldly landscape of Melnik's sand pyramids. See p.162

▸▸ **Karlovo to the Stara Reka gorge**. Climb from Karlovo up into the ravine-scarred heart of the Central Balkan National Park. See p.288

▸▸ **Trigrad to Yagodina**. Traverse dramatic karst-scapes and lush highland meadows in the western Rhodopes. See p.354

Pamporovo

PAMPOROVO (ПАМПОРОВО), the "Gem of the Rhodopes", has been undergoing intensive development in recent years, mostly in the form of massive luxury hotel and apartment complexes that are springing up at an astonishing rate. One of the most popular destinations for package tours, it's become known as the "Sunny Beach" of winter tourism and is frequently overrun with groups of English and Irish tourists on cheap holidays who party rowdily most nights. That said, it's a stunning location, and is still a user-friendly ski resort where mild weather and good snow-cover make skiing conditions near perfect from mid-December to mid-April, with a range of classes and pistes to suit everyone from absolute beginners to the pros. Over summer it is marketed as a mountains-and-lakes resort, with a number of organized walking and cycling tours on offer – though hikers would do better elsewhere – but in May and from September until the start of the skiing season Pamporovo is pretty forlorn, with only a few hotels and facilities open.

Buses drop you at the junction of the Plovdiv to Smolyan road and the slip road to the main complex of hotels. The beginners' slopes are just below the outlying *Malina* chalet complex, reached by bus or a thirty-minute walk from the centre of the resort. **Equipment** can be rented here, at the bus depot, or at the Studenets waystation (accessible by chair lift from *Malina* or the bus station). Chair lifts also run from Ardashlar (just below *Malina*) and from Studenets to the 1926-metre-high summit of Mount Snezhanka, the starting point of many of the **ski runs**. Advanced skiers can take a draglift from Studenets up the side of "The Wall", the most difficult and demanding run at Pamporovo.

The **TV Tower** on Mount Snezhanka (daily 9am–4.30pm) has a café and an observation gallery with a marvellous view of the Rhodope Mountains and, on clear days, parts of the Pirin and Rila. It also makes a useful landmark for hikers. Twenty minutes' walk from here, the **Orpheus Rocks** (*Orfeevi Skali*) overlook a superb panorama of the mountains surrounding the Smolyan Valley.

Accommodation

As independent travellers are charged considerably more for rooms, tuition and equipment than people on **package holidays** (and they might find that everything's booked up anyway), would-be skiers are strongly advised to take one of the cheap deals offered by foreign tour operators (see p.33), plus the optional "ski pack" which covers all rentals and lift rides. If you do just turn up on spec, the *Finlandia* (☎03095/8367, ⓦwww.hotelfinlandia.com; ❻), *Perelik* (☎03095/8405, ⓦwww.pamporovoresort.com; ❺) and *Snezhanka* (☎03095/8316; ❻) are the least expensive hotels and include breakfast and use of swimming pool and fitness facilities. The ⌖ *Malina Village*'s chalets with underfloor heating and satellite TV (☎03095/8388, ⒺΜmalina.villages@mail.bol.bg; ❻ with four people sharing) work out to be the cheapest beds at the resort. For a touch more luxury, you could try the plush *Orlovets* (☎03095/9001, ⓦwww.pamporovoresort.com; ❽) or the pristine *Grand Hotel Murgavets* (☎03095/8310, ⓦwww.murgavets-bg.com; ❽). You could also stay in Chepelare (see opposite) or down the valley in Smolyan (see p.346), from where there are regular buses up to the pistes of Pamporovo during the winter season. If you have your own transport, the tiny village of **STOIKITE** (СТОЙКИТЕ), 5km to the west, has its fair share of **private rooms** available from its tourist office on the main square (officially Tues–Sat 9.30am–12.30pm & 3–8pm; ⓦwww.stoikite.com). The *Sveta Elena* hotel (☎03095/8570; ❸), 3km above the village, has more comfortable accommodation.

Eating and drinking

Traditional Rhodope dishes like spit-roasted lamb (*cheverme*), stuffed vine leaves (*sarmi*), white bean stew (*Smolenski bob*) and a local variation on the cheese-filled *banitsa* are on offer at central "folk-style" **restaurants** such as the *Chanove* and *White House* – and at the restaurant of the *Rhodopa Tourist* hotel in the village of Stoikite – all of which feature music and dancing. Otherwise **entertainment** consists of the usual après-ski parties and bar crawls, and discos in the larger hotels till the small hours.

Momchilovtsi

Around 6km to the east lies **MOMCHILOVTSI** (МОМЧИЛОВЦИ), though it's best reached by bus from Smolyan, a further 8km south. Set on a steep slope with gorgeous views in all directions, it's certainly a very peaceful place: on a hazy summer afternoon the silence is interrupted only by the occasional cock-crow and the intermittent buzzing from the couple of saw mills, which still form an important part of the village economy. Though Momchilovtsi may, at first glance, seem little more than a rustic backwater, it's also a popular retreat for wealthy Bulgarians, and in recent years there's been a spate of building work, with modern apartments and villas arising amongst the chicken-coops and wood sheds. There are a few family-run hotels scattered around, including the *Shipkata*, at ul. Stamboliiski 22 (☎03023/2204; ❷) and the *Rodopchanka*, at ul. Byalo More 40 (☎03023/2863; ❷), both of which have cosy, traditionally furnished rooms. The eponymous *Momchilovtsi*, just down the road from the bus station (☎03023/2311; ❷), is a smart modern place offering large, comfortable apartments sleeping either three or four people, and has its own restaurant. You can also rent bikes and book private rooms (❶–❷) and hotel accommodation through the local **tourist office** (Mon–Fri 8.30am–5pm; ☎03023/2240, at weekends call ☎0888/147991). There's a small local history **museum** just below the main square, as well as an **art gallery**, both of which can be opened by staff at the tourist office.

Nine kilometres away, next to the *Momchil Yunak* chalet (see p.342), is a recently opened **snowboard park** with jumps and slopes, where you can rent equipment from 30Lv per day.

Smolyan

A conglomerate of three villages (Smolyan, Raikovo and Ustovo) that stretches for 15km along the banks of the River Cherna, **SMOLYAN** (СМОЛЯН), the administrative and cultural capital of the central and western Rhodopes, embodies Communism's attempt to mould the mixed Christian–Pomak agrarian population of Bulgaria's southern margins into the urbanized citizens of a modern socialist state. Situated 1000m above sea level, it's one of the highest towns in Bulgaria, which means that the climate in summer is a lot fresher and more bearable than much of the rest of the country. Attractively squeezed between pine-clad peaks, the modern housing estates perched above the centre have maintained something of the region's traditional highland architecture, giving the whole place a rural feel, underscored by the goats and piles of logs in the backstreets.

Arrival and information

Smolyan has two bus stations, at opposite ends of town. Coming from Sofia, Plovdiv or anywhere north or west you'll probably **arrive** at Avtogara Smolyan on ul. Minyorska, just downhill from the upper end of bul. Balgariya, which runs down into the centre. You can walk it in ten minutes or wait for buses #1, #2 or #3, which run from one end of Smolyan to the other via the modern centre, terminating at Avtogara Ustovo, the station that serves Kardzhali and other points east. However, some buses from Plovdiv that bypass Pamporovo and come via the Rozhen Pass arrive at Ustovo, while private buses from Plovdiv drop passengers outside the *Hotel Smolyan*, smack in the centre, every hour.

Beside the hotel, the helpful **tourist information centre** (Mon–Fri 9am–5.30pm; ℡0301/62530, ⓦwww.smolyan.com) can advise on trips and activities in the Smolyan region and books **private rooms** (❶–❷).

There are two **post offices** (both Mon–Fri 8am–6pm, Sat 8am–11pm), one on bul. Balgariya, next to the *Olimp* café, and another in the administrative complex, just around the corner from the **telephone office** (daily 7am–10pm). **Internet** access is available next to the museum (see p.348).

Accommodation

Just a couple of minutes' walk from Avtogara Smolyan is ⚐ *Triti Eli*, approached down a flight of steps from bul. Balgariya at ul. Srednogorets 1 (℡0301/6862, Ⓔ Dreitannen_h@yahoo.com; ❷), a small, family-run place with a friendly English-speaking owner who's a mine of local information and also runs guided coach tours around the region. The *Babylon*, located uphill at ul. Han Presian 27 (℡0301/63268, Ⓔbabylon@digsys.bg; ❷), is a bigger establishment with its own restaurant. The large three-star *Hotel Smolyan* is a little out of the way at the bottom of bul. Balgariya (℡0301/62053, ⓦwww.hotelsmolyan.com; ❸), but has comfy rooms with TV and bath, as well as a restaurant, bar and pool. Next door is the bright red *Kiparis Alfa* at bul. Balgariya 3 (℡0301/64040, ⓦwww.hotel-kiparis.com; ❹), a new complex with smart air-conditioned rooms, Wi-Fi, a spa centre and fitness facilities.

Alternatively, you could base yourself in the picturesque mountainside suburb of **Smolyanski Ezera**, where several small lakes surrounded by crags and forests provide a setting for the *Smolyanski Ezera* mountain chalet (℡0301/63458; ❶) and the *Panorama* **campsite** – accessible by bus #4 from Avtogara Smolyan – which enjoys a truly spectacular view and is open all year. Accessed by a rough track is the cosy family-run *Villa Chapov* (℡0301/64286; ❷), which rents out bikes and snowshoes and provides

The Rozhen Observatory and festival

Visible for miles around, the lofty white dome of **Rozhen Observatory** contains a mammoth optical telescope manufactured at the Zeiss works in Germany, which has scanned the cosmos since the 1970s. The site was chosen because of the clear skies and absence of background light; besides the main telescope, there are three smaller ones on other hilltops. As they only work at night, people who take the trouble to fix a **visit** (book in advance on ℡03021/8357) are denied the thrill of stargazing, but may still enjoy the telescope and its vintage early 1960s computer hardware, which is mainly used for checking astronomical maps.

The Rozhen peak near the observatory is the setting for the largest folklore festival in the Rhodopes – the **Rozhenski sabor** – where almost every village in the area is represented by dancers, singers or musicians. It's usually held on the last weekend in August, but check with the tourist office in Smolyan to be sure (see above). One or two buses a day from Plovdiv cross the Rozhen Pass en route to Smolyan (and vice versa), running past the slip road to the observatory, or you can walk here from Progled in an hour cross-country (or a couple of hours along the road).

transport to the ski lifts; the nearby *Pamporova Kushta* (℡0301/68043, Ⓦwww.pamporov.hit.bg; ❷) is equally attractive.

You could also stay in the charming, laid-back little town of **SMILYAN** (СМИЛЯН), halfway between Smolyan and Mogilitsa. The number of private rooms and small hotels in Smilyan is increasing each season, and the best of these is the *Dairy Inn* (℡03026/2241; ❸), which, as its name suggests, is attached to a working dairy, where guests can sample some of the milk and cheese made here, or even try their hand at working some of the machinery. You could also try the spotless *Dangulevi* (℡03026/2356; ❶) just along the road. The only time when rooms may be scarce is during the annual **Milk Festival**, on the last weekend of August, when local cattle breeders parade their finest beasts, dressed in flowers, beads and bells, to compete for the coveted title of "Miss Cow". Another local outfit, run by a British couple, offers a range of outdoor activities in the region that can be booked through either Ⓦwww.balkantraks.com or Ⓦwww.bulgarianventures.net.

The Town

A four-lane boulevard carrying so little traffic that its overhead walkway is practically redundant runs through the **civic centre**, passing a lead-domed **planetarium** whose shows (Mon–Sat; Ⓦwww.planetarium-sm.org; 5Lv) are available in foreign languages once a day at 2pm and include footage from Rozhen Observatory (see p.347). The post office, the town hall, the Rhodope Drama Theatre and other public buildings are all massed on the hillside, in a sprawling concrete complex which also houses a couple of cafés and a supermarket.

Several flights of steps behind the post office lead up to Smolyan's **History Museum** and **Art Gallery** (both Tues–Sun 9am–noon & 1–5pm; 5Lv). The museum has a superb collection of artefacts from the Bronze Age onwards, including a restored Thracian helmet with elaborate cheek-guards, and "secret" Christian gravestones resembling Muslim ones but carved with crosses underneath. There's also a large collection of traditional local instruments, such as bagpipes (*gaidi*) and lutes (*tamburi*), and colourful carpets (*chergi*) and tufted goat's-hair rugs (*halishta*) – all of which are still manufactured around Smolyan. Best of all are the grotesque *kukeri* costumes; fashioned from animal skins and adorned with horns, wooden swords and belts of cow bells, they are worn by celebrants at New Year in the Rhodope and Pirin regions. Another room on the top floor is devoted to photos and models of traditional architecture in villages such as Shiroka Laka and Mogilitsa – especially the Agushev konak (see opposite). The **art gallery** across the way is likewise worth a visit, with Rhodope landscapes by Dechko Uzunov and Vasil Barakov, Nensko Balanski's iconic *Woman with a Cup of Coffee*, and temporary exhibitions of graphics or photography. Perhaps because of their elevated position, neither place appears to receive many visitors and you may have to knock to gain access.

Moving on from Smolyan

Chances are you'll be catching a **bus** out of Avtogara Smolyan, which not only serves Plovdiv but Laki (see p.342), Mogilitsa (see opposite), and Devin in the western Rhodopes. Except for the 5.30am service via the Rozhen Pass, all buses to Plovdiv pass through Pamporovo and Chepelare. If you're heading towards Kardzhali, you can take a state bus from Avtogara Ustovo. There are also **minibuses** from *Hotel Smolyan* to Plovdiv and Ustovo to Kardzhali.

The older quarters of town contain a few more sights such as a sixteenth-century **mosque** that's visible on the way in from Pamporovo; the National Revival-style **Pangalov House** on ul. Veliko Tarnovo (not open to visitors); the churches of **Sveta Nedelya** and **Sveti Todor Stratilat** in Raikovo; and **Ustovo**, which, in parts, still resembles the village it once was, sited higgledy-piggledy on the hillsides around the confluence of the Cherna (Black) and Byala (White) rivers.

Eating and drinking

Bulevard Balgariya is lined with **restaurants** and pavement **cafés**, such as the *Otmora* at no. 35, which serves a good range of national and international dishes and offers some splendid mountain views from its terrace. Perched high above the town at ul. Snezhanka 16 is the *Riben Dar*, a fish restaurant with over a hundred different dishes. There are numerous places to **drink**, including *Café Luxor* at no. 51, which does a good range of cakes and cocktails, and *Starata Kashta*, a National Revival-style house dating from 1840, reached by steps up from the main drag at ul. Studenska 2. **Nightlife** in Smolyan consists of commercial pop and folk at *Topstars*, and slightly better dance music at *Buksy*. Both are on bul. Balgariya.

Mogilitsa, Arda, and Gorna Arda

Having seen the model of the Agushev konak in Smolyan's museum, you may want to check out the original in the otherwise unremarkable village of **MOGILITSA** (МОГИЛИЦА), 26km south of town. You can do this in a day by taking the bus from Avtogara Smolyan terminal to Arda (the next village up the valley), which stops in Mogilitsa en route, then catching the bus back to Smolyan. Alternatively, you could catch the evening Arda bus, and stay at the *Babachev Guest House* (☎03036/330; ❶) or the *Golevi kashta* (☎0887/438389; ❶), both in Mogilitsa, and visit the konak next day. The owner of the latter is a hiking guide and arranges horse riding. Alternatively you could stay at the *Milchovata kashta*, perched on a hill in the tiny hamlet of **Bukata** immediately to the east (☎03036/297; ❶). The *Milchovata* arranges horse riding, bike rental and wood carving demonstrations, as does Mogilitsa's tourist information centre (officially daily 9am–5.30pm; ☎03036/331 or 315).

The **Agushev konak** is no longer open to the public, but can be viewed from outside. It's a splendid example of the fortified manor houses built by rich Rhodope merchants in Ottoman times, when villages like Mogilitsa owned vast herds of sheep and were far wealthier than today. As the largest sheep-owners in the region, the Agushevs could afford to build a winter residence in Mogilitsa (1812–42) and a summer one in the hills (which hasn't survived). Divided into three walled compounds (for Agushev's household and the families of his eldest sons), the complex is visually unified by its thick slate tiles and pinnacled chimneys, with latticed screens designed to preserve the privacy of the women's quarters while allowing air to circulate (it has 86 doors and 221 windows altogether).

Just 3km east of Mogilitsa, at **Sinite virove** ("the Blue Pools"), is the stunning **Uhlovitza Cave** (Wed–Sun 9am–5pm), one of twenty or so in the Mogilitsa region, and best known for its curious rock formations. The bus from Smolyan to Arda will stop nearby. **Arda** itself is a tranquil village 6km south of Mogilitsa and has a small tourist information centre (officially Mon–Fri 9am–noon & 1–5pm; ☎03028/235 or 0889/651232). The *Kashta Argirovi* guesthouse (☎03028/466, ⓦkyshti-argirovi.com; ❷) offers comfortable accommodation with shared bathrooms and excellent food. They also organize hiking, mountain biking and horse riding in the region. From Arda a narrow road winds its way 2km to the remote hamlet of **Gorna Arda**, which sits next to the Greek border and consists of homesteads scattered between potato and bean fields still ploughed by horses. The neatly renovated guesthouse *Bilyanska kashta* (☎0887/638974; ❷) occupies a lovely spot high above the village, while lower down is the homely *Kosovi kashta* (☎0889/445331 or 0887/415188; ❷). Its owners also run the *Geranitsa Komplex*, a fairytale assortment of wooden buildings, waterwheels, swings and hammocks in the woods just short of the border. It's a great place to kick back for a while. Guests can sleep at the complex in cosy rooms (❶) and can feast on a range of Rhodopean dishes including plenty of grilled meat and fish. There are several good walks in the vicinity.

The western Rhodopes

Despite an average altitude of only 1000m, the western Rhodopes offers some of the finest **walking** in Bulgaria. The perfectly proportioned gorges and crags are covered with aromatic pines and spruces, with lizards and bluebirds flashing among the rocks, as hawks and eagles soar overhead. Around **Trigrad** there are some fabulous caves such as the Devil's Throat, plus there's an annual bagpipe festival at the picturesque villages of **Shiroka Laka** and **Gela**.

Shiroka Laka makes a popular excursion from Pamporovo or a pleasant stopover en route to the sleepy hill towns of **Devin** and **Dospat**. From Dospat you can head north to the historic town of **Batak** and on to the spa resorts of **Velingrad** and **Yundola** – which can also be reached by bus from Plovdiv, or on the narrow-gauge railway running between Septemvri and the Pirin mountain town of Bansko. Unfortunately, public transport in the region is particularly poor, with infrequent and unreliable bus connections. Unless you have plenty of time – and patience – you would do better to rent your own transport; if you do get stuck somewhere, though, **hitchhiking** is a common and acceptable option, for tourists and locals alike.

Travelling through the region you're struck by the degrees of separation between its Christian and Pomak (Slav Muslim) inhabitants, with some villages exclusively one, others a mixture of both. Broadly speaking the area is Christian as far west as Devin but the majority of villages thereon are Pomak. While a mosque or a church is an obvious sign, many Pomak villages weren't allowed to build mosques during Communist times and have only begun to do so recently. Most feature a boxy prayer hall and a white pencil-minaret in the Ottoman style. Although Pomak women cover their heads and bodies, this stipulation is variously interpreted in different villages: some wear a headscarf (*zabradka*) and a long dress or pantaloons (*shalvari*), with others sporting a white wimple and a dun-coloured smock, or even a half-veil (*feredzhe*).

Shiroka Laka and around

SHIROKA LAKA (ШИРОКА ЛЪКА), nestling in the deep and narrow valley of the Shirokolashka River, is a popular destination for coach parties from Pamporovo, wanting to see a genuine Rhodope village. Its name means "broad meadow", and with its humpbacked bridges and asymmetrical half-timbered houses topped by their distinctive flagstone tile roofs, this remarkably unspoilt settlement of two thousand people could have been lifted off a postcard. The advantage of coming on a tour is that you get to see a performance by local musicians at the **National School of Folklore Arts** – something you would miss should you turn up on spec. The **Sgurovski konak** (containing the local Ethnographic Museum; 9am–noon & 1–6pm; closed Wed; 2Lv) is another local attraction and gives an idea of life as it would have been for a wealthy local family in the nineteenth century. The walled **Church of the Assumption** at

▲ Houses with tiled roofs, Shiroka Laka

the western end of the village tends to stay closed until a tour bus arrives, but does open until 1pm on Sundays. It dates from 1834 and worshippers are greeted by a sobering fresco of a funeral procession surrounded by prancing demons. Inside, the church walls are adorned with more wonderfully naive frescoes, including one of Elijah ascending to Heaven in a smoking chariot, a trail of black smoke billowing in its wake. Note also the iconostasis, with its series of panels, painted in the same "rustic" style, relating the story of Adam and Eve and the Fall.

Essentially, however, Shiroka Laka is a place to stroll around the cobbled lanes and enjoy picnics in the surrounding meadows – unless you happen to be around for the first weekend of March, when there's a *kukeri* **carnival** of dancers and musicians in weird costumes, playing out an ancient fertility rite. It also hosts the **International Bagpipe Festival** (Ⓦwww.gaidaland.com) in August, Bulgaria's largest such gathering and a rare chance to hear the awesome sound of *Sto kaba gaidi* – sixty to one hundred bagpipers playing together. The festival kicks off with a procession of dancers and musicians on the Saturday morning, followed by performances at the National School of Folklore Arts, with more playing and festivities at nearby Gela (see below) on Sunday.

Accommodation

Gaida Inn Main square ☏03030/758 or 227. Set in a characterful old house, with a cosy *mehana* downstairs. ❷
James kashta ul. Churshishka ☏0887/136207, Ⓦwww.shirokalaka.com. A spruced-up old house with several comfortably furnished rooms and an affable South African host offering excellent home-cooked cuisine. Breakfast costs 5Lv per person. ❸

Kalina Just off the main square ☏03030/675. Has pleasant rooms and a *mehana* that boasts live bagpipes every evening. ❷
Shiroka Laka ☏03030/341. On the hill above the music school, this is the largest and least appealing of the village's hotels. It has its own restaurant. ❸
Zgorovska kashta On the main road at the Pamporovo end of the village ☏03030/277. Has comfortable rooms and a good restaurant. ❷

Practicalities

The *Shiroka Laka* **restaurant** on the main square has a reasonable choice of Bulgarian standards. The helpful **Rhodopi tourist centre** (daily 9am–noon & 1–7pm; ☏03030/233 or 0887/118711, Ⓦwww.rhodope.net) can provide maps, brochures, timetables and details of accommodation throughout the region, including **private rooms** in the town (❶–❷).

Gela

If you're looking for an even quieter spot to rest up, the nearby village of **GELA** (ГЕЛА) – legendary birthplace of **Orpheus** – has several private rooms to rent, generally in cosy, modern chalet-style accommodation. One bus a day serves Gela, leaving Shiroka Laka in the morning and returning in the evening. The *Gela Hotel* (☏03030/308; ❷) has great views, or you could try the cosy two-star *Gerust* (☏03030/760 or 0897/837700; ❷). Otherwise Kalinka Draganova (☏03030/560) can arrange **private rooms** (❶–❷). With only a few dozen inhabitants, it's a lovely, peaceful place, whose origins go back over 3300 years, and where the calm is broken only by Shiroka Laka's international bagpipe festival, which moves up to Gela on the first Sunday of August (see above). Look out for the *silivriak*, otherwise known as the Orpheus Flower, an endemic Balkan species whose small pink bells are said to have been formed from the blood of the mythical musician after the Bacchantes threw his butchered body into the river.

Devin

Thirty-four kilometres west of Shiroka Laka, **DEVIN** (ДЕВИН) is a pleasant enough town in a bowl between rugged mountain ranges, famous for its bottled water and spa centres. There's a big military garrison here, and despite the presence of a firing range in the surrounding hillls, there are various hiking possibilities. In the absence of a **tourist office**, Travel Escape at ul. Orpheus 1, just off the main square (Mon–Sat 9am–5pm; ☎03041/2411) has an English-speaking manager who provides local information and arranges excursions with Konna baza Devin (☎0885/252737 or 0889/246909), which runs **horse riding** tours of varying length as well as hunting and fishing trips. Aside from a mosque and a church, the only official "sight" is a display of Rhodope folklore in the **museum** on the main square (Mon–Sat 10am–noon & 1.30–5.30pm; 2Lv).

Practicalities

Beyond the square, at ul. Osvobozhdenie 50, is the *Manolov* (☎03041/2269; ❷), the cheapest of Devin's **hotels** and comfortable enough. The *Ismena* at ul. Guritsa 41 (☎03041/4872, ⓦwww.ismena-hotel.com; ❹) has a great position overlooking the town, a small pool, various spa therapies, and is the most preferable of the town's hotels. The central *Spa Hotel* at ul. Druzhba 2A (☎03041/2498, ⓦwww.spadevin.com; ❺) is smart but somewhat sterile, has a hot pool, sauna and fitness centre, but is no match for the enormous *Orpheus* at ul. Tzvetan Zangov 14 (☎03041/2041, ⓦwww.orpheus-spa.com; ❻), a new 250-room spa complex with a wonderful outdoor pool that's open to the public.

Six **buses** a day leave Avtogara Smolyan for Devin, passing through Shiroka Laka en route, from where up to seven local services a day also go to Devin. From Devin, two or three daily buses head westwards to Dospat (see p.355).

Trigrad and around

The star attraction in the southwestern Rhodopes is the locality of **Trigrad**, with its awesome **gorge** and **caves**. Getting here without a car can be a challenge, as it's reached by only one bus a day from Devin (Mon–Fri; 5.30pm). Hitching is an option: quite a lot of traffic runs the 9km along the main Devin to Dospat road to Teshel, from where you could walk to Trigrad (10km) or **Yagodina** (8km), along minor roads, both of which run through gorges noted for their caves. Once there, you could easily **hike** round all the sites in the area within two to three days. The region is covered by Cartographia's (ⓦwww.cartographia-bg.net) Rhodope map series.

Trigrad

The **TRIGRAD GORGE** (*Trigradsko zhdrelo*) is one of the most spectacular vistas in Bulgaria, its sheer walls overhanging the foaming River Trigradska, which disappears into a stupendous cave called the **Devil's Throat** (*Dyavolsko garlo*), accessible via a 150-metre-long tunnel at ground level (daily 9am–5pm; hourly tours; 3Lv). The thunder of water is audible long before you sight a huge waterfall that vanishes into the bowels of the earth; objects swept into the cave are never seen again. As big as two cathedrals, the cave is traversed by stairways, and bats flit around the shaft of light entering through a mossy fissure overhead. On leaving, you can walk uphill to a viewing platform above the void where the Trigradska goes underground – in legend, the entrance to the underworld used by Orpheus (see box on p.356) – or scramble down beside the mouth of the road tunnel to find a placid pool at the bottom of the gorge, where the river reappears.

Fifteen minutes' walk beyond the Devil's Throat lies the sprawling village of **TRIGRAD** (ТРИГРАД), whose mosque and tiny church reflect the relative size of its Muslim and Christian communities – and their closeness. The village was wealthy during Turkish times (when one landowner alone had twelve thousand sheep), but is nowadays something of a sleepy backwater, disturbed only once a year by the **Orphic Mysteries Folk Music Festival**, on the last weekend in July, which attracts hundreds of visitors from miles around. One of the best places **to stay** in the village is at the *Silivriak Hotel*, on the highest street to the right above the main square (℡03040/220; ❷). It's run by the custodian of the Devil's Throat cave, Kostadin ("Kotse") Hadzhesky, one of Bulgaria's foremost cavers and the person to ask about serious speleology. There are a few more small, family-run hotels in the village such as the *Zdravets* (℡03040/391; ❷), which also runs organized excursions, and the *Izgrev* (℡03040/545; ❷). Alternatively, you could stay at the *Chairite* cottage (℡03040/220; 100Lv per night for up to 6 people), located in the protected lake district of the same name, 19km east of the village – a superb place to study the local flora and fauna. The atmosphereic *Kaminata* **restaurant**, just below Trigrad's main square, is the best place to eat traditional Rhodopean dishes and has a roaring open fire in winter. For **horse riding** in the region contact Arkan Tours (℡032/640205, Ⓦwww.arkantours.com).

Yagodina and around

The road to **Yagodina** runs through the longer but less precipitous **Buzhnov Gorge**, past the mouth of a side canyon that's great for hiking and caving. Only 2km long and 2–4m wide, the **Haidushki dol** ("Outlaws' Ravine") ascends in cascades to its watershed between two peaks connected by a natural rock bridge called the **Devil's Bridge**, after a legend that only he can cross it. This wild karst terrain abounds in caves – 102 have been found so far – which are mostly only accessible to cavers. However, Kotse (see above) can arrange a trip to the **Haramiiska Cave** (around 30Lv per person) that needs more nerve than skill, where you crawl into one chamber before being lowered 42m in a harness into another cavern – an awesome but safe experience, as the guides take every precaution.

The **Yagodina Cave** (*Yagodinska peshtera*), 2km up the road, is an established attraction, with 45-minute tours (daily 10am–5pm; 5Lv) covering 1km of the 10-kilometre labyrinth, the largest cave system in Bulgaria. You'll need warm, waterproof clothing, as the temperature is 6°C and water drips constantly, enlarging the stalactites at a rate of one centimetre every fifty to a hundred years. Don't miss the **cave pearls** formed by drops falling on tiny pebbles, gradually coating them with a lustrous shell; and the **Devil's Face** on the wall. Look out also for the **Newlyweds** formation, where 21 weddings have taken place between Bulgarian caving enthusiasts, who also host an annual Speleologists' Party in the cave on January 1.

While the lowest of the cave's three levels was flooded 300,000 years ago, the uppermost later served as a **Prehistoric cave dwelling**, where excavations have unearthed Stone and Bronze Age kilns, potsherds and grindstones that can be seen *in situ* after finishing the tour of the lower cave. It's thought that groups of twenty to thirty people lived here, using several hearths as the direction of the draught varied with the seasons, blowing in the mouth of the cave or out of a hole at the back. Head down the road past the entrance to the lower cave, cross a wooden bridge and then a concrete one to regain the road to Yagodina, which is all uphill but has a path that cuts the walk to under an hour. Hikers refresh themselves at a *cheshma* inscribed with a paean to water by

Saint-Exupéry, before entering **YAGODINA** (ЯГОДИНА), a purely Pomak village with a smart new mosque. Visitors can stay at a number of small hotels: the *Yagodina* (✆030419/310; ❷) is the most central and has its own restaurant; further along is the *Snezhana* (✆030419/263; ❷), which can organize fishing and riding trips, as well as some live folk music, or you could try the small *Iglika* chalet (✆030419/263; ❶) in the hills. Both the *Snezhana* and *Iglika* have cooking facilities, though meals can be arranged on request. Alternatively, you could hike to Trigrad (1hr 45min) and sleep there. To get to Trigrad, continue straight ahead on entering the village, past the post office, until you see a barn. The path beside it joins a track that soon reaches the junction of many paths; the one to the right that disappears behind a rock leads to a wide highland meadow, where you pick up a trail near the left-hand scarecrow, which, after an uphill slog, levels out in the woods. Turn left when you come to a broad path and you'll start descending the heights above Trigrad, to enter the village near the *Silivriak Hotel*.

Dospat

Three daily buses connect Devin with **DOSPAT** (ДОСПАТ), 40km west. You'll pass through lots of Pomak villages en route before descending into this small town once noted for its folk costumes and festivities but now known for its reservoir and clean mountain air. Downhill from the bus station is a small square with a mosque, where a right turn takes you towards the jade-green **reservoir**, distantly overlooked by a nice **hotel**, the *Tihiyat kat* (✆03045/2082; ❷). To reach it, head uphill from the bus station and fork left – it's at the far end. Fork right and you'll find the *Panorama* (✆03045/2183; ❷), which has a pool, sauna, and excellent views. The most central option is the bright new *Laguna* at ul. Trakiya 3A (✆03045/2078; ❷).

Dospat is a turning point, where you can either head north along the desolate route to Batak (see below), or **continue westwards** past the turn-offs for Dolen and Kovachevitsa, towards Gotse Delchev in the Mesta Valley and the Pirin Mountains beyond (see p.138). This route passes through some of the loveliest countryside in Bulgaria, with an ever-changing panorama of gorges, forests and meadows dotted with a succession of highland villages, where tobacco farming is the main source of income. Be warned, though, that there's no **bus** between Dospat and Gotse Delchev, and only one to Batak, and this can be erratic; check times in advance. The Batak bus is signposted for Pazardzhik, as it terminates there.

Batak

The highlands to the north of Dospat are as thickly wooded and thinly populated as any in the Rhodopes, with not a single village on the road to Batak – only hunting lodges, the socialist-era *Rai* hotel (✆0898/818463; ❶) and the nearby *Loven Dom* (✆03553/2048; ❶), signposted after crossing the dam at Golyam Beglik reservoir. In such a lonely, peaceful setting, it's hard to imagine that **BATAK** (БАТАК) was once a byword for infamy that reverberated across Europe. During the April Rising of 1876 the Turks unleashed *bashibazouks* and Pomaks from other settlements to rape, pillage and slaughter the populace. Five thousand people – nearly the entire population – were hacked to death or burnt alive, an act for which the Pomak commander responsible was decorated. Britain's Prime Minister Disraeli cynically dismissed the **atrocities** to justify the continuing alliance with Turkey, until the weight of reports by foreign diplomats and J. A. MacGahan of *The Daily News* became impossible to ignore. Yet only a sustained campaign by trade unions, Gladstone and public figures like Victor Hugo and Oscar Wilde prevented Britain's support of Turkey in the Russo-Turkish War of 1877–78. Although the defeated Turks were obliged to concede an independent Bulgaria under the Treaty of San Stefano, Disraeli ensured at the Congress of Berlin that Macedonia and Thrace were returned to the Ottomans, and the half of Bulgaria south of the Balkan range became the Turkish protectorate of Eastern Rumelia – in return for which Turkey rewarded Britain with Cyprus.

The Town

As a bloody milestone on the road to liberation, the massacre is still commemorated in April, and the town echoes with memories of the dead. One wall of the **museum** on the main square (daily 8.30am–5pm; 2Lv for this, the church and the Ethnographic Museum; free Mon) is inscribed with a seemingly endless roll-call of those who died, and sepia photographs show old women who survived sitting beside piles of skulls and bones – some set out on a table to form the words *Ustanak ot 1876* (Rising of 1876). Display cabinets are filled with press reports and denunciations of the Turks or those who seemed to lend them support – including Turgenev's attack on Disraeli and Queen Victoria, *Croquet at Windsor*. A burnt tree trunk commemorates local rebel leader Trendafil Kerelov, who was lashed to it before it was set alight. Exhibits upstairs relate to Batak's contribution to the Balkan and World Wars, including documents from the nearby partisan camp of Tehran – so-named in honour of the Allies' summit in 1943 – and a gruesome photograph of heads left on a wall in the village.

The Orphic mysteries

The **legend of Orpheus** originated in ancient Thrace, where he was supposedly born in the vicinity of Gela, son of a Muse (perhaps Calliope, patron of epic poetry) and King Oeagrus of the Odrysae tribe (Apollo in other versions of the story). His mastery of the lyre moved animals and trees to dance, and with his songs – which had previously enabled the Argonauts to resist the Sirens' lure – Orpheus tried to regain his dead wife, Eurydice, from the underworld. His music charmed Charon, the ferryman, and Cerebus, the guardian of the River Styx, and finally Hades himself, who agreed to return Eurydice on the condition that neither of them looked back as they departed – but emerging into the sunlight of the overworld, Orpheus turned to smile at Eurydice and so lost her forever. Thereafter, Orpheus roamed the Rhodopes singing mournfully until he was torn apart by "the women of Thrace" (whom Aeschylus identifies as followers of Dionysus – the "Bacchantes"). His head continued singing as it floated down the River Mesta to Lesbos, where it began to prophesy until its fame eclipsed that of the Oracle at Delphi.

Despite having its origins in Thracian religion, the myth of Orpheus had a bigger effect in Greece, where an **Orphic cult** rich in mysticism was well established by the fifth century BC. Itinerant priests offering initiation into the Orphic mysteries traversed the Greek world, and Orphic communities arose in southern Italy and Sicily. Original texts codifying Orphism's basic tenets have been lost, although later Hellenistic writers held that initiates were vegetarians and that they regarded the material world as evil (describing the body as a "prison", according to Plato), and the spiritual world as divine. Little is known about the cult's practices, but it's thought that the ritual involved the mimed – or actual – dismemberment of a person representing Dionysus, who was then "reborn" as a free soul after death. Another theory has it that the cult's true, secret purpose was to bestow upon its adherents longevity, or even physical immortality.

Immediately opposite the museum lies the low, roughly hewn **Church of Sveta Nedelya**, where MacGahan found naked corpses piled one metre deep. Its bare interior contains stark reminders of the violence: the bloodstains on the walls have never been expunged; signs point to bullet holes in the walls; a glass case holds one of the heavy woodsmen's axes used to bludgeon the locals into submission; while in a sunken chamber at the end of the church lie the bones of the massacred.

After all this you may not have much stomach for further sightseeing, though there's a small **Ethnographic Museum** with an exhibition of antique farm tools and local outfits.

Practicalities

Batak's **bus station** is at the eastern end of the main street, **ulitsa Apriltsi**. The town has a smart new **hotel**, the *Unikat* at ul. Apriltsi 24 (℡03553/2326, ⓦwww.unikatbatak.com; ❹), which also has a decent restaurant; the only other **accommodation** is around the Batak Reservoir (*Yazovir Batak*), about 6km from town. Here you'll find the *Panorama Hotel* (℡03553/2064; ❸), which is open year-round and offers hovercraft and boat rides on the lake as well as off-road 4WD trips and bike rental. *Rositsa Vilno Selishte* (℡0897/963107; ❸) is a pleasant development of bungalows with a restaurant and lake views. Numerous signs along the road advertise **private rooms** (❶–❷), or you can pitch a tent beside the lake for free. Try *Yoana mehana* just off the main road for traditional Bulgarian fare, or continue towards the lake to *Ostrava mehana*, which offers similar dishes and has a lakeside cocktail bar. Buses to Velingrad pass by here.

Velingrad and around

With its diverse springs, excellent climate and leafy parks, **VELINGRAD** (ВЕЛИНГРАД) is one of Bulgaria's most popular spa towns, although those not intent on taking a cure will find little else to do here. It consists of three villages originally named Kamenitsa, Ladzhene and Chepino – lumped together in 1948 and renamed after local partisan heroine Vela Peeva. Both the train and bus stations are a few minutes' walk east of the modern centre, which in turn lies just to the east of **Ladzhene**, where Velingrad's oldest baths, the **Velyova banya** (founded in the sixteenth century, although the buildings are modern), stand in a park beside the Yundola road. Just to the north of the centre is **Kamenitsa**, fringed by wooded parks that harbour the town's open-air baths, most of the modern spa facilities, and a small Ottoman-period *hammam*, the **Kremachna banya** or "Flint Baths". The small **Historical Museum** (Mon–Sat 9am–5pm; 2Lv), at ul. Vlado Chernozemski 2 in the Kamenitsa quarter, features a range of antiquities and an extensive display of painted eggs.

Velingrad's third cluster of baths lies 2km south of the centre in the **Chepino** quarter (bus #1 from the centre), where mineral water flows free from taps in the streets. Above Chepino to the south lies the Kleptuza spring, waters from which flow down to the **Kleptuza lake**, just east of Chepino: with pedalos, rowing boats and lakeside walkways, this is the most popular of Velingrad's resort areas.

Accommodation

Abeer pl. Svoboda ℡ 0359/57100, ⓦwww .abeerhotel.com. Has a spa centre and a hot pool. ❺

Dvoretsa ul. Tosho Staikov 8 ℡0359/56200, ⓦwww.dvoretsa.com. A five-star affair in the woods just outside the centre, boasting indoor and outdoor hot pools and over a hundred therapies. ❺

Kamena ul. Edelvais 4 ℡0359/5853, ⓔkamena @velingrad.com. The cheapest option in the area, with indoor and outdoor pools, tennis courts, a nightclub and spa therapies. ❸

Markita ul. Tsar Ivan Asen II ☎0359/58994 or 58974, ⓦmarkita.net. Small and not that central, but it does have an outdoor pool and a bar. ❹

Olymp ☎0359/56100, ⓦwww.olymp.velingrad .com. High-class hotel that dominates the hillside

towards Ladzhene and offers a slightly less comprehensive list of treatments than *Dvoretsa*. Its outdoor pool has a terrace with superb views of the town. ❺

Rich bul. Saedinenie ☎0359/57803, ⓦwww .hotel-rich.com. A new hotel with a pleasant outdoor pool that's open to the public. Also offers spa treatments. ❹

Practicalities

The central **tourist information centre** on pl. Svoboda (Mon–Fri 8am–6pm, Sat & Sun 8am–2pm; ☎0359/51667, ⓦwww.velingrad.com) can organize various local excursions including one to a nearby factory producing handmade rugs. It also arranges accommodation in **private rooms** (❷–❸) and hotels, and has Internet access. All the hotels listed above have very good restaurants, while Velingrad's main square has no shortage of places to **eat** and **drink**. The *Omar* at the *Rich* hotel is regarded as one of the town's best, and puts on a nightly floorshow featuring Bulgarian and western music.

Local **mountain bike** enthusiasts (ⓦwww.bikearea.org) have mapped and marked several biking routes in the surrounding area and can organize guided tours here and in other parts of the country. Their **map** should be available from Velingrad's tourist centre or from Odysseia-in in Sofia (see p.75).

There are three **buses** a day running between Velingrad and Plovdiv, four daily buses to Velingrad from Sofia, and regular services between Yundola and Batak. Moving on, however, many travellers opt for the three daily **trains** to Bansko in the Pirin range (see p.142). The narrow-gauge line switchbacks through glorious pine forests and subalpine meadows, calling at Avramovi Kolibi, the highest station on the Balkan peninsula, before descending to the logging town of Yakoruda and skirting the southern flanks of the Rila Mountains en route to Razlog (see p.142) and Bansko.

Yundola and Dorkovo

A 16km bus ride to the northwest of Velingrad, **YUNDOLA** (ЮНДОЛА) is another small health resort 1390m above sea level, set amid rounded hills and copses of trees. It used to be popular with trade unionists and Young Pioneers, but is chiefly remarkable for its inhabitants' longevity. The prevalence of centenarians in Bulgaria is ascribed to features of life in the highlands, where "Nature takes years off the weak and adds them to the strong" – as Leslie Gardiner was told. Human longevity is supposedly extended by pure air, climatic extremes, a lack of stress, and a spartan diet with little meat and plenty of yoghurt. The only **accommodation** is at Yundola's *University Complex* (☎0359/28436; ❶), which has mostly dorm rooms and a few double rooms.

Goats in the Rhodopes

Goats are still the basis for life in many Rhodope communities. Every family owns several, which are entrusted to the village goatherd, or *manzardzhiya*. Their milk is drunk or turned into yoghurt and cheese, which together with salted goat's meat (*pastarma*) forms the villagers' wintertime staple. Goats' hair is woven into rugs that can last for eighty years, and their skin can be made into everything from wine-sacks and sandals to bagpipes (*gaidi*). During the Ottoman occupation, when Bulgarians were forbidden to carry arms, goats' horns served as daggers, and many of the country's most famous *haiduks* (including the female outlaw Rumena Voivoda) started their careers as goatherds.

The village of **DORKOVO** (ДОРКОВО), 14km east of Velingrad, is notable for its annual **international folklore festival** on the last weekend of July, which attracts up to fifteen thousand visitors and aims to represent the blend of three cultures – Christian, Pomak and Vlach – that characterizes the Chepino Valley. There's a strong Macedonian element, as most of the villagers are descended from Macedonians who came here as refugees after the Congress of Berlin in 1878. Before then Dorkovo was a Pomak village, but many of the inhabitants fled after 1877, fearing reprisals for their participation in the slaughter at Batak. There are hourly buses from Velingrad and **private rooms** can booked through the municipality offices on the main square (℡03543/222; ❶).

The eastern Rhodopes

The **eastern Rhodopes** were the Ottomans' first conquest and their last foothold in Bulgaria before the Balkan Wars of 1912–13, and to this day many of the inhabitants are of ethnic Turkish origin. Geographically it is distinguished by 2500 hamlets and villages (far more than in either the central or the western Rhodopes) and comparatively low highlands (the average altitude is 329m). Traditionally, this was the poorest, least developed region of Bulgaria – a condition that only began to be remedied after dams and non-ferrous metal plants were established in the 1950s, and which seems likely to relapse as these industries collapse today.

From a tourist's viewpoint the **chief attractions** are birdwatching at the nature reserve on the River Arda near Madzharovo, the rock-hewn hilltop temple and fortress at Perperikon, and the variety of strange rock formations in the Kardzhali region. However, as the reserve is only accessible by bus from Haskovo and the widely scattered rocks can only be reached by car, anyone coming from Smolyan and reliant on buses is limited to hiking around Belite Brezi or a visit to Kardzhali, a town whose past is more intriguing than its present.

Heading east from Smolyan to Kardzhali

Fairly regular buses run from Smolyan to Kardzhali, passing Pomak and Turkish villages and the entrance to the **Arda Gorge** (a lovely spot for walking and picnicking if you have your own transport), en route to the mainly Turkish mining town of **ARDINO** (АРДИНО). A few kilometres further on, the *Belite Brezi hizhai* (℡03561/2982 or 0889/676981; ❶) and campsite is the starting-point for many fine **hikes**, including a seven-hour trail to the 90m-high **Ardino waterfall** on the River Arda. From there, it's only another hour's walk to the **Devil's Bridge** (*Dyavolskiyat most*), one of the humpbacked bridges built by the Turks on the Arda's tributaries along the route from Plovdiv to the Aegean. Though you wouldn't think so from its meagre source near Mogilitsa, the Arda is vital to the region, flowing through serpentine gorges to feed the reservoirs and power stations near Kardzhali, Madzharovo and Ivailovgrad.

Another road from Smolyan approaches Kardzhali by way of Momchilgrad, running closer to the Greek border, through the mining centres of **Madan** (МАДАН; from the Arabic word for "ore") and **ZLATOGRAD** (ЗЛАТОГРАД; "Gold Town"). Like **Rudozem** (РУДОЗЕМ), nearer Smolyan, they did well under Communism, but the 1990s saw the mining industry crippled by spiralling energy costs and the collapse of the lev and the price of non-ferrous metals on the world market. The last mines closed in 1999, while plans to kick-start trade with Greece by opening a new border crossing near Rudozem have been in the pipeline for years, but have so far come to nothing.

Zlatograd's fortunes have been recently revived, however, by the opening of the **Ethnographic Museum complex** (Thurs–Mon 9am–noon & 2–5pm; 2Lv), a marvellous collection of beautifully renovated nineteenth-century buildings 1km west of the bus station. Within the main complex are three guesthouses, two *mehana*, the traditional workshops of a cutler, a goldsmith, a tailor and a woodcarver, and the **Ethnographic Museum** itself, which displays local costumes, tools and functioning vertical and horizontal looms. A traditional café serves coffee made from rye and boiled on a bed of hot sand, while a little beyond is the **Education Museum** with a mocked-up classroom and a collection of faded photographs and dog-eared books. Across the river is the *Vodenitsata* or **Water Mill Museum**, a stone millhouse containing an intriguing water-powered contraption (*tepavitsa*) made of four massive wooden hammers that full rough woollen material with deafening regularity.

The complex's **tourist information centre** (℡03071/2169) sells a ticket covering all the sites, and can arrange accommodation in the region as well as excursions to Thracian remains in the locality. You can stay within the complex at the lavishly furnished 130-year-old *Pachilovska kashta* (❸), the less luxurious, but equally atmospheric *Krucheva kashta* (❷), or the *Alexandrovi kashta* (℡03071/4166; ❸), which serves as a reception area for all the houses. In a concrete block the other side of the river is a budget alternative, the *Grebentsi*, at ul. Evgenya Pachilova 4 (℡03071/2158), which has simple but clean dorm rooms (10Lv per person) downstairs, or more comfortable doubles with cable TV upstairs (❶).

Kardzhali and around

Founded by the seventeenth-century Turkish general Kardzhi Ali on the site of a much older settlement, **KARDZHALI** (КЪРДЖАЛИ) was one of the last towns to remain in Ottoman hands – old photos and paintings of the town depict a maze of lanes thronged with hawkers in fezzes, veils and pantaloons, mingling with Bulgarian peasants, brigands and Turkish officers. When it finally fell to the Bulgarian army in 1912, however, it had fewer than three thousand inhabitants, and only a trace of its erstwhile exoticism lingers in the bazaar quarter today. Other than to visit the excellent Historical Museum, there are few reasons to spend more than an afternoon before moving on. However, for those with a car, it can serve as a base for trips to the ruins of **Perperikon** as well as numerous **rock formations** – the nearest is 4km from town – or a stopover en route to the nature reserve at Madzharovo.

The Town

The train and bus stations are at the eastern end of town, from where you can catch any bus along the broad sweep of bul. Balgariya into the centre, where the **municipal garden** (*Gradska gradina*) with its elegant floral arrangements, makes a useful focal point. North of here is the commercial quarter, where butchers, fruit sellers and artisans ply their trades in shacks beside a **mosque**, whose Ottoman minaret is all that distinguishes it from the dwellings in the area. The nearby riverside offers a view of the suburbs on the far bank of the Arda, connected by a bridge to bul. Availo, which cuts across town from east to west.

The town's most interesting sight by far is the **Historical Museum**, the largest in the Rhodopes and one of the best collections in Bulgaria, on a nameless street some four blocks east of bul. Republikanska (Tues–Sun 9am–noon & 1–5pm;

4Lv) and housed in a vast Moorish edifice built in the 1930s as a Muslim college, though never used as such. The ground-floor history section includes a reconstruction of a locally excavated 6000-year-old dwelling-workshop, a curious jasper pendant in the form of a zoomorphic swastika and delicate gold jewellery discovered in a Thracian necropolis. Other artefacts on show here include fragments of tenth-century church murals and a fearsome-looking medieval catapult, covered in plate armour. The first floor is given over to displays of minerals, crystals and the natural history of the eastern Rhodopes, including photos of some of the nearby strange rock formations (see p.362). Above this, on the top floor, is a truly absorbing exhibition illustrating traditional local crafts, industries and folk rituals, including reconstructions of a leather workshop, smithy and dairy, as well as the more usual domestic set-ups. There's also a fine collection of ritual costumes, with the monstrous *kukeri* again stealing the show. Note also the *survakar* costume, worn by a young boy who would go from house to house at New Year, striking people with a stick, for good luck. The local tobacco industry is represented by stacks of the dried leaves, cut into several different shapes, and a collection of sepia photographs showing nineteenth-century peasants working on the crop, in scenes which you will see along roadsides, virtually unchanged, today. The museum is also the best place to find leaflets and information about the nearby sites of **Perperikon** and **Tatul** (see p.366).

The **art gallery** at ul. Republiska 53 (closed for renovation at the time of writing) contains an exhibition of icons, and works by Bulgarian artists including Vladimir Dimitrov-Maistor, Ivan Mrkvichka, and Yaroslav Veshin. In the southern suburbs is the **Assumption of the Virgin Mary Monastery**, built between 2000 and 2003 as a jubilee monastery. The sturdy exterior walls and hefty wooden gate emphasize the incongruity of such a building in a predominantly Muslim town, though within is a peaceful sanctuary of neat lawns, flowerbeds and colourful murals, where visitors can stay in comfortable en-suite rooms (see below). The complex surrounds a mid-twentieth-century church which houses a casket containing what are thought to be fragments of the holy cross discovered at Ahridos near Perperikon in 2002.

Practicalities

In the absence of a tourist information centre, the Kardzhali Regional Economic Development Agency in the municipal offices at bul. Balgariya 41 (℡0361/66966) can provide limited information on local sights, as can staff at the Historical Museum.

Accommodation options in and around Kardzhali include the partially refurbished three-star high-rise *Hotel Arpezos* (℡0361/60200; ❸), not far from the riverside at bul. Republikanska 46, which has an indoor swimming pool and top-floor bar. Conveniently located opposite the bus station at bul. Belomorski 68 is the smart new *Kurdzhali* (℡0361/82354, ⓦwww.hotel-kardjali.com; ❸), which is air-conditioned and has wireless Internet. For an unusual place to stay, try one of the comfortable en-suite rooms at the Assumption of the Virgin Mary Monastery (℡0361/62494; ❷). Further from the town just after the village of **ENCHETS** (ЕНЧЕЦ) and reachable only by taxi or car, there's floating accommodation on the lake at Kardzhali dam (*yazovir Kardzhali*). Small wooden bungalows (℡0889/822783; ❶) with common bathrooms are crammed onto a pontoon anchored to the *Pristan* restaurant, which chugs across the lake most nights on impromptu fishing trips. Next door is a similar structure supporting the *Moby Dick,* a restaurant that blares out noisy commercial folk music, while on the other side the *Emona* restaurant is housed on a small ship.

There are several **bars** and **cafés** behind Kardzhali's municipal offices on ul. Exarch Yosef, while you can sample good local **food** at the restaurant in the *Hotel Arpezos*, noted for regional specialities such as mutton, sausages (*suzdurma*), *baklava* and figs, along with Armira wine from the Ivailovgrad district. You could also try the well-regarded *Smokinite*, a traditional-style *mehana* serving good-quality Bulgarian cuisine, though it's a little out of the way at ul. Dimitar Madzharov 9, on the edge of the industrial zone south of the river.

Kardzhali is a good point from which to head on to **Turkey**, with around seven daily buses to Istanbul and Bursa, as well as daily services to Izmir and Odrin.

Perperikon and Ahridos

Mistakenly listed as a medieval stronghold in the 1930s, the spectacular rock-hewn ruins of **PERPERIKON** (ПЕРПЕРИКОН) failed to attract world interest until 2001, when an excavation team lead by Professor Nikolai Ovcharov began collecting evidence that proved the hilltop site dates back to between 6000 and 5000 BC. Professor Ovcharov put forward the hypothesis that here was the long-lost Rhodopean temple to Dionysus, closely linked to the ancient cult of Orpheus and referred to by Greek and Roman historians. The site was conquered, abandoned, and rebuilt by successive civilizations, resulting in the current gradual unearthing of a kaleidoscope of remains that have yet to be fully excavated and conclusively pieced together. The complex's main features are a 4m-wide **stone passage** cut 8m into the rock at places and leading steeply up to a **stone throne** within the once towering **great palace.** At either end of the palace's vast hall are the eastern and western **crypts** – the latter containing fifteen sarcophagi covered by stone slabs. Just above is the circular **altar** positioned in the centre of what is thought to have been an open-roofed oval temple dedicated to Dionysus, where high priests predicted the future by reading the flames from wine poured onto the altar fire. Beyond the temple, a steep path leads up to the hilltop, where a series of stone foundations surrounds the **acropolis**, a colonnaded fortress with walls three metres thick. To the west lie the foundations of the **small palace** and a deep **reservoir** cut into the rock, the largest to have been found in the Rhodopes. At the edge of the site, at its highest point, are the remains of a **medieval tower**. An information centre next to the car park sells maps of Perperikon and runs guided tours of the ruins whenever people turn up (10Lv per person). The excellent website ⓦ www.perperikon.bg gives details of the latest discoveries at the site.

In the neighbouring village of Chiflik (1km south of Perperikon) lie the excavated foundations of **AHRIDOS** (АХРИДОС), thought to have been the wealthy administrative capital of the eastern Rhodopes between 900 and 1200 AD, with earlier Thracian finds at the site dating back to 500 BC. The major building of the complex is a ninth-century church, which was elegantly decorated and entered by crossing a partially surviving mosaic made of square and triangular marble blocks depicting a cross. In 2002 archeologists discovered what are thought to be fragments of the holy cross at the site, which are now stored in the church at Kardzhali's Assumption of the Virgin Mary Monastery.

Buses run twice a day from Kardzhali to Stremtsi via Chiflik.

Rock formations in the Kardzhali region

Most of the odd **rock formations** in the Kardzhali region originated in the volcanic eruptions that raised the land from the sea forty million years ago, and whose ashes solidified into the porous golden-coloured rock known as tufa, which is easily eroded – the same process that created the "fairy chimneys" of

THE RHODOPES AND THE PLAIN OF THRACE | The eastern Rhodopes

Cappadocia in Turkey. Kardzhali's formations are far smaller, but diverse enough to appeal to geologists or anyone with more than a passing interest in such things. As all except one are near out-of-the-way villages, you'll need a **car** and Cartographia's (ⓦwww.cartographia-bg.net) East Rhodopes **map** (which doesn't show all of the sites, but identifies the localities).

The nearest rock formation to Kardzhali is marked on maps as the *Piramidite* (Pyramids) but known to locals as the **Stone Wedding** (*Vkamenenata svatba*), after a legend that a wedding party was turned to stone by the gods to punish the bridegroom's mother for envying his bride's beauty. The clusters of pink and red-tinged tufa do indeed resemble a procession frozen in mid-motion, but the villagers of Zimzelen, just uphill, have no qualms about using clefts in the rock as goat pens. This is the only formation within walking distance of Kardzhali (about 1hr) – take the road uphill past the Bulgarian and Turkish cemeteries, then follow the surfaced fork and the rocks are visible at a distance – though it's easier to take a taxi than risk getting lost.

Further afield, the **Stone Mushrooms** (*Kamenite gabi*) stand about 2.5m high, their brown-spotted stalks and pink caps with green undersides coloured by traces of manganese and other minerals. Legend has it that they represent the heads of four sisters decapitated by Turkish brigands for stabbing their chief when he tried to rape them. A large dark rock nearby is known as the Murderer. The Mushrooms are located near Beli Plast, 20km north of Kardzhali, along the minor road to Haskovo (not the E85).

Spectacularly suspended in the air by two green tufa columns (a third has been destroyed) and a limestone "bridge", the **Rock Window** (*Skalen prozorets*) stands 10m high, 15m long, 7m wide and 1.5m thick. It's situated between the hamlets of Zranche and Krushka just beyond Kostino, about 15km northwest of Kardzhali.

Just outside the village of Tatul, roughly 20km northeast of Momchilgrad, the **Stone Forest** (*Vkamenenata gora*) consists of a dozen charred-looking stumps up to 1.5m high and 4m in diameter, which are marked with rings and may actually be prehistoric trees, covered in lava.

The ridge of the **Broken Mountain** (*Yanuk tepe*) looks like someone has taken a cleaver to it, terminating midway in a precipitous drop with rhyolite columns strewn around – the result of a landslide late in the nineteenth century, near Vodenicharsko. Nearby, the fantastic **Rocks at Ustra** (*Skalite na Ustra*), huge purple pillars in the form of prisms, cones or stairways, perch on the hillside above Ustren. Both formations are in the vicinity of the small town of Dzhebel, 21km southwest of Kardzhali.

The **Mushroom** (*Gabata*) and the **Lion** (*Lavat*) are examples of two kinds of tufa formation in the vicinity of Benkovski, on the road to Zlatograd. Shaped like a giant puffball mushroom, with a stalk that narrows at the bottom and a brown, flattened cap 3m in diameter, the Mushroom lies 1.5km southwest of Benkovski. The Lion – which resembles a lion's head and gets its texture and colour from particles of gritstone – is in the same area, but closer to the village of Kitna (or Kitka).

The Madzharovo nature reserve

For birdwatchers, the chief attraction of the eastern Rhodopes is the **nature reserve** on the River Arda, established in 1994 under the Bulgarian-Swiss Biodiversity Conservation Programme. The gorges of the Arda are one of the few breeding grounds in Europe for three different **vultures** (the Egyptian, Griffon and Black), and the habitat of eight kinds of **falcons**, and nine kinds of

woodpecker, as well as black storks, bee-eaters and other species. Falcons catch mice, lizards, suslik, snakes, large insects and birds, while the vultures feed only on carrion, cleansing the environment of pathogenic micro-organisms. You may also catch sight of the now scarce **karakachan sheep**, an endemic Bulgarian strain, once herded in large numbers by the nomadic Karakachan people, who would drive them to winter pasture in northern Greece. Stricter border controls and collectivization under the Communist regime led to their decline, but they

▲ Madzharovo nature reserve and River Arda

are now being successfully bred on the reserve, along with the traditional breed of sheepdog, to protect them from prowling wolves.

Guided tours are arranged through the **Nature Information Centre** (daily 9am–5pm; ℡03720/345 or 0887/389121, ⓦwww.bspb.org), off the road by the bridge across the River Arda, near Madzharovo. Besides photos of the birds, mammals and flowers within the nature reserve (named in Bulgarian and Latin), there is a **restaurant** and three cosy double bedrooms (❷) for the use of visitors, which should be reserved well in advance. If the birdwatchers' chalet is full, try the pleasant, three-star *Rai* (℡03720/230, ⓦwww.hotelraibg.com/index_engl.html; ❷) at ul. Dimur Madjarov 48, in nearby **MADZHAROVO** (МАДЖАРОВО), which has its own restaurant and café. Eight kilometres away in the hills above Madzharovo is the remote hamlet of **Gorno Pole**, where the *Divata Ferma* guest house (℡03720/438 or 0886/963512, Ⓔwildfarm@tourism.bg; ❸) offers tranquil rural accommodation and delicious organic food. The owners can arrange horse riding, hiking, gold-panning and honey-making trips with advance notice.

Buses from Haskovo (see p.335) are the only means of reaching the reserve without a car. There are two services daily to Madzharovo. While there are no buses from Krumovgrad to Madzharovo, there are two from Krumovgrad to **Studen Kladenets**, a village set in a lunar landscape 30km upriver from Madzharovo, where the ravines of the Valchi Dol are home to another **vulture colony**. Though there is no visitor centre nor anywhere to stay here, staff at Madzharovo nature reserve can arrange access to two birdwatching hides.

From Momchilgrad to Ivailovgrad

The only reason for travelling this far east is to experience the most **Turkish region** of Bulgaria. In Momchilgrad and Krumovgrad you'll hear more Turkish spoken than Bulgarian (which isn't even *understood* by some people), and satellite dishes, trade and transport are oriented towards Turkey. People have ruddier skins, broader faces and stockier physiques than the inhabitants of the western Rhodopes – as sure a sign of their Turkish ancestry as their names (written in Turkish, rather than Cyrillic, on the tombstones). While being able to speak Turkish will help, people are generally reserved towards outsiders due to the region's long history as an embattled borderland and the vicissitudes of ethnic–state relations (see "Bulgaria's Muslim Minorities" in Contexts, p.456) having inculcated habits of clannishness and isolation.

The landscape is characterized by eroded, deforested expanses which, seen by moonlight, resemble deserts or lunar surfaces. With its dry sandy soil and Mediterranean climate, it has always needed irrigation to produce crops, and the minerals in the mountains – zinc, lead, gold and silver – made mining more profitable than agriculture until the Turks introduced the cultivation of tobacco, which is still the main crop. They chiefly grow an aromatic strain called *dzhebel basma*, a name deriving from *djebel*, the Arabic word for hill, and you will often see little old women selling bunches of the dried leaves by the roadside.

MOMCHILGRAD (МОМЧИЛГРАД), 10km south of Kardzhali, marks the start of the highlands, encrusted with **ruined fortresses** built by both Bulgaria and Byzantium, when the area was contested by the two empires. A stunning

The inhabitants of the small dreary town of Madzharovo are known as "Thracians" by the Bulgarians, due to their being descended from refugees from Aegean Thrace who fled during the Greek civil war of 1945. The town's **Thracian Festival**, which takes place in the last week of September, is a lively affair involving two days of dancing, music, wrestling and fireworks.

example lies 8km from Momchilgrad on the edge of the tiny village of **TATUL** (ТАТУЛ), served by seven daily buses that stop on the way to Nanovitsa from Momchilgrad. Thought to have originally been a Thracian hilltop temple dating back to 2000 BC, fortifying walls suggesting a change of use were added around 600–500 BC. A circular stone altar similar to that at Perperikon (see p.362) lies atop the hill close to a massive grain store. Most striking is the single **tomb** carved into the flat surface of the highest rock, reached by a series of steps, and accompanied by a similar tomb slightly below – both with drainage channels hinting at the possibility of human sacrifice rather than burial, or perhaps the production of sacred wine. Very little is known of the site despite recent excavation work, but a popular theory suggests that the rocky grave could be that of Orpheus, who allegedly once expressed a desire to be buried somewhere between the earth and the sky. Comfortable **accommodation** is available in Nanovitsa at the *Hizha Nanovitsa* (☎0887/959197, ⓦwww.nanovica.hit.bg; ❶).

More recently, it was in Momchilgrad that the worst violence of the "name-changing campaign" occurred, when about forty people died in clashes between protestors and the militia in the winter of 1984–85. These days, relations between the two communities are good, with Christians and Muslims working together in local politics and business. Should you wish to **stay**, your best bet is the *MG* hotel (☎03631/6034; ❷), which occupies a fine hilltop site on the eastern side of the village, has an outdoor swimming pool, and an excellent terrace **restaurant** with panoramic views of the eastern Rhodopes. They can also provide information about Tatul and other local attractions. Another option is the new *Konak* (☎03631/6127; ❷), just off the road to the *MG*, which features the town's best nightclub. From Momchilgrad it's now possible to continue south and cross the border into Greece via the Makaza Pass.

The succession of Muslim villages over the next 30km east culminates in an elegant, isolated **mosque** before the road descends to **KRUMOVGRAD** (КРУМОВГРАД), a smaller town with some cafés for a pit stop and the *Ahriga Hotel* (☎03641/7383; ❷), should you need to spend the night before catching a bus to Istanbul, Haskovo or Plovdiv. Buses depart from a vaguely marked stop in the market opposite the *Ahriga*.

Beyond Krumovgrad lies splendid open rolling countryside, planted with wheat and dotted with copses where livestock graze around waterholes, but eerily devoid of human settlements so far as you can see. There are, in fact, dozens of Turkish hamlets in the hills that are so small and isolated that none of the children go to school, which explains why the Ivailovgrad region has the highest illiteracy rate in Bulgaria (60 percent). Fifty-nine kilometres east of Krumovgrad, **IVAILOVGRAD** (ИВАЙЛОВГРАД) marks a return to the Slav, Christian areas of settlement, and boasts the impressive remains of the **Armira Roman Villa**, a 22-room complex built around 130 AD for the Roman noblemen and army officers who used the region for rest and recreation. Invading Goths destroyed it some 240 years later, but several mosaic floors have survived, including a depiction of the owner and his two children. Motorists

5

can also visit the Thracian tomb at **Mezek** as a detour off the road to Svilengrad (see p.337), though be sure that all your documents are in order, as there's a **checkpoint** at the hydroelectric dam on the Arda Reservoir. Ivailovgrad's **tourist information centre** (Mon–Fri 9am–noon & 1–6pm; ☎03661/8042, can arrange trips to both sites and can also open up the **Historical Museum**, which has an exhibition about the town's now defunct silk industry. **Accommodation** is available at either the *Bor-Hasienda* (☎03661/6511; ❷), or the *Ahrida* (☎0898/628653; ❶). Despite its proximity to Greece and Turkey, there's nowhere to cross the **frontier** until you reach Svilengrad.

Travel details

Trains

Asenovgrad to: Plovdiv (14 daily; 25min).
Dimitrovgrad to: Harmanli (4 daily; 1hr); Haskovo (4 daily; 30min); Kardzhali (4 daily; 2hr); Momchilgrad (3 daily; 2hr 15min–2hr 45min); Plovdiv (7 daily; 1hr 30min); Svilengrad (4 daily; 1hr).
Harmanli to: Dimitrovgrad (4 daily; 1hr); Plovdiv (4 daily; 2hr–3hr 30min); Simeonovgrad (4 daily; 15min); Svilengrad (5 daily; 30min).
Haskovo to: Dimitrovgrad (4 daily; 30min); Kardzhali (4 daily; 1hr–1hr 45min); Momchilgrad (4 daily; 2hr–3hr 15min); Plovdiv (4 daily; 2hr); Sofia (3 daily; 5hr); Stara Zagora (4 daily; 1hr 30min–2hr 30min).
Kardzhali to: Dimitrovgrad (4 daily; 2hr); Haskovo (3 daily; 1hr–1hr 45min); Momchilgrad (4 daily; 30min); Plovdiv (4 daily; 4hr 30min); Podkova (3 daily; 50min); Sofia (2 daily; 6hr); Stara Zagora (3 daily; 3–4hr).
Momchilgrad to: Dimitrovgrad (4 daily; 2hr 15min–2hr 45min); Haskovo (4 daily; 2hr–3hr 15min); Kardzhali (4 daily; 30min); Plovdiv (1 daily; 5hr); Podkova (4 daily; 20min); Stara Zagora (2 daily; 2hr 15min–4hr 30min).
Pazardzhik to: Plovdiv (15 daily; 30–45min).
Plovdiv to: Asenovgrad (hourly; 25min); Burgas (6 daily; 3hr 45min); Dimitrovgrad (7 daily; 1hr–1hr 30min); Hisar (3 daily; 1hr); Karlovo (5 daily; 1hr 45min); Momchilgrad (1 daily; 5hr); Pazardzhik (hourly; 30–45min); Septemvri (10 daily; 45min–1hr); Sofia (14 daily; 2hr–3hr 30min); Stara Zagora (13 daily; 1hr 30min-2hr); Svilengrad (3 daily; 2hr); Varna (3 daily; 6hr); Yambol (9 daily; 1hr).
Podkova to: Dimitrovgrad (4 daily; 3hr 30min); Kardzhali (4 daily; 50min); Momchilgrad (4 daily; 20min).
Septemvri to: Bansko (3 daily; 5hr); Plovdiv (6 daily; 45min–1hr); Sofia (8 daily; 1hr 30min–2hr 15min); Velingrad (5 daily; 1hr 30min).
Svilengrad to: Harmanli (6 daily; 30min).

Buses

Asenovgrad to: Bachkovo (7 daily; 30min); Laki (4 daily; 45min); Plovdiv (hourly; 30min).
Bachkovo to: Asenovgrad (7 daily; 30min).
Batak to: Pazardzhik (3 daily; 1hr 20min); Plovdiv (2 daily; 1hr 30min); Sofia (1 daily Mon–Fri; 2hr 30min); Velingrad (3 daily; 1hr).
Devin to: Dospat (2–3 daily; 1hr); Plovdiv (4 daily; 2hr 15min); Smolyan (6 daily; 2hr 30min); Trigrad & Yagodina (1 daily Mon–Fri; 30min).
Dimitrovgrad to: Haskovo (every 30min; 25min).
Dospat to: Batak (1 daily; 1hr 30min); Pazardzhik (1 daily; 3hr); Plovdiv (1 daily; 3hr 15min); Smolyan (1 daily; 3hr).
Harmanli to: Haskovo (every 30min; 40min); Ivailovgrad (3 daily; 2–3hr); Sofia (3 daily; 5hr); Plovdiv (4 daily; 2hr); Stara Zagora (5 daily; 1hr); Svilengrad (hourly; 45min).
Haskovo to: Dimitrovgrad (every 15min; 25min); Harmanli (hourly; 40min); Ivailovgrad (3 daily; 3hr); Kardzhali (hourly; 50min); Krumovgrad (3 daily; 4hr); Madzharovo (2 daily; 2hr); Plovdiv (14 daily; 1hr 30min); Sofia (14 daily; 4–5hr); Svilengrad (hourly; 1hr 20min).
Ivailovgrad to: Haskovo (2 daily; 3hr); Kardzhali (1 daily; 3hr).
Kardzhali to: Stremtsi via Chiflik/Perperikon (2 daily; 20min); Haskovo (hourly; 50min); Ivailovgrad (2 daily; 3hr); Krumovgrad (hourly; 30min); Momchilgrad (every 30min; 30min); Plovdiv (hourly; 2hr 30min); Sofia (7 daily; 5–6hr); Smolyan (2 daily; 3hr); Varna (2 daily; 5hr); Zlatograd (5 daily; 1hr).
Krumovgrad to: Kardzhali (6 daily; 30min); Plovdiv (1 daily; 3hr); Sofia (1 daily; 8hr); Stara Zagora (1 daily; 4–5hr); Studen Kladenets (2 daily; 2hr).
Laki to: Asenovgrad (4 daily; 45min); Belitsa (2 daily; 15min); Manastir (1 daily; 30min); Plovdiv (1 daily; 1hr 15min); Smolyan (1 daily; 1hr 15min).
Madzharovo to: Haskovo (3 daily; 1hr 15min); Plovdiv (1 daily; 2hr 30min).

Manastir to Laki (1 daily; 30min).
Pamporovo to: Plovdiv (6 daily; 2hr 30min);
Smolyan (hourly; 30min).
Pazardzhik to: Batak (2 daily; 1hr 20min); Dospat
(3 weekly; 3hr); Gotse Delchev (1 daily; 4hr);
Panagyurishte (hourly; 1hr 30min); Plovdiv
(18 daily; 40min); Septemvri (3 daily; 30min).
Plovdiv *Avtogara Yug* to: Asenovgrad (every 30min;
30min); Blagoevgrad (1 daily; 4hr); Burgas (2 daily;
4hr); Dupnitsa (1 daily; 5hr); Hisar (hourly; 1hr);
Karlovo (hourly; 1hr 15min); Kyustendil (2 weekly on
Mon & Fri; 4–5hr); Pazardzhik (hourly; 40min); Sliven
(6 daily; 3hr 15min); Sofia (hourly; 2hr); Varna
(2 daily; 5hr); Velingrad (1 daily; 1hr 15min).
Avtogara Rodopi to: Devin (2 daily; 2hr 15min);
Dospat (2 daily; 3hr 15min); Gotse Delchev (1 daily;
6hr 30min); Haskovo (13 daily; 1hr 30min); Luki
(1 daily; 1hr); Kardzhali (hourly; 2hr 30min);
Krumovgrad (1 daily; 3hr); Madan (3 daily; 3hr
30min); Pamporovo (8 daily; 2hr 30min); Rudozem
(3 daily; 2hr); Shumen (1 daily; 4hr); Smolyan (5
daily; 3hr); Zlatograd (3 daily; 4hr). *Avtogara Sever*
to: Burgas (4 daily; 4hr); Gabrovo (3 daily; 3hr);
Kazanluk (3 daily; 2hr); Koprivshtitsa (1 daily; 2hr
30min); Panagyurishte (2 daily; 2hr); Pleven (1 daily;
4hr 30min); Ruse (1 daily; 7hr); Sevlievo (1 daily;
4hr); Troyan (3 daily; 3hr 30min); Veliko Tarnovo
(3 daily; 4hr).
Shiroka Laka to: Devin (5–7 daily; 2hr); Smolyan
(3 daily; 1hr 20min).
Septemvri to: Pazardzhik (5 daily; 30min).
Smolyan *Avtogara Ustovo* to: Kardzhali (2 daily;
3hr); Madan (hourly; 30min); Momchilovtsi (10
daily; 40min); Rudozem (hourly; 20min); Sofia
(6 daily; 5hr) Zlatograd (6 daily; 1hr). *Avtogara
Smolyan* to: Devin (6 daily; 2hr 30min); Gela

(1 daily Mon–Fri; 1hr 40min); Mogilitsa (2 daily;
1hr); Pamporovo (hourly; 30min); Plovdiv (hourly;
3hr), via Rozhen Pass (1 daily; 4hr); Shiroka Laka
(6 daily; 1hr 20min); Sofia (4 daily; 5hr).
Svilengrad to: Dimitrovgrad (1 daily; 2hr);
Harmanli (hourly; 45min); Haskovo (hourly;
1hr 30min); Kapitan Andreevo (9 daily; 20min);
Mezek (2 daily; 20min); Plovdiv (2 daily; 2hr); Sofia
(3 daily; 4hr).
Velingrad to: Batak (2 daily; 1hr); Blagoevgrad
(1 daily; 3hr); Plovdiv (3 daily; 1hr 15min); Sofia
(4 daily; 2hr); Yundola (3–4 daily; 30min).
Zlatograd to: Kardzhali (1 daily; 1hr); Plovdiv
(3 daily; 3hr 30min); Podkova (2 daily; 40min);
Smolyan (2 daily; 1hr 15min); Sofia (3 daily;
5hr 30min).

International trains

Plovdiv to: Istanbul (1 daily; 8hr 30min).
Svilengrad to: Alexandropolis (1 daily; 6hr);
Bucharest (1 daily; 21hr); Istanbul (1 daily; 7hr);
Thessaloniki (1 daily; 13hr).

International buses

Haskovo to: Istanbul (6 daily; 5hr).
Kardzhali to: Bursa (7 daily; 10hr); Izmir
(4–5 daily; 12–15hr); Istanbul (7 daily; 7hr);
Odrin (7 daily; 3–4hr).
Krumovgrad to: Istanbul (1 daily; 6–8hr).
Plovdiv to: Athens (1 daily; 23–26hr); Berlin
(4 weekly on Mon, Wed, Fri & Sat; 21hr); Istanbul
(6 daily; 6hr); Paris (3 weekly; 2 on Wed & 1 on
Sat; 27hr); Thessaloniki (2–3 daily; 14hr); Xanti
(2 weekly on Wed & Sat; 12–14hr).

6

The Black Sea Coast

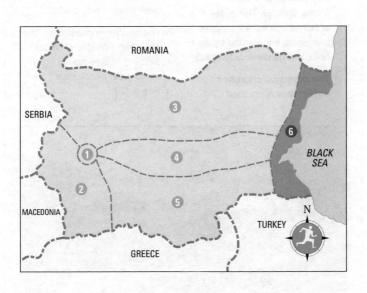

CHAPTER 6

Highlights

✳ **Varna Archeological Museum** One of Europe's finest collections of Thracian artefacts, and Bulgaria's largest array of Roman-era funerary sculpture. See p.379

✳ **The northern coast** Cliffscapes, coastal heaths, rocky inlets and bird-infested lagoons make this the Black Sea's most mysterious stretch. See p.392

✳ **The Palace of Queen Marie, Balchik** The queen of Romania's former summer residence, surrounded by lush botanical gardens. See p.395

✳ **The medieval churches of Nesebar** A unique assemblage of medieval churches, influenced by both Bulgarian and Byzantine cultures. See p.405

✳ **Sozopol** The old town features charming cobbled streets, a wealth of wooden houses and tiny chapels. See p.416

✳ **Lozenets** DJ-driven beach bars turn this unassuming fishing village into the Black Sea's party capital during the peak season.See p.425

✳ **The southern coast** Beautiful white sand beaches – most dazzling at Sinemorets – and some great beach bars. See p.427

▲ Shoreline, Sozopol

6

The Black Sea Coast

The Bulgarian **Black Sea coast** is one of the fastest developing tourist destinations in Europe. Blessed with blissfully long stretches of white-sand beach, Bulgaria's coast was intensively developed during the Communist period, when its purpose-built holiday complexes served as the summer playground of the entire eastern bloc. Despite a slump in the 1990s, the Bulgarian seaside is currently undergoing a dramatic construction boom, driven by rising visitor numbers and the real-estate dreams of outsiders eager to take advantage of Bulgaria's (so far relatively cheap) property prices.

While still a holiday paradise in some senses, rapid growth has also turned the Bulgarian Black Sea into a potential ecological nightmare. Parts of the coast can seem like an endless procession of high-rise hotels and dusty building sites. Once you get away from the big resorts, however, there is still much to be discovered, with plenty of not-quite-crowded sandy beaches, exhilarating rocky seascapes in both the far north and the far south, and lush virgin forests in the coast's immediate hinterland. For the hedonistically inclined, Bulgaria's beach-bar scene provides some magnificent opportunities for unrestrained partying.

The ideal base for exploring the northern coast is the riviera town of **Varna**, which, after Sofia, is Bulgaria's most animated metropolis. Varna's northern suburbs run into the mega-resorts of **Sveti Konstantin** and **Golden Sands**, fringed by an almost unbroken sequence of sandy bays and seductive beach bars. Beyond here, crumbling rock formations and imposing cliffs characterize the coast around **Balchik**, **Kaliakra** and **Kamen Bryag**. The central Black Sea coast comprises a mixture of quiet seaside backwaters and major tourist complexes, of which **Sunny Beach** – probably the most artificial of the Bulgarian resorts – is the biggest. Just south of Sunny Beach, the peninsula-hugging town of **Nesebar** is noted for its ruined Byzantine churches and half-timbered fishermen's houses. Controlling access to the southern half of the Black Sea coast is the relaxed riviera town of **Burgas**, not far from which is the formerly Greek fishing village of **Sozopol**. The coast beyond Sozopol offers a succession of glorious white-sand **beaches** and a wide variety of flora and fauna, ranging from the near-tropical forest around the **River Ropotamo** to marshes rich in birdlife.

The tourist **season** runs from late May to late September, and is at its height in August, when transport and accommodation are overburdened. From October to April the coast can be freezing cold, and a number of hotels close down entirely. Outside Varna and Burgas, many museums and tourist attractions open only during the summer, and hours become erratic as tourist numbers begin to slacken off in September.

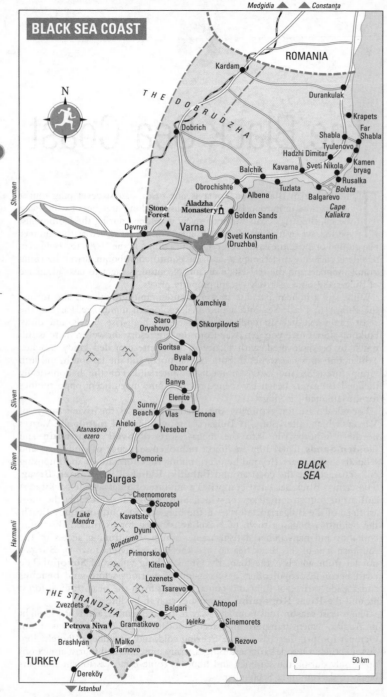

BLACK SEA COAST

However you travel, your likely **point of arrival** on the coast will be either Varna or Burgas, from where **buses** can take you to the smaller towns and resorts. It's also possible to travel **on from Bulgaria** to destinations elsewhere in the Black Sea region, with regular buses to Istanbul, and seasonal bus services to Odessa and Kiev.

Varna

Nowhere is the modernizing face of the Bulgarian Black Sea coast more evident than in **VARNA** (BAPHA), a bustling metropolis where Roman ruins, dainty churches and leafy nineteenth-century residential districts jostle cheerfully with new shopping malls and speculative real-estate developments. A booming economy has boosted the city's population to an estimated half a million, making Varna – unofficially at least – Bulgaria's second-largest city. The commercial and business centre of the Bulgarian coast, Varna is also a resort town in its own right, with a fine stretch of beach and an impressive repertoire of restaurants, cafés and clubs. The city's beachside suburbs stretch northwards to envelop the resort complexes of Sveti Konstantin and Golden Sands, creating a 20km-long pleasure zone of non-stop bathing, boozing and bopping opportunities.

As well as being a party city, Varna can also boast an excellent historical and cultural pedigree. The Archeological Museum displays some of the oldest jewellery in the world, while a second-century Roman bath complex provides visitors with an enjoyable open-air history lesson. The annual **Varnensko lyato** (Varna Summer) festival offers top-quality orchestral music and ballet in June and July, while international theatre, folklore and jazz festivals throughout the summer help to broaden the cultural menu.

Some history

Highly skilled goldsmiths and coppersmiths lived around the Gulf of Varna six thousand years ago, and their Thracian descendants littered the interior with burial mounds. Varna's importance as a port, however, really dates from 585 BC, when a mixed bag of Apollonians and Milesians established the Greek city-state of **Odyssos**. The town's best years came in the second and third centuries AD, when it was the Roman province of Moesia's main outlet to the sea, a bustling place where Greek and Thracian cultures mingled. Devastated by the Avars in 586 AD, and repopulated by Slavs (who were probably responsible for renaming it Varna, or "Black One"), it nevertheless remained the region's biggest port and an important staging post for the Byzantine fleet on its way to the Danube. The city declined somewhat under the Turks, but recovered as an important trading centre in the nineteenth century, when a population of Bulgarians, Greeks, Turks and Gagauz (Turkic-speaking Christians, see p.386) made it one of the coast's more cosmopolitan centres. Tourism in Varna first took off in the 1920s, when Czechs made up the majority of summer visitors. The holiday business was given a further boost in the 1950s, when Varna was developed as a riviera town serving the Communist states of central and eastern Europe. Tourist revenue took a dive with the collapse of east-European economies after 1989, only to recover again in the run-up to Bulgaria's acceptance by the European Union. Nowadays Varna is very much at the centre of the economic transformation of Bulgaria's Black Sea coast, with corporate headquarters, car showrooms, cinema multiplexes and real-estate offices springing up throughout the city.

Arrival, information and city transport

Varna **airport** is 10km west of town just off the main Sofia-bound highway. Most scheduled airlines arrive at the main airport building (which contains the rather misleadingly named Terminals 1, 2, 3 and 4 – not really separate terminal as such, since they're all next door to each other), while an increasing number of package and charter flights use a new building ("Terminal 5") two kilometres further west. A shuttle minibus connects Terminal 5 with the main airport building. Bus #409 (pay the conductor; 1–2Lv depending on distance) runs from the main airport building to the Golden Sands resort, passing Varna bus station, Varna city centre and Sveti Konstantin on the way. A taxi from the airport to the centre will set you back roughly 10Lv.

The main **train station** is just south of the centre, a ten-minute walk up ul. Tsar Simeon into town. Bus #109 connects the train station with Golden Sands, passing through the city centre and Sveti Konstantin en route.

Inter-city buses arrive at either the **main bus station** or the smaller **Mladost bus terminal**, both of which are 2km northwest of town on either side of bul. Vladislav Varnenchik. All of the municipal bus services heading east from here pass through the centre; of these the most useful are the #1, #10, #18 and #22 (city centre–train station) and the #409 (city centre–Sveti Konstantin–Golden Sands).

Orientation and information

The city's main point of reference – and central drop-off point for almost all major bus routes – is the **Cathedral of the Assumption** (Katedrala), a few paces north of the main downtown area. From here it's a short walk south to the municipal-run **tourist information centre**, in a pavilion just off Knyaz Boris I near the junction with ul. Musala (June–Sept: daily 9am–7pm; Oct–May: Mon–Fri 9am–6pm), which provides advice on accommodation and sightseeing, and has a modest stock of brochures about the region. The Varna Chamber of Commerce runs another tourist information centre at bul. Tsar Osvoboditel 36B (Mon–Fri 9am–7pm, Sat 9am–1pm), which handles reservations in selected hotels, sells maps and tourist publications, and may have a free city guide to give away. Most reliable and entertaining of the locally published **English-language guides** is the seasonally updated *Varna In Your Pocket* (⊛ www.inyourpocket .com), available free from hostels, hotels, restaurants and cafes. The 1:10,000 Domino **map** of Varna covers public transport routes and is available from bookshops and street stalls.

Local transport

Central Varna is easy to explore on foot, although **local buses and trolleybuses** come in handy if you're heading for the suburbs or the seaside resorts to the north – most stop either in front of or behind the cathedral. **Tickets** are bought from the conductor, with a flat fare of 0.80Lv covering most central city destinations. Trips between the city centre and Sveti Konstantin and Golden Sands cost 1Lv and 2Lv respectively. Buses run from around 6.30am until 11pm (June–Sept), or until 10pm (Oct–May).

Taxis leave from the train station, the cathedral or at main junctions throughout the city. Rates are roughly 0.60Lv initial fee and 0.80Lv per kilometre after that (fifty percent more at night), although many drivers will quote an (often inflated) fare in advance – especially if you're travelling to the northern beach resorts. Some of the more reputable taxi firms are listed on p.391.

Accommodation

While there's an ample stock of accommodation in Varna throughout the year, all but the most expensive hotels in Sveti Konstantin and Golden Sands operate on a summer-only basis (May to mid-October being the norm). Several accommodation bureaux offer **private rooms** (①) throughout the city, many of which are reasonably central, though the cheapest tend to be very grotty. Isak (Mon–Fri 7am–6pm, Sat 7am–2.30pm; ☎052/602 318) and Astra Tour (daily 7am–9.30pm; ☎052/605 861) both have offices in the train station; Isak also has an office at the bus station (☎052/505 747).

Hostels

With only a handful of hostels on the whole Black Sea coast, bunk-space is at a premium in July and August, and it's important to phone or email in advance if you want to be certain of a space.

Flag Hostel ul. Sheinovo 2 ☎0897 408 115, ⓦwww.varnahostel.com. The Bulgarian coast's first-ever hostel, occupying a city-centre apartment with a trio of cosy dorms and a communal kitchen-cum-lounge area. Beds 20Lv.

Gregory's Backpackers Hostel ul. Feniks 82, Zvezditsa ☎0897 634 186, ⓦwww.hostelvarna .com. Located in a village 15km south of Varna, but don't let that put you off: the hostel itself is a lively social centre with a bar for drinkers (and plenty of chill-out space for those that don't), affordable excursions and free minibus trips into town, ensuring that you'll be far from isolated. Accommodation consists of a couple of four-bed dorms, a couple of six-bed dorms and a self-contained double. There's also camping space (10Lv per person) out back. Open May–Sept. Double room ③, dorm beds 20Lv.

Yo Ho Hostel bul. Saborni 44 ☎0887 933 340 and 0887 601 691, ⓦwww.yohohostel.com. Hiding beyond a graffiti-covered hallway just beyond the cathedral, this is a cute and intimate hostel with two four-bed and one six-bed dorms. There's a small kitchen, a sitting room and a pleasant tree-shaded yard. Beds 20Lv.

Hotels

You'll find no shortage of **hotels** to choose from in Varna and the resorts to the north, with styles ranging from swish designer to family-run B&Bs. Where you stay will depend on what you want to do: the central hotels are within walking distance of downtown sights, while those places northeast of the centre are more suburban in atmosphere and offer easy access to the beaches.

Central Varna

Akropolis ul. Tsar Ivan Shishman 13 ☎052/603 108, ⓕ052/603 107, ⓔhotel_akropolis@yahoo .com. A row of bungalow-type constructions in the courtyard of an apartment block just east of the train station, this looks like a motel but has the feel of a friendly B&B. Rooms are reasonably spacious (most will sleep three if necessary) and come with TV, WC and Bulgarian-style open showers. Breakfast is available in the café area for an extra charge. Wi-Fi available in the cafe. ③

Antik ul. Ohrid 10 ☎052/632 167, ⓦwww .galia-online.com/antik. Medium-sized hotel just uphill from the station, offering functional but snug en suites with TV, many featuring small balconies. ③

Aqua ul. Devnya 12 ☎052/639 090, ⓦwww .aquahotels.com. Large modern building near the train station with smart fully equipped rooms, views of Varna's dockside cranes, and an on-site spa centre that offers massages, beauty treatments and reinvigorating soaks. ⑥

Dionis ul. Buzludzha 13 ☎052/655 630 and 0899 021 122, ⓦwww.hoteldionis.com. A functional-looking modern building on a quiet street just uphill from the train station harbours a soothing family-run B&B, with neat and reasonably spacious en suites above a bright reception-cum-breakfast-room area. ⑤

Divesta ul. Hristo Samsarov 1 ☎052/684 747 and 684 748, ⓦwww.hoteldivesta.com. Modern, medium-sized hotel offering sizeable doubles with TV and minibar, many enjoying good views of the nearby cathedral. Right beside an animated market area and within easy walking distance of the central sights. ⑦

Modus ul. Stefan Stambolov 46 ☎052/660910, ⓦwww.modushotel.com. Brash new temple to contemporary design right opposite the Sea Gardens, with rooms featuring bold colours, sleek surfaces, flat-screen TVs and moody lighting. Wi-Fi throughout. ⑧

Musala Palace pl. Musala 2 ☏052/664 100, Ⓦwww.musalapalace.bg. Five-star bastion of luxury offering spacious rooms with deep carpets, lush fabrics and reproduction Baroque-style furnishings. Lavish breakfasts and outstanding service. Fully equipped gym and a wellness centre provide extra opportunities for pampering. Doubles start at 340Lv. ⑨

Panorama bul. Primorski 31 ☏052/687 300, Ⓦwww.panorama.bg. Solid upmarket choice at

Bus Station, Shumen, Dobrich, Park of Fighting Friendship & Airport

VARNA

BULEVARD VL. VARNENCHIK

OSMI PRIMORSKI POLK

Dentists' Clinic

Archeological Museum

City Art Gallery

Vectra Travel

SABORNI

UL. ANTIM I

LYUBEN KARAVELOV

KNYAZ BORIS I

City Hospital

Cathedral of the Assumption

MARIYA LUIZA

Mustang Cinema

Balgaran Cinema

Alfa Tour

SLIVNITSA

Festival Hall

PL. MITROPOLIT SIMEON

Clock Tower

Market

Theatre & Opera House

KNYAZ BORIS I

PL. NEZAVISIMOST

Armenian Church

PL. EKZARH IOZIF

BULEVARD PRIMORSKI

Ethnographic Museum

Church of Sveta Bogoroditsa

Roman Thermae

Church of Sveti Atanas

Aquarium

Navy Museum

PLEVEN

KRALI MARKO

DEBAR

GABROVO

Astra Tour

Train Station

Isak Accommodation Bureau

City Historical Museum

Roman Baths

BULEVARD PRIMORSKI

Port

Varna Lake

Asparuhovo, Galata & Minibuses to Albena

0   200 m

Hydrofoil Station

the western end of Varna's beach, featuring en suites with deep carpets and sturdy furnishings. Views of both port and beach from all but a couple of rooms. 7

Plaza bul. Slivnitsa 10 Ⓣ052/684 060, Ⓦwww.hotelplazabg.com. Chic medium-sized establishment right on the main strip. Rooms are on the functional side, although comfy leather sofas and small balconies add a bit of distinction. Fills up quickly so reserve well in advance. 6

Splendid ul. Bratya Shkorpil 30 Ⓣ052/681 414, Ⓕ052/681 415, Ⓔsplendid@cityplanethotels.com.

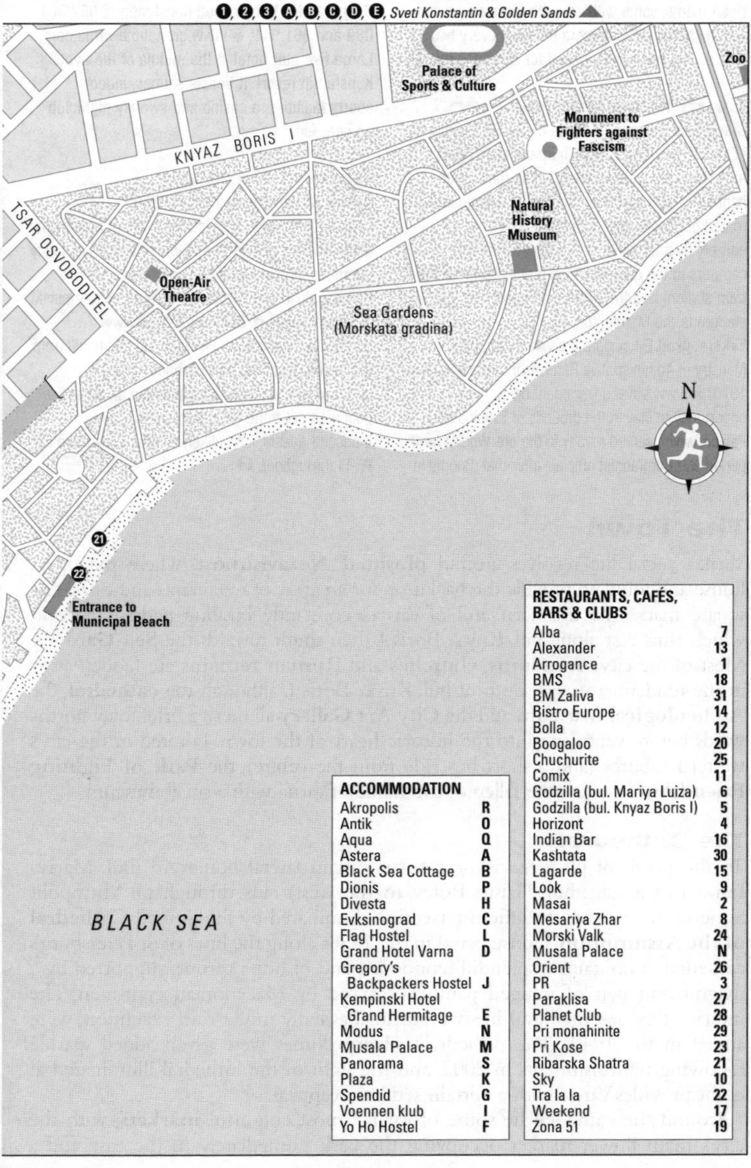

1, 2, 3, A, B, C, D, E, Sveti Konstantin & Golden Sands
Zoo
Palace of Sports & Culture
Monument to Fighters against Fascism
4, Dolphinarium & Terrarium
KNYAZ BORIS I
TSAR OSVOBODITEL
Natural History Museum
Open-Air Theatre
Sea Gardens (Morskata gradina)
N
21
22
Entrance to Municipal Beach
BLACK SEA
ACCOMMODATION
Akropolis R
Antik O
Aqua Q
Astera A
Black Sea Cottage B
Dionis P
Divesta H
Evksinograd C
Flag Hostel L
Grand Hotel Varna D
Gregory's Backpackers Hostel J
Kempinski Hotel Grand Hermitage E
Modus N
Musala Palace M
Panorama S
Plaza K
Spendid G
Voennen klub I
Yo Ho Hostel F
RESTAURANTS, CAFÉS, BARS & CLUBS
Alba 7
Alexander 13
Arrogance 1
BMS 18
BM Zaliva 31
Bistro Europe 14
Bolla 12
Boogaloo 20
Chuchurite 25
Comix 11
Godzilla (bul. Mariya Luiza) 6
Godzilla (bul. Knyaz Boris I) 5
Horizont 4
Indian Bar 16
Kashtata 30
Lagarde 15
Look 9
Masai 2
Mesariya Zhar 8
Morski Valk 24
Musala Palace N
Orient 26
PR 3
Paraklisa 27
Planet Club 28
Pri monahinite 29
Pri Kose 23
Ribarska Shatra 21
Sky 10
Tra la la 22
Weekend 17
Zona 51 19

Fine nineteenth-century building opposite the cathedral, offering en-suite rooms with wine-red carpets, TV, minibar and electric kettles. Internet access (either wireless or cable) throughout. ❻

Voennen klub bul. Vladislav Varnenchik 2 ☎052/617 965, ✉varna@eamci.bg. Hotel on the top two floors of a cultural centre for the Bulgarian armed services, with slightly decrepit but perfectly clean rooms, some with en-suite facilities, others with a shared WC/bathroom between every two rooms. Very reasonably priced for central Varna. ❷

Sveti Konstantin i Elena

Black Sea Cottage ul. 20-ta 67 Sv. Sv. Konstantin i Elena ☎052/648 877. Suburban house uphill from the main Varna-Golden Sands road, offering a handful of self-contained doubles – which can be rented out separately on a B&B basis or in their entirety by a family or group. Tent space for campers in the garden. Catch bus #109 (from the train station) or #409 (from the airport and bus station) to the Marek stop. ❸

Evksinograd Evksinograd; bookings through Ministry of Administrative Reforms in Sofia ☎02/940 1370, ✉www.travel.government.bg. A great opportunity to stay in the grounds of Evksinograd Palace, which served royalty in the pre-World War II period and Communist officials after that. Rooms in

the complex's *Hotel Tunela* (so named because there's an archway in the middle of the building) are spacious affairs with parquet floors, 1980s furnishings and big bathrooms. There's a café-restaurant with a sea-facing terrace, and secluded beaches are a short walk away. Often booked solid with official government guests in July & Aug. Hotel rooms ❻, two-person bungalows ❼

Grand Hotel Varna Sveti Konstantin ☎052/361 089 and 361 941; ✉www.grandhotelvarna.com. Large five-star hotel in the middle of the Sveti Konstantin resort. It boasts saunas, indoor sports facilities, a casino and swanky nightclub on site. ❽

Golden Sands

Astera Golden Sands ☎052/359 777, ✉asterahotel.com. Nine-storey seafront hotel with contemporary design throughout, plus casino, fancy international restaurant and spa centre. ❽

Kempinski Hotel Grand Hermitage al. Kempinski 1 Golden Sands ☎052/333 222, ✉www .kempinski-varna.com. Five-star slightly uphill from the beach, featuring plush fabrics, roomy bathrooms, a spa centre on site, and an attractive pool area out front. With room for over one thousand guests, it's unlikely to offer cosy intimacy. Wi-Fi throughout. ❽

The Town

Varna's social life revolves around **ploshtad Nezavisimost**, where the opera house and fountain provide the backdrop for an array of restaurants and cafés. The square marks the northern end of Varna's constantly bustling pedestrian zone, which runs east along bul. Knyaz Boris I then south towards the **Sea Gardens**. Most of the city's **museums**, **churches** and **Roman remains** are hidden away in the residential streets south of bul. Knyaz Boris I, although the **cathedral**, the **Archeological Museum** and the **City Art Gallery** all merit a brief foray northwards before venturing into the historic heart of the town. Located in the city's western suburbs (and a short bus ride from the centre), the **Park of Fighting Friendship** honours the fallen of the Battle of Varna with a small museum.

The Cathedral

To the north of pl. Nezavisimost, Varna's main lateral boulevard (bul. Mariya Luiza to the east; bul. Hristo Botev to the west) cuts through pl. Mitropolit Simeon, an important traffic intersection dominated by the domed **Cathedral of the Assumption**. Constructed in the 1880s along the lines of St Petersburg's cathedral, it contains a splendid iconostasis and bishop's throne, supported by a magnificent pair of winged panthers, carved by Macedonian craftsmen. The interior frescoes, medieval in style but unabashedly modern in execution, were added in the 1940s. The cathedral's silvery domes were given added sparkle following refurbishments in 2002, and the sight of the cathedral illuminated at night provides Varna with a certain seductive appeal.

Around the cathedral lie some of Varna's most colourful **markets**, with the city's main flower market occupying the park immediately to the east, and a huge expanse of stalls selling fruit, vegetables, mushrooms, herbs and souvenirs stretching away south on the far side of bul. Hristo Botev.

The Archeological Museum

Five minutes' walk east of the Cathedral, the **Archeological Museum** (Tues–Sun 10am–5pm; 4Lv) occupies Varna's former girls' high school on the corner of bul. Mariya Luiza and ul. Antim I. There's a fine display of nineteenth-century icons upstairs, but it's the archeological collection on the ground floor, scattered throughout innumerable halls, which commands most attention.

The Chalcolithic necropolis

Bulgaria's claim to be one of the cradles of European culture was bolstered by the discovery of a **Chalcolithic** (the era when Neolithic man began to smelt copper) necropolis on the outskirts of town in 1972. Dating from the fourth millennium BC, the necropolis was unusual in that it contained many graves in which effigies, rather than human dead, were buried – probably to ensure the continuing health of the living. The gold baubles, bracelets and animal-shaped pendants with which these symbolic corpses were adorned are displayed extensively throughout the museum. Many pieces are simply executed; others display an incredible degree of skill considering they were made six thousand years ago. They're possibly the oldest examples of gold jewellery ever discovered, and have led many to assume that metalworking techniques were developed in Bulgaria independently of other early civilizations of the Near East. There's also an intriguing collection of pottery from the Neolithic period on show, including a small clay human head, presumably a ritual object, recovered from the settlement of Arsenala, which is now submerged beneath Varna Lake.

Thracian, Roman and Bulgarian artefacts

No less impressive than the Chalcolithic collection is the **Hellenistic-era jewellery** from Odyssos. On one gold earring, found in the grave of a Thracian lady from the fourth century BC, is a superbly detailed figure of a

---

The Thracian horseman

Even the smallest of Bulgaria's historical museums devotes at least some space to a display of stone tablets portraying the principal deity of Thrace during the Roman era, the **Thracian horseman** (*Trakiiski konnik*; sometimes also translated as the "Thracian rider" or the "Thracian hero"). In ancient times, in the lands bordering the Black Sea, the **cult of horse and rider** was common among the Thracians and the plain-dwelling Scythian nomads to the north, as well as Asiatic peoples across the Bosphorus to the east. The horse was regarded as an animal capable of reaching the underworld and communicating with the dead, while the rider was deemed a protector of both nature and the souls of the departed.

Stone tablets bearing reliefs of a spear-wielding horseman, often accompanied by a hunting dog, began appearing in Thrace in the third century BC, and soon became universal throughout the eastern Balkans. Tablets were placed in sanctuaries and sacred caves, often those linked with deities associated with health or the protection of nature like Asclepius and Apollo; and they were increasingly used as **funerary monuments**, implying that bereaved families were eager to identify the deceased with the person of the rider god himself. The stylized iconography of the Thracian horseman probably found its way into the subsequent Christian art of the Balkans, with the familiar, spear-wielding, mounted hero re-emerging in medieval icons of **St Demetrius** and **St George**.

winged Victory, clothed in wispy, billowing drapery, which can be viewed through a magnifying lens. The assemblage of artefacts from the **Roman period**, meanwhile, provides vivid evidence of the city's high status and Romanized culture: strigils used by citizens to scrape themselves clean in the public baths, lamps decorated with gurning theatrical masks, fine surgical equipment and a fragment of a marble plaque carrying a public announcement of upcoming gladiatorial bouts, dated to 221 AD. As well as documenting their comfortable lives, the museum's collections also record the deaths of the well-to-do in Roman Odyssos, with the finest display of Roman-period **funerary sculpture** in Bulgaria. Prominent Greek and Roman citizens were honoured with a tombstone depicting scenes of funeral feasts, usually showing the deceased reclining on a couch attended by a spouse, children and servants. Townsfolk of Thracian origin preferred a grave plaque decorated with a relief of the so-called **Thracian horseman** (see box, p.379), the rider god whose worship became universal among the natives from the Hellenistic era onwards.

Bulgarian gold and silver from the fourteenth century introduces a collection of **medieval weaponry, jewellery** and fine **pottery**, including some later examples of colourful faïence ware, imported from Venice and Asia Minor. The extensive collection of **icons** on the top floor includes some high-quality examples of the Tryavna school, and is complemented by a display of ecclesiastical plate and vestments.

The City Art Gallery

A couple of hundred metres to the east of the Archeological Museum, on Lyuben Karavelov, is the **City Art Gallery** (Tues–Sun 10am–6pm; 2Lv), which hosts high-profile temporary exhibitions in the summer as well as harbouring a wide-ranging permanent collection. There are some splendid portraits of self-possessed nineteenth-century locals by Ivan Mrkvichka (1856–1938), the Czech painter who became a naturalized Bulgarian, as well as a few lionizations of the Bulgarian peasantry courtesy of Vladimir Dimitrov-Maistora (see p.121) and Stoyan Venev.

From bulevard Knyaz Boris I to the sea

Many of Varna's attractions are to be found amid the crumbling early-twentieth-century buildings that lie between **bulevard Knyaz Boris I** and the **port**, where the commercial bustle of the city centre gives way to quiet residential streets lined with chestnut trees. Huddled among the townhouses are several excellent museums, a couple of churches and the best of Varna's Roman remains. Careful map-reading is often required to find them, but it's worth the effort.

The Armenian church and the Church of Sveta Bogoroditsa

From the Archeological Museum, bul. 27 Yuli leads south to pl. Ekzarh Iosif, where elderly *Varnentsi* gather for an evening chat, and locals bring jerry cans and flagons to collect the hot mineral water gushing from a public fountain. Just beyond, at the junction of Koloni and Kliment, is a small nineteenth-century **Armenian church**, squeezed into the corner of a schoolyard. Serving a local population of about three thousand, the church contains naive icons covered in Armenian script. Outside, a small tablet commemorates the genocide of 1915, when up to one and a half million Armenians lost their lives at the hands of the Ottomans – suggesting a shared history of suffering in which both Armenians and Bulgarians find common cause.

Of more historical value, however, are the intricately carved iconostasis and bishop's throne of the seventeenth-century **Church of Sveta Bogoroditsa** at Han Krum 19, a partly sunken church whose tower was added later once Ottoman restrictions had been removed.

The Roman thermae and the Church of Sveti Atanas

Across the road from the Church of Sveta Bogoroditsa stands a vast tower of crumbling red brick, once the western wall of the **Roman thermae** (daily except Mon 10am–5pm; 3Lv), a sizeable complex thought to have been built in the late second or early third century – coins found on the site bear the image of the emperor Septimius Severus (193–211 AD). Scrambling among the ruins, it's possible to imagine the ritualized progress of the bathers from the *apodyterium*, or changing room, through the rising temperatures of the *frigidarium*, *tepidarium* and *caldarium*; and then back again. The daily visit to the baths was an important part of social life, and bathers would circulate and exchange gossip in a large central hall, or *palaestra*, which also served as a venue for athletic contests and daily workouts.

The adjacent **Church of Sveti Atanas** (daily 9am–5.30pm) is a classic example of National Revival architecture. An arcaded porch precedes a sumptuous interior, with a rich gilt iconostasis, carved wooden ceiling and painted marble-effect pillars. The icons on display here contain many of their original Greek inscriptions, which is unusual in that in most churches they were scratched off once the Bulgarians took control.

The Ethnographic Museum

A ten-minute walk west from here brings you to the **Ethnographic Museum** (daily 10am–5pm; 4Lv) occupying a National Revival house on ul. Panagyurishte. It's an interesting and attractively arranged collection, but one that concentrates exclusively on Bulgarian ethnography, despite the fact that Varna was a predominantly Greek, Turkish and Gagauz town until the Liberation.

Downstairs lie reminders of the region's traditional trades and occupations: among them a variety of fishing nets, wine barrels, wattle-and-daub beehives and a nineteenth-century *yamurluk* or hooded cloak, as worn by the shepherds who roamed the hills of the interior. On the first floor, there's a display of **regional costumes**, showing great diversity of styles, largely because the area inland of Varna was a crossroads of migrating peoples. One distinct local group were the *chenge*, represented here by a wedding scene from the village of Asparuhovo, 50km west of Varna. Faceless costumed dummies are grouped around a ceremonial wooden wedding sledge, with the bride surrounded by men in black hats wreathed with flowers. Items relating to regional folk beliefs include the embroidered **masks** worn during *kukeri* (spring) and *survakari* (New Year) rites, and a couple of the **New Year camels** paraded through the streets in some areas – approximations of the humped beast made from sheepskin and mounted on skis. Also on display are a variety of **ritual loaves** baked to mark specific occasions: the *kravai* for New Year or St John's Day; the "pony" (*konche*) for Todorovden (the feast day of St Theodore, patron of horse-breeding); or the *proshtupalnik* – shaped like a baby's foot – to celebrate a child's first steps. On the topmost floor are the inevitable restored living rooms, comprising an elegantly furnished salon, drawing room and bedroom, offering an insight into the lives of the new urban middle classes of *fin-de-siècle* Varna, some of whose fashionable costumes are also on show.

Bearing southeast from the Ethnographic Museum along Han Omurtag will bring you to ul. 8 Noemvri and the **City Historical Museum**, at no. 5 (Tues–Sat 10am–5pm; 3Lv). A collection of photos, documents and holiday brochures traces the development of Varna from nineteenth-century Balkan backwater to the comfortable bourgeois European town and seaside resort it had become by the 1920s. The top floor contains the recreated shop-fronts of a typical mid-twentieth-century street, while the basement contains a reconstructed tailor's workshop of the 1940s, plus a few period magazines and more photos. Just outside is the rusted hulk of a nineteenth-century British-made steam roller, and immediately to the south are the overgrown remains of more **Roman baths**, this time dating from the late fourth century AD, and far less extensive than the better-preserved *thermae* on Han Krum.

The Sea Gardens

The massed flowerbeds of Varna's extensive *Morskata Gradina,* or **Sea Gardens**, were laid out at the end of the nineteenth century by Czech horticulturalist Anton Novak, who supposedly modelled them on the Baroque palace gardens of Belvedere and Schönbrunn in Vienna. The park's tree-lined pathways are patrolled from dawn to dusk by young families, courting couples and skateboarding teens, and there's the usual scattering of street vendors, offering the ubiquitous corn on the cob and packets of sunflower seeds. During the summer a road train leisurely shuttles passengers back and forth through the park from the Dolphinarium to just below the *Odesos* hotel for 0.50Lv.

The Navy Museum and the Aquarium

At the western end of the park, the gunboat responsible for the Bulgarian navy's only victory lies honourably embedded outside the **Navy Museum** (Mon–Fri 10am–5.30pm; 3Lv). The boat in question, the *Drazhki* (Intrepid), sank the Turkish cruiser *Hamidie* off Cape Kaliakra during the First Balkan War of 1912. Since Bulgaria's navy was subjected to enforced cut-backs by the Neuilly Treaty of 1919, and later collaborated with Hitler's *Kriegsmarine*, there's little else for it to take pride in, and the museum itself houses a musty collection of naval relics, mostly from the nineteenth and twentieth centuries, including model ships, uniforms and various ship fixtures, all labelled in Bulgarian only.

Just beyond is the **Aquarium** (Tues–Sun 9am–5pm; 2Lv), a small collection of freshwater and seawater creatures, whose habits are explained in Russian and German translations only. The most interesting specimens are the sea-needles, who reproduce when the female of the species deposits her eggs in a pouch on the male, who is expected to do the brooding; the Black Sea turbot, a denizen of the sea bed which assumes the colour of rocks to disguise itself against predators; the translucent ghost shrimps; and the freshwater sturgeon, which can grow to a length of 9m in the wild, although those confined here are rather smaller.

A little way to the east, pathways descend to Varna's *Morski bani* or municipal **beach**, where bathers can look out at the shoals of tankers and cargo vessels anchored in the bay. The beach stretches northwards for a couple of kilometres, lined with a succession of outdoor bars, clubs and restaurants which, in summer, remain buzzing well into the early hours. At the far end of the beach, steaming mineral water spews out of the hillside, collecting in a pool often used by elderly bathers well into winter.

Back in the park, tree-lined avenues stretch eastwards towards the Socialist-Realist **Monument to Fighters against Fascism**, to the south of which lurks an unassuming **Natural History Museum** (Tues–Sun 10am–5pm; 3Lv), providing a useful introduction to the coast's flora and fauna, if you can make out the Bulgarian captions. The small **zoo** nearby (daily 8am–6pm; 1.50Lv) features camels, lions, wolves, ostriches and pelicans among others. A little further on is the **Dolphinarium** (Tues–Sun: box office opens at 9am; shows at 10.30am, noon & 3.30pm; 16Lv), where the highly trained creatures are put through their paces in entertaining shows. The **Terrarium** (daily 9am–9pm; 2Lv) lies just beyond, an unassuming building that hosts a fascinating collection of live creatures including black widow and tarantula spiders, several rare chameleons, various deadly snakes and a crocodile. Over on the northern side of Knyaz Boris I looms the **Palace of Sports and Culture**, an oval of concrete and glass that looks a bit like a futuristic circus tent – it serves as the venue for concerts, trade fairs and indoor sports events.

The Park of Fighting Friendship

Among the housing estates that mark the city's northwestern margins lies the bizarrely named **Park of Fighting Friendship** (bus #22 from the cathedral), where a granite monument atop a Thracian tumulus marks the site of the **Battle of Varna**. An army of thirty thousand Crusaders made their way here in November 1444, intending to meet a fleet of Venetian and Genoese ships before sailing on to Constantinople. Unfortunately, the fleet had already abandoned the intended rendezvous, in a vain attempt to stop Sultan Murad II and his forces from crossing the Bosphorus. Murad rapidly made his way up the coast and during the subsequent clash, King Wladyslaw III of Poland and Hungary recklessly led a charge to capture Sultan Murad in his tent, but was cut down in the attempt. His army wavered, forcing János Hunyadi to order an inglorious retreat, marking the end of Christendom's last attempt to check the Ottoman advance.

A small **museum** (officially daily 9am–5pm; 3Lv) in the corner of the park displays replica medieval armour and weapons wielded by the various East European peoples that made up Wladyslaw's army. Within the mound itself, a domed memorial chamber contains a recumbent statue of Wladyslaw – a copy of the fifteenth-century original, which can be seen adorning his grave in the Wawel Cathedral in Kraków.

The resort sprawl north of Varna

North of Varna lies a 20-kilometre-long stretch of seaside suburbia, where villas and holiday cottages cling to vine-covered hillsides overlooking a succession of long sandy bays. Interspersed among the suburbs are a sequence of purpose-built resorts developed from the 1950s onwards to boost Bulgaria's tourist industry – **Sveti Konstantin i Elena** (Sveti Konstantin for short), **Sunny Day** and **Golden Sands** (Zlatni pyasatsi). Alongside the big resort areas are a host of smaller hotel developments scattered on either side of the main coastal road. With garish hotels and gritty building sites standing beside nouveau-riche mansions and lush areas of greenery, it is an area of stark and often bizarre contrasts.

Most people come here for the beaches and the beach-bar nightlife, although the former royal palace at **Evksinograd**, the **Botanical Gardens at Sveti Konstantin**, and the **Aladzha rock monastery** above Golden Sands provide plenty in the way of sightseeing interest.

Shuttling around the area is easy enough: **buses** #109 (from the train station or the cathedral) and #409 (from the bus station or the cathedral) run along the main coast road as far as Golden Sands, passing Evksinograd and Sveti Konstantin on the way. Additionally, bus #8 from in front of the cathedral goes to the centre of the Sveti Konstantin resort. **Taxis** are an affordable way of getting around the area during the day, although at night drivers will demand a flat fee of 20–30Lv for trips between the resort areas and central Varna.

Evksinograd Palace

Roughly 3km beyond the northeastern extremities of Varna's Sea Gardens, the main coastal road runs past the entrance to **Evksinograd Palace**, a French-style chateau surrounded by landscaped park. Built under the name of "Sandrovo" by Prince Alexander Battenberg in 1882, and renamed (combining the Greek word *euxine* – "hospitable" – with the Slavonic *grad* – "town" or "fortress") by his successor Ferdinand, the palace subsequently served as the holiday home of the Bulgarian Politburo. It is still used as the main summer venue for government receptions, meaning it's difficult to visit during July and August. At other times of year members of the public can **stay** in the palace's outlying villas (see "Varna accommodation", p.378), or embark on a **guided tour** of the palace grounds – providing you can drum up a big enough group (minimum ten people; 5Lv each; book on ℡052/393 140 or 393 150). It's easy to get to, with buses #7, #8, #109 or #409 running past the palace complex's (unmarked) green gates.

Tours lead past the vineyards where Bulgaria's most sought-after white wines and brandies are produced, and descend towards the seafront through the botanical gardens laid out for Ferdinand by French horticulturalist Edouard André (who also worked at Liverpool's Sefton Park) at the begining of the twentieth century. The Communist Party hierarchy stayed in a deluxe villa complex in the woods overlooking the shore, complete with state-of-the-art health clinic and sports hall – the latter including a bowling alley. Party Secretary Todor Zhivkov had two villas, one of which ("Magnolia") is nowadays hired out as a corporate conference centre, while the other (the beachside "Sunny Bungalow") accommodates holidaying dignitaries such as Bulgaria's president and prime minister.

Whether you sign up for a tour or not, the Evksinograd estate's fine **wines** are on sale to all comers from the vineyard shop beside the palace gates (Mon–Fri 9am–6pm, Sat & Sun 9am–2pm).

Sveti Konstantin and beyond

Immediately beyond Evksinograd, the suburb of **SVETI KONSTANTIN I ELENA** (СВЕТИ КОНСТАНТИН) sprawls on either side of the main coastal highway, with its characteristic Black-Sea mixture of villas, holiday homes, apartment blocks and construction sites. At its heart is the **Sveti Konstantin resort**, the first of the great tourist complexes built in the postwar drive to develop the coast. Originally named Druzhba ("friendship"), it first admitted Western tourists in 1955, and has since served as a prototype for others.

Centred on the swish *Grand Hotel Varna* (see p.378), the resort has a park-like feel, with an abundance of oaks and cypresses, several small beaches and coves, and hot mineral pools on the seafront. There's a good choice of restaurants and bars, although the pace of nightlife is less frenetic than in central Varna or Golden Sands. The elite trade union rest-homes which used to grace the northern end of Sveti Konstantin are now hotels operating under the banner of the **Sunny Day** (Slanchev den) resort.

On the northern side of the coastal highway from the Sveti Konstantin resort lie the **Sofia University Botanic Gardens** (Botanicheska gradina; April–Oct daily 9am–6pm; 2Lv), a well laid-out expanse of roses, cacti and desert plants, with plenty of meadow space for the garden's small family of horses.

Moving northeast from Sveti Konstantin along the coastal highway (also traversed by the #109 and #409 buses), **Kabakum beach** some 3km beyond (get off at the "Zhurnalist" bus stop) is one of the nicest stretches of sand in northern Varna, and gets fewer package tourists than its neighbours in Sveti Konstantin and Golden Sands. A few hundred metres northeast of the Zhurnalist stop, steps lead down behind the *Trifon Zarezan* restaurant to another stretch of wonderful beach.

Golden Sands (Zlatni pyasatsi)

Tourists generally balk at pronouncing Zlatni pyasatsi, so most Bulgarians along the coast will understand if you say "Goldstrand" or **GOLDEN SANDS** (ЗЛАТНИ ПЯСЪЦИ) instead. The resort's many hotels occupy a wooded, landscaped strip behind Zlatni pyasatsi's greatest asset, its **beach**: a soft, pale golden expanse 4km long, sloping gently into an undertowless sea. The strolling areas behind the beach feature well-tended gardens, outdoor pools and plenty of sports facilities for children.

Golden Sands also offers a wide range of bars, restaurants and discos, as well as **activities** such as scuba diving, waterskiing and paraskiing. A group of hotels at the southern end of the resort operates separately under the name of the Riviera Holiday Club.

Uphill from the centre of the resort, the **Aquapolis water park** (June–Sept daily 10am–7pm; adults 25Lv, children 9Lv) offers a sequence of outdoor pools surrounded by bars and restaurants, with long snaking waterslides at the far end.

The Golden Sands Nature Park and Aladzha Monastery

Rising immediately to the west of Golden Sands is a ridge covered in verdant forest, thick with oak, chestnut and lime. Now under the protection of the **Golden Sands Nature Park** (Priroden park Zlatni pyasatsi), the forest can be traversed by a trio of well-marked trails, each of which starts on the far side of the main road that marks Golden Sands' eastern boundary. A **Nature Park Visitors' Centre** (Mon–Fri 9am–4.30pm; ☎052/355 591) stands beside the main road at the northern end of the resort, although it's rarely open during its advertised hours.

Leading uphill through dense woodland, the trails converge after about an hour's walk on **Aladzha Monastery** (АЛАДЖА МАНАСТИР; daily: May–Oct 9am–6pm; Nov–April 9am–4pm; 5Lv) – if approaching by car, it's clearly signed from the Varna–Golden Sands road. The monastery is a medieval foundation comprising dozens of cells and chapels hewn from natural caves in a chalky cliff; occupied since the Stone Age, the site served as a place of refuge during the Dark Ages. A Christian church may have existed here as early as the fifth century AD, though the monastery itself was probably established during the thirteenth century, in the same way as the rock monasteries of Ivanovo (see p.204).

Aladzha's monks were *hesychasts*, striving to attain union with God by maintaining physical immobility and total silence. However, they did get round to painting several exquisite murals in the chapels, which can be seen at the end of the first and second galleries. Nowadays they're scrappy and faded, although in olden times they were sufficiently impressive to earn the monastery its name – *Aladzha* means "multicoloured" in Turkish.

A **museum** at the entrance displays models of how the monastery used to look when occupied, alongside ornaments, weapons and other artefacts dating from around 5000 BC, discovered in a Chalcolithic necropolis on the western

The Gagauz

Bulgaria's Black Sea shore hosts several communities of **Gagauz**, a Turkish-speaking Christian people whose origins remain the subject of much controversy. Turkish sources maintain that they are descended from the **Seljuk Turks** of Sultan Izzedin Kaykaus, who came to the area in 1261 and soon converted to Christianity under pressure from their Bulgarian neighbours. This is disputed by Bulgarian ethnologists, who suggest that they are descended from the original **Bulgars**, the Turkic nomads who descended on the Balkans in the eighth century. Perhaps the most likely theory is that they are descended from the **Cumans**, another Turkic tribe who started moving into eastern Bulgaria in the twelfth century, and formed the backbone of the short-lived fourteenth-century coastal empire of Balik and Dobrotitsa, which was centred on the towns of Balchik (see p.394) and Kavarna (see p.396).

Although many Gagauz were Islamicized and assimilated by their Turkish conquerors during the Ottoman era, enough of them remained Christian to ensure their continued existence as a distinct community. Many emigrated to Bessarabia, where they could practise their Christian faith more freely than they could under the Ottomans. They still retain a strong presence in the former Soviet republic of Moldova, where the Gagauz lands around the provincial town of Komrat enjoy autonomous status. Those Gagauz who remained in Bulgaria found themselves increasingly torn by the **national struggles** of the nineteenth century, when many identified themselves with Varna's Greek population to distinguish themselves both from their Turk overlords and from the Bulgarian peasants who were increasingly moving into the city. Most Gagauz joined the Greeks in opposing the opening of Bulgarian-language schools and churches, and therefore received little sympathy from the Bulgarians after the Liberation. Unlike the Greeks, however, the Gagauz had no other national homeland to emigrate to, and despite their small numbers, they still retain a distinctive presence in Vinitsa, Kichevo, and a succession of villages strung out over the hills north of Varna. Older Gagauz still speak a dialect of Turkish among themselves, but a literary version of the Gagauz tongue never developed in Bulgaria, and knowledge of the language is slowly dying out among the young.

outskirts of Varna in 1972. You might enjoy poking around the various catacombs and surrounding woods – the latter a place of many **legends**. Its mythical guardian, Rim Papa, is said to awake from a cotton-lined burrow every year to ask whether the trees still grow and women and cows still give birth, and go back to sleep upon being answered in the affirmative.

The Stone Forest

Roughly 15km west of central Varna, the desolate scrubland on either side of the Devnya road is interrupted by scores of curious stone columns standing as high as 7m, known as *pobiti kamani* or "standing stones", usually translated as the **Stone Forest** (ПОБИТИ КАМЬНИ; 3Lv if the roadside pavilion is manned). These strange formations were created around fifty million years ago when fragments of two chalk strata gradually bonded together in the intervening sand layer, by a process analogous to stalactite formation. Nowadays the area is a popular spot for picnics and leisurely hikes. The site is difficult to get to by public transport, but for those travelling by car it is well signed from the westbound A2 highway or from the Varna–Devnya road which runs parallel.

Eating, drinking and nightlife

The majority of Varna's places to eat and drink are along the route of the evening *korso*, which stretches east from ploshtad Nezavisimost along bul. Knyaz

Boris I, before turning down Slivnitsa towards the Sea Gardens. There are plenty of **cafés** and **restaurants** lining the route, although the Varna restaurant scene changes so rapidly that it's sometimes difficult to provide precise recommendations. The strip of eateries, beach bars and clubs along the beach is particularly prone to changes from one season to the next, although there will always be something lively going on here between June and September. In general the places along this main strip are more expensive than elsewhere in Bulgaria, but not prohibitively so.

Vampires and vampire hunters

The ugly, industrial town of **Devnya**, 30km west of Varna, is now known only for its highly noxious chemical industry, but during the nineteenth century its reputation was widespread as Bulgaria's **vampire** capital. Reports brought back from the Black Sea region by contemporaneous travellers reveal that belief in vampires was widespread among the Bulgarian peasantry of the time. Travelling in the 1880s, the Czech Balkanologist Konstantin Jireček found a wealth of vampire lore in the isolated rural communities west of Varna. Inexplicable illnesses among humans, and particularly sheep – the region's main source of income – were attributed to a visitation by some bloodthirsty demon, and local wise men (known as *vampirdzhiya* or *dzhadzhiya*) were paid handsomely by villagers to drive the fiends away. According to Jireček, the vampire hunters of Devnya were considered the best in eastern Bulgaria.

The belief was that people became vampires if proper burial customs were not observed or if certain portentous events happened before their death: for example, a shadow passing across their body, or a dog or cat jumping across their path. After burial, an invisible spirit would rise up from the grave each night, feeding off local flocks and bringing listlessness and ill health to the human population. Vampires could also assume solid form, often living among humans for many years, getting married and having children before being detected. To chase the vampires away, a *dzhadzhiya* would be summoned to walk among the flocks, holding an icon aloft. The icon also came in handy when trying to identify the resting place of the vampire. If it began to tremble when held above a particular grave, it meant that the culprit had been found. The best way to deal with a vampire was to exhume the body, stab it through the heart with a hawthorn branch, then burn it with kindling taken from the same shrub. If the vampire was in spirit form, it could be driven into a bottle which was then thrown onto a fire.

The beliefs noted by Jireček were by no means isolated cases. The British travellers St Clair and Brophy, who lived in a village south of Varna in the 1860s, wrote of a boy forbidden from marrying his sweetheart because locals earnestly believed that he was of vampire descent. They also relate how peasants in a neighbouring village burned a man alive for vampirism, because he was fond of nocturnal walks and was "found to have only one nostril".

According to Jireček, the best vampire hunters were thought to be descended from *valkodlatsi*, literally **werewolves**, who resulted from the sexual union of a vampire and a young maiden, and were the only living beings who could see vampire spirits. The *valkodlatsi*'s vampire-hunting descendants were also thought to have another supernatural power: the ability to detect buried treasure. In an area full of ancient Thracian, Roman and Byzantine remains, it's not difficult to see why the idea of hidden hoards of goblets and coins – all waiting to be unearthed by the lucky peasant – exerted such a hold on the popular imagination.

Another associated piece of local lore concerns the Lake of Varna (a fjord-like inlet stretching west from the city), which used to be known as **Vampire Lake**. According to popular belief, the lake required an annual human sacrifice, the last recorded instance of which was in 1933, when one Ana Konstantinova went swimming there despite warnings, and was duly sucked underwater.

Eating

There are plenty of cafés around pl. Nezavisimost and along bul. Knyaz Boris I serving tea, coffee and a selection of pastries. Pizzerias are scattered liberally throughout town, and there is a line of fast-food stalls serving burgers, kebabs and chips beside the park at the junction of bul. Slivnitsa and Knyaz Boris I.

Cafés, fast food and pizzerias

BMS corner of bul. Knyaz Boris I 42 and ul. 27 Yuli. Order-at-the-counter canteen serving tasty ready-made Bulgarian dishes and plenty of salads. Daily 8am–11pm.

Godzilla bul. Mariya Luiza 37A and bul. Knyaz Boris I 66. Home-grown chain that serves unexciting but filling pizzas and huge salads in fun, bar-like surroundings. Inexpensive, and enduringly popular with the locals. Open 24hr.

Lagarde bul. Knyaz Boris I 46. Delicous croissants, cakes, tarts and fresh baguettes from a French-influenced bakery. Ideal for picking up eat-on-your-feet breakfasts and daytime snacks. Standing-room only inside, although there's a small area of outdoor seating in summer. Daily 8am–10pm.

Mesariya Zhar bul. Knyaz Boris I 64. Inexpensive self-service canteen offering the full range of Bulgarian grills, stews and salads. The functional interior is comfy enough for a sit-down lunch. Mon–Sat 8am–10pm, Sun 9am–9pm.

Sky ul. Pushkin 1. Takeaway burgers, toasted sandwiches and *katmi* (Bulgarian pancakes) from a good-value snack-bar that remains busy day and night. Daily 8am–4am.

Restaurants

Bistro Europe bul. Slivnitsa 11. Boasting an enviable position near the entrance to the sea gardens, this smart café-restaurant's main claim to fame is the menu of mussels from the Dalboka seafood farm (see p.398), with a pan full of the shellfish selling for about 12Lv a portion. There's also a good choice of grilled local fish and (expensive) international meat dishes, and plenty in the coffee-and-cakes line too. Daily 8am–1am.

BM Zaliva South beach (Yuzhen plazh). Solid Bulgarian fare in a shore-side setting, with outdoor seating positioned on decking terraces looking out towards the sea. Offering dependable grills and plenty of seafood options, this is a good place to eat before moving on to nearby beach bars. Daily 8am–2am.

Chuchurite ul. Panagyurishte 15. Traditional-style *mehana* opposite the Ethnographic Museum, decked out with folksy textiles, stuffed animal heads, cattle bells and other rustic decorations. The menu covers pretty much everything in the Bulgarian culinary repertoire, from skewer-grilled pork kebabs to baked lamb and stewed-in-a-pot cheese and vegetable dishes. There's a wide choice of Bulgarian wines and prices are moderate. Daily noon–midnight.

Horizont in the Sea Gardens beyond the zoo. Stylish restaurant with an eager-to-please menu that covers Bulgarian, Chinese and modern European recipes without always pulling it off – but the middle-of-the-park location complete with sea-facing terrace makes it a great location for a meal. There's a lawn-side café on the ground floor that transforms itself into a club at night. Daily 11am–1am.

Kashtata ul. 18-ti Noemvri. Just uphill from the Roman Thermae and the City Museum, Kashtata offers traditional pork dishes and grilled Black-Sea fish in an atmospheric dining room crammed with traditional textiles and agricultural implements. Moderate prices and a good choice of Bulgarian wines. Daily 10am–midnight.

Morski valk ul. Odrin 21. Housed in a stone-clad basement packed tightly with wooden tables, the "Sea Wolf" is a popular hangout for the local alternative crowd, serving generous portions of Bulgarian favourites – mostly grilled meats and clay-pot *kavarma* stews – at rock-bottom prices. Daily noon–1am.

Musala Palace pl. Musala 3 ☏052/664 100. Lavishly decorated in the manner of a nineteenth-century Parisian salon, the restaurant of the *Musala Palace Hotel* (see p.376) offers a small but exquisite menu of European classics and Bulgarian favourites. Main courses are reasonable at around 36Lv each, although you can always splash out extravagantly on the international wine list. Daily 11am–11pm.

Orient ul. Tsaribrod 1. Street-corner snack bar that turns into an outdoor restaurant in summer, serving moderately priced Turkish food including the full repertoire of grilled-lamb kebab fare and some delicious oriental sweets. Daily 8am–midnight.

🏃 **Paraklisa** ul. Yoan Ekzarh 8, ☏052/639 735. Some of the best and most imaginative traditional Bulgarian food in Varna, served up in a tree-shaded courtyard. There's a huge choice of classic vegetarian dishes you won't find elsewhere, alongside home-baked bread, quality grilled meats and pot-baked stews. With mains rarely exceeding the 12Lv mark, it's good value too. Mon–Sat 11am–11pm.

Pri Kose ul. Arhimandrit Filaret 4A. Intimate two-storey restaurant with an Iberian theme – expect Spanish omelettes, succulent paellas, juicy steaks and a good choice of international wines. Slightly more expensive than the Bulgarian places, but unlikely to disappoint. Daily 11am–11pm.

Pri monahinite corner of Paraskeva Nikolau and bul. Primorski. Indoor seating in a small stone-clad space and a tree-shaded terrace outside. A big selection of traditional Bulgarian fare, with grilled fish and roast lamb dishes figuring strongly. There's a handsome choice of vegetarian dishes, although portions are modest – so ordering a few and dipping in seems a good idea. Mains in the 15–20Lv bracket. Daily 11am–11pm.

Ribarska shatra Kraybrezhna aleya. Located on the beachfront below the Sea Gardens, this is one of the few shore-side fish restaurants which remains open year-round. It's also a nice spot for a drink, with its great sea view. Daily 10am–midnight.

Drinking and nightlife

For **evening drinking**, most of central Varna's cafés serve alcohol well into the night, and, in summer, a string of seemingly numberless outdoor **bars** lines the municipal beach, accessible via pathways that lead down from the Sea Gardens.

There's a sprinkling of all-year-round **clubbing venues** in central Varna, and a whole host of summer-only, drink-and-dance-til-dawn beach bars in Sveti Konstantin, Kabakum and Golden Sands to the north. Having a few drinks in central Varna before hitting the clubs in the suburban resorts is perfectly feasible, providing you don't mind forking out for taxis.

Bars

Alba bul. Mariya Luiza 34. Beer hall-cum-restaurant serving rather ordinary food: fortunately the Czech beers on draught and wooden-table pub atmosphere more than compensate. Pool tables and live big-screen sport upstairs. Daily 11am–2am.

Bolla ul. Al. Malinov 1. Basement-level bar with moody lighting, party-hungry patrons and a long list of shots and cocktails. Daily 9am–4am.

Boogaloo bul. Knyaz Boris I 20. Enter the unmarked hallway at no.20 and head downstairs to find one of Varna's cult nocturnal hideaways, the walls of which are decorated with the owner's vinyl LP collection. Jazz, rock or reggae on the sound system. Daily 8pm–4am.

Indian Bar ul. Parchevich 4. Intimate neighbourhood bar with friendly pub feel, decorated with Native-American memorabilia and football-related

▲ Beach bar, Varna

souvenirs. Decent blues, rock and soul in the background. Daily 10am–11pm.

Look bul. Knyaz Boris I 60. Minimally decorated tunnel of a bar with outdoor seating spread over two neighbouring streets, constantly buzzing with daytime coffee-sippers, evening drinkers and the pre-clubbing crowd. Imaginative menu of afford-able shots and cocktails. Daily 9am–3am.

Planet Club ul. Tsar Simeon I 26. Classy café-bar just above the railway station with a big outdoor terrace, extensive list of wines and cocktails, and a menu of fancy pasta dishes and sandwiches. Daily 9am–3am.

Weekend ul. Stefan Stambolov 2. Über-cool black box of a bar sporting the odd loungey sofa and a late-drinking crowd eager to shake a limb or two to pounding house and techno rhythms. Frequent DJ-led events in the basement bar. Daily 6pm–4am.

Zona 51 ul. Ruse 33. Friendly home-from-home for the city's alternative rock, metal and ska-punk communities, with reassuringly grungy décor and a stage for live bands at the back. Daily noon–1am.

Clubs

Alexander *Hotel Cherno More*, bul. Slivnitsa 33. Varna's leading "mix" club – which basically means that it is primarily a gay venue but people of all sexual persuasions are welcome. Nightly DJs, occasional cabaret performances. Tues–Sat from 10pm.

Arrogance *Hotel Astera*, Golden Sands ⓦwww .arroganceclub.com. State-of-the-art mega-club featuring four floors of music – one each for techno, R&B, chillout and *chalga* (Balkan pop-folk). Open nightly in the summer season and on most weekends throughout the year – check the website for schedules.

Comix Hristo Samsarov 3. Central Varna's longest-running house and techno venue, regularly packing in revellers with a weekend mix of local and international DJs. Often moves to a beach-bar venue in July & Aug: keep your eyes peeled for posters.

Masai Golden Sands. Club with Aftrican-themed décor on one of the hillside streets above the beach area, with DJ-led house, techno and retro events. Open nightly in summer, weekends throught the year.

PR Golden Sands ⓦwww.prclub-bg.com. Beach-side club pulling in an impressive number of international techno and house DJs. The adjacent *PR Beach* is one of Golden Sands' coolest beach bars. Summer only.

Tra la la Kraybrezhna aleya. One of several clubs standing side-by-side on Varna's beach-side alley, *Tra la la*'s uncomplicated play-anything-if-it-fills-the-floor DJ policy pulls in a broad and hedonistically inclined public.

Entertainment

The **Opera House**, on pl. Nezavisimost (box office: Mon–Fri 10.30am–1pm & 2–7.30pm; ☎052/223 388, ⓦwww.operavarna.bg) is Varna's main cultural institution, with operatic and other musical performances put on year-round. The **Stoyan Bachvarov State Theatre**, at pl. Nezavisimost 1 (☎052/613 002), is the main venue for top-quality drama in Bulgarian. Challenging theatre from Bulgaria and abroad is showcased during the **Varna Theatre Festival** (ⓦwww.theatrefest-varna.org) in early June.

Many other major events, including orchestral concerts, take place in the open-air theatre (*Leten teatar*) in the Sea Gardens; the modern Festival Hall (*Festivalen tsentar*) on Slivnitsa 2; or, on occasion, the Palace of Sport and Culture out on bul. Knyaz Boris I. All the above are pressed into service during the annual **Varnensko lyato**, or "Varna Summer", featuring symphonic, operatic and chamber music (June–July; ⓦwww.varnasummerfest.org), which attracts a healthy sprinkling of international guest musicians. The Varna Summer also comprises an international **ballet competition**, which puts promising young stars through their paces in the second half of July. The Varna **jazz festival** (ⓦwww.vsjf.com) attracts top musicians from around central and eastern Europe in early August. Later the same month, the Varna International Folk Festival (ⓦwww.varnafolk.org) celebrates traditional music and dance from around the world.

There are two **film festivals** of note: the annual Love is Folly (usually Aug–Sept) involving an international menu of movies, mostly with a romantic theme; and the Zlatna Roza ("Golden Rose"; even-numbered years only; usually Sept or Oct), which hands out prizes to the best Bulgarian pictures. Schedules and tickets for the above festivals are available from the ground floor of the Festival Hall itself.

The **cinema** in the Festival Hall shows the best range of first-run and cult films, although Kino Balgaran, at bul. Mariya Luiza 1, boasts its fair share of recent Hollywood releases. Films are shown in their original language, with Bulgarian subtitles.

For children, there's a **puppet theatre** at ul. Dragoman 4 (☏052/607 844), although it takes a summer break in July and August.

Listings

Airlines Bulgaria Air, bul. 8-mi Primorski polk 55 ☏052/651 101, ⓦwww.air.bg.

Airport information ☏052/573 323, ⓦwww.varna-airport.bg.

Car rental Avis, at the airport ☏052/500 832; City Rent, at Varna Business Park ☏052/960 044 or through Vectra Travel (see "Travel Agents", below); Hertz, at the airport ☏0899 855 034; Sixt, at the airport ☏052/599 490 and at the *Kempinski Hotel* in Golden Sands ☏0885 705 090. In addition, several travel agencies in town deal with car rentals – try City-Rent through Vectra Travel (see right).

Dentist Dental polyclinic at bul. Saborni 24.

Hospital bul. Saborni 40. In emergencies call ☏150.

Internet Doom, ul. Petar Enchov 23.

Laundry Peralnya, ul. Opalchenska 23, does service washes and dry cleaning.

Pharmacies Sanita, bul. Vladislav Varnenchik 14, is open 24hr.

Police ul. Panagyurishte 1 ☏052/611516.

Post office The main post office is at bul. Saborni 36 (Mon–Sat 7.30am–7pm).

Taxis Lasia ☏052/500 000; OK Trans ☏052/500 500.

Telephones At the main post office (see above).

Travel agents Alfatour, at bul. Mariya Luiza 26 (☏052/616 080, ⓦwww.alfatour.bg) handles airline tickets and international bus travel; Vectra Travel, at bul. Knyaz Boris I 75 (☏052/655 778, ⓦwww.vectratravel.com) sells airline tickets and hotel bookings; USIT Colours, at bul. Tsar Osvoboditel 11 (☏052/631 701, ⓦwww.usitcolours.bg) specializes in youth and student travel.

Moving on from Varna

Varna has two **bus stations**, both 2km west of the centre. The main bus station on bul. Vladislav Varnenchik handles most inter-city routes plus local services to Dobrich, Albena and Balchik; while the smaller Mladost bus station on ul. Dobrovoltsi handles minibus services to Dobrich and Balchik and buses heading south to Nesebar and Burgas. Luckily the bus stations are within five minutes' walk of each other, so you can probably check timetable information at both before deciding which service to buy a ticket for.

The main bus station also handles **international buses** to Istanbul, Odessa and Kiev, as well as regular departures to France, Italy, Greece and many other European destinations.

Domestic and international **train bookings** can be made from BDZh/Rila, at ul. Preslav 13 (Mon–Fri 8am–5pm, Sat 8am–noon; ☏052/632 348).

Varna **airport** is 10km west of town at the end of bus route #409. Most airlines use the main terminals 1, 2, 3 and 4, although some charter flights use the new terminal 5, which is 2km away and reachable by additional shuttle bus – so allow plenty of time if terminal 5 is where you're heading for. For international **airline tickets** try Alfatour or Vectra Travel (see "Listings", above).

Leaving Varna **by sea,** there is a passenger catamaran service to Odessa in Ukraine twice a week from June to mid-September. Tickets (180Lv one way) can be purchased from a small kiosk at the port. Citizens of the EU, USA and Canada no longer need a visa to visit Ukraine. Nationals of other countries should enquire at the Ukrainian Consulate in Varna at ul. General Skobelev 44 (☏052/601 280, ©gc_bg@ mfa.gov.ua; Mon–Fri 9am–noon).

The northern coast

North of Golden Sands lie a couple more sandy-beach resorts in the shape of **Kranevo** and **Albena**, after which the landscape becomes steadily more dramatic. Chalky coastal hills provide a picturesque perch for the lively town of **Balchik**, while the ruddy wave-bashed cliffs around **Kaliakra** and **Kamen Bryag** provide much for fans of moody maritime landscapes. Beyond here, rocky stretches of coast alternate with isolated sandy bays, while a colourful patchwork of grain, sunflower and watermelon fields stretches inland. In the extreme north, rustic settlements like **Shabla**, **Krapets** and **Durankulak** offer an uncommercialized, get-away-from-it-all atmosphere and plenty in the way of uncrowded beaches, clifftop paths and wildfowl-inhabited wetlands.

Although the coast itself remains the star attraction, the region also offers at least one not-to-be-missed sightseeing destination in the shape of the **Palace of Queen Marie** (and surrounding botanical gardens) at Balchik. There's also a handful of museums in the inland city of **Dobrich** – useful if bad weather forces you away from the beaches.

Getting around the region is fairly easy, with regular minibuses shuttling between Varna, Albena, Balchik, Dobrich and Kavarna. Beyond here public transport begins to thin out, with a handful of services from Varna and Dobrich to Shabla, but only the odd bus per day to sleepy Kamen Bryag, Krapets and Durankulak.

Kranevo

Just beyond the northern end of Golden Sands, **KRANEVO** (КРАНЕВО) is a rapidly expanding village sitting at the southern tip of a glorious curve of beach that extends onwards towards the mega-resort of Albena, some 4km distant. Kranevo's growing number of private rooms and family-run hotels make it a useful budget alternative to its more package-oriented neighbour, although there is little here in the way of sights or entertainment: but you can always walk along the sands to Albena if you fancy using the facilities there. The main E87 coastal road forges through the eastern fringes of Kranevo, and it's here that Varna–Albena and Varna–Balchik buses pick up and drop-off. A 1km walk downhill brings you to what passes for the village centre, a parade of hastily constructed cafés and restaurants leading down towards the beach.

Rooms (❶) are available throughout the village for those prepared to ask around, with prices around 10Lv per person depending on proximity to the shore. One of the best **hotels** is the *Apolon*, on the main road near the southern entrance to the village (☏05722/66646; ❸), which offers comfy, characterful en-suite rooms with TV and telephone. A cheaper option is the two-star *Magia* (☏05722/66412; ❶), close to the beach. Both have good restaurants, although there are plenty of places offering grilled fish in the village centre. Food and drink in Kranevo is significantly cheaper than in neighbouring Albena up the road.

Albena

The step-pyramid architecture of the hotels in **ALBENA** (АЛБЕНА) marks it out as one of the more architecturally inventive of Bulgaria's purpose-built resorts; it's also efficiently run and clean, with well-tended flowerbeds and lawns lying behind an extensive and usually crowded beach, lined with bars and grill-food restaurants.

Bordering the resort to the south is an area of swamp-like semi-submerged forest known as the **Balta**; access to this alluring landscape is via the asphalted track to the *Gorski kat* restaurant.

Albena is bypassed by the main road, but well served by minibuses from Varna (departing from a stop 200m west of the cathedral) and buses from Balchik (see p.394). Arriving at the terminal at the eastern end of the resort, you'll find a small **tourist bureau** (June–Sept: daily 8am–8pm; ℡0579/62920, ⓦwww .albena.bg), where you can get rooms in any of the resort's forty **hotels**, with prices (❹–❽) depending on star rating and nearness to the seafront. Albena also has a good **campsite** (off the entrance road to the left; ℡0579/62961) with well-shaded areas for tents, and en-suite four-person bungalows (❸), some of which have self-catering facilities. **Food and drink** in Albena are among the most expensive in Bulgaria and, unless you periodically escape to neighbouring Kranevo or Balchik, this may not prove the inexpensive holiday destination you anticipated. There are plenty of al fresco restaurants, bars and cafés along the resort's main thoroughfares and beside the beach, most catering to the German package tourists: individual recommendations are impossible, though, as things change considerably from one season to the next.

Albena boasts at least five **sailing and windsurfing** schools strung out along the beach, offering boat and board rental from about 10Lv per hour, as well as week-long courses (around 240Lv for fourteen hours' tuition). There's also a **scuba-diving** centre, with prices starting at 60Lv for an introductory session and 500Lv for a week-long course. The resort's **riding** centre is one of the best in Bulgaria, with twelve hours of tuition costing around 250Lv, and a variety of rides (ranging from one-hour "gallops" to day-long picnics) offered for all abilities.

The Tekke at Obrochishte

Beyond the vast roundabout marking the western fringe of Albena, the E87 darts briefly inland through the village of **OBROCHISHTE** (ОБРОЧИЩЕ), overlooked from a hillside by a partially ruined Dervish monastery or **Tekke**, dedicated to the semi-legendary local holy man **Ak Yazula Baba.** This sixteenth-century foundation consists of two seven-sided structures roughly 50m apart, with the smaller of the two, on the right, containing the still-intact *turbe,* or **tomb**, of Ak Yazula Baba himself. A fourteenth-century mystic who became an object of veneration for local Muslims, Yazula Baba attracted Dervish communities to the area and, although the latter have long since departed, the Tekke is still a powerful draw for Muslims and Christians alike. Bulgarians believe it to be the last resting place both of St Athanasius (patron saint of lost sheep), and of the country's first Christian ruler, Knyaz Boris I. Pious shepherds used to sacrifice hundreds of sheep here on St George's Day – hence the name Obrochishte, which means "place of sacrifice".

Even today local Muslims and Christians observe common holidays and join in each other's **rites**, assembling here to eat a sacrificial meal (followed inevitably by drinking and dancing) on four important dates of the year: Atanasovden (St Athanasius's Day, Jan 19), Gergyovden (St George's Day, May 6), Kurban bayram and Sheker bayram (both moveable Muslim feasts, see p.51 for details). The *turbe* is open daily between 9.30am and 4pm (2Lv entrance), and visitors can thrust their hands through a special opening in the building to acquire good fortune from the head of the saint buried within. Pilgrims also hang clothes or strips of cloth on neighbouring trees to ensure good health and protection from evil. The roofless ruin to the left of the *turbe* is the old Dervish *imaret*, or refectory, where people gather on the four main holy days to cook vast cauldrons of meat.

Only 3km from the Albena roundabout, Obrochishte is an easy walk from the resort itself: an asphalt path runs parallel to the road on the left-hand side. Otherwise, half-hourly Albena–Dobrich buses pass through the village.

Balchik

Occupying a succession of sandy cliffs and crumbling sugar-loaf hills, the whitewashed cottages of **BALCHIK** (БАЛЧИК) hover precipitously above a series of ravines running down to the sea. It's the kind of scene beloved of artists, and Balchik-inspired seascapes are a regular sight in provincial galleries throughout Bulgaria. Founded by the Milesians in the sixth century BC and named Krounoi ("The Springs"), the town was a valued haven for Greek merchants attempting to pass the treacherous waters around Cape Kaliakra, as well as an important centre for viniculture – hence its later name, Dionysopolis, honouring the god of the vine. By the sixth century AD, the harbour had silted up, and the Turks were subsequently to dub the town Balchik, or "Town of Clay".

Balchik has been largely saved from mass-tourist development because it lacks a really good beach, but there's a handful of smart hotels and holiday apartments on the waterfront, and plenty of private accommodation in the streets above. Balchik's popularity with day-trippers is ensured by the lush **botanical gardens** that surround the **summer palace of Queen Marie of Romania**, a reminder of the interwar years when Balchik was ruled from Bucharest.

The Town

Assuming that you arrive at the **bus station**, any exploration of Balchik should begin with the **National Revival Complex** at Hristo Botev 4 (officially Mon–Fri 9am–noon & 2–5pm; 2Lv): head uphill from the bus station and take a left when you see the whitewashed church bell tower. The complex consists of a reconstructed nineteenth-century schoolhouse (note the cage for unruly pupils), which shares a pleasant garden with the Church of Sveti Nikolov, built in 1845 by local National Revival architect Koyu Raichov. The iconostasis is decorated with pictures by itinerant artists from Galichnik in western Macedonia, and there's a splendid gold-suffused portrait of the saint himself, patron of seafarers, on the left side of the nave as you enter. There is no entry fee for the church but its opening hours are erratic; you may need to ask staff at the History Museum (see below) to open it.

Heading downhill from the bus station you'll soon come across the **History Museum** on pl. Nezavisimost (Mon–Fri 8am–noon & 1–4.30pm; 2Lv), which contains marble and bronze statuary from Dionysopolis, including a torso of the deity himself. Opposite is a small **Ethnographic Museum** (same times; 2Lv) displaying traditional local costumes and reconstructed nineteenth-century peasant interiors. From here the main thoroughfare, ul. Cherno More, winds down to the port, passing on the way a flight of steps leading up to an **art gallery**, at ul. Otets Paisii 4 (officially Mon–Fri 9am–noon & 1–5pm; 2Lv), which features icons from local churches. At the bottom of the hill, a small whitewashed mosque stands inland from the port, where grain silos loom over a lively seafront square. From here an esplanade stretches westwards towards Balchik's **beach** area, although there's only a thin strip of sand – most sunbathers position themselves on the various piers and jetties protruding into the bay.

The palace of Queen Marie and the botanical gardens

Overlooking the shore 2km west of town, the **Palace of Queen Marie** (daily: May to mid-Oct 8am–8pm; mid-Oct–Dec & March–April 8.30am–6pm; Jan & Feb 9am–5pm; 10Lv for both the palace and the gardens) was begun in 1924 to serve as the summer residence of Queen Marie of Romania. A granddaughter of Queen Victoria of England, Marie ordered the construction of a central villa for herself, with a number of smaller villas ranged across the hillside for her family and guests. The surrounding parkland was taken over by the Bulgarian Academy of Sciences in 1955, and the resulting **botanical gardens** now constitute an unmissable horticultural attraction. The palace and gardens can be approached from the southern entrance on Balchik's seafront esplanade, or from the northern entrance (the one used by private cars and tourist coaches) just off the Balchik–Albena road – best reached by following ul. Primorska westwards from the port. Balchik–Albena buses pick up and drop-off passengers near the northern entrance: ask to be put down at *dvoretsa*, "the palace".

If you arrive at the seafront end of the complex, you'll first come face to face with the "**palace**" itself, a whitewashed villa which sprouts spindly balconies and a tower in the form of a minaret (the reconciliation of her Christian and Muslim subjects was one of Marie's pet projects, inspired either by her adherence to the Baha'i faith or by her Turkish lover). The villa is a relatively modest affair as far as royal residences go: the ground floor is taken up with an art gallery and souvenir shop while the first floor shows Marie's hammam-like bathroom, boudoir, bedroom and salon as well as a two-room museum. Behind the villa is an intriguing labyrinth of steeply ascending narrow terraces, each symbolizing one of Marie's children – the sixth one (truncated by the cliff) represents Mircea, who died of typhus at the age of two. To the east of the villa are several set-piece follies, including a water mill, a rose garden, a Roman bath

▲ Palace of Queen Marie

and a small chapel, where vivacious frescoes include a picture of Marie herself in Byzantine garb.

The queen left instructions for her heart to be buried within the **chapel** in a jewelled casket – the latter was hurriedly removed from Balchik in 1940, when Bulgaria regained the southern Dobrudzha. Any number of paths wind up the hillside towards the upper reaches of the gardens, where you'll find more than six hundred varieties of trees and shrubs, yet more enchanting villas (some of which you can stay in; see below), lovingly tended flowerbeds and, up towards the northern entrance, a fantastic parade of enormous cacti.

Practicalities

Balchik's bus station is on the high ground above the town centre, just over 1km from the seafront. From here ul. Cherno More winds down the hill to the town centre and the port, to the west of which lies the main beach. Albena–Balchik buses pick up and drop-off at pl. Ribarski, by the port, where you'll find a small but helpful **tourist information centre** (July & Aug: daily 8am–8pm; June & Sept: Mon–Fri 8am–4.30pm; ⓣ0579/76951, ⓦwww.balchikinfo.org). The Chaika tourist office, on the port-side square at pl. Ribarski 1 (daily 8am–8pm; ⓣ and ⓕ0579/72053 and 75629, ⓦwww.chaikabg.com), can arrange **private rooms** (❷) graded according to their distance from the sea; expect to pay around 15Lv per person for something 1km away, slightly more for something central. Otherwise, the coolest place to stay is in one of the seven **villas** in the botanical gardens behind Queen Marie's palace (book them in advance on ⓣ0579/74452, ⓦwww.dvoreca.com; ❸–❹), a mixed bag of simply decorated en-suite doubles and four-person apartments all set in fantastic surroundings.

Comfortable **hotels** include the *Byala Kashta*, five minutes west of the port at Geo Milev 18 (ⓣ0579/73822 and 73951; ❺), which has lovely pine-floored rooms with sea views, satellite TV and breakfast included. The nearby *Mistral* at ul. Primorska 8B (ⓣ0579/71130 and 71140, ⓦwww.hotelmistralbg.com; ❼) offers fancier furnishings, thick carpets and sea-facing rooms.

Opportunities for **eating and drinking** in Balchik tend to be concentrated on the seafront path west of the port, where several outdoor restaurants and cafés serve grilled fish, coffee and spirits until late. Best of the sit-down venues is the *Korona*, serving excellent grilled fish and steaks in an old mill which once formed part of Queen Marie's palace complex. *Planeta Payner*, just east of the palace, offers Mediterranean-influenced food, fancy cocktails and dancing in a garden-shrouded shoreside villa. You can drink well-kept ales and watch big-screen sports in the *Irish Rover* on the port-side square.

Kavarna

Spread across an inland plateau 18km along the coast from Balchik, **KAVARNA** (КАВАРНА) is a relatively frumpy market town that owes its summer-resort status to the Chirakmana beach area 3km south of the centre. Like almost all the places along this stretch of coast, Kavarna has a long pedigree, having been founded by Greeks from Mesembria in the fifth century BC. A predominantly Greek and Gagauz town up until the nineteenth century, Kavarna was burned to the ground by marauding Circassians (Turkic Muslims from the Caucasus) in July 1877, and at least a thousand of its townsfolk murdered. Nowadays Kavarna is at the centre of a hotel and real-estate boom, boosted by the construction of a string of **golf courses** along the coastal road out of town.

Kavarna also enjoys a growing reputation as the heavy-rock capital of Bulgaria, thanks to the **Kavarna Rock Fest** in the last weekend of June, when thousands converge on the town's sports stadium to enjoy tight-trousered histrionics from the kind of international big names that older readers may recognize – Robert Plant, Whitesnake and various ex-members of Black Sabbath, Deep Purple and Uriah Heep have all played Kavarna in recent years.

The Town

Ulitsa Dobrotitsa heads from the bus station into the town centre, where steps behind the *Julie* hotel descend to a fourteenth-century Turkish *hammam* on ul. Chirakman containing the **Marine Museum** (summer Tues–Sun 8am–noon & 2–6pm; winter hours unpredictable; 3Lv), where visitors can see a 3000-year-old anchor as well as a collection of other treasures from the sea. Nearby at ul. Chernomorska 1B, the **Historical Museum** (Tues–Sun 8am–noon & 2–6pm; 3Lv) houses an exhibition telling of the local noble Balik, who set up an independent principality based on Kavarna in the 1340s, extending his power southwards as far as the River Kamchiya.

A couple of blocks west of here lies an **Ethnographic Museum** (Mon–Fri 8am–noon & 1–5pm; 3Lv), housed in a former schoolhouse, its classrooms now decorated in the style of a typical family home of the nineteenth century. Among the oddities on display is a mirror framed by fine lacy curtains: the curtains were drawn for forty days in the event of a death in the family.

Practicalities

Kavarna is served by regular buses from Varna, Dobrich and Balchik. As for **accommodation**, the *Juli* B&B at ul. Dobrotitsa 6 (☎0570/85889; ❷) is modern and comfortable with a bar and restaurant. A little further from the centre, several hillside hotels overlook the newly built Chirakmana area on the seafront, among them the *Venera* (☎0570/84878; ❷), which has a cosy atmosphere and an excellent restaurant. The cafes and beach-bars that make up the Chirakmana area are reached by regular buses from town; there's also a cluster of places serving seafood and Bulgarian dishes. Finally, there are a couple of very tranquil alternatives 4km before Kavarna on the road from Balchik. The *Sveti Georgi* (☎0570/8058 and 0889 626 639; ❷) is a slightly run-down complex of two hotels, a restaurant and a tree-shaded campsite (5Lv per person) with a great view of the bay. Nearby, the single track road after the turning to the *Sveti Georgi* leads to the luxury hotel and villa complex of *Byalata Laguna* (☎0579/76917; ❻), which occupies an idyllic and isolated spot on the coast with outdoor restaurants, a swimming pool and fitness facilities.

Cape Kaliakra

Twelve kilometres southeast of Kavarna the sheer reddish crags of **CAPE KALIAKRA** (НОС КАЛИАКРА; 3Lv admission if the kiosk on the road to the cape is manned) rear dramatically above the sea. The slender point of the cape was fortified by successive Roman, Bulgarian and Byzantine rulers, with Kaliakra reaching its zenith during the fourteenth century, when the *bolyari* Balik and Dobrotitsa ordered shafts dug through the rock so that the garrison could be supplied by sea. Legend has it that during the Ottoman conquest forty women tied their hair together and jumped from the rocks rather than be raped by the Turks. Kaliakra is now an extensive archeological site, covered in evocative ruins dating from Dobrotitsa's time, beginning with a monumental gateway above the road-end car park. More dramatic still are the stunning views of the ruddy cliffs running north and west from the point of the cape.

An easy drive from Kavarna, Kaliakra is more difficult to get to by public transport: four buses per day run to the Gagauz village of **Balgarevo** (БЪЛГАРЕВО), from where the cape is a one-hour walk across a coastal heath covered in prickly shrubs and wild flowers. However, the asphalted track is unshaded, and the going can be tough at the height of summer.

Around the cape

A **museum** in one of the caves (mid-May to mid-Oct daily 10am–7pm) commemorates Russian Admiral Ushkov's defeat of the Turkish fleet in 1791 and the sinking of the Ottoman gunboat *Hamidie* by the Bulgarian navy in 1912. There's also some delicately wrought medieval jewellery on display, and gaming dice used by thirteenth-century soldiers. The cave is said by Muslims to contain the grave of **Sari Saltuk**, a mythical Turkish hero who, in the style of St George, came here to kill a seven-headed dragon and thereby free two of the sultan's daughters. Christians claim that it is the last resting place of St Nicholas, who saves seafarers from shipwreck and guides fishermen towards their prey.

There's a **café–restaurant** in a cave next to Kaliakra's museum, but no **accommodation**. For those willing to go a little further to eat, 1km west of Balgarevo on the Kavarna road is a signed turning which descends steeply towards the **mussel farm** that doubles as an idyllic and incredibly popular seafront restaurant, *Dalboka* (☎0899 911 377, ⓦwww.dalboka.com).

The best place **to swim** in the vicinity of Kaliakra is **Bolata**, a small and relatively uncommercialized beach popular with in-the-know tourists, squeezed between cliffs about 2km north of the cape. To get there, take the side road midway between Kaliakra and Balgarevo.

Rusalka and the coastal steppe

From Balgarevo, a minor road runs northeast to the one-horse town of **Sveti Nikola** (СВЕТИ НИКОЛА), where the Vodasport centre (☎05744/601 and 0888 397 160, ⓦwww.vodasport.com) offers various **underwater experiences** in the Bulgarian Black Sea's most impressive diving waters. These range from a two-hour "try-a-dive" (55Lv) to a full PADI Open Water Diver Course (600Lv), all of which need to be booked in advance. The road out of Sveti Nikola towards the coast leads sharply downhill to Taouk Liman, the Bay of Birds, better known as the **RUSALKA HOLIDAY VILLAGE** (РУСАЛКА). A villa complex accompanied by the usual bars and restaurants, Rusalka is a quieter alternative to the bigger resorts to the south, a temptingly isolated place whose two shingle beaches are framed by moody, crumbling cliffs. Rusalka is a small enough resort to have an intimate, family feel, with plenty of supervised activities to keep young children busy, while older holidaymakers can enjoy scuba diving, windsurfing, tennis or horseriding. Accommodation in Rusalka's villas (☎02/962 4215) is relatively expensive (❺), but all food and most activities are included in the price. Buses to Rusalka leave Kavarna every thirty minutes.

Rusalka stands in the middle of one of the last surviving stretches of uncultivated **steppe** in Europe, a thin coastal ribbon rich in wild grasses, herbs, insects and bird life. Carpeted by wild flowers in May, the steppe is taken over by hardier, though no less alluring, thistles as the summer progresses. Group walks and 4WD safaris, led by expert guides in the local flora and fauna, are sometimes on offer from Rusalka; otherwise it's a question of just heading north or south out of the resort and exploring. Resist the temptation to pick any plants; most are protected by law.

Kamen Bryag

The coastal steppe can also be accessed from the village of **KAMEN BRYAG** (КАМЕН БРЯГ), 5km up the coast from Sveti Nikola and reachable by one early **bus** a day from Kavarna (Mon–Fri only). A track leads east out of the village onto a heath-covered clifftop, where you're bound to come across one of the many family graves hewn out of the rock here, remnants of a second-to-fifth-century AD **necropolis** thought to be the work of Sarmatians – a northern Black Sea tribe who travelled down from the Crimea before intermarrying with local stock and disappearing for ever. Work your way south from here to find a path leading down to the ruins of a late-Roman fortress and a grass-tufted clifftop meadow known as **Yailata**, a sublime spot from which to survey the northern coastline.

Two **restaurants** and a barely stocked shop service the village, which has long been a popular summer hangout for adventurous young Bulgarians. **Accommodation** can be found by asking the village's elderly residents if they have rooms available (●); the *Trita Kestena* restaurant (☎05744/759) also has **private rooms** and **bungalows** (●). **Camping** on the clifftop is free, though there are no toilets or washing facilities other than those provided by the restaurants.

The potholed road north of Kamen Bryag passes a landscape littered with rusting metal containers that once stored oil pumped from the ground; now mostly derelict, they spew out a constant stream of hot sulphurous water that locals and tourists alike use as showers. In the next village north, **TYULENOVO** (ТЮЛЕНОВО), a small **restaurant** nestles on rocks overlooking a tiny natural harbour, and just up the road the *Delfina* **hotel** (☎0885 095 931; ●) has a restaurant and clean modern rooms looking out to sea.

Shabla and beyond

The majority of traffic heading north from Kavarna sticks to the main E87 road further inland, passing through the melon-growing village of **Hadzhi Dimitar** (you'll see the fruits piled high at roadside stalls) before arriving at **SHABLA** (ШАБЛА), a small farming town made up of the neat, whitewashed one-storey houses so typical of the Dobrudzha. In summer local minibuses offer a shuttle service from here to the seafront at **Shablanska Tuzla** ("Shabla Mudflats"), 5km northeast of town, where a long sandy beach stretches in both directions. The *Panorama* **campsite** directly above the beach offers comfortable bungalows for rent (●) and accepts campers for 5Lv per person. There are a couple of beach bars and a restaurant serving grilled fish, but this relatively little-visited part of the coast seems a world away from the packed beaches of Varna, Golden Sands and Albena. Immediately north of the campsite are two lakes shrouded in bullrushes, the **Shablensko ezero** and the **Ezerechko ezero**, frequented by many varieties of birds, principally ibises, herons and grebes. Beyond here an enticing landscape of deserted beaches and crumbling ochre cliffs carries on for kilometres.

East of Shabla a minor road wheels south towards Kamen Bryag (see above), hitting the coast after 5km at **Far Shabla** ("Shabla Lighthouse"), a cluttered mix of ramshackle fishing huts and newly built villas. A kilometre or so to the south, next to a memorial to some Soviet airmen who crashed hereabouts during World War II, lies an attractive part-sandy, part-rocky bay that's popular with local bathers. Back in the middle of Far Shabla, the 🍴 *Bai Pesho* **restaurant** serves up delicious *ribena chorba* (fish soup) and grilled fresh fish in an unpretentious bar-cum-dining room perched above the seafront. There's a handful of simply decorated **rooms** above the restaurant (☎0888 221 771; ●).

Krapets

Served by a single daily bus from Shabla, the seaside village of **KRAPETS** (КРАПЕЦ), 10km north, is a sleepy place sprawling along a line of low sea-facing cliffs. There's a small uncommercialized beach at the northern end of the village, and a small resort complex (the Yanitsa) with a popular outdoor pool to the south. Otherwise Krapets remains locked in rural solitude, and is an ideal place to get away from it all. Hidden behind a garden wall on the northwestern fringe of the village, the ⚐ *Villa Kibela* (☎0888 880 281, ⓦwww.villakibela .com; ❸) is one of the cosiest places **to stay** on the northern coast, offering neat en suites with TV, a fabulous garden with small outdoor pool and delicious home-cooked lunches and dinners for a few extra leva.

Durankulak

Further up the coast is **DURANKULAK** (ДУРАНКУЛАК), famous as the epicentre of the 1900 peasant rebellion against the *desyatak*, a crippling tax imposed on agricultural produce by the Radoslavov regime. Lying just east of town is the Durankaluk lake **nature reserve**, where the entire population of the globally threatened red-breasted goose winters; white pelican, pygmy cormorant and the bittern, among many other bird species, can also be spotted here. The lake's largest island, accessible by mud track, is home to the Durankulak **Archeological Park** (open site; no fee), where remains of some of Europe's first stone-built architecture can be found, dating back to 7000 BC, alongside a 1200-grave prehistoric necropolis, the scant remains of a temple to the goddess Kibella, and a proto-Bulgarian village from 900–1000 AD.

A gravel road from the northern end of Durankulak village leads to the lake's northern shore, where the popular *Zlatna Ribka* **restaurant** (closed Mon) serves fresh fish from the lake in an attractive modern pavilion facing the reedy shore. The *Zlatna Ribka* also offers en-suite **rooms** (☎0898 777 072; ❸) in the three modern villas beside the restaurant. Just beyond Durankulak's northern limits, another side road heads east to the seafront, where you'll find a curving beach backed by sandy cliffs. The *Kosmos* **campsite** right by the beach (☎05748/263; bungalows ❶, camping 5Lv per person) has adequate facilities and a well-positioned restaurant. Two kilometres further north, the shore-side *Progress* **holiday camp** (☎02/870 9119 and 0886 852 741) is primarily intended for corporate team-building events but welcomes all-comers if space is available, offering en-suite doubles (❸) in comfy bungalows with TV, plus a restaurant, kids' playground, swimming pool and Internet access.

Crossing **the border** to Romania 6km north of Durankulak is reasonably straightforward, although it is not served by public transport. Taxi drivers on the other side will take you to the resort town of **Mangalia**, 10km away, where you can link up with the Romanian public transport system.

Dobrich

Thirty-five kilometres inland from Balchik, **DOBRICH** (ДОБРИЧ) is the main transport hub for the settlements of the northern coast. The town started life as Hadzhioglu Bazardzhik, supposedly named after itinerant merchant Hadzhi Oglu Bakal, who built the first house here in the sixteenth century. Circassians and Tatars formed the majority of the pre-Liberation population, and although many families fled south to avoid advancing Russian armies in 1877, the area retains a strong Muslim element. Present-day Dobrich is a somewhat workaday provincial town, although a clutch of museums and a delightful town park make it worth a half-day of sightseeing time.

The Town

Travelling through Dobrich in the 1870s, Felix Kanitz said that he knew of no other town in Bulgaria whose "Asiatic character … was so typical and unadulterated in appearance". Nowadays central Dobrich is resolutely modern, with stark concrete piles and plazas, although something of the nineteenth-century artisans' quarter has been rather antiseptically recreated in the **Stariya Dobrich** (Old Dobrich) quarter just off the central pl. Svoboda. You can watch demonstrations of traditional crafts in some twenty workshops, including pottery, blacksmithing, woodcarving, bookbinding and jewellery. The unmarked **Archeological Museum** (Mon–Fri 8am–noon & 1–5pm; 2Lv), within the courtyard of the complex, houses a small but impressive collection of 7000-year-old gold treasures and pottery discovered at Durankulak's 1200-grave necropolis, as well as Greek and Roman jewellery and artefacts including a ceramic baby's bottle. A hundred metres west of pl. Svoboda at bul. Balgariya 14 is the **Regional Art Gallery** (May–Oct: Mon–Sat 9am–12.30pm & 1.30–6pm, Nov–April: Mon–Fri 9am–12.30pm & 1.30–5pm; ⓦ www.dobrichgallery.org; 2Lv), one of provincial Bulgaria's best collections, and a good place to catch up on the leading quartet of twentieth-century Bulgarian painters – Vladimir Dimitrov-Maistora, Vasil Stoilov, Zlatyu Boyadzhiev and Dechko Uzunov – who tried to combine modernist styles of painting with indigenous Bulgarian traditions.

Bulevard 25 Septemvri heads south from pl. Svoboda towards an excellent **Ethnographic Museum** (daily 9am–noon & 2–6pm; 2Lv) where folk costumes, agricultural tools and weaving machines cram the rooms of a restored nineteenth-century merchant's house. The upstairs dining room and *chardak* – a south-facing verandah that the family used as a sitting room during the summer months – provide some idea of the elegant

lifestyles enjoyed by those who grew rich on the Dobrudzhan wool trade a century ago.

Two more museums lie further south at the junction of 25 Septemvri and Otets Paisii. The **Yordan Yovkov Museum** (Mon–Fri 8am–noon & 1–5pm; 2Lv), a concrete-and-glass pavilion dominating the crossroads, is easiest to spot. The museum's collection of sepia family portraits and Bulgarian-language captions fails to communicate much about the work of the Zheravna-born novelist and poet (1880–1937) who spent many years in the Dobrudzha as a schoolteacher, and was renowned for conjuring up the lost world of nineteenth-century Bulgarian village life. At the **Dobrich Historical Museum** in the park opposite (officially Mon–Fri 8am–noon & 1–5pm; 2Lv), a similar words-and-pictures display attempts to shed light on Dobrudzhan history. The region passed from Bulgarian to Romanian rule on numerous occasions between 1913 and 1945, and the endless black-and-white photographs showing armies of different hues marching in and out of Dobrich give some idea of the area's confused past.

South of the museum stretch the lovingly tended flowerbeds of **St George's Park**, a popular strolling area that boasts tennis courts, a boating lake and densely wooded areas in its further reaches.

Practicalities

Dobrich's **train and bus** stations are on the western and eastern edges respectively of the downtown area, and both involve a pretty straightforward ten-minute walk into the centre. There is a **tourist information office** inside the City Art Gallery (see p.401), although it is not always open during its advertised hours.

Of the town's **hotels**, the eleven-room *Stariya Dobrich*, located in the old quarter at ul. Konstantin Stoylov 18 (☎058/601 590; ❷), is the cosiest place to stay in town, its simple doubles and triples boasting hardwood floors and traditional fabrics, but it soon fills up. The only real competition comes from the high-rise *Dobrudzha*, just northwest of the main square at ul. Nezavisimost 2 (☎058/601 351; ❹) which offers smart if somewhat loudly decorated en suites with desk space and satellite TV; and the *Sport Palace* in the city park (☎058/603 622; ❹), which has a swimming pool and sauna. Best of the **restaurants** are the *Splendid*, at ul. Ohrid 8, which offers grilled meats over an open fire; and the *Krachma pri Vancho* next to the *Stariya Dobrich* hotel, which serves traditional Bulgarian fare in folksy surroundings. Dobrich's pedestrianized centre is overrun with pavement **cafés** during the summer, when a certain *joie-de-vivre* fills the otherwise sterile flagstoned centre.

The central Black Sea coast

South of Varna, the E87 highway winds its way across coastal hills before hitting the Bulgarian Black Sea's second-biggest city, **Burgas**, after 130km or so. Along the way you'll pass Bulgaria's biggest – and most garish – package resort in the shape of **Sunny Beach** (Slanchev bryag), sited somewhat incongruously next to the

UNESCO-protected churches of medieval **Nesebar**. Strung out to the north and south of Sunny Beach are some spectacular stretches of sand: some beaches, like those at **Kamchiya**, **Karadere** and **Irakli**, retain a relatively un-commercialized, desert-island feel, while the shorefronts at **Byala** and **Obzor** are quickly filling up with real-estate opportunities and apartment blocks.

The whole route makes for a highly scenic **drive**, while regular Varna-Burgas **buses** provide easy public-transport access to the settlements along the way.

Kamchiya

From Lake Varna, the highway swings inland to climb the Momino plateau, and you won't catch sight of the sea again for another 55km unless you take one of the minor roads that branch off towards the coast. The first of these, approximately 25km out from Varna just beyond the village of Bliznatsi, descends to the mouth of the **Kamchiya** (КАМЧИЯ), a slow-moving silt-laden soup of a river where you'll find a small resort beside the wooded estuary. The main attraction here is the **Kamchiya nature reserve**, an area of marshy forest and luxuriant vegetation known as the Longoza, which covers about thirty square kilometres. The waters are rich in pike and carp, and wild pigs run free in the woods. In high season **boat trips** (6Lv per person; 45min) commence from the road end just short of the river's mouth, although the Longoza's elusive pelicans, kingfishers and waterfowl tend to make themselves scarce when they hear the tourists coming. Just north of the estuary there's a lovely 3km-lomg stretch of **beach**, which remains blissfully uncrowded despite the presence of a couple of small-scale hotel developments on its upper reaches.

Only two **buses** a day run from Varna to Kamchiya, making it just about feasible as a day-trip. There are several riverside food-and-drink shacks near the boat jetties, while the *Kamchiya Park* **hotel** (☎05144/320 and 05144/329, ⓦwww.kamchia.net; ③) has its own swimming pool, restaurant and nightclub. Most of the campsites signposted off Kamchiya's maze of narrow roads don't actually cater for campers, but offer Communist-era bungalows of varying standards: *Camping Rai* (☎05144/262) has comfortable two-storey villas sleeping four (80Lv), two-person bungalows with en-suite bathrooms (②) and allows camping for 7Lv per person.

Byala

Returning to the main E87 and continuing south for 17km brings you to **BYALA** (БЯЛА), a small wine-producing town facing Cape Atanas. There are plenty of private rooms here, a long sandy beach, and a sprinkling of largely Bulgarian tourists. The **tourist information centre** (Mon–Sat 8am–8pm; ☎05143/2406) on the main street can arrange private rooms (①). On the edge of town and with great views of the coast is the *Hotel Laguna* (☎0888 310 012; ②). A couple of kilometres south, the excellent *Chayka* fish restaurant overlooks the bay and Byala's harbour.

Best of the local beaches is **Karadere** just north of town, a majestic stretch of (as yet) unspoiled beach popular with wild-camping young Sofians. It's a bit difficult to get to, lying at the end of unmarked roads which head east from the E87 between Byala and Gotitsa.

Obzor and around

The small resort of **OBZOR** (ОБЗОР) is 5km south of Byala. Known to the Greeks as Heliopolis, or City of the Sun, the town's heyday came in the Roman period, when, under the name of Navlohos, it became a fortified trading settlement. The broken columns of the Temple of Jupiter can still be seen in the large park to the left of Obzor's main square, but its principal asset nowadays is the broad sandy beach which runs northwards towards Byala. Obzor is currently in the throes of a major construction boom, with package hotels and apartment developments spreading inexorably along the shoreline. With a fair number of family-run cafés and restaurants, and bustling streets jammed with traders selling plastic souvenirs, it's a fun place to spend a day. **Private rooms** (➊) are available from the Soti-Sis tourist office (daily 9am–8pm; ☎0554/32887) at the bus station, and incoming buses during the summer are also met by a cluster of locals eager to rent rooms. The *Paraiso Beach* **hotel** on the seafront at ul. Chernomorska 16 (☎052/644 490 and 0897 975 682; ➍) is a modern medium-sized place with shore-facing balconies in many of its rooms; further up the scale and a little further along the same road is the 280-room *Riu Helios Bay* (☎0554/33022, ⓦwww.riu.com; ➐), a fully-equipped four-star used by international travel companies and boasting its own complex of restaurants and bars, an outdoor pool and a fitness centre.

South of Obzor: Irakli and Emona

Heading south, 4km out of Obzor, a left turn leads to *Chayka Camping* (open July & Aug only), one of the few remaining seaside **campsites** in the region with bungalows (➊) and camping for 4Lv per person. The road then turns inland once more, ascending the ridge of a mountain that slopes down to Nos Emine, Bulgaria's stormiest cape, where a signpost for **Irakli** points left off the main road and leads you to a small beach bar and campsite (☎0554/37267) offering basic bungalows (➊). The as yet unspoiled beach beyond the bar is popular with Bulgarian naturists who pitch tents here for free and use the campsite's facilities. A rough track from Irakli winds its way several kilometres to the tiny hillside village of **EMONA** (ЕМОНА), which has fantastic views of the cape, and where the only disturbances are goat bells and the occasional howl of a jackal. Most of the clean modern rooms at *Hotel Emona* (☎054/37093; ➊) have sea views and its **restaurant** serves decent Bulgarian cuisine; the only alternative is the characterful *Zayek* restaurant a few streets below, again with good Bulgarian cuisine as well as great home-made *rakiya*.

Back on the road from Obzor you'll pass through **Banya** (БАНЯ), a pleasant highland village presiding over a carpet of vineyards. From here there is a slow climb through dense forest, after which the main road descends for a magnificent view of Nesebar, the southern coastline and the distant Strandzha massif.

Sunny Beach

Slanchev bryag (СЛЬНЧЕВ БРЯГ) – called Sonnenstrand by the Germans and **SUNNY BEACH** by the Brits – is Bulgaria's largest, and least atmospheric, coastal resort. Massive investment in recent years has fuelled a surge of development, stretching the resort north and south towards Sveti Vlas and Nesebar. It's a vast, only partly shaded expanse of gaudy oversized hotel and apartment blocks interspersed with restaurants, shopping malls, bars and other places to spend money, and on (rare) rainy days, its soullessness quickly becomes apparent. Its main drawback is its sheer size: it's impossible to explore the resort's facilities without shuttling up and down the main strip by bus, and the grid layout of the place can be disorientating. Independent travellers would be better off staying in nearby Nesebar, a perfectly handy base from which to make use of Sunny Beach's admittedly excellent eight-kilometre-long stretch of sand – which has received the coveted international Blue Flag award – and for taking advantage of some of the liveliest nightlife to be found on the Black Sea coast. Of the numerous **clubs**, *Cacao Beach* is the choice of hip Bulgarians, while *Lazur* is a giant complex that attracts vast numbers of partygoers. The clubs pump out booming dance music until 6am every morning, so nearby hotels are best avoided.

Though Varna–Burgas buses pass through Sunny Beach, most people approach the resort from Burgas, from where there are bus services every twenty minutes. You'll be hard-pushed to find accommodation in high season if you just turn up on spec, and it's best to make enquiries in advance: Kometa 2 is a well established **tourist office** just north of the central post office (daily 9am–9pm; ℡0554/22176, Ⓦwww.kometa2.com), which arranges **accommodation** in hotels (❹–❼) and self-catering apartments (❺–❽). Otherwise, tourist offices in Burgas or Nesebar should be able to help. The websites Ⓦwww.sunny-beach .com and Ⓦwww.nesebar.com are also a useful source of information.

Sveti Vlas and Elenite

Half-hourly buses head from Sunny Beach to **SVETI VLAS** (СВЕТИ ВЛАС), 6km away on the northern shoulder of the bay. Increasingly popular as a tourist venue, the original village is now surrounded by an astonishing number of ambitious new apartment blocks and resort complexes. A reasonable beach lies 1km away from the centre. Kometa2 tourist bureau has another office here (daily 9am–9pm; ℡0554/68294; Ⓕ0554/68112) and can arrange private rooms (❶–❷) as well as hotel accommodation. One of the best of the **hotels** is the four-star *Sineva* (℡0554/68934, Ⓕ0554/68308; ❼), which offers very comfortable air-conditioned rooms as well as fitness facilities and a swimming pool overlooking the sea. A cheaper option is the *Santorini* (℡0554/68894; ❹), which has a decent restaurant and is close to the beach. The website Ⓦwww .sveti-vlas.co.uk is a useful source of local information.

Buses continue northwards to the holiday village of **ELENITE** (ЕЛЕНИТЕ), 6km further up the coast, a predominantly package destination divided into two villa colonies sharing restaurants, bars and discos. It's a well-run resort with pristine two- and three-storey villas, a good beach, good sporting facilities, and childcare provision in a central kindergarten, although it can seem rather isolated if you're after more than just a beach holiday. A central reception desk beyond the main gates (℡0554/68960, Ⓦwww.elenite.com) allocates all-inclusive room packages, including food, drink and use of all facilities for 300Lv per double per night.

Nesebar

Three kilometres south of Sunny Beach, a slender isthmus connects the old town of **NESEBAR** (НЕСЕБЪР) with the mainland, ensuring a constant stream of visitors to what was once undoubtedly a tranquil spot. Harbouring the best of the coast's nineteenth-century **wooden architecture**, as well as a unique collection of **medieval churches**, it's easy to see why Nesebar has become the most publicized (and commercialized) of Bulgaria's Black Sea attractions. At the height of summer the town can be more than a little oppressive, its narrow cobbled streets crammed with packs of tourists, countless tacky souvenir stalls and persistent restaurant touts, but a willingness to put up with the crowds is rewarded by Nesebar's many fine sights.

A thriving port in Greek and Roman times, Nesebar really came into its own with the onset of the **Byzantine** era, when it became the obvious stopover for ships sailing between Constantinople and the Danube. The Byzantines used Nesebar as a base from which to assail the **First Bulgarian Kingdom** during the eighth century, provoking Khan Krum (see p.438) to seize it in 812. The bellicose Bulgar captured tons of booty in the process, including the formula for "Greek Fire", an explosive mixture which the Byzantines relied on for their military superiority over the "barbarians".

Nesebar passed from Byzantine to Bulgarian ownership several times throughout the Middle Ages, and was one of the last outposts remaining in the hands of the beleaguered Byzantine Empire in its dying days, but it continued to thrive regardless. Under the Ottomans, it remained the seat of a Greek bishopric and an important centre of Greek culture, which is why so many medieval churches have survived here. In the long run, however, Varna and Burgas were to grow at Nesebar's expense, hastening its decline into a humble fishing port. After the Russo–Turkish War of 1828, when the bulk of the

The Black Sea Greeks I: Ancient Colonists

Why, or precisely when, the ancient Greeks first ventured north into the Black Sea remains the subject of much conjecture. The vast, mysterious body of water, which they initially called the *Axeinos*, or "inhospitable" sea, lay on the very fringes of the known world, and was regarded as a treacherous and forbidding place even for experienced mariners, who were more used to island-hopping in the Aegean. Herodotus tells us that from one end to the other was a voyage of nine days, while the lands around were home to "the most uncivilized nations in the world". Heroic legends such as the tales of the **Argonauts**, the intrepid band of Golden-Fleece-seeking adventurers who sailed to Colchis (modern Georgia) on the far coast, and the **Amazons**, the wild tribeswomen whose domain lay beyond the northern shores, emphasize the awe in which the sea was held in antiquity. By the seventh century BC, however, Greeks from Asia Minor were beginning to establish a string of colonies in the region, first along the coast of northern Turkey, and subsequently moving on to the shores of what is now Bulgaria, Romania and Ukraine.

Overpopulation and political upheaval at home obviously helped to precipitate this sudden burst of outward migration, but opportunities for trade played a part too – the lands around the sea had an almost mythical reputation for wealth, and a wide variety of goods was traded. Pioneers in colonizing the Black Sea were the Greeks of **Miletus** (a city-state on the Aegean coast of Turkey), although some Bulgarian historians argue that they merely followed in the footsteps of their neighbours the Carians, a race from Asia Minor (closely related to Bulgaria's Thracians) who had developed mercantile contacts in the Black Sea several generations earlier.

Apollonia (now Sozopol) was Miletus's first colony on the Bulgarian coast, soon followed by **Odyssos** (Varna), **Anchialos** (Pomorie) and **Krounoi** (Balchik). In many cases the colonists settled on or near an existing Thracian port: this was certainly the case with **Mesembria** (Nesebar), where the natives were ejected by newcomers from the Greek mainland city of Megara and its colony of Byzantium. Having settled down and established a network of maritime trade, the Greeks optimistically renamed the sea *Euxinos*, or "hospitable" – which remained its name throughout the Classical era.

These colonies couldn't have survived without friendly contacts with the Thracians, and a mutually beneficial system of **trade** developed. The Thracians obtained wine and salt (salt-pans are still a feature of the regional economy, especially around Pomorie) in return for grain and livestock – which the Greeks then re-exported at a tidy profit. **Intermarriage** must have been common from the earliest days, and cities such as Odyssos developed a thriving hybrid culture where colonists and natives lived cheek-by-jowl, observing each other's customs and paying homage to each other's gods.

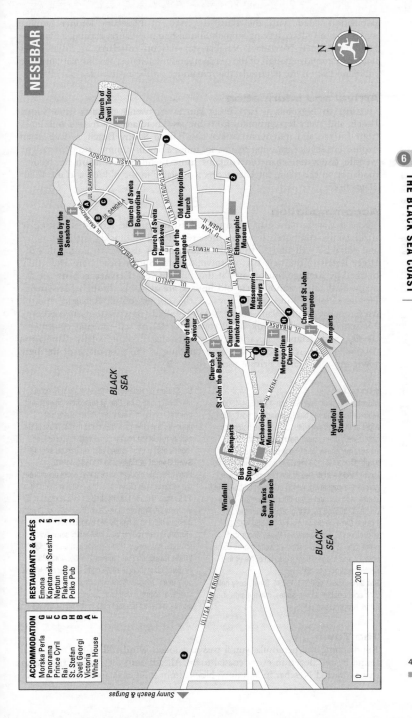

NESEBAR

ACCOMMODATION
Morska Perla G
Panorama E
Prince Cyril C
Rai D
St. Stefan B
Sveti Georgi H
Victoria A
White House F

RESTAURANTS & CAFÉS
Emona 2
Kapetanska Sreshta 5
Neptun 1
Plakamoto 4
Polko Pub 3

BLACK
SEA

BLACK
SEA

Church of Sveti Todor

Church of Sveta
Bogoroditsa

Basilica by the
Seashore

Church of Sveta
Paraskeva

Church of the Archangels

Old Metropolitan
Church

Ethnographic
Museum

Messemvria
Holidays

Church of St John
Aliturgetos

Ramparts

Church of Christ
Pantokrator

New Metropolitan
Church

Church of the
Saviour

Church of
St John the Baptist

Archeological
Museum

Ramparts

Hydrofoil
Station

Windmill

Bus Stop

Sea Taxis
to Sunny Beach

UL. VASIL TODOROV
UL. SLAVYANSKA
UL. KRAYBREZHNA
UL. SANDALA
ULITSA MITROPOLSKA
UL. IVAN II
UL. ASEN II
UL. HEMUS
UL. MESEMBRIYA
UL. AHELOI
UL. PARTIZANSKA
UL. RIBARSKA
UL. MENA
ULITSA HAN KRUM

N

Sunny Beach & Burgas

200 m

population sided with the Russians, most of Nesebar's leading families emigrated to Odessa, leaving a much diminished population earning a living by building caïques. Nowadays Nesebar depends on **tourism**, its fishing fleet unable to employ enough of the ten thousand inhabitants, of whom about three thousand live on the peninsula, the remainder on the mainland.

Arrival and information
Getting to Nesebar is easy: buses run every twenty minutes from Sunny Beach, and every forty minutes from Burgas. There are also regular minibuses from Burgas, and infrequent "water taxis" from Sunny Beach, as well as an express bus service, running five or six times a day in summer, from Varna. The website ⓦ www.nesebar.com contains some useful **information** on accommodation in the town. Internet access is available in the old town at the *White House* hotel.

Accommodation
There is a wide choice of **accommodation** available, largely consisting of small, family-run hotels; however, these tend to fill up quickly during summer, and you'd be well advised to book in advance. It's also worth noting that the larger hotels in the new part of town, towards Sunny Beach, are often fully booked by package tour groups at this time of year. **Private rooms** (❷–❺), many of them in atmospheric old houses, are available through Messemvria Holidays, located in an alleyway on the corner of ul. Ribarska and ul. Mesembriya (daily 9am–8pm; ☎0554/45880, ⓦwww.messemvria.com). Messemvria can also book hotel rooms (❹–❺) or self-catering apartments (❺–❼), and arrange a variety of excursions. Ecotour (daily 8am–9pm; ☎0554/43200) is based in the same building as the post office of the new town and can arrange private rooms there (❷).

Hotels
Morska Perla ul. Tsar Simeon 4 ☎0554/45606. Modern three-storey block behind the post office. Most of the neat en-suite rooms have balconies, and there's one ground-floor apartment. ❻
Panorama corner of ul. Vasil Levski and ul. Han Krum ☎0554/44236, ⓦwww.hotel-panorama-bg .com. Modern high-rise in the new part of town, across the causeway, which offers small balconied rooms with a/c and a top-floor restaurant. Tends to be block-booked by tour groups in summer. ❹
Prince Cyril ul. Slavyanska 9 ☎0554/42220, ⓔprincecyril_hotel@abv.bg. Nicely decorated hotel, whose pine-furnished en-suite rooms come with TV and fridge. There's also a couple of four-person apartments. ❹
Rai ul. Sadala 7 ☎0554/46094. Small, cosy hotel with comfortable, a/c en-suites, down a side street off ul. Kraybrezhna. ❸

St. Stefan ul. Ribarska ☎0554/43603, ⓔhotel. sstefan@gmail.com. One of Nesebar's newest and priciest hotels, in a very central location, just opposite the church of the same name. Most of the plainly furnished rooms come with balconies, and there's also a gym, sauna and Jacuzzi on site. ❻
Sveti Georgi ul. Sadala 10 ☎0554/44045. Unremarkable modern place a few doors down from the *Victoria*, with clean en-suites and a communal TV lounge. Usually fully booked by tour operators. ❹
Victoria ul. Kraybrezhna 22 ☎0554/46000. Stylish modern hotel in a typical old wooden house, offering smart rooms with balconies, some with splendid sea views. Has a restaurant on site. ❻
White House ul. Tsar Simeon 2 ☎0554/42488, ⓦwww.white_house-13.8k.com. Modern block next door to the *Morska Perla*, with clean en suites and a couple of roomy apartments sleeping up to four people. It has an Internet café in the lobby. ❹–❻

The Town
Approaching the peninsula, you'll pass a wooden **windmill** of the type once found by the dozen in every coastal town. Ahead loom the massive **ramparts** that protected Nesebar in antiquity; blocks from the Greek fortifications of the

fourth century BC served as foundations for the masonry and brick walls of Roman and Byzantine times. Just inside the gateway, an **Archeological Museum** (Mon–Fri 9am–7pm, Sat & Sun 9am–1pm & 2–6pm; 4Lv) houses an interesting collection of votive plaques, tombstones, coins and other evidence of Nesebar's classical past (captioned in English). One of the more intriguing artefacts on show is a small statue showing three separate images of Hecate, goddess of witches and fertility, dating from the second century BC. Other items include pottery imported from Greece, and gold jewellery such as some finely crafted earrings decorated with lions' heads, from the Hellenistic period. The basement, meanwhile, holds a small display of icons, dating back to the sixteenth and seventeenth centuries, as well as an eighteenth-century bishop's throne; the sixteenth-century icon of *Christ and the Pharisees* is particularly well-preserved.

A rash of shops and outdoor cafés along ul. Mesembriya masks the transition into the **old town**, a maze of cobbled lanes and wooden houses juxtaposed with many of Nesebar's antique churches. The Muskoyanin House, at ul. Mesembriya 34, contains an **Ethnographic Museum** (daily 10am–1pm & 2–6pm; 2.50Lv), with a disappointing lack of information on the Black Sea Greeks (see boxes, p.406 and p.420). For those interested in local architecture, it's perhaps worth visiting to see the cunningly asymmetrical interior of the house, whose cosy wooden living quarters overhang a sturdy ground floor of undressed masonry.

Nesebar's churches

Though usually termed "Byzantine" by foreign art historians, Nesebar's **churches** are understandably regarded by the locals as masterpieces of Bulgarian culture. Most of them are the result of three waves of building that corresponded with the era of Byzantine rule (1018-1185) and the First (632-1018) and Second (1185-1386) Bulgarian Kingdoms (which naturally drew upon Byzantine traditions). As they date from a period when control of the town changed hands frequently, and the ethnicity of the people who built them is hard to discern, it's probably fairest to regard them as products of a great Orthodox civilization – both Slav and Greek – which flourished in the Balkans during the late Middle Ages.

You first encounter an example from the reign of Tsar Ivan Aleksandar (1331–71), who was responsible for several of Nesebar's churches. A chunky, ruddy-hued structure of stone and brick, the **Church of Christ Pantokrator** (daily 9am–11pm), on ul. Mesembriya, is notable for its exterior decoration, with blind niches, turquoise ceramic inlays and red-brick motifs – all redolent of late Byzantine architecture. An unusual feature is the frieze of swastikas (an ancient symbol of the sun and continual change) on the apses. Currently used as an "art gallery" – basically a small shop selling mediocre works by local artists – the church is usually accessible during the daytime.

Just downhill from here, on ul. Mitropolska, lies the **Church of St John the Baptist**, whose plain, undressed stone exterior dates it to the eleventh century. Also converted into an art gallery, only one of its frescoes now survives: dating from the seventeenth century, it depicts St Marina pulling a devil from the sea before braining it with a hammer – possibly representing local merchants' hopes that their patron saint would deal with the Cossack pirates who raided Nesebar in those days.

Better-preserved frescoes can be seen in the early seventeenth-century **Church of the Saviour** (Sveti Spas; Mon–Fri 10am–5pm, Sat & Sun 10am–1.30pm; 2Lv), whose dull exterior conceals colourful frescoes commissioned by local merchants of the time – evidence that a thriving and wealthy culture existed in Nesebar even at the height of the Ottoman occupation. Scenes from the lives of Christ and the Virgin predominate, defaced by centuries-old graffiti of sailing vessels – an art form common to Nesebar's churches, executed by those praying for safety on the seas. One of the prettiest parts of town lies beyond, its cobbled alleys overhung by half-timbered houses carved with sun-signs, fish and other symbols. Here you'll find the ruined **Church of the Archangels Michael and Gabriel**, featuring a chequered pattern of brick and stone on its blind niches, and the recently restored **Church of Sveta Paraskeva** (daily 10am–10pm), studded with green ceramics, which now houses an art gallery. Both date from the same period as the Christ Pantokrator church. Further northeast is the comparatively plain, nineteenth-century **Church of Sveta Bogoroditsa**, whose unremarkable facade hides an interesting collection of icons, some dating back to the seventeenth century. Also worth a look is the bishop's throne, with its armrests carved in the form of smiling fish.

The historic centre of town is now a small plaza occupied by picture-sellers, surrounding a pit containing the ruined **Old Metropolitan Church** (Starata Mitropoliya), built in the fifth or sixth century AD. It was here that bishops officiated during Nesebar's heyday as a city-state, when Byzantine nobles demonstrated their wealth and piety by endowing more than forty ecclesiastical edifices between 1018 and 1185. Several were concentrated at the northern tip of the peninsula, where the **Basilica by the Seashore** proved to be so vulnerable to raids by pirates that a fortified keep was added. Both are now in ruins, as is the old windmill in the vicinity, while the thirteenth-century **Church of Sveti Todor** (daily 9am–10pm) nearby has become a gallery.

To wrap up Nesebar's churches in some kind of chronological order, head back along ul. Mesembriya, then turn left down ul. Ribarska to find the **Church of Sveti Stefan**, also known as the **New Metropolitan Church** (daily 9am–6pm; 4Lv). Founded in the tenth or eleventh century during the First Kingdom, the church was enlarged under the Second Kingdom, then supplanted the Old Metropolitan Church in the fifteenth century. Most of the frescoes that you see today were added in the sixteenth and seventeenth centuries. So similar are the faces of the seven handmaidens who accompany the Virgin to the Temple (on the southwest pillar) that legend has it that the unknown artist was infatuated with his model. The patron who financed the church's enlargement is given pride of place among the *Forty Martyrs* on the west wall. Also note the bases of the marble columns, which originally formed the capitals of pillars in a pagan temple, and the opulently carved eighteenth-century bishop's throne, one of the best of its kind in Bulgaria.

It's fitting to end with the ruined **Church of St John Aliturgetos**, in splendid isolation by the shore, at the bottom of ul. Ribarska. Though never consecrated, St John's represents the zenith of Bulgarian–Byzantine church architecture, achieved during the Second Kingdom. Its exterior decoration is strikingly varied, employing limestone, red bricks, crosses, mussel shells and ceramic plaques, with a representation of a human figure in limestone blocks embedded in the north wall.

Eating and drinking

There's a surfeit of **places to eat** on the peninsula, from summertime harbourside kiosks selling mackerel, mussels and other snacks, to dozens of restaurants trying to attract foreign tourists with pizzas, *bratwurst* and roast-beef lunches. As you might expect, many of these establishments are pretty ropey and overpriced tourist traps, though it's still possible to get a decent meal in town; as a general rule, it's best to avoid those places that employ touts to hassle passers-by. If it's seafood you're after, the *Kapetanska Sreshta* fish restaurant is a nice enough place, with a shaded terrace overlooking the harbour. You can also try any of the restaurants with sea-facing terraces along the southern side of the peninsula: water features and flower beds lend appeal to *Emona*, just beyond the Ethnographic Museum, while *Neptun*, towards the far end of town, is a reliable option. *Plakamo*, just down from the New Metropolitan Church at Ivan Aleksandar 8, is family-run and relatively sheltered. In the centre, opposite Messemvria Holidays, *Polko Pub* serves an extensive range of pizzas.

Pomorie

Continuing south from Nesebar, beyond **Aheloi** (АХЕЛОЙ), the road passes the salt-pans surrounding Lake Pomorie, one of Bulgaria's main sources of salt, and renowned for its therapeutic **mud baths**. Sited upon a peninsula beside the lake, **POMORIE** (ПОМОРИЕ; pronounced "Pah-mor-ye") would probably resemble Nesebar if it hadn't been gutted by fire in 1906 and rebuilt in concrete during the 1950s. The recent property boom has provided the town with some incongruous new landmarks, including several vast apartment complexes with typically kitsch facades. Pomorie's ancient precursor, Anchialos, was founded by the Apollonians, became rich through the export of salt and wine, and found favour in the Roman era as an exclusive health resort. Despite its dilapidation the lakeside sanatorium

▲ Pygmy cormorants

remains important to the local economy, as does another speciality of long standing, the locally produced aromatic dry *Pomoriiski dimyat* **wine**. Apart from an abundance of private rooms and an underused stretch of beach, however, there's little in modern Pomorie to justify a stopover.

The Town

Pomorie's **bus station** is separated from the centre by a three-kilometre stretch of grotty industrial suburbs, best avoided by catching bus #1 (every 20–30min) to *centralna spirka* (central bus stop) in the town centre. Pomorie's **beach** occupies a four-kilometre-long sand bar which stretches north from the tip of the peninsula, and separates the town's famous salt-pans from the open sea. This is a prime spot for **bird-watching**, with a number of rare species – such as the pygmy cormorant and the corncrake – frequenting the long strip of salty water, where artificial breeding platforms have been set up to encourage the large numbers of avocets and other wetland birds which come here. It's also the site of the **Salt Museum** (Mon–Sat 10am–6pm; 2Lv) which features a working salt-pan and a small exhibition covering the ancient history of Pomorie's trade in "white gold".

Private rooms (❶–❷) can be rented from Pomerie's numerous accommodation bureaux: Try Lilit Tourist Agency (daily noon–9pm; ☎0596/24905) on Knyaz Boris I, the main road into town. *Interhotel Pomorie* on ul. Yavorov 3 (☎0596/22440, ⓦwww.pomorie.com/ih-pomorie/new_intro.html; ❺) is the town's best hotel; down the road at number 15, the *St George* is a smart new seafront affair with a fully equipped spa centre (☎0596/24411, ⓦwww.st-george-bg.com; ❹). The nearest **campsites** are the *Evropa* (4Lv per person, 5Lv per tent), 2km along the Burgas road, where there's another popular stretch of sandy beach; and *Kamping Aheloi* (☎0596/85588; 4Lv per person, 4Lv per tent), occupying an isolated coastal spot just south of the town of Aheloi on the road to Nesebar (Burgas–Nesebar buses drop off by the entrance). Further information can be found at ⓦwww. bulrest.com/pomorie.

The Burgas lakes

Midway between Pomorie and Burgas the road passes **Atanasovsko ezero**, the largest and most ecologically important wetland reserve in Bulgaria. This ten-kilometre-long stretch of shallow inland water is frequented by more than three hundred species of **birds** – representing nearly three-quarters of the country's total – including such rare visitors as the Dalmatian pelican, corncrake and pygmy cormorant, as well as thousands of more common birds. The lake serves as the midway point on the "Via Pontica" – the route used by birds migrating between Scandinavia and Africa – and tens of thousands of white storks have been recorded circling the area on their way south. Plant life is equally varied and abundant, while Europe's smallest mammal, the Etruscan shrew, also makes its home here. Immediately west of Burgas is **Burgasko ezero**, which has been transformed over recent years from an almost hopelessly polluted body of water into an important nature reserve, and a protected breeding site for night herons, squacco herons and little egrets. Just south of here is the final major reserve, **Poda Lagoon**, where you'll find the only colony of spoonbills on the Black Sea coast, which nest here between May and June.

The **Poda Information and Visitors Centre** (☎056/850540, ⓦwww.bspb-poda .de), at the edge of the lagoon, is open daily, and arranges tours of the site for 3Lv per person, whenever there is interest. Further Information can be found at ⓦwww .pomonet.bg/bourgaslakes.

The southern Black Sea coast

The main transport hub for the southern Black Sea coast is the city of **Burgas**, a likeable and easy-going port which has good transport links to nearby resorts and beaches. The most alluring of the seaside towns south of Burgas is **Sozopol**, a rapidly expanding settlement which still retains something of its former fishing-village charm. Beyond Sozopol lie some spectacular beaches, and a string of towns that offer an invigorating sense of high-season tourist bustle – but without the charmless concrete high-rise hotels of the mega-resorts further north. Places like **Primorsko**, **Kiten** and **Ahtopol** offer reasonably inexpensive lodgings and proximity to good beaches, while **Lozenets** has become the Black Sea's hot spot for well-heeled Bulgarians and prices are accordingly higher. From Ahtopol a lonely coast road continues to **Sinemorets**, a middle-of-nowhere village whose stunning main beach has been blighted by recent hotel developments, though unspoilt beaches can be found a little further south and north.

Transport is straightforward with regular buses trundling southwards from Burgas to Sozopol, with less frequent services continuing onwards to Lozenets, Ahtopol and beyond.

Burgas

Overlooked by most tourists and often dismissed as a polluted industrial zone, **BURGAS** (БУРГАС) is a surprisingly attractive city, and makes a welcome break from the crowds and commercialism of the nearby seaside resorts. Though the city's suburbs are certainly dreary, the centre is pleasantly urbane and tourist-friendly. Recent efforts to improve its seedy image have resulted in a surge of new visitors, and smart hotels and restaurants have sprung up to cater for them. As the site of an oil refinery and associated chemical plants, Burgas is far more industrial than any of its neighbours on the coast, and its deep harbour is home to Bulgaria's oceanic fishing fleet. The presence of visiting ships and passing tourists gives the town a certain cosmopolitanism – especially in late August, during the **folk festival** – but nothing to compare with the cultural life of Varna.

Road traffic southwards is borne by a thin finger of land that separates the gulf itself from the land-locked Burgasko ezero to the west (see box, opposite), while further down lie the picturesque freshwater resevoir of **Mandrensko ezero** (Lake Mandra) and the **Poda Lagoon** (see box, opposite), lying beside the main E87 road 10km south of Burgas.

Arrival

Both the **train** station and the main **bus** station (Avtogara Yug) are just south of the centre on Garov Ploshtad. The half-hourly bus #15 from the airport ends up here too, and it's the best place to pick up a taxi. There's a left-luggage office behind the bus station. An additional bus station, Avtogara Zapad, lies 3km northwest of the centre (bus #4 from the centre), although you're only likely to use it if you're travelling to or from Malko Tarnovo.

Accommodation

Private rooms (①) in downtown apartment blocks are available from Dimant, at bul. Tsar Simeon 15 (summer daily 8am–10pm, winter Mon–Fri 9am–6.30pm; ℡056/840779, ✉dimant91@abv.bg). Primorets Travel, opposite the bus station at Garov Ploshtad 3 (daily 7am–7pm; ℡056/842727), also arranges rooms (①). The nearest **campsite** is *Kraimorie*, 14km south of town and 2km off the coastal road: any bus heading south can drop you at the turn-off.

Hotels

Bulair ul. Bulair 7 ℡056/846232, ⓦwww .hotelbulair.com. A modern hotel offering comfortable a/c rooms. Let down by its proximity to a busy street. ❸

Bulgaria ul. Aleksandrovska ℡056/842820, ⓦwww.bulgaria-hotel.com. Despite its refurbishment, this imposing sixteen-floor hotel has been eclipsed by several smart new competitors – though none can beat its unrivalled views. ❻

Fors ul. K. Fotinov 17 ℡056/828852, ⓦwww .hotelfors-bg.com. Brand new central hotel with smart a/c rooms, Wi-Fi and a pizza restaurant. ❸

Fotinov Guest House ul. K. Fotinov 22 ℡0897/834130, ⓦwww.hotelfotinov.com. A pleasant family-run affair with Wi-Fi, fitness facilities and a sauna. ❸

Luxor ul. Bulair 27 ℡056/847670, ⓦwww .luxor-bs.com. High standards and facilities including sauna, steam bath, fitness centre and Wi-Fi. Its restaurant serves good Italian food. ❺

Plaza ul. Bogoridi 42 ℡056/846294, ⓦwww.plazahotel-bg.com. In terms of style and luxury, this is probably the best hotel in town and certainly offers a more intimate experience than the *Bulgaria*, though it lacks additional facilities.

Primorets at the south end of the Sea Gardens at pl. Aleksandar Batenberg 2 ℡056/843137, ℻842934. A well-established hotel in need of refurbishment that nevertheless offers good value and is just a short walk from the beach. ❷

The Town

Social and commercial life in Burgas centres on **ulitsa Aleksandrovska**, the long boulevard that scythes north–south through town. The upper part is sedate, shaded by trees and largely residential, while the lower end of the avenue is brash and colourful, lined with cafés and thronged with people. Everyone comes here to stroll in the evening, walk their dogs or just sit and drink a coffee or two. Midway along is a spacious plaza whose surprisingly spruce, marble Soviet war memorial has been outclassed by the gleaming white stone and bronzed glass of **Burgas Free University**, Bulgaria's first privately funded fee-paying college, offering courses in marketing.

The other axis of social life in Burgas is **bulevard Aleko Bogoridi**, which turns off by the towering *Hotel Bulgaria*, in the direction of the Sea Gardens to the east. Narrower than ul. Aleksandrovska, but likewise full of shops and cafés, it runs past the small **Armenian Church** of St Hach, a modern structure with an elaborate bell tower, ministering to the needs of the town's few hundred Armenian residents. A third of the way along bul. Bogoridi is an **Archeological Museum** (Mon–Sat 10am–7pm; 2Lv) housing a display of Roman-period votive tablets, Thracian jewelley and Neolithic pots. One block south of the museum at ul. Mitropolit Simeon 22, a Moorish-style former synagogue contains an **Art Museum** (Mon–Fri 9am–noon & 2–6pm; 2Lv), with a fine display of eighteenth- and nineteenth-century icons and a range of work by contemporary Bulgarian artists.

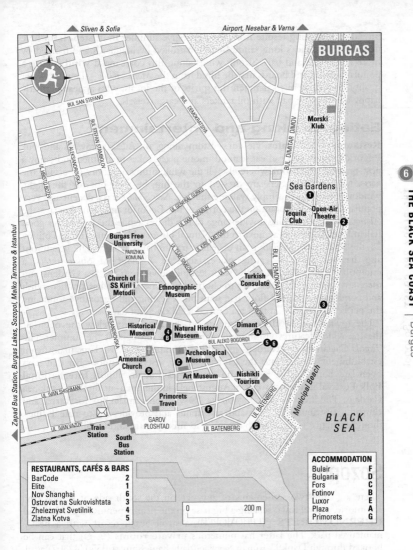

North of bul. Bogoridi, residential streets huddle around the **Church of
SS Kiril i Metodii**, built between 1894 and 1905. The saints are depicted in
peeling murals above the entrance, framed by Art Nouveau stained glass. A
couple of minutes' walk east, the **Ethnographic Museum**, at ul. Slavyanska 69
(Mon–Sat 10am–7pm; 2Lv), exhibits (with commentary in Bulgarian only)
fishing paraphernalia, regional textiles and fearsome *kukeri* costumes. Just south
of here, the **Natural History Museum**, at ul. Konstantin Fotinov 30 (Mon–
Sat 9am–7pm; 2Lv), has the usual collection of stuffed animals.

Bulevard Bogoridi ends near the attractive and well-kept **Sea Gardens**, laid
out with flowerbeds, statues and fountains, and dotted with cafés. There are
some splendid views of the sea from the terraces, while the shady avenues

provide a refreshing respite from the oppressive summer heat. Steps from here descend to the city's long sandy **beach**, patrolled by lifeguards and fringed by more restaurants and bars. Strong winds along this coast make **windsurfing** a popular activity, and boards may be hired from the *Morski Klub* – the poor water quality doesn't seem to dampen the spirits of the locals, who appear perfectly happy to share the bay with oil tankers and cargo vessels.

Eating, drinking and entertainment

Restaurants and **cafés** vie for custom along ul. Aleksandrovska and bul. Bogoridi, where you can eat seafood in one place, cakes in another, and enjoy a post-prandial drink somewhere else, all the while sitting outdoors, observing the *korso*. Most promenaders are dressed to the hilt, be they out for the night, window-shopping, or simply walking the dog. *Nov Shanghai* is a decent and very popular Chinese restaurant on the corner of bul. Bogoridi and Demokratsiya; the *Zlatna Kotva* opposite has a wide range of fish dishes, while the *Luxor* does good Italian food. Tucked away next to the Natural History Museum at ul. K. Fotinov 28, the *Zheleznyat Svetilnik* is an excellent traditional restaurant. The beachfront also has its share of eating places, such as *Ostrovat na Sukrovishtata*, a traditional-style *mehana* near the steps leading down from the Sea Gardens, and there are several beach-hut **bars** to choose from. The *Bulgaria* has a rather stylish and comfortable ground-floor bar, with plush seating and decorative fountains, the perfect setting for an iced tea or a cocktail on a hot day.

The town's coolest **club** is *BarCode* on the beach just below the open-air theatre, which features visiting international DJs throughout the summer. The *Tequila Club* in the Sea Gardens, just off bul. Dimitar Dimov, is a large mainstream establishment; further into the gardens is *Elite*, a stylish outdoor bar that stays open late. Some of the best music can be heard at the annual **International Folk Festival** in the last week of August, held in the open-air theatre in the Sea Gardens. The free weekly *Programata* (Ⓦ www.programata.bg) for Varna and Burgas is distributed in bars and restaurants and provides up-to-date listings, though patience is required to decipher its mix of Latin and Cyrillic text.

Sozopol

There are only two settlements of any size on the south side of Burgas bay: Kraimorie, a naval town serving a big base on the nearby peninsula of Aitia, and **CHERNOMORETS** (ЧЕРНОМОРЕЦ), a small beach resort with a neatly manicured park. The latter has numerous **private rooms** (❶–❷) that can be booked through Dank93 Tourist Service (daily 8am–8pm; ℡ 0550/42307) at ul. Sveti Nikola 34 opposite the bus station and a **campsite**, the *Gradina* (℡ 0550/22524; double bungalows ❶, 5Lv per tent and 4Lv per person), located on the beach to the south.

Both towns are served by half-hourly buses on the Burgas–Sozopol route, but it's better to press on to the small fishing port of **SOZOPOL** (СОЗОПОЛ), the favoured resort of Bulgaria's literary and artistic set since the beginning of the nineteenth century, popular with German and eastern European package tourists since the 1970s and now with British holidaymakers and investors buying into the current property boom.

With an engaging huddle of nineteenth-century houses on a rocky headland, two fine beaches, scores of bars and restaurants, and a lively promenade, Sozopol is fast overtaking Nesebar as the coast's prime attraction. Somewhat incongruously,

Burgas is the transport hub for the whole coastline from Nesebar down to Rezovo. If you miss one of the **buses** to Sozopol, Nesebar or Sunny Beach, private buses depart in-between times from the eastern side of Garov Ploshtad. Nisikli Tourism runs five buses a day to **Istanbul** from its office at ul. Bulair 39 (daily 9am–noon; ☏056/841261) and numerous centrally located travel agents – such as Dimant at Tsar Simeon 15 – also handle reservations for Istanbul-bound buses. Eurolines has an office at the bus station (☏056/845722) and several other agencies clustered nearby offer tickets to destinations all over Bulgaria and Europe. International air tickets can be booked through Blue Sky travel agency on ul. Bogoridi 42 (☏056/840809, ✉bluesky@infotel.bg), which also arranges accommodation and car rental. Travellers heading for Turkey should be able to get a visa at the border crossing; in case of any difficulty, there's a **Turkish Consulate** north of the Sea Gardens at bul. Demokratsiya 38 (Mon–Fri 9am–1pm & 3–5pm; ☏056/42718).

its harbour also serves as one of Bulgaria's chief naval bases, with ranks of gunboats anchored off the neighbouring island of Sveti Kirik.

For the first ten days of September, Sozopol hosts the **Apollonia Arts Festival**, comprising classical music, jazz, theatre and poetry, and frequent open-air pop concerts take place throughout the summer. Be warned that finding accommodation can be difficult in July and August, when the tourist season is at its height. The website ⓦwww.sozopol.com is a useful source of information.

Some history

Stone anchors in the local Archeological Museum suggest that traders from the Aegean visited Sozopol harbour as early as the twelfth century BC, although the identity of these early seafarers remains the subject of much conjecture. More certain is the town's status as the first of the **Greek colonies** along the coast, founded around 610 BC by a party of adventurers from Miletus, who included in their number the philosopher Anaximander, who is credited with making the first world map (now lost) and being the first theoretical astronomer. His speculations on the nature of the universe, including the then revolutionary notion that the earth floats free and unsupported in space, formed the basis of modern cosmology. The Greeks named the town Apollonia Pontica after Apollo, the patron of seafarers and colonizers, and prospered by trading Greek textiles and wine for Thracian honey, grain and copper. Apollonia's major customer was Athens, and the decline of the latter in the fourth century BC ended the town's brief reign as a minor maritime power.

Having spent several centuries existing quite happily on the fringes of more powerful Thracian and Macedonian states, the Apollonians flirted with various anti-Roman alliances in the first century BC to try and stave off the inevitable advance of Latin power. In 72 BC, their attachment to the Black Sea empire-builder Mithridates of Pontus was punished by the Roman general Marcus Lucullus, who sacked the town and carried off the treasured statue of Apollo that had graced its harbour.

Apollonia disappeared from the records of chroniclers during the latter stages of the Roman Empire, re-emerging in 431 AD as **Sozopolis**, the "City of Salvation". Under the Byzantines the town soon developed a reputation for the good life, and rebellious nobles and troublesome bishops were "retired" here by emperors unwilling to see their peers too harshly punished. However, marauding armies returned during the fourteenth and fifteenth centuries, and following the Turkish invasion Sozopol sank into anonymity, replaced by Burgas as the area's major port.

Arrival and accommodation

Just 35km south of Burgas, Sozopol is easily accessible by **bus**. Direct buses from Burgas and from coastal towns south of Sozopol tend to come and go from the old town's bus station on pl. Han Krum, whereas buses arriving from other Bulgarian cities usually arrive and depart from the new town at pl. Cherno More. At either place you may be approached by locals offering **private rooms**, although these could well be overpriced, especially in high season, when you'll find it near impossible to get accommodation of any kind unless you book in advance. The most reliable local tourist agency is Lotos (daily 8am–8pm; ℡0550/23925, ⓦwww.aiatour.com) at ul. Musala 7, which offers rooms ranging from old houses on the peninsula to the more spacious chalet-style buildings of the Harmanite district (❶–❸). It's worth noting that many places will charge more for shorter stays at busy times of year. The *Zlatna Ribka* **campsite** (℡0550/22427; 4Lv per tent and 5Lv per person, double bungalows ❶), 3km north of town, is one of the south coast's best, situated on a part-sandy, part-rocky coastline – the bus from Burgas passes the site on its way into town.

Hotels

Art ul. Kiril I Metodii 72 next to the Art Gallery ℡0550/24081, ⓔart_plaza_sbh @abv.bg. On the northern edge of the old town peninsula, with spacious rooms with lovely sea views and a great restaurant. ❸

Lola ul. Vihren 32 ℡0550/22412, ⓦwww.thotels .bg. Modern hotel with smart, clean rooms with a/c. Most have balconies with sea views ❹

Orion ul. Vihren 28 ℡0550/23193, ⓦwww .hotel-orion.net. High above town and quite a walk from the centre, this hotel offers good value. Its small but comfortable a/c en-suite rooms have balconies – some with quite spectacular views – and there are several four-person apartments. Doubles ❸; apartments ❺

Rusalka ul. Milet 36 ℡0550/23047. One of the few old-town hotels, the *Rusalka* sits on the eastern edge of the peninsula and all of its comfortable a/c rooms overlook the bay. ❸

Sveti Nikola ul. Boruna 1 ℡0550/23333, ⓦwww.hotel-svetinikola.com. A friendly place with a great rooftop terrace and an excellent location perched on the rocky seafront. ❹

Voennomorski Klub or Navy Club, ul. Republikanska 17 ℡0550/24362. A drab yet reliable, year-round source of cheap if unexciting en-suite rooms. ❷

The Town

Sozopol is divided into two parts: the **old town** on the peninsula, and the modern, **Harmanite** district on the mainland (whose name means "The Windmills"). There are two **beaches** with a small admission charge: one nestling within the curve of a sheltered bay where the peninsula joins Harmanite; the other further south, beyond a headland. Walking between the two entails a foray into the backstreets of Harmanite, uphill from a solitary wooden **windmill** that now serves as a bar.

The touristic hub of Sozopol is a cobbled **concourse** between the peninsula and Harmanite, flanked by souvenir stalls and portrait artists, always thronged with strollers and bombarded by loud rock and pop music. Alongside runs a shady municipal **park**, carpeted with cottony wads of blossom during early summer; east of this is the beach. Sheltering among the trees, the pale sandstone **Chapel of Sveti Zosim** is staffed by an indomitable old lady from 7am until 10pm and honours the patron saint of seafarers, the Orthodox Church's answer to Apollo.

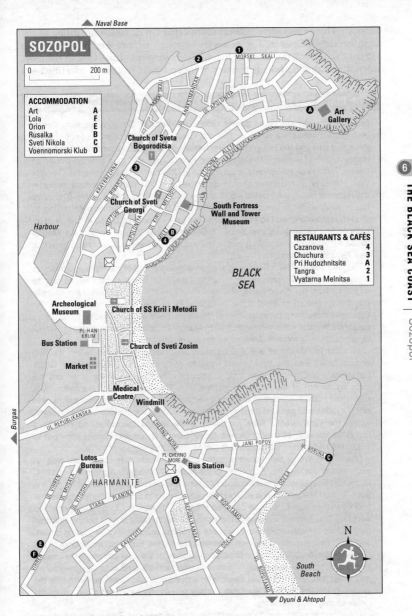

The Archeological Museum

On the other side of the concourse from the church, Sozopol's municipal library forms the backdrop for an **amphitheatre**, erected for use during the Apollonia Festival and serving as a concert venue throughout the summer. Hidden around the side of the library, the **Archeological Museum** (summer daily 8am–6pm; winter closed Sat & Sun; 3Lv) displays an extensive collection of ancient amphoras and barnacle-encrusted anchors, dredged from the sea off

Sozopol. There's also some colourful imported Greek tableware, dating to the sixth century BC, as well as examples of rough Bronze Age pottery from a range of sites along the coast, including Kiten and Varna Lake. One of the more interesting exhibits, though, is a tiny wooden figure, tentatively identified as a

The Black Sea Greeks II: the modern era

Occasionally you still come across elderly residents of Sozopol speaking **Greek** among themselves – a reminder that the Greek population of the coast remained influential well into the last century. The Greeks of the coastal towns had maintained some degree of wealth and status under Turkish rule, and thus seemed poised to take advantage of the upsurge in commerce in Ottoman lands following the Crimean War. However, the decline of Turkish power and the rise of **modern national movements** had a detrimental effect on the cosmopolitan culture of the Black Sea towns, whose ethnic groups squabbled among themselves, rather than uniting to challenge the moribund Ottoman Empire. The Greeks, inspired by the existence of an independent Greek state ever since 1830, came under the influence of the **Megáli Idhéa** (Great Idea) of liberating all the Hellenes within Turkish territory and forging a new Byzantine empire.

The idea that the Black Sea towns formed an integral part of the Hellenic world was anathema to the **Bulgarians**. Increasingly numerous in the coastal towns due to migration from the countryside, they saw the Greeks – who controlled the Church, education, and most local trade – as agents of the ruling Ottoman elite. The Ottomans played one group off against the other, eventually acquiescing to Bulgarian demands for the establishment of a Bulgarian Orthodox Church independent of Greek control – a move that infuriated the Greeks.

With the foundation of a Bulgarian state after 1878, mistrust between the two groups faded into the background, only to re-emerge in 1906 when the Greek patriarchate in Constantinople tried to appoint a new bishop of Varna without the prior agreement of the Bulgarian government. The new bishop, Neophytos, was prevented from disembarking at Varna's harbour by a hostile crowd, and a donkey in priest's robes was paraded through the streets. Things took an uglier turn in Pomorie, where the local Greeks were rumoured to be arming themselves to prevent a Bulgarian takeover of their churches. Greek-owned shops and houses were put to the torch, and many Hellenic families fled to Greece.

After World War I, both governments agreed to settle their differences with an exchange of populations. According to the **Mollov-Kafandaris Agreement** of 1924, Black Sea Greeks would quit the coastal towns and be replaced by ethnic Bulgarians from Aegean Macedonia and southern Thrace. Greeks in Sozopol, Pomorie, Nesebar and elsewhere had to choose between declaring themselves to be Bulgarians and adopting Slav names, or leaving. The poorer Greek families stayed behind because they lacked the resources to contemplate uprooting themselves and starting afresh, and their descendants were largely assimilated by the Bulgarian majority over the next seventy years. Despite the population exchange, the atmosphere of the coastal towns didn't change that much – most of the new arrivals tended to be vine-growers and fishermen, very much like those who moved out, and locals still joke that the incoming Bulgarians from southern Thrace usually spoke better Greek than the Hellenes they were replacing.

The bitterness that used to characterize relations between Greeks and Bulgarians on the coast has these days largely disappeared, especially now that the straitjacket of Communist educational policy – which trumpeted Bulgarian achievements at the expense of everyone else's – has been cast aside. Many Bulgarian families on the coast can dredge up a Greek ancestor or two, who are nowadays the subject of fond reminiscences rather than ethnic angst.

representation of Apollo, dating to the fifth century BC and discovered in Sozopol harbour. All exhibits are labelled in English as well as Bulgarian.

The old town

The **old town** begins beyond the post office, where three cobbled roads thrust into a labyrinth of alleys and vine-shaded houses, and tourists are ambushed by old ladies brandishing lace tablecloths for sale. The best examples of traditional architecture lie towards the head of the peninsula along ul. Apoloniya and Kiril i Metodii. In winter, boats and fishing tackle are kept inside the stone lower storeys; families occupy the creaking wooden rooms upstairs, which extend so far out that they threaten to touch the houses on the other side of the street. Some of their eaves are carved with suns or fish, for good luck.

Several shed-like *paraklisi* or **chapels** can be found scattered throughout the old town, usually bare inside save for a picture of the saint to whom they're dedicated. Despite its central location, it can be difficult to find the **Church of Sveta Bogoroditsa** (daily 10am–1pm & 2–6pm), hidden within a walled courtyard on ul. Anaksimandar. Surrounded by noisy bars and cafés just south of here, the **Church of Sveti Georgi** (daily 9am–1pm & 3–8pm), on ul. Apoloniya, offers at least some respite from the general hubbub and holiday crowds, and is open year-round. It houses a colourful nineteenth-century iconostasis, including an arresting image of the Archangel Michael trampling a sinner.

Sozopol's former high school, at the far end of ul. Kiril i Metodii, now contains an **Art Gallery** (Mon–Sat 10am–7.30pm; 2Lv). Downstairs are works by local marine artists Aleksandar Mutafov and Yani Chrisoupolus, which document pre-World War II Sozopol and the working lives of its fisherfolk, while the first floor hosts temporary exhibitions.

Positioned on the east of the peninsula above the sea, the **South Fortress Wall and Tower Museum** (daily 9.30am–7.30pm; 4Lv) is the largest building to have been excavated in Sozopol. The restored section of the town's original wall and tower is impressive, but the museum's use of shipping paraphernalia to top up its scant collection of ancient objects is disappointing.

Eating, drinking and nightlife

There are dozens of **cafés** and snack stalls beside both beaches and along the concourse leading to the old town, while most of the residents of Harmanite seem to be converting their garages and front gardens into *café-apéritif* **bars**. As for **restaurants**, places come and go and standards are variable, so some trial and error is inevitable. Sozopol offers the widest and freshest selection of fish on the coast, although you can't always tell whether your fillet has been recently grilled or merely heated up in a microwave. Sea views can be enjoyed at the numerous places along Morski Skali or Istochna Aleya, the path along the eastern side of the peninsula. The *Chuchura*, at ul. Ribarska 10, and the *Vyatarna Melnitsa*, at Morski Skali 27, are both touristy folk-style places with outdoor seating and easy-listening live music, while the *Tangra*, at Morski Skali 25, is as good a place as any to enjoy standard Bulgarian fare. The *Art* hotel's restaurant *Pri Hudozhnitsite* has fantastic sea views from both indoors and outdoors, and serves a good range of fish. For something slightly more upmarket, the *Cazanova*, on Istochna Aleya, is an Italian-influenced joint built into an overhanging portion of coastal cliff and flanked by similar eateries. In the uphill part of Harmanite, the restaurant of the *Hotel Orion* has an inviting east-facing terrace.

Evenings can be spent promenading in the old town or attending a **concert** in the amphitheatre. The *Art Club Michel* on ul. Apolonia 39 occupies an atmospheric old building and has nightly live jazz sessions until midnight. Sozopol's nightlife continues at several overcrowded **discos** open from 10pm until dawn: venues tend to change, although they're usually to be found in Harmanite near the south beach.

South of Sozopol

South of Sozopol, the coast offers some of Bulgaria's most glorious stretches of **sandy beaches**. A whole string of semi-deserted beaches are punctuated by areas of coastal wetland, notably the lush woodlands around the estuary of the **River Ropotamo**, while the coastal hills are covered with prickly conifers. Hugging the Turkish border just west of the coast are the mountains of the **Strandzha**, covered by Bulgaria's deepest and least-explored **forests**.

Those with private transport can cruise the area and pick their ideal bathing spot; travellers reliant on local buses will have to time things carefully. There are hourly **buses** from Sozopol to Kavatsi, Dyuni, Ropotamo, Primorsko, Lozenets, Kiten and Tsarevo. From Tsarevo buses connect with Ahtopol, Sinemorets and Rezovo. In high season, services fill up quickly and drivers won't stop to pick up travellers at roadside halts if the vehicle is already packed. In addition, frequent private buses service the coastal stops between Burgas and Ahtopol.

Kavatsi and Dyuni

Four kilometres down the coast from Sozopol, the highway descends towards a long sandy bay backed by two campsites. The well-run **Kavatsi** (КАВАЦИ) is a vast wooded campsite (6Lv per tent and 6Lv per person), with an abundance of ageing bungalows (❷), the odd restaurant, and direct access to a huge sweep of sandy beach. The Siroko Surf School (☎0888 835 561) next to the campsite offers windsurfing lessons for 35Lv per hour, kitesurfing lessons for 50Lv per hour and catamaran trips for 45Lv per hour; it also has schools on the beaches at the *Zlatna ribka* (see p.418) and *Gradina* campsites (see p.416). The southern reaches of Kavatsi run straight into the shaded and usually overcrowded *Smokinya* site close to the sea (☎0550/24356; 5Lv per person and 5Lv per tent), where makeshift beach bars fuel a busy outdoor party scene. At the southern end of the bay is a dune-punctuated stretch of beach, popular with naturists, where Bulgarians often pitch tents for free. Coastal bus services will drop you off at the entrance to Kavatsi on request, as will the hourly open-sided tourist buses that run between Sozopol and Dyuni in season.

The luxurious **Royal Dyuni Resort**, 4km beyond Kavatsi, is a somewhat sterile resort offering all-inclusive packages, divided into a seaside marina and two hillside colonies (☎0550/22356, ⓦwww.duni.bg; ❽). Dyuni's chief attraction is the marvellous sandy **beach** that extends southwards for 3km, protecting an inland plain of marsh and reed, and **Lake Alepu**, a lagoon surrounded by dunes and sand lilies. The area is vastly popular with beach-hoppers, although it has a tendency to become increasingly litter-strewn as the season progresses – unfortunately, only those portions of the beach within the orbit of Dyuni are regularly cleaned.

Arkutino and the River Ropotamo

Four kilometres south of Dyuni, **ARKUTINO** (АРКУТИНО; the name refers to an area rather than a precise settlement) is the isolated site of a pleasant hotel, the *Arkutino* (☎0550/33194; ❸), and an inviting moonscape of shifting, scrub-covered coastal **dunes**. From here several unmarked walking trails run south along the coast, picking their way over shrub-carpeted clifftops before emerging at the estuary of the Ropotamo River, where there's an attractive stretch of near-deserted sand which can only be reached on foot. On the opposite side of the main road from the hotel, there's a small area of coastal swamp accessed by wooden walkways (daily 8.30am–5.30pm; 2Lv), allowing glimpses of **giant waterlilies** that bloom in late summer.

The River Ropotamo

A few kilometres south of Arkutino, the highway crosses the **River Ropotamo**, whose estuary has been designated a **nature reserve**. Local tourist agencies imbue the Ropotamo with the mystique of the Florida Everglades, especially its **waterlilies**, although the reality can be something of a letdown. Boat trips (daily 7am–7pm; departures depend on the volume of custom; 7Lv) cover the stretch from the highway to the estuary, missing the best of the flora and fauna. This lies beyond the waterlily lake along the banks upriver, which are lined with oaks, beech, willows and creeping lianas. The river attracts fishermen because of its abundance of whitefish, barbel, grey mullet and carp; dragonflies, small black turtles and (non-poisonous) watersnakes are also found here. To the south of the river mouth rises **Cape Maslen**, where the sea has hollowed out caves that are sometimes frequented by **seals**.

The easiest way to see the river is to book an **excursion** with one of the many travel agents in Sozopol (see p.417 for operators; 15–25Lv per person). Otherwise, Sozopol–Tsarevo **buses** stop at the bridge from where boats take off, but drivers seem reluctant to pick up passengers here – so be prepared to hitch back.

▲ River Ropotamo

Primorsko

On the other side of the cape, the peninsula village of **PRIMORSKO** (ПРИМОРСКО) commands the northern approaches to another glorious curve of a **beach**, running along the bay to the south. It's a dusty place blighted by holiday-house construction, but its popularity as an inexpensive resort for Bulgarians and Czechs gives the place an appealing vigour. Most of the accommodation is in **private rooms** (❶–❷) available from the Demin tourist agency at the bus station (daily 8am–10pm; ☎0550/32866), although there are a several smallish **hotels** in the grid of streets that form the village centre. The *Sunarita* at ul. Treti Mart 29 (☎0550/33222, ⓦwww.sunarita.com; ❹) offers high standards, while the *Flamingo*, ul. Mart 8 (☎0550/33031, ⓕ32272; ❸), at the eastern end of the peninsula, is small but modern and comfortable. The *Metropol* (☎0550/33166; ❸) is a stylish, modern villa containing smart rooms with TV. Snack bars, restaurants and shops flank ul. Treti Mart, Primorsko's main street, and local nightlife is centred on the open-air bars and clubs at pl. Treti Mart. Paths lead downhill from the square to the beach, where you'll find a cluster of grilled-fish **restaurants**.

Around Primorsko

Just north of Primorsko, in what was once Communist President Zhivkov's private hunting reserve, is the much heralded **Beglik Tazh** (daily 9am–7pm; 2Lv), a jumble of enormous boulders thought to have been used by the **Thracians** as a sacred sanctuary. Excavated in 2004, very little is known about the site. The few signs available hint at the mysterious practices that may have taken place – such as the "Wedding Bed", a massive slab of stone where the priest and priestess supposedly performed a sexual ceremony to symbolise the unification of sun and earth. Nearby is a sacrificial stone, a sacred cave and a sun clock consisting of sixteen stones that were once vertical with an obelisk at the centre. The Thracians created the sanctuary by digging out the volcanic ash between the boulders and then cutting the rocks by hand. To reach the site, follow signs from Primorsko towards the north beach and into the forest.

Two kilometres south of Primorsko lies **Camping Druzhba**, known until recently as the International Youth Centre and originally intended as a holiday camp for Eastern Bloc students. With the demise of fellow socialist regimes, the centre lost its *raison d'être* and fell into stagnation for a few years before being absorbed by the Albena group (ⓦwww.albena.bg), which renamed it and is now in the process of modernizing the uninspiring facilities. It commands direct access to the southern end of Primorsko beach and currently has a bungalow settlement in place (☎0550/30105, ⓦwww.primorskoclub.com; triples ❹).

Kiten

Barely a kilometre beyond *Camping Druzhba*, the coast road runs into **KITEN** (КИТЕН), another peninsula village girdled with beaches, the attractive and sheltered **Atliman bay** to the north garnering more bathers than the slightly scruffier, wind-whipped expanse of sand to the south. Less chaotic and more inviting than Primorsko, it's a family-oriented resort popular with Bulgarians and ex-Eastern Bloc tourists. Most private houses in the village offer **rooms** (❷) through the Kiten Kvartirno Bureau just beyond the bus station at ul. Piren 5 (daily 8am–10pm; ☎0550/36965). In addition, there's a number of good **hotels**: the *Elit* on the seafront (☎0550/36998; ❸) has comfortable en-suite doubles with air-conditioning, TV and fridge. Next to the south beach *(yuzhniya plazh)* at ul. Urdoviza 2, the upmarket *Marina Hotel* occupies a great spot and offers a range of fitness facilities (℡0550/36984; ❸). Of the two **campsites**, the *Atliman* (℡0550/36864; 3Lv per tent and 4.50Lv per person) at the northern entrance to the village is small and quiet, while the *Kiten* (℡0550/36924; 4Lv per tent and 5Lv per person) at the far end of *yuzhniya plazh* is a larger affair and has the usual dilapidated bungalows (❶). With virtually every garage and garden in Kiten transformed into a rudimentary café or restaurant, you're unlikely to have any problem finding somewhere to **eat** or **drink**; the fish restaurants along ul. Urdoviza are particularly worth trying.

Lozenets

LOZENETS (ЛОЗЕНЕЦ), the next town down the coast, has become a massive hit with well-to-do Bulgarians in recent years. The once deserted main street is now frequently jammed with expensive cars, while smartly dressed holidaymakers throng the pavements. Windy beaches to the north attract water sports enthusiasts and the well-established Oxo Surf School offers **windsurfing** lessons for 35Lv per hour (June–Sept daily 8.30am–7pm; ℡0887 601 694 and 0888 308 630).

During the summer season locals meet incoming buses to offer **private rooms**, which can also be booked through the Tourist Agency at the bus station (daily 9am–7pm; ℡0550/52744; ❷–❸). Of the many new **hotels**, *Friends* at ul. Ribarska 43 (℡0550/57250, Ⓦwww.friendshotel.org; ❹) is a particularly pleasant choice with a tree-shaded garden. Right on the beach, the *Sunrise* (℡0550/57207; ❹) has a great position but suffers from the noise of kids playing nearby. To escape the bustle of the centre, try the *Phoenix* (℡0550/57332, Ⓔhotel_feniks@mail.bg; ❸) on the northern edge of town, which has modern air-conditioned doubles and a small pool; the central *Lozenets* at ul. Veleka 8 (℡0550/57546; Ⓕ57545; ❹), with a pool and air-conditioned rooms, is larger and a little less cosy. *Villa Alba* on the outskirts of town arranges tailor-made activity holidays through its website (Ⓦvillaalba.clubextreme.org), including horse riding, diving, windsurfing and mountain biking. One kilometre south of Lozenets, *Oasis Camping* (℡0550/52171; 4.50Lv per person and 3lv per tent) has reasonable facilities next to the beach.

The coolest **bar** in town is *By the Way* on ul. Ribarska, where trendy Bulgarians sample its vast array of cocktails before moving on to *Alcohol* on the beach, a temporary two-floor structure hung with billowing white drapes and pristine leather couches – currently considered the Black Sea's most fashionable **nightclub**. Another popular hangout is the *Tarfa Beach Bar* at the southern end of Lozenets, where singers entertain the clientele with Bulgarian favourites. Just up the street, the *Friends* hotel has a good **restaurant** and sushi bar in a garden. Further on, the *Starata Kushta* is a busy traditional-style restaurant that also offers clean air-conditioned rooms (℡0550/57257; ❸). All the restaurants require reservations for dinner in high season.

Tsarevo (Michurin)

A century ago, tsars Ferdinand and Boris used to enjoy bathing near the Greek-populated village of Vasiliko, now known as **TSAREVO** (ЦАРЕВО). In 1948 the Communists renamed it "Michurin" (in honour of the Soviet plant-breeder), by which name it is still known to many of the locals, despite having officially reverted to its prewar title. The old town is calm and quiet, with a Holy Trinity National Revival-style church that houses a small **History Museum** (Sun–Fri 9am–noon & 3–9pm; free). The lively main street of the new town runs downhill to a park, with the harbour to the south and a small beach on the other side of the rocky promontory. **Private rooms** (❶–❷) are available from the Tsarevo tourist bureau (☎0550/52162, ⓦwww.tzarevo.net) at ul. Michael Gerjikov 18, down the road from the bus station; of the many **hotels** available, *Skritiya Muzhe* (☎0550/52357; ❸) *in the old town* is small and snug, and has a decent restaurant. The nearby *Vesiliko Complex* at ul.Vesiliko 136 (☎0550/54022, ⓦwww.wasiliko .bginvent.net; ❸) offers great value for money with chalet-style rooms and apartments right on the seafront. **Campers** can head for the *Arapya* site, 3km north of town, an appealingly isolated but very busy spot with a good beach.

The far south

Beyond Tsarevo the E87 swings inland towards the Strandzha and the frontier crossing at Malko Tarnovo (see p.429), while a well-surfaced minor road continues along an increasingly rocky coastline before reaching the next town of any size, **Ahtopol**. Occasionally forced inland, the road dives between coastal hills, where herders watch over grazing sheep and pigs. Eight kilometres beyond Tsarevo the road passes through **VARVARA** (ВАРВАРА), a sleepy village built around a small shingle cove which is popular with urban Bulgarians eager for a taste of seaside rusticity. On the edge of the village, the smart *Family* **hotel** (☎0550/62166, ⓦwww.hotel-varvara.com; ❸) has air-conditioned rooms with sea views. There are a couple of guesthouses in the centre and numerous houses offering **private rooms** (❶).To the north of the village is *El Borracho*, a Mexican-style **restaurant** with a pool and tennis courts, while overlooking the square is *Pri Dimo* – a popular outdoor eatery that also offers rooms (☎0899/928851; ❷).The beach at Ahtopol is just about walkable from here; there are plenty of grassy clifftops to explore in the vicinity, and the rocky shore provides excellent snorkelling territory. From here the lonely coast road continues to Sinemorets, a middle-of-nowhere village whose stunning main beach has been blighted by a grotesque seven-storey hotel, though unspoilt beaches can be found a little further south and north. A worsening road weaves its way to the quiet border village of **Rezovo**, where visitors can gaze at pristine Turkish beaches beyond their reach.

Ahtopol

Surrounded by a girdle of trade-union rest homes, **AHTOPOL** (АХТОПОЛ) is a tranquil, sea-battered little place whose peninsular position echoes that of Sozopol and Nesebar. From the bus station, situated at the western end of town, the main street leads down towards a small fishing harbour. Just above is a small **museum** (Tues–Sun, irregular hours; 2Lv), which recalls the original Greek settlement of Agathopolis. At the head of the peninsula, surrounded by well-tended flowers, stands the **Hram Vasnesenie Gospodne** (Chapel of the Ascension), a low, unadorned structure with vivid nineteenth-century frescoes behind its icon screen.

The peninsula has several tiny shingle **beaches** separated by rocky headlands, with a much larger sandy one to the north, beyond the rest-home colony. A tourist bureau (daily 9am–noon & 4–6pm; ☎0550 62224) next to the bus station rents out **rooms** (❶), while the *Boruna* hotel at ul. Briz 8 (☎0897/931073; ❷) has similarly priced rooms with magnificent sea views and an outdoor restaurant. *Hotel Valdi* (☎0550/62320, ⓦwww.hotelvaldi.com; ❸) at ul. Cherno More 22A has air-conditioned rooms and Internet access, and offers a free daily boat trip to Sinemorets (9.30am, returns from Sinemorets at 5.30pm; non-guests 5Lv).

Overlooking the harbour on ul. Briz, the *Chetirimate Kapitane* **restaurant** has a great terrace and a decent range of fish dishes, while the unnamed Chinese restaurant on the main street offers a refreshing change of cuisine. You'll find **cafés** and a **market** on the street across the park from the bus station. Crowded on the edge of the village are numerous Communist-era bungalow sites offering accommodation (❶), but if you don't mind the walk, *Camping Delfin*, 2km north, is far more picturesque, with a couple of rows of basic bungalows (❷) perched on a hilltop facing Ahtopol across the bay.

Sinemorets

From Ahtopol the coast road heads south through a forest thick with Strandzha oak, before dropping down to cross the reed-shrouded **River Veleka**. On the opposite bank stands the windswept hilltop settlement of **SINEMORETS** (СИНЕМОРЕЦ), a village that until 1989 was out of bounds to outsiders due to its proximity to the Turkish border. Since then it's been discovered by beach-hoppers, as well as wealthy city-dwellers building seaside villas and second homes. It's a strange mixture of bucolic village and building site, the kind of place where expensive cars trundle down the dirt tracks that serve as streets, and shepherds wander by with flocks of sheep. Sinemorets's fame rests on its **beaches**: the south beach, reached by a road which leads eastwards through the village towards the headland before veering south, has sadly been monopolized by package tourists staying at the monstrous 700-bed *Bella Vista* hotel. A rough track leads further south to another beach, only accessible by foot or 4WD, which offers a far less crowded expanse of fine white sand bordered by rocky promontories. More spectacular is the beach to the north, a kilometre-long sandbar that slows the progress of the River Veleka towards the sea. Framed by low green hills, it's one of the most beautiful spots on the Black Sea coast and is the kind of place that attracts younger, liberal-leaning Bulgarians – bathing nude here will hardly raise an eyebrow.

Practicalities

During summer Sinemorets is well connected with the outside world by buses travelling from all the towns south of Burgas. Almost all the houses in the village offer **rooms** (❶) – just ask around or knock on a few doors. There are also several modern **hotels** to choose from: the *Villa Philadelphia* (☎0550/66106, ⓦ www.villaphiladelphia.com; ❸) is a comfortable, modern place with Internet access that arranges guided birdwatching tours of the Strandzha Nature Park (see p.428), while the *Sinyata Akula*, otherwise known as the *Blue Shark* (☎0550/6623; ❷), is a well-regarded family pension with TV and fridge in every room. Closer to the beach, the pleasant *Domingo* (☎0550/66093, ⓦ www .casadomingo.info; ❸) has comfortable rooms around a swimming pool, and can arrange canoeing trips on the Veleka River. *Zafo Camping* (☎0550/66141), towards the end of ul. Botamyata, has clean double bungalows (❶–❷) and a new air-conditioned hotel (❸), while *Bella Vista* (ⓦ www.resortbellavista.com) offers all-inclusive accommodation to package tourists (❾) and has its own diving school. *Blue Shark, Domingo* and *Zafo* have their own **restaurants**, while at the bottom of town looking out over the sea is *Home Bar Koraba,* perfect for outdoor evening drinks.

Rezovo

From Sinemorets two buses a day cover the 10km south to the village of **Rezovo** on the Turkish border – passports are checked upon entry - though it's not possible to cross the frontier here. Plenty of houses have signs advertising rooms. The *Panorama* **restaurant** has a terrace offering sweeping views of the Turkish coastline and can also arrange **private rooms** (❶) if you intend to stay, but there's not much to keep you here once you've climbed down the steps to the river borderline and seen the national flags on either side.

The Strandzha Nature Park

The interior west of the south coast is dominated by the wooded **Strandzha Nature Park** (СТРАНДЖА), a region of plateaux and hills interrupted by rift valleys, and watered by the Ropotamo and Veleka rivers. It's a captivating area of untouched forests, thick with beech, alder, elm and the ubiquitous Strandzha oak, and would be perfect hiking territory were it not for the fact that distinct paths are few; fortunately good maps of the area are available from the Strandzha Nature Park Administration in Malko Tarnovo (see p.430). It is also home to significant early Bronze Age **dolmens**, known locally as dragons' dens, which can be located through the **Historical Museum** in Malko Tarnovo (see opposite). Week-long **horse riding tours** of the region are run by *Arkan Tours* (ⓦwww.arkantours.com), based in Plovdiv.

The most direct route into the region **from Burgas** is the road which works its way over the western shoulder of the Strandzha massif. The four daily buses from Burgas's Avtogara Zapad stop at Brushlyan and Gramatikovo before arriving at Malko Tarnovo, 10km short of the Turkish border. **From the south coast**, a minor road branches off the main E87 highway and winds its way inland from Tsarevo towards Malko Tarnovo, passing some of the region's most picturesque villages on the way – although buses only travel as far as Bulgari and Kosti (twice daily) on this route. If you want to explore the Strandzha in depth, you'll definitely need your own transport.

South from Burgas

Immediately south of Burgas the main inland route to Malko Tarnovo begins to ascend through wooded hills, passing a sequence of rustic, half-abandoned villages. Fifty-three kilometres out of town, at the village of **ZVEZDETS** (ЗВЕЗДЕЦ), a minor road forks left towards **Petrova Niva**, a hilltop overlooking the river Veleka, which serves as a popular spot for picnics and short hikes. Bulgarian insurgents met here in 1903 to launch the **Preobrazhenie Uprising** against the Turks (so called because it was launched on *Preobrazhenie* – Transfiguration – an important Orthodox holy day falling on August 6). The event is still marked by an annual *sabor* or "gathering" on the weekend nearest to *Preobrazhenie*, which involves folk music, feasting and dancing.

Continuing along the main route from Zvezdets, a right turn after 10km leads to the tiny village of **BRASHLYAN** (БРЪШЛЯН; all Malko Tarnovo buses from Burgas Zapad call in here), site of the Strandzha's best-preserved ensemble of traditional peasant houses and an architectural reserve. It's a charming spot imbued with rural calm. The village is centred on the sunken church of **Sveti Dimitar**, built, according to Ottoman restrictions, behind a wall high enough to render it inoffensive to any passing Muslim. The restored **church school** (*kiliino uchilishte*; daily 8am–1pm & 2–6pm; 0.50Lv) has a small room where the wealthier village children once sat on goatskin rugs and wrote on wax tablets, erasing their work by holding the tablets up to the heat of the nearby fireplace. There's a small **ethnographic collection** (due to relocate at the time of writing) showing the woollen cloaks once worn by Brashlyan's menfolk – predominantly herders who wintered their flocks on the shores of the Aegean to the south. A map next to the church school shows the locations of fourteen old houses offering **accommodation**: the well-established *Seeka Yankova* (☎05952/4929; ❷) can also arrange food for guests; *Gergana Nakova* guesthouse (☎05952/4144; ❸) is more comfortable and is one of the few houses with en-suite rooms. Two unnamed **restaurants** serve decent Bulgarian fare.

Inland from Tsarevo

The other main route into the region, the E87, heads inland from Tsarevo, winding its way slowly over the hills. The first village of any note is **BALGARI** (БЪЛГАРИ), renowned for the still-practised custom of *nestinarstvo* or **fire dancing**. Traditionally associated with the feast day of SS Konstantin and Elena (which falls on May 21 in most parts of Bulgaria, but is celebrated here on June 3 and 4, or the nearest weekend), the ritual involves initiates falling into a trance and dancing on hot embers, to furious bagpipe and drum accompaniment. The secret lies in the low thermal conductivity of the embers, whose heat is transmitted slowly enough for the walkers to avoid injury by moving at a fast pace. Preparations for the fire-dancing last all day, with icons of the saints paraded round the village, and the inevitable sacrifice of sheep prior to communal feasting. The local **bar** behind the church sells basic provisions and can direct visitors to several houses in the village that offer **private rooms** (❶) with meals included; one such is the homely *Lapchev* (☎055069/322 and 0887 665191; ❶).

From Balgari, a minor road heads off towards **KOSTI** (КОСТИ), another bucolic spot lying 7km south, on the banks of the River Veleka. There's a wealth of (mostly unmarked) hiking paths heading up and down the river, with the most inviting being the eight-hour **trek** downstream to Sinemorets (see p.427). An easier option is the thirty-minute walk (follow the blue and white markings from Sasho Pankovski's house – see below) to a tiny chapel (*paraklisa*) built over an ancient spring and surrounded by 250-year-old oaks. It's dedicated to Sveti Ilya, Kosti's patron saint. From here an unmarked path branches north uphill for 4km to Bulgari, though it's inadvisable to attempt any unmarked routes without a compass and a local map available from the Strandzha Nature Park Administration in Malko Turnovo (see below). A **restaurant** on the vast main square serves simple dishes and is frequented by inebriated locals most of the time. The best **accommodation** is just off the main road into Kosti at the renovated stone house owned by Sasho Pankovski, an affable Burgas politician, (☎055069/433 and 056/823948; ❶), who offers small but comfortable rooms and good home-cooked food. Maria Uzuova, who speaks English and German, has a guest house nearby (☎056/534992 and 0887/890331; ❶) and can arrange guided walks.

Back on the main road, **GRAMATIKOVO** (ГРАМАТИКОВО) lies midway between Balgari and Malko Tarnovo, offering a smattering of traditional buildings and a **Nature Museum** (Mon–Sat 9.30am–5.30pm) covering the history of forestry in the region. Several **restaurants** cluster around the main square, and the municipality office (Mon–Fri 9am–12.30pm & 1.30–4.30pm; ☎05958/266) can arrange **private rooms** in the village.

Malko Tarnovo and the border

All roads in the Strandzha lead to **MALKO TARNOVO** (МАЛКО ТЪРНОВО), a former copper-mining town lying in a bowl surrounded by hills. It's a quiet place where tourism was never encouraged in the past, due to the proximity of the border. A small collection of National Revival buildings huddles above the main square, three of which together serve as a **Historical Museum** (Mon–Fri

8am–5pm, weekends 9.30am–1pm & 2–5pm; 2Lv), including regional archeological discoveries such as a pair of early Iron Age clay idols, and historical, ethnographic and icon collections. With advance notice the museum can arrange trips (20–40Lv per person) to the nearby **Mishkova Niva complex** consisting of a megalithic grave site and a temple to Apollo; it can also provide information about the numerous hard-to-reach Thracian, Roman and prehistoric sites that are scattered throughout the locality. The **Strandzha Nature Park Administration** (*Upravlenie na naroden park Strandzha*; Mon–Fri 9am–5pm; ☎05952/2896, ⓦwww.bg-parks.net), in a marked office block just off the main square at Yanko Maslinkov 1, is the place to book **private rooms** (❶–❷), and there are a couple of **cafés** and a **restaurant** around the square.

Travelling on from Malko Tarnovo **by car**, traffic at the frontier is pretty light and clearing Bulgarian customs should be straightforward. Things can be more time-consuming on the Turkish side, however, where you'll have to wait behind files of bus passengers in order to buy an entry visa, which will cost £10 for UK citizens, and US$10 for US citizens.

Bus passengers may have longer delays, as border officials tend to give baggage a thorough going-over, but the wait is worthwhile – the descent into Turkey through the scrub-covered southern slopes of the Strandzha is highly scenic.

Travel details

Trains

Burgas to: Kazanlak (7 daily; 3hr 15min); Plovdiv (5 daily; 4hr 30min); Sliven (7 daily; 1hr 30min–2hr 30min); Sofia (7 daily; 6hr 30min); Stara Zagora (5 daily; 3hr).
Varna to: Dobrich (1 daily; 2hr 45min); Plovdiv (3 daily; 6–7hr); Ruse (3 daily; 4hr); Sofia (6 daily; 8–9hr).

Buses

Ahtopol to: Burgas (8 daily; 2hr 15min); Sinemorets (8 daily; 15min); Sofia (4 daily; 8hr); Sozopol (3 daily; 1hr 30min); Tsarevo (5 daily; 20min).
Albena to: Balchik (every 20min; 30min); Dobrich (every 30min; 40min); Golden Sands (every 15–30min; 30min); Varna (every 30min; 30min).
Balchik to: Albena (every 20min; 30min); Dobrich (every 30min; 50min); Kavarna (8 daily; 30min); Shabla (7 daily; 1hr); Varna (every 30min; 1hr).
Burgas *Avtogara Yug* to: Ahtopol (3 daily; 2hr 15min); Kiten (9 daily; 1hr 30min); Lozenets (9 daily; 1hr 40min); Nesebar (every 40min; 50min); Obzor (hourly; 1hr); Pomorie (every 30min; 20min); Primorsko (9 daily; 1hr 20min); Rezovo (2 daily; 3hr); Ruse (5 daily; 4hr); Sinemorets (2 daily; 2hr 30min); Sofia (hourly; 6hr 30min); Sozopol (every 30min; 50min); Sunny Beach (every 10min; 45min); Tsarevo (hourly; 2hr); Varna (hourly; 3hr).
Avtogara Zapad to: Malko Tarnovo (4 daily; 2hr).

Chernomorets to: Burgas (every 30min; 30min); Sozopol (every 30min; 15min).
Durankulak to: Balchik (3 daily; 1hr 20min); Kavarna (2 daily; 50min); Shabla (4 daily; 20min).
Golden Sands to: Albena (every 15–30min; 30min); Sveti Konstantin (every 10–30min; 20–25min); Varna (every 10–30min; 30min).
Kavarna to: Balchik (every 30min; 30min); Balgarevo (5 daily; 20min); Dobrich (hourly; 1hr 30min); Durankulak (2 daily; 50min); Kamen Bryag (1 daily; 40 min; Mon-Fri only); Shabla (4 daily; 30min); Varna (hourly; 2hr).
Kavatsi to: Sozopol (hourly; 15–30min).
Kiten to: Burgas (hourly; 1hr 30min); Plovdiv (4 daily; 5hr 30min); Sofia (6 daily; 7hr); Sozopol (hourly; 45min); Stara Zagora (8 daily; 3hr 30min); Veliko Tarnovo (1 daily; 6hr 30min).
Kosti to: Tsarevo (2 daily; 40min).
Lozenets to: Ahtopol (7 daily; 30min); Burgas (hourly; 1hr 40min); Kiten (6 daily; 10min); Plovdiv (2 daily; 5hr 40min); Primorsko (6 daily; 20min); Rezovo (2 daily; 1hr); Sinemorets (2 daily; 40min); Sofia (6 daily; 7hr 10min); Tsarevo (hourly; 15min); Varvara (7 daily; 20min); Veliko Tarnovo (1 daily; 6hr 40min).
Malko Tarnovo to: Brashlyan (4 daily; 20min); Burgas *Avtogara Zapad* (4 daily; 2hr).
Nesebar to: Burgas (every 40min; 50min); Pomorie (every 40min; 30min); Sofia (7 daily; 6hr 30min); Sunny Beach (every 15–20min; 15min).
Obzor to: Burgas (1 daily; 1hr); Sunny Beach (1 daily; 25min); Varna (7 daily; 1hr 30min).

Pomorie to: Burgas (every 30min; 20min); Nesebar (every 40min; 30min); Sofia (5 daily; 7hr); Sunny Beach (every 40min; 30min).

Primorsko to: Burgas (hourly; 1hr 20min); Plovdiv (7 daily; 5hr 30min); Sofia (8 daily; 7hr); Sozopol (hourly; 30min); Stara Zagora (hourly; 3hr 30min); Tsarevo (2 daily; 30min); Veliko Tarnovo (1 daily; 6hr 30min).

Shabla to: Balchik (4 daily; 1hr); Durankulak (2 daily; 20min); Kavarna (4 daily; 30min); Krapets (1 daily; 15min).

Sofia *opposite Central Station* to: Burgas (4 daily; 6hr 30min); Sozopol (2 daily; 7hr 15min); Varna (5 daily; 8–9hr).

Sozopol to: Ahtopol (1 daily; 1hr 30min); Burgas (every 30min; 50min); Dyuni (hourly; 20min); Kavatsi (hourly; 15min); Kiten (hourly; 45min); Plovdiv (5 daily; 5 hr); Primorsko (hourly; 30min); Sofia (7 daily; 7hr 15min); Veliko Tarnovo (1 daily; 4hr).

Sunny Beach to: Burgas (every 30min; 45min); Elenite (hourly; 20min); Nesebar (every 15min; 15min); Obzor (6 daily; 25min); Pomorie (hourly; 30min); Sveti Vlas (hourly; 10min); Varna (7 daily; 2hr 10min).

Sveti Konstantin to: Golden Sands (every 10–30min; 20–25min); Varna (every 10–30min; 25min).

Tsarevo to: Ahtopol (8 daily; 20min); Burgas (hourly; 1hr 10min); Kiten (8 daily; 20min); Kosti (2 daily; 40min); Plovdiv (2 daily; 5hr); Rezovo (2 daily; 1hr); Sinemorets (4 daily; 35min); Sofia (10 daily; 7hr); Sozopol (every 30 min; 40min); Varvara (1 daily; 15min).

Varna *central bus station* to: Balchik (8 daily; 1hr 30min); Burgas (5 daily; 3hr); Byala (1 daily; 1hr 20min); Dobrich (every 30min; 50min); Golden Sands (every 20–30min; 30min); Kamchiya (2 daily; 50min); Kavarna (8 daily; 2hr); Obzor (hourly; 1hr 30min); Ruse (4 daily; 4hr); Shabla (5 daily; 2hr 30min); Shumen (2 daily; 2hr); Silistra (4 daily; 3hr); Sunny Beach (5 daily; 2hr 10min); Sveti Konstantin (every 10–30min; 20min); Veliko Tarnovo (hourly; 4hr). *Varna Mladost bus station* to: Balchik (hourly; 1hr); Burgas (hourly; 3hr); Dobrich (every 30min; 50min); Nesebar (7 daily; 2hr 10min); Shumen (4 daily; 2hr); Sunny Beach (7 daily; 2hr).

Flights

Burgas to: Sofia (1 daily; 1hr).
Varna to: Sofia (2 daily; 1hr).

International trains

(mid-June to mid-Sept only)
Varna to: Budapest (3 weekly; 24 hr); Bucharest (3 weekly; 8hr); Kiev (3 weekly; 36hr); Minsk (1 weekly; 4 days); Moscow (3 weekly; 36hr); Prague (3 weekly; 36hr); Rostov (1 weekly; 3 days).

International buses

Burgas to: Istanbul (5 daily; 6hr); Athens (2 weekly; 21hr).
Varna to: Athens (2 weekly; 24hr); Istanbul (4 daily; 8hr); Kiev (2 weekly; 26hr); Odessa (2 weekly; 30hr); Paris (2 weekly; 36hr); Rome (2 weekly; 30hr); Thessaloniki (2 weekly; 12hr).

International boats

Varna to: Odessa (June to mid-Sept: 2 weekly; 9hr).

Contexts

Contexts

History

National history is a serious business in a country that was virtually effaced for five hundred years – when this part of the Ottoman Empire was referred to by Westerners as "European Turkey". Since the Liberation in 1877–78, successive regimes have tried to inculcate a sense of national pride among their citizens, emphasizing historical continuity between the modern state and the medieval Bulgarian empires of the past.

Neolithic beginnings

Despite several Paleolithic finds in the caves of the Balkan Mountains, the early inhabitants of the Bulgarian lands don't really enter the limelight of history until the sixth millennium BC, when the Balkans were a major centre of the so-called **Neolithic Revolution**. This came about when Stone Age hunters began to be replaced by a more settled, agricultural population – probably the result of a wave of migration from the Near East. This sudden flowering of organized culture is best observed at the recently excavated Neolithic village at **Stara Zagora** (see p.298), famous for its decorated pottery, clay figurines and fertility symbols. By the fourth millennium BC mining and metallurgy took off in a big way: copper and gold objects found in the **Chalcolithic necropolis** near **Varna** (see p.373) show that the Balkan peoples were developing smelting techniques independently of the civilizations of the Near East.

Chalcolithic culture went into decline at the end of the fourth millennium BC, a process hastened by a worsening of the climate. Civilization in the Bulgarian lands was revitalized by the arrival of newcomers from Central Europe, bringing with them the metalworking techniques of the **Bronze Age**. By the end of the second millennium BC these migrant groups, together with the original tribes of the eastern Balkans, were coalescing into an ethnic and linguistic group subsequently known to history as the **Thracians**.

The Thracians

Ruled by a powerful warrior aristocracy rich in gold treasures, the ancient Thracians inhabited an area extending over most of modern Bulgaria and northern Greece. Close ethnic links with their neighbours in both the Danube basin to the north and in Asia Minor to the east placed them at the centre of an extensive Balkan–Asian culture. Despite their subsequent absorption by a whole host of invaders and their eventual assimilation by the Slavs, the Thracians are regarded as one of the **bedrock peoples** of the Balkans whose ethnic stock (though much diluted) has endured – and the present-day Bulgarians are proud to claim them as ancestors. We're largely dependent on ancient Greek authors – notably Herodotus, Xenophon and Strabo – for knowledge of the Thracian world. Herodotus, in a famous passage you'll see quoted in museums throughout Bulgaria, claimed that the Thracian population was "greater than that of any country in the world except India", and would have been a force to be reckoned with had it not been for their tribal disunity.

Although the Thracians were admired for skills such as archery and horse-manship, many of their **customs** seemed slightly barbaric to their southerly neighbours. Certain tribes practised polygamy, others allowed their young women unlimited sexual freedom before marriage, while tattoos for both males and females were *de rigueur* in most areas. Strabo relates how one group of Thracians was nicknamed the *Capnobatae* (literally the "smoke treaders"), suggesting that they burned hemp seeds indoors and got high on the fumes. Dope-crazed hopheads or not, the Thracians practised an ecstatic, **orgiastic religion**, honouring deities closely linked with the Greek god Dionysus. Themes of death, rebirth and renewal figured highly in their religious rites, providing a corpus of belief from which the Greeks borrowed freely – most notably in the case of the legendary Thracian priest-king **Orpheus**.

Greeks, Persians and Macedonians

Certain Thracian tribes developed close links with the **Greek colonists** who began settling the Black Sea coast from the seventh century onwards. The Greek presence turned the Black Sea into an extension of the Mediterranean world, and while bounteous harvests of wheat and fish were shipped south-wards to the Aegean to feed cities like Athens, exquisite sculpture and pottery came in the other direction, enriching the culture of the eastern Balkans.

The **Persians** invaded the area in the late sixth century BC, disrupting the lively system of trade that linked the Black Sea Greeks with the Thracians inland. However, their departure allowed the emergence of powerful Thracian tribal kingdoms such as that of the **Odrysae**, which brought stability to the region in the mid-fifth century BC and allowed Greek–Thracian mercantile contacts to flourish anew.

The Odrysae briefly threatened to become the nucleus of a powerful Balkan empire, but this role was taken up a century later by the neighbouring **Macedonians** under Philip II – who invaded Thrace and founded Philippopolis (present-day **Plovdiv**). It took Philip and his son Alexander the Great (who marched to the Danube in 335 BC) a lot of time and men to subdue the Balkans, but their empire (under Alexander's successors the Antigonids) proved lasting. It was during this period that the Thracian interior was opened up fully to the ideas, goods and culture of the Hellenistic world, and the **tombs** of local Thracian rulers (most notably those at **Kazanlak**; see p.290) and **Sveshtari** (p.264) were sumptuously kitted out with Greek-inspired frescos and luxurious furnishings.

Rome and Byzantium

The **Romans** became the dominant power in the region after their defeat of Macedonia in 168 BC, but it took almost two centuries for the empire to subdue the Thracians, who were in constant revolt. It wasn't until about 50 AD that the conquerors were finally able to carve out secure administrative units, creating the province of **Thrace** to the south of the Balkan range and **Moesia** to the north. Using slave labour, the Romans built garrisons, towns, roads and bridges across their domain, and conscripted many Thracians into their legions.

Military strongholds and neighbouring civilian settlements sprang up along the **Danube frontier** (relics of which can today be seen in the museums of Vidin, Pleven and Sofia), while prosperous new towns like Nicopolis ad Istrum commanded the trade routes inland. Many of the old Greek towns along the coast continued to thrive, and although they now hosted a population of mixed Greek and Thracian descent, Greek language and culture remained dominant throughout the region.

From the third century onwards the empire's contraction and decline was hastened by recurrent invasions of the Danubian provinces by the Goths (238–48 AD), Visigoths (378 AD), Huns (447 AD) and other so-called **barbarians** – civilization in Moesia and Thrace suffered greatly as a result. However, the division of the empire into two parts, with **Byzantium** inheriting the mantle of Rome in the east, meant that the authorities in nearby Constantinople could (for a while at least) concentrate their military resources more effectively here.

Both the Danubian frontier and the stronghold of Thrace were reinforced by Emperor **Justinian** in the sixth century, allowing urban life in the region a brief reprieve. Both Philippopolis (Plovdiv) and **Serdica** (Sofia) flourished during his reign. Even under Justinian, however, the **sklaveni** (ancestors of the Balkan Slavs) found a way of breaching the empire's defences, and indulged in big looting trips into Thrace in the 540s. By the seventh century, increasing numbers of Avars and Slavs were crossing the river with impunity, leaving the Byzantines with little choice but to allow them to settle and employ them as irregular frontier troops.

Slavs and Bulgars

The **Slavs** who migrated into the Balkan peninsula from the late fifth century onwards were one of the indigenous races of Europe, the distant forebears of the Russians, Poles, Czechs, Slovaks, Slovenes, Croats and Serbs – and, of course, the Bulgarians. Many of them came in the wake of the Avars, a warlike Central Asian people who briefly forged a Central European empire in the sixth century and pressganged the Slavs into their all-conquering armies. However they got here, the Slavs who settled south of the Danube soon began to outnumber any remaining Thracians in the area and established a linguistic and cultural hegemony over the region.

The Slavs were later to fuse with a new wave of migrants, the warlike **Bulgars**. These mounted nomads, possibly originating deep in Central Asia, swept down towards the Balkans after being driven out of "Old Great Bulgaria" – a swath of territories over which they briefly ruled lying between the Caspian and the Black seas. They were a Turkic people, ethnolinguistically akin to the Huns, Avars and Khazars. Under pressure from the latter, the Bulgars began a great **migration** into southeastern Europe, where the largest group (some 250,000 strong), led by **Khan Asparuh**, reached the Danube delta around 680 and shortly afterwards entered what would soon become Bulgaria.

The First Bulgarian Kingdom

Theophanes the Confessor records that in 681 the Byzantine emperor Constantine IV was forced to recognize the independence of a "new and vulgar people" north of the Balkan range. Asparuh's new **Bulgar Khanate**, subsequently known as the *Parvo Balgarsko Tsarstvo* – the **First Bulgarian Kingdom** – was centred at **Pliska** and ruled over a Danubian state that stretched from the Carpathians in the north to the Balkan Range in the south. Although the Khanate was very much reliant on Slav strength, the Bulgars – whose semi-nomadic society was geared to movement and war – definitely provided the impetus for its expansion over the next 150 years.

The Khanate – and the growth of Christianity

The Khanate's growth was greatest during the reign of **Khan Krum** "the Terrible" (803–14), who collected goblets fashioned from the skulls of foes, and pushed his boundaries as far as the Rila Mountains in the west and the Rhodopes in the south. His successor **Khan Omurtag** (816–31), having conquered all that he could, signed a thirty-year treaty with the Byzantine Empire, and in the ensuing peace the Bulgar state was increasingly opened up to Byzantine culture. The most obvious manifestation of this was the decision of **Khan Boris** (852–89) to adopt Orthodox **Christianity** as the official state religion in 865. The move was a pragmatic one, recognizing that a rapprochement with Byzantium was in the First Kingdom's long-term diplomatic interests, but Boris's son **Simeon** feared that the Orthodox Church could be used as a vehicle for Byzantine interests in Bulgaria: he therefore established a separate **Bulgarian Patriarchate**, thus ensuring the Bulgars full ecclesiastical autonomy.

The **majority Slav population** over which the Bulgars ruled was largely Christianized well before 865, and Boris's decision to adopt the new religion bolstered the growing influence of the Slavs in the Bulgar state. Many Bulgar nobles agitated for a return to **paganism**, and their defeat only served to confirm the gradual eclipse of the Turkic culture of the original Bulgars – although the name of the former ruling class has been perpetuated in the name Bulgaria.

Language and the Cyrillic alphabet

The position of Slavs in the Bulgarian kingdom was also enhanced by the decision to adopt the **Slav tongue** (rather than Greek) as the official language of the Bulgarian Church. The Byzantines themselves were eager to promote this, as they thought that their missionaries, armed with a Slavonic translation of the Gospels, would be able to go forth and convert the entire population of Central and Eastern Europe. Thessaloniki-based missionaries **Cyril and Methodius** began the job of creating an alphabet suited to the needs of the Slav language, initially opting for a rune-like script subsequently known as Glagolitic. However, the task was completed by their disciples **Kliment** and **Naum**, who named the script (still used in varying forms by the modern Bulgarians, Serbs, Ukrainians and Russians) **Cyrillic** in honour of their mentor.

Zenith and decline

Armed with the Cyrillic alphabet, Bulgaria became the main centre of **Slavonic culture** in Europe. The "golden age" of literature and arts coincided with the reign of **Tsar Simeon** (893–927), whose defeat of the Byzantine army at Aheloi in 917 allowed him to annex sizeable chunks of Macedonia and Thrace, and to claim haughtily to be "Tsar of all the Bulgarians and Byzantines".

Frequent wars and rising taxes bred discontent with the feudal order, aiding the rise of the **Bogomils** (see box, p.236), a heretical sect whose doctrines eroded the authority of both church and state. Bogomil ideas gradually spread throughout the Balkans, and went on to influence like-minded movements in France and Italy during the twelfth and thirteenth centuries.

The reigns of Petar I (927–69) and Boris II (969–71) were also marked by increasing threats from Byzantium, and an invasion by Prince Svyatoslav of Kiev gave the Byzantines the pretext they needed to launch a full-scale onslaught. Bulgaria was reduced to a territory known as the **Western Kingdom**, governed from Ohrid in Macedonia. **Tsar Samuil** was partly successful in restoring the old kingdom, until the Byzantine emperor Basil Bulgaroctonos – the "**Bulgar-Slayer**" – defeated his army at Strumitsa in 1014 and blinded the fourteen thousand prisoners taken. Samuil died of horror after seeing the maimed horde fumbling its way into Ohrid.

Following Ohrid's capture in 1018 the whole of Bulgaria fell under **Byzantine domination**. As a result, the Orthodox Church was largely Hellenized, and Bulgarian architecture and art were increasingly influenced by Byzantine styles. The authorities in Constantinople visited savage repression upon heretics like the Bogomils, and retaliated violently to various eleventh-century rebellions. However, their power didn't extend to protecting the local populace against marauding **Magyars** and **Pechenegs**, the latest group of warlike migrants from Central Asia, who plundered south of the Danube in the eleventh and twelfth centuries.

The Second Kingdom

In 1185 leading nobles Petar and Asen led a successful popular uprising against Byzantium, proclaiming the **Second Kingdom** in Veliko Tarnovo, henceforth Bulgaria's capital. Byzantine forces under Emperor Isaac Angelus confidently expected to be able to crush the rebel state at birth, but after two attempts in 1187 and 1190, were finally forced to accept Bulgarian independence. Asen's brother and successor **Tsar Kaloyan** (1197–1207) extended Bulgaria's borders further, recapturing Varna and parts of Macedonia and Thrace from Byzantium. However, it was the **fall of Constantinople** to the **Crusaders** in 1204 that gave the Second Kingdom the chance it needed to consolidate and grow. Exiled Byzantine aristocrats, having established statelets in Epirus and Nicaea, proceeded to make war on both each other and the Crusaders' self-styled **Latin Empire of the East**. Tsar Kaloyan sought to exploit this fragmentation of Byzantine power in the Balkans, dreaming of one day setting up a Slav–Greek empire of his own.

Kaloyan succesfully negotiated **union with the Catholic Church** in 1204 in the hope that the pope would support Bulgarian expansion, although at grass-roots level Bulgaria's Church remained Orthodox in all but name. Widely admired in his own time (the name *Kaloyan* was derived from the Greek for "John the Handsome"), Kaloyan was also mercilessly cruel, notoriously razing Plovdiv to the ground and flaying its leading citizens alive in 1205, and hostile chroniclers were subsequently to dub him *Skiloyan* – "John the Dog".

Kaloyan inflicted a stunning defeat on the Latin rulers of Constantinople in 1205, capturing Emperor Baldwin and holding him prisoner in Tarnovo (see p.235). Before he could take advantage of this success, however, Kaloyan was murdered in a palace coup – as were almost all of Bulgaria's thirteenth-century tsars. A period of anarchy ensued under Tsar Boril before **Ivan Asen II** (1218–41) could restore order and continue the expansion of Bulgaria's frontiers. His victory over Theodore Comnenus of Epirus at **Klokotnitsa** in 1230 won him territories from the Adriatic to the Aegean, and ushered in an era of prestige and prosperity that marked the zenith of medieval Bulgaria's development. Ivan Asen also brought an end to the union with Rome, allowing a vibrantly Orthodox, Bulgaro-Byzantine culture to flourish.

The Mongols

This period of plenty was cut short by an unexpected disaster. After 1240 **Mongol hordes**, fresh from their campaigns in Central Europe, withdrew through Serbia and Bulgaria, desolating the countryside. The ensuing chaos provided the Byzantines with an opportunity to win back some of the ground they had lost in the plain of Thrace.

One batch of Mongols – subsequently known as the **Tatars** – settled in southern Russia and the Crimea, whence they mounted continual raids on the lands bordering on the Black Sea. The presence of this powerful and unpredictable warrior-state on its northeastern borders considerably weakened Bulgaria's freedom of manoeuvre – perpetually threatened by enemies on both sides, the Second Kingdom increasingly had to compromise with its neighbours in order to avoid their wrath.

The late thirteenth century

The latter half of the thirteenth century saw a return to internecine feuding and punitive taxation, producing a **peasant rebellion** that led to the crowning of **Ivailo the Swineherd**, whose brief reign (1277–80) was largely devoted to fighting off the Tatars. Referred to as "the Cabbage" by Byzantine historians eager to accentuate his humble origins, Ivailo was a messianic figure who mobilized a hitherto docile peasantry by claiming to have been inspired by miraculous visions. Despite early successes against the Tatars, Ivailo was incapable of meeting the aspirations generated by his rebellion, and the Bulgarian nobility mounted a counter-coup. Ivailo fled to the court of the Tatar khan Nogai, expecting to secure an alliance that would return him to power, but was instead put to death.

He was replaced by the first of the **Terterids**, a dynasty whose only remark-able tsar, Todor Svetoslav (1300–21), succeeded in making peace with the Tatar khans. By threatening to secede from the kingdom, the feudal ruler of Vidin, **Mihail Shishman**, managed to have himself crowned tsar in 1323, inaugurating the new **Shishmanid dynasty**. However, Mihail was fatally wounded at the battle of Velbazhd (modern Kyustendil) in 1330, when the Bulgarian army was smashed by that of **Serbia** – by now the ascendant power in the Balkans.

Ivan Aleksandar and the Turkish conquest

During the reign of Mihail's successor, **Ivan Aleksandar** (1331–71), Bulgaria almost regained the prosperity and level of civilization attained during Asen II's time, with literature, sculpture and painting displaying a harmonious fusion of Bulgarian and Byzantine styles. However, the rest of the fourteenth century was a confused story of disintegration and decline. Overpowerful *bolyari* asserted their autonomy from Tsar **Ivan Shishman** (1371–96), weakening the central authority of the kingdom just when it was needed to organize resistance to a new threat: the **Ottoman Turks**.

Possessing a disciplined war machine and superior numbers, the Turks proved unstoppable; mutual distrust between Balkan and Byzantine rulers prevented any meaningful concerted action against the invaders, and the defeat of a powerful Serbian army at **Kosovo** in 1389 effectively sealed the fate of the whole Balkan peninsula. Most of Bulgaria had been overrun by 1393 and the anti-Turkish **crusades** of 1394 and 1444 failed to reverse the situation. With the fall of Constantinople, last bastion of the Balkan Orthodox world, in 1453, any remaining hope of outside help against the Turks disappeared for good.

"Under the yoke"

Although the transition to Ottoman rule was surprisingly peaceful by the standards of the time, it was accompanied by swift and far-reaching changes to Bulgarian society. Muslim colonists occupied the most fertile land and prosperous towns, while Bulgarian peasants became serfs of the Turkish *Spahis* (land-holding knights). In northern Bulgaria and the Rhodopes some Bulgarians converted to Islam, gaining rights denied to the Christian *Rayah* or "Herd", notably exemption from the **blood tax** or *devshirme*, whereby the oldest boys were taken from their families and indoctrinated before joining the elite Ottoman janissary corps. The Turks subordinated the native **Orthodox Church** to the Patriarchate of Constantinople, which imposed Greek bishops and ignorant, grasping clergy on the faithful.

Ottoman power in Bulgaria was occasionally challenged by popular **rebellions**, which tended to break out whenever Turkish armies were beaten back by those of their European neighbours. Austrian and Moldavian advances encouraged an uprising in Tarnovo in 1598, and the successful Austrian and Polish campaigns of the 1680s led to widespread revolt throughout northern Bulgaria. For the most part, however, life under Ottoman rule settled down to something approaching normality in the seventeenth and eighteenth centuries. Highland settlements such as Koprivshtitsa, Elena and Kotel were accorded privileges and allowed to accumulate wealth through trade, merchants sank their money into the renewal of churches, and the *devshirme* system gradually withered away. It was only with the disintegration of Ottoman provincial government in the late eighteenth century, and the emergence of the rapacious Turkish bandits known as the **kardzhali**, that the idea of Turkish rule as something fundamentally unjust and corrupt once again gripped the popular imagination. The partiality of the Ottoman legal system was one reason why many Bulgarians took to the forests to became **haiduti**, or outlaws.

Meanwhile, spiritual and artistic values predating the conquest were nurtured in the **monasteries**, which remained important repositories of Slav learning at a time when regular parish priests conducted services in Greek only. After the sixteenth century, the Bulgarian monasteries had restored contacts with **Russia**, a newly resurgent and rapidly expanding Orthodox power that came to be viewed as the great hope of the subject Christians of the Balkans.

The National Revival

The role of Bulgaria's monasteries in preserving ancient traditions ensured that memories of the medieval empire never died out altogether. Interest in Bulgaria's past began to express itself with the publication (outside Ottoman territory) of a *History of Bulgaria*, written by Peter Bogdan Bakshev, seventeenth-century Catholic bishop of Sofia, and a *History of the Serbs and the Bulgarians*, written by Hristofor Zhefarovich a century later. However, neither of these had the impact of **Paisii of Hilendar**'s *Slav-Bulgarian History*, written in 1762. Circulated in manuscript form (because the Greeks who controlled the Church wouldn't countenance the printing of Bulgarian-language texts), Paisii's work inspired a generation of nationalists, and became the spiritual cornerstone of the Bulgarian renaissance, the **National Revival**.

The material base for such an upsurge in national feeling was provided by the economic changes of the nineteenth century. Bulgaria increasingly supplied the Ottoman Empire with wool, cloth and foodstuffs, giving rise to a prosperous **mercantile and artisan class** based in the towns and villages of both the Balkan Mountains and the Sredna Gora. Economic development speeded up after the Crimean War, when Turkey's French and British allies demanded that the Ottoman Empire be opened up to Western European trade.

Bulgaria's cultural reawakening expressed itself in protests against the **Greek Church**, which controlled all ecclesiastical affairs in the country and ran most of the schools. The Greeks opposed Bulgarian efforts to establish churches and schools of their own. **Riots**, in which the local Greek priest was chased out of town, became a regular feature of mid-nineteenth-century life.

Community leaders had to bargain hard with the Ottoman authorities to gain concessions on the issue of Bulgarian-language schooling, but by the 1840s Bulgarian **education** was beginning to take off. The growing middle class endowed schools offering a modern, secular education; in addition, there were *chitalishta* or "reading rooms" – cultural centres that offered courses for adults. The campaign for church autonomy was rewarded in 1870, when a decree from the sultan permitted the foundation of the **Bulgarian Exarchate** – a semi-independent institution nominally subject to the Greek Orthodox patriarch of Constantinople, but capable of enforcing use of the Bulgarian language in churches and church schools. This emboldened the Bulgarians to extend their struggle further into the political sphere.

Whereas their elders had sought reforms, "second generation" nationalists increasingly pursued Bulgarian independence through armed struggle, and émigrés in the Serbian capital Belgrade, led by **G.S. Rakovski**, began organizing a **Bulgarian Legion** in 1861. Its members fought alongside Serbia in its wars with the Ottoman Empire, while other Bulgarian exiles formed *cheti* or armed groups that raided Turkish-controlled territory from sanctuaries in Serbia and Romania.

The revolutionary underground and the April Rising

The *cheti* received little support from the Bulgarian peasantry, however, and their unpopularity convinced **Vasil Levski** and the Bucharest-based **Bulgarian Revolutionary Central Committee (BRCK)** that a mass uprising could only be inspired by an indigenous **revolutionary underground**, which they set about creating. Levski himself led the way, travelling the length and breadth of the country to establish clandestine revolutionary cells. Levski and the other agents charged with setting up the BRCK network were henceforth known as the **apostles** due to the almost evangelical nature of their work. Levski himself was captured and executed in 1873, a setback that nevertheless provided the liberation struggle with its first great martyr, inspiring idealistic and patriotic youngsters everywhere to rally to the cause.

The culmination of the BRCK's organizational efforts was the **April Rising of 1876**, which after exhaustive (but, as it turned out, insufficient) preparation was launched in the Balkan Mountains and the Sredna Gora – a heroic attempt answered by savage Ottoman reprisals, which took an estimated 29,000 Bulgarian lives.

The "Eastern Question"

Despite these valiant efforts, the fate of Bulgaria didn't really rest with the Bulgarians themselves. The gradual stagnation of Ottoman power in Europe had raised the problem – dubbed the **"Eastern Question"** by contemporary politicians and journalists – of who would profit from the empire's demise. The main contenders in the area were Austria–Hungary and tsarist Russia, the latter nursing a long-standing ambition to extend its influence as far south as Constantinople and thereby gain control of the Bosphorus. Both the French and the British were horrified by the prospect, and tended to support Turkey in order to frustrate Russian expansion. The British establishment was notoriously hostile to any Bulgarian aspirations that involved Russian backing, with Queen Victoria herself remarking that the Bulgarian people "hardly deserved the name of real Christians". In the cynical environment of Great Power diplomacy, the aspirations of the nationalities languishing under Ottoman rule counted for little.

The Russians exploited the ideology of **Pan-Slavism** – the belief that Slav peoples everywhere should be freed from foreign domination and united under the authoritarian guidance of the Russians – in order to stir up anti-Ottoman sentiment in the Balkans and exert control over the liberation movements thus produced. It was therefore taken for granted by Russia's opponents that any future Bulgarian state would merely be a vehicle for the Balkan ambitions of its big Slav brother. However, the Western powers found it difficult to give the Turks their unqualified support: public opinion in the West was often deeply sympathetic to the demands of the Ottoman Empire's Christian subjects – of which Russia fancied itself to be the protector.

Russian troops had temporarily expelled the Ottomans from parts of Bulgaria during the 1810–11 and 1828–29 **Russo-Turkish wars**, but were consistently unwilling to provoke the Western powers by pressing their advantage in the region too far. Britain and France had even laid siege to Russia's Black Sea ports in the **Crimean War** of 1854–56 to demonstrate their support for the Ottoman Empire – which they hoped would survive in its present form if only they could persuade it to introduce reforms.

The War of Liberation

In 1876, however, the **massacres** that followed the April Rising sent a wave of revulsion throughout Europe, and the Russian army prepared to teach the Turks a lesson. The British and French, faced by an angry public enraged by tales of Ottoman atrocities against Bulgarian civilians, were no longer in a position to back the Turks. The British tried to diffuse the situation by bringing the Turks to the negotiating table, but after assenting to the **Constantinople Conference** in November 1876, the Ottoman government rejected its draft proposals for an autonomous Bulgarian province.

The Russians were initially cautious about embarking on a war with Turkey because they feared an armed response from Austria. By the time the Constantinople Conference broke up, however, the Russians had reached a secret agreement with the Austrians; promising them Russian support for their claim to Bosnia-Herzegovina if they remained neutral in any Russo-Turkish conflict. Free to act, the Russian Tsar Alexander II (subsequently known to Bulgarians as **Tsar Osvoboditel** – the "Tsar-Liberator") declared war on Turkey in April 1877.

Romanians and Bulgarian volunteers fought alongside the Russians in the 1877–78 **War of Liberation**, which would have been a total rout had the Turks not fought belated rearguard actions at the siege of Plevna (modern-day Pleven) and the battle of the Shipka Pass.

The defeated Turks signed the **Treaty of San Stefano** in March 1878, recognizing an independent Bulgaria incorporating much of Macedonia and Thrace. This so-called **"Big Bulgaria"** was too much for the Western powers to swallow, and was promptly broken up by the speedily summoned **Congress of Berlin** (July 1878). The outcome of the Congress reflected the desire of British prime minister Benjamin Disraeli to "keep the Russians out of Turkey, not to create an ideal existence for Turkish Christians". Macedonia and southern Thrace were returned to the Turks, and the rest of Bulgaria was split into two chunks: land south of the Balkan Mountains became **Eastern Rumelia**, an autonomous province of the Ottoman Empire; while land to the north became an independent **Principality of Bulgaria**, owing nominal suzerainty to the Turks and paying annual tribute to the sultan.

From Independence to World War II

In the immediate post-Liberation years, attempts to build a stable **democracy** in the principality were hampered by continuing Great Power interest in Balkan affairs. The Russians still regarded Bulgaria as a potential instrument of tsarist policy, provoking tension between pro- and anti-Russian elements within the country itself.

Russian advisers were responsible for drafting an autocratic constitution for the fledgling state, but this was rejected by the Constituent Assembly which met at Tarnovo in 1879. Dominated by the Liberal Party (in which many leading lights of the liberation struggle were gathered), the Assembly drew up the so-called **Tarnovo Constitution**, which envisaged a single chamber parliament elected by universal male suffrage. This went down badly with Bulgaria's newly chosen prince, the autocratically minded Alexander Battenberg (Aleksandar Batenberg to the Bulgarians), a German aristocrat who had served with the Russian army during the War of Liberation. The prince suspended the constitution and convened a special assembly – which he blackmailed into voting him emergency powers by threatening to abdicate if they refused. Aleksandar accepted a partial return to democratic government in 1883.

Unification and the Serbo-Bulgarian War

Many of the Liberal politicians who fled Aleksandar's so-called **personal regime** ended up in Eastern Rumelia, which since 1878 had been ruled by local governor-generals eager to advance the Bulgarian cause in the region, despite its continuing status as a province of the Ottoman Empire. Growing popular agitation for **unification with Bulgaria** culminated in an uprising within Eastern Rumelia and the declaration of union in September 1885; a *fait accompli* that Turkey accepted after much sabre-rattling.

Serbia, offended that changes of Balkan borders could be made without its permission, and afraid that Bulgarian unification would be followed by territorial gains elsewhere, launched a punitive attack on Bulgaria. In the ensuing

Serbo-Bulgarian war of 1885 a ramshackle Bulgarian army successfully routed the Serbs at Slivnitsa.

International intrigue

More serious, however, was the displeasure expressed by Russia at Bulgaria's failure to consult its big Slav cousin on the issue of unification. In a **turn-around of international attitudes**, Bulgarian expansion was now opposed by the Russians, because they were constrained by an agreement with Germany and Austria promising to preserve the status quo in the Balkans. The British, slowly becoming aware that Bulgaria wasn't necessarily the subservient Russian creature they had feared it to be, responded to Bulgarian unification with glee. The Russians withdrew their advisers and troops from Bulgaria, expecting the principality to collapse. When this didn't happen, pro-Russian officers in the Bulgarian army deposed Prince Aleksandar and spirited him out of the country in 1886, before themselves falling victim to a counter-coup organized by leading Liberal politician **Stefan Stambolov**. Stambolov secured Aleksandar's return, but the fawning way in which Aleksandar attempted a reconciliation with the Russian tsar enraged Stambolov, and the prince was forced to abdicate in September 1886. The Russians prepared to mount a takeover of Bulgaria but misjudged local opinion, as parliamentary elections produced an anti-Russian, pro-Stambolov majority. Acting as the head of a **Council of Regents**, Stambolov attempted to sever the Russian connection entirely by realigning Bulgaria's foreign policy with Austria and Germany, and inviting the Habsburgs' favourite German toff **Ferdinand of Saxe-Coburg-Gotha** to become the new monarch.

Stambolov, however, had to initiate a repressive regime in order to get these changes accepted by the country, and an uprising by Russophile army officers in 1887 was mercilessly suppressed. Stambolov's **dictatorship** lasted until he was ditched by former protégé Ferdinand in 1894. Ferdinand sought a rapprochement with Russia, and set about creating a more **absolutist monarchy**. Stambolov, the only politician with the stature to challenge the court, was killed by Macedonian terrorists – possibly with Ferdinand's connivance – in 1895.

The Balkan wars

By 1900 growing turmoil in the Ottoman Empire left the Great Powers of Europe increasingly unable to control events in the region – however desperate they were to do so – giving the small states of the Balkans more room for independent action. Ferdinand exploited the chaos created by the **Young Turk** revolution in July 1908 to declare Bulgaria's full independence from Ottoman suzerainty, crowning himself tsar in the same year. Political crisis in the Ottoman lands meant that the future of **Macedonia and southern Thrace** was once more back on the agenda, and Bulgaria and its neighbours began discussing ways of driving the Turks from the area for good.

The **First Balkan War** of 1912 gave Bulgaria the chance it had been waiting for to try and reclaim some of the territories taken away by the Congress of Berlin. In alliance with Serbia and Greece, Bulgaria launched an attack on Turkey, capturing the fortress of Edirne and advancing on Istanbul. The war created a good deal of excitement in Western Europe, with journalists and artists travelling with the Bulgarian army to witness modern conflict at first hand. Italian futurist poet F. T. Marinetti wrote his epochal poem *Zang Tumb Tumb!* after watching the Bulgarian artillery bombardment of Edirne.

Bulgarian forces were initially so confident of capturing Istanbul that Tsar Ferdinand ordered his state carriage to be sent to the front line so that he could enter the city in triumph – but bad weather and a cholera outbreak saved the Turks from defeat. Bulgarian troops succeeded in occupying the Pirin region of eastern Macedonia, but found that the Serbs and the Greeks had beaten them to the rest. Unable to agree on an equitable division of the spoils, the former allies fell out, Greece and Serbia defeating Bulgaria in the **Second Balkan War** of 1913.

Bulgaria was forced to renounce claims on the bulk of Macedonia and surrender the southern Dobrudzha to Romania, but still managed to finish the Balkan Wars with a positive balance. Allowed to keep the Pirin, it also obtained Thracian lands in the south, including access to the Aegean Sea at the port of Dedeagach (now the Greek town of Alexandroupolis).

World War I

Following the outbreak of **World War I**, much of Bulgarian opinion sided with the Entente Powers of Britain, France and Russia, largely due to ties of Slavic kinship with the Russians and a common dislike of the Turks. However, the Entente's commitments to Bulgaria's major Balkan rival, Serbia, dissuaded Bulgaria from joining the alliance. Instead, German promises to restore **Macedonia** persuaded King Ferdinand and Prime Minister Radoslavov to enter the war on the side of the Central Powers.

Hoping to gain large amounts of territory at very little human cost, Bulgaria waited until September 1915 before joining the action, with Radoslavov confidently boasting to his compatriots that it would all be over by Christmas. Three years of agony ensued: anti-war politicians like the leader of the Agrarian Party, **Aleksandar Stamboliyski**, were jailed; and countless thousands of Bulgarians were dispatched to die in the trenches and mountains of Macedonia.

1918–1944

With the country bled white, Bulgaria's army collapsed beneath the Allied offensive along the Salonika front in September 1918. Deserting soldiers hoisted red flags and converged on Sofia, while the cabinet declared an **armistice** and released Aleksandar Stamboliyski, hoping to avert a revolution. Though the mutineers were swiftly crushed, Ferdinand was forced to abdicate in favour of his son, **Boris III**, leaving Stamboliyski's **Bulgarian Agrarian National Union** or **BZNS** the most powerful force in the country.

The Agrarians emerged as the largest party in the 1919 election – the general desire for radical change was reflected in the fact that the Communists came second – and Stamboliyski became prime minister of a country whose wartime allegiance to the Allies punished with the **Treaty of Neuilly** (1919). Under its terms, Bulgaria was bound to pay crippling war reparations, Romania reoccupied the southern Dobrudzha, Yugoslavia claimed most of Macedonia, while southwestern Thrace – and with it, access to the Aegean – went to Greece.

Unlike previous governments, the **Agrarians** favoured the countryside rather than the towns, exalting "peasant power" to the dismay of Bulgaria's traditional elite. The bourgeoisie became alarmed by Stamboliyski's dictatorial radicalism, and nationalists everywhere were outraged by his attempts to build peaceful relations with neighbouring Yugoslavia – a policy that entailed renouncing Bulgarian claims on Macedonia. Bulgaria had been flooded with Macedonian refugees since the end of the war, many of whom owed their allegiance to the

Internal Macedonian Revolutionary Organization, or **IMRO** – a group committed to liberating Macedonia from Yugoslav control and therefore implacably opposed to Stamboliyski's new direction in foreign policy.

The 1923 Coup

In June 1923, right-wing military officers supported by IMRO gunmen staged a bloody **coup d'état** against the Agrarians, assassinating Stamboliyski in the process. The reactionary **"Democratic Concord"** coalition under Aleksandar Tsankov assumed power, which it monopolized until 1931. Having failed to come to Stamboliyski's aid in June, the **Communists** staged a hastily planned **uprising** in September 1923, provoking the army and police to savage repression and anti-Communist terror. The Communist Party was banned, and many of its leaders who fled to the Soviet Union later perished during Stalin's purges.

The 1930s

The 1930s were a time of stagnation and political unrest, epitomized by the murderous feuds within IMRO. The June 1931 election brought to power a left-of-centre coalition, the "People's Bloc", but faced by the constraints of the **Great Depression**, the new government was unable to carry out its radical social programme. Economic slump provoked an increase in political extremism, which mirrored the growth of authoritarianism elsewhere in Europe. The Communists re-emerged in the shape of a front organization, the **Bulgarian Workers' Party**, which was banned by the government in 1932; while Aleksandar Tsankov made up for the demise of the Democratic Concord by forming the Hitler-inspired **National Socialist Movement**.

Disintegration of the body politic encouraged the **Military League** to assume power in May 1934 in a coup inspired by the ideas of **Zveno** (Link), another elitist organization whose programme included the customary hotchpotch of militant left- and right-wing ideologies. Parliament was dissolved, all parties were abolished and IMRO was brought to heel: Bulgaria was "depoliticized". But in government the League proved as faction-ridden and ineffectual as its civilian predecessors, and after November 1935 **Tsar Boris III** established his own **dictatorship**, periodically erecting a parliamentary facade.

World War II

Nazi Germany's economic penetration of the Balkans during the late 1930s provided the Third Reich with considerable influence over Bulgaria and its neighbours, and despite the country's declaration of neutrality on the outbreak of **World War II**, Bulgaria inexorably succumbed to the Reich, which required it as a "land bridge" which German troops could cross in order to mount the invasion of Greece. In return for Hitler's offer of Macedonia, Boris III committed Bulgaria to the Axis in March 1941, although he balked at declaring war on the Soviet Union due to Bulgaria's traditionally good relations with the Russian people.

Many Bulgarian Communists exiled in Moscow returned home to foment resistance, but Bulgaria's wartime **partisan movement** was a relatively small affair. However, the Communists did manage to infiltrate and manipulate other opposition groups, combining them into the **Fatherland Front** (*Otechestven Front*) in 1942. Events moved towards a climax with the Red Army's advance and Romania's escape from the Axis in August 1944. On September 8 the

USSR declared war on Bulgaria and crossed the Danube; that night, junior officers acting with the connivance of the minister of defence, Gregoriev, seized strategic points in Sofia, while partisan brigades swept down from the hills. This virtually bloodless putsch was repeated across Bulgaria the next day, making September 9 **Liberation Day**.

The People's Republic

After September 9, the **Bulgarian Communist Party** emerged from two decades of clandestine existence to become the leading political force in the country. Initially their radicalism was hidden behind the ostensibly moderate **Fatherland Front government** led by political veteran Kimon Georgiev, principal architect of the 1934 coup. However, the Communist Party's domination of the Front was never in doubt. Manipulating the ministries of Justice and the Interior to cow right-wing collaborators, and driving the left and centre parties into opposition by repeated provocations, the Party increased its membership from 15,000 to 250,000 in six months. Dominant in government, they then staged a referendum on the **monarchy**, abolished it, and proclaimed the **People's Republic** on September 15, 1946.

Now controlled by **Georgi Dimitrov**, **Vasil Kolarov** and **Anton Yugov**, the state apparatus was turned against the opposition. Many of the political parties left outside the Communist-controlled Fatherland Front had boycotted Bulgaria's first postwar elections in 1945, convinced that the presence of the Red Army on Bulgarian soil would intimidate voters into backing the Front.

A more organized campaign was mounted for the general elections of October 1946, producing a parliament that included a small but vociferous number of anti-Communist MPs. The opposition centred on the Agrarian party or **BZNS**, heir to the popular radical tradition of Stamboliyski, and leaders of peasant resistance to enforced collectivization of the countryside. The Communists claimed that they were traitors sabotaging the economic recovery of the nation: hundreds of BZNS party workers were purged and their leader, **Nikola Petkov**, was hanged for "treason" after a show trial in 1947. Other parties outside the Front were snuffed out at the same time. The same year, Bulgaria acquired the new "Dimitrov" **Constitution** (modelled on the USSR's) and the **nationalization** of 2273 enterprises struck the "bourgeoisie" a mortal blow.

Some of the more patriotic Bulgarian Communists criticized the terms of Bulgaro-Soviet trade (eighty percent of Bulgaria's tobacco crop was purchased at below market prices and then undersold abroad), leaving themselves open to accusations of nationalism at a time when blind loyalty to the Soviet Union was the order of the day – as good a reason as any to launch a purge of "Titoists". Ten ministers, six Politburo members (including **Traicho Kostov**, shot after renouncing his "confession" to having been a fascist spy since 1942) and 92,500 lesser Party members were arrested or dismissed in the purge of 1948–49, while the nation was paralysed by **police terror**. Stalinism pervaded Bulgaria, and for his total sycophancy the Party leader who succeeded Dimitrov, **Valko Chervenkov**, was dubbed "little Stalin".

The era of "Socialist Construction"

With opposition both outside and inside the Party effectively crushed, the government could embark on the transformation of Bulgaria into a modern industrial state. Average Bulgarians, however, gained little from the first **Five-Year Plan**, though this gave a great boost to heavy industrial production (up 120 percent from 1949 to 1955). While factories mushroomed, workers were expected to meet ever-rising production targets, and consumer goods and foodstuffs grew increasingly scarce. Agricultural production remained at roughly its 1939 level, despite an increase in the population and Bulgaria's acquisition of the grain-producing southern Dobrudzha. Unlike elsewhere in Eastern Europe, there were few large estates to be expropriated – on the contrary, economists bemoaned the mass of smallholdings and the individualism of their owners.

Following the **death of Stalin** (1953), Moscow gradually withdrew support from hardliners in the satellite states, and advocates of less spartan policies replaced them. In Bulgaria, Chervenkov lost the position of Party Secretary (1954) and prime minister (1956) to **Todor Zhivkov** and Anton Yugov. The separation of these offices reflected the Kremlin's new policy of "collective" leadership, and Bulgaria's dutiful purge of "anti-Party" elements in 1957 followed their example by avoiding bloodshed. China, however, seemed to have inspired Zhivkov's sudden announcement of the **"Big Leap Forward"** in October 1958, whereby the economy aimed to fulfil the Five-Year Plan in three years, and smallholdings were pooled into 3290 **collective farms**. Industrial dislocation was considerable, but the effect on agriculture was mitigated by the private plots that peasants were allowed to retain.

The Zhivkov era

For much of the **Zhivkov era**, Bulgarian conformity to Soviet wishes became a cliché of East European politics, with the country jokingly referred to – even by Bulgarians themselves – as the sixteenth republic of the USSR. However, this pliability did have its advantages: Bulgaria obtained cut-price Soviet oil, electricity and raw materials, and was relieved of the duty of hosting significant Soviet garrisons.

With access to education and employment denied to people who failed to conform, most Bulgarians grudgingly accepted rigid Party control of public life, although this passivity was made easier to bear by the Communist system's achievements in the social sphere. Given adequate food, guaranteed work, schooling and medical care, and the prospect of an apartment in the future, people were generally prepared to tolerate low wages, shortages of consumer goods and the lack of liberal freedoms.

The West's image of Bulgaria under Zhivkov was almost wholly negative, coloured by the country's slavish adherence to Soviet foreign policy, and the fearsome reputation of the *Darzhavna Sigurnost* or DS, the state security police. The assassination of dissident writer **Georgi Markov**, who died after being stabbed by a poison-tipped umbrella on London's Waterloo Bridge in 1978, gave the Bulgarian security services a reputation for subterfuge and cruelty. Subsequent allegations that the DS had abetted a **plot to kill Pope John Paul II** in 1981 suggested that Bulgaria did the kind of dirty work with which not even the KGB would wish to soil its hands.

However, it was the Party's manipulation of **nationalism** that seemed to Western eyes to be the most distasteful aspect of the regime. On the surface, attempts by the Party to present socialist Bulgaria as a homogeneous national state, the logical culmination of centuries of struggles for freedom, seemed to start off innocently enough. Vast amounts of money were spent on the monuments and festivities celebrating the **1300th anniversary of the founding of the Bulgarian state** in 1983, and resources were channelled into the restoration of historical monuments associated with Bulgaria's past greatness.

However, there wasn't much room in Zhivkov's Bulgaria for people of different ethnic origin. Ever since the 1950s smaller minorities like the Vlachs and Islamicized Gypsies had been encouraged to drop their traditional names and adopt Bulgarian ones. The campaign moved on to the **pomaks** (Muslim Bulgarians) in the 1970s, and to the million-strong **Turkish minority** in the 1980s. Those who refused to Bulgaricize their names were refused work, housing, or worse still, sent to concentration camps such as Belene and Lovech. Opposition to the **name-changing campaign** sparked violence in 1984, and led to a mass exodus of Bulgarian Turks in summer 1989, provoking outrage from human rights groups across the world. All this led to a further deterioration of relations between Bulgaria and the outside world – even Bulgaria's socialist allies were increasingly embarrassed to be associated with it.

The demise of the Communist regime

Bulgaria's socialist economy was beginning to stall well before the emergence of **perestroika** in the Soviet Union began to raise fundamental questions about the continuing viability of the whole system. Summer droughts in 1984 and 1985 had harmed agriculture and reduced hydroelectric power (which usually accounted for much of Bulgaria's supply) at a time when Soviet oil supplies were cut back, causing widespread energy shortages. Prices skyrocketed with hardly any corresponding wage increases, and for the first time in many years a note of testiness entered Bulgaro–Soviet relations.

As Gorbachov increasingly toyed with the idea of wide-reaching reform in the USSR, the hardline leaders of his Soviet bloc allies became more and more of an embarrassment. Zhivkov was particularly unpopular with the new Soviet leadership, not least because they found his anti-Turkish policies repugnant.

The Bulgarian Communist Party was initially slow to respond to Gorbachov's innovations, but by January 1988 Bulgarians were being allowed to form private firms providing that they employed no more than ten people, and the government increasingly advocated a departure from rigid state planning and a tentative move towards **market economics**. Enthusiasm for political change continued to be lukewarm, however, and for some time Bulgarians moved in a strange political limbo, where talk of *glasnost* and *perestroika* was officially sanctioned, but any practical application of them merely invited the usual hassles from the security police.

Protest

Ecological protesters from the city of **Ruse** were the first independent citizens to organize themselves into pressure groups outside Party control in spring 1988. Encouraged by their example, intellectuals in Sofia formed the **Club for the Support of Glasnost and Perestroika** in November of the same year, an organization that united both dissidents and moderate Party members, but the Club's supporters were subjected to petty harassment, denied meeting space and forbidden to use photocopiers.

The Communist Party itself was split between those around Zhivkov who favoured caution, and those eager to rush ahead with political change. Throughout 1989 opposition organizations like **Podkrepa**, the new independent trade union federation formed in February 1989, and **Ecoglasnost**, a green pressure group (which did much to unite disparate strands of the opposition around a cause which they could all share), were allowed to operate after a fashion, but their members never knew from one day to the next what the precise limits to their political freedom were. As the year progressed Zhivkov attempted to win support by stoking up nationalist fervour, with renewed repression of Bulgaria's Turks. The resulting **mass exodus** of Bulgarian Muslims into neighbouring Turkey merely served to convince many in the country that the Communist regime had finally lost all legitimacy to rule.

The fall of Zhivkov

In October 1989 Sofia's police were still beating up members of Ecoglasnost with impunity on the capital's streets, but in the end the forces of conservatism were overtaken by events. On **November 10, 1989** (the day after the Berlin Wall came down), reformers within the Party seized their chance and called a meeting of the Central Committee, which forced Zhivkov's resignation. The former dictator was arrested on charges of inciting racial hatred and, soon afterwards, embezzling state funds; new Party leader **Petar Mladenov** promised free elections, market reforms and an end to the corruption and gangsterism of the past. Opposition leaders took advantage of the new atmosphere to form the **SDS** or *Sayuz na demokratichnite sili* (Union of Democratic Forces) on December 7, an impressive assemblage of dissidents, greens and human–rights activists which non-Communist Bulgarians everywhere pressed forward to join.

Post-Communist Bulgaria: a slow start

The reformist wing of the Bulgarian Communist Party had obviously thought that by ditching Zhivkov and committing themselves to the idea of a multi-party system, they stood a good chance of being perceived as the authors of democratic change. Separation of party and state was symbolized when Petar Mladenov became state president and relinquished the Party chairmanship to **Aleksandar Lilov**, previously the victim of one of Zhivkov's purges. Former hardliners were removed from government, Mladenov's protégé **Andrei Lukanov** became prime minister, and the Party itself changed its name to the **Bulgarian Socialist Party** (**BSP**).

Multiparty elections were called for **June 1990**, too early for either the BSP or the opposition SDS to establish themselves as credible democratic movements. The BSP, despite verbal commitments to democratic socialism, still included far too many dyed-in-the-wool Communists for people to take its new identity seriously; while the SDS, a loose coalition of newly formed parties and citizens' pressure groups, could agree on little save for a hatred of Communism and a desire to speed up market reforms.

Public uncertainty over the economic changes proposed by the SDS played into the hands of the BSP, which garnered 45 percent of the vote and an absolute majority in the *Veliko Narodno Sabranie* or **Constituent Assembly**.

Much of this success was attributed to the conservative nature of the Bulgarian countryside, where the Socialist Party machine was far more effective in reaching potential voters than its cash-starved opponents. The other main beneficiary of the poll was the **Movement for Rights and Freedoms** – *Dvizhenieto za prava i svobodi* or **DPS**. Formed to protect Bulgaria's Muslims, the DPS gained solid support from the country's Turks and pomaks, giving it 23 MPs in the new chamber. However, Bulgaria's urban population had voted en masse for the SDS, and many suspected that the BSP's majority had been artificially inflated by **vote rigging**.

The summer of 1990 and after

The SDS leadership was split on the issue of whether to accept the election result or stage some kind of protest, but the potentially volatile nature of Bulgarian society persuaded them to refrain from anything that might provoke violence. Nevertheless, **discontent** smouldered on throughout June, with regular street demonstrations in the capital, and student-manned **barricades** outside Sofia University. Frustration at the BSP's victory boiled over with the discovery of an old **video tape** that showed President Mladenov threatening to use tanks against opposition demonstrators in Sofia the previous December. Mass meetings called for his resignation, a demand echoed by Socialist Party members themselves.

Mladenov bowed to pressure and resigned on July 7, but this only encouraged further demonstrations by opposition groups dissatisfied with the slow pace of change. In Sofia, university lecturers and students established the **"City of Truth"** – a tent settlement near the mausoleum of Communist Bulgaria's founder, Georgi Dimitrov – to demand a removal of all former Communist MPs and a speeding-up of the criminal proceedings against Todor Zhivkov. Similar "cities" soon sprang up in provincial capitals. In the meantime, **conservative forces** egged on by hardline Communists continued to protest against the new freedom accorded to Bulgaria's ethnic Turks, outraged by the thought that national unity might be compromised by the presence of Turkish deputies in parliament.

By the time the Constituent Assembly convened in Veliko Tarnovo in mid-July, political authority within the country was in a serious state of disintegration. The Assembly's most urgent task was to elect a new president who could somehow hold the country together. After more than a month of deadlock, the Assembly awarded the presidency to the leader of the SDS, **Zhelyu Zhelev**, a respected dissident academic who had been sent into internal exile by the former regime for writing a book entitled *What is Fascism?* – a work that embarrassed Bulgaria's erstwhile rulers by demonstrating the similarity between both left- and right-wing forms of totalitarianism.

Zhelev faced a potentially dangerous breakdown in public order almost immediately upon his election. A decision by parliament ordering the removal of Communist symbols from all public buildings was interpreted by the Sofia mob as an invitation to **set fire** to the Socialist (Communist) **Party headquarters** – where a big red star was prominently displayed – on August 26. Zhelev denounced the vandals, and things began to calm down.

Plummeting confidence in the socialist system had, however, produced a crisis in the Bulgarian **economy**. The cabinet of BSP prime minister Andrei Lukanov courted the likes of Robert Maxwell in an attempt to attract foreign investment into the country, but unwillingness to adopt necessary market reforms soon led to the government's collapse. Made nervous by a nationwide wave of **strikes** and **student protests**, the socialist-dominated Assembly consented to the formation of an all-party **coalition government** in December 1990. Stiff medicine was applied to the Bulgarian economy with the **liberation of prices** in February 1991. Subsequent massive inflation and high interest rates caused bankruptcies, growing unemployment and widespread **social misery**.

October 1991 and after

Early 1991 saw Bulgarian society as divided as at any time in its history. The most visible results of post-Zhivkov change – rising prices, declining social services and the ostentation of those who grew fat on the proceeds of private enterprise – were an affront to people on fixed incomes, especially pensioners and employees of ailing state firms. The BSP tapped these resentments by proposing a slowed-down model of economic reform and the retention of some measure of state planning. For the SDS and other non-socialists, however, Bulgaria's salvation depended on a total **purge of Communist influence**, and the wholesale adoption of a **free market** – whatever the social cost.

Elections in October 1991 gave the SDS a wafer-thin majority, but the new government's crash programme of economic reform led to social hardship and polarized the country even further. The winter of 1991/92 was characterized by extensive **power cuts**, after former Soviet republics began to demand hard currency for the electricity they used to supply so cheaply.

The government's reluctance to give aid to the economically depressed tobacco-producing regions of the south lost it the support of the DPS, who held the balance of power in parliament, and Bulgaria's first post-Commnist government fell after barely a year in office – to be replaced by an administration of non-party technocrats.

Towards the winter of discontent

The next parliamentary **elections**, in **December 1994**, resulted in a crippling defeat for the SDS and handed an absolute majority to a rejuvenated BSP. Led by the young and popular **Zhan Videnov**, the BSP was by now an odd grouping of genuine social democrats, old-style Communists and out-and-out careerists, supported by industrial workers, pensioners and rural Bulgarians bewildered by the changes of the last few years.

The Videnov administration was soon brought down by its own economic incompetence. Market reforms ground to a standstill, and all levels of the economy became infected with corruption – often with government connivance. BSP elder statesman Andrei Lukanov – who had himself become a byword for shady dealings – was gunned down by mystery assailants in October 1996 for threatening to blow the whistle on government corruption. As **winter 1996** approached, foreign investors fled the country, the lev plummeted against the dollar, and food shortages re-emerged.

The presidential elections of November 1996 saw Zhelev replaced by the SDS lawyer **Petar Stoyanov**. Prime minister Videnov resigned in December, ushering in a period of acute instability. With the economy worsening, a wave of anti-government demonstrations swept the country, and SDS-inspired crowds mounted an assault on parliament in mid-January 1997. The SDS won the elections of April 1997 by a landslide, with suave technocrat **Ivan Kostov** becoming prime minister.

Another false dawn

Bulgaria's **economy**, however, had been left in such bad shape by the departing administration that the new government had little choice but to swallow the medicine offered by the International Monetary Fund – by now the real power in Bulgarian affairs. An economic austerity programme was introduced, and inflation was brought under control by pegging the lev to the Deutschmark (and, after 2002, the Euro). The privatization of state-controlled industries was speeded up once more, but this only led to renewed accusations that enterprises were being sold off cheaply to government supporters, with the officials responsible for negotiating the deals pocketing hefty commission fees. A series of much-vaunted **anti-corruption drives** aimed to restore public confidence in big business, but often had the opposite effect – those under investigation invariably tended to be linked to the BSP, while SDS supporters escaped scrutiny.

The return of the king

Despite Kostov's success in stabilizing Bulgaria's finances, the majority of citizens continued to eke out a living on meagre wages. With the lack of any real improvement in living standards, support for the government gradually withered away. However, the BSP, still tainted by the economic incompetence of the Videnov years, was badly placed to profit from widespread disillusionment with the SDS – leaving a political vacuum ready to be exploited by a new and unexpected force.

Ever since 1990, the idea of a return to the **monarchy** had occasionally been floated by those disillusioned with Bulgaria's frequently unstable post-Communist political setup. The Madrid-based **Tsar Simeon II**, who had been chased out of the country by the Communists at the age of nine, was in regular contact with Bulgarian politicians throughout the 1990s, but initially showed little real interest in coming back. By the turn of the millennium, however, events were inexorably moving in his favour. Tired of investing their hopes in successive governments that failed to deliver, ordinary Bulgarians needed a figurehead who could restore some level of confidence in the country. They were joined by many educated, professional Bulgarians who traditionally voted for the SDS, but felt betrayed by its descent into corruption.

Simeon's backers formed a new political organization, the **National Movement of Simeon the Second** (*Natsionalnoto Dvizhenie Simeon Vtori*; or **NDSV**), and prepared to fight the parliamentary elections of June 2001 with Simeon himself heading their list of candidates. Having lived in exile for the last 55 years, Simeon was perceived to be untainted by the corruption endemic among Bulgaria's political elite. Simeon himself kept his cards close to his chest, studiously avoiding the question of whether he was using the parliamentary elections as a platform from which to regain his throne.

In the event the NDSV won a landslide, Simeon assembling a cabinet which included figures from across the political spectrum, as well as young financial experts who had been lured away from highly paid banking jobs abroad by the possibility of forging high-profile political careers at home.

Sitting president Petar Stoyanov was politically damaged by the scale of the SDS parliamentary defeat, and decided to stand in the **presidential elections of November 2001** as an independent, depriving himself of an effective campaigning machine. After a remarkably low turnout, Stoyanov was pipped at the post by the BSP's **Georgi Parvanov**.

The political present

The government of Simeon – still known officially by his family name of **Simeon of Saxe-Coburg-Gotha** (Simeon Sakskoburgotski in Bulgarian) even though many of his supporters refer to him simply as "The Tsar" – continued the work of its SDS-led predecessor, pursuing financial stabilization policies advocated by international organizations such as the IMF and the EU. Simeon's biggest foreign-policy success was Bulgaria's admittance to the **NATO** alliance in April 2004. As with previous administrations, however, popular support for Simeon ebbed away as voters realized that their living standards were not going to improve with any great speed. Simeon himself was increasingly seen as the grey tool of his ministers rather than as the charismatic saviour people had hoped for.

With the class-based BSP and ethnic-Turkish DPS remaining the only political parties capable of commanding a solid electorate, Bulgarian politics entered a fluid and unpredictable phase, with the centre-right fragmenting into a host of minor parties – often tied to a particular leader rather than a coherent set of policies.

Elections of August 2005 produced a narrow majority for the BSP under youthful leader Sergei Stanishev, who formed a coalition government with NSDV and DPS support. The election also witnessed the emergence of **Ataka**, a rabidly right-wing anti-European, anti-Turkish and anti-Gypsy party which won nine percent of the vote. Stanishev presided over his country's **entry into the EU** on January 1, 2007, although the governments of his predecessors Kostov and Saxe-Coburg-Gotha had done most of the preparatory work for Bulgaria's accession.

Although Bulgaria's entry into the EU has injected new dynamism into the country's economy, many of the problems which dogged Bulgaria throughout the 1990s remain. Economic growth in Sofia, Varna and other cities often stands in stark contrast to decay and depopulation in rural areas. Young, educated Bulgarians from all parts of the country are increasingly seeking employment abroad, leading to a shortage in skilled workers and a worrying decline in the birth rate. Above all, government corruption and organized crime have eroded popular faith in state institutions and political parties, giving rise to a new breed of non-ideological, populist politicians. Nowhere has this been more pronounced than in Sofia, where mayoral elections in November 2005 produced a victory for **Boyko Borisov**, a former fireman, bodyguard and interior-ministry chief who seemed to epitomize the kind of straight-talking, politically neutral figurehead for whom most Bulgarians craved. Borisov's new party **GERB** ("Citizens for the European Development of Bulgaria") soon replaced both the SDS and the NDSV as the great hope of right-of-centre Bulgarians, although it remains difficult to see what – aside from personal loyalty to Borisov himself – GERB actually stands for.

Bulgaria's minorities

Despite a proud Slavonic heritage forged through centuries of national struggle, Bulgaria is far from being an ethnically homogeneous state. As well as Vlachs, Armenians, Jews and Karakachani, the country contains about a million Muslims (many of whom are ethnic Turks), and just under half a million Gypsies.

Muslims

Some sources estimate that Muslims constituted up to a third of Bulgaria's population on the eve of the Liberation. Many of them fled in the wake of the Ottoman collapse, but the descendants of those who stayed are scattered throughout the country. Today, the **heaviest concentrations of Muslims** are found near the Turkish border around Kardzhali, Harmanli and Haskovo; near the towns of Shumen, Razgrad, Targovishte and Isperih in the Rhodope mountains; northwest of the Balkan range; between Burgas and Varna on the Black Sea coast; and north of Varna in the Dobrudzha.

Origins

Many of Bulgaria's 745,000-strong **Turkish population** are likely to be descended from **Yörük tribespeople**, nomadic sheep-rearers from central Anatolia who were introduced to the Balkans by the Turkish sultan to guard the frontiers of his European domains. These newcomers settled throughout Bulgaria, especially in lowland regions where the native Christian population was either wiped out or put to flight.

Tatars had been frequenting the Dobrudzha and the Black Sea coast since the thirteenth century, and their Islamic religion and Turkic language made them natural allies of Bulgaria's Ottoman conquerors. Their numbers were augmented in the nineteenth century by refugees fleeing from Turkey's wars with tsarist Russia. Large numbers of Crimean Tatars were settled here in the 1850s, but they found it hard to adapt to a sedentary lifestyle, continued to practise nomadism, and in lean years pillaged Christian and Muslim farmers alike. Similarly unruly were the **Circassians**, also refugees from the tsarist empire, who were given lands along the southern banks of the Danube. The Circassians were recruited as irregulars by the local Ottoman gendarmes, and soon earned a reputation among the local Bulgarians for arbitrary cruelty. Both Tatars and Circassians were gradually assimilated by the more numerous Turks, and soon lost many of their specific racial characteristics – indeed nowadays, Dobrudzhan Tatars are usually referred to as Turks by the local Bulgarian population.

Some fifteenth-century Bulgarians **renounced Christianity** in favour of Islam. It's unclear whether these conversions were forced, or whether landholding peasants willingly adopted Muslim ways in order to retain their privileges under a new regime. In many cases village priests went over to Islam and took their flock with them, despairing at the way in which Balkan Christianity had collapsed so quickly. Subsequently known as **pomaks** (derived from the word *pomagach*, or "helper" – they were viewed as collaborators by their Christian neighbours), about 300,000 of these Slavic Muslims still live in compact communities throughout the western Rhodopes. Under the Ottoman Empire, *pomak* irregulars were often used by the authorities to police the local Christians. It was a *pomak* leader from Dospat, Ahmed Aga Barutanliyata, who was allegedly responsible for the **Batak** massacre in 1876 (see p.355).

Muslims under the modern Bulgarian state

Muslims tended to occupy a privileged position under Turkish rule, and fear of Bulgarian reprisals caused many of them to flee during the War of Liberation in 1877. The Turkish Muslim population of Sofia, for example, evacuated en masse in 1878, and most of their mosques were either demolished or put to other uses. The Bulgarian government undertook to preserve the religious rights of those Muslims that remained, paying for the upkeep of surviving mosques and providing Turkish-language teaching in some schools. Numerous cases of **revenge** did occur, with ethnic Turks being forced from their villages by irate Slavs, but few of these incidents are documented.

During the **interwar years** Muslims were left largely unmolested by the state, although several Turkish settlements were awarded Bulgarian names in the 1930s – the northwestern town of Targovishte, Eski Dzhumaya until 1934, is one example. Local government officials habitually doled out Slavonic names to ethnic Turks when registering births, although there was no consistent, government-sponsored campaign to do so.

The Soviet-inspired **constitution of 1947** paid lip service to minority rights, although Bulgaria's Communist bosses seemed eager to facilitate **emigration** of Muslims to Turkey during the immediate postwar years. Around 155,000 Turks departed between 1949 and 1951, and were followed by a second wave in the late 1960s.

Turning Muslims into Bulgarians

Turkish-language schooling and cultural facilities were provided by the Bulgarian government up until the late 1960s, when there was a radical change in policy towards Bulgaria's minorities. From now on the emphasis was to be on outright **assimilation**. Bulgaria's atheist leaders were frustrated by the way in which Turks and *pomaks* clung to religious traditions, and began to wonder whether they could ever be turned into loyal citizens of the socialist state.

The *pomaks* were the first to experience the effects of the **name-changing campaign**, which aimed to coerce the bearers of traditional Islamic names into adopting Bulgarian alternatives. Beginning in 1971, official ceremonies took place in villages throughout the western Rhodopes, in which *pomaks* were awarded fresh identity papers bearing their new Bulgaricized names. Riots in Pazardzhik, in which two Communist Party officials were reportedly killed by an angry mob, resulted in mass arrests and deportations. **The winter of 1984** saw the full force of the campaign directed against Bulgaria's ethnic Turks, combined with a full-scale attack on Muslim traditions. Mosques were closed down or demolished, local religious leaders were replaced with Party stooges, circumcision was discouraged, and use of the Turkish language in public places was forbidden.

Going under the sanitized name of the *Vazroditelniyat protses* or **"Regeneration Process"**, the campaign was presented to the Bulgarian public as another glorious chapter in the country's progress towards national rebirth. Sycophantic academics were employed to argue that the Turkish minority had in fact been Bulgarians all along: forcibly Islamicized in the fifteenth century, they were merely fulfilling their destiny by adopting Bulgarian names and returning to the fold. Repressive aspects of the campaign were often conducted under the smokescreen of social progress. Well-intentioned Bulgarians were led to support the measures against the Turks when it was argued that Muslim women, denied access to educational and career opportunities by the bonds of patriarchal society, would benefit from forced assimilation.

The campaign met with **fierce resistance** from the Turks themselves. Numerous demonstrations in towns in the Kardzhali district ended with security forces firing on angry crowds; and eight civilians were shot dead during one peaceful protest in Momchilgrad in December 1984. Such events soon attracted the attention of human rights organizations abroad, but the regime turned a deaf ear to foreign criticism. The government turned the crisis to its own advantage, garnering domestic support by accusing Amnesty International and the Western press of participating in a plot to destabilize socialist Bulgaria.

Summer 1989: the "Great Excursion"

With the Zhivkov regime increasingly relying on nationalist excesses in order to distract attention from the Communist system's failings, anti-Turkish policies were stepped up in the **spring of 1989**. Growing numbers of Turks sought to emigrate rather than change their names. By June 1989 the Bulgarian–Turkish border was jammed with people trying to leave, many taking their entire worldly possessions with them. Official sources claimed that the crowds gathering at the frontier were "tourists" (*ekskurziyanti*) taking advantage of the new freedom of travel, unintentionally providing the phrase by which 1989's exodus of Turks came to be known – the *golyama ekskurziya* or **"Great Excursion"**.

Between May and August up to 300,000 Turks and *pomaks* crossed the border, a population movement that had serious consequences for Bulgarian society. Whole areas had been depopulated, and entire towns and villages deprived of trained professionals like teachers and doctors. Most importantly, the economically vital **tobacco crop**, traditionally concentrated in areas of Muslim settlement, lay unharvested in the fields. Urban Bulgarians were organized into work brigades and sent to the countryside to save the crop – for many of them, this was their first experience of the havoc wrought by Todor Zhivkov's nationality policies.

Inspired by the progress of *glasnost* in the Soviet Union, Bulgarian intellectuals were increasingly eager to join persecuted Turks in denouncing the totalitarian nature of the state, and organizations like the **Independent Committee for the Defence of Human Rights** brought leaders of both groups together for the first time. Sharing a common hatred of Communism, Bulgaria's ethnic Turks and urban liberals seemed to be at the start of a fruitful political friendship when the Zhivkov regime came to an end on November 10, 1989.

The post-Zhivkov era

Conditions for Bulgaria's Muslims have radically improved since November 1989. Their interests are represented by the so-called "Movement for Rights and Freedoms" (*Dvizhenieto za prava i svobodi* or **DPS**), a political party which has established a firm hold on the Turkish- and *pomak*-inhabited areas of Bulgaria. The DPS has frequently held the balance of power in the Bulgarian parliament, leading some to argue that the Muslim minorities in Bulgaria now wield too much influence and have the power to dictate policy at a national level. There is also a widespread belief that Muslims are given preferential treatment in areas under DPS control. This is especially true in the region around Kardzhali, which is to all intents and purposes a DPS-controlled fiefdom. Such concerns have led to a rise in right-wing political activity, with the openly racist party **Ataka** winning strong support in the presidential elections of 2006. However, the fact that Bulgaria's Muslims are entitled to political representation is now largely taken for granted, and a return to the anti-Muslim policies of the past is unlikely.

The Gypsies

One of Bulgaria's minorities with no political muscle, largely ignored and abused by their neighbours, are the **Gypsies** (*Roma* in their native tongue; *Tsigani* in Bulgarian). Descended from a low-caste Indian tribe, they made their way into Eastern Europe in the late Middle Ages, and, although many urban Gypsies converted to Islam and adopted Turkish as their mother tongue during the sixteenth and seventeenth centuries, on the whole they have remained remarkably isolated from the communities around them. Intermarriage with other groups is rare, and they still tend to live in their own *mahala* or quarter of town – usually run-down suburbs which have become virtual no-go areas for the local Bulgarians. These Gypsy **ghettos** exist in every major Bulgarian city, with some of the biggest being in Sliven, Lom and Sofia – where they are known colloquially as "*Cambodia*" and "*Abyssinia*". In Kazanlak and Plovdiv, large roadside screens have been erected in order to prevent passing travellers from seeing into the Gypsy *mahalas*.

According to the 2001 census there were 370,000 Gypsies in Bulgaria, although this figure doesn't take account of the many Gypsies who, in the hope of avoiding racial discrimination, declared themselves as Bulgarians or Turks. Unlike the Turks however, Gypsies have never developed political organizations capable of defending their interests. This is largely because they lack a common sense of identity, and think of themselves as members of specific Gypsy **tribes** rather than a larger unified whole. These tribes are named after the trades with which they were once associated, and remain a valuable badge of identity for Gypsies even if the trades themselves are no longer practised. Predominant among these are the *kardarashi* (coppersmiths), *kalaidzhii* (tinners), *ursari* (bear tamers) and *kalburdzhii* (sieve-makers). Originally they would travel the country selling their wares, or working in the supply train of the Ottoman army, although **nomadism** had largely died out by the time of the Liberation, and was in any case outlawed by the Communists.

After World War II most Gypsies joined the industrial workforce or were employed as **labourers** on collective farms. The economic stagnation of the 1980s and 1990s hit the Gypsy community especially hard, and high unempoyment has been a feature of Gypsy life during the last decade, increasing their isolation from other sections of Bulgarian society. This background of non-integration and social deprivation, coupled with only fifty percent of Gypsy children regularly attending school, helps to explain why Gypsies tend to be blamed for the **increase in crime** which has taken place in Bulgaria since 1989. Indeed, some tribes regard pickpocketing as a legitimate trade, and the involvement of Gypsies in petty crime and theft has increased over the past two decades – in 1986, ten percent of crimes in Bulgaria were attributed to Gypsies; by 1994 the figure had risen to 37 percent – but this shouldn't hide the fact that most criminal acts in the country are still committed by non-Gypsies.

Even educated Bulgarians still show open disdain for Gypsies, regarding them as second-class humans incapable of benefiting from any social programmes designed to help them. Bulgarians often blame Gypsies for landing their country with a negative image abroad: Gypsies, they argue, migrate to Western countries with the sole intention of living off social security benefits or petty crime, thereby earning Bulgaria a bad name. (They often omit to mention that non-Gypsy Bulgarians do this as well.)

Bulgaria's Gypsies currently enjoy a much higher birth rate than any other group in the country, suggesting that they will become an increasingly large proportion of the national population in the years to come. However, the failure of successive governments to engage with Gypsy grievances can only serve to store up social problems for the coming decades.

Books

There is more writing on Bulgaria than you might initially imagine – though, as a rule, it appears more in books on the Balkans as a whole rather than forming the central subject of either travel writing or fiction. Sadly, many of the best books are no longer in print. What follows is a collection of books about the country either currently in print, or out of print (o/p), and available in larger libraries or specialist secondhand bookstores. Titles marked 🏃 are particularly recommended.

Travel books and general accounts

Frank Cox *Bulgaria* (o/p). The *Morning Post*'s Bulgaria correspondent during the Balkan Wars, Cox was impressed by a well-organized country that seemed to have imposed order on this hitherto chaotic corner of southeastern Europe. He found Sofia rather staid though, commenting that "the system of partial seclusion of the womenfolk kills all social life, and the absence of a feminine element in the restaurants and other places of social resort deprives them of all convivial charm".

Leslie Gardiner *Curtain Calls* (o/p). East European travelogue of 1960s vintage, the last six chapters of which deal with Gardiner's experiences in Bulgaria – including a slow-burning flirtation with his Balkantourist guide, Radka – recounted in an amusing style.

Claudio Magris *Danube*. This highly praised account of the

Danubian countries interweaves history, reportage and highbrow literary anecdotes in an ambitious attempt to illuminate their cultural and spiritual backgrounds. Only one section is devoted to Bulgaria, naturally enough, but the rest is a fascinating read.

S.G.B. St Claire and Charles A. Brophy *Residence in Bulgaria* (o/p). These two former British army officers lived in a village south of Varna in the late 1860s, returning to write a book on a country "which although but five or six days distant from England, is as little known as the interior of Africa". Their account is largely pro-Ottoman and anti-Bulgarian, although their characterization of the Bulgarians as a surly bunch who overcharge foreigners will be familiar to those holidaying on the Black Sea coast today. Worth tracking down for the folkloric anecdotes alone.

History and politics

J. D. Bell *Peasants in Power* (o/p). Before, during and after World War I, the Agrarians were the largest radical opposition party in Bulgaria and the "Greens" of southeastern Europe. Bell discourses on the brief period of Agrarian government and their charismatic leader, Stamboliyski, in a scholarly but uninspiring manner.

Stephen Constant *Foxy Ferdinand* (o/p). Readable and impeccably researched biography of Bulgaria's unlamented tsar, who privately referred to his subjects as *mes bufles* – "my buffalos". Deals candidly with Ferdinand's bisexuality – a subject that contemporary Bulgarian historians still shy away from.

R.J. Crampton *A Short History of Modern Bulgaria*. Probably the definitive work on the subject: an informed, well-balanced and easy-to-read account widely available from bookshops and public libraries. Especially good on the intrigues of Bulgarian political life after the Liberation.

John V.A. Fine *The Early Medieval Balkans: a Critical Survey From the Sixth to the Late Twelfth Century*. Up-to-date and sophisticated analysis of the formation of Slav states in south-eastern Europe, revealing just how formidable an entity the First Bulgarian Empire actually was. Contains revealing ruminations on the true nature of the Bogomil heresy (see p.236).

Misha Glenny *The Balkans: Nationalism, War and the Great Powers, 1804–1999*. Wide-ranging history written in a breezy accessible style, but backed up with prodigious research. The narrative zooms around from Croatia to Constantinople and all points between, but just about everything you ever wanted to know about the region is in here somewhere.

Richard C. Hall *The Balkan Wars*. Good academic history of the cycle of wars which engulfed the region in 1912–13, providing the curtain-raiser for World War I. Packed with insights into the national rivalries which still plague the region to this day.

R.F. Hoddinott *The Thracians* (o/p). Thorough introduction to the Bulgarians' ancestors, although descriptions of archeological evidence are sometimes a bit too technical for the lay reader.

Dennis P. Hupchik *The Balkans: From Constantinople to Communism*. Accessible narrative which functions well as a general introduction to the main themes of Balkan history.

Machiel Kiel *Art and Society of Bulgaria in the Turkish Period*. Pretty much the definitive work on the development of churches, monasteries and religious painting between the fourteenth and nineteenth centuries. Kiel adopts a refreshingly even-handed approach to both Bulgarian and Ottoman sources, debunking the national myth-making perpetrated by both sides.

Elizabeth Kwasnik *Bulgaria: Tradition and Beauty* (o/p). The catalogue to an exhibition that toured several provincial museums in the UK, with essays on carpet-weaving, traditional costumes and rural celebrations, accompanied by excellent colour pictures.

D.M. Lang *The Bulgarians* (o/p). Traces the Bulgars from Central Asia until the Ottoman conquest, neatly complementing Macdermott's history (see below). Illustrated.

Mercia Macdermott *A History of Bulgaria, 1393–1885* (o/p); *The Apostle of Freedom* (o/p); *Freedom or Death* (o/p); *For Freedom and Perfection* (o/p). Written sympathetically and with obvious enjoyment; all in all, probably the most engaging histories of Bulgaria in the English language. The last three are biographies of famous nineteenth-century revolutionaries – Vasil Levski, Gotse Delchev and Yane Sandanski – which, despite being tinged with hero worship, are impeccably researched and eminently readable.

Georgi Markov *The Truth that Killed* (o/p). Disillusioned by constraints on his literary career in Sofia, Georgi Markov defected for a new life in England, where he began working for the BBC World Service. Collected here are some of the autobiographical pieces broadcast by Markov on the BBC Bulgarian service. They so enraged the Politburo that they ordered his murder. Jabbed with a poison-tipped umbrella on Waterloo Bridge, Markov died of a rare fever a few days later.

Mark Mazower *The Balkans.* Masterful, readable study which tackles the broad sweep of Balkan history in thematic rather than narrative style. Displaying empathy for the various peoples who live in southeastern Europe, Mazower avoids many of the clichés and preconceptions that tend to mar other writings on the subject.

Dimitri Obolensky *The Byzantine Commonwealth.* Classic work on the spread of Christianity and Byzantine culture in the Balkans during the Middle Ages; it's particularly good on the medieval Bulgarian church.

Nikolai Ovcharov *The Shortest History of Bulgaria.* Accessibly written and beautifully illustrated, this is your best bet if a quick introduction to the main themes of the nation's history is what you're after. Ovcharov is one of the country's leading archeologists, but (unlike other Bulgarian historians) refrains from boring the reader with his own discoveries and obsessions. Published by Letera in Bulgaria and available from bookshops throughout the country.

Duncan M. Perry *Stefan Stambolov and the Emergence of Modern Bulgaria.*

A political rather than personal biography of the most talented and charismatic of Bulgaria's post-Liberation politicians, which makes a good introduction to the period as a whole. The same author's *The Politics of Terror: the Macedonian Revolutionary Movements 1893–1903*, is a thorough and readable account of the genesis of IMRO.

E.P. Thompson *Beyond the Frontier* (o/p). Heartfelt account of the Allied mission to aid Bulgarian partisans in World War II, led by the author's brother Major Frank Thompson.

Tzvetan Todorov *The Fragility of Goodness.* Bulgaria's Jews were saved from the Holocaust during World War II, largely as a result of popular pressure on Bulgaria's pro-German government. This book offers a thought-provoking account of this unique episode in European history, and asks what it is that encourages ordinary members of the public to embark on altruistic protests.

Maria Todorova *Imagining the Balkans.* Seminal work of cultural theory which argues that the concept of the Balkans – as an unstable and backward area populated by crazy people – was largely the invention of Western travellers and writers who aimed at the promotion of exotic images rather than real understanding. A stimulating read.

Balkan Gypsies

Garth Cartwright *Princes Amongst Men.* Music journalist Cartwright travels the Balkans in search of gypsy beats, interviewing Romanian brass bands, Serbian balladeers and the big stars of Bulgarian gypsy music as he goes – and coaxing great stories from pretty much everyone he

talks to. Zestful, entertaining, frequently moving but never sentimental, this is as good as musical travelogues get.

Isabel Fonseca *Bury Me Standing.* Part travelogue, part social enquiry, presenting a sympathetic description of contemporary Gypsy life in Eastern Europe. The one chapter on Bulgaria concentrates on the town of Sliven, where Gypsies and ethnic Bulgarians are more integrated than anywhere else in the country.

Fiction and poetry

Georgi Gospodinov *Natural Novel*. Fragmented, postmodern novel from one of Bulgaria's leading contemporary poets and critics, with entertaining prose-morsels addressing subjects as diverse as life on Sofia's housing estates, the sources of literary inspiration, and the importance of the toilet in the domestic life of extended families.

Nikolai Haitov *Wild Tales*. Short stories set in the rural communities of the Rhodope Mountains, from a popular contemporary Bulgarian author.

Geo Milev (trans. Ewald Osers) *Roads to Freedom*.

Milev's death at the hands of the reactionary Tsankov regime in 1925 made him into one of socialist Bulgaria's favourite left-wing martyrs, but it's often forgotten that he was a ground-breaking modernist poet who borrowed from expressionism and other Western styles.

Viktor Paskov *A Ballad for Georg Henig* (o/p). Acclaimed Bulgarian novel of the 1980s, recounting, in mildly Kafkaesque manner, the story of an elderly Sofia violin-maker who has somehow managed to be overlooked on all official state records.

Bulgaria in foreign literature

Boris Akunin *Turkish Gambit*. Genteel espionage novel in which tsarist-era civil servant Erast Fandorin unearths a double agent at the heart of the Russian general staff. Set in Bulgaria during the Russo–Turkish War of 1877–8, this is a satisfying holiday read.

Julian Barnes *The Porcupine*. Political satire centring on the trial of deposed Communist dictator Stoyo Petkanov – a fictional character based on Bulgaria's Todor Zhivkov. A telling account of how democratic revolutions can soon degenerate into cynicism and disillusionment.

Malcolm Bradbury *Rates of Exchange*. Comic novel recounting the misadventures of an English academic sent by the British

Council to lecture in the imaginary Communist state of Slaka, loosely based on countries like Bulgaria. As a Westerner's view of the absurdities of life under Communism, it's extremely funny. The same author's *Why Come to Slaka?* (o/p) was a less successful send-up of the kind of propagandist tourist literature published by Communist states before 1989 – although anyone with experience of Bulgaria in those days will find it curiously familiar.

Robert Littel *October Circle* (o/p). Cold War thriller concerning a group of young Bulgarian Communists who fall foul of the regime in the aftermath of the Warsaw Pact's 1968 invasion of Czechoslovakia. Breezy, undemanding, and with plenty of local colour.

Bulgarian music

Though Bulgaria is a small country, there are several clearly defined regional styles: the earthy, almost plodding dances from Dobrudzha are quite different in character from the lightning-fast dances of the Shop people around Sofia, while the long heart-rending songs from the Thracian plain contrast with the sweet and pure melodies from the northeast. In the remote mountains of the Rhodopes, in the south, occasionally you can still hear the distant sound of a shepherd playing the bagpipe to his flock on a summer evening, and in the villages or small towns of the valleys groups of people sing slow, broad songs to the accompaniment of the *kaba gaida,* a large, deep-voiced bagpipe.

Vocal styles and complex rhythms

To the Western ear one of the most immediately recognizable characteristics of Bulgarian music is the vocal timbre of female singers – a rich, direct and stirring sound, referred to in the West as **"open-throated"**. In fact the throat is extremely constricted and the sound is forced out, which accounts for its focus and strength. Very often these female singers perform without accompaniment, or with (at most) a simple drone such as that of a bagpipe. Nonetheless, in some districts a most extraordinary system of **polyphonic performance** has grown up. In the Shop area near Sofia, women in the villages of Plana, Bistritsa and others sing in two- and three-part harmony, though not a harmony that Western ears readily recognize, as it is full of dissonances. In the Pirin district, in the southwest, the villagers sometimes sing two different two-voiced songs with two different texts simultaneously, resulting in a four-part texture. Although this polyphonic style is normally the domain of women, men in the Pirin region also sing in harmony, but with a different repertoire and in a rather different and simpler style.

The other striking thing about Bulgarian music is its **rhythmic complexity**. To the Hungarian composer and collector of folk songs **Béla Bartók** (1881–1945), the discovery of these irregular rhythms was a revelation. The most widespread is probably the *Ruchenitsa* dance, three beats arranged as 2 2 3, closely followed by the *Kopanitsa* (2 2 3 2 2). More complex patterns like 2 2 2 2 3 2 2 (*Bucimis*) or 3 2 2 3 2 2 2 2 3 2 2 (*Sedi Donka*), are also common. These patterns, foreign to us, are ingrained in the Bulgarian people, who snap their fingers in such rhythms while waiting for a bus or hanging around on the corner of the street.

Ritual music

The yearly round of peasant life was defined by the rhythm of the seasons, sowing and harvest, and many of the **ancient rituals** intended to ensure fertility and good luck still survive, though more as a folk tradition than in the belief that they will produce any kind of magical effect. All these customs, such as *Koleduvane*, which normally involves groups of young men going in procession around the village and asking for gifts from the householders; *Laduvane* at New Year; and *Lazaruvane* on St Lazarus' Day in spring (the most important holiday for the young women, when they take their turn to sing and dance through the streets) have particular songs and dances connected with them. The songs are usually simple, repetitive and very old. The most startling of these rites, *nestinarstvo* – from the villages of Bulgari, Kondolovo and Rezovo in Strandzha – has died out in its original form, when its exponents would fall into a trance and dance on hot coals to the sound of bagpipe and drum to mark the climax of the feast of SS Konstantin and Elena, but it's sometimes presented at festivals and folklore shows. The wild stirring music remains the same.

These days the two most important rites of passage in Bulgarian life, be they in the country or in the town, are **getting married** and **leaving home** to do military service. Both occasions are marked by music. Every aspect of a wedding – the arrival of the groom's party, the leading out of the bride to meet it, the procession to the church and so on – has a particular melody or song associated with it. The songs sung at the bride's house the night before the wedding are by no means joyful celebrations of marriage: on the contrary, they are the saddest songs in the whole body of Bulgarian music, because the bride is leaving home, never to return to her parents' house.

Parties to see the young men off to the army are more cheerful. In the town the family of the recruit hires a restaurant and a band (normally some combination of accordion, keyboard, electric guitar, clarinet/saxophone and drum kit), which plays a haphazard mix of folk, pop and other melodies while the guests eat, drink and dance.

Bands and instruments

Traditional bands usually consist of *gaida* (bagpipe), *kaval* (end-blown flute), *gadulka* (a bowed stringed instrument) and *tambura* (a strummed stringed instrument), sometimes with the addition of the large drum, the *tapan*. They were always common throughout the country, but when after World War II the state founded its own ensembles for folk songs and dances, these instruments were the ones chosen to make up the huge orchestras thought necessary to accompany them.

The **gaida** is maybe the most famous of all these instruments, although it's fairly simply made: a chanter for the melody, a drone and a mouth-tube for blowing, all attached into a small goatskin that acts as a reservoir for air. In the Rhodopes the huge, deep-voiced *kaba gaida* is played as dance music or to accompany singing. On special occasions bagpipe players from the southwestern Rhodopes team up to perform as *Sto kaba gaidi* (one hundred *kaba gaidi*), producing a unique and undeniably impressive cacophony which has to be heard to be believed.

Like the *gaida,* the **kaval** was originally a shepherds' instrument, and some of its melodies go by such names as "Taking the herd to water", "At noon" and "The lost lamb". The modern *kaval* is made of three wooden tubes fitted together, the topmost of which has a bevelled edge that the player blows against on the slant to produce a note. The middle tube has eight finger holes and the last has four more holes that affect the tone and the tuning. They are sometimes called **Devil's holes**: the story goes that the Devil was so jealous of the playing of a young shepherd that he stole his *kaval* while he was sleeping and bored the extra holes to ruin it. Of course, they only made the instrument sound sweeter and the Devil was, as usual in folk tales, discomfited once more.

The **gadulka** is a relative of the *rebec*, with a pear-shaped body held upright on the knee, tucked into the belt or cradled in a strap hung round the player's neck. It has three or sometimes four bowed strings, and as many as nine sympathetic strings that resonate when the instrument is played, producing an unearthly shimmering resonance behind the melody. The *gadulka* is unbelievably hard to play – there are no frets and no fingerboard, the top string has to be stopped by fingernails and the whole thing keeps wriggling out of your grasp like a live fish. This makes the *gadulka* players' habit of showing off by playing virtuoso selections from the popular classics both startling and irritating.

The **tambura** is a member of the lute family, with a flat-backed pear-shaped body and a long fretted neck. Its original form, found in Pirin and in the central Rhodopes, had two courses of strings, one of which usually provided a drone while the melody was played on the other. These days the common form of the instrument has four courses tuned like the top four strings of a guitar, and in groups it both strums chords and plays melodies.

Around the end of the nineteenth century factory-made instruments like the accordion, clarinet and violin appeared in the country and were soon used to play dance music and to accompany songs.

Ensembles and festivals

During the Communist period, folk music was treated as a pillar of Bulgaria's cultural heritage, and state-financed song and dance ensembles were formed to perform a national folk repertoire. At the same time, specialized music schools in both Kotel and Plovdiv taught traditional instrument-playing skills to successive generations of musicians.

The most famous of Bulgaria's folk ensembles is the **Filip Kutev Ensemble** founded in the 1950s by Kutev, an extraordinarily talented composer whose style of writing and arranging became the model for a whole network of professional and amateur groups across the country. His great gift was the ability to take the sounds of village singers, drone-based and full of close dissonances but essentially harmonically static, and from this forge a musical language that answered the aesthetic demands of Western European concepts of form and harmony, without losing touch with the Bulgarian feeling of the original tunes. The methods cultivated by Kutev are what you hear in the albums that have made Bulgarian folk music famous in the West, most notably recordings by "Le Mystère des Voix Bulgares" and by the Trio Bulgarka.

Another crucial factor in the growth and encouragement of Bulgarian music is the series of regional competitions and festivals held around the country. The **Koprivshtitsa festival** (see p.274) is particularly important, not merely because of its size (there are literally thousands of performers bussed in from all over the country) but because it is the only one devoted to amateur performers. Practically the only recordings of genuine village music that the state record company, Balkanton, has ever released were made here: *Koprivshtitsa '76* and the double album *Koprivshtitsa '86* are among the most beautiful and valuable recordings of Bulgarian songs and dances ever made.

The other major festivals, at Predel in the Pirin mountains and at Rozhen in the Rhodopes, take place every two years or so; there is also a huge number of smaller annual festivals in many parts of the country – see "Festivals" (p.49) for a full list.

Wedding bands

Wedding bands are an extremely important part of Bulgarian musical life, hired to play at weddings, the seeing-off of recruits and various village festivities. During the Communist period, wedding bands existed outside official ideas of what folk music was supposed to be, and were therefore free to experiment with new instrumentation, fusing folk instruments such as the *gaida* and *kaval* with electric guitar, synthesizer and drums. Indeed it was only in the mid-1980s that officialdom realized the existence of wedding band music, and through the efforts of some quite brave and far-seeing musicologists was persuaded to recognize them as worthy of public support and recording. A tri-yearly festival was set up in the town of **Stambolovo** (hence their alternative name *Stambolovski orkestri*) which presented them in a somewhat bowdlerized form – they were subjected to the "assistance" of approved musical directors – but the Balkanton record *Stambolovo '88* gives a very good impression of the amazing revelation of this kind of music.

Ivo Papazov is the best known of these musicians in the West, thanks to the work of Hannibal Records, who managed to record him with his electric band after a long struggle with the bureaucracy. His flirtations with jazz following his work in the late 1970s and early 1980s with the Plovdiv Jazz-Folk Ensemble are maybe less successful than his startling transformations of traditional Thracian music, but some of his most intriguing achievements lie in the performance of **Turkish music**. He is of Turkish origin, and even in the period just prior to the fall of the Zhivkov regime, when the very existence of a Turkish minority in Bulgaria was denied, you could get home-made recordings of Papazov playing Turkish melodies with a small band of the type common today in Istanbul. His second Hannibal release, *Balkanology*, begins with a Turkish dance and also includes Macedonian and Greek material. Papazov's most recent release *Fairground/Panair* (2003), on Bulgarian label Kuker, has a very heavy jazz influence.

New sounds

It is not only the *Stambolovski orkestri* who have been pushing back the boundaries. Particularly worth investigating is the work of the *kaval* player **Teodosii Spasov**, who has not only recorded a very beautiful and practically avant-garde folk album, *Dalag Pat* (*The Long Road*) in collaboration with composer Stefan Mutafchiev, but also played to great acclaim with the well-known Bulgarian jazz pianist Milcho Leviev. Spasov's subsequent albums *The Sand Girl, Welkya, Beyond the Frontiers, Titla* and *Nestardartni Standarti* represent a successful folk-jazz fusion from one of Bulgaria's most exciting players.

Modern Bulgarian music is currently experiencing a commercial boom. During the 1990s Bulgarians took to a new form of music that mixes Balkan folk motifs with Western and Oriental pop – **popfolk** (commonly referred to as **chalga**). Popfolk is heard everywhere and is big business, complete with video clips, catchy-but-disposable songs and teenybopper starlets. Amidst all this, two (Gypsy) *chalga* performers stand out: the strong voice of **Sofi Marinova** and Bulgaria's most controversial, gender-bending phenomenon **Azis**, whose Roma origins, open homosexuality and flamboyant cross-dressing have done much to break down taboos in a traditionally conservative society.

The past few years have seen Bulgarian **Romany music** make a mark for itself outside of the country. Leading the way, former *chalga* singer **Jony Iliev** has taken Gypsy roots music out of the *mahala* and onto the world stage, sticking to acoustic instruments while producing a modern sound.

As for the future of Bulgarian roots music, the appetite for experimentation between different genres of music is on the increase. Sofia-based band **Bulgara** mix traditional instruments with jazz virtuosity, and are a great live act into the bargain. The **Karandila Orchestra** from Sliven mix a traditional Balkan gypsy repertoire of hip-shaking, *darbuka*-driven beats with jazz and Latin styles. Perhaps most impressively of all, Vienna-trained accordionist **Martin Lubenov** mixes Bulgarian folk melodies with Gypsy tunes, modern jazz and Argentinian tango. Led by musical mutations such as these, Bulgarian music is entering a very interesting phase indeed.

Discography

The best place to find Bulgarian music is, of course, Bulgaria, especially since some of the most interesting labels are not easily available outside the country. Balkanton, the one-time state record company, still has an enormous amount of wonderful material – it's hard to go wrong with them if you stick to the folk side of things, but not much is available on CD. And keep an eye open for productions by the more modern Kuker and Gega records as well; although hard to get hold of they're consistently good. Popfolk and wedding band music is available at the many CD shops and market stalls throughout Bulgaria but is rarely found abroad. However, you should be able to get hold of most of the recordings below without too much trouble.

Various

Anthologie de la Musique Bulgare Vols. 1–5 (Le Chant du Monde LDX 274970, 274975, 274977, 274979, 274981). Recorded by an ethnomusicologist on several field trips through the length and breadth of the country, and including styles that are often passed over, this is undoubtedly the most comprehensive survey of folk and traditional music available.

Song of the Crooked Dance (Yazoo 7016). Vintage recordings of songs and instrumentals, well chosen and well remastered. There are some breathtaking performances here and a wealth of material, mostly of village music, all with excellent notes.

Two Girls Started to Sing (Rounder #1055). Amateur recordings of village musicians made by an enthusiast from the USA, perhaps a little ragged but a wide-ranging and effective selection.

Vocal Traditions of Bulgaria (Saydisc CD-SDL 396). A lovely selection of songs by professional and amateur performers taken from the radio archives, displaying enormous authority and covering the whole

country. Once again though, the emphasis is on the village rather than the town.

Individual artists

Azis *Na Golo* (Sunny Records, Bulgaria 2003). To experience the *chalga* superstar at his best, go for this camp classic. Azis's Gypsy roots, Bollywood-flavoured vocal acrobatics and shuffling of Balkan melodies gives the listener an aural sugar rush. Huge fun and the sound of modern Bulgaria at play.

Balkana *The Music of Bulgaria* (Hannibal HNCD 1335). The Trio Bulgarka are joined here by members of the Trakiiskata Troika and friends in the first major project by a Western label to record material afresh rather than pick over the archives. Both a historic step and a fine recording, it came as a revelation when it was first released in the mid-1980s.

The Bisserov Sisters *Three Generations of the Bisserov Sisters* (PAN Ethnic Series 2080). Although the Bisserov Sisters have been performing professionally for a long time, they remain very close to their roots. They're at their best when singing local music to their own accompaniment of *tarabuka* drum and long-necked *tambura* lute, as here.

Bulgara *Bear's Wedding* (Sound Project/Ethnic Art MK 21418). Thrilling exercise in jazz-folk genre-bending from one of Bulgaria's best live bands. Song titles like "Balkan Flamenco" and "Romanian Tango" give you some idea of what to expect.

Bulgari *Bulgarian Folk Music* (Latitudes LAT 50613). Bulgari have taken the small-band folk-instrument tradition and pushed it to the limits – fast, intricate and harmonically interesting, they are probably the best

of this particular bunch at the moment, although this recording finds them a little on the staid side.

The Bulgarian Voices Angelite *Melody Rhythm and Harmony* (Jaro 1993–2). The amoeba-like development of Bulgarian female choirs, splitting, reforming, changing directors and record companies, with legal action always lurking in the background, is not easy to disentangle. The particular incarnation known as Angelite ("The Angels") is caught here live on a double CD – there are fine performances of all the old favourites, and the instrumental playing is immaculate.

The Bulgarian Voices Angelite *Mercy for the Living* (Jaro 4220–2). A CD dedicated to performances of Orthodox Christian religious music, ranging from reconstructions of medieval chant to big nineteenth-century compositions by Bulgarian and Russian composers, this provides an excellent introduction to this very rich, if specialized, field.

Jony Iliev *Ma Maren Ma* (Asphalt Tango). Amazing Bulgarian Roma roots music straight from the poor Gypsy quarter of Kyustendil. Jony sings the Balkan blues and his family band plays with real fire.

Kanarite *Izbrano – chast 1* (Payner PNR 2412830 –49). A collection of the best numbers by Bulgaria's most popular and successful wedding band. This album covers most styles of wedding music found throughout Bulgaria.

Karandila Orchestra *Cyclops Camel* (Messechina MMK01). Seriously funked-up Gypsy brass from Sliven.

They also appear on *Gypsy Summer* (Kuker KP/R 01), the soundtrack album of Milan Ognyanov's documentary film of the same name. Both CDs can be picked up in record shops in Sofia.

Martin Lubenov & Jazzta Prasta Band *Veselina* (Connecting Cultures CC50026). Accordion virtuoso Lubenov leads piano-, base- and drum-wielding colleagues on an exhilarating journey round the fringes of Bulgarian folk, producing a sensuous tango–Balkan mix-up.

Le Mystère des Voix Bulgares *Le Mystère des Voix Bulgares* (Disques Celliers CD 008). Cellier's ground-breaking release of what he had trawled from the state archives remains one of the best available. There isn't much more to say.

Le Mystère des Voix Bulgares *Ritual* (Elektra Nonesuch 7559-79349-2). Although this could be described as "more of the same", it's a very good same, and includes interesting arrangements of songs from Bulgaria's Sephardic Jewish tradition.

Ivo Papazov *Fairground/Panair* (Kuker, Bulgaria). After a thirteen-year recording break, Ivo Papazov's latest album showcases his mix of Bulgarian wedding music with Eastern-Bloc jazz elements that often overtake and dominate. Overall, Papazov's wedding music style is very "Eighties" (his prime years), but a BBC World Music award testifies to his appeal to the Western audience.

Philip Koutev Ensemble *At Daybreak* (Gega New GD 304). Koutev was a brilliant arranger and composer, and his ensemble was the vehicle for displaying his ideas. This recent CD of mostly old favourites show that they have lost none of their magic, and at least some ears will find the clean and well-balanced modern sound an improvement on

their reverb-drenched earlier recordings.

Theodosii Spassov *Fish are Praying for Rain* (Traditional Crossroads TCRO 4298). Spassov's collaboration with a jazz pianist and drummer is either a fascinating exploration of the boundaries or an egregious example of a dog walking on its hind legs, depending on taste. In any case, it can't be ignored. If you are lucky enough to come across his 1986 collaboration with composer Stefan Mutafchiev on Balkanton, *The Long Road*, try that for a bit more experimentation with a bit less self-indulgence.

Theodosii Spassov and Nikola Iliev *Na Trapeza* (Gega New GD 207). Spassov is undoubtedly the finest and most startling player of the notoriously intractable shepherd's flute, the *kaval*, and here he is joined by clarinetist Iliev in an extraordinary mixture of spontaneous invention and disciplined unison playing. A fine disc.

Trakia Folk Ensemble Plovdiv *Grozdana* (Gega New GD 228). The Trakia Ensemble was always the most experimental and exciting of the large-scale regional ensembles, and the sweeping orchestral and choral arrangements, leavened by a couple of tracks in which the instrumentalists get a chance to cut loose, show it at its best.

Trio Bulgarka *The Forest is Crying (Lament for Indje Vojvoda)* (Hannibal). For many people the Trio Bulgarka remain the best vocal group to come out of Bulgaria. The three soloists manage to blend their highly individual voices beautifully, and they had the cream of composers and arrangers writing for them.

This article – an edited extract from *The Rough Guide to World Music* – was researched and written by **Kim Burton** and updated by **Nick Nasev**.

C

Language

Language

Bulgarian

Bulgarian is a South Slavonic tongue closely related to Croation and Serbian, and more distantly to Russian, which most Bulgarians learned at school before 1989. Since then, English language studies have become increasingly popular, but you'll still find that English is widely understood only among young people and urban professionals, or in the ski and beach resorts favoured by British holiday-makers. Those who acquire some Bulgarian will find that even the smallest effort reaps great rewards.

Two widely available **self-study courses** offering an accessible introduction to the everyday language are *Colloquial Bulgarian* (Routledge) and *Teach Yourself Bulgarian* (Hodder & Stoughton), both of which are accompanied by optional cassettes. Once in Bulgaria itself, you'll find an increasing number of Bulgarian-English **dictionaries** and phrase books at bookshops and street stalls.

The Cyrillic alphabet

Most signs, menus and so on are in the **Cyrillic alphabet**, but along highways you'll also see signs in the Roman alphabet. For easy reference in the course of this guidebook, you'll find the Cyrillic version of **town names** in parentheses after the Roman spelling.

There are different ways of **transcribing** Cyrillic into Latin script (for example, "Cherven Bryag" or "Červen Brjag" for ЧЕРВЕН БРЯГ; "Tarnovo" or "Tûrnovo" for ТЬРНОВО) but – with a few notable exceptions like "Bulgaria" and "Sofia" instead of "Bûlgariya" and "Sofiya" – we've tried to adhere to the following system. This shows Cyrillic characters in capital and lower-case form, with their Roman transcription and a roughly equivalent sound in English.

It's useful to know that putting the word *da* before **verbs** makes an infinitive (*iskam da kupya*, "I want to buy"), while *ne* is used to form the negative (*ne iskam*, "I don't want"). Use of the particle *li* turns the sentence into a question – *imate li…?* is "do you have …?"

А а	a as in bad	К к	k as in kit
Б б	b as in bath	Л л	l as in like
В в	v as in vat	М м	m as in met
Г г	g as in gag	Н н	n as in not
Д д	d as in dog	О о	o as in got (never as in go)
Е е	e as in den		
Ж ж	zh like the 's' in measure	П п	p as in pot
		Р р	r as in rasp
З з	z as in zap	С с	s as in sat
И и	i as in bit (or "bee", at the end of a word)	Т т	t as in tap
		У у	u as in rule
Й й	i "y" as in youth	Ф ф	f as in fruit

Х х	h as in loch (aspirated)	Ь ь	(this character softens the preceding consonant)
Ц ц	ts as in shuts		
Ч ч	ch as in church	Ю ю	yu as in you
Ш ш	sh as in dish	Я я	ya as in yarn
Щ щ	sht like the last syllable of sloshed		
Ъ ъ	a, but pronounced a bit like the u in but		

In practice there are the odd exceptions to this pronunciation: Bulgarians pronounce ГРАД (town) as "grat" instead of "grad", for example. But the system generally holds good and if you follow it you'll certainly be understood.

The most important thing is to work on the **pronunciation** of certain sounds (Ж,Х,Ц, Ч, Ш, Щ, Ъ, Ю and Я in the alphabet) and attuning your ear to Bulgarians' throatily mellow timbre. Most Bulgars sway their heads sideways for "**yes**" and nod to signify "**no**", but a few do things "our way", increasing the possibility of misunderstandings which can leave both parties floundering through *da*s and *ne*s.

Bulgarian words and phrases

Basics

dobar den	hello/good day	molya – izvinete	please – excuse me
dovizhdane	goodbye	blagodarya (or merci)	thank you
Govorite li angliiski/ nemski/ frenski?	Do you speak English/ German/ French?	nyama zashto	you're welcome
		kak ste?	How are you?
da – dobre	yes – OK	kakvo ima?	What's up?
ne	no/not	zdravei	hi!
ne vi razbiram	I don't understand	lek den!	Have a good day!

Requests

Imate li…?	Have you got…?	Kade moga da si kupya …?	Where can I buy …?
Staya s edno leglo/dve legla	a single/double room	Smetkata, molya	The bill, please
Kolko se plashta na vecher za leglo?	How much for the night?	Kolko?	How many/how much?
		Daite mi… molya	Please give me …
Mnogo e skapo	It's too expensive	For more on accommodation and eating, see p.40 and p.43.
Nyamate li poevtina staya?	Do you have a cheaper room?	

Reactions

dobro, loshe	good, bad
skapo, evtino	expensive, cheap
trudno, interesno	difficult, interesting
hubavo, spokoino	beautiful, calm
golyamo, malko	big, little/few
novo, staro	new, old
rano, kasno	early, late
toplo, studeno	hot, cold

moe, nashe, vashe	my/mine, ours, yours
kakvo?	what, which?
kak?	how?
tova, onova	this, that

NB. If you're uncertain about a noun's gender it's easiest to give the qualifying adjective or pronoun a neuter ending (as above).

Signs

vhod, izhod	entrance, exit ВХОД, ИЗХОД
otvoreno, zatvoreno	open, close ОТВОРЕНО, ЗАТВОРЕНО
svobodno, zaeto	vacant, occupied СВОБОДНО, ЗАЕТО
vhod svoboden	admission free ВХОД СВОБОДЕН

pochiven den	day off ПОЧИВЕН ДЕН
pochivka	pause/lunch break ПОЧИВКА
na remont	closed for repairs НА РЕМОНТ
vnimanie	attention/danger ВНИМАНИЕ
pusheneto zabraneno	no smoking ПУШЕНЕТО ЗАБРАНЕО

Getting about

tuka	here
tam	there
Kak moga da otida do tam?	How can I get there?
S koi avtobus moga da otida v tsentra?	Which bus to the centre?
Tozi li e avtobusat za...?	Is this the bus for...?
Tozi li e vlakat za...?	Is this the train to...?
Za kade patuvate?	Where are you going?
Blizo li?	Is it near?

Na koya spirka da slyaza za...?	Where do I get off for...?
Spri!	Stop!
Ima li vrazka za...?	Are there connections for...?
tryabva li da se prehvarlyam?	Do I need to change?
Molya, zapazete mi...	Please reserve me...
dve legla/mesta	two sleepers/seats
Na koi kolovoz se namira vlakat za...	Which platform for the ... train?

See p.35 for more help with transport.

Time and dates

Kolko e chasat?	What's the time?
Koga?	When?
dnes, utre	today, tomorrow
(za)vchera	(the day before) yesterday
sutrinta	in the morning
sled obed	in the afternoon

tazi sedmitsa	this week
ot ... do ...	from ... until ...
Yanuari	January
Fevruari	February
Mart	March
April	April

Mai	May	sryada	Wednesday	
Yuni	June		СРЯДА	
Yuli	July	chetvartak	Thursday	
Avgust	August		ЧЕТВЪРТЪК	
Septemvri	September	petak	Friday	
Oktomvri	October		ПЕТЪК	
Noemvri	November	sabota	Saturday	
Dekemvri	December		СЪБОТА	
ponedelnik	Monday	nedelya	Sunday	
	ПОНЕДЕЛНИК		НЕДЕЛЯ	
vtornik	Tuesday			
	ВТОРНИК			

Numbers

edin, edna, edno	1	sedemnaiset	17
dve, dva	2	osemnaiset	18
tri	3	devetnaiset	19
chetiri	4	dvaiset	20
pet	5	dvaiset i edno	21
shest	6	triiset	30
sedem	7	chetiriiset	40
osem	8	petdeset	50
devet	9	shestdeset	60
deset	10	sedemdeset	70
edinaiset	11	osemdeset	80
dvanaiset	12	devetdeset	90
trinaiset	13	sto	100
chetirinaiset	14	petstotin	500
petnaiset	15	hilyada	1000
shestnaiset	16		

Useful slang terms

Borets (pl. bortsi)	Literally "wrestler"; strong man employed by gangsters	Mente	Fake (as applied to cigarettes, designer clothes, watches, etc).
Chenge	Policeman, "cop"	Mutra (pl. mutri)	Gangster (literally "thick-necked")
Gadzhe	Girlfriend or boyfriend		
Krachma	Literally "tavern"; a real dive.		

Bulgarian food and drink terms

Basics

Imate li...?	Do you have...?	Nazdrave!	Cheers!
Az sam vegetarianets/ vegetarianka	I am a vegetarian	Hlyab	bread хляб
		Kifli	rolls кифли
Ima li postno yadene?	Do you have any vegetarian dishes?	Kiselo mlyako	yogurt кисело мляко
		Maslo	butter масло
Ima li neshto bez meso?	Do you have anything without meat?	Med	honey мед
		Mlyako	milk мляко
Molya, donesete mi/ni...	Please bring me/us....	Piper	pepper пипер
		Sol	salt сол
Listata	the menu	Yaitse	egg яйце
Smetkata, molya	The bill, please	Zahar	sugar захар
Dve biri	two beers		

Appetizers, soups (supi) and salads (salati)

Bob	spicy bean soup Боб	Postna supa	vegetable soup постна супа
Bulyon	consommé бульон		
Chorba	broth, thick soup чорба	Salata shopska	mixed salad, topped with grated cheese шопска салата
Kyopoolu	aubergine, pepper and tomato salad кьопоолу		
		Shkembe chorba	tripe soup шкембе чорба
Lyutenitsa	piquant sauce of red peppers and herbs лютеница	Tarator	yogurt and cucumber soup таратор

Meat (meso)

Drebolii	giblets дреболии	Kyufteta	meatballs кюфтета
Ezik	tongue език	Mozak	brains мозък
File	fillet филе	Musaka	moussaka мусака
Gyuvech	meat and veg stew baked in a pot гювеч	Parzhola	grilled cutlet пържола
		Pileshko	chicken пилешко
		Ptitsi	poultry птици
Imam Bayaldi	stuffed aubergines (lit. "the Imam burst") Имам Баялди	Salam	salami салам
		Shishcheta	lamb or pork shish kebabs шишчета
Kare	fillet or loin chop каре	Slanina	bacon сланина
Kebapcheta	grilled, sausage-shaped meatballs кебапчета	Svinsko (s kiselo zele)	pork свинско (and sauerkraut) (с кисело зеле)

Terms

cheverme	barbecue чеверме	parzheno	fried пържено
divech	game дивеч	pecheno	roast печено
na skara	grilled на скара	zadusheno	braised задушено

Fish (riba)

Byala riba	pike perch бяла рива	Kefal	grey mullet кефал
Chiga	sterlet чига	Lefer	bluefish лефер
Esetra	sturgeon есетра	Midi	mussels миди
Haiver	roe хайвер	Palamud	tuna паламуд
Kalkan	turbot калкан	Pastarva	trout пъстърва
Karagyoz	Black Sea herring карагьоз	Sharan	carp шаран
		Skumriya	mackerel скумрия
		Som	sheatfish сом

Vegetables (zelenchutsi)

Chesan	garlic чесън	Parzheni kartofi	chips/french fries пържени картофи
Chushki	peppers чушки		
Domati	tomatoes домати	Praz	leeks праз
Gabi	mushrooms гъби	(Presen) luk	(spring) onions (пресен) лук
Grah	peas грах		
Karfiol	cauliflower карфиол	Sini domati	aubergines сини домати
Kartofi	potatoes картофи		
Krastavitsa	cucumber краставица	Spanak	spinach спанак
Luk	onions лук	Tikvichki	courgettes тиквички
Maslini	olives маслини	Zelen fasul	runner beans зелен фасул
Morkovi	carrots моркови		

Fruit (plodove) and cheese (sirene)

Chereshi	cherries череши	Vishni	morello cherries вишни
Dinya	watermelon диня		
Grozde	grapes грозде	Yabalki	apples ябълки
Kaisii	apricots каисии	Yagodi	strawberries ягоди
Krushi	pears круши	Kashkaval	hard, Edam-type cheese кашкавал
Limon	lemon лимон		
Malini	raspberries малини	Pusheno sirene	smoked cheese пушено сирене
Praskovi	peaches праскови	Sirene	salty, feta-type cheese сирене
Slivi	plums сливи		

Drinks (napitki)

Goreshti napitki	hot drinks горещи напитки	**Voda**	water вода
Kafe	espresso кафе еспресо	**Sok portokal**	orange juice сок портокал
Neskafe	instant coffee нескафе	**Aperitivi**	aperitifs аперитиви
Chai	tea чай	**Rakiya**	brandy ракия
Bezalkoholni napitki	soft drinks безалкохолни напитки	**Vino**	wine вино
		Shardone	Chardonnay Шардоне
		Bira	beer бира
		Nalivna	draught наливна

Glossary

Alafranga Term for the combination of native woodwork and textiles with Western fashions in nineteenth-century interior design (from *à la française*); or painted niches and walls in National Revival-style houses.

Banya Public bath or spa.

Bashibazouks Murderous bands of *pomaks* (see opposite) and Turks, employed to punish rebellions against Ottoman rule.

Bey Turkish provincial governor.

Blato Marsh or reed-encircled lake.

Bolyarin Medieval Bulgarian nobleman (a *bolyarka* is a noblewoman).

Caravanserai Hostelry for merchants in Ottoman times.

Chardak Balcony or porch.

Charshiya A bazaar or street of workshops, once a typical feature of Bulgarian towns.

Cherga Handwoven rug. With a simpler design than a *kilim*, and often taking the form of a long thin runner.

Cherkva Church (see also *Tsarkva*).

Cherno More Black Sea.

Cheshma Public drinking fountain.

Cheta Unit of resistance fighters or guerrillas.

Chetnik Member of a *cheta*.

Chiflik Farm or small administrative unit in Ottoman times.

Chorbadzhii Village headmen (literally, "soup makers") or rich landowners; also pejorative term for those who collaborated with the Turks during the Ottoman occupation.

Dere Stream.

Dupka Hole, den or cave.

Dvorets Palace.

Dzhamiya A mosque (also spelt *Djami* or *Dzhamija*).

Esonarthex Short porch before the narthex of a church.

Ezero Lake.

Firman Sultan's seal of authorization.

Gora Forest, hill or mountain (Sredna Gora – Central Range).

Grad City or town. The oldest quarter is often known as the *Stariya grad* or the *varosh* (see opposite).

Gradina Garden.

Guber Fleecy rug.

Hadzhi Man who has made the pilgrimage to Mecca (if a Muslim), or to Jerusalem (if a Christian).

Haiduk Outlaw, bandit.

Haidutin Outlaw, freedom fighter. Plural: *haiduti*.

Hali Market hall.

Halishte Soft blanket or fleecy rug.

Han Inn or *caravanserai*.

Hisar Fortress.

Hizha Hikers' hostel or mountain hut.

Igumen Father-superior of a monastery.

Izvor A spring.

Janissaries Elite military fighting corps raised from foreigners whom the Turks abducted during childhood under the hated *devşirme* system, and indoctrinated with fanatical loyalty to the sultan.

Kardzhali Turkish outlaws, particularly active in the late eighteenth and early nineteenth centuries.

Kashta House.

Kaza Small Ottoman administrative unit.

Khan (or *Han*) Supreme ruler of the Bulgar tribes and, later, the first Bulgarian state; the title is of Central Asian origin.

Kilim Woollen carpet, featuring a complex central design within a border.

Kitenik See *Guber*.

Kobilitsa Yoke used for carrying buckets.

Koleda Christmas.

Koledar Christmas carol singer.

Komitadzhi Another word for *Chetnik* (see above).

Konak Headquarters of an Ottoman *chiflik* or region; including the governor's residence, a garrison and a prison.

Korso Evening promenade.

Kozek See *Guber*.

Kozyak Goat-hair rug.

Krepost Fortress.

Kuker Mummer; a man dressed in carnival costume to celebrate winter nearing its end, a ceremony that usually takes place in January, although in some areas it is associated with the beginning of Lent.

Kvartal Suburb.

Kvartira Room (*chastni kvartiri* – private rooms).

Liberation, The The attainment of Bulgaria's independence from Ottoman rule, following the Russo-Turkish war of 1877–78.

Magistrala Main highway.

Mahala Quarter or area of town, often occupied by a particular ethnic or religious group (*tsiganskata mahala* – the Gypsy quarter).

Malko Small, little or minor (Malko Tarnovo – Tarnovo Minor).

Manastir Monastery.

Minder Couch or seat built into a room (plural, *minderi*).

Mogila Burial mound.

Most Bridge.

Naos Innermost part of an Orthodox church.

Narthex Entrance hall of Orthodox church.

National Revival Nineteenth-century upsurge in Bulgarian culture and national consciousness. Sometimes called the Bulgarian renaissance.

National Revival Style Architecture developed during the eighteenth and nineteenth centuries, characterized by the use of oriels and decorative features such as carved wooden ceilings, stylized murals and niches. Best seen in Koprivshtitsa, Tarnovo, Tryavna and Plovdiv.

Nos Cape.

Odyalo Blanket.

Oriel Angular or curved bay window projecting from the upper floor of a house.

Osvobozhdenieto The Liberation (see above).

Pametnik Monument or memorial.

Pat Road.

Pazar Market.

Peshtera Cave (see also dupka).

Planina Mountain.

Ploshtad (Pl.) Town square.

Pomaks Bulgarians who converted to Islam during the Turkish occupation, or their descendants; mainly resident in the Rhodopes.

Pop Orthodox priest.

Prohod Mountain pass.

Prolom Gorge or defile.

Rayah (or *Raya*) "The Herd", as the Ottomans called and treated the non-Muslim subjects of their empire.

Reka River.

Sabranie Parliament, assembly.

Selo Village.

Shose Avenue or highway.

Sofra Low table with a circular top of copper or brass.

Survakar Boy who goes from house to house wishing people a happy new year by hitting them on the back with a *survaknitsa*.

Survaki New Year.

Survaknitsa Decorated twig borne by a *survakar*.

Sveti (Sv.) Saint; blessed or holy. *Sveta* is the feminine form: *Sveta Bogoroditsa* is the Holy Virgin; *Sveta Troitsa* is the Holy Trinity.

Tekke Dervish lodge.

Tell Mound of earth left by successive generations of human settlement. Tells in the Plain of Thrace provide evidence of Bulgaria's Neolithic and Bronze Age inhabitants.

Thracians Inhabitants of Bulgaria during the pre-Christian era.

Tsarkva Church.

Turbe Small Islamic mausoleum.

Turisticheska Spalnya Tourist hostel, providing cheap dorm-type accommodation.

Ulitsa (Ul.) Street.

Varosh Central quarter of old Balkan town.

Vazrazhdane National Revival (see above).

Velikden Easter.

Veliko Great (Veliko Tarnovo – Great Tarnovo).

Vilayet Large Ottoman administrative unit; province.

Voyvoda Leader of a *cheta*.
Vrah Summit or peak.

Yazovir Reservoir, artificial lake.

Acronyms

BKP Bulgarian Communist Party.

BSP Bulgarian Socialist Party (successor to the BKP).

BZNS Bulgarian Agrarian National Union.

DPS (Dvizhenieto za prava i svobodi). The Movement for Rights and Freedoms – a party supported by Bulgarian Muslims and ethnic Turks.

DS (Darzhavna Signurnost). State security police under the Communists.

IMRO (Internal Macedonian Revolutionary Organization). Macedonian separatist

organization, predominantly terroristic from 1893 to 1934. In Bulgarian it's VMRO – Vatreshnata Makedonska Revolutsionna Organizatsiya.

NDSV (Natsionalnoto Dvizhenie Simeon Vtori). The National Movement of Simeon II: the political platform created to support Simeon of Saxe-Coburg-Gotha in the general elections of 2001.

SDS (Sayuz na demokratichnite sili). Union of Democratic Forces – a coalition of right-of-centre groups.

Travel
store

Avoid Guilt Trips

Buy fair trade coffee + bananas ✓

Save energy - use low energy bulbs ✓
- don't leave tv on standby ✓

Offset carbon emissions from flight to Madrid ✓

Send goat to Africa ✓

Join Tourism Concern today ✓

Slowly, the world is changing.
Together we can, and will, make a difference.

Tourism Concern is the only UK registered charity fighting
exploitation in one of the largest industries on earth: people forced
from their homes in order that holiday resorts can be built,
sweatshop labour conditions in hotels and destruction of the
environment are just some of the issues that we tackle.

Sending people on a guilt trip is not something we do. We know as
well as anyone that holidays are precious. But you can help us to
ensure that tourism always benefits the local communities involved.

Call 020 7133 3330
or visit **tourismconcern.org.uk** to find out how.

*A year's membership of Tourism Concern costs just £20 (£12 unwaged)
- that's 38 pence a week, less than the cost of a pint of milk, organic of course.*

Fighting
Exploitation
in Tourism

TourismConcern

www.roughguides.com

Information on over 25,000 destinations around the world

- **Read** Rough Guides' trusted travel info
- **Access** exclusive articles from Rough Guides authors
- **Update** yourself on new books, maps, CDs and other products
- **Enter** our competitions and win travel prizes
- **Share** ideas, journals, photos & travel advice with other users
- **Earn** points every time you contribute to the Rough Guide community and get rewards

Small print and Index

A Rough Guide to Rough Guides

Published in 1982, the first Rough Guide – to Greece – was a student scheme that became a publishing phenomenon. Mark Ellingham, a recent graduate in English from Bristol University, had been travelling in Greece the previous summer and couldn't find the right guidebook. With a small group of friends he wrote his own guide, combining a highly contemporary, journalistic style with a thoroughly practical approach to travellers' needs.

The immediate success of the book spawned a series that rapidly covered dozens of destinations. And, in addition to impecunious backpackers, Rough Guides soon acquired a much broader and older readership that relished the guides' wit and inquisitiveness as much as their enthusiastic, critical approach and value-for-money ethos.

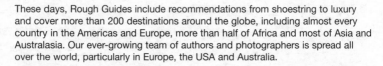

These days, Rough Guides include recommendations from shoestring to luxury and cover more than 200 destinations around the globe, including almost every country in the Americas and Europe, more than half of Africa and most of Asia and Australasia. Our ever-growing team of authors and photographers is spread all over the world, particularly in Europe, the USA and Australia.

In the early 1990s, Rough Guides branched out of travel, with the publication of Rough Guides to World Music, Classical Music and the Internet. All three have become benchmark titles in their fields, spearheading the publication of a wide range of books under the Rough Guide name.

Including the travel series, Rough Guides now number more than 350 titles, covering: phrasebooks, waterproof maps, music guides from Opera to Heavy Metal, reference works as diverse as Conspiracy Theories and Shakespeare, and popular culture books from iPods to Poker. Rough Guides also produce a series of more than 120 World Music CDs in partnership with World Music Network.

Visit www.roughguides.com to see our latest publications.

Rough Guide travel images are available for commercial licensing at www.roughguidespictures.com

Rough Guide credits

Text editor: James Rice
Layout: Ankur Guha
Cartography: Ashutosh Bharti
Picture editor: Sarah Cummins
Production: Rebecca Short
Proofreader: Stewart Wild
Cover design: Chloë Roberts
Photographer: Gregory Wrona
Editorial: **London** Ruth Blackmore, Alison
Murchie, Karoline Densley, Andy Turner, Keith
Drew, Edward Aves, Alice Park, Lucy White,
Jo Kirby, James Smart, Natasha Foges, Róisín
Cameron, Emma Traynor, Emma Gibbs, Kathryn
Lane, Christina Valhouli, Monica Woods, Mani
Ramaswamy, Joe Staines, Peter Buckley,
Matthew Milton, Tracy Hopkins, Ruth Tidball;
New York Andrew Rosenberg, Steven Horak,
AnneLise Sorensen, April Isaacs, Ella Steim,
Anna Owens, Sean Mahoney; **Delhi** Madhavi
Singh, Karen D'Souza
Design & Pictures: **London** Scott Stickland, Dan
May, Diana Jarvis, Mark Thomas, Chloë Roberts,
Nicole Newman, Emily Taylor; **Delhi** Umesh
Aggarwal, Ajay Verma, Jessica Subramanian,
Pradeep Thapliyal, Sachin Tanwar, Anita Singh,
Nikhil Agarwal
Production: Vicky Baldwin
Cartography: **London** Maxine Repath, Ed
Wright, Katie Lloyd-Jones; **Delhi** Jai Prakash
Mishra, Rajesh Chhibber, Rajesh Mishra, Animesh
Pathak, Jasbir Sandhu, Karobi Gogoi, Amod
Singh, Alakananda Bhattacharya, Swati Handoo
Online: Narender Kumar, Rakesh Kumar,
Amit Verma, Rahul Kumar, Ganesh Sharma,
Debojit Borah, Saurabh Sati, Ravi Yadav
Marketing & Publicity: **London** Liz Statham,
Niki Hanmer, Louise Maher, Jess Carter, Vanessa
Godden, Vivienne Watton, Anna Paynton, Rachel
Sprackett; **New York** Geoff Colquitt, Katy Ball;
Delhi Ragini Govind
Manager India: Punita Singh
Reference Director: Andrew Lockett
Operations Manager: Helen Phillips
PA to Publishing Director: Nicola Henderson
Publishing Director: Martin Dunford
Commercial Manager: Gino Magnotta
Managing Director: John Duhigg

Publishing information

This sixth edition published June 2008 by
Rough Guides Ltd,
80 Strand, London WC2R 0RL
345 Hudson St, 4th Floor,
New York, NY 10014, USA
14 Local Shopping Centre, Panchsheel Park,
New Delhi 110017, India
Distributed by the Penguin Group
Penguin Books Ltd,
80 Strand, London WC2R 0RL
Penguin Group (USA)
375 Hudson Street, NY 10014, USA
Penguin Group (Australia)
250 Camberwell Road, Camberwell,
Victoria 3124, Australia
Penguin Books Canada Ltd,
10 Alcorn Avenue, Toronto, Ontario,
Canada M4V 1E4
Penguin Group (NZ)
67 Apollo Drive, Mairangi Bay, Auckland 1310,
New Zealand

Cover concept by Peter Dyer.

Typeset in Bembo and Helvetica to an original
design by Henry Iles.

Printed and bound in China

© Jonathan Bousfield and Dan Richardson 2008

No part of this book may be reproduced in any
form without permission from the publisher except
for the quotation of brief passages in reviews.

504pp includes index

A catalogue record for this book is available from
the British Library

ISBN: 978-1-85828-068-4

The publishers and authors have done their best
to ensure the accuracy and currency of all the
information in **The Rough Guide to Bulgaria**,
however, they can accept no responsibility for
any loss, injury, or inconvenience sustained by
any traveller as a result of information or advice
contained in the guide.

1   3   5   7   9   8   6   4   2

Help us update

We've gone to a lot of effort to ensure that the
sixth edition of **The Rough Guide to Bulgaria** is
accurate and up to date. However, things change
– places get "discovered", opening hours are
notoriously fickle, restaurants and rooms raise
prices or lower standards. If you feel we've got it
wrong or left something out, we'd like to know,
and if you can remember the address, the price,
the hours, the phone number, so much the better.

Please send your comments with the subject
line "**Rough Guide Bulgaria Update**" to ©mail
@roughguides.com. We'll credit all contributions
and send a copy of the next edition (or any other
Rough Guide if you prefer) for the very best
emails.

Have your questions answered and tell others
about your trip at
® community.roughguides.com

Acknowledgements

Jonathan would like to thank Lyuba Boyanina, Ani Hadzhimisheva, Krasimir Kostov, Athony Georgieff, Polly Mihailova, Petya Milkova, Andy Whiteman, Max Breeds and Matt Willis – all of whom contributed in some way to turning this edition into a longer and stranger trip than was originally intended. Thanks are also due to Georgi Dimitrov at Odysseia-In, James and Vanya in Bansko, Veselina Sarieva in Plovdiv, Matt

and Jenny in Bansko, and Mark and Amy in Bansko. Finally thanks to Marijana, without whom chapter 6 just wouldn't have been the same. Thanks also to James Rice for unflagging enthusiasm and patience, Stewart Wild for proofreading, Sarah Cummins for picture research, Ankur Guha for layout and Ashutosh Bharti for maps.

Readers' letters

Thanks to all the readers who took the trouble to write and email with their comments and suggestions. In particular, thanks to:

Michael Adams, Keith Arnold, Gavin Bell, Mike and Jerry Black, Michael Dennehy, Lew Graham, Bronwen Griffiths, Jon and Ann Higgins, Ariel Jacob, Steve Maher, Andrew Middleton, Nadrian Seeman,

Ann-Marie Sinclair, Todd Vance, Geert Vanhoovels and Annemie Van Linthoudt, Lynne Van Wyngaarden, Mrs Ware, Robin Wheeler, Nedyalko Yordanov.

SMALL PRINT

Index

Map entries are in colour.

INDEX

O

W

Y

Z

Map symbols

maps are listed in the full index using coloured text

-----	National border	▣	Restaurant
- - - -	Chapter division boundary	♦	Point of interest
	Motorway	ⓘ	Tourist office
	Main road	ℂ	Telephone
	Minor road	⊠	Post office
	Pedestrianized road	♥	Museum
	Underpass	⊙	Statue
	Steps	⛫	Monument
- - - - -	Path	∴	Ruin
	Railway	⛷	Ski area
	River	⛰	Mountain refuge
	Wall	⛰	Ranger station
	Bridge	⸸	Church (regional maps)
≈	Pass	⛪	Monastery
	Gorge	⛌	Mosque
⛾	Waterfall	✡	Synagogue
▲	Mountain peak	☐	Market
⋀	Mountain range	◯	Stadium
⤜	Cliff	▮	Building
◠	Cave	⊞	Church (town maps)
♣	Tree	⁺₊⁺	Cemetery
✈	Airport	▦	Park
★	Transport stop	▧	Forest
◉	Accommodation	▨	Beach

503

ROUGH GUIDES Travel Insurance

Visit our website at www.roughguides.com/website/shop or call:

COLUMBUS DIRECT
Travel Insurance

ROUGH GUIDES

ⓣ UK: 0800 083 9507

ⓣ Spain: 900 997 149

ⓣ Australia: 1300 669 999

ⓣ New Zealand: 0800 55 99 11

ⓣ Worldwide: +44 870 890 2843

ⓣ USA, call toll free on: 1 800 749 4922

Please quote our ref: *Rough Guides* books

Cover for over 46 different nationalities and available
in 4 different languages.